MARRIAGE TODAY

MARRIAGE TODAY

PROBLEMS, ISSUES AND ALTERNATIVES

Edited by
James E. De Burger

Schenkman Publishing Company, Inc.

A Halsted Press Book

JOHN WILEY AND SONS

New York • London • Sydney • Toronto

Copyright © 1977
Schenkman Publishing Company, Inc.
Cambridge, Massachusetts 02138

Distributed solely by Halsted Press, a Division of John Wiley and Sons, Inc., New York

Library of Congress Cataloging in Publication Data

Main entry under title:

Marriage today.

   Bibliography: p.
   1. Marriage—Addresses, essays, lectures.
2. Sex—Addresses, essays, lectures. 3. Family—
Addresses, essays, lectures. I. DeBurger, James E.
HQ734.M413   301.42   75-8664
ISBN 0-470-20465-6
ISBN 0-470-20466-4 pbk.

To
Clifford Kirkpatrick

CONTENTS

PART FOUR: MARITAL RELATIONSHIP CRISIS: PROBLEM-SOLVING RESPONSES

UNIT NINE. TERMINATION AND REMARRIAGE: THE AMERICAN PATTERN

UNIT TEN. IMPROVING THE MARITAL RELATIONSHIP

PART FIVE: PROSPECTS AND POSSIBILITIES

UNIT ELEVEN. ALTERNATIVES, CHANGE, AND THE FUTURE OF MARRIAGE

SELECTIVE BIBLIOGRAPHY

ACKNOWLEDGMENTS

The author wishes to thank the following writers and publishers for generously granting permission to reprint their material:

Robert R. Bell, "Parent-Child Conflict in Sexual Values," *Journal of Social Issues* 22 (No. 2, 1966): 34-44.

Miriam Berger, "Trial Marriage: Harnessing The Trend Constructively," *The Family Coordinator* 20 (January 1971): 38-43.

Jessie Bernard, "Marriage: His and Hers," *Ms* 1 (December 1972): 46ff. Excerpted From *The Future of Marriage* © 1972 Thomas Y. Crowell Co., Inc.

Eleanor Stoker Boll, "Should Parents or Cupid Arrange Marriages?," *New York Times Magazine* (December 13, 1959): 15. © 1959 by the New York Times Company. Reprinted by permission.

James H. S. Bossard and Eleanor Stoker Boll, "Childrearing in the United States," pp. 535-541, 544-549 in *The Sociology of Child Development*, Fourth Edition. Copyright 1966 by Harper and Row, New York.

Urie Bronfenbrenner, "Parents Bring Up Your Children!," *Look* 35 (January 1971): 45-46.

Donald J. Cantor, "A Matter of Right." This article first appeared in *The Humanist*, May/June 1970 issue and is reprinted by permission.

Ronald Chen, "The Dilemma of Divorce: Disaster or Remedy," *The Family Coordinator* 17 (October 1968): 251-254.

Harold T. Christensen, "Children in the Family: Relationship of Number and Spacing for Marital Success," *Journal of Marriage and the Family* 30 (May 1968): 284-288.

Sylvia Clavan, "Women's Liberation and the Family," *The Family Coordinator* 19 (October 1970): 317-323.

Joan Cook, "Marriage," *Ladies Home Journal* (September 1971): 192-197. Reprinted by permission of Transworld Feature Syndicate, Inc.

Kingsley Davis, "Jealousy and Sexual Property," *Social Forces* 14 (March 1936): 395-405.

James E. De Burger, "Sex in Troubled Marriages," *Sexual Behavior* 2 (May 1972): 22-26. Reprinted by permission of Interpersonal Publications, Inc.

Susan Edmiston, "To Love. Honor, and Negotiate," *Woman's Day* (July 1972): 14ff. By permission of Woman's Day Magazine. © 1972 by Fawcett Publications, Inc.

Richard Farson, "Why Good Marriages Fail," *McCall's* (October 1971): 110ff.

Gloria Tishler Hirsch, "Non-Sexist Childrearing: De-Mythifying Normative Data," *The Family Coordinator* 23 (April 1974): 165-170.

Charles W. Hobart, "Commitment, Value Conflict and the Future of the American Family," *Marriage and Family Living* 25 (November 1963): 405-412.

John W. Hudson and Lura F. Henze, "Campus Values in Mate-Selection: A Replication, *Journal of Marriage and the Family* 31 (November 1969): 772-775.

Morton Hunt, "Is Marriage in Trouble?," *Family Circle* (January 1971): 25-27 and "Sex Games Married People Play," *Family Circle* (October 1972): 108-112.

Morton Hunt, "The Future of Marriage." Originally appeared in *Playboy* Magazine. Copyright © 1971 by Morton Hunt.

Joan K. Jackson, "Alcoholism and the Family," from Vol. 315 of *The Annals of the American Academy of Political and Social Science.*

Jurate Kazickas, "Couples Believe A Few Punches Make A Marriage," *Courier-Journal* (September 27, 1970). By permission of Associated Press.

Lester A. Kirkendall and Roger W. Libby, "Interpersonal Relations: The Crux of the Sexual Renaissance," *Journal of Social Issues* (April 1966): 45-59.

Clifford Kirkpatrick, "The Family in Transition—Impact of the Scientific Revolution," from *The Family: As Process and Institution,* pp. 126-128, 137-145. Copyright © 1963 The Ronald Press Company, New York.

Mirra Komarovsky, "The Effects of Poverty on Marriage," from *Blue-Collar Marriage,* pp. 284-310. Copyright © 1967 by Random House, Inc.

Michael Korda, "If you Look to Marriage as an Instrument for Personal Growth . . .," *Glamour* (March 1972) 194ff. Copyright © 1972 by the Condé Nast Publications, Inc.

Judson T. Landis, "The Trauma of Children When Parents Divorce," *Marriage and Family Living* 22 (February 1960): 7-13.

E. E. LeMasters, "Parenthood as Crisis," *Marriage and Family Living* 19 (November 1957): 352-355.

Lionel S. Lewis and Dennis Brissett, "Sex as Work: A Study of Avocational Counseling," *Social Problems* 15 (Summer 1967): 8-18.

Violette S. Lindbeck, "The Cost of Sexual Apartheid," pp. 91-107 from *Sexuality: A Search for Perspective* by Donald L. Grummon and Andrew M. Barclay. © 1971. Reprinted by permission of D. Van Nostrand Co.

Eleanor D. Macklin, "Heterosexual Cohabitation Among Unmarried College Students," *The Family Coordinator* 21 (October 1972): 463-472.

Vincent D. Mathews and Clement S. Mihanovich, "New Orientations on Marital Maladjustment," *Journal of Marriage and the Family* 25 (August 1963): 300-304.

Margaret Mead, "Trial Parenthood." Reprinted from *Redbook Magazine* (June 1973), copyright © The Redbook Publishing Company.

Richard Meryman, "Counseling A Troubled Marriage," *Life* (April 28, 1972): 51-60. © 1972 Time Inc. Reprinted by permission.

Roger McIntyre, "Parenthood Training or Mandatory Birth Control: Take Your Choice," *Psychology Today* 7 (October 1973): 34ff.

Wenda Wardell Morrone, "The Most Common Sex Problems in New Marriages," *Glamour* (May 1972): 192ff and "How to Make A Good Marriage Better," *Glamour* (July 1972): 114ff. Copyright © 1972 by the Condé Nast Publications, Inc.

B. Jeanne Mueller, "Reconciliation or Resignation: A Case Study," *The Family Coordinator* 19 (October 1970): 345-352.

Ellis G. Olim. "The Self-Actualizing Person in the Fully-Functioning Family," *The Family Coordinator* 17 (July 1968): 141-148.

David H. Olson, "Marriage of the Future: Revolutionary or Evolutionary Change?," *The Family Coordinator* 21 (October 1972): 383-393.

Nena O'Neill and George O'Neill, "Open Marriage: A Synergic Model," *The Family Coordinator* 21 (October 1972): 403-409.

Nena O'Neill and George O'Neill, "Open Marriage: Implications for Human Service Systems," *The Family Coordinator* 22 (October 1973): 449-456.

Herbert A. Otto, "Has Monogamy Failed?," *Saturday Review* (April 25, 1970): 23ff.

Nick Panagakos, "The Biological Revolution," *Courier-Journal and Times Magazine* (June 6, 1971): 12-21. Reprinted by permission of NEA.

James W. Ramey, "Communes, Group Marriage, and the Upper-Middle Class," *Journal of Marriage and the Family* 34 (November 1972): 647-655.

Ira L. Reiss, "Sexual Codes in Teen-Age Culture," from Vol. 338 of *The Annals of The American Academy of Political and Social Science.*

Karen Renne, "Health and Marital Experience in An Urban Population," *Journal of Marriage and the Family* 33 (May 1971): 338-350
  Maslow, Abraham. *Religions, Values, and Experiences.* Columbus: Ohio State University Press, 1964.
  O'Neill, Nena and George O'Neill. *Shifting Gears: Finding Security in A Changing World.* New York: M. Evans & Co., 1974.
  Packard, Vance. *A Nation of Strangers.* New York: David McKay Co., 1972.

xvi

David M. Rorvik, "You Can Choose Your Baby's Sex," *Look* 34 (April 21, 1970): 88-94.

Vicki L. Rose and Sharon Price-Bonham, "Divorce Adjustment: A Woman's Problem?," *The Family Coordinator* 22 (July 1973): 291-297.

Isadore Rubin, "Transition in Sex Values: Implications for The Education of Adolescents," *Journal of Marriage and the Family* 27 (May 1965): 185-189.

Virginia Satir, "Marriage As a Human-Actualizing Contract," pp. 57-66 from Herbert A. Otto, Ed., *The Family in Search of A Future.* © 1970 by Meredith Corporation. Reprinted by permission of Prentice-Hall, Inc., Englewood Cliffs, New Jersey.

Barbara Seaman, "Do We Need to Know More About Sex?—An Interview with Dr. Rollo May," *Family Circle* (January 1971): 30-32.

Barbara Seaman, "The Liberated Orgasm," pp. 49-70 from *Free and Female* © 1972 by Barbara Seaman. Reprinted by permission of Coward, McCann & Geogehegan, Inc.

Philip E. Slater, "Sexual Adequacy in America," *Intellectual Digest* 4 (November 1973): 17-20.

Susan Sontag, "The Double Standard of Aging," *Cosmopolitan* 174 (March 1973): 208ff.

Charles B. Spaulding, "The Romantic Love Complex in American Culture," *Sociology and Social Research* 55 (October 1970), 82-100.

Robert Staples, "Public Policy and the Changing Status of Black Families," *The Family Coordinator* 22 (July 1973): 345-351.

Bernhard J. Stern, "The Family and Cultural Change," *American Sociological Review* 4 (1939): 199-208.

Time, "The New Woman—Where She Is and Where She's Going," (March 20, 1972): 26-28. Reprinted by permission from Time, The Weekly Magazine; Copyright Time, Inc.

Time, "Human Potential: The Revolution in Feeling," (November 9, 1970): 54-58. Reprinted by permission from Time, The Weekly Newsmagazine; Copyright Time, Inc.

John W. Weiss, "A Peaceable Revolution in Parenthood," *Parents' Magazine* (May 1973): 44ff.

Introduction to the Study of Modern Marriage

Studying Problems and Issues

Social historians of the future are likely to identify *change* — dramatic, rapid, and pervasive change — as the most salient characteristic of family life and marriage in the twentieth century. Of course, we need not in fact wait for the future historians nor speculate as to what they will be saying; for there are many living "witnesses" who can testify in word and deed to the patterns of change which have occurred during their own life span. Below are some quotations reflecting various notions about marriage and family life which were compiled from an interview study of persons aged seventy-five and over.[1] Each subject had been asked to describe "how things were in their youth."

> "A husband and wife worked together — they *had* to. Making a living, feeding a family took a lot of work.
>
> My parents would have been terribly embarrassed if any of us children had caught them embracing or kissing.
>
> If you wanted to court or keep company, you asked the young lady's parents. It was the only decent thing to do.
>
> Women were entitled to a lot of respect — but they knew their place.
>
> Mostly what we learned about sex was what was sinful about it.
>
> Small children were raised to obey their parents and to not bring shame on their family.
>
> Having children was regarded as the normal, natural thing to do — even maybe doing God's will. When a couple didn't have children, they just didn't have much respect from the community.
>
> When married people had trouble, they usually just toughed it out."

To even the most casual observer, a comparison of today's norms and values in each of the areas of familial experience touched on by these selected statements would suggest that striking change has occurred since the turn of this century.

In the study of problems and issues surrounding modern marriage and family life, the matter of *social* (or sociocultural) *change* takes on immense importance. Sociologists believe that individual character or personality structure is intimately linked through socialization to the technology, the prevailing behavior forms, and the cultural or normative content of the environing society. From this perspective it would be surprising if significant change in familial-marital process and structure did not flow from the altered or changing patterns of personalities currently forming new familial-marital units. For the prevailing conditions in this society epitomize change and alteration.

Sometimes, however, we are rather hesitant to make the connection between societal conditions and individual character. Let us take an example. Much comment has been given to the "lack of commitment," the "tentativeness" accompanying the formation of marriage partnerships in contemporary society. Many people, evidently still positively valuing the mores of an earlier and presumably more stable period in national history, abhor the somewhat casual attitudes held toward marriage by many young men and women. And yet, observation suggests that if individuals of this generation have had the opportunity to learn any one thing well about human relations, surely it is that change is inevitable. Economic, social, and political experiences on a nationwide scale provide little assurance that there really are eternal verities, that one can place great faith in the durability of meaningful relations, or that there are durable, over-arching values on which one can depend. In discussing the significance of sociocultural change for the emerging character of individuals in this society, Wheelis has pointed out that:

> "The social character now coming to prevail seems sculptured to fit a culture of change. In order to survive, it would appear that the individual must become progressively more able to modify himself, to alter his values, to change his reactions. The currently developing social character is equipped with precisely this potential. In it the light touch supplants the firm grip; the launcher of trial balloons replaces the committed man. One avoids final decisions, keeps everything subject to revision, and stands ready to change course when the winds change."[2]

While "tentativeness" in social relations is but one example of the connection between societal factors and emergent individual character, it clearly would have potential significance for every aspect of familial and marital experience.

The process of social change is itself frequently regarded as a "problem" for society among those who place a premium on stability of institutions and relationships. This view holds that, at best, social change produces more problems than it solves. It follows, from this position, that as social policy we should attempt to hold societal conditions in equilibrium, that we should closely limit the impact of technology on institutions such as the family, and that we should resist changes in the morality, norms, values, and behavioral forms characteristic of our society's past. On the other hand, an increasing number of people in this society see change not as an enemy but as a positive force for improvement. From this perspective, the old traditional values, norms and behavioral forms are not bad simply because they are old, but because they are unworkable and inappropriate to a vastly changed societal setting. Policy-wise then, if marriage and the basic values undergirding it are to be viable, the society must enhance, not inhibit, exploratory or purposive patterns of change in intimate human relations. This view would suggest, then, that society can benefit from experimentation in human relations generally, and specifically that there can be value in the formulation and testing of new values, norms, and behavior patterns in marriage.

The divergence in points-of-view regarding change and its implications discussed above is illustrative of a basic *issue* connected with marriage in modern society. As we shall see later, there are issues, both general and specific, involved with each of the areas of life-experience typically encountered in the processes leading to and following the formation of a marital partnership.

It is clear from both scholarly writing and the mass media that the problems and issues confronting contemporary marriage are extensive. It is hardly surprising that both the novice and the seasoned student sometimes experience bewilderment as they get into serious study in the field of marriage. For American marriage today is a scene which displays a welter of interconnected but conflicting norms, values, and behaviors. Consider, for example, the high rates of both marriage *and* divorce in this society; over ninety percent of our adult population does eventually marry, but it seems that of those who take the conjugal vows a large proportion are later as anxious to get out of marriage as they were earlier to get into it. Add to this the curious fact that in the quest for love-based partnerships, Americans ". . . try, try, and try again:" thus, marriage rates are as high for some age-groups of divorced people as for those marrying for the first time. Again, while there is widespread discussion of the limitations inherent in conventional monogamous marriage, the evidence is that most Americans attach high value to it and continue to form principally this kind of marital bond. Look at the variety and number of demands laid on contemporary marriage; never before in Western history has so much been expected of the conjugal relationship. On the one hand there are widespread and persisting expectations that marriage will provide a principal source of life-satisfaction for the individual; specifically, it is expected that marriage will prove to be personally rewarding, affectionally and sexually-gratifying, and emotionally sustaining for the partners. This belief system, on the other hand, is confronted by rather vague but widely-held suspicions that there may be some truth to the critical claims that marriage is constricting to personality development, emotionally crippling to one or both partners, and is a setting for mutual exploitation. Finally, we can add to these dilemmas the puzzlement resulting from a listing of the well-advertised differences among the "experts" regarding the optimal forms, the desirable functions, and even the basic question of the worthwhileness of family groups and marriage! Marriage today is thus a confused scene; this confusion adds up to difficulties of functioning for individuals within the partnership as well as to larger social problems stemming from the ambiguous relationship of the marriage to its surrounding social context.

The prospect that marriage and family life may in themselves be so disorganized as to constitute a social problem for society can be threatening, irritating, or downright unbelievable for many. However, when one considers the terms of the social scientist's definition of a social problem, the possibility takes on substance. Sociologically, a *social problem* exists when a situation is characterized by the perception among a significantly large proportion of the population of deep and pervasive value conflicts or threats to basic values; accompanying this perception are varying levels of dissatisfaction and the emergence of a belief that "something ought to be done" — indeed, must be done on a large scale for the society. To many students of the family, it thus appears that the widespread malfunctioning typical of so many contemporary marriages quite adequately qualifies it for classification as a social problem. To consider marriage as a social problem implies that its structure and processes have ramifications far beyond the particular pair relationship quality. Research suggests that the quality of marriage may have implications for such things as mental and physical health of partners and their offspring, dependency patterns, economic sufficiency, work roles, and community involvement; these and other aspects of behavior related to marital functioning are thus significant because they affect the structure and processes of society itself.

The study of problems and issues in modern marriage thus involves consideration of its partnership or pair aspects and its larger social dimensions. We have mentioned pair or group problems and social problems above. Now we can briefly comment on the third focal point for study: individual or personal problems. In this society, the individual perspective assumes great importance since marital problems specifically (and family problems generally) are defined in terms of perceptions of the marital situation held by the individuals involved. Writing almost two decades ago on the cultural configurations of family life and marriage in this society, Sirjamaki pointed out a major configuration: The criterion of success for a marriage is the personal happiness of the individuals involved.[3] Evidence accumulated since that time suggests that this cultural norm has intensified rather than abated over the years.

The significance of personal happiness as a determinant of the quality of interaction in a family group or marriage is recognized by leading researchers. Kirkpatrick, in this vein, provided a systematic definition of *family problem* using unhappiness as a central standard. Thus, a family problem involved a situation implying family-related maladjustment (unhappiness): (1) for a certain number of individuals, (2) extended over a certain period of time, (3) with a certain intensity in the experiences of conflict, frustration, deprivation, and disapproval.[4]

As we have seen in earlier discussion, it is very likely that the way in which a family or marriage functions may have extensive implications for the environing society. There is a big difference, however, between a "family problem" and a "problem family." For example, a particular family group might be classified as a "problem family" because its members are economically dependent on the state. For American society, however, with its tradition of individualism in the pursuit of happiness, the term "family problem" with its connotation of personally-experienced distress within the family group is of much greater significance. There are comparatively few problem families; there are doubtless individuals beyond number who experience family problems. It seems clear that the personal "definitions of the situation" constitute the major determinant of the forms and quality of functioning typical of both individuals and groups.

Following the definitional scheme developed by Kirkpatrick, we could say that a *marital problem* consists in the experiencing by one or more partners of unhappiness associated specifically with one's interaction, status, and roles within an ongoing marital situation. This definition of marital problem is assumed, even if not specifically stated, in virtually all of the materials included in this anthology.

The study of problems and issues, then, is a first step in getting a fuller view of where we are in American marriage today. The picture that emerges may not be particularly edifying — indeed, it may prove unsettling to us since marriage as an approved and desired state is strongly internalized by most people in this society. It is unlikely, however, that we shall be able to improve the quality of marriage or heighten the human potentials for individual happiness within the marital partnership if we ignore the widespread problems and distress associated with contemporary marriage. Through careful analysis and objective study we may be able to identify significant sources of maladjustment and explore courses of action which may lead to the reduction of problems and the amplifying of positive interaction between mates. Some elements of objective study and their possible contribution to these goals will be discussed in the following section.

SYSTEMATIC STUDY OF MODERN MARRIAGE

Social scientists have for many years engaged in the systematic study of family life and marriage. *Systematic study,* which may be regarded as a relatively disciplined, orderly search for knowledge bearing on the object under analysis, has focused on family life in both its institutional and group aspects. From the viewpoint of the social scientist, systematic study must be objective and should approximate the scientific method as closely as possible. Recent decades have seen a rapid acceleration in the collection and codification of empirical evidence on human behavior patterns. Corresponding to this general development, and despite the family group's rather strong resistance to the analytical probings of the social scientist, there is an emerging and continuously expanding body of objective knowledge on familial and marital behavior.

Certain cautions may be mentioned at this point. First, as is apparent from the earlier discussion, the notion of systematic study as presented here leans heavily toward the scientific, objective approach. It is not the intent, however, to suggest that this approach constitutes the only practical or meaningful mode of study. Indeed, to many people, the security and stability associated with the theological system of familial ideas and doctrines may make a great deal more sense and prove to be personally more functional than the tentativeness and questioning attitude associated with the social scientist's seemingly insatiable desire to classify and explain familial behavior. Science is but one pathway to truth, since, at bottom, truth is socially-defined. A second question concerns the usefulness, the practical contributions of the scientific enterprise to ongoing family life and marriage. There is probably some ground for guarded optimism concerning the dawning of a more rational era in family relations and human problem-solving. It would be quite erroneous, however, to assume that we have already entered an epoch characterized by universal and readily available scientific prescriptions for otpimizing the quality of human relations — especially is this true when we are considering the patterns of intimate relations found within the family group and marriage. Scientific, objective study can, and has, provided data useful to individuals and groups engaged in the process of coping with the everyday dynamics of familial experience.

Ultimately, of course, the degree to which social science can make a positive, lasting contribution to the quality of family life will be determined by the extent to which it gains acceptance as a valid guide to a wide variety of life-experiences. Writing in an optimistic vein over two decades ago, Burgess stated the problem and the prospects quite clearly:

"In a changing, complex, and complicated society, the family and its members need the findings of psychological and sociological research. Young people of today are willing to participate in this research. They are not so much asking for advice as for the scientific knowledge which they can use to plan the patterns of family relationships which will give self-expression to the members of the family and promote their personal development. It is the sum total of this enlightened planning and experimentation by individual families that will perhaps play a part in making the findings of research effective in determining future family trends.[5]

As is the case with any major field of interest, the study of the family has been characterized by a variety of systematic approaches. Sociologists are one, if not the largest, of several kinds of social scientists conducting research which directly involves the testing of hypotheses or the gathering of empirical data specifically bearing on family forms and processes. Important contributions to the body of knowledge on familial behavior have, of course, come from many points within the social and behavioral sciences. Kirkpatrick identified six different sources of knowledge; these included the historical, the familial-societal-interrelational, the family functions, the psychoanalytical, the personality-culture, and the role-process approaches.[6] Other authors have included the disciplines of economics, anthropology, Western Christianity, and law in their classification of approaches.[7]

Depending on the criteria of classification, we could obviously depict numerous different "approaches." Thus, systematic study of marriage could be viewed in terms of its characteristics as a "pure" or as an "applied" science; the former is primarily knowledge-oriented while the latter is action-oriented. Or distinctions could be made between research focii; thus, some approaches emphasize form or structure; others are more interactional — concentrating on the articulation of social and cultural systems through the intra-familial structure of statuses and roles; still others are social-psychological in approach, emphasizing the study of individual behavior within the familial group as that behavior is limited, controlled, and influenced by the social context. The kind of approach used by the social scientist is of fundamental importance, since it determines the kind of data collected in an empirical, systematic study and it also serves to guide the interpretation of the research findings. In short, then, there are currently numerous competing approaches. But a very significant feature of the various approaches, especially those within the social science framework, consists in their systematic approach and their growing tendency to insist upon scientific method in the acquisition of data and the building of knowledge. Inter-disciplinary research and the corollary refinement of competing explanatory schemes may some day produce an empirically-based general theoretical approach to familial forms and processes. Such a development may help to reduce the puzzlement produced in the public by differences among the "experts."

To a large extent modern sociological study of marriage is distinctive in its attempt to ascertain the significance of the dynamic interrelationship between the individual, the group, and society. Indeed, there are few, if any other, situations outside the familial group or marriage where this tripartite juncture assumes as great an importance for human behavior. This feature especially adds much challenge and excitement to the sociological study of contemporary familial and marital experience. Thus it seems that the major areas of interaction between marital partners (e.g., intimacy, economic decision-making, child-rearing, etc.) could be best understood by simultaneously analyzing the impact of individual, group, and societal variables on these interaction areas. In practice, we would begin the study of a problem, say in the area of intimate behavior, by analyzing *individual* habit patterns, prior selective experiences, personality structure, self-concept, etc. The individual would then be related analytically to the structure of roles and statuses characterizing the *group*; this would entail considering the group's identity-conferring and perspective-conferring processes, its socialization processes, its structure of power and rank, its system of rewards and punishments, etc. The group would finally be examined with reference to the derivation of its norms, identity, and purposes from the environing *society* and its relation to the network of institutions, culture, and groups which comprise society. Each facet of the analysis would be directed toward understanding of the forms and processes at work in the definition of the situation as a "problem." Even though this is a very sketchy account, it is obvious that such an analytical approach is likely to be very time-consuming. However, a serious attempt to interrelate rather than isolate these variables in research can yield a comparatively richer set of data for explaining and possibly treating problems in the marital partnership.

It was suggested earlier that there may be considerable resistance on the part of familial groups to the analytical probings of the social scientist. At this point it may be profitable to identify some difficulties confronting the systematic study of familial experience. These have been defined by Kirkpatrick in terms of two kinds of obstacles: emotional and intellectual. Emotional difficulties consist of:

> ". . . the biases, fears and wishful preconceptions which blur the vision of persons observing the family behavior about them. Some students rebel against detached, scientific observation of family life. A person frequently insists on generalizing with emotional fervor from one case, namely, his own family group. Four difficulties deserve special mention. The conservative attitude . . . , the romantic complex . . . , surviving sex taboos . . . , and the conception of sexual, marital, and family relationships as essentially comic . . ."[8]

By "intellectual obstacles," Kirkpatrick meant that there exists, external to the rational student, ignorance, dogmatism, and complexity which make objective inquiry and understanding difficult. For example, generalizations regarding familial experience may be biased by pre conceptions; there may be a serious lack of accumulative, validated principles of familial behavior; or adding to the difficulties of a lack of knowledge may be the existence of false and inconsistent beliefs about family life which are held with great tenacity.

Some aspects of family experience may prove to be very disproportionately surrounded by obstacles to study. One such area may be the study of *alternatives* to current patterns of family life and marriage.

These obstacles stem mainly from our emotional and intellectual commitment to past, established patterns and somewhat to the fear of change itself. Below we will explore some dimensions of the question of alternatives to our present patterns in marriage and consider some positive outcomes from their serious study.

An implicit theme in the organization of materials in this anthology is that human relationships are susceptible to improvement and that we should direct knowledge into that effort. If, in other words, patterned human relations are vexing, troublesome, and maladjusting due to their organized structure and processes, then rationality impels us to consider alternative structures and processes which may produce better functioning. Increasingly, social critics are contending that it shows social irresponsibility to merely contemplate and bemoan the welter of problems confronting marriage today. For, given the intellectual, economic, and personal resources at our disposal in this society, we have the opportunity, the challenge of developing ". . . new forms of marriage and family which might conceivably add more warmth and intensity to human existence than we ever dreamed possible."[9] As Otto has further pointed out,

> "It is only with the advent of modern anthropological research and sociological theory that man has recognized his institutions, not as eternal verities, but as defined ways of being social. For the first time, he is now free to examine such institutions as marriage and the family with a certain amount of objectivity and to restructure these institutions, not in blind compliance to social pressures and economic sanctions, but in full consciousness of his needs and potentialities.
>
> After five hundred thousand years of human history, man is now at a point where he can create marriage and family possibilities uniquely suited to his time, place, and situation."

Based on the notion that science should contribute to the sum total of human happiness, a similar argument holds that it is insufficient for the social scientist merely to observe, classify, and theoretically explain the malfunctioning of contemporary marriage. If intrinsic value is seen in intimate, rewarding human relations and if the basic premise of the malleability and modifiability of individual and group behavior patterns is accepted, then it seems imperative that scholarly effort be directed to the study of behavioral alternatives which could possibly provide more satisfying and constructive familial and marital relations.

As we have noted in earlier discussion, we are likely to encounter emotional and intellectual obstacles to the study of alternatives. The foundations of these obstacles lie both within us and within the institutional structures of our society which have furnished our norms, our prescriptions of approved behavior. Perhaps we should remember that, at this point, our commitment as students is to explore, study, and analyze possible alternatives and their likely effects on familial and marital behavior. With rare exceptions, most of us are concerned mainly with enlarging our knowledge about the actual and potential functioning of the family and marriage rather than committing our-selves to the task of radically changing existing institutions overnight. This is not to say that our major institutions should be left intact, as is; for most of them, drastic change is long overdue. More importantly, we are not saying that serious, careful study of this field should leave the student unchanged in attitudes and values or, in other words, as a person. Perhaps it comes down to a question of relative activism as contrasted to introspection. Our activist inclinations should be tem-pered with the realization that knowledge, too, is power. For whatever our particular motivation may be in academically probing the prob-lems, issues, and alternatives confronting contemporary marriage, our endeavor holds considerable potential for personal development. Not the least of these benefits may be the enlargement of our "relative freedom" to function as individuals. Such freedom, as Allport has so cogently portrayed it,[10] depends on:

> ". . . the individual's possession of multiple possibilities for be-havior. To state this point paradoxically, a person who harbors many determining tendencies in his neuro-psychic system is freer than a person who harbors few. Thus a person having only one skill, knowing only one solution, has only one degree of freedom. On the other hand, a person widely experienced and knowing many courses of conduct has many more degrees of freedom."

The principle embodied in Allport's idea was an underlying assump-tion at work in the organization of materials for this book. In the following section, we will discuss some of the other assumptions which influenced the organization and selection of materials.

NATURE AND ORGANIZATION OF THE MATERIALS

In recent years, a veritable torrent of writing on the problems of family and marriage has poured forth. Popular publications, profes-sional journals, monographs and books, and numerous newspaper columns have contributed to the swelling stream of discussion on the condition of the American family and marriage. The assumptions and values behind current writing on this topic are varied and inspection shows that they represent a wide range of opinions. At one pole, the tone of expressed views seemingly reflects a tendency toward myopic problem-denial. An example: "There's nothing basically wrong with the institution of marriage — we're just generating problems by asking too many questions about it." At the other pole, we find a deadly, sometimes cynical pessimism: "The family is the source of most social ills in this society, and marriage is a wretched institution which has outlived its usefulness." Since this book will also convey perspectives on American marriage and its prognosis, it would seem fair to ask what assumptions and perspectives governed the selection of its contents.

We can begin by observing that many students in marriage and family courses contributed to the selection process by providing evaluations and reactions to the articles. If there was one dominant editorial motivation, it can probably be best described as realistic optimism. This meant that there should be no problem-denial and also no "doom-saying." But this probably puts it too simply. In reality there were several assumptions, beliefs, and themes that not only influenced the conscious selection of materials, but which also appear for discussion within the readings themselves. Following a suggestion made by many students, we have listed below, in very sketchy form, some of these assumptions and themes.

1. Marriage, in both its forms and processes, is in serious trouble; as a consequence of currently inadequate forms and processes there exists a massive amount of personal suffering.

2. Most serious problems in contemporary marriage are integrally related to processes of change occurring throughout the institutional network of society.

3. The current marriage scene is especially and deeply affected by two important and interrelated social movements occurring in this society. The first of these is the *sexual equality movement* which is but one aspect of an even broader social movement in the direction of human equality — social, political, and otherwise. The core of the sexual equality movement is found in its concern with women's roles and status, its effort to humanize the man-woman relationship, and its drive to eliminate sexism. The second can, for lack of a better term, be called the *human potentials movement*. It reflects the emergence of a wave of new, humanistically vital, and socially aware individualism and is oriented toward enhancing the worth and dignity of the individual. Its impetus is gained from an ideology urging the individual's potential or capacity for love, maximal growth, and satisfying productive self-awareness. The movement is fundamentally humanistic; in one breath its ideology stresses self-actualization, acceptance of and trust in one's fellow humans, and the development of meaningful-but-responsible relationships with others.

4. Personal happiness, or the quest for it, is the most dominant individual factor: (a) in the initial formation of the marital partnership, (b) in determining the quality of its processes, and (c) in predicting its stability.

5. Each individual has inherent worth and most have undeveloped potentials; futhermore, each person's capacity for growth toward more adequate personhood can be drastically affected by the conditions of existence in the environing society.

6. American society has a family history strongly affected by patriarchal tradition and conservative attitudes; but it also has a

tradition of pragmatic experimentation which may lend some validation to the quest for alternatives to unsatisfactory contemporary patterns of marriage. Ambivalence and confusion result from this bifurcation of motives.

7. The judicious use of evidence derived from objective, scientific research can aid the understanding of marital problems and issues and can contribute to the problem-solving processes.

8. Change over time in the individual behavior patterns associated with marriage and in the approved forms of marriage itself is certain; such change-processes take place in the context of a changing, dynamic society.

9. Meaningful group relationships are a potentially significant source of change for individual behavior and values.

10. Change, for both individuals and relationships, need not be either accidental or deteriorative; change may be planned or purposive and beneficial in its outcomes.

For the most part, this listing gives a preview of some of the more important assumptions and themes occurring in the materials which you will be reading. It is probable, of course, that careful reading will reveal other values and assumptions not specified here. One such inexplicit assumption is that marriage is here to stay, that this form of intimate partnership will continue to be highly valued. Still another is that for the foreseeable future, the predominant type of marital partnership will continue to take the form of a pair-relationship rather than polygyny, polyandry, or group marriage.

OVERVIEW OF THE MATERIALS

The materials you will be reading have been, for the most part, organized from the perspective of the married pair or of the individuals comprising the marital partnership. The *marital partnership* is conceptualized as an interpersonal bond emerging from a social-biophysical-cultural context through a process of selective contacts between persons. Following initial contact between persons, the potential partnership moves typically through a variety of encounters in family-related experiences. Ultimately, what happens to any family group, in terms of the structures and processes it develops, is largely determined by the manner in which the marital partners perceive and respond to the various kinds of demands encountered in the course of their shared life-experiences. It is this on-going construction of reality through continuous definition of life situations which will, of course, determine whether the partnership is beset by "marital problems," and whether the partnership itself will continue to be maintained by the individuals involved or be broken by them. It ought to be noted that despite the current attention being paid to the phenomenon of marital disintegra-

tion, the marriage bond is one of the most enduring intimate relationships in the society. It clearly qualifies, on the average, as the most
enduring primary relationship within the family system.

Although the married-pair perspective predominates, it is clear that
an understanding of the problems and issues confronting marriage
today depends upon a comprehension of what is happening in the
society. *Part One* introduces material illustrative of some sweeping
social changes occurring in this society and shows how they are related
to changes in family life and marriage. Further materials then call
attention to the implications of the sexual equality movement and the
human potentials movement for modern marriage. In all subsequent
reading, there are opportunities to ask how these two movements are
related to the interaction of partners in each of the basic areas of
encounter in marriage.

In *Part Two* we will first explore some ways in which individual,
group, and societal factors interact to define and shape the process of
partner-selection. Some of the problems and issues connected with
human sexuality and sexual expression are then explored. The matter
of sexuality is quite important, since the culturally shaped human sex
drive seems increasingly important in shaping the quality of interpersonal relations between potential mates.

Part Three, dealing with basic encounters in marriage, begins with
materials which review some of the factors associated with the
problem-experiencing of married persons. Attention is then given to
some of the assumptions and foundations upon which a marital partnership is typically based in this society. Issues surrounding the marriage choice and the functioning of the relationship are discussed along
with a view of some alternatives to contemporary marital forms and
processes. In the remainder of Part Three, this same pattern is followed. In each of the basic areas of encounter for the marriage partners we will consider problems, issues, and alternatives.

In *Part Four,* materials are devoted first to one of the most widely-
discussed patterns in American family life: the tendency to dissolve
and re-form marital partnerships. Following materials deal with a form
of behavior which holds the attention of practitioner and researcher
alike, namely, the problem-solving responses and patterns of persons
within an ongoing marriage. As we know, the mass media coverage of
the family scene frequently portrays — and probably over-emphasizes
— the high incidence of marital break-up. Standing in contrast to the
admittedly high frequency of marital disintegration is the fact that
there are many more cases in which persons in a troubled but valued
relationship try to solve their problems and develop techniques for
improving their marital partnership.

The concluding selections in *Part Five* deal with the interconnected
questions of alternatives to traditional marital modes, the processes of
social change, and the future of the family and marriage. While in
earlier discussion alternatives are viewed in a fairly positive light with

considerable hope for their efficacy, some important questions are raised here regarding the merits and feasibility of certain alternatives proffered as new answers to the old problems of unsatisfactory relationships in family and marriage. While this note of caution is sounded, there is found in the concluding material a somewhat optimistic note on the continued existence of marriage as a viable human relationship with as-yet-unrealized assets for enriching the lives of those within this oldest of all human partnerships.

SUGGESTIONS FOR USE

Knowledge begins with questions and it grows through questioning. This notion is as applicable to the study of contemporary marriage as to any other field. In your reading of this book, you will find a mixture of materials, including scientific research reports, scholarly speculation, accounts of current happenings, critiques, philosophies of living, etc. Your greatest gain will probably come through approaching the selections in a constructively questioning manner, rather than approaching them in a quest for ready-made answers to the problems of coping with your own familial experience.

Of course, granted that you are concerned with improving family life experience and marriage, it is very likely that some practicable answers and personally applicable alternatives will emerge from your pursuit of knowledge. As we have suggested earlier, this is perhaps the least we should expect from the knowledge-building process. But we must remember that familial and marital forms and processes are in flux; the most accurate prediction we could make about family life and marriage is that they will certainly change. We will have to be on guard against treating answers or solutions as final and unchanging; in this connection, to attend seriously only to those proposed solutions or ideas that reinforce our preconceptions is to ensure that our understanding of contemporary marriage will be incomplete if not inaccurate. It has been pointed out by therapists that the most rewarding forms of human interaction seem to be characterized by considerable openness. Perhaps this gives a clue to deriving optimum benefit from serious study; thus our quest for knowledge in this field may turn out to be most rewarding if we cultivate intellectual openness toward the exciting variety of materials available to us.

A few practical suggestions can be made. First, make use of the selective bibliography and the unit study guides; they should prove to be a rich source of ideas for papers, projects, discussion, and further study. Secondly, devise your own technique for "opening up" your mind for the reading. Some students do this by preparing, prior to reading each section, a list of their private feelings, attitudes, values, and opinions about the topic at hand. This listing is then set aside temporarily. Getting one's personal concepts "out front" can prove to be a means of generating a meaningful and often-rewarding analysis of the bases of one's ideas; this is the case especially when we compare our reasoning with that expressed by others both in dialogue and in serious writing. The third and final suggestion is that you involve yourself with others in a process of positive change. Perhaps the minimal point of entry into positive change lies in the discussion of significant topics with meaningful others. What you do beyond that will depend upon a variety of factors including your own particular levels of energy or other personal resources and your level of commitment to improving human relations generally and family life specifically.

REFERENCES

1. DeBurger, James E. "Family and Marital Values: An intergenerational Study." Unpublished research paper, 1967.

2. Wheelis, Allen. *Quest for Identity* (New York: W.W. Norton, 1958), p. 14.

3. Sirjamaki, John. "Culture Configurations in the American Family." *American Journal of Sociology* LIII (May 1948): 453-459.

4. Kirkpatrick, Clifford. *The Family: As Process and Institution*, 2nd Edit. (New York: Ronald Press, 1963), p. 180.

5. Burgess, Ernest W. "The Family and Sociological Research." *Social Forces* 26 (October 1947):1-6.

6. Kirkpatrick, *op. cit.*, pp. 18-20.

7. Nye, F. Ivan and Berardo, Felix. *Emerging Conceptual Frameworks in Family Analysis* (New York: MacMillan, 1966); also cf. Christensen, Harold (Ed.). *Handbook of Marriage and the Family* (Chicago: Rand-McNally, 1964).

8. Kirkpatrick, *op. cit.*, pp. 8-10.

9. Otto, Herbert A. (Ed.). *The Family in Search of A Future* (New York: Appleton-Century-Crofts, 1970), p. 9.

10. Allport, Gordon W. *Becoming* (New Haven: Yale University Press, 1955), pp. 84-85.

UNIT STUDY GUIDE

A. *Terms to Review*

Institution	Social problem	Culture
Group	Marital problem	Problem family
Primary group	Science	Social change
Society	Systematic study	Social movement
Marriage	Theory	Issue, social

B. *Questions for Discussion and Study*

1. Discuss and give examples of intellectual and emotional obstacles to the study of family groups.
2. Describe the operating assumptions of science (eg. amorality) and discuss the extent to which these assumptions are valid in the scientific study of the family.

xxxii Marriage Today

3. In your opinion, which area of family life or marriage is most difficult to study objectively? Show why you think this is so.

4. Can study of familial behavior be systematic without being scientific? Discuss.

5. In what ways can scientific study of the family provide ways of improving familial and marital experience? Discuss   d give specific examples.

6. "Take the role" of a social scientist and respond to the following critical assertion: "Marriage and family relations and the love between a man and woman are sacred things . . . scientists should quit meddling with such things!"

7. Suppose you wanted to do a field study of the effectiveness and functioning of some alternative to current marriage patterns (eg. group marriage). What arguments would you use to induce the participants in this situation to cooperate in your research?

C. *Topics-Ideas for Papers and Projects*

1. The problem of ethical neutrality in scientific study of marriage.

2. Common elements in planned and unplanned social change.

3. Do a survey of local mass media to determine salient issues associated with family and marriage in your community.

4. Survey the holdings of your school library on the topics of family, marriage, divorce, etc.

5. Scientific versus intuitive study of the family and marriage: procedures, assets, and liabilities of each approach.

PART ONE

THE CHANGING
SOCIAL CONTEXT
OF MARRIAGE

Unit 1
Sources of Change in Family Life and Marriage

Man's yesterday may ne'er be like his morrow;
Naught may endure but Mutability. – Shelley

Introduction

In our previous discussion we concluded that family life and marriage exist today in a context of profound, pervasive, and rapid societal change. Most would concede that the rapidity of social change constitutes one of the most conspicuous features of twentieth-century culture. So rapidly is the pace of change accelerating that, according to some predictions, the 1970's will witness as much change as occurred in the previous four decades.[1] This aspect of change has given rise to a large variety of books and articles dealing with its effects on both the institutional structure of society and the individual psyche. Illustrative of the growing concern with this topic is Alvin Toffler's writing, in which the term "future shock" is coined to describe the individual's disorientation and inability to cope with stresses induced by the continuous flow of cultural change in contemporary society.[2]

Family life and marriage have clearly experienced their share of the stresses arising out of large-scale sociocultural change. It seems that the effects of change are seldom, if ever, limited to merely one component of the society. In fact, change in one institutional or normative segment of the society may serve as a powerful impetus to change in other parts of the social system. Thus, much of the observed change in contemporary family life reflects basically a process of accommodation or adjustment between the familial institution and other institutional segments of the society (political, economic, legal, religious, etc.). New and sometimes radically different answers to problems confronting family and marriage may emerge from this interaction. As Hunt says, ". . . The signs of grave disorder in modern marriage are actually a series of alternatives to conventional, old-style monogamy."

We can now reiterate the significance of the social context in our changing family life by briefly commenting on the nature of the familial-societal interrelationship. One point is that the image con-

3

noted by the notion of the isolated nuclear family may bear little resemblance to reality. The nature and functioning of the family, considered either in the abstract as an institution or, concretely, as the patterns of relationship existing in millions of groups, is integrally bound up with the very nature and ongoing processes of the environing society and culture. Furthermore, marriage — considered either in the abstract as a sub-institution or, concretely, as the typical patterns of meaningful relationships bonding the partners together — is dependent upon the larger familial institution for fundamental definition of its *raison d'etre*. The sociological principle here is that which postulates the interdependence of all components in the social system. While the fiction of the independently acting individual or of the isolated nuclear family may be widely held and have some analytical or social value, the fact is that nothing and no one stands truly alone in the mass society.

There are other principles deserving of comment. One is that sociocultural change is the rule rather than the exception in society.[3] In considering modifications in family life and marriage which have occurred in the past few decades, we should also remember that such changes have not always been in direct response to specific events or changes occurring in the family's sociocultural setting. Some observed changes in family life may clearly be tied to alterations in the environing society; but as many more may be found to emanate from exploratory, trial-and-error familial behaviors which are likely to have been facilitated *but not determined* by changes in the family's social context.

While a comprehensive listing and treatment of the societal sources of change in family life and marriage would doubtless fill a volume in itself, we can mention several here that seem very important. Science, for example, and the rapidity with which its accompanying technology is diffused throughout society (through application to transportation, communication, medicine, etc.) constitutes a potent base for change in family life. This is especially true in American society where the value systems surrounding the major institutions are varied, confusing, and often in conflict. The culturally approved pluralistic value situation generally characterizing American society is of itself an undoubtedly rich source of varietism in familial forms, processes, and conflicts. One other major potential source of change can be identified, namely, culturally approved social policies which have specific implications for the behavior of individuals and groups. Such policies reflect cultural norms as manifested through economic, political, and other organizational structures. In short, I am saying that existing norms may be discriminatory and they may have serious implications for individuals' familial roles and behavior when implemented through legal, economic, religious, or other organizational policies. Historically, the familial roles of women and minority group individuals have been significantly affected (and usually deleteriously so) by the existence of culturally based and organizationally implemented discrimination. In this connection, it is only very recently that the federal government has begun to acknowledge that every bit of legislation and policy affects the American family for better or worse.

What of the issues surrounding change itself? I will list below some that are frequently mentioned. Note that, as issues regarding change, each could apply to the larger phenomenon of change in the society or, specifically, to the area of family life and marriage.

1. *Purposive versus fortuitous change.* Should we set out to make purposive, planned changes in societal or institutional structures and processes? Do we have adequate knowledge for intervening and controlling? Will "natural processes" govern changes that take place if no attempts to intervene occur?

2. *The vehicle of change: organization or individual.* Should change-processes operate on a one-by-one basis for the individuals involved, or should planned change be carried out through the organization?

3. *The durability of changes.* Should we strive toward ultimate, final answers — permanent solutions? Or, should short-run change and goal formulation be our objective? What are the costs and benefits of each approach to planned change? How do these elements emerge in fortuitous change?

4. *The scope of change: systematic or component-oriented.* Objectively, as change occurs, is the entire social unit (society, institution, etc.) affected or only one or more components of a larger social unit? In purposive change, should change-efforts be directed toward the social unit as a whole (eg. the family institution) or toward one of its components (eg. child-rearing norms)?

5. *The speed of change: rapid or gradualistic.* What is the optimum pace at which change should proceed, either planned or fortuitous?

This is but a brief listing of some general issues surrounding social and cultural change. The list could easily be extended and could be broadened to include specific issues current in the society. Some of these more specific issues will be discussed in the readings for this unit.

REFERENCES

1. Cornish, Edward. "Future Shock," reviewed in *The Futurist* 4 (October 1970), pp. 175-180.

2. Toffler, Alvin. *Future Shock* (New York: Random House, 1970).

3. Moore, Wilbert. *Social Change* (Englewood Cliffs: Prentice-Hall, 1963), p. 2.

The Family in Transition: Impact of the Scientific Revolution

CLIFFORD KIRKPATRICK

THE SCIENTIFIC REVOLUTION AND THE FAMILY

Science is the dynamic influence which has dramatically transformed the world. It has the utmost significance in terms of content, method, and applications. As to content, science is in essence a conceptual pattern common to a considerable body of men by virtue of similar sensory impressions and similar rules of logical thought, this pattern being constantly checked and modified for consistency with new observations.[1] The rich content of modern science is a product of the scientific method. The scientific method is a way of observing nature and man as a part of nature, in order to gain more complete understanding, prediction, and control. It is skeptical, amoral, and often disturbing when applied to areas not previously regarded as susceptible to scientific study. The scientific method has acquired prestige, however, because of the mechanical marvels that it has produced. It enriches not only pure science but technology, the workday companion of science. Technology is the direct source of the mechanical revolution which has brought the family to a state of transition.

The Mechanical Revolution. The term *industrial revolution* is commonly applied to the tremendous change which came through the scientific application of power to machinery in the late eighteenth and early nineteenth centuries in Europe. Perhaps more properly the term *mechanical revolution* could be used because industry, in the sense of large aggregations of workers, was not new. In the beginning of the new era, power had to be closely connected in space to machines. This meant that factories developed in areas where a source of power was convenient. Later, electricity often replaced steam, with the result that the power generated at a distance from machines could be carried by wires rather than by belts, chains, or gears. This fact is pertinent to decentralization of industry and the possible restoration of economic functions to the home.

It is well known that all sorts of secondary consequences flowed from the application of power to machines; for example, accentuation of the factory system, urbanization, and improved transportation. Especially significant for the family institution are the transformed means of transportation and communication.

Transportation and Communication. Control of space is an outstanding consequence of the scientific revolution. The dramatic story of modern magic carpets has often been told. With incredible speed masses of men move about the surface of the planet. In the United States 35.5 million persons, living in a particular house in March 1960, had moved to a different house by March 1961. About 29.7 million had moved within the same state, and approximately 5.8 million moved to a different state.[2]

Mobility facilitated by modern means of transportation can bring family members in close and convenient contact, but it also may separate them. It is indeed hard to evaluate the centrifugal as compared with the centripetal influence of improved transportation.[3] Family members can assemble from the ends of the earth for family reunions with speed and convenience. A pioneer space traveler can circle the earth repeatedly and return to kiss his wife for the photographers. On the other hand, family members may be separated by ever-greater distances in wartime. Work at a distance from home is facilitated by the automobile, the airplane, modern trains, and buses. Perhaps our machines are more likely to take family members away from each other than toward each other.

The development of modern media of communication is closely related to the improvement in transportation. Communication by mail, for example, is tremendously accelerated by modern means of transportation. While George Washington and John Adams found it difficult to communicate with Martha and Abigail during the Revolutionary period, participants in World War II communicated with relative speed and convenience. The more distinctive agencies of modern communication are, of course, cheap printing, the telegraph, the telephone, the movies, the radio, and television, which has acquired an intercontinental range.

Just as the improvement in transportation may have a twofold effect, either separating or bringing people together, so may revolutionized communication media have a twofold effect. On the one hand, they make for a uniformity of ideas because of press services, newspaper chains, nation-wide radio broadcasts, syndicated columns, propaganda, and mass advertising. On the other hand, the opinion climate may be made diverse by the varied points of view expressed through media of communication. The old, simple, generally accepted ideas concerning the family institution have been replaced by a confused cultural heritage which leaves many persons bewildered.[4]

Scientific knowledge concerning the family is widely available; but, on the other hand, every newsstand displays scores of magazines portraying some distorted aspect of family life. Science and romanticism, conservatism and radicalism are expressed on the printed page and on the air. It is no wonder that people are confused about the family institution.

The Biological Revolution. The scientific revolution in the biological sphere has special significance for family members. The original need for scientific control of biological forces was great. During the Middle Ages matters of health were enmeshed in superstition. Some 25 million inhabitants of Europe died from bubonic plague. Probably one out of every two or three infants died before reaching the first year of life. Survivors were commonly orphaned at an early age. Research progress which ultimately met this original need for health and survival was achieved by Vesalius, Harvey, Jenner, Pasteur, Koch, and more recent microbe hunters. Control of forces of life and death has been amply demonstrated, as data to be given in this book will show.

It is interesting to contemplate the future possibilities of biological knowledge on family life. Improved contraceptives and better information in regard to control of fertility are to be expected. There may be increasing use of sterilization processes. Artificial insemination already produces each year more "test tube" babies. With improved techniques for preserving the human sperm, artificial fertilization on eugenic grounds may be further developed. There is reason to think that control of sex of offspring may eventually be achieved in some degree.[5] Not only may sperm be preserved and used for artificial fertilization, but it is conceivable from animal experiments that ovaries might be transplanted to other organisms and thus acquire a longer reproductive function.[6] A fertilized ovum was grown in a glass container for 29 days then baptized and killed.[7]

Mothers now have less fear that polio will strike their children. German measles which may cause pregnant women to have defective children is being brought under control.[8] The difficulties of menopause can be alleviated. Menstrual tension and cramps in many cases can be controlled. Women need not be "witches every month." Tranquilizers, for all their dangers, may prevent or calm many a family quarrel. Family sociologists are aware of the implications of a continuing biological revolution.[10]

SOCIAL CONSEQUENCES OF
THE SCIENTIFIC REVOLUTION FOR THE FAMILY

There is no sharp line of demarcation between economic and social consequences. For purposes of convenience, however, a distinction will be made. Social consequences will be considered with reference to the familial group, the home, the family institution, and the marriage relationship.

The Familial Group. In general it may be said that the familial group in present-day United States has become a small primary group, relatively independent of extended kinship ties, and vulnerable because of this very independence. For the sake of simplicity, we shall present certain clearly demonstrated changes in familial groups and then proceed to explanations and analysis of derivative consequences.

Decline in the size of household is an outstanding fact that can be clearly demonstrated. It will be recalled that a household, in distinction to a biological nuclear family, may include persons unrelated by blood, marriage, or adoption. The available facts for the United States concerning the size of the household go back to 1790. In 1790, the average number of persons in a household was 5.7; by 1890 it was 4.9; and by March 1960, 3.6.[11]

A decline in the extended family is another social consequence. The family as a group composed of husband and wife, numerous children, children's children, and dependent relatives is increasingly inappropriate to modern life. Spinsters and widows now find employment, and hence to a lesser extent seek refuge with the male head of an extended residential family group. Given urbanism, the hired man and his wife, constituting a secondary family, are less likely to be members of an extended family group. Married children under the present tradition of neolocal residence are less likely to acquire shares of a family estate and to continue residence with parents.

It is possible to go too far in portraying the nuclear family as isolated under modern industrial and bureaucratic conditions. Litwak suggests that the extended family may operate in spite of class and occupational barriers.[12] Sussman has shown that related nuclear families may live close together and carry on interdependent activities.[13] From the research of Zimmerman and Cervantes there is reason to think that friends of the family are meaningful, similar, and perhaps supportive in maintaining family success and stability.[14]

A decline in fertility is a significant long-range trend. The reproductive function is now less significant as a basis for family life than was formerly the case. Glick suggests that during the last 150 years there has been a decline in the number of children under 21 per family from 3.0 to only 1.3.[15] By 1959 there was clear evidence of an upward trend in fertility. Yet in view of improved conditions as to health and home facilities it is certain that modern American women carry a vastly lighter reproductive burden than did their grandmothers.

Decline in the association of generations is a fourth change in the family group, somewhat interwoven with the changes already discussed. One could think of the volume of the association between generations as dependent upon the number of persons, the intimacy of interactions, and the duration of association in relation to total life span of the individuals concerned. Certain items of information pertaining to the composition of family and household groups imply a decreased volume of contact between children and parents. The facts given in Table 8 are highly significant. We note that only 57.0 per cent of the families included one or more children.

The more general picture of declining association between generations is revealed by Glick in his comparison of the family life cycle in

Table 8

Type of family and presence of own children under 18 years,
March 1960.

Type	Families		
	Number		Per cent
Total Families 45,062,000			100.0
Husband-wife familles 39,335,000			87.3
One or more own children	23,333,000		51.8
No own children under 18	16,002,000		35.5
Other Families 5,727,000			12.7
One or more children under 18	2,329,000		5.2
Other children (no own children under 18)	3,398,000		7.5

Source: U. S. Bureau of the Census, "Household and Family Characteristics: March,"
Current Population Reports, Series P-20, No. 106 (January 2, 1961) p. 14 (adapted).

1890 with that in 1940 and in 1950. The difference in generation
association between these periods is due to earlier marriages, fewer
children, and longer life of adults in later periods. His analysis is
summarized in Table 9.

There does seem a convergence of evidence that the degree of
association between generations is now surprisingly small. Notably

Table 9

Median age of husband and wife at each stage of the family cycle,
1950, 1940 and 1890.

Stage of the Family Cycle	Median Age of Husband			Median Age of Wife		
	1950	1940	1890	1950	1940	1890
First marriage	22.8	24.3	26.1	20.1	21.6	22.0
Birth of first child	—	25.3	27.1	—	22.6	23.0
Birth of last child	28.8	29.9	36.0	26.1	27.2	31.9
Marriage of first child	—	48.3	51.1	—	45.6	47.0
Marriage of last child	55.3	52.8	59.4	47.6	50.1	55.3
Death of husband or wife	64.1	63.6	57.4	61.4	60.9	53.3
Death of husband, if last	71.6	69.7	66.4	—	—	—
Death of wife, if last	—	—	—	77.2	73.5	67.7

Sources: Paul C. Glick, "The Family Cycle," *American Sociological Review,* XII (1947),
165. For criticism, see Theodore Caplow, "A Note on Glick's Family Cycle," *American
Sociological Review,* XIV (1949), 150-52. Paul C. Glick, "The Life Cycle of the Family,"
Marriage and Family Living, XVII (1955), 4.

significant is the considerable period of the life span remaining, especially to women, after the marriage of children. The implication is that women decreasingly can claim justification for themselves on the ground of an assumed lifelong reproductive and child-rearing function. To some extent, as we have seen, justification for existence has been rewon by employment outside the home.

The degree of association between siblings is likewise reduced by the present smaller size of family. Brothers and sisters also spend a smaller proportion of their lives in contact with each other, partly because of a longer life expectation.

The Home. The home as the situation in which the familial group functions has felt the impact of the scientific revolution. Mention will be made of the educational function, the religous function, the recreational function, the security function, devaluation of homemaking, a possible reversal of trends, and stress on family companionship.

Formal educational relationships in the home between the parents and their children have declined, although basic habits of language, manners, and morals are still transmitted. The length of educational experience is certainly prolonged by formal education outside the home in school and college. The day is long past in which the full vocational training of the son was the duty of the father.

Religious activities are less characteristic of the home than formerly. It is a far cry from the hurried, movie-going family of the present day to the patriarchal family of the Romans in which the father performed a priestly function. There is every reason to think that Bible reading and family prayers now provide less basis for family unity in the home. Modern transportation makes church and Sunday School more readily available to take over the religious function.

A declining recreational function has been stressed. The automobile, the night club, the theater, the movies, and the general expansion of commercial recreational facilities have, it is claimed, drained recreational activity out of the home. The influence of technology, however, may not operate in a single direction.

The decline of the security function is symbolized by the absence of a rifle over the fireplace and the presence of a social security card in the pockets of family members. The state rather than a father must defend a home from atomic attack. Social workers rather than relatives offer help in time of trouble.

The home as an area for womanly work commanding sentimental respect has increasingly been devalued. The modern woman is likely to refer to herself in self-deprecation as a mere housewife. She is less likely than her grandmother to take pride in housekeeping as a means to status. The pecuniary valuation of things in the modern world means a lack of prestige for woman's activity as a homemaker. She contributes thousands of dollars in service to the home, but since she receives no pay check, the value of these innumerable services can readily be underestimated.

Countertrends may partially reverse the weakening effect of technology and of substitute agencies on family functions. It has been customary in writings concerned with the family to analyze the influence of technology as progressively removing functions from the home. The can opener rather than the spinning wheel is alleged to be the domestic symbol. Technology, however, can reverse its previous influence upon economic, reproductive, child-rearing, educational, religious, recreational and protective functions. Since power can be transmitted by electricity rather than by belts, gears, or chains, some restoration of the family economic function is taking place. The "do-it-yourself" activity is often familial activity. The automatic washing machine is counteracting the trend toward commercial laundries. Modern heating units such as stokers, oil burners, and gas furnaces clear the basement for small workshops. Modern devices give stimulus to home canning and freezing. The electric sewing machine makes sewing and mending easier and the new kitchen ranges and automatic dishwashers reduce the demand for eating in restaurants. Religious influences can operate in the home through the radio and television. Cheap printing and other media of communication can facilitate the educational process in the home. The same can be said of the so-called recreational function. Increasingly there are possibilities of unified recreational activities of family members with the aid of modern devices. The most conspicuous recent example, of course, is television. Technology takes from the home, but it can likewise restore.

Impersonality of contacts outside the family tends to stimulate a yearning for warm companionship within the family circle. There is a qualitative aspect to the home atmosphere which is not fully considered in statistics concerning increased use of canned goods, bakery products, and ready-made clothes. When all factors are taken into account, the home has by no means completely lost its attraction or its capacity for yielding intense human satisfactions. Intensity of interpersonal relations within the home may compensate for loss of functions and for casual association in the external world.

Social Consequences for the Family Institution. The family institution is part of a larger social structure involving other institutions which regulate varied aspects of social life. When certain components of the social pattern are modified, they produce effects upon the more static aspects of the social structure. The family institution was once rigidly interwoven into an institutional framework, but now various institutions are changing, with a resulting lapse of institutional support. We shall consider lapse of institutional support and mode of decline of institutional support. Lapse of institutional support involves economic institutions, law, morality, government, education, and, very definitely, religion.

Social agreements concerning property have changed. Formerly, the transmission of property was an important function of the family. Now the family is less integrated by the bond of common interest in tangible property. Personal gain now replaces collective pride in possessions accumulated by generations. A family member is less motivated to support the traditional family institution when property symbolism, property accumulation, and property transmission have acquired new nonfamilial meanings.

Law is another institution which has reinforced and upheld the family institution. It is true that we still have a law of domestic relations, but it differs from state to state, court interpretations vary, and it is not always enforced. There is no clear-cut legal definition of family duties and obligations.

Morality is also an important part of the supporting institutional framework. Family relationships have been rigidly defined in terms of right and wrong. This is less true at the present time. It can almost be said that in the modern world, every man is his own moralist. The blurring of a clear-cut definition of right and wrong is especially notable in the field of sex conduct. Conceptions of morality may vary widely between husband and wife, and between parent and child.

Government is another component of social structure which in the past has lent support to the family institution. The phase "For God, your home and country" implies an integration of loyalties. Civil marriage representing control by the state gave some support to the family institution. Governments, however, vary from country to country, and here in the United States confusion due to fifty state jurisdictions weakens the traditional family structure.

Educational institutions have also been part of the supporting institutional framework. The growing strength of public and secular education now threatens to rob the family institution of its control over child rearing, and often values are imposed at variance with those taught in the family group.

Religion, in the past, has given important support to the family institution, but in many ways its influence has now declined. There is profound significance for the family institution in disunity of religious organizations evidenced by 259 denominations in the United States in 1960[16]. Such differentiation in the religious structure weakens authority in regulation of family life. In general, it may be said that there has been increasing secularization of family life.[17]

It is not sufficient to argue in general terms that the family is subject to a lapse of institutional support, for a weakening influence in the social structure is not simple or direct. The weakening operates in at least three different ways, which should be distinguished.

Weakness and redirection in related institutions would mean one type of decline in institutional support. It is probably true that morality and religion have both weakened, thus reducing their influence on the family institution. The institutions of property and law probably have become redirected rather than weakened, and in that sense fail to provide institutional support for the family.

The appropriation of functions of the family by other expanding institutions is a second mode of decline in institutional support. Government and education have increased in strength and have steadily appropriated traditional functions of the family group. The increasing provision of social security by the government would be a case in point. In regard to education, there is ample evidence that the training of children is increasingly carried on in the school. In 1940 the median years of schooling was 8.7, while in 1959 it had increased to 10.9. In 1940 the proportion of persons over fourteen having completed four years of high school was 15.9 in contrast to 26.4 in 1959.[18]

Finally, as a consequence of the two processes mentioned, there tends to be increased variability of familial behavior. This has a weakening effect, since an institution implies a pattern of expectations in regard to the behavior of others. The culture controlling family life tends to be the common culture of the family group, rather than the common culture of the community. Families therefore differ increasingly one from another with this restriction of a common culture to the familial group. An increase in variable behavior on the part of individuals, which is sometimes called individuation, takes place. There are more different ways of being a family member than there were in an earlier period. Variability engenders variability. Once the great institutional uniformities crumble, the consequent variability in family behavior makes further variation inconspicuous and respectable.

Social Consequences for Marriage. Marriage was defined as a socially sanctioned relationship between men and women potentially enduring beyond the birth of offspring. Various implications of the scientific revolution for marriage can be pointed out as distinct from implications for the familial group, the home, and the family institution.

One of these implications would be relative freedom of the married couple from the control of kindred. At one time, as we have seen, marriages were arranged and controlled by kindred groups. At the present time, the interference from in-laws or relatives is regarded as a violation of human rights.

The intensity of the bond between husband and wife is in some respects increased under modern conditions. Since so many other ties are absent or weakened, greater stress is laid upon love and emotional interaction between members of the marriage group.

The relationship between a modern married couple involves total personality contact. At one time, it was merely one role, say that of wife-and-mother, which was interwoven with one role of the husband — namely, that of father-provider. Now a more inclusive comradeship is expected and often obtained. There is contact not only in regard to the home and children, but likewise in regard to literature, politics, music, philosophy of life, and many other things.

Higher expectations in regard to personal happiness characterize the modern marriage relationship. Perhaps too much emphasis is laid upon "happiness in marriage," for a high aspiration level predisposes to disillusionment.

PATTERN OF FAMILY CHANGE

Changes in family life have been described from various points of view. It may be that family change comes first in certain areas, and that certain components of social structure spearhead the process of change. Certain tentative hypotheses will be ventured.

Hypotheses Concerning Family Change. One plausible hypothesis is that the modifications in family structure tend to come first in urban rather than rural areas. A backward rural area tends to reveal a picture of family life such as existed at an earlier historical period.

Space is lacking in which to marshal all available evidence bearing on the hypothesis. Certainly negative evidence should not be excluded. Sewell found, for example, little influence of the size of the community upon attitudes toward the family as measured by the Sletto-Rundquist scale.[19] It may be that his group of college students was too homogeneous to bring out the expected differential.

The younger generation spearheads family change. This second tentative hypothesis is from the point of view of time rather than space. From this hypothesis one would expect the younger generation to be more modern than their parents in attitudes toward the family.

An interesting study based on a sample of 307 State College of Washington students and their mothers presents questionnaire evidence which bears upon both the space (rural-urban) and the time (generation-comparison) factors. The schedule dealt with attitudes toward divorce and other issues related to the family. The evidence does not, however, consistently support the hypothesis that family change is spearheaded by urban areas and the younger generation. Possibly the urban and younger-generation groups were leading a reversal of opinion on certain issues.[20]

Changes in regard to the family may be spearheaded at the upper levels of the social structure and involve the more intelligent and highly educated people. The early feminists came from the middle or upper classes. There is good evidence that educated groups made use of contraceptives in planning family size before lower-class groups. Emancipation in regard to traditional values is likely to come first among the more educated.

Intellectual changes tend to precede emotional changes. Emancipated young people, while intellectually convinced of the advisability of a break with the established family pattern, may find in themselves a residue of emotionalized attitudes which prevents an easy conscience in the practice of their experiments.

A final hypothesis would be that private behavior, representing a deviation from established patterns, would tend to precede public behavior. It is one thing to violate existing sex taboos in private, and another to flaunt the rebellion publicly. It is probable, for example, that women smoked in private long before they appeared in public with cigarettes hanging from their lips.

These hypotheses are presented merely as challenges to reflection. Only the application of scientific research methods can confirm or refute.

Cultural Inconsistency. It is to be expected that the changes in the family — in its group, institutional, and marital aspects — would bring about cultural inconsistencies. Certainly there are features of family life which have changed less dynamically than others, thus producing the discrepancy termed *culture lag.* If, for example, our preceding hypothesis were correct, the attitudes of parents concerning family life would lag behind the attitudes of offspring. The second type of cultural inconsistency, namely, cultural conflict, would be expected as a result of the juxtaposition of incompatible cultures. The family system of Polish peasants would probably be at variance with the family practice of native-born Americans. Conflicting creeds and philosophies of marriage do meet head on in the present age, sometimes in the same family group. The difference between lag and conflict is one of degree, depending upon the time and space relationships in the juxtaposition of incompatible culture components.

Summary Table of Family Transition. It seems desirable to compile a summary of some of the concepts that have proved useful in charting the trend of family change. In Table 10 contrasts are presented between the family of the past and the family of the future. In other words, the table contrasts the "trend from" with the "trend toward." Family change is partly shifting of choice with respect to alternative goals. In Part II of the table will be found a collection of descriptive labels. These express dichotomous categories with respect to family patterns — those that were, and those now in the process of becoming.

Transition and Decline. Popular writers bewail the present-day degeneration of family life as compared with family life known in the past. There are certainly recurrent problems concerned with family life, to be solved by the cultures of various groups. The fact that some new solution is found, appropriate to changed conditions, does not mean that the family is moving toward a state of decay. It seems more appropriate to regard changed conditions and changed patterns as subject to new and detached evaluations. The decline of authority within the family group may seem to be a loss from the point of view of order, but a gain from the point of view of freedom. The independent behavior of children may seem to be rebellion, but it also signifies the development of individuality and maturity. Family change is often a matter of grasping different horns of old dilemmas.

Amid the cries of protest against change, it should not be forgotten that there are certain universal characteristics of the family institution. Extreme deviations from these universals are unlikely because of biological and sociological resistance. It is conceivable that civilization and mankind may be destroyed by an atomic war; but, while mankind survives, there will continue to be cultural regulation of sex, reproduction, child rearing, and the relationships of sex, age, and kinship groups.

Table 10

Trend chart of family change.

Trend from (past)	Trend toward (future)
Part I: (Dilemma) Goals	
1. Order and efficiency	1. Freedom in family experience
2. Love-reproduction	2. Work achievement
3. Devoted child rearing	3. Personal self-expression
4. Rigid, specific training	4. Flexible, general training
5. Realistic expectations	5. High aspiration level for children
6. Family loyalty	6. Community loyalty
7. Extensive, casual association	7. Restricted, intensive association
8. Love safety	8. Love experience
9. Sex restraint in support of family values	9. Free sex expression
10. Mature, discriminating mate selection	10. Early marriage
Part II: Descriptive Dichotomies	
11. Extended	11. Nuclear
12. Lineage-local	12. Neolocal
13. Unilateral descent	13. Bilateral descent
14. Family property	14. Individual property
15. Consanguineal	15. Conjugal
16. Kindred	16. Marriage
17. Polygamous marriage by purchase	17. Unstable monogamy with marriage by consent
18. Sharp division of labor	18. Blurred division of labor
19. Trustee-domestic	19. Atomistic
20. Authoritarian	20. Democratic
21. Institution	21. Companionship
22. Familism	22. Individualism
23. Rural	23. Urban
24. Sacred	24. Secular
25. Patriarchal	25. Equalitarian
26. Traditional	26. Developmental
27. Institution	27. Primary group
28. Cultural behavior	28. Variable behavior
29. Sex segregation	29. Sex mingling
30. Duty	30. Happiness
31. Marriage a sacrament	31. Marriage a contract
32. Respect	32. Love
33. Dependent	33. Independent
34. Integrated function	34. Declining function
35. Ecclesiastical marriage	35. Civil marriage

REFERENCES

1. Clifford Kirkpatrick, "A Methodological Analysis of Feminism in Relation to Marital Adjustment," *American Sociological Review,* IV (1939), 325-34.
2. U.S. Bureau of the Census, "Mobility of the Population of the United States, March 1960 to March 1961," *Current Population Reports,* Series P-20, No. 118 (August 9, 1962), p.12.
3. Gerald R. Leslie and Arthur H. Richardson, "Life-Cycle Career Pattern and the Decision to Move," *American Sociological Review,* XXVI (1961), 894-902.
4. See Wilbur Schramm, Jack Lyle, and Edwin B. Parker, *Television in the Lives of Our Children* (Stanford: Stanford University Press, 1961).
5. *Science Newsletter,* LV (1949), 387.
6. *Ibid.,* LVI (1949), 419.
7. "Test-Tube Tempest," *Newsweek,* February 6, 1961, p. 78.
8. "Virus Cornered," *Time,* August 3, 1962, p. 30; "Rubbing Out Rubella," *Newsweek,* August 6, 1962, p. 52.
9. "Witches Every Month," *Time,* October 22, 1956, p.71.
10. W. F. Ogburn and M. F. Nimkoff, *Technology and the Changing Family* (Boston: Houghton Mifflin Company, 1945), Chapter 13.
11. *The American Family, a Factual Background Report of Inter-Agency Committee on Background Materials* (National Conference on Family Life, 1948), p. 8; U.S. Bureau of the Census, "Marital Status and Household Characteristics, March: 1950," *Current Population Reports. Population Characteristics,* Series P-20, No. 33 (February 12, 1951), pp. 12-15; U.S. Bureau of the Census, "Household and Family Characteristics: March 1960," *Current Population Reports, Population Characteristics,* Series P-20. No. 106 (January 9, 1961), p. 2. (There is a slight change in definition.)
12. Eugene Litwak. "The Use of Extended Family Groups in the Achievement of Social Goals. Some Policy Implications," *Social Problems,* VII (1959-60), 177-87. Eugene Litwak "Occupational Mobility and Extended Family Cohesion, *American Sociological Review.* XXV (1960), 9-21: Eugene Litwak "Geographic Mobility and Extended Family Cohesion," *American Sociological Review.* XXV (1960), 385-94.
13. Marvin B. Sussman and Lee Burchinal. "Kin Family Network: Unheralded Structure in Current Conceptualizations of Family Functioning," *Marriage and the Family Living.* XXIV (1962), 231-40.
14. Carle Zimmerman and Lucius Cervantes. *Marriage and the Family* (Chicago: Henry Regnery Company, 1956).
15. Paul C. Glick. "The Family Cycle," *American Sociological Review,* XII (1947), 164-74.
16. *The World Almanac 1962* (New York: New York World-Telegram and the Sun, 1962), p. 705.
17. See Carl E. Reuss, "Research Findings on the Effects of Modern-Day Religion on Family Living," *Marriage and Family Living,* XVI (1954), 221-25.

18. U.S. Bureau of the Census, "Educational Attainment of the Civilian Population: April, 1947," *Current Population Reports,* Series P-20, No. 15 (May 4, 1948), pp. 7-11; U.S. Bureau of the Census, "Literacy and Educational Attainment: March 1959," *Current Population Reports,* Series P-20, No. 99 (February 4, 1960), p.13.

19. William H. Sewell and Eleanor E. Amend, "The Influence of Size of Home Community on Attitudes and Personality Traits," *American Sociological Review,* VIII (1943), 180-84.

20. Arlene Sheeley, Paul H. Landis, and Vernon Davies. "Marital and Family Adjustment in Rural and Urban Families of Two Generations." *The State College of Washington Institute of Agricultural Sciences, Agriculture Experiment Stations Bulletin* No. 506 (May, 1949), pp. 1-26.

Is Marriage in Trouble?

MORTON HUNT

Not since the early days of Christianity, when the idealization of celibacy was leading scores of thousands of men and women to remain single or to flee from their mates into the Egyptian desert, has marriage shown so many signs of being in serious trouble as it does today in America. Among those signs:

The divorce rate, climbing steadily ever since 1962, after some years on a plateau, is now almost back to the all-time high of 1946. That high, however, was only a temporary phenomenon — a burst of postwar housecleaning — while today's rate (nearly one divorce for every three marriages) represents a chronic, growing, far more profound condition. Young people think of divorce as a possible, or probable, part of their future, even before marrying. Many of them approach marriage in the spirit, "We'll try it for a while. If it doesn't work . . ."

Infidelity is also on the rise. When Dr. Alfred Kinsey gathered data on it a generation ago, he found about half of all husbands and a quarter of all wives were unfaithful to their mates at some time during their marriages. Today his successors estimate the present percentages to be 60 and 30-35 respectively. More than that, many prominent people, and some who are not, hardly bother nowadays to conceal extramarital activities. Though the general public still condemns such behavior, it does so with less severity than formerly. Less than a generation ago, Ingrid Bergman was forced to leave America when her affair with Roberto Rossellini became known. Today the disclosure of an actress's infidelity does her box-office appeal little, if any, harm.

"Living together" — or common-law marriage, as it used to be called — is becoming more and more common among the young and the middle-class, who formerly wouldn't have dreamed of it or dared it. Couples who live together can now be found on a great many campuses, and although their numbers are still small, what is important is that only a few years ago the practice was isolated, newsworthy and concealed, where today it is widespread, unremarkable and fairly open. The same is true among older adults.

Homosexuals used to hide their tendencies and most lived within the concealment of conventional marriages. Today a rapidly growing number openly admit their preference, demonstrate publicly for fair treatment and remain single or live in homosexual unions.

The Women's Liberation Movement is demanding equal status for women in the world of work, social relationships and within marriage. Some of their spokeswomen have urged that women receive pay for homemaking, or that husbands and wives each work only half a day and each perform homemaking duties half a day on an equal basis. The movement's chief theoretician, Kate Millett, seems to feel that marriage might be replaced by purely voluntary unions.

From all the foregoing, one is justified in wondering whether something is terribly wrong with modern marriage. One may even agree with those alarmists, or extremists, who claim it is on its deathbed and will disappear altogether in a generation or two.

First, what, if anything, is amiss? What is the nature of the disorder? Basically this: We are living in an era of rapid and drastic social change; the basic model of American marriage was designed long ago and was meant to serve purposes other than our present ones and to operate under very different conditions.

Only a century or two ago — and much less in some parts of the country — marriage was, above all, economic and life-supporting in its goals. A man's food and clothing were, in large part, made at home; a woman's only source of support was her husband; and even the children were worth more economically (thanks to the labor they contributed) than it cost to rear them, according to no less an authority than the great economist, Adam Smith.

But factories, freezers and supermarkets have drastically reduced the time and labor spent on cooking and sewing. As for support, four-fifths of all women work before they marry, and 40 percent do so afterwards — and it is perfectly clear to all of them that even if they should prefer to be supported by a man, they don't have to be. This knowledge makes it unnecessary for them to be subservient or docile within marriage; it changes the whole interaction betweeen man and wife.

The situation is somewhat similar with the child-rearing function of marriage. Although parents still have a great deal of influence over their children and can make themselves felt in the schools, the schools nonetheless teach children much of their basic skills and give them much of their knowledge of the outside world. Play groups, camps and other outside agencies have replaced the social atmosphere provided by the large family of old. And instead of being worth a good deal in terms of the labor they used to contribute, children now impose a huge economic burden on their parents. Unquestionably, children give their parents a sense of purpose and completion, but more and more couples are finding sufficient emotional satisfaction in a few, rather than several, children.

Thus, the form of marriage that once was meaningful is no longer so to some. For our great-grandfathers married later than we do and barely outlived the time when their children reached maturity, while we marry younger, live far longer and are only halfway through adult life when our children clear out. Our ancestors hardly had time to become emotionally or sexually bored by marriage. A model of marriage based on lifelong total fidelity worked more or less well when people shared

20 or so years of married life; it is now being applied to marriages that can stretch on for 50 years.

If the loss of the former values in marriage were the whole story, one could confidently write its obituary. But this is not the whole story, for even though marriage has not been modified enough to function smoothly under present circumstances, it has been acquiring new meaning in recent decades and serving, however imperfectly, certain profound needs we cannot seem to satisfy elsewhere today.

The most important of these is the need to feel intimately joined to some other human being. In the past, husbands and wives rarely were intimate friends; men felt closer to their business partners or fellow soldiers, and women to their female relatives. The closeness of husband and wife was more a matter of location than of emotional and intellectual rapport. In our time, however, it is not easy for us to find lasting intimacy outside the home. Our cities are too vast and cellular; our suburbs too fluid and impermanent; our corporations too huge and impersonal. Our lives are planned by computers; our names replaced by numbers; our friends (or we ourselves) are always on the move, and the result is that we are *friendly* with many but *friend* to none. In Professor David Riesman's classic phrase, we are members of a lonely crowd.

To whom, then, can we turn? Who can be friend, confidant, comforter, leisure-time companion, nurse when we are ill, helper in our work, reliable pal and object of our sexual passion? Only one person: our mate. Marriage today is a tiny inner world in which we can make good the shortcomings of the great outer one.

We hear much talk of today's troubled male-female relationships; we hear that men and women do not trust each other, are angry at each other, fear each other. But even if all this is true, they still want and need each other desperately — far more than friends of their own sex. They want and need love; and even today love does not feel authentic and complete to most of them unless it becomes official and legalized as marriage. For whatever emotional security a love affair yields, marriage — for all its present fragility — yields much more.

And, therefore, a remarkable paradox exists: *In the very era when marriage is in grave difficulty and is even said by some to be dying, it is more popular than ever.* There were 2,146,000 marriages in America in 1969 — almost equaling the all-time high of 1946 — and the marriage rate, far from declining, has been climbing ever since 1959. A larger share of adults marry today than they did in the family-oriented days of our great-grandparents, and even the young, for all their sexual freedom and premarital experimenting, are marrying in proportions comparable to those of a generation ago. Those who subsequently divorce haven't turned against marriage as such, but only against the marriages they had, for nearly six out of seven remarry. Even the unfaithful are not hostile to marriage; most of them either try to keep their marriage intact, despite their affairs, or break up their marriages only to contract others, sometimes to their lovers.

Yet if marriage is more desired than ever, it is also more often disappointing and subject to disruption. In the days when economic and practical goals were primary in marriage, a man and woman could remain married all their lives without being particularly close. For us, who marry primarily to find intimate, loving companionship, marriage seems intolerable if it fails to yield just that.

But this is a great deal to ask of it. Throughout most of human history, men and women have depended on a whole network of close relationships to satisfy their many emotional needs. Today we depend on a single relationship to do so. Margaret Mead has suggested that we place a greater burden upon marriage than any people have ever done. Marriage so often fails us today not because it no longer has any value for us, but because what we demand of it is so complex and difficult to achieve.

All this began to be true a couple of generations ago. It is merely — and suddenly — a great deal more true today, when social change has become explosive and the evolution of marriage has not kept pace. Yet only a minute percentage of Americans propose to cast it on the junkheap of history; the great majority are busily tinkering with it, modifying it, redesigning it, rebuilding it, to make it work for them under present conditions.

What look like signs of disintegration are, therefore, actually signs of adaptation and experiments in survival:

Those who divorce and remarry a second time, or even a third or fourth, are adjusting the ethics of monogamy to fit the emotional realities and the long life expectancy of today. Some sociologists even see this as a significant departure from monogamy and jokingly call it "serial polygamy."

Those who are unfaithful, whether in mere brief sexual escapades or in serious love affairs, are making good the shortcomings of their own marriages. This is not to say that their marriages are all unhappy. A half or more of these people, indeed, consider their marriages satisfactory — without being completely satisfying — and view their infidelities as a realistic way to deal with the problem.

Those who live together unwed are trying to reconcile their need for emotional attachment with their desire to remain free or to preserve sexual equality. They think themselves revolutionaries of a sort — especially the young among them — but, in truth, the great majority are living a monogamous, home-based, mutually supportive life — a new variety of informal apprenticeship marriage.

Those women who are demanding full equality within the home and in the job market and fighting for day-care centers and other ways of dealing with home-making and child-rearing are, for the most part, anything but anxious to do without marriage. They want to be married — but under terms and conditions which will permit them to be full and equal citizens of their world.

Thus, the signs of grave disorder in modern marriage are actually a series of alternatives to conventional, old-style monogamy. The big question, then, is: which of these alternatives is the best suited to contemporary men and women and can serve them most successfully? Which will be the choice in the future?

None — or, to put it another way, all. For our society is so divided and polymorphous, so lacking in common purpose or unifying beliefs, that no one form of marriage is currently best for all of us. Every one of the preceding alternatives — and, of course, conventional monogamy itself — is presently best for some people, but not for all the rest, and I expect this will be the case for quite some years. Some, I would think, will remain tied to the classic pattern; some will practice the "serial polygamy" of marriage-divorce-remarriage; about half or more will modify monogamy by infidelities of one sort or another; and some will choose nonlegal trial marriage, at least for a few years; a fair number of men and women will openly live in homosexual unions which may even, some day, win legal status; and all these forms will be compounded by a series of variations in role specialization and in the division of labor, ranging from the old-fashioned allocation of tasks to man and to woman all the way to a virtual identity of the tasks undertaken by each.

Though I cannot, therefore, say which form of marriage is best for contemporary men and women or which will function best in the society of the future, I feel certain that marriage is not going to expire soon unless civilization itself expires or mankind exterminates itself. If some day our society grows more coherent and we find common purposes and values, one of the alternatives now existing — or even one not yet thought of — may become the dominant form. Which one it will be I cannot guess without knowing what shape society will assume; but in almost any shape that seems likely, we will probably continue to need some special connectedness and loving relationship to keep us from being alone in a crowded world.

Commitment, Value Conflict and the Future of the American Family

CHARLES W. HOBART

There are many attempts to characterize the nature of modern society: the affluent society, the other-directed society, the managerial society, the mass society, the expert society, the pluralistic society, the achieving society, the insane society. Most of these characterizations share at least one underlying assumption, that as a society we tread where man has never trod before, that there are qualitative differences between our society and earlier ones which make extrapolation on the basis of earlier societal experience unreliable at best, and often completely invalid.

One consequence is that the continued utility of many features fundamental to earlier societies becomes problematic. Examples include the segregation of sex roles, homogeneity of culture, widespread status ascription. It is both important and difficult to speculate about what further structural modifications may be in the offing. So long as an institution provides functions prerequisite to the survival of any human social system we must think in terms not of the disappearance of the institution but of the evolution of functional alternatives.

It is in this context that the following discussion of the future of the family is set. This paper deals first with the argument that the family as we know it is becoming obsolete, and with some recent changes in social structure which are contributing to this apparent obsolescence. Second there is a discussion of value conflicts and of future societal development given continued pre-eminence of materialistic values. Finally there is consideration of bases for anticipating a value revolution which would facilitate renewed commitment to family relationships.

There is no need to cite the varied evidence which seems to suggest the progressive obsolescence of the family as we know it. Some maintain that the family, no longer an economic necessity, is an inefficient, artificial, arbitrary, outmoded structuring of relationships. Barrington Moore, in his provocative "Thoughts of the Future of the Family" protests such "obsolete and barbaric features" as "the obligation to give affection as a duty to a particular set of persons on account of the accident of birth," "the exploitation of socially sanctioned demands for gratitude, when the existing social situation no longer generates any genuine feeling of warmth."[1] Moore concludes that "one fine day human society may realize that the part-time family, already a prominent part of social landscape, has undergone a qualitative transformation into a system of mechanized and bureaucratized child rearing" since "an institutional environment can be . . . warmer than a family torn by obligations its members resent."[2]

In contradiction to this position, it is the thesis of this paper that though the family is from some value perspectives an outdated structural unit, defined in terms of responsibility and commitment it remains a necessary condition for the development and expression of humanity. Furthermore, if it in fact is such a necessary condition, concern for its effective survival should help to shape the course of the future development of society.

It must be admitted that the family is undergoing changes, both within itself and in relation to the rest of society, which tend significantly to weaken its solidarity. At least four of these changes may be mentioned: 1) loss of functions; 2) increased personal mobility within society; 3) the decline of status ascription and the increase in status achievement; and 4) the ascendency of materialistic values.

1. In regard to loss of family functions, note that not only has the emergence of separate and distinct institutions accomplished the functional depletion of the once omnifunctional family, but active family membership has become optional in our day. Social status placement is primarily based on occupational achievement, rather than family ascription. There are now no imperious deterrents to a solitary family-alienated existence; all necessary services are available commercially. In fact, family responsibilities today distract and detract from single-minded pursuit of highly prized personal success in most occupations — scholarly, commercial, or professional.

Americans *are* getting married with greater frequency than ever before, a reflection, perhaps, of the increasing significance of companionship and emotional security within the family for people today. But if they marry for companionship and security, the high level of divorce rates[3] suggests that Americans seek divorce when they fail to attain these goals.

2. The rate of spatial mobility of Americans today is remarkable: in the last decade one half of all families in the States have moved every five years. Some consequences of this unprecedented movement have been: 1) increase in the number and variety of readjustments which a family must make; 2) radical loss of support of the family by neighborhood, friendship, and kinship primary groups; and 3) weakened discouragement of separation and divorce by these groups. Thus increased mobility may be seen as 1) precipitating more crises and adjustment difficulties within the family, 2) stripping the family of external supports at the very time of heightened stress, and 3) weakening the opposition to traditionally disapproved means of resolving difficulties, such as divorce.

Since mobility involves physical removal from the informal controls exercised by primary groups, Howard S. Becker's conceptualization of commitment becomes relevant to this discussion. Becker conceives of commitment as an act, consciously or unconsciously accomplished, whereby a person involves additional interests of his ("side bets") directly in action he is engaged in, which were originally extraneous to this action. Becker emphasizes that the process is relative to the values or valuables of the person.[4] I am emphasizing its relativity to the importance of the reference groups in whose eyes he stands to gain or lose on his "side bets."

In Becker's terms, then, commitment in marriage was once strengthened by making side bets staking one's reputation on one's trustworthiness, loyalty, fidelity in marriage. These bets were secured by the scrutiny of unchanging reference groups: close neighbors, fellow parishioners, occupational associates. The increasing speed of physical mobility as well as the growth of value confusion and of heterogeneous sub-cultures have tended to sharply depreciate the coin with which side bets to marital commitment were once made. This devaluation further weakens the stability of marriage.

3. Another trend in American society which appears to have a powerful potential for further weakening the family is suggested by the phrase "proliferation of associations," "personality market," "individuation." These suggest a growing contrast with the recent past when most close relationships with people were traditionally defined ascribed relationships with mate and children, with other kin, with neighbors, with fellow parishioners. Today, more and more relationships are achieved. They are "cultivated" in school, at work, in voluntary associations; they are promoted through friends and professional or business contacts.

The significant point is that rather than being ascribed, and thus traditionally defined and delimited, relationships are now more often achieved and thus more idiosyncratic and potentially boundless. Herein lies their threat to the family, for they, like many other aspects of contemporary life, may readily infringe upon family claims, may alienate members from the family. Note that at one time only men, as sole breadwinners of the family, were vulnerable to these possibilities, in work and voluntary association situations. Their colleagues in these situations were other men, thus posing no threat to devotion to the wife at home. But with the spectacular increase in the employment of married as well as unmarried women, both sexes are vulnerable, and increasingly their work and voluntary association relationships *may* endanger the marriage bond. With this bond under greater stress, the decline of the primary group discouragements to divorce becomes increasingly consequential.

The proliferation of achieved, and thus potentially unlimited, relationships for both men and women is by no means exclusively dysfunctional. Restriction of "close" relationships to a small circle of sharply limited ascribed relationships tends to be delimiting as far as growth of the person is concerned. Mead and others have demonstrated that the personality is a social product, and personality growth can occur only in relationships. Hence a small circle of ascribed relationships tends to be stultifying in at least three ways. In the first place, since the limits of an ascribed relationship are traditionally defined in terms of convention and appropriateness, the personality potential in an ascribed relationship is far more limited than in the more open, uncircumscribed achieved relationship. Second, since the circle of ascribed relationships is more homogeneous than the range of possible achieved relationships, the latter may awaken a broader range of latent potentialities within the person. Third, the circle of ascribed relationships may soon be rather thoroughly explored and exhausted, especially given geographical immobility, early in life. By contrast, the opportunities for new achieved relationships may last until death and may be limited only by the activity and involvement of the person. Thus it seems that the increase in proportion of achieved relationships is a necessary condition for actualization of more human potential in society.

I noted above that any achieved relationship, particularly a cross sex one, may jeopardize the marriage bond and perhaps parental responsibilities. Yet, given extensive and rapid spatial and vertical mobility, almost all relationships tend to be shifting sand, lacking in dependability and security, providing no basis on which to build a life. The very impermanence of these manifold relationships heightens the need for *some* relationships which are dependable; which can be, invariably, counted on; which will not be weakened or destroyed by the incessant moving about of people. Such secure relationships can only be found, given the structural peculiarities for our society today, within the family. Actualization of this security within the family depends upon commitment, a commitment symbolized in the phrase "in sickness and in health, for better or for worse, for richer or for poorer, till death do you part."

4. A final source of instability within the family is the value confusion which appears to be one of the hallmarks of our age. The crucial significance of values depends upon the fact that man is a being who must *live* his life since it is not lived for him by imperious drives or instincts, as Fromm says.[5] Man, thus emancipated from the security of nature's control, needs human community to humanize him and to structure his choice between the alternatives which confront him. The basis for choice is a set of values, generated in society, in terms of which choice priorities may be assigned.

One linkage between values and the family lies in the fact that the original unit of human community and the universal humanizing unit of all societies is the family. It is in the family that many of the most important values, bases for choice, are learned. The family not only transmits values; it is predicated on, and in fact symbolizes, some of the distinctively "human" values: tenderness, love, concern, loyalty.

Man's capacity for consistent and responsible action depends on his being able to orient himself and to act on the basis of commitment to values; thus a certain level of value consistency is important. But a prominent feature of American society today is a pervasive value conflict. The family depends upon and symbolizes "inefficient values" of being, knowing, caring, loving, unconditionally committing oneself. These values are incompatible with the urban industrial values of production, achievement, exchange, quantification, efficiency, success. Simultaneous unlimited commitment to people — in love and concern — and to achievement, success, prosperity, is impossible. The resultant tension in a society which pays uncritical lip-service to both sets of values is disruptive and potentially incapacitating. It tends toward resolution in favor of the "inhuman" urban values. Fromm has noted that as a society we tend to *love things,* and *use people,* rather than the reverse. And Whyte has remarked that the "organization men" he interviewed seemed to prefer to sacrifice success in marriage to career success, if forced to choose between them.

This value confusion is, of course, a source of instability within the American family. A family presumes unlimited commitment between family members: "till death do you part" between husband and wife, "all we can do for the kids" on the part of parents toward children. But the priority of these love and concern values is directly challenged by success and achievement values which may imply that status symbols are more important than babies; that what a child *achieves* is more important than what he *is;* that what we *own* is more important than what we *are.* Thus the stage is set for conflict between a success oriented husband and a child-people welfare oriented wife, or for a rather inhuman family which values things over people, and which may raise children who have difficulty living down this experience of worthlessness.

The question may be raised whether what one does versus what one is are polar characteristics, or is not what one does a part of what one is? Purely logically the latter is of course true. But social-psychologically speaking, there are significant differences in the way these two value emphases influence the process and consequences of parent-child interaction. Briefly, parents who emphasize *doing* respond to their children in terms of conditional love, and the child comes to feel that he is unacceptable unless he conforms, and also unless he meets certain "production quotas." By contrast, parents who emphasize *being* respond to their children in terms of unconditional love, and their children come to feel that they are intrinsically acceptable and loveworthy. Successful performance is thus a matter of much more anxious preoccupation for the former than for the latter ideal type of child.

This review of some changes in family and society — loss of functions, increased mobility, increased status achievement, and ascendancy of materialistic values — has pointed out that some of these changes have functional as well as dysfunctional consequences. What are the likely prospects for the future? Which way will the value conflict be resolved? What are the preconditions, the prospects, and the probable consequences of more explicit self-conscious commitment to the family?

Let us look first at some futher consequences of the value predicament in our society today. Consider the emerging character type in America. Torn from family commitments by the demands of urban living — dedication to efficiency, success, etc. — modern man is often alienated from himself and from others.[8] To escape the anxious awareness of his inability to express his humanity and to relate to others through his role as a functionary in a bureaucratic system, he is tempted to identify with the system, becoming, in Mills' terms, a "cheerful robot."[7] In Riesman's terms he is the "other-directed," [8] forever adapting to the demands of the situation, of the people at hand; in Fromm's terms he is the "personality package," an exchangeable commodity to be sold for success.[9]

The ecology of the American city likewise reflects this value pattern and has important consequences for the family. Most cities can be characterized as central places for the merchandizing of goods and credits. They are the center of great webs of communication and transportation through which our economy of exchange functions. The natural areas of the city are determined by land values: the allocation of people and facilities is in accord with who can pay. Thus it is not for the family that the city functions, and it is not in accord with the values foundational to the family that people and facilities are located. Because the city is not a livable habitat for family units, families have fled to the suburbs. Here children can play, but here too, mothers are often stranded, driven to distraction by childish babbling from which there is no escape, and fathers are missing, early and late, commuting.

From an institutional perspective the family is weakening, and again our value confusion is involved. No longer a necessary economic unit, the family continues to provide for the socialization of children and for companionship. Yet even in these two remaining areas the family is losing significance. Children have more and more been turned over to schools, and, in some instances, nursery schools and Sunday schools, for a major portion of their socialization as parents occupy themselves with other activities. More significant than the time turned over to such institutional socialization of children is the responsibility that parents more than willingly relinquish or do not recognize as theirs. There appears to be little concern in America today that the shaping of a human life, a human personality, a future of happiness or hell, which is best accomplished in a primary group, is turned over ever earlier and for longer periods to secondary, impersonal, social, agencies. In these agencies children can only be "handled" and manipulated in groups, rather than cared for as individuals.

Leisure time is used by some to cultivate companionship with wife and children. But for many it appears that what time is spent together is seldom spent primarily in *being* together, but rather in *doing* simultaneously: watching T.V., going someplace, being entertained. Leisure is thus often an escape from the tension of urban life which pulls people in different directions, a distraction from "the great emptiness."[10]

The family persists because people want and need the family. The problem is that, having often lost the family in its meaningful sense as a primary commitment, people want a fantasy; they compulsively seek security. They get disillusionment.[11] Pulled apart by the value conflict of our society they want both personal loving involvement and social efficient achievement, and often they can commit themselves to neither. Thus straddling both ways of life, they can only distract themselves from their predicament.

This admittedly pessimistic overview forces us to confront a further question. What kind of a *future* is in store for our society? Will time tolerate the tension of values, will it tolerate the embarrassing persistence of the family? Some current trends suggest the resolution of the tension in favor of materialistic urban values which place a premium on man, the efficient doer.

To be more explicit, the character type of the future, according to some, will be the true functionary, the "cheerful robot." "Human engineering" seems determined to insuring that man is socialized into this mold, his human anxieties conditioned out. The power structure of the society will be even more centralized than the current structure. The city will rid itself of remaining small shops and other lingering evidences of human sentiment, so that where there is now variety and diversity, there will be functional monotony. With the rapid increase in urban population there is the prospect that the inefficiency of suburban living will be eliminated and people will be housed in compact apartments or even in some collective arrangement.

The family as we know it will be eliminated from this society, Moore has suggested,[12] and Skinner, in *Walden II*,[13] agrees.[14] Children, housed separately, will not endanger the efficiency of adult activity. They will not be left to the haphazard care of their accidental parents but will be socialized by behavioral conditioning experts. Couples will have no use for life-long commitments and will often tend to go their separate ways. Each man for himself by himself will escape into the mass of interchangeable associates. Such is the vision of the future that some foresee.

But it seems undeniable that such a future would, in one sense, mean the end of human society. Human society is not an automatic process as are subhuman spheres of life. There is reason to believe that man, *as we know him,* has to care enough to carry on,[15] and to care enough he has to have a reason; life has to have some meaning. Without at least the illusion, the vision, of human ends that today's contradiction of values yet provides man, what would keep him going? Thus it seems impossible to conceive of the future of man in the above terms. Something more or less than man might emerge to carry on something more or less then human society, but such speculation is best left to science fiction writers.

But while the inhuman potential in current trends is not only sober-ing but frightening, the *human* possibilities are also unparalleled. An alternative future depends upon a value revolution in American soci-ety—not just the emergence of an unambiguous value hierarchy, but a displacement of the now preeminent success, efficiency, productivity, prosperity values by the more human oriented being, knowing, caring, loving values. This revolution is in fact overdue; it is prerequisite to our continued societal survival. It is heralded by Winston White's provoca-tive discussion *Beyond Conformity* which maintains that we are even now undergoing "a shift from emphasis on the development of economic resources to the development of human resources — particularly the capacities of personalities."[16] A society of scarcity must encourage pro-ductivity and efficiency upon pain of greater scarcity, poverty and starvation. But in an affluent society, plagued not by *underproduction* but by *underconsumption,* production-increasing values *are in fact dysfunctional,* aggravating the chronic overproduction problem. In the affluent society, the implementation of "human" values is not only possible as it is not in a society of scarcity, it is also functional in the sense of diverting initiative and energy from the productive sphere, where they threaten to aggravate existing over-production, to other areas where they may serve to free people to be more themselves.

A key to this value change lies in renewed commitment to the family and in thus re-establishing the centrality of the commitment to ineffi-cient, human values which the family relationship symbolizes. There are some who would try to solve the problems of our heterogeneous society in terms of restructuring (Fromm's work communities for ex-ample), of eliminating structurally some of the diversity and complex-ity of our society. But this is the kind of shortsightedness that tries to move forward by moving backward. To look wistfully at the beauty and relative simplicity of the rigidly structured life in a primitive society without at the same time realizing that our human potentialities are greater than would be realized in such a society is the kind of irrespon-sibility that evades the task at hand. This is the most significant point made in *Beyond Conformity.* White sees human personality as emanci-pated from ascriptive ties in contemporary society. Since man is no longer *determined* automatically by family, church, or occupation, grea-ter individuality of personality is possible. In the absence of automatic structural determinants, man is "indeed, forced to be free," to become more individualistic.[17]

It follows from this that the family of the future must not be defined in terms of more structure, but in terms of less explicit structure. It must at once be flexible enough for increasingly individuated people, yet a stable basic unit for human life. The family as a commitment implies freedom in the definition of the marital relationship in order to meet the demands of the particular way of life of the two people involved. For its members, family relationships should be a part of a larger pattern of meaningful, involving relationships. Only thus, indi-vidually defined and not exclusive, can the family tie avoid being a trapping, arbitrarily binding, stultifying commitment for its members. Defined in this way, the family would be a sustaining, liberating, and humanizing influence; it would invest life in modern society with context, continuity, and direction. As a commitment, a limiting choice, an orienting value complex, it would permit a decisive stance in the urban sea of alternatives, not an artificial reduction of the alternatives.

Are there any alternative side bet possibilities in our day to shore up the marriage commitment, which have not suffered the erosion of effectiveness noted earlier in contemporary society? I think that the answer is yes. It is an answer which is not only compatible with, but dependent on, the fact that, since *doing* is inescapably becoming less important in contemporary society than *being*, husbands and wifes are increasingly chosen because of the persons that they *are* rather than what they can *do*. Increasingly mates may be known deeply and loved for what they are. To know and love the person in this way is to feel for and care for the person. Love in this sense, then, involves the inadvertent side bet of deeply feeling with and for caring about this person. A risking of the marriage vows involves immediate apprehension of the pain this causes my mate, as my own pain. My empathy with and ego involvement with my mate guarantees a "side bet penalty" which is likely to be heavier than the attractiveness of what I stand to gain from my breach of commitment.

Here is a basis for a new, deeper commitment to the family, in so far as couple members dare to invest themselves to this extent, in each other. And in this deeper commitment, more of meaning in life would be discovered in the experience of human values; the intrinsic values of being, becoming, knowing and being known, caring and being cared for, in contrast to the values of doing and achieving. And out of this profound experiencing of human values might come the basis for the slow revolution in values which would further facilitate deeper commitment to the family, and in time the reorientation of contemporary society.

The implications of such a changed significance of the family and such a value revolution for future society are many. The character type which could emerge in this kind of family setting would be neither the chameleon-like other-directed nor the rigid, artifically dogmatic inner-directed, to use Riesman's terms. Instead there could emerge the autonomous individual who is able to see and consciously choose between the alternatives; who knows himself and can express himself in decisive, directed action; who retains his sense of identity discovered *beyond* role, in the various roles he must play. Not merely functioning, having sold his soul "true believer" fashion, not living oblivious of alternatives, he could consciously exercise the greatest sense of free-dom and responsibility that man has ever known; he could live Winston White's vision.[18]

With renewed emphasis on *being* rather than on *doing*, the family and the concern with human relationships which it symbolizes could once again be an organizing principle in society. With less emphasis on over-efficiency our society could significantly cut down the length of the working day. Such a work schedule would make possible an enriched home life. While older children were in school both men and women could work, if they chose, and thus perhaps develop specialized interests. The specialization of their work could be balanced by the vocations of homemaking and greater involvement in parenthood for both men and women, and by the opportunity to develop other interests in their leisure time. A shorter work day would mean that children could once again be socialized more within the family primary group. The school could accomplish its distinctive function of transmitting knowledge in half a day, leaving the humanization responsibility to the home. Here the inefficient process of growing up could take place in a context where there is time for each child, and where each child is valued and known as an individual. In the home children need not be collectively handled, regimented and manipulated as they must be at school, but might be better freed to become, to find themselves, to develop their unique potentials.

In addition to assuming the responsibility for socializing children, such a family could provide meaningful and sustaining relationships which are a prerequisite to open, undefended, loving relationships with others. As I noted above, it is inevitable that most relationships in an urban society will be timebound, that the demands of complex and highly mobile living will pull people apart, but the family can offer the element of permanence which other relationships cannot. And thus safeguarded by their family-centered security against being left unbearably alone when the hour of separation came, people could dare to invest themselves in a number of invaluable but often short term relationships whose dissolution would otherwise be unbearable. Increased leisure time would enable individuals to develop these relationships both within and without the family.

The question arises, could people really bear to spend more time with their families than they now do? To this a number of things can be said. In the first place, people presumably would not have the same need that they do today to escape the emptiness of shallow family-togetherness by constantly doing or being with different people. Time spent together could be on a more meaningful level than it can now be. Secondly, time would also be spent in other meaningful, involving relationships with non-family members which would mean that the family would not seem a trap and would not degenerate into a stagnating aggregate of individuals. The family would lose the compulsive exclusive security which makes it dull for those who spend most of their leisure time with their family and dare not do otherwise. Assuming a commitment of family members to each other more profound than any based merely on exclusion or external structure, family members could tolerate an element of genuine insecurity in their relationships which would not have have to be evaded and would keep the relationship from being static and dull.

Finally young people, no longer stranded, disoriented, alienated from parents would not have to escape compulsively, haphazardly into marriage.

There are a few shreds of evidence that the American family may in fact be evolving in the direction advocated in this paper. Hilsdale, in a rather sensitive interviewing study, sought to discover whether subjects entered marriage with an absolute commitment to marriage, or merely a commitment to trial of marriage. He found that 80% entered with an absolute commitment. This commitment was, significantly, associated with an "almost total absence of starry-eyed Hollywood-type 'romantic love.' "[19] Another finding of this study was the preoccupation of his subjects with communication: they felt that their marriage would last "because we can talk to each other, because we can discuss our problems together."[20] Hilsdale terms this faith "magical," but it can also be seen as a reaction to the fact that in an increasingly impersonal society, people cannot talk with each other. In this light it appears as both awareness by people of their need to really communicate with another, and a commitment to safeguard this highly valued and important aspect of the marriage relationship. Moreover, there is evidence that communication is related to marital adjustment.[21]

In this paper I have argued that if an affluent society is to survive, it must undergo a value revolution which will make what we have called human values preeminent over production values. Such a society-wide evaluation would eliminate a major source of the compromised commitment, of the value conflict between and within the family members, and of the inadequate and distorting socialization of children, which exist in the American family today. There seems to be reason for hoping that such a value revolution may come out of the changing pattern of husband-wife relationship. If this should continue such that the family were restructured along the lines suggested by these values, people could find the security and sustenance which they need, but often cannot find, in today's world. The nature of contemporary urban society makes this increasingly necessary for a number of reasons. Earlier alternative bases of family solidarity are disappearing, and thus commitment is an increasingly crucial bond. Increasing, the family is the only security base available to man today. Where a commitment-based family security is dependably available to man, he will have a basis for relating fearlessly to the greater varieties of people available to him in a society organized in terms of achieved statuses, deepening and enriching himself and others in the process.

REFERENCES

1. Barrington Moore, "Thoughts on the Future of the Family," in Maurice R. Stein, Arthur J. Vidich and David M. White, *Identity and Anxiety*, Glencoe, Ill.: The Free Press, 1960, pp. 393-94.

2. *Ibid.*, p. 401.

3. See, for example, U.S. Bureau of the Census, *Statistical Abstract of the United States*, Washington, D.C., 1961, p. 48.

4. Howard S. Becker, "Notes on the Concept of Commitment," *American Journal of Sociology*, 66 (July, 1960), p. 35.

5. Erich Fromm, *The Sane Society*, New York: Holt, Rinehart, and Winston, 1960, p. 24.

6. A few recent titles in the growing literature on alienation in modern man include: *American Journal of Psychoanalysis*, A Symposium on Alienation and the Search for Identity, Vol. 21, no. 2, 1961; Eric and Mary Josephson, *Man Alone, Alienation in Modern Society*, New York: Dell Publishing Co., 1962; Robert Nisbet, *The Quest for Community*, New York: Oxford University Press, 1953; Fritz Pappenheim, *The Alienation of Modern Man*, New York: Monthly Review Press, 1959; Maurice Stein, *The Eclipse of Community*, Princeton: Princeton University Press, 1960; Maurice Stein, Arthur Vidich and David White, Eds., *Identity and Anxiety; Survival of the Person in Mass Society*, Glencoe, Ill.: Free Press, 1960; Allen Wheelis, *The Quest for Identity*, New York: W. W. Norton, 1958.

7. C. Wright Mills, *The Sociological Imagination*, New York: Oxford University Press, 1959, p. 171.

8. David Reisman, Nathan Glazer, Reuel Denny, *The Lonely Crowd*, New York: Doubleday Anchor Books, 1956.

9. Erich Fromm, *The Art of Loving*, New York: Harper and Bros., 1956, p. 3.

10. Robert MacIver, "The Great Emptiness," in Eric Larrabee and Rolf Meyersohn, Eds., *Mass Leisure*, Glencoe, Illinois: The Free Press, 1958, pp. 118-122.

11. Charles W. Hobart, "Disillusionment in Marriage and Romanticism," *Marriage and Family Living*, Vol. 20 (May, 1958), pp. 156-162.

12. Barrington Moore, *op. cit.*

13. B. F. Skinner, *Walden Two*, New York: The Macmillan Co., 1948.

14. But note that the evolution of child handling procedures in the Jewish communal kibbutzim is in the direction of granting parents more access to their children and permitting children to spend more time in their parents' apartments. John Bowlby, *Maternal Care and Mental Health*, Geneva: World Health Organization, 1952, pp. 42-43.

15. William H. R. Rivers, "The Psychological Factor," in W. H. R. Rivers, ed., *Essays on the Depopulation of Melanesia*, Cambridge, England: The University Press, 1922.

16. Winston White, *Beyond Conformity*, New York: The Free Press of Glencoe, Ill., 1961, p. 162.

17. *Ibid.*, p. 164.

18. Winston White, *op. cit.*

19. Paul Hilsdale, "Marriage as Personal Existential Commitment," *Marriage and Family Living,* 24 (May, 1962), p. 142.

20. *Ibid.*, p. 143.

21. Charles W. Hobart and William J. Kausner, "Some Social Interactional Correlates of Marital Role Disagreement and Marital Adjustment," *Marriage and Family Living*, 21 (Aug., 1959), p. 263.

The Family and Cultural Change

BERNHARD J. STERN

From the beginnings of culture there has been an intimate web of interrelationships between the family and other institutions because the persons who make up the family are also participants in the economic, religious, and other social activities of a community. Never has the family lived alone. The family as an isolated institution is as unrealistic as the individual economic man of the classical economists and the abstract ego of the Freudian man.

The exigencies of the struggle for survival from primitive to contemporary societies have required not only that individuals have the additional security which economic and psychological participation in the family life affords, but have demanded as well that several families cooperate in economic activities. Moreover, families have always commingled on ceremonial occasions, whether religious or political, and have combined into larger groups in feuds and warfare. The family members, therefore, bring to the family group the social attitudes, the patterns of behavior and the knowledge of technologies that reside in the larger community. Within the family there is, in varying degrees, not only a merging and funding of joint property but also of attitudes and experiences through the reciprocal intercommunion of family members. The impact of personality upon personality through common residence, and the intimacy between family members rooted in affectional relations give fertile soil for a relatively cohesive family tradition, which is a composite of cultural aspects derived from the larger community. The family in turn, while functioning as an agency for joint economic activity or for joint sharing or products of labor earned outside the home, and for the transmission of property, has served also as the unit through which the larger community inculcates attitudes of authority and of loyalty to traditional ideas and ideals.

One effective method of studying the impact of culture on the family is through an analysis of how cultural change affects the status and role of woman as wife and mother and, consequently, how it affects family form and function. Woman, by her ability to bear and nurture children and by definition in our culture, is the nucleus of family life. Historically, cultural changes, and in particular, economic changes have had decisive effect upon women's place in society and in the family. Women's rights have been inextricably bound up with the broader problem of human rights, and improvements in the status of the masses, through changes in productive relations, have had repercussions on the status of women. When the dominint ideology of an era has been humanitarian and rationalistic and geared to the enlargement of freedom and the release of human potentialities, woman's status has advanced, if not always formally through legislation, none the less in practice. On the other hand, in periods of cultural retrogression, as under fascism, when human rights are curtailed, the earlier institutionalized restrictions which sanctioned and enforced the subordinate status of women are revived and intensified.[1] The relative freedom accorded woman in economic and political life and in other forms of social activities has immediate and decisive influence on intrafamilial relationships, on the husband-wife roles, and on parent-child authority. I shall illustrate this for modern times in brief historical perspective.

In western society, the patriarchal social organization prevailed for centuries. Although there had been permutations in degrees of dominance, women unquestionably had been subordinate to men within the family throughout the ancient[2] and medieval[3] world. When in early modern times the bourgeoisie began to develop its attitudes, the subjection of women was accepted by both the Church and aristocracy. The exalted formalism and passionate eroticism of romantic chivalry were merely veneer that did not interfere with the application of corporal punishment to wives as permitted by canon law. It was a manifestation of woman's changing relations when, beginning with the thirteenth century, the bourgeoisie began to exhibit in some respects more regard for the personality of the woman than did either the aristocracy or the Church. The wives of the bourgeoisie had entered into trade, both independently and as shopmanagers and assistants, and also the wives of artisans were admitted to some guilds on an equal footing with men. As a result, borough regulations permitted them to go to law and provided that their husbands were not to be held responsible for their debts. The middle class and artisan husband was, moreover, dependent upon his wife's assistance in these days of family and domestic industry. Neither husband nor wife could prosper without each other's help and it was to his interest that she be trained in some skill which would make her economically proficient. Traditional attitudes were tenacious but by the sixteenth century the cloistered life of woman of feudal days had begun to disappear.

These changes in outlook towards women cannot be ascribed to the Reformation, although it liberalized the canonical view of divorce. Luther still regarded marriage as "a physic against incontinence" and declared that women "should remain at home, sit still, keep house, and bear and bring up children."[4]

That women's prestige had not been greatly heightened among the clergy in England, is illustrated by Bishop Aylmer's characterization of them in a sermon before Queen Elizabeth:

> Woman are of two sorts; some of them are wiser, better learned, discreeter, and more constant than a number of men; but another and a worse sort of them, and the most part, are fond, foolish,

wanton flibbergibs, tattlers, triflers, wavering, witless, without counsel, feeble, careless, rash, proud, dainty, nice, tale-bearers, eavesdroppers, rumor-raisers, evil-tongued, worse-minded, and in every wise doltified with the dregs of the devil's dunghill.[5]

The improved position of women in the family that came with the rise of the middle class resulted in a large part from the desire of the thrifty citizen to make his life a success according to mercantile ideals. As Wright declares of the citizen:

> Like all true believers in the divine right of property, he was aware of the positive service rendered by so important a functional unit as the home to the organization of that society which made his goods safe and gave his accumulated possessions continuity. Hence, he was seriously concerned to maintain a code fostering ideals useful in the efficient conduct of the household, so that the home might make the greatest possible contribution to the happiness of its component parts, without friction and waste, either material or emotional. In this middle class code of domestic relations, the husband was recognized as the primary earner of wealth while upon the wife devolved the duty of the thrifty utilization of the income for the comfort of her household. Therefore the wife became, acknowledged or unacknowledged, the factor determining the success of the individual home. If the wife were a railing shrew, a slattern, an extravagant, gossipy, or faithless creature, the domestic efficiency and happiness so earnestly desired by every worthy husband would be jeopardized."[6]

The Elizabethan tradesman considered it his duty to be well informed on the domestic relations that might lead to the stability of the home. There arose a vast literature of handbooks and printed guides which gave advice to the middle class on family happiness and crystallized attitudes independent of the tradition of the aristocracy.[7] In these manuals, a gradual improvement in women's position is discernible. They repeatedly insist that the woman must be treated as the lieutenant of her husband, sharing his confidence and trust, and not as his chattel slave. The husband retained his powers of discipline and his authority, but there was an increased emphasis on woman's rights. Family industry and domestic economy, however, by its very nature offered a limited horizon to women and perpetuated men's dominance in all essential respects.

With the introduction in England of industrial capitalism which broke away from the family system and dealt directly with individuals, husbands were freed to some extent from whatever economic dependence they had had on their wives. The ideal of the subjection of women to their husbands could be put into practice without the husband fearing the consequent danger of his wife's inefficiency. Women no longer were given specialized training with the result that one of the first fruits of capitalist individualism was their exclusion from the journeymen's associations. Excluded from the skilled trades, the wives of the men who became capitalists withdrew from productive activity and became economically dependent and to a large degree parasitic. The wives of journeymen either were obliged to confine themselves to domestic work, or to enter the labor market as individuals in competition with their male relations. The competition which had previously existed only between families in which labor and capital had been united within the family group, was now introduced into the capitalist labor market where men and women struggled with each other to secure work and wages. Capitalist organizaton tended to deprive women of opportunities for sharing in the more profitable forms of production and confined them as wage workers to the trades where they were obliged to accept lower wages than men and thus to depress labor standards.[8]

As a reflection of the development of capitalist economic life, the political theories of the seventeenth century regarded the state as an organization of individual men only, or of groups of men, not as a commonwealth of families. Consequently, educational, scientific, economic, and political associations formed for public purposes did not include women as members, which underscored their postulated inferiority and made their functioning in the larger community difficult.

It is erroneous to overestimate the rapidity with which domestic industry and the family life which centered around it disintegrated. As late as the mid-eighteenth century, the population of England remained mainly rural and women continued to be engaged in productive work in their homes and in some form of domestic industry, but from that time forward, agrarian and industrial changes deprived them of their employment. There was great distress and unemployment among women as well as men at the turn of the century. The laborer's wage remained below the level of family subsistence, and women and children were urgently obliged to work to supplement the father's income. In rural areas, a new class of women day laborers developed in agriculture, and the infamous Gang System for the exploitation of women and children developed. As urbanization was accelerated concomitant with the introduction of power-driven machinery of the industrial revolution, women came to the cities in increasing number to sell their labor power as factory workers.[9] The conditions under which they were obliged to work aroused the shocked indignation of the Victorian writers who became nostalgic for a return to the feudal family.[10] It is to the credit of Marx and Engels that they anticipated the advances in family life that these technological changes implied, identifying the distress occasioned by factory employment to the exploitative nature of capitalism rather than to the use of machines.[11]

Development of the family in the United States paralleled in many respects that of the Old World. With the culture of colonial New England dominated by the Puritan clergy, the patriarchal regime of

Biblical tradition prevailed. Woman's status is clearly defined by a seventeenth century document:

> The dutie of the husband is to travel abroad to seeke living: and the wives dutie is to keepe the house. The dutie of the husband is to get money and provision; and the wives, not vainly to spend it. The dutie of the husband is to deale with many men: and of the wives, to talk with few. The dutie of the husband is, to be enter-medling: and of the wife, to be solitarie and withdrawne. The dutie of the man is, to be skilfull in talke: and of the wife, to boast of silence. The dutie of the husband is, to be a giver: and of the wife, to be a saver . . . Now where the husband and wife perfor-meth the duties in their house we may call it College of Qyietness: the house wherein they are neglected we may term it a hell.[12]

According to Calhoun, for nearly 150 years after the landing of the Pilgrims there were practically no women wage earners in New England outside of domestic service. Later, however, theory and practice did not always coincide, for some women of the poor classes went outside of the home to work and others of the middle class engaged in independent enterprise. An analysis of advertisements from 1720 to 1800 reveals that women were teachers, embroiderers, jellymakers, cooks, wax workers, japanners, mantua makers, and dealers in crockery, musical instruments, hardware, farm products, groceries, drugs, wines and spirits. Hawthorne noted one colonial woman who ran a blacksmith shop, and Peter Faneuil's account books show deals with many Boston tradeswomen.[13] Mrs. Spruill has recently shown that the same situation prevailed in the southern colonies where women's function was likewise conceived as being limited to that of childbearing and serving as housekeeper.[14]

Whatever distinctive characteristics the American family assumed were derived from the fact that the frontier areas of the United States were settled by individual families rather than by groups as in the agricultural villages of Europe. Their relative isolation tended to develop, therefore, a pronounced functional ingrown economic and affectional pattern. In the United States, moreover, diverse family forms were constantly being brought to these shores by different immigrant groups. These persisted as long as ethnic communities retained their strength but gave way, as their communities gave way, to the standardizing effects of industrial society. The adaptation of the second and third generation immigrants to the dominant family pattern repeatedly developed frictions in intrafamily relations based on divergent outlooks between parents and children. The clash of national family traditions merely intensified the conflicts that arose in native families from the fact of the existence of alternative patterns of behavior in a complex society undergoing rapid economic and political transitions.

The ferment created by the discussion of human rights that accompanied the American revolution penetrated into the home. Abigail

Adams asked her husband that he see to it that the new government should not "put such unlimited powers into the hands of the Husbands." In John Adams' jesting response there was recognition of the fact that the problem of woman's rights was but a part of the larger problem of minority rights. He expressed surprise that the British ministry, after stirring up "Tories, land-jobbers, trimmers, bigots, Canadians, Indians, negroes, Hanoverians, Hessians, Russians, Irish, Roman Catholics, Scotch renegadoes," had also stimulated women to demand new privileges.[15] It is significant that the organized woman's rights movement in the 1840's was associated with the antislavery movement, which was women's recognition of the fact that their own inferior status has sociological implications comparable to the oppression of the Negro people. The campaign for the removal of woman's disabilities in the home as well as in the state became a part of a broader program for the extension of democratic rights.

As in Europe, it was the factory system that accelerated changes in the functions of the family by bringing women from the household into the larger industrial world, for the majority of the employees of early American factories were women. The basis was thus laid for a changed status of women in the family derived from the fact that she contributed to the family income, and in some instances was the major source of family support. While the process tended to disintegrate the patriarchal family which yielded slowly but surely to industrial trends, the shifting of production from the home to the factory formed the basis of a new type of family.

As technological changes have proceeded apace, there has been no turning back to the preindustrial family here or abroad. The accompaniments of industrialism have made this impossible. Concentration of production has led to the increase of urban communities which have permitted wider social contacts for men and women, offering greater variety of possibilities for the manifestations of an individual's potentialities. Centralization of wealth in cities has increased educational opportunities, decreased illiteracy, and provided recreational opportunities outside of the home. Modernization of housing and the mechanization of the home have tended to lighten the drudgeries which thwart and frustrate the housewife.[16] Advances in public health and sanitation and the control of epidemic diseases have to some degree lessened the anxieties of family life.[17]

There is no intention here to suggest that advances have been uniformly distributed over the entire population. Divergences are so pronounced that to discuss adequately the nature of the family, it is imperative to differentiate between the forms and functions of the family as they are found in different social classes, and not merely to limit oneself, as has often been done, to the middle class. The family situation is markedly different among the 65 percent of the families in the United States whose annual incomes were less than $1,500 in 1935 from what it is among the 32 percent between $1,500 and $5,000 and the 3 percent above $5,000.[18] The findings of the President's Committee on Farm Tenancy,[19] of the National Emergency Committee on Conditions in the South,[20] of recent housing surveys,[21] and of the National Health Survey,[22] should dissipate the complacent assumptions that modern science as utilized by capitalism has improved the living standards and lightened the burdens of the household so that the American family of the masses can feel secure. Family insecurity, never eliminated from the American scene, was even further intensified by the social changes concomitant with the recent economic crisis.[23]

Recent economic developments have not checked the increase in women's participation in industrial life. Contrary to the judgment of sociologists such as A. J. Todd, who predicted that reduced wage levels and a surplus labor force would check the economic tendency of women to enter industry,[24] the number of women workers has increased considerably since the crisis. The unemployment census revealed that between 1930 and 1937, 2,740,000 additional women workers had entered the country's labor market.[25] Women are not merely entering industry in larger numbers than ever before, but more of them are remaining in industry permanently.[26] There is, as a result, an unprecedented approach of equality between the sexes and a less coercive discipline of the children. The participation of women in industry has, however, not resulted in actual equality for women in the United States because women have been at a disadvantage in their bargaining power with men and they have had the double burden of home and work. Traditionally, women have been paid less for their labor and have been obliged to combat historically derived attitudes that they are less capable than men of developing skills and attaining man's level of productivity. There have been many impediments to women's social equality both in law and in practice, and social services and legislation have been insufficient to cushion the effects upon the family of women's entrance into industry.

The reinterpretations of family roles which recent social changes have produced may perhaps best be illustrated by comparing Levy and Munroe's *The Happy Family* and *A Plan for Marriage* edited by Folsom, both contemporary guides to successful marriage for the middle classes of today, with their Elizabethan counterparts discussed earlier in this paper. There have been marked realignments of authority between the sexes to the advantages of wives, and a pronounced less doleful stress on the duties of parents and children. Reciprocal responsibilities receive important attention, but the family is conceived as existing for the welfare of its members rather than they for the family. The family is not sacrificed to a strident individualism, but its very important function is as a training ground for personalities capable of adjustment to society. It soon becomes apparent that in the redefined family few of its earlier functions have been completely relinquished. The modern urban family is clearly no longer a productive unit, but that it has an economic function as a property sharing agency has been decisively underscored by the manner with which family members assumed mutual responsibilities during the last crisis even when not obliged to do so by law.[27] Although a child's formal education is as a rule acquired through public schools, the participation of the family in the educational process in conjunction with the school is decisive in the formation of personality and in the building of social attitudes. Recreational activities outside of the home have supplemented rather than replaced family gatherings, especially since the radio has brought the world into the home. The emphasis on the individuality and personality of the constituent members of the family has enhanced rather than minimized the difficult family function of giving emotional security and a sense of adequacy, through reciprocal affection, in order that the maturing child will be able to cope with the impact of a competitive society with its inevitable insecurities.[28]

For all of its limitations, this form of the modern family which few families as yet share, has undeniably superior values as compared to earlier forms. To the degree that it prevails, it has been made possible by the improvement in living standards and by the advances in the status of women. Its survival and extension is contingent upon these conditions, and whatever social and political conditions affect them affect the family.

The modern family is reinforced by developments in the Soviet Union, where industrialism and urbanism and the mechanization of collectivized rural areas are now involving women in all phases of economic, social, political, and cultural life. Women's equality is implemented by its legalization in the Soviet constitution and facilitated by a vast network of state social services that relieve tensions and anxieties that have been the traditional lot of the working woman. Through these services, the difficult problem is solved of how women can enter industry on a par with men, and at the same time be the nucleus of satisfying family life. With economic security and improved living and working standards assured in an expanding collectivist economy, the basic cause of marital unhappiness is removed. The family is thus more firmly established, with its cohesive force resting primarily on the affectional relations between parents as equals and parental authority over children derived not by force but by responsible guidance. These advances in the status of women, associated as they have always been historically with the extension of rights to other submerged groups such as national minorities, are penetrating remote areas, although they involve drastic shifts in older institutionalized values.[29]

The threat of retrogression in family comes from fascist countries, where monopoly capitalism in crisis has abolished democratic forms. There has been an outspoken and organized effort to subordinate women once more to an inferior status and to confine them to childbearing and domestic work under the indisputable authority of the male members of the family. In spite of its announced plan, it has not been able to eliminate women from industry, for in a highly industrialized country like Germany, women are required in economic life, but the fascist program has worked to their detriment. Employment of women in civil service, in the professions, and in skilled trades is barred. Men have displaced women at their lower wages with the result that the entire wage structure is depressed and insecurity is intensified. The patriarchal family is glorified, and family life, dominated by the husband and father, reinstitutes those qualities of coercion the elimination of which had been the achievement of centuries of progressive thinking. The regressive developments in women's role in the family and society are but a part of a larger picture which includes as well the denial of rights to minority peoples.[30]

At the present juncture of human history, sociologists and others interested in the preservation of the family, must therefore determine which form of family they wish to preserve. There are those in the United States who are finding hitherto unsuspected and eminently suspicious values in the families of the Ozark and Appalachian mountaineers. Minimizing the pathology of such isolated rural families, well portrayed in Cadwell's *Tobacco Road* and for New England in O'Neill's *Desire Under the Elms*, these sociologists hanker after the stability of the mountaineer families as contrasted with the more loosely knit modern family.[31] There are, moreover, powerful forces in the United States which would eliminate from our culture those democratic rights that give sustenance to the modern family, and in particular, resent the rights which women have acquired. Civilized family living is in the balance. Its future rests with the preservation and extension of democracy.

REFERENCES

1. I have documented this thesis more fully and from a different angle in "Women, Position of, in Historical Societies," *Encyc. Soc. Sci.,* 15: 422-450, and in my book, *The Family: Past and Present,* New York, 1938.

2. L.T. Hobhouse, *Morals in Evolution,* chap. 5, New York, 1916; F. Warre Cornish, "The Position of Women," in Leonard Whibley, ed., *A Companion of Greek Studies,* Cambridge, 1905.

3. Eileen Power, "The Position of Women," in C. G. Grump and E. E. Jacobs, eds., *The Legacy of the Middle Ages,* Oxford, 1926; C. G. Coulton, *Medieval Panorama,* 614-628, New York, 1938.

4. Martin Luther, *Table Talk* 298 ff. (1566), trans. by William Hazlitt, London, 1857.

5. Daniel Neal, *The History of the Puritans* 1: 218, London 1843-44.

6. Louis B. Wright, *Middle Class Culture in Elizabethan England,* 201, Chapel Hill, N.C., 1935.

7. Chilton L. Powell, *English Domestic Relations, 1487-1653,* New York, 1917.

8. Alice Clark, *Working Life of Women in the Seventeenth Century,* London, 1919.

9. Ivy Pinchbeck, *Women Workers and the Industrial Revolution, 1750-1850,* London. 1930.

10. Wanda F. Neff, *Victorian Working Women,* New York, 1929.

11. Karl Marx, *Capital,* 527-529, trans. from 4th ed. by Eden and Cedar Paul, New York, 1929; and Frederick Engels, *The Origin of the Family,* 196, Eng. trans., Chicago, 1902.

12. Quoted by Katherine DuPre Lumpkin, *The Family: A Study of Member Roles,* xiv-xv, Chapel Hill, N.C., 1933.

13. A. W. Calhoun, "The Early American Family," *Amer. Acad. Pol. and Soc. Sci.,* March 1932, 155: 7-12, also A. W. Calhoun, *A Social History of the American Family from Colonial Times to the Present,* Vol. I, Cleveland, 1917.

14. J. C. Spruill, *Women's Life and Work in the Southern Colonies,* Chapel Hill, N. C., 1938.

15. Charles Francis Adams, ed., *Familiar Letters of John Adams and his Wife Abigail Adams During the Revolution,* 155, New York, 1876.

16. William F. Ogburn and Clark Tibbitts, *Recent Social Trends in the United States,* vol. I, chap. 8, New York, 1933; William F. Ogburn, "The American Family Today: Its Trends," *The New York Times,* August 27, 1933.

17. M. C. Buer, *Health, Wealth and Population in the Early Days of the Industrial Revolution,* 59-60, London, 1926.

18. National Resources Committee, *Consumers Income in the United States,* 18, Washington, D.C., 1938.

19. National Resources Committee, *Farm Tenancy,* Washington, D.C., 1937.

20. National Emergency Council, *Report on the Economic Conditions of the South,* Washington, D.C. 1938.

21. E. E. Wood, *Slums and Blighted Areas in the United States,* Washington, D.C., 1935; L. W. Post, *The Challenge of Housing,* New York, 1938.

22. U.S. Public Health Service, *The National Health Survey, 1935-36,* "Illness and Medical Care in Relation to Economic Status," Washington, D.C., 1938. See also Interdepartmental Committee to Coordinate Health and Welfare Activities, *The Need for a National Health Program,* Washington, D.C., 1938.

23. Samuel A. Stouffer and Paul F. Lazarsfeld, *Research Memorandum on the Family in the Depression,* Social Science Research Council Bulletin 29, New York, 1938; R. S. Caven and K. H. Ranck, *The Family and the Depression,* Chicago, 1938; E. Franklin Frazier, "Some Effects of the Depression on the Negro in Northern Cities," *Science and Society,* Fall, 1938, 489-499; R. S. and H. M. Lynd, *Middletown in Transition,* chap. 5, New York, 1937.

24. A. J. Todd, "Limits to the Changing American Family Functions," *Essays in Social Economics in Honor of Jessica Blanche Peixotto,* 314, Berkeley, Calif., 1935.

25. Census of Partial Employment, Unemployment and Occupations: 1937, *Final Report,* Washington, D.C., 1938.

26. M. E. Pigeon, "The Employed Woman Homemaker in the United States," U.S. Dept. of Labor, *Women's Bur. Bul. No. 148*, Washington, D.C., 1936.

27. Howard M. Bell, *Youth Tell Their Story*, Washington, D.C., 1938, and citations in Note 23.

28. For an excellent analysis of the difficulties which the family under capitalism has in fulfilling this important function, see Francis H. Bartlett, "The Limitations of Freud," *Science and Society*, Winter, 1939, 87-98.

29. M. Fairchild and Susan Kingsbury, *The Family, Factory and Woman in the Soviet Union*, New York, 1935; M. Fairchild, "The Russian Family Today," *J. Amer. Assn. Univ. Women*, April, 1937, 142-148; S. and B. Webb, *Soviet Communism: A New Civilization?* 2: 812-838, New York, 1938; F. Halle, *Women in the Soviet East*, New York, 1938.

30. Alfred Meusel, "National Socialism and the Family," *The Brit. Sociol. Rev.*, 1936, 182-183, 389-399; Clifford Kirkpatrick, *Nazi Germany: Its Women and Family Life*, New York, 1938. For evidence of the progress of women in Germany prior to the advent of Hitler, see H.W. Puckett, *Germany's Women Go Forward*, New York, 1930.

31. C.C. Zimmerman and M.E. Frampton, *Family and Society*, New York, 1935. These writers get their inspiration from LePlay, whose work receives plaudits as well of Nazi writers on the family. See C. Kirkpatrick, *op. cit.*, 101.

UNIT STUDY GUIDE

A. *Terms to Review*

Commitment	Factory system	Serial polygamy
Culture lag	Family institution	Spatial mobility
Domestic economy	Industrial revolution	Status, ascribed
Extended family	Monogamy	Trial marriage
Nuclear family	Patriarchal family	Value conflict

B. *Questions for Discussion and Study*

1. Discuss the impact of the "biological revolution" on the modern family. Show its significance for changing marital relationships.

2. "The basic model of American marriage was designed long ago and was meant to serve purposes other than our present ones." What are these "other purposes" and "present ones?" How do purposes become defined?

3. Discuss the significance of personal mobility for change in family life and marriage.

4. Identify and discuss some functional and dysfunctional aspects of these changes in family and society (with regard to marriage): loss of family functions, increased status-achievement, and ascendancy of materialistic values.

5. In the light of Stern's article written over three decades ago, discuss the significance of the present-day economic system in the U.S. for family life and marriage. In what ways has history supported or failed to support Stern's major conclusions?

6. A senate subcommittee on the effects of legislation and federal policy was recently established. Find out what action the committee has taken, what its findings were, whether it still exists, etc.

C. *Topics-Ideas for Papers and Projects*

1. Form a debate on this: "The family remains a necessary condition for the development and expression of humanity."

2. Develop a list of specific family issues to accompany each of the five general issues regarding change which were given in the introduction to this unit.

3. Do a content analysis of attitudes toward changes in family life and marriage as revealed in advice columns in your local newspaper during the last three years.

4. Select and interview a sample of clergy in regard to their views on changes in family life over the last decade.

Unit 2

Current Social Movements and Modern Marriage

Challenging the meaning of life . . . is the truest expression of the state of being human . . . – Frankl

The self-actualized man and woman can never be alien to or thwart one another. What they share in common is immensely more important to them than what separates them as male and female. – Lindbeck

Introduction

The purposes of this unit are to examine two social movements which have developed recently in American society and to explore their implications for contemporary marriage. One, which we have already termed "the sexual equality movement," has been variously described as "Women's Liberation," or "The Women's Movement." The other has been rather loosely labeled the "human potentials movement." These, of course, are not the only social movements which have emerged in this society during the twentieth century. They were selected for focus here because they constitute a highly potent source of stress and change in the norms, values, and behavior patterns on which conventional marriage is built. As we shall see in later units dealing with specific problem areas in marriage, many of the difficulties currently experienced by marital partners are increasingly defined in terms of ideals and norms reflecting the ideology of the sexual equality and human potentials movements.

At this point we can ask what the term *social movement* means to the student in social sciences. King, in setting out what he considers the basic distinguishing features of a social movement, notes that the social movement — along with institutions, local events, and various kinds of organizations — is marked by group activity, social relationships, and some sort of objectives. But there are certain features of the social movement which distinguish it from other phenomena. These distinguishing features would include: 1) the kind of goal to which a movement is committed (its prime purpose is *change*), 2) employment of organization as a means of achieving goals, and 3) their geographical scope (transcending the local community). These are distinguishing features of a social movement when it is in a mature stage, and:

> Each of these three features, to be sure, characterizes many associations and agencies, but the convergence of all three is the distinctive mark of social movements.

In summary, then, King understands a social movement to be ". . . a group venture extending beyond a local community or a single event and involving a systematic effort to inaugurate changes in thought, behavior, and social relationships."[1]

Sociologist Clifford Kirkpatrick, who was an eminent student of both the family and collective behavior, formulated a rather precise descriptive statement which summarized features contained in several other conceptualizations of the social movement. Thus, according to Kirkpatrick, a social movement is a wave of emergent behavior directed toward change or defensive maintenance of a social structure; it is characterized by these features:

1. A *situation* defined as unsatisfactory;

2. An *idelology* involving goals, means, justifications, assumptions, and vision;

3. *Selective grouping,* in terms of leadership, organization, interaction, and motivation;

4. *Strategy and tactics* with reference to barriers and counter-movements; and

5. *Progression* through phases and stages, resulting usually in a compromise institutionalization.

Kirkpatrick's formulation also takes into account the social order within which the social movement takes place. We would thus need to consider *carrier groups* in terms of social class, ethnic, and age-sex factors which identify recruits to the movement, and *institutions* (such as political, religious, economic, educational, familial, welfare, etc.) which represent the social movement's targets. The envisioned change in the social order may be examined in terms of both the direction and the orientation of the particular social movement. Thus, direction may be against, toward, or away from existing organization and culture; and the movement may be described in terms of whether it has mainly a value, control, or participation orientation.[2] Each of the movements discussed in this unit could be analyzed meaningfully using the formulation provided by King and Kirkpatrick.

Now that we have examined the term itself, we can turn to the related question of how the sexual equality and human potentials movements precipitate and nurture changes in the nature of marriage. It must be acknowledged that, for the great majority of people in this society, there is no direct connection with the mechanics of these two movements; for most, no membership is held in a movement-related organization, and identification of changed beliefs and aspirations toward marriage and family life is not consciously tied to the ideology emanating from the sexual equality and human potentials movements. However, as the readings in this unit suggest, much of the stress, conflict, and impetus to change in marriage which we have observed in recent years is traceable to the growth among the masses of ideas and aspirations toward interpersonal relations which reflect the influence of these two movements' ideologies.

Change in the social order is fueled by the emergence of new ideas and proposed alternatives to existing structures. But what is the mechanism by which these factors induce change in patterned social relations? Our earlier reading on the impact of scientific technology suggests an answer. Specifically, the dramatic growth of mass media holds the answer. Mass media constitute probably the most important vehicle of new ideas and concepts regarding marriage. We can list below what seem to be major functions of the mass media as they re late specifically to family life and marriage.[3]

1. *Linkage function.* This is the process by which individual familial groups gain an internal perspective which sees the group as standing in a close relationship to other systems in the environing society. The linkage function operates to heighten social interdependence generally and induces a lessening of the familial group's tendency to maintain its "boundaries," its own sense of uniqueness. Concretely, mass media may provide informational guidelines which pave the way for individual family members to engage in activities which effectively link the group, however circuitously, to the social movement. Some examples: joining a local chapter of a women's movement organization, enrolling in a "self-actualization" course, attending a marriage-enrichment retreat.

2. *Defining-classifying function.* The content of certain mass media, containing various values and tenets of the sexual equality and human potentials movements, may function to identify and label the individual's heretofore rather vague marriage-related difficulties and psychological discomforts. For example, non-specific annoyance at continuously being expected to perform certain household chores because of one's ascribed sexual status may be sharpened by this process into a definition of a problem of coping with sexism.

3. *Behavior-modeling function.* Mass media frequently convey ac-

counts of actual problem-solving and coping behavior engaged in
by individuals and groups seeking to re-organize their lives along
the lines suggested in the value systems of the sexual equality and
human potentials movements. Thus, mass media informs, channels problem-solving motives, and provides models for implementation of the movements' ideologies in individual behavior.

In addition to these, mass media research suggests the likelihood of
certain social-psychological functions. These would include mass
media's potential for reinforcement of attitudes or behavior patterns,
its possible tension-reduction effects through identification processes,
and the provision of a source of authority or reference for individual
behavior.[4]

While much has been made here of the impact of these two social
movements upon contemporary marriage and of the seemingly crucial
role of mass media in their effectiveness, certain cautions should be
mentioned. First, mass media do not typically or universally reflect the
leading edge of change-movements in society; usually they reflect the
societal tendency to maintain the status quo. Secondly, counter-
movements or organizational activity designed to thwart the movements we have been considering may make it very difficult to assess
fairly their impact at this point in history. Thirdly, among the mass
media there is much variation in the extent to which these movements
may be presented in a negative light or in the extent to which they will
receive a fair, balanced coverage. Finally, we might consider the proposition that the problems addressed by the sexual equality and human
potentials movements may have been identified *but not created* by
them. Clearly, the thrust of these two movements has been to catalyze
action toward human problem-solving and problem-prevention processes in aspects of marital experience whose significance have too long
been ignored or whose forms have been taken for granted as "the
natural and right way." With these thoughts in mind, we can turn to the
readings.

REFERENCES

1. King, Wendell C. *Social Movements in the United States* (New York:
Random House, 1956), pp. 25-26.

2. Kirkpatrick, Clifford. Drawn from unpublished notes and lecture materials provided to the author.

3. De Burger, James E. "Mass Media and Marital Problem-
Solving." Unpublished research paper, 1970.

4. Dexter, Lewis A. and David M. White, Eds. *People, Society, and
Mass Communications* (New York: The Free Press, 1964). Melvin L. De
Fleur, *Theories of Mass Communication* (New York: David McKay Co.,
1970). Charles R. Wright, *Mass Communication: A Sociological Perspective*
(New York: Random House, 1959).

Women's Liberation and the Family

SYLVIA CLAVAN

The current efforts to win more equitable status on the part of many women in American society have emerged as a significant movement. Its potential for changing major social institutions, particularly that of the family, should not be underestimated. This paper is a statement on the present nature of the Women's Liberation Movement, the issues involved, and the implications it has for the future.

Transformation of the structure of the family as an institution in American society is underway. Changes in the role of the female, the role of the male, and the relationship between them are both cause and effect of the transformation. The potential for greater change in these areas is contained in the ideology and goals of the Women's Liberation Movement. An editorial from *Women: A Journal of Liberation* (vol. 1, no. 3) states, "Traditionally, women have been most oppressed by the institution of the family . . . To be free, women must understand the source of their oppression and how to control it." Another editorial (vol. 1, no. 2) discussing the limited goals of earlier feminists states, "It is significant that the common phrase which describes the present women's movement is the word 'liberation.' This word implies a deep consciousness of the significance of our struggle: Women are asking for nothing less than the total transformation of the world."

Often it is the atypical or the deviant social phenomenon that points future change. Jessie Bernard (1968, 6) suggests this when she writes:

> "In discussing changes over time, it is important to remind ourselves of the enormous stability of social forms. The modal or typical segments of population show great inertia: they change slowly . . . What does change, and rapidly, is the form the nontypical takes. It is the nontypical which characterizes a given time: that is, the typical, which tends to be stable, has to be distinguished from the characteristic or characterizing, which tends to be fluctuating. When we speak of the 'silent generation' or the 'beat generation' or the 'anti-establishment generation', we are not referring to the typical member of any generation but to those who are not typical."

It is suggested that some of the various actions and ideas of the Women's Liberation Movement might be considered as possible "nontypical behavior anticipating the norm."

The available material on the Women's Liberation Movement mainly consists of articles and journals prepared by women in the movement, a few studies underway, and recent coverage by the mass media including national magazines and local newspapers. The earlier feminist movements are part of history, and source materials pertaining to them are more readily available.[1]

The literature dealing with the family does contain some reference to the relationship between a changing female role and possible changes in the present family structure. In general, these references have to do with the effects of role conflict on modern women in American society. Most often the role conflict is depicted as the outcome of antagonism between female needs and desires and the behavior expected of her. At other times the problem is presented as conflict inherent in the way modern women are socialized. That is, they are formally educated about the same as men, but are expected to assume the more traditional female roles of wife-mother-homemaker upon marrying. These types of references almost always apply to educated, middle-class women. They are mostly found in descriptive studies using general knowledge of role theory rather than in studies testing hypotheses. Dager's discussion (1964, 757-759) of sex-role identification point to factors frequently alluded to in these studies. Other studies of the female role treat the effects of the working wife or mother on the family. One example would be Nye's (1967) discussion of possible changing trends in the family occurring from women's increasing participation in the occupational world. Nye and Hoffman's (1963) *The Employed Mother in America* also looks at these effects. Goode's (1963, 373) *World Revolution and Family Patterns* touches on the possibility of the revolutionary idea of full equality for women, and he states:

> "We believe that it is possible to develop a society in which this would happen, but not without a radical reorganization of the social structure."

In general, the sociological literature does not seem to recognize any incipient and rapid change in the roles of women in American society

---

1. The primary sources of material on the current movement are the many articles written by members of the various organizations and distributed through them. *Women: A Journal of Liberation* is sporadically available in private book stores, particularly those serving university students. The author examined many bibliographies suggested by the movement literature as pertinent to understanding the modern feminist. Simone de Beauvior, *The Second Sex*, New York: Knopf, 1953 (originally 1949) and Betty Friedan, *The Feminine Mystique*, New York: W. W. Norton, 1963, are referred to consistently. Fredrich Engels, *The Origins of Family, Private Property, and the State*, New York: New World, originally 1884, is also mentioned often. For an historical background, Mary Beard, *Women As Force in History*, New York: Macmillian, 1946; Eleanor Flexnor, *A Century of Struggle: The Woman's Rights Movement in the U. S. A.*, Harvard: 1959; and Aileen S. Kraditor, *Ideas of the Woman Suffrage Movement*, 1890-1920, New York: Columbia University, 1965 are helpful. For examples of journalistic coverage, see *The Atlantic*, March, 1970, 18-126; *The Saturday Review*, Februrary 21, 1970, 27-30 and 55; "Sisterhood is Powerful," *New York Times Magazine*, March 15, 1970; and the special report, "Women's Liberation: The War on 'Sexism' ", *Newsweek*, March 23, 1970.

as either an impetus for change or a predictor of change in other social sectors.

THE ISSUES INVOLVED

At the present point of its history, Women's Liberation Movement is an "umbrella name" covering a proliferation of women's groups, some more highly organized than others, but all dedicated to some aspect of improving women's status in this society. The current resurgence of active interest in the status of modern American women is often traced to the publication in 1963 of Betty Friedan's *The Feminine Mystique*. The book examined the post-World War II "back to the home" movement of American women and attacked as a myth the picture of the American woman as a fulfilled and happy housewife. Friedan established the National Organization for Women (NOW) in 1966 as a parlimentary style organization emphasizing improvement for women through legislative change.

Following the appearance of NOW, other feminist groups began to emerge. Among those frequently alluded to are the New York Racial Women, Women's International Terrorist Conspiracy from Hell (WITCH), Redstockings, the Feminists, and Female Liberation. Many of the young women comprising these groups came out of the civil rights and/or peace movements where, ironically, they found that they were treated as inferiors because of their sex.

For purpose of analysis, the Women's Liberation Movement may be conceptualized in two ways. First, it may be viewed as part of an ongoing process that results from industrialization or modernization of a society, of movement toward more equal status for men and women. Thus, in the United States, it may be seen as reactivation of the earlier feminist movement.

Second, the movement may be conceptualized in a more narrowly political sense as emerging out of the revolutionary spirit that characterized the 1960's. This view would hold that oppression of women is but one manifestation of a society that needs complete restructuring. Proponents of this view see female liberation as secondary to the primary focus of social revolution.[2] Although the ideology of the political approach is still nontypical in the American social world, many of its ideas such as experiments with leaderless societies, rejection of traditional roles and institutions, self-determination, communal living, and shared responsibility for child-rearing, are pertinent to American family structure.

The aims of the different feminist groups are varied and often contradictory. The lack of an organized program can be attributed to newness of the movement, to organizational difficulties encountered at the outset of any new program, or probably most important, basic

2. See Roxanne Dunbar, "Female Liberation as the Basis for Social Revolution," article published by the New England Free Press, Boston, Mass., 1969.

divisiveness as to an agreed upon goal or goals. It is possible, however, to pick out several ideas common to most groups. All of the groups see the present conjugal family structure with its traditional division of labor as destructive to full female identity. Much of the focus has been on trying to alleviate the burdens of housework and to get help through free collective child care. The work world it attacked because of its sexual discriminatory practices. The traditional male-female relationship is viewed on a continuum ranging from a point that advocates some changes in sex roles to one that demands complete new definitions. For purposes of discussion, the areas generally considered by women liberationists to be in need of change fall roughly into economic and familial categories. Crossing both of these categories are questions of legal rights. Rights of women under law, however, have been and continue to be gained both worldwide and nationwide. Attempts to implement these rights are part of the feminist struggle.

The Economic Dimension of the Common Goal. Economic discrimination against women takes many forms, some overt and some covert. The argument for broader rights under the law overlaps the economic area, particularly for the single woman. The impetus for redress and amelioration is coming primarily from the highly educated, professional, semiprofessional, or upper-ranked occupational segment of women in the labor force. Their particular situation can best be described as that of second-class citizens in a world of men, if they are permitted to enter that world at all. Although their grievances might appear strange to a female factory worker, they are visible and real and, to some extent, have been documented. (Rossi, 1970; Berman and Stocker, 1970) With an increasing number of women earning college degrees and seeking further professional training, action toward attaining a balance between men and women in the higher reaches of occupations will probably become intensified.

Two structural factors have been important in the increase of interaction of women and the economy, industrialization and the conjugal family unit. Goode (1963, 369; 1964, 110) has noted that with industrialization the family structure of a society tends toward a conjugal system. He suggests that both modern industrialization and the conjugal structure offer women more economic freedom. Some substantiation for this can be based on the figures given in the President's Commission on the Status of Women (1965, 45) to the effect that in 1962 there were 23 million women in the labor force. In 1967, the Federal Bureau of Labor Statistics (Report No. 94) reported that the number of women working was 27 million, and in the June, 1970 issue of the BLS *Employment and Earnings,* that the figure had grown to 30,974,000. Approximately three out of five women workers are married and among married women, one in three is working. While it is possible to infer from this that discrimination and prejudice against women in the world of work have lessened, the reality is that traditional women's jobs are accorded lower status, earnings are lower than those for men in equivalent jobs, many industries use women as an expendable work force, and men are given preference in hiring where qualified women are available, to name but a few common discriminatory practices. The complete disregard of the female as a member of the work force in her own right is underlined when one notes that they are rarely mentioned, if at all, in the literature dealing with work and occupations. When they are considered, it is almost always within the context of the family structure, i.e., characterized as *still* single, the secondary jobholder in an *organized* family, or the major jobholder in a *disorganized* family. Caplow and McGee (1958, 95 and 194) succinctly speak to the point:

> ". . . women tend to be discriminated against in the academic profession, not because they have low prestige but because they are outside the prestige system entirely . . ."

And:

> "Women scholars are not taken seriously and cannot look forward to a normal professional career. This bias is part of the much larger pattern which determines the utilization of women in our economy."

Johnstone (1968, 103), in considering what economic rights are for women, summarizes them as follows:

> ". . . the right of access to vocational, technical, and professional training at all levels; the right of economic life without discrimination and to advancement in work life on the basis of qualifications and merit; the right to equal treatment in employment, including equal pay; and the right to maternity protection."

And Rossi (1970, 99-102), exploring the problems of job discrimination suggests that women:

> ". . . have numerical strength, and a growing number of women's rights organizations to assist them in tackling all levels of discrimination in employment."

She predicts that unless protections are forthcoming, there will be an increased militacy by American women. She suggests further that:

> ". . . it must be recognized that such militant women will win legal, economic, and political rights for the daughters of today's traditionalist Aunt Bettys, just as our grandmothers won the vote that women can exercise today."

The Familial Dimension of the Common Goal. Although strengthening women's economic and legal positions would affect other changes in American society, social acceptance of Women's Liberation goals regarding the family has greater far-reaching implications. The assumptions underlying the President's Commission's Report on the Status of Women and its recommendations for improving women's economic, political, and legal positions presented only five years ago are summarized by Margaret Mead (1965, 183-184) in an epilogue to that report. In part, they assume "that both males and females attain full biological humanity only through marriage and the presence of children in the home . . ." Americans feel that "a life that includes a legal and continuous sex relationship is the only good life." The typical woman is depicted as marrying early, having several children, and living many years after her children are grown. Mead goes on to say:

> "Here it (the Report) makes the following assumptions: all women want to marry; marriage involves having (or at least, rearing) children; children are born (or adopted) early in marriage; the home consists of the nuclear family only; and special attention must be given to women not in the state assumed to be normal — the single, the divorced, and the widowed."

Women's Liberation questions and challenges these traditionally held ideas about the ideal American woman. Not all liberationists favor destruction of the conjugal family system, but most view the expected role structure of the husband as provider and the wife as homemaker and child's nurse as the basis of their oppression. It is possible that the movement heralds a revolutionary change in the American family. The movement's proposals generate many questions and reconceptualizations of existing family organization. Some of these are suggested below:

1. The conjugal family system has often been presented as congenial to the mode of life in modern industrialized societies. However some have suggested that American society has entered a new socio-economic era. For example, a decade ago Galbraith (1958) spoke of the need for less emphasis on production, and the society is frequently referred to as a post-modern society. Within this context, it is possible to speculate that the conjugal unit may be outmoded. If upper strata women can be considered to have reached a post-modern economic level, then the traditional family arrangements may no longer suit their needs. This may partially explain the phonemenon of the protest coming from this socio-economic level.

2. Change has occurred in the American family since the early Colonial period. There has been no serious suggestion, however, that child-rearing be made a public rather than a private responsibility so that women could pursue their own goals. In the past, instances of interest in public child rearing have been closely allied to political and/or economic goals. The most frequently cited examples are the Hebrew kibbutz, the Chinese commune, and the Russian system of state nurseries for children.[3] It may be argued that the change to public responsibility has been going on with the transfer of the educational, religious, and recreational functions from the family to other social

institutions. However, the functions of the family are most often stated to be the socialization of the child and the psychological function of providing emotional support for its members. Seen in this way, extended public child care would seriously weaken the basis for maintenance of a conjugal system.

Seeking an alternative mode of child care as a means of freeing women bears an inherent conflict. The basic premise is that the job is oppressive and demeaning. It is accorded low status and attracting competent men and women to the job might prove difficult. It is possible, however, that what is considered oppressive in private family settings may not be so considered should the task be accorded some professional ranking. Women in the movement are aware that a satisfactory solution to the problem will not be easy.

3. The institutionalized normative expectations of the female in American society today require that she regard her wife-mother-homemaker role as primary. Any employment that she may participate in is considered to be secondary to her basic role. A consequence of these prescribed behaviors is that an increasing number of women, particularly those who have enjoyed a higher education, find marriage and the home a source of discontent and unhappiness. They conform to expectations of them as women, but find that there is no social acceptance of their desire to participate fully in the world of work. The result is guilt on the part of those who pursue careers or unhappiness on the part of those who continue to conform. If, as Women's Liberation proposes, the career role moved to primary position and were socially sanctioned, would those women who find their present traditional roles acceptable become the new disaffected group? Put in another way, would exchange of one set of prescribed and proscribed behaviors liberate one segment of the female population but inhibit another segment?

4. If nothing else, the aims of Women's Liberation necessitate some degree of restructuring of the traditional roles of the male and female and the relationship between them. Jessie Bernard (1968, 14) described this problem area as somewhat like a "zero-sum game". For instance, on a material level when women are given rights such as the right to vote, men lose nothing. But when women are given property or employment rights, men are deprived of what was theirs. The same theory could be applied on a socio-psychological level. The emphasis on changes in the female role tends to hide the necessary corresponding changes in the male role. Bernard states, "For women, the relevant problems have to do with the implications of sexuality for equality; for men, with the implications of equality for sexuality." What is often referred to as the "emasculation of the male" has been given attention

3. For a discussion of the relationship between economic and political factors and public child-rearing, see Jesse R. Pitts, The Structural-Functional Approach, in H. T. Christensen (Ed.), *Handbook of Marriage and the Family,* Chicago: Rand McNally and Co., 1967, 110-111.

from time to time in both the professional literature and in fiction. This, of course, refers to to emasculation within the context of the socio-cultural definition of masculinity. Margaret Mead (1935) suggested that different definitions exist when she detailed different cultural manifestations of sexuality such as the unaggressive males and females of the Arapesh tribe, the "male-like" males and females of the Mundugumor, and the reversal of sex attitudes that were found in the Tchambuli tribe, as compared to American sexual definitions.

The Women's Liberation Movement views men in varying ways. All of the views emphasize the present differences and the drive toward equality. This emphasis tends to obliterate the many attributes that men and women have in common, common needs, feelings, desires, emotions, etc. If society's prescriptions for approved female behavior have inhibited full realization of her potential, then those same prescriptions for the male have affected him similarly. The suggestion is that in a network of inter-dependent role relationships, it is unrealistic to emphasize one role over the other.

WHERE WILL IT LEAD?

As women begin to attain some of the goals toward which their efforts are directed, changes in family structure can be anticipated. The nature of the changes cannot be predicted with any degree of certainty. In general, the movement has emphasized the necessity for change in social expectations of the female without giving much attention to the attendant effects on the family that such change would bring. The exception to this is the stand taken by the most extreme liberationists who hold that the present family structure is not acceptable. If, however, the nuclear family unit is still viewed as functional and desirable, then efforts can be made toward accommodating future changes. While attention is focused on the demands for change in sexual roles, an opportunity exists also for bringing into closed correspondence the needs of both men and women for self-realization and the broader societal need for a healthy viable family form.

The kinds of action needed as steps toward this end open a new area of inquiry for those in the applied family services. It would seem that whatever the course the implementation takes, the underlying directional philosophy should be to permit choice. Oppression appears to exist where there is no choice of acceptable alternatives for the individual. It has already been suggested that freedom to choose a life style within marriage is an important indicator of happiness in that relationship (Orden and Bradburn, 1969; and Janeway, 1970). The freedom to choose alternative patterns of behavior in the other role relationships within the nuclear family unit may well prove to be a source of strength for that unit.

Industrialization, advanced technology, and higher levels of education may spell the end of traditional division of labor by sex. Societal recognition and acceptance of variation in sex role patterns would be living proof of a social revolution fashioned by the Women's Liberation Movement of the 70's.

REFERENCES

Beard, Mary. *Woman As Force in History.* New York: Macmillan, 1946.

Berman, J. and E. Stocker. Women's Lib in the American Psychological Association. *Women: A Journal of Liberation,* 1970, 1, 52-53.

Bernard, Jessie. The Status of Women in Modern Patterns of Culture. *The Annals,* 1968, 375, 3-14.

Caplow, Theodore and R. J. McGee. *The Academic Marketplace.* Garden City, N.Y.: Doubleday and Co. Inc., 1958.

Dager, Edward Z. Socialization and Personality Development in the Child. In H. T. Christensen (Ed.) *Handbook of Marriage and the Family.* Chicago: Rand McNally and Co., 1967.

de Beauvior, Simone. *The Second Sex.* New York: Knopf, 1953 (originally 1949).

Dunbar, Roxanne. Female Liberation as the Basis for Social Revolution. Boston: New England Free Press, 1969.

Engels, Friedrich. *The Origins of Family, Private Property, and the State.* New York: International Publishers, original date 1884.

Flexnor, Eleanor. *A Century of Struggle: The Women's Rights Movement in the U.S.A.* Cambridge: Harvard, 1959.

Friedan, Betty. *The Feminine Mystique.* New York: W. W. Norton, 1963.

Galbraith, John K. *The Affluent Society.* Boston: Houghton Mifflin Co., 1958.

Goode, W. J. *The Family.* Englewood Cliffs, N. J.: Prentice-Hall, Inc., 1964.

Goode, W. J. *World Revolution and Family Patterns.* New York: Free Press, 1963.

Janeway, Elizabeth. Happiness and the Right to Choose. *The Atlantic,* March, 1970, 118-126.

Johnstone, Elizabeth, Women in Economic Life: Rights and Opportunities. *The Annals,* 1968, 375, 102-114.

Komisar, Lucy, The New Feminism. *Saturday Review,* February 21, 1970, 27-30 and 55.

Kraditor, Aileen S. *Ideas of the Woman Suffrage Movement, 1890-1920.* New York: Columbia University, 1965.

Mead, Margaret. *Sex and Temperament in Three Primitive Societies.* New York: William Morrow, and Co., Inc., 1935.

Mead, Margaret and F. Kaplan (Eds.). The Report of the President's Commission on the Status of Women and Other Publications of the Commission. *American Women.* New York: Charles Scribner's Sons, 1965.

Nye, F. Ivan. Values, Family, and a Changing Society. *Journal of Marriage and the Family,* 1967, 29, 241-248.

Nye, F. Ivan and Lois W. Hoffman. *The Employed Mother in America.* Chicago: Rand McNally and Co., 1963.

Orden, S. R. and N. M. Bradburn. Working Wives and Marriage Happiness. *American Journal of Sociology,* 1969, 74, 392-407.

Pitts, Jesse R. The Structural-Functional Approach. In H. T. Christensen (Ed.), *Handbook of Marriage and the Family.* Chicago: Rand McNally and Co., 1967.

Rossi, Alice S. Status of Women in Graduate Departments of Sociology, 1968-1969. *The American Sociologist,* 1970, 5, 1-12.

Rossi, Alice S. Job Discrimination and What Women Can Do About It. *The Atlantic* March, 1970, 225, 99-102.

U.S. Bureau of Labor Statistics. Employment and Earnings, June, 1970.

U.S. Bureau of Labor Statistics. Report Number 94, 1967.

Anon. Sisterhood is Powerful. *New York Times Magazine,* March 15, 1970.

Anon. The War on "Sexism." *Newsweek.* March 23, 1970.

Anon. *Women: A Journal of Liberation,* Winter, 1970, 1; and Spring, 1970, 2.

The New Woman—
Where She is and
Where She's Going

TIME

There is a tide in the affairs of
women,
Which, taken at the flood, leads
—God Knows where.
—Byron, *Don Juan*

By all rights, the American woman today should be the happiest in history. She is healthier than U.S. women have ever been, better educated, more affluent, better dressed, more comfortable, wooed by advertisers, pampered by gadgets. But there is a worm in the apple. She is restless in her familiar familial role, no longer quite content with the homemaker-wife-mother part in which her society has cast her. Round the land, in rap session and kaffee-katsch, in the radical-chic salons of Manhattan and the ladies auxiliaries of Red Oak, Iowa, women are trying to define the New Feminism. The vast majority of American women stop far short of activist roles in the feminist movement, but they are affected by it. Many of them are in search of a new role that is more independent, less restricted to the traditional triangle of *Kinder, Küche, Kirche* (children, kitchen, church).

The most lordly male chauvinist and all but the staunchest advocate of Women's Liberation agree that woman's place is different from man's. But for the increasingly uncomfortable American woman, it is easier to say what that place is not than what it is. Most reject the Barbie-doll stereotypical model of woman as staple-naveled Playmate or smiling airline stewardess. Marilyn Goldstein of the Miami *Herald* caught the feeling well when she wrote about the National Airlines' celebrated "Fly me" advertising campaign: "If God meant men to 'Fly Cheryl,' he would have given her four engines and a baggage compartment."

The New Feminism includes equality with men in the job market and in clubs, though it is not restricted to that. Already, women have invaded countless dens once reserved exclusively for the lion; there are women at McSorley's Old Ale House in New York, women in soapbox derbies and stock car races, women cadets in the Pennsylvania state police. Women have come to protest what seems to them to be the male chauvinism of rock music. An all-female group in Chicago belts out:

Rock is Mick Jagger singing
'Under my thumb, it's all right'
No, Mick Jagger, it's not all right
And it's never gonna be
All right again.

The New Feminism has increasingly influenced young women to stay single, and it has transformed — and sometimes wrecked — marriages by ending once automatic assumptions about woman's place. In the first issue of *Ms.*, New Feminist Gloria Steinem's magazine for the liberated woman, Jane O'Reilly writes of experiencing "a blinding click," a moment of truth that shows men's preemption of a superior role. An O'Reilly example: In New York last fall, my neighbors — named Jones — had a couple named Smith over for dinner. Mr. Smith kept telling his wife to get up and help Mrs. Jones. Click! Click! Two women radicalized at once. The terms Ms. itself, devised as a female honorific that, like Mr., does not reveal marital status, is winning wider acceptance: for example, the Republican National Committee and the federal Equal Employment Opportunity Commission now use it.

American men and women are looking at each other in new ways — and not always liking what they see. Reactions are ambivalent. Men feel threatened; yet sometimes, by marginal amounts, they appear more favorable than women do toward strengthening women's status in society. A Louis Harris poll taken for Virginia Slims cigarettes ("You've come a long way, baby") indicates that men favor women's rights organizations 44% to 39%, whereas women narrowly oppose them (42% to 40%). But unquestionably, consciousness has been raised all around, particularly among the more liberal and better educated. *Psychology Today* got almost 20,000 replies to a questionnaire that sampled men, women not associated with a women's group and women who were. Of the men, 51% agreed that "U.S. society exploits women as much as blacks." Nongroup women agreed by 63%, group women by 78%.

Second-Class. The New Feminism has touched off a debate that darkens the air with flying rolling pins and crockery. Even *Psychology's* relatively liberated readers are not exempt. Male letter writer: "As far as Women's Lib is concerned, I think they are all a bunch of lesbians, and I am a male chauvinist and proud of it." Female: "It's better to let them think they're king of the castle, lean and depend on them, and continue to control and manipulate them as we always have."

Activist Kate Millett's scorching *Sexual Politics* (TIME, Aug. 31, 1970) drew a frenetic reply in Norman Mailer's celebrated *Harper's* article, "The Prisoner of Sex," which excoriated many of Millett's arguments but concluded in grudging capitulation: "Women must have their rights to a life which would allow them to look for a mate. And there would be no free search until they were liberated." Arthur Burns, chairman of the Federal Reserve Board, complained last month: "Now we have women marching in the streets! If only things would quiet down!" Washington Post Co. President Kay Graham left a recent party at the house of an old friend, Columnist Joseph Alsop, because her host insisted upon keeping to the custom of segregating the ladies after dinner. Other social habits are in doubt. A card circulating in one Manhattan singles bar reads: IF YOU'RE GONNA SAY NO, SAY IT NOW BEFORE I SPEND ALL OF MY GODDAM MONEY ON YOU!

Many currents of social change have converged to make the New Feminism an idea whose time has come. Mechanization and automation have made brawn less important in the marketplace. Better education has broadened women's view beyond home and hearth, heightening their awareness of possibilities—and their sense of frustration when those possibilities are not realized. As Toynbee had noted earlier, middle-class women acquired education and a chance at a career at the very time she lost her domestic servants and the unpaid household help of relatives living in the old, large family; she had to become either a "household drudge" or "carry the intolerably heavy load of two simultaneous fulltime jobs."

A declining birth rate and the fact that women are living increasingly longer—and also longer than men—has meant that a smaller part of women's lives is devoted to bearing and rearing children. The Pill has relieved women of anxiety about unwanted pregnancies.

All of this helped ensure a profound impact for Betty Friedan's *The Feminine Mystique,* published in 1963. In it, she argued that women lose their identities by submerging themselves in a world of house, spouse and children. The book came just at the height of the civil rights movement in the South; the pressures to give blacks a full place in society inevitably produced a new preoccupation with other second-class citizens. The Viet Nam War also led to far-reaching questions about traditional American assumptions and institutions, to a new awareness of injustice.

First in Wyoming. The 1960s were not the first time in American history that civil rights and feminism were linked. Early American woman was conventionally seen, and conventionally saw herself, as the frontiersman's help meet in building the new nation—wife and mother of pioneers. It was the Abolitionist movement before the Civil War that helped get American feminism under way. In working against slavery, women emerged as a political force. The 1848 Women's Rights Convention at Seneca Falls, N.Y., was the first of several to demand the vote, equal opportunity in jobs and education and an end to legal discrimination based on sex.

The 14th Amendment in 1868 enfranchised blacks, but not women. In 1913 some 5,000 women, many of them bloomer-clad, marched down Washington's Pennsylvania Avenue carrying placards addressed to Woodrow Wilson: MR. PRESIDENT! HOW LONG MUST WOMEN WAIT FOR LIBERTY? About 200 women were roughed up by unsympathetic bystanders, and 169 were arrested for obstructing traffic in front of the White House. Anger over the shabby treatment of the demonstrators, plus the momentum of state women's suffrage movements—Wyoming in 1890 was the first to enfranchise women—finally got women the vote throughout the U.S. with ratification of the 19th Amendment in 1920.

"The golden psychological moment for women, the moment at which their hopes were highest, was in the 1920s and 1930s, when they won the vote and began to go to college in considerable numbers, with the expectation of entering the professions," says Clare Boothe Luce, politician, diplomat and author. "Women then believed that the battle had been won. They made a brave start, going out and getting jobs." World War II made Rosie the Riveter a figure of folklore, and many women never before in the work force found that they liked the independence gained by working. The postwar reaction was the "togetherness" syndrome of the Eisenhower era, a doomed attempt to confer on suburban motherhood something of the esteem that pioneer women once enjoyed. From the affluent housewife's suicidal despair in J. D. Salinger's "Uncle Wiggly in Connecticut," it was not far to *The Feminine Mystique.*

Oddly, women characters have never had a particularly important place in American literature; as a rule they have had smaller roles than in English, Russian or French fiction. In *Love and Death in the American Novel*, Critic Leslie Fiedler argues that U.S. writers are fascinated by the almost mythological figures of the Fair Maiden and the Dark Lady, but "such complex fullblooded passionate females as those who inhabit French fiction from *La Princesse de Clèves* through the novels of Flaubert and beyond are almost unknown in the works of our novelists." There are memorable figures, of course: Hawthorn's Hester Prynne, John O'Hara's Grace Caldwell Tate and Gloria Wandrous, Fitzgerald's Dasiy Buchanan, Dreiser's Sister Carrie, Steinbeck's Ma Joad, Margaret Mitchell's Scarlett O'Hara, Nabokov's Lolita, Roth's Sophie Portnoy.

Still, Fiedler finds American writers displaying at least covert hostility to women. Probably none has matched in misogynist invective Philip Wylie's diatribe in *Generation of Vipers* (1942): "I give you mom. I give you the destroying mother . . . I give you the woman in pants, and the new religion: she-popery. I give you Pandora. I give you Proserpine, the Queen of Hell. The five-and-ten-cent-store Lilith, the mother of Cain, the black widow who is poisonous and eats her mate, and I designate at the bottom of your program the grand finale of all soap operas: the mother of America's Cinderella." It is a mark of the wondrous sea change of public attitudes that in a scant three decades Wylie's castrating bitch has become, in much popular mythology if not in fact, part of the wretched of the earth.

Twenty Years Older. Just where is American woman today? In a statistical overview, she is nearly 106 million strong, at the median age 30 and with a bit more than a twelfth-grade education. She is likely to be married (61.5%). She makes up more than a third of the national work force, but according to a Department of Labor survey, she generally has a lower-skilled, lower-paying job than a man does. In many jobs she does not get equal pay for equal work. (Her median earnings have actually declined relative to men.) In a recession she is, like blacks, the first to be fired. Because of the instability of marriage and a growing divorce rate, women head more and more households; 20 million people live in households depending solely on women for support.

As Patick Moynihan pointed out in his controversial report on black family life, black women tend to be the center of households more often than white women. Black women, interestingly, are more likely to go to college than black men are. According to Christopher Jencks and David Riesman in *The Academic Revolution*, "Among other things this reflects the fact that at least until recently they have had a better chance than their brothers of getting a professional job once they earned a degree."

Early in 1964, Lyndon Johnson sent out a presidential directive pushing for more women in Government. Only in 1967 did the federal civil services start making full-scale reports on the numbers of women at the upper civil service levels of the U.S. Government. In the top grades, at salary levels beginning at $28,000 a year, 1.6% of the jobs were held by women in 1966 *v.* 1.5% four years later. Midway in his present term, President Nixon promised to appoint more women, and to that end he created a brand-new position on the White House staff for a full-time recruiter of women. She was Barbara Franklin, 32, a Harvard Business School graduate who was an assistant vice president of New York's First National City Bank. She claims to have more than doubled the number of women in top Government jobs within a year.

But women in Washington seldom scale the highest reaches of power like the National Security Council. There has never been a woman Supreme Court Justice, though both Pat Nixon and Martha Mitchell lobbied for one before Nixon wound up nominating William Rehnquist and Lewis Powell. Only two women have ever sat in the Cabinet: Frances Perkins under F.D.R. and Oveta Culp Hobby under Eisenhower. Ten years ago, there were two women in the U.S. Senate and 18 women Representatives; now there are only Senator Margaret Chase Smith and eleven women in the House. The first woman in Congress, Jeannette Rankin, elected from a Montana constituency in 1916 and still starchy at 91, ventured recently that if she had it to do it all over again she would, with just one change: "I'd be nastier."

At the state and local levels, women have yet to make much impression on government. New York is the only state that has a special women's advisory unit reporting to the Governor, but its head, a black ex-newspaperwoman named Evelyn Cunningham, readily confesses· "We're a token agency." There are 63 separate agencies in the New

York State government, she notes, and only 13 of them have women in jobs above the rank of secretary. Round the U.S. there are a few woman mayors—among them Anna Latteri in Clifton, N.J., Patience Latting in Oklahoma City, Barbara Ackerman in Cambridge, Mass.

The last female state Governor was Lurleen Wallace in Alabama, a stand-in for her husband George, forbidden by the state constitution to succeed himself. (The first: Nellie Tayloe Ross was elected Governor of Wyoming in 1924.) The legislatures of the 50 states have a total membership of more than 7,000—including only 340 women. Few of these women have much influence, though there are stirring exceptions: New York Assembly Member Constance Cook, for example, represents a small upstate county, but led a successful fight for liberalizing the state's abortion law in 1970.

In a man's world, women still have only a ritualized place: they are received regularly and warmly only in woman-centered trades like fashion or in acting. As Clare Luce puts it, "Power, money and sex are the three great American values today, and women have almost no access to power except through their husbands. They can get money mostly through sex—either legitimate sex, in the form of marriage, or non-married sex." Sexual freedom is not enough; "what leads to money and power is education and the ability to make money apart from sex."

It is not an easy goal to achieve. Many women fear it: they want to have their cigarettes lit and their car doors opened for them. Far more seriously, they are afraid that, as working mothers, they simply would not be able to give their children the necessary personal care and attention. Ann Richardson Roiphe, a novelist with five children, worries about the de-emphasis of the family. She has written: "These day I feel a cultural pressure not to be absorbed in my child. Am I a Mrs. Portnoy sitting on the head of her little Alex? I am made to feel my curiosity about the growth of my babies is somehow counter-revolutionary. The new tolerance should ultimately respect the lady who wants to make pies, as well as the one who majors in higher mathematics."

Utopian. In a sense, if the feminist revolution simply wanted to exchange one ruling class for another, if it aimed at outright female domination (a situation that has occurred in science fiction and other fantasies), the goal would be easier to visualize. The demand for equality, not domination, is immensely complicated. True equality between autonomous partners is hard to achieve even if both partners are of the same sex. The careful balancing of roles and obligations and privileges, without the traditional patterns to fall back on, sometimes seems like an almost utopian vision.

While nearly everyone favors some of the basic goals of the New Feminism—equal pay for equal work, equal job opportunity, equal treatment by the law—satisfying even those minimum demands could require more wrenching change than many casual sympathizers with the women's cause have seriously considered. Should women be drafted? Ought protective legislation about women's hours and working conditions be repealed?

Still, American women cannot be forced back into the Doll's House. More and more, American women will be free to broaden their lives beyond domesticity by a fuller use of their abilities; there will be fewer diapers and more Dante. Anatomy is destiny, the Freudians say. It is an observation that can hardly be dismissed as mere male chauvinist propaganda, but it is simply no longer sufficient. The destiny of women and, indeed, of men, is broader, more difficult than that—and also more promising.

The Cost of Sexual Apartheid

VIOLETTE S. LINDBECK

They marched through city streets and demonstrated before civil authorities. Powerful business interests were arrayed against them; cultural leaders deplored their claims. They were spat upon, stoned, jeered at, and jailed.

Blacks in the 1960s? No, women in the suffrage movement of the 1920s. The movement itself inspired the *Saturday Review* of August 28, 1920, to write that suffrage

> is man's last stand against the subversion of his rights of virility by a tyranny which . . . will prove to be at once humiliating and dangerous. Humiliating, because it is the submission of the superior to the inferior sex. Dangerous because, if pushed beyond a certain point, it will be overthrown by an appeal to physical force.

If we read "black" for "women" and "white" for "men," this quote rivals in vitriol the most extreme racist diatribes of today.

The similarity between racial and sexual prejudice, now a common topic in the literature, is not surprising, for prejudice is everywhere the same in its nature and its fruits. Just as we attempt to "explain" perceived differences between blacks and whites as racial, so that we can believe the self-fulfilling prophecy that blacks are "naturally" lazy, shiftless, artistic, immoral, and dependent, so we maintain that women are "naturally" sensitive, tender, weak, emotional, patient, impulsive, and illogical. For blacks and for women, physiological differences in the human species are warrant for assigning to them mutually exclusive cultural roles, personality traits, intellectual and emotional capacities, and different interests and pursuits. And just as minority groups in America have yet to achieve full civil, economic, and social equality, so are women denied the full equality for which they fought in the twenties. In fact, there is documented evidence that the position of women in America has declined since the 1940s, and a muted, but very real, anti-feminist sentiment has pervaded American life and literature ever since.[1]

In general, we remain the heirs of a tradition of Western patriarchalism and androcentrism rooted in Hebraic, Greek, and Roman cultures and reaching full bloom in the Victorian era. As a result, traits labeled "masculine" and "feminine" — indeed, a whole ideology of male and female — were divided in yin-yang fashion in the name of a theological order of creation, a romantic-dialectic philosophy, or the

Freudian theory that masculinity and femininity are physiologically determined. This heritage endures today to retard personal growth, hinder effective communication between men and women, reinforce the sexual apartheid of women, interfere with the potential social contributions that both men and women can make, and, I will argue, make difficult needed social, civil, and economic reforms.

It may be that the overall social, political, and economic conservatism marking the American way of life in the 1960s has caused it to fall behind other nations such as Sweden, Israel, and the Soviet Union in providing public services as well as public opportunities for all its people. Especially may this conservatism be a factor in the persistence of the still powerful and pervasive prejudice, both racial and sexual, in America today. But just as it is unrealistic to talk about a "black" problem in the United States, since it is mostly a "white" problem, in origin and in resolution, so do we confront not a "women's problem" *per se* but the problem of how men and women can learn to regard themselves and one another in ways that are both personally and socially constructive.

We must remember that sexual prejudice works two ways. If, as one group of reformers would have it, women are suffering from the "feminine mystique," men are the victims of a like "masculinity trap." The ideology that defines men and women over and against one another catches both in the web of conflicting claims of old versus new and makes life either a prison for both or a source of unwarranted privilege or immunity from responsibility for some.

Our social values are now changing. Our economy, the effects of education, the new pattern of family living and its consequent new demands on men and women now blur the lines that formerly defined the relationship between them. The old notions, however, have not died easily.

Masculinity and femininity, the social roles assigned to men and women, have little to do with what is "bone of our bone and flesh of our flesh." They are not simply givens but are chiefly cultural products, learned responses, as diverse in social conception and dispensation as are kinship systems, political regimes, or religious ideologies. Yet even though some of our institutions are changing or have now changed to meet new societal needs, our culture has not yet reached a new consensus on what it means to be a man or a woman in the latter third of the twentieth century.

What are the reasons for America's intransigence to changing the status and roles of women? Why has the mythology of feminine versus masculine taken hold with such persistence? And what is the resulting conflict for men, the so-called masculinity trap, that threatens them?

For thousands of years, a natural inequality among men was assumed, made the first social premise. Social harmony, concord, justice itself were thought to depend upon a hierarchical order for all human relations — rule and ruled, master and slave, patriarch and family, man and woman. An androcentric bias in this classical consensus developed religious and philosophical ideologies to rationalize woman's social inferiority. Religiously, she was said to have been created after man and for him, the weaker vessel in mind and morality. Aristotle was echoed by the medieval Aquinas: woman was matter, man was form in which the divine spark of reason and will predominated. St. Augustine declared that the only possible reason for her creation was as a sexual means for procreation — unfortunate, but there it was. For any other relation, however, for friendship or assistance, a man would better turn to another man.

Further, as the sexual being *par excellence,* women was also dangerous, the temptress, seeking to drag man down from his higher calling. Here begins the Western ambivalence toward woman: she was either sinful Eve or blessed Mother, witch or lady. And it was but a short step to the noble Kant, Hegel, Weiniger, and Freud. If not the hand of God, nature itself intended woman as the defective, "misbegotten" creature. The steps from the medieval moralists who talked of "the use of a woman's body" to the gay blades of the Age of Reason who "took their pleasure" to Hugh Hefner's "playmates" are equally short ones. The Victorian honoring of woman as the "angel in the household," "the eternal feminine that leads us upward," is but the Protestant version of the medieval honoring of divine motherhood, the earth that nurtures the growth of new humanity.

With the Romantics came a change in ideology that rejected women's inferiority and substituted the doctrine of "separate but equal." Woman was not simply measured against man and found wanting; her full humanity was affirmed, but she was said to be a "different kind" of human being. Maleness and femaleness were said to constitute a mutually complementary bi-humanity. This is the ideology that has gained ground today and represents for many the last word, the great step forward from the traditional ideology of woman's inferiority.

What the Romantics intended was a challenge to the masculine definition of human worth and wholeness. Confronting the beginnings of the industrial, scientific, technological era, they extolled women for supposedly possessing those qualities of being that seemed to be threatened by this new age — instinctiveness, emotionalism, closeness to nature, distance from abstract modes of thought and exploitative activity — just those qualities for which she had been held in low esteem by the Rationalists. What happened, of course, was that this "new" ideology stressed distinct, innate differences between male and female and hence, for all practical purposes, converged with the old. Man's domain remained that of the impersonal world, the public sphere, the life of reason, of transforming action and mastery over nature and history. Woman's domain remained the personal, private world of feeling and receptivity, of holding together and preserving the natural and the social.

This notion of woman's "peculiar humanity" still flourishes. America is still fixated on the validity of masculine-feminine apartheid because, after the initial political idealism that established our nation, we quickly settled down to its real business — Business, as Calvin Coolidge said. Amassing wealth and increasing economic productivity became ends in themselves to which all else in our cultural life was to be subordinated.

The Victorian era, coinciding with industrialization and the growth of laissez-faire capitalism, saw the emergence of two new and distinct classes of women. One was the female proletariat whose labor was exploited in the rising factories and mills; the other was a middle-class woman who became a symbol of the conspicuous consumption made possible by the rise of the new commercial class. Both were genuinely new phenomena.

Previously, most women had worked alongside their men as economic partners in the home, in the fields, and in the family shops. Now the separation of home and work made wives and children an economic liability to men in the working class and superfluous as economic partners to men in the growing middle class. The Victorian ideology of male-female differences worked to rationalize the new position of both groups of women. Their lower pay, restricted entry into higher positions, and relegation to menial, routine, simple-minded tasks in factories and offices could be rationalized by the myth of the feminine lack of competence, mental and emotional. Thus was made available a continuous supply of cheap labor. On the other hand, the myth of frail, fainting femininity, ever reaching for the smelling salts, sanctioned the restriction of middle-class women to the home, where they were kept idle as status symbols of the husband's new economic position. The "my wife doesn't *have* to work" pride of the American middle-class man was born here.[2]

In America a new man was being bred as well. Not only has America's middle-class culture been a thoroughly masculine one, but it has been marked by a narrower conception of "masculinity" than were the Continental cultures. The roots of the condition may well be in our pioneer past, so that to the image of man as the strong, rugged, reckless conqueror of nature and the savage hordes on the Frontier was added that of man as the aggressive, ruggedly individualistic competitor in the commercial world. Both enterprises had little place for the "soft" man and little but scorn for the man with sensibilities and interests that could better blossom in a more cultivated climate. Those traits that could assure success in business enterprises came to be considered peculiarly "masculine": competitiveness, aggressiveness, cold intelligence, lack of crippling emotional sensitivities to others, and the ability to put work and economic advancement at the center of one's value system and to subordinate other roles to this one. As Margaret Mead has pointed out, bookishness, passivity, artistic propensities, emotional sensitivity, and an interest in cultural pursuits (except for sports, which would "make a man of him") were not encouraged but disparaged in boys. Men measured themselves and their sons by this commercial yardstick, and conversely they measured their daughters.

This division of masculine versus feminine is nowhere more visible than in our sexual standards — the traditional "double standard." Men gave the accolade of moral superiority to women, in sexual matters as well as in other spheres of life, and thus gave them the whole responsibility for sexual morality. Girls were "good" (which really meant "better") and therefore were the ones to say "no." The boy could press on, and the girl had to call the halt. By making the girl his moral guardian as well as her own, the boy is then always off the hook. No matter what pressures he may bring to bear, the blame for any adverse consequences is always placed squarely in her lap — sometimes literally, if she makes the mistake of getting pregnant.

In sexual matters, there are no "bad" boys, only "bad" women: Recall that prostitutes are arrested, but their customers are not. If a girl refuses to engage in intercourse, she is guilty of breaking off what would have been a "meaningful relationship." If she consents to intercourse and suffers guilt feelings, pregnancy, abortion, she is at fault for saying "yes," or for not taking the proper precautions (especially today, since she has "the pill"). Either way, the "double-standard man" is relieved of making his own moral decisions by placing the major responsibility for all acts on the girl. If he suffers guilt feelings from his sexual encounter, he can blame her for "leading him on." She should not have let him continue. Paradoxically, the "double-standard woman" can always blame her own misfortunes on the amoral importunities of the male.

We can see the results of this traditional training of the sexes wherever we look. The division of labor according to sex forced women, particularly middle-class women who were not satisfied with their enforced restriction to the home, into those areas that did not place them in direct economic competition with men: the arts, literature, and social welfare and cultural organizations. In the 1940s, for example, Talcott Parsons wrote that women in America have only three socially approved roles: domestic, glamour girl, and companion or adjunct to men. Those who broke through these culturally approved roles received little encouragement, let alone approbation, from men. They were, as Samuel Johnson observed about the woman preacher, like the dog who walked on its hind legs: It didn't do it very well, but one was surprised to find it doing so at all.

Prevented from entering or participating fully in the privileges and responsibilities of "the man's world," women have countered in many ways. As the Negro was forced to adopt the protective coloration of the

"Uncle Tom," so have women adopted the mask of the feminine ideal
that hides their real feelings, submerges their own individuality, and
renounces their abilities. Or like the Negro they have internalized a
sense of personal and social-inferiority subtly nurtured from infancy.
If education or experience cracks the mask or calls into question the
assimilatied self-image, woman, like the Negro, may very well react
with aggressive self-assertion, with perhaps a parody of the stance and
tone of the favored group or with a fierce challenge to compete. In
turn, such behavior is often interpreted as further evidence that full
cultural participation is "unnatural" for them, their "uppityness" or
temerity a further sign of their lack of rational competence and emotional restraint. Rarely is it rightfully interpreted as the natural human
reaction of submerged groups still struggling with a sense of inferiority, still defensive about their status, still lacking in full self-confidence.

Sometimes, the woman may counter with a contempt for masculine
life equal to the contempt of many Negroes for the proclaimed virtues
and values of the middle-class white. The themes are part of our
folklore. Men are only little boys to be managed, coaxed, and cajoled
into doing what mama knows best; business and politics are games big
boys play while women deal with the really nitty-gritty issues of life.
And where women have achieved social strength, they may resent and
seek to limit the participation of men, whether it is in the home, with
the children, or in the traditional feminine occupations such as school
teaching or nursing. Prejudice and apartheid bear the same fruits
wherever practiced.

Meanwhile, back in the home, the hot-house intimacy of the nuclear
family has taken its toll. The propaganda of the feminine mystique that
woman should find all her fulfillment and sense of achievement in the
context of her family has made for an unprecedented heightening of
the emotional involvement between mother and child. Many women
live vicariously through their children and try to produce the "perfect"
offspring, who will be their badge of success; but in so trying, they may
actually spoil their children for independent, mature adult lives.

Women also strive to live vicariously through their husbands, pushing them, nagging them through the mazes of the vocational rat-race.
In our society a woman's social status is measured by her husband's job,
the title he has and how much he can pay for. Hence the race of
conspicuous consumption: "keeping up with the Joneses." For many
writers of popular literature, "Momism" is the bugaboo of our society:
Molochs of mothers busily swallowing up husbands and sons with their
too-aggressive presence in the home. For these women, personal
achievement comes only from the reflected glory of the husband's job
or the children's achievements, and they succeed only in alienating the
one and emasculating the other.

Working at cross-purposes to this threat of the consuming matriarch
are the economic interests that glorify the woman as consumer. The

billion dollar cosmetic and fashion industries began by telling women from three to thirty-three that sexual attractiveness was their chief source of public approval, indeed, their social duty. They also made housekeeping the woman's chief occupation by putting back into the home the tasks that modern technology could do equally well. Consequently, while laundries, communal housekeeping services, bakeries, and restaurants are allowing European and Asian women to leave the home in increasing numbers, our washers, dryers, mixers, and floor polishers are keeping more and more women in the home. And the home thereby becomes the focus of the woman's attention, so much so that husbands and children appear as intruders and despoilers.

To what degree has this stress on the consumer role contributed to what Galbraith has called the peculiar American phenomenon of private affluence and public squalor? Have women, convinced that their proper social role is circumscribed by attention to personal enhancement and home betterment, furthered the growth in our society of a private value-centeredness to the neglect of public expenditures for the community's well being?

Until recently, we could laugh at our Lady Bountifuls with their Thanksgiving basket social work, our garden club beautifiers, our lady Culture Vultures, a la Helen Hokinson cartoons, dragging bored and resisting husbands to concerts, galleries, and community welfare projects. Now we are aware to our sorrow of public ugliness, poverty, and cultural deprivation grown to such proportions that we despair of denting them.

As the woman has become trapped by these conflicting roles, so also has the man. The masculine *paterfamilias* role inherited by men has also taken its toll. The middle-class marriage especially has become a vocational and economic trap for men who are regarded chiefly as the breadwinner, the unresting goose who lays the golden eggs that are gobbled up by the family as fast as they can be laid. Husbands experience only too well what a recent survey among middle-class women revealed: when asked to list the important roles of their spouses, these wives put bread winner first, father second, and husband a poor third. "How do I love thee? Let me count the ways, First, as a meal ticket . . ."

Reduced solely to his economic function, the husband becomes identified with and circumscribed by those qualities that make for vocational success. In the aggressive competitiveness of his occupational world, the man must practice the insensitivity to others that makes for his own commercial success. Judge others by what they can do to you or for you; practice emotional restraint, keep a stiff upper lip, for it will not do to alienate boss or customer, particularly when they are hurting you or you them. Men who must "bring home the bacon" must concentrate on developing their powers of cold, analytic intelligence — what Erich Fromm and others call "exploitative reason" — to dissect, quantify, and reduce all things to their pragmatic functions.

Consider the pressure on the man who must then go home to his family — for the conquering hero of the business world is also husband

and father. How can the Dr. Jekyll of corporate finance turn into the Mr. Hyde of East Suburbia, successful father and husband, who cherishes wife and children for what they are, not for their achievements or their economic or social contributions to the family unit? In the home the man must develop his capacity for "receptive reason," the ability to see and respect those around him for their unique abilities and characteristics.[3] Husband and father are roles that call for emotional warmth and sensitivity to others. Yet, from childhood, he has been trained in those qualities regarded as "masculine" — the very qualities, ironically, that make him ill-suited for his roles as husband and father.

One means used to ease this conflict of roles is to invoke the myth that home and work are incommensurable and not to be "mixed." Home is where you forget about work; work is where you leave your private life behind you. But myth it is, for worker and householder are one man, and the desire not to mix home and work often has serious repercussions on the husband-wife relationship. The husband typically invests the major portion of his time, emotional energy, and ego-involvement in his job, but he may not share it with his wife, partly because, by staying at home, she may little understand or contribute to his attempts at sharing, but also because he wishes to make home a shelter and refuge from the demands of the job. This kind of reticence is often misunderstood by the wife, particularly if she has few interests outside the marriage. She makes demands on his time, energy, or ego that the husband is unable or unwilling to fulfill. His failure to talk with or respond to her, in effect, estranges them both by feeding the wife's jealousy and resentment of the time and interest he takes in his work.

The psychological distance between home and work also aggravates the man's problem of projecting the nature and significance of the "masculine role" to his children. We hear charges against "the vanishing American father" who fails to supply an image in the family of masculine protector, educator, and moral authority, but the validity of this charge is debatable since it is often made in the name of an already outmoded image of "masculinity." These rules and tasks, which were once the traditional province of the man in the family, have been largely taken over by other social agencies in our advanced culture. What is left to the family, as the specialized social unit it has become, are the affectional, companionship, child-care, and socializing roles, which were traditionally thought the duty of women. It is unrealistic to "hop on pop" for failing a role that made sense only in a previous era when the patriarchal father had life and death power over his wife and children, was responsible for initiating his children into the adult world of work, had individual control over their economic destinies, and generally served as the final voice of authority in the family.

The irrational nostalgia for an idealized image of the *paterfamilias* where "father always knows best" is as little helpful in the domestic sphere as is the image of man as "master of his fate and captain of his soul" in the vocational realm. Just as the sedentary "organization man" with at most only indirect control over his fortune and future cannot identify except in fantasy with the rugged and self-reliant pioneers of the past, so today's father cannot see himself, except in fantasy, as the patriarchal master of his household. Because his training in "masculinity" makes success in the new role of father and husband psychologically difficult, many men respond to this confusion in roles by giving up the struggle, by "copping out" as their children would charge. Acquiescence is easier: if a woman's place is in the home, let her reign there while he finds satisfaction elsewhere and preserves his own image of the proper masculine pursuit. This pattern of the too passive, too indifferent, or too absent father combined with a too dominant, too present, too possessive mother is at least a partial source of male homosexuality and the new phenomenon of totally alienated middle-class youth.[4]

Some men, nevertheless, try to play the traditional masculine role, but with equally detrimental effects upon family life. One wonders if the communications gap between generations would have become the unbridgeable abyss it is were it not for the inhibiting effect of the masculine stereotype. Sharing confidences and free discussion are not encouraged by the masculine stance of self-sufficiency, all-knowing authority, and the stiff-upper-lip emotional restraint that fears the display of doubts, dependency, and affection as somehow "feminine" and "unmanly." Why should not men show themselves to their children as human beings with the usual human complement of wisdom and folly, strengths and weaknesses, fears and hopes? Would not communication across generations become more possible if parents, particularly fathers, could drop their Olympian masks and admit to their own doubts and anxieties, could confess to their own hesitancies in facing a world with such intense and intricate social problems that few if any know all the answers, few if any are sure of their footing, and certainly few can read the signs of the times clearly enough to guide the next generation into the future? As the panacea to our youth problems some suggest that fathers should assume more authority in the home by representing in their own persons the objective standards and obligations of and to the outside world. They are kidding themselves. Can anyone represent a moral consensus that is no longer present? Facing a time of rapid social change and moral confusion in the wider society, what father dares say that he embodies rectitude and wisdom devoid of all ethical ambiguity and personal confusion? These are not the times to play the parental "heavy" role. There is nothing easy about being a father today, but it would be easier nonetheless if fathers worried more about their full humanity and less about their projected image of "masculinity."

In addition to creating stresses around the father role, the masculine stereotype subverts genuine communication between husband and wife and makes hollow the companionship desired and needed in marriage. Middle-class men find it difficult to express their inner fears and desires, to discuss their problems with their wives of twenty years or more because to do so seems to present one's self as less of a man. Little boys don't cry; men never show inadequacies. But the stiff upper lip leads to the stiff *in toto*! Psychiatrists point to the masculine training in emotional restraint and the inability to express dependency and anxieties as an important cause of the early male mortality rate from psychosomatic illnesses. It is the men who now have the "lethal" role in our society, who are killing themselves off.[5] The increased life-span given to women by our culture has not been matched by men, and it's a bad bargain, most women would agree.

Male conflicts over the masculine stereotype wreak other kinds of havoc on wedded bliss. Whereas in the Victorian era female frigidity appeared to be the chief sexual neurosis, now there is an apparent increase in male impotence, either partial or total.[6] The trauma of proving potency as a sign of one's masculinity appears to be too much for some men, especially those schooled to believe that the male is the sexually dominant partner and is alone responsible for intitiating and satisfactorily concluding the sexual act. The Victorians believed that the male's sexual needs were the more urgent, while the woman was the indifferent, or at most the passive, instrument for their satisfaction. Gone now is this kind of role security.

Research publicized in the mass media on feminine sexuality and its diverse expressions in our own and other cultures has made the American woman aware of what she has been missing and has educated her to consider her own sexual nature and to demand her own sexual satisfaction. It has shown her that sex is a game two can and ought to play, in both its initiation and its pleasurable consequences. The Victorian myth that sex was a man's province meant that he could not feel threatened in his sexual role: whatever he did had to be all right with his wife. But now men are threatened, because they are unable to understand or respond to the new demands made by their wives, or they are unable to accept marriage as a partnership in this area as in others. Hence, the sexually emancipated women are putting many men to a test that their "masculinity" training ill equips them to pass. Already under the competitive pressure of their vocation, they cannot accept the challenge to compete in bed, too, and they resign by becoming sexually passive. In their uncertainty over their sexual role, they come to expect the wife to take the initiative, or they find their sexual kicks in the untouchable "bunnies" or the acquiescent call girls who allow them to pretend to be the sexual aggressors.

Despite the ominous tone of this discussion, we can look at this situation in another light. Let us for a moment look at all this conflict and anxiety in a positive way, as the necessary condition for change. For example, the myth of the "eternal feminine leads us upward," of women as the sensitive possessors of vast, natural reservoirs of kindness, tenderness, compassion, forbearance, patience, and understanding (all that the New Testament, incidentally, lists as gifts of the Holy Spirit) can be dismissed as Tommyrot. Why allow sensitivity, emotional warmth, sympathy, compassion, and the rest to be labeled "feminine" traits in the first place? Any husband, father, lover, or friend worth his salt possesses these characteristics; any teacher, minister, doctor, lawyer, or poet lacking them will fail his vocation completely.

Suppose we declared that aggressiveness, competitiveness, pugnaciousness, that old "do or die" spirit, were un-American. Then the male stereotype, the "model of masculinity" inculcated in little boys, can include "blessed are the peace-makers," a notion we seem to have forgotten in the raising of our children. The gentle courtesy of Thai boys, the self-control and poise of the Chinese, the grave decorum of the Indians stand in marked contrast with the pushing, shoving, and tussling of American boys. We are responsible for this difference because we have taught our sons that the fist — and its extensions, the knife and the gun — will settle disputes. "What! Johnny punched you? Well, what did you do to him? You go out there and give it to him. No son of mine is going to grow up a coward!" This "chip on the shoulder" is the "manly" way in America, and it ill becomes us, especially when we compare ourselves with others. The French mastery of high intense but rational political debate reinforces their conviction that the pen is, indeed, mightier than the sword. (Would that ink were the ultimate weapon in all nations' arsenals.) And the Chinese teach their children that he who strikes the first blow is not the manly but the craven one, for only those who have not reason nor right on their side resort to blows.[7]

Be reminded that aggressiveness, anger, hostility, and brutality are the dark *human* potentials, present in woman as well as man. Only historical ignorance can account for our propensity to regard them as peculiarly male traits. Women as well as men throughout history have stormed the barricades and screamed for the heads and blood of traitors or blasphemers. With this knowledge, in fact, Margaret Mead has opposed the drafting of women into the armed forces on the ground that wars would be fought more fiercely, without quarter, and would be more difficult to end.

"Our duty, our task in this human generation, is to find a moral substitute for war," said William James. We can be grateful that such sentiments are still voiced today, but we cannot reach this goal so long as smoothing over feelings and creating harmony are labeled peculiarly "feminine" traits, on which women alone have the monopoly. Nor can we reach this goal so long as the myth of what is manly continues to provide men with the opportunity to prove their virility through physical violence. If men do not become the blessed peace-makers who alone are to inherit the earth, we may not, in the near future, have any earth for anyone to inherit.

Perhaps the current student protest against middle-class American mores and social pressures are, in part, a rightful protest against the perpetuation of this myth of masculine-feminine differences and its accompanying apartheid. Isn't that what the dressing alike, the flourishing of refurbished male plumage, the lengthened hair is all about? Isn't that what the protest against the hypocrisy and sham of the older generation in sexual matters proclaim? I have my doubts that it will work, doubts heightened by reading that women in the New Left movements are quitting to form "liberation" groups for themselves and rejecting the roles assigned to them to act as secretarial — and sex — pools for the male leaders. Even today, young women are still rushing into early marriages like lemmings into the sea. Women are still quitting school to put husbands through college or graduate school because they are even today influenced by the continued emphasis on sex-typed roles. Many students are retreating into the same privatism of values, the same exalting of the sexual relation and the private goods of domesticity, as does Suburbia, although in other forms. The "make love, not war" movement may only further the Eros-imperialism of our society if it neglects those other forms of love that provide purpose and value in human existence and contribute to human fullness: the love of truth, the love of beauty, of goodness, of friends, of humanity, of God. It may well be that the increasing eroticism of our culture presages a new and healthier consensus on the meaning and proper avenues of sexual expression; but it may also be one more evidence that our society has failed to give enough meaning and value to other aspects of our cultural life.

In an area such as this, which is so much a matter of our own self-images as men and women and deeply ingrained habits of thought and feeling, emotional fireworks in public discussions are inevitable. As Pogo put it, "We have met the enemy and they is we." The degree of personal and public defensiveness and offensiveness in the discussion thus far threatens often to turn it into yet another skirmish in the poverbial "battle of the sexes." But this will not do. It is a genuinely new situation we face, and our response also must be genuinely new.

What will the new fashion bring? First of all, gone will be the economic exploitation of men, which the dating and mating game entails. When full partnership is accepted, men and women together will share the price of a mutually enjoyable time, whether they are married or not. Wife and husband will share the economic burden of the family and will support one another and their children according to their individual needs and abilities. If they are separated or divorced, the woman will be compensated financially for her services to the family, but the man will not be required to support an idle but employable former wife.[8]

No longer will a man need to feel vocationally trapped by his marriage, because his wife will be willing, if able, to work to support him and the family while he goes back to school or is retrained for another job. Indeed, the man could even choose to stay at home with his children, the house, and his hobbies and let his wife assume the role of breadwinner or student for a time — as some men do even now. This sharing of the financial burden and newly flexible roles will take a good deal of the pressure off a man so that he need not feel harassed and resentful in marriage, so that he no longer is forced into the narrow role of breadwinner and wage slave to justify his existence.

Woman, who now have twenty-five to thirty years of prime life left to them after their children have grown, will come to regard this "second life" as a blessing, not a curse. From the beginning, we will raise our daughters to know and understand this idea, and we will teach them that marrying and raising a family is but one stage in their lives. Then, those millions of physically active women who were made to think of their role as wife and mother as their *raison d'être* will be better prepared to face this time of their lives. They will prepare themselves for other meaningful work and will cease to fritter away their years in multiple, unsatisfying activities: bridge clubs, night courses, trips to the beauty parlor — anything to fill the hours. Girls must be taught that there is more to being a person, leading a full human life, than being a sexual partner and mother. Then, perhaps, women will take their educations seriously and will see their contribution to the world outside the home as equally important to marriage and the family.

The sharing of economic responsibility will go hand in hand with a wider sharing of family responsibilities. The traditional division of home labor into women's and men's chores will be totally discarded. Each will do necessary tasks on the basis of who has the time, energy, interest, and competence as individuals to do them. The man will not be threatened if the woman wields a better hammer than he; the woman will not be threatened if his cooking is better than hers. They will relate to each other as the unique persons they are, not according to some impersonal image of maleness and femaleness and what is deemed proper to each.

Women, allowed to be full partners outside the home, will respond by allowing men to be full marital and parental partners and will no longer jealously guard their home and children as solely their own. Fatherhood in all its dimensions will then be as important to a man's identity and esteem as are his other roles, and he will be as concerned with cultivating the mental and emotional qualities needed for fatherhood as with cultivating those needed for his vocation. Perhaps, some day, society will give him more support for his role as a father by providing courses in family living for schoolboys and by making work schedules more flexible so that men can be more nearly full-time fathers when their children are growing up.

The relationship between husband and wife will be further enhanced as they become full partners in all endeavors, share common interests, concerns, values, and perspectives, and communicate, as it were, on the same wave length, the human. Only then can we realize the unique and valuable possibilities of our preferred form of marriage — marriage for love and companionship.

Sex is not enough to create a bond of long-lasting affection and mutual respect, care, and empathy. Children cannot be strong enough to bind a couple together over the years. Both are rather the "embodiments" of a love that grows through commitment and sharing in the expectation of a total life together. Sexual relations in marriage will increase in spontaneous enjoyment as they become, not the cause of a couple's coming together (especially not the arena for proving one's manhood or womanhood, a test of proficiency with an "A" for orgasm), but the fun and games that accompany the genuine sexual reciprocity possible in a marriage.

This reciprocity is possible only between equals, between friends, as it were. Where genuine and mutual friendship is lacking, sexual relations will suffer. Sex becomes rather a kind of marital "prostitution," an impersonal exchange of bodily service for other services rendered; it becomes mutual masturbation. Or it becomes a power play wherein each attempts to subjugate the other by yielding or not yielding, however they define it. Sex can also be used to release hostility or resentment built up in other areas of marital life. But where there are genuine reciprocity and open communication there need not be any trauma about potency, nor any inhibitions about who does what and when. All these are replaced by the delight in delighting the other, the kind of self-giving that gains in the gift of self.

With this goal in mind, we can then say, first of all, down with the double standard of sexual morality. Men and women are equally responsible here, as elsewhere, for it does take two to play.

Men and women can then engage in a more honest, albeit painful, attempt to understand themselves and to communicate more candidly and genuinely with one another. They can say to each other with the poet:

> I want your warm body to disappear
> politely and leave me alone in the
> bath
> Because I want to consider my destiny.

Then they can arise from their baths crying, "Eureka! We have found it. Our destiny lies in a common humanity, co-responsibility for all things human."

Is not the recognition of common humanity, of co-responsibility, the answer to all prejudice and apartheid? It is not the last word to be spoken about human interrelatedness, but must it not be the first? C.S. Lewis has written that a belief in equality is not food, but medicine; without it no human relationship can be healthy, no human alienation cured. Or, as Simone Weil expressed it, a man must claim in justice first his impersonal humanity, his right to be treated and to act as a man alongside other men. Only then can he accept himself truly as an individual and find acceptance by others as the singular person he is with the individual, natural endowment, the personal history, and the life situation that have made him unique.

Marriage today is often only a trap and an agonizing one at that. Desiring intimacy, acceptance, companionship, we find ourselves wedded to a strange and alien creature conditioned to separateness, unable to share in our experiences or our perspectives. That segment of the student generation now forswearing marriage might, however, be guilty of doing the right thing for the wrong reasons. At fault is not our form of marriage so much as its substance, especially when it includes the masculine-feminine mythology inculcated by our society. We should rejoice that our present culture and socio-economic conditions permit many for the first time to marry not for the state, family convenience, or economic necessity but for love and companionship, a personal choice freely made. For most in our highly mobile society, marriage holds the only possibility of a lasting relationship with another person, the only schoolhouse for continued growth in empathy, aid, and comfort. Severed as we are from our families of birth and our childhood friends, this possibility is not to be taken lightly. We can marry because we find a person with whom we can share our whole future, all of ourselves, who will accept us for what we are — warts, wrinkles, and all.

This form of marriage is not outmoded as some would have it; rather, it has barely been tried, and for the first time, for the many, there is the possibility of its being truly tried. For the first time, as men and women approach genuine equality, full partnership, and the acceptance of one another's common humanity and personal uniqueness, the traditional words of the marriage service can be given full meaning and the exchange of vows a reality:

> I, John (this singular fellow) take thee, Mary (this unique individual), to have and to hold from this day forward, for better, for worse (you won't let me down), for richer or poorer (we'll take care of each other), in sickness and in health (I'll not be cast off when I'm disabled) as long as we both shall live (I never need be alone or lack for someone).

Add to this pledge the words of an even older service: "And with my body I thee worship" (my sexuality has now found its very human and personal reason for being). This, if you will forgive the phrase, is a hell of a romantic notion. Here is someone who says he commits himself to me as I to him, no holds barred. This is an incredible affirmation of one's selfhood and an equally incredible affirmation of another's.

But can it come off? Granted that nothing is given automatically with the recitation of the words; it is really only an opportunity, one among others, in fact. But is is, and remains, a fascinating and fruitful adventure in humanity to take the opportunity seriously. Perhaps only now can we begin to take it seriously.

The masculine fashion of the past must become a thing of the past. Freedom must be granted to men (as to married couples and to women) to fashion for themselves their own life styles, to realize their unique capacities and talents, to choose their own interests and occupations without the nay-saying of some arbitrary rule of sex typing. It is doubtful that anyone can predict with absolute certainly the shape of things to come; but I believe the new fashion in manhood and womanhood, only barely sketched here, could ensure a healthier, more creative future for men and boys, for women and girls, and for our society generally as the concept of what it means to be a man or a woman expands to embrace and express a fuller humanity for both.

Maslow's self-actualizing people, those he designates as the "norm" for a genuine humanity are, he admits, only a tiny percentage of the present population. Understandably so, for this is a culture whose ideology of masculinity and femininity served in the past to produce sufficient male drones, inculcated with the supremacy of their worker role and conditioned to accept the demands and pressures of their honey-money gathering without question; and sufficient queen bees conditioned to ever higher standards of consumption to ingest all that might be garnered by the drones and to expend it on their offspring and the home wax works. Thus did we keep our economic hive buzzing. What we failed to do was to produce sufficiently full human beings, male and female, whose horizons transcended the hive and who refused to let their personhood and life patterns be molded into the honeycomb of the commercial-consumer ethos in which they lived.

Ironically enough, now that even industry and business, and with them governmental and educational agencies, are beginning to question the results of sex typing and the fruits of sexual prejudices on the employment of men and women, we find that the momentum is increasing to grant full equality to women, to return men to hitherto "feminine" occupations such as school teacher, and to recruit women for hitherto "masculine" jobs such as mathematician. There is more concern for providing child-care facilities for working mothers and for re-educating men to manage better in their personal relations on the job. But dare we let a reshuffling of economic roles be the key to a new fashion of manhood and womanhood? Rather, must we not re-think, from the roots up and on the basis of the fullest scientific, sociological, psychological, historical, and ethical understanding we can muster, what role, within the whole range of human potential for individual personality development and social relations, sexuality really does play? Should we not ask what difference, where and when, sexual identity *per se* does make in the education of men and women and in the socially significant roles they acquire?

I am convinced that, when all the evidence is digested and past sexual prejudices discounted, we will see an increase in the number of Maslow's self-actualizing people. They will seem singularly devoid of past, sex-typed roles; they will have a pressure within "toward spontaneous expressiveness, toward full individuality and identity, toward seeing the truth, . . . toward being creative, toward being good, . . . pressing toward what most people would call good values, toward serenity, kindness, courage, knowledge, honesty, love, unselfishness, and goodness." The self-actualized man and woman can never be alien to or threaten one another. What they share in common as human beings is immensely more important to them than what separates them as males and females.

Maslow's "healthy human specimens" will have a "clearer, more efficient perception of reality, more openness to experience, an increased aliveness, autonomy, objectivity, transcendence of self, recovery of creativity, the ability to fuse concreteness and abstractness, a democratic character structure, the ability to love . . ." [9] Such men and women will exult in their freedom to be themselves and to accept the other in his or her unique but co-humanity. When more such full, healthy specimens are nurtured among us, we need no longer worry about the fashion in manhood and womanhood prevalent in society. The fashion will be to be human.

REFERENCES

1. Government figures as of 1968 on the employment of women indicate that "the relative position of women in the labor force has deteriorated rather than improved. In 1940 they represented 53 percent of those in clerical positions; by 1967 this ratio had risen to 72 percent. During this same period there has been a steady decline in the percentage of women in the more privileged occupations — professional, technical, and kindred jobs — a decline of 16 percent since 1940." Willa Player, "Facts and Trends in Educational Opportunities for Women in Higher Education," Bureau of Higher Education, U.S. Office of Education, unpublished paper.

Other significant data from this report include the following: In 1940, 28 percent of all college faculties were women; in 1964, 22 percent. In 1920, 68 percent of all high school teachers were women; in 1964, 46 percent. In 1928, 55 percent of all elementary school principals were women; in 1968, only 22 percent; and only 4 percent of all secondary school principals are women. Of those in the professions in the U.S. in 1968, 1 percent are women in engineering, 3 percent are women in law, and 6.7 percent are women in medicine. (In Great Britain in 1951, 16.5 percent of the doctors were women.) In 1966, the median income earned by women workers employed year-round, full-time was only 58 percent of that earned by men — a decline of 7 percent from 1955.

These figures remain little changed in the latest government report, *Background Facts on Women Workers in the United States* (Washington, D.C.: U.S. Department of Labor, Wage and Labor Standards Administration, Women's Bureau, 1968). However, these data also suggest that changes in the relative occupational positions of women may be forthcoming. In 1930 women earned 39.9 percent of Bachelor's or first professional degrees granted. In 1950, they earned only 24 percent of such degrees, but received 40.4 percent of them in 1966. Similarly, 40.4 percent of Master's degrees were earned by women in 1930, 29.2 percent in 1950, and 33.8 percent in 1966; in 1930 they earned 15.4 percent of Ph. D. degrees, in 1950 9.6 percent, and in 1966 11.6 percent.

2. Viola Klein, *The Feminine Character – History of an Ideology* (New York: International Universities Press, 1948).

3. See Norman Bell and Ezra Vogel (eds.), *Modern Introduction to the Family* (New York: Free Press, 1960).

4. D. J. West, *Homosexuality*, 3rd ed. (London: Duckworth and Co., 1968), Ch. 9; and Kenneth Keniston, *The Uncommitted: Alienated Youth in American Society* (New York: Harcourt, Brace and World, Dell Publishing Company, 1965).

5. Sidney M. Jourard, *The Transparent Self* (New York: Van Nostrand Reinhold, 1964).

6. Myron Brenton, *The American Male* (New York: Coward-McCann, Inc., 1966).

7. Margaret Mead and Martha Wolfenstein (eds.), *Childhood in Contemporary Cultures* (Chicago: University of Chicago Press, 1955), II, Ch 7.

8. Caroline Bird, *Born Female: The High Cost of Keeping Women Down* (New York: David McKay Company, 1968), Ch. 10.

9. Abraham H. Maslow (ed.), *New Knowledge in Human Values* (New York: Harper & Row, 1959), pp. 119-121.

Human Potential:
The Revolution in Feeling

TIME

In an Evanston, Ill., high school, students of English Teacher Thomas Klein shrouded themselves in bed sheets and crawled blindly around the floor. At a body-movement session in Beverly Hills, Calif., participants took turns pummeling a sofa pillow with feral ferocity. From a four-story midtown Manhattan brownstone, the sound of screaming can be heard all day long. It comes from patients of Psychiatrist Daniel Casriel, who believes that such release is therapeutic. In Escondido, Calif., a group of naked men and women, utter strangers, step into what their leader, Beverly Hills Psychologist Paul Bindrim, calls a "womb pool" — a warm Jacuzzi bath. They are permitted to hug and kiss each other, but intercourse is out.

To many Americans, these activities typify a leaderless, formless and wildly eclectic movement that is variously called sensitivity training, encounter, "therapy for normals," the bod biz, or the acidless trip. Such terms merely describe the more sensational parts of a whole that is coming to be known as the human potentials movement — a quest conducted in hundreds of ways and places, to redefine and enrich the spirit of social man.

To reach man's unawakened resources, the movement focuses on the actions and interactions of individuals in a group. In this, it has borrowed freely from psychology's past, from such extenders of Freudian theory as Karen Horney and Harry Stack Sullivan, who realized that no individual can be defined, and no emotional disorder healed, without an examination of the interchange between one man and all the others in his life. Society itself is defined by the group. The movement's exponents argue that by expanding the individual's self-awareness and sense of well-being within the group, a new feeling of community develops that strengthens both the individual and the group.

Weekend Marathon. The human potentials movement has already touched the major social institutions: church, factory, school and state. In a study for the Carnegie Corporation, Donald H. Clark, associate professor of education at New York's City University, reports that the movement has permeated every level of education, from kindergarten to graduate school and beyond. Encounter sessions or T (for training) groups have been held, sometimes as parts of the curriculum, in dozens of colleges and universities, among them Harvard, Columbia, Boston

University and the New School for Social Research. Big business has enlisted its employees in human potentials centers in ever increasing numbers, and many companies now operate programs of their own. In some, white employees don blackface, black employees whiteface, presumably to encourage the feeling that the difference in the races is, after all, only skin-deep.

Aided by widespread publicity, including the movie *Bob and Carol and Ted and Alice* and Jane Howard's best-seller, *Please Touch,* the movement is spreading explosively. Two years ago, when California's Esalen Institute first sought to export its own brand of the new gospel east, 90 curious New Yorkers showed up for a five-day encounter group in Manhattan. A similar event last year drew 850; last April, 6,000. Since January 1969, when Donald Clark counted 37 "growth centers" — established sites for the development of human or group potentials — the census has risen past 100.

To Esalen in San Francisco and Big Sur, the institute's beautiful Pacific retreat south of Carmel, come 25,000 people a year — and if the pilgrim is turned away there, he can find similar sanctuaries in San Diego (Kairos), New York (Aureon, Anthos, GROW), Chicago (Oasis), Houston (Espiritu), Austin, Texas (Laos House), Washington, D.C. (Quest), Decatur, Ga. (Adanta), Calais, Vt. (Sky Farm Institute), and scores of other communities. The groups can vary in size from half a dozen friends meeting in a big-city apartment to hundreds and even thousands of complete strangers at a psychological convention. The gamut is as wide as the cost, which can run anywhere from $30 or less for a weekend marathon encounter session in a church basement to $2,100 for a seven-week training program at the National Training Laboratories.

Even though the movement's advocates deny that it is therapy, many people visit the new growth centers or attend informal group sessions in quest of precisely that. The American Psychiatric Association estimates that in California, more troubled individuals already seek help from the human potentials movement than from "traditional sources of psychotherapy." Yet the human potentials group sessions are largely valueless, and even dangerous, for the severely disturbed. Psychologist Carl Rogers, one of the movement's charter members, and many others consider it a learning experience for "normals" rather than a therapeutic experience for the sick — who are too engrossed in their own emotions fully to feel another's.

Targets of Criticism. Psychologist Rogers calls the new group movement "the most significant social invention of this century." It may not be quite that, but even the American Psychiatric Association has bestowed guarded approval in a 27-page task-force report: "The intensive group experience is intrinsically neither good nor bad . . . If properly harnessed, however, the experience may be a valuable adjunct" to psychotherapy.

Critics have accused the movement of everything from Communist-style brainwashing to sedition. Dr. Joseph T. English, formerly head of the Health Services and Mental Health Administration of the U.S. Department of Health, Education and Welfare, thinks that it has "been oversold to an unaware public." U.S. Representative John R. Rarick of Louisiana, its most voluble enemy, has filled pages of the *Congressional Record* with unrestrained rhetoric: "Organized thought control and behavior programming . . . a perversion of group therapy that makes healthy minds sick . . . obvious degeneracy."

One of the more frequent targets of this criticism is the Esalen Institute, the creation of two Stanford psychology graduates, Michael Murphy and Richard Price. In a San Francisco ashram, or Hindu retreat, where Murphy spent eight meditative years and was later joined by Price, the two dreamed of a university without academic trappings, which would combine the best of Western humanistic psychology and Eastern thought.

A Social Oasis. Murphy's father left him a 60-acre tract on Big Sur, and in 1962, Esalen Institute opened. "We only knew that a forum was needed for all these new ideas," Murphy said. "We had no idea where it would all lead to. We didn't care." The statement is characteristic of the part of the human potentials movement that Esalen represents. It and its many imitators are analogous to the so-called "free university," which eliminates the traditional boundaries between students and faculty, one academic discipline and another, the cognitive (knowing) process and the affective (feeling) process.

The encounter group, as it evolved at Esalen, is first of all a vehicle to provide an intense emotional experience. It is usually kept small enough — half a dozen to 20 members — to generate intimate response. Its focus is on the "here and now," on what the group members experience as they sit, lie or touch together. It demands complete openness, honesty and cooperation. As described by the American Psychiatric Association, the encounter group is "a social oasis in which societal norms are explicitly shed. No longer must facades of adequacy, competence, self-sufficiency be borne." Indeed, just the opposite kind of behavior is encouraged. "The group offers intimacy, albeit sometimes a pseudo intimacy — an instant and unreal form of closeness . . . one which has no commitment to permanence."

All of this applies to Esalen at Big Sur. The scene itself inspires strong emotions: a verdant reach of craggy coastline dropping precipitously into the Pacific. A row of small rustic bungalows that house Big Sur's 60 "seminarians" — its own name for clients — is dominated by the main lodge. Other emotions, some of them hostile to Esalen, have been aroused by the institute's most notorious and over-publicized attraction: its hot sulphur baths, where seminarians of both sexes soak blissfully in the nude during breaks in their sessions.

Shocking Experience. Esalen's curriculum, like that of most human growth centers, is wide. The fall 1970 catalogue offers a smorgasbord of workshops, labs and seminars, among them group sessions for millionaires ("On Becoming Rich"), couples, divorcees and dentists ("The manner in which the professional approaches his patients and practice is, in general, a reflection of the way he approaches life").

There are also numerous workshops in Gestalt therapy, an approach devised by the late German Psychiatrist Frederick S. Perls. One of the newest and most rebellious branches of psychology, Gestalt theory seeks to celebrate man's freedom, uniqueness and potential. This is markedly different from conditioning his behavior, after the manner of B. F. Skinner and other behaviorists, who argue that man is infinitely malleable, or from probing his subconscious and his past, like Freud. The "here and now," according to Perls, is all that matters: the mind and body are inseparably one; converts are commanded to "lose your mind and come to your senses." This is implied by the very word *Gestalt,* which means configuration, or the whole, and which, as applied in therapy, insists on the unity of mind and body. Hence it places great emphasis on the body as a part of the whole; and it is this emphasis, widely practiced by human potentials groups, that has helped earn the movement a reputation for being anti-intellectual. The accusation is not entirely true, but a casual visitor to Esalen could be forgiven for believing it.

To the uninitiated, an Esalen encounter group can be a shocking experience. As TIME's Andrea Svedberg, who herself attended one, reports: "People touch, hold hands, kiss, throw each other up in the air, fight, use all the dirty words, tell each other cruel truths. Every aspect of so-called proper behavior is discarded. Every emotion is out in the open — everybody's property." Feelings are not spared. In time, the group develops a tribal loyalty, as fiercely protective as it is critical.

Over the years, Esalen has evolved, mostly by trial and error, dozens of ways by which group members can learn to communicate with their bodies rather than with their minds. Each procedure has its purpose. When, for instance, the spirits of some grouper noticeably sag, he may be rocked tenderly in the air on the hands of the others. Tears are a summons to "cradle": the moist-eyed one is warmly and multiply embraced. An extension of cradling is the hero sandwich: the whole group, often as many as 35 persons, cuddle together in a formation rather like the football huddle, but far more intimate. Esalen has also elevated massage to something of an art. The body is kneaded, not gently, from neck to foot; to some seminarians, the massage becomes an emotional bath — what insiders call a "peak experience."

Exciting Feedback. All such exercises are calculated to awaken in the grouper a new awareness of and respect for the purely physical side of his being. In a way, it is an extension of the flush of well-being that is one of the rewards of the exercise, an attempt to recruit all of the senses — not just the mind — into the act of living.

Although no one man dominates the human potentials movement, its contemporary origins can be traced to the late psychologist Kurt Lewin, who fled to the U.S. from Nazi Germany in 1933. With him he brought a fascination with the dynamics of the group, society's basic unit. Lewin's work convinced him that no amount of telling people what to do — the standard educational approach — could be half so instructive as letting them find out for themselves.

It was this principle that, by accident, gave rise to the National Training Laboratories, the first serious entrant in the human potentials movement. In 1946, the Connecticut Interracial Commission sought Lewin's advice in solving the state's interracial problem. With three colleagues, Lewis brought black and white leaders together to discuss their differences.

But because of Lewin's interest in the dynamics of group behavior, he also appointed four observers, with instructions to record their comments after each meeting: how things went, why things went wrong, etc. The conferees insisted that they be allowed to participate in these post-mortems. "What happened was that they found the feedback more exciting than the actual event — the conference," says Leland Bradford, former executive director of N.T.L.

At its Main retreat, opened in 1947, the N.T.L. began applying the feedback process to what has become an entirely new educational approach: the T group. Uninstructed and agenda-less, the group begins to coalesce in a highly charged emotional atmosphere. At first, group members are reserved; but eventually they remove their social masks. Says Bradford: "People come as lonely people — we're all lonely people — and find they can finally share with somebody. One statement I've heard 300 or 400 times from T-group members is, 'You know, I know you people better than people I've worked with for 30 years.' "

Intense Encounter. T groups are now conducted internationally by 600 N.T.L.-trained leaders and are designed to improve corporations, government agencies, churches and other institutions. They differ from encounter groups in that they tend to be less emotional, place more reliance on verbal than on nonverbal communication, and are less concerned with the individual's growth per se than with his development within his group. T groups improve relationships within organizations by trading what the late Douglas McGregor of M.I.T. called management's "X" approach (do as I say) for the "Y" approach (join with me so that we can work things out together). Obviously, that does not and cannot make equals of the boss and the factory hand; if that is the unrealistic goal, the "Y" approach will fail. But by making the president and the factory hand more aware of each other it can vastly improve the employee's sense of his own value and place.

The pervasiveness of the human potentials movement is demonstrated by the inroads it has made even in relatively conservative cities like Cincinnati, where T groups and encounter groups have become an integral part of business·and civic activities. Procter & Gamble and Federated Stores, for example, both use human potentials groups to increase the effectiveness and morale of their staffs. After hours, some of the employees, inspired by their office training, conduct private encounter groups of their own. Methodist and Episcopal church leaders regularly schedule group training sessions for their laity, and the University of Cincinnati sponsors sensitivity groups both to improve the workings of its own departments and to aid the community at large. Even the police department is involved. Next month new recruits will be given 40 hours of group sensitivity training to give them a better understanding of the problems and ways of the city's minorities. N.T.L.'s approach represents what might be called the conservative end of the human potentials movement. At the other, or liberal end are Esalen and all its imitators and derivatives. Somewhere in between lies the Center for Studies of the Person in La Jolla, Calif., a loose confederation of 53 psychologists, sociologists, anthropoligists, philosophers, educators, clergymen and journalists.

Its informal objective might be described as that of the movement's interpreter to those who have heard of it and want to know more.

The very eclecticism of the human potentials movement has brought it criticism even from within its own ranks. Robert Driver, founder and operator of Kairos, San Diego's human growth center, has compared it to "a tree which is growing too fast without putting down proper roots." The movement also attracts a great many persons who join it for the wrong reasons: "Already," says Driver, "we see some growth experiences that are used merely to blow out tubes every six months or so."

Re-entry Problem. There is genuine concern as well at the lack of follow-up procedures to determine the long-term effect of the group experiences. Says Psychologist Richard Farson, an Esalen adviser, "All research shows that people have the most tremendous subjective reaction after it is over — as a rule, more than 80% say they are overwhelmingly responsive. But the objective results — testing — show virtually no lasting effects. It is difficult to show as much as a 5% change in anybody even after the most intense encounter." The movement admits the need to learn why the benefits appear to be short-lived. But follow-up procedures cost big money and the movement is still a deficit operation. This year, for example, Esalen broke even for the first time since its gates opened in 1962.

There are more disturbing aspects of the proliferating group sessions. Among some 200 Stanford University undergraduates exposed to a wide variety of personal growth workshop experiences, the overall "casualty rate" — those who suffered psychological impairment — was 8%. Perhaps even more significant was the discovery that a so-called charismatic leader, or trainer, within the movement produced a casualty rate of 14%. Psychiatrist Louis A. Gottschalk of the University of California, after participating in one encounter group of eleven, diagnosed "one borderline acute psychotic withdrawal reaction" and "two severe emotional breakdowns with acute anxiety" within that group. Irving D. Yalom, chairman of the American Psychiatric Association's Task Force on encounter groups, reports that after one T group session 10% to 15% of the members consulted a resident psychiatrist for such adverse responses as anxiety, depression, agitation and insomnia.

The explanation could lie in the possibility that some leaders themselves may desperately need what they preach. At most growth centers, anyone can join the movement as a trainer with little experience. He learns on the job. Many such trainers are unequipped to recognize the casulties they produce. Their approach tends to be simplistic. "If expression of feelings is good," says the A.P.A. report sarcastically, "then total expression — hitting, touching, feeling, kissing and fornication — must be better."

The movement is also well aware of what it calls the "re-entry problem." Writes Jane Howard in *Please Touch,* the result of a year's participation in the human potentials movement: "Just as it is hard to be sober when nobody else is, I found what thousands of other veterans of groups have found: that it is hard to re-enter 'back-home' reality after the intoxicating communion of a successful encounter or T group." Sometimes recognition that the world has not changed is more than the returning grouper's new sensory awareness can take . . . in which case he either turns into a "T-group bum," endlessly circuiting the growth centers, or into a cop-out. An alarming number of such refugees from reality leave their wives, families, jobs and communities.

Youth's Disaffection. The dangers are real. But the human potentials movement cannot be dismissed as a passing fad. "There is increasing concern for the humanization of organizations," says Dr. Vladimir Dupre, executive director of N.T.L., "an increasing desire by people to feel more connected with each other, to act on their own environment rather than feeling acted upon."

In education, where man's affective aspect is largely overlooked, the movement is probing a long-neglected area. Max Birnbaum, associate professor of human relations at Boston University, who believes that this neglect is in large part responsible for the counterculture subscribed to by the younger generation, feels that the answer to youth's disaffection might lie in the new movement. He sees the day when the learning experience will involve a group of peers, "in contrast to the traditional classroom, with the teacher as an authority figure and the students as charges." This model is already taking shape in many of the human potentials movement's group sessions.

It is too soon to assess the true value of the movement. According to Donald Clark, it does "not lead to old answers but to new puzzles, new problems, new models of experience, new perspectives, and subsequently may provide a possible — though not guaranteed — footing from which one may reach for new answers and new skills."

A WEEKEND ENCOUNTER: STRENGTH FROM THE GROUP

Senior Editor Leon Jaroff recently spent a weekend with a Cleveland encounter group. Here he reports on his experiences:

About the only thing that the dozen participants in Personal Growth Lab had in common was their need for the giant-size box of Kleenex conveniently placed on a round table littered with coffee cups and cigarette butts. Nearly everyone was in tears at least once during the emotionally charged weekend encounter in the basement activities room of the Methodist Church of the Redeemer in Cleveland Heights, Ohio, and two of the women wept almost continuously. Otherwise, we represented a diverse group: a married couple, an internal revenue employee, a few housewives, a physical-ed instructor, a secretary, a lawyer, a college student, and a commercial artist with a polio-crippled arm. Some of us had been attracted by the excellent reputation of the group leader Sylvia Evans, a psychologist and therapist with the Gastalt Institute of Cleveland. Some had registered (fee only $30 for the weekend) at the suggestion of their ministers or their therapists.

The setting was informal. We sat on chairs, benches and a sofa, or sprawled on the floor in a large circle. Our attire was equally casual: sports shirts, slacks, or dungarees. Unlike members of the more highly publicized encounter groups, none of us took off any more than his shoes. But before the session was over (four hours Friday evening, eleven hours on Saturday and nine hours on Sunday), many façades and illusions had been stripped away.

Sylvia, an attractive blond woman with three grown children, used a number of well-tested psychological devices to draw all of us fully into the sessions. We did yoga deep-breathing exercises, and sat back-to-back in pairs, talking to each other only about our immediate feelings, the "here and now" that is all-important to Gestaltists. We looked long and often uncomfortably into each other's eyes, then walked around in silence with our eyes closed, making physical contact with each other — clasping hands, embracing, caressing — whatever we were moved to do.

After each exercise, Sylvia asked: "Does anyone want to share his experience with us?" When one of us made a revealing response, she deftly turned the group's attention — like a movie director shifting a camera — toward him, moving in for a closeup that was soon followed by flashbacks and moments of drama.

One of those moments occurred on Saturday, while Barbara, a housewife, was nearing the end of a tearful recital about her husband. Suddenly she turned to a trim, young, redheaded girl, and said: "Frances, I wish I could be strong like you." Her envy was understandable. In the first two days of the encounter, Frances had seemed confident, sensitive to the problems of others, familiar with psychiatric jargon, and articulate almost to the point of being glib.

But Frances responded unexpectedly: "Don't call me strong, not now. Not now." Sylvia turned to look at Frances. "Why do you say *now?*

Perhaps you should close your eyes and fantasize. Tell us what you visualize, whatever comes into your head."

"I see a lot of black, sticklike shapes," Frances began. "They are moving around, but one is becoming more prominent. It represents today, and it is very important."

"Frances," one of the girls interrupted, "I don't know what the hell you are talking about."

Frances paused, swallowing. "All right, I'll tell you what I'm really talking about. Last April, my husband shot himself and left me with seven children — and I can't go on, I don't have the strength to go on." She put her head down on the sofa, sobbing convulsively. All of us, shocked and concerned, looked to Sylvia for help. She was silent, watching Frances compassionately. "If you let us," she said, "maybe we can help." At Sylvia's suggestion, Frances, still sobbing, lay on her back in the middle of the floor. We all knelt around her, placed our hands under her, lifted her above our heads and began to rock her back and forth. It all seemed rather silly at first, but Frances' face soon began to relax and the sobbing stopped.

After a few minutes we gently lowered Frances back to the floor, then placed comforting hands on her. "Now, one at a time," Sylvia said softly, "please return to your seats." (She explained to me later that had we all left simultaneously, Frances might have associated our departure with her earlier tragedy, in which all of her support was withdrawn at once.) Frances rose slowly, lit a cigarette and turned to look at us. "Thank you all," she said, her face breaking into a radiant smile. "I feel much better."

There were other emotional outbursts. Bob, a tall, powerfully built man, who had been largely reticent for most of the weekend, suddenly began to talk after I had expressed my enthusiasm for tennis. When competing in tennis, he said, or in other athletics, against someone not as good as he was, he often let up so much that he lost.

Sylvia saw her opportunity and seized it. The camera swung to Bob, and he was soon talking about how his father had often beaten his stepmother. "Are you still angry at your father?" Sylvia asked. Only disappointed, Bob insisted. Sylvia nodded knowingly. She instructed Bob to place a sofa cushion on the floor, to pretend that it was his father, and to express his "disappointment" to the pillow while he was hitting it. Bob took a few halfhearted swipes, and unconvincingly remonstrated with his father. Sylvia spoke sharply: "Say you're angry, not just disappointed — say it!" Suddenly Bob was pounding the pillow ferociously, half sobbing: "I'm angry at you, angry because you were so brutal. Why did you have to do it? Why?" Then he was in control again, looking a little sheepish.

Sylvia did not relent. "I want you to pick someone here and do something with them," she suggested. Bob looked around, chose the other big man in the group — Bernie — and suggested that they wrestle. At first the bout was only mildly competitive. But suddenly the two big men were ricocheting angrily from wall to wall while the rest of us scrambled for cover. It was obvious that Bob was a stronger and more experienced wrestler. But suddenly, as Bernie was squeezing him in a scissors grip, Bob went limp and gave up. "What's the matter, strong man," Bernie taunted, "You're not so strong after all, are you?" We all tensed, waiting for Bob's reaction, but there was none.

With Sylvia's guidance, we all talked to Bob about his problems, gradually bringing them into focus. Bob, conditioned by his father's brutality, is afraid of the damage his own strength can cause if he brings it to bear — or worse yet, if he loses control. Thus he strives to maintain complete control of his emotions and even of his speech.

By Sunday evening, Sylvia's camera had focused on everyone. Linda, uncertain of her femininity, sat opposite an empty chair representing her mother and accused her of always wanting a boy. She was reassured by several of us that she seemed feminine, indeed. Bernie, whose wife was leaving him, and Barbara, who was leaving her husband, each took the part of the other's mate and got deeply involved in an angry, accusative pushing match. Barbara, usually very controlled, was able to express her feelings freely for the first time in years. Carl, unaware of his pent-up anger, which Sylvia and several group members had sensed, was asked to walk around the circle, stopping in front of each of us and making a hostile remark. Sylvia had to drag his first statement from him. But his anger quickly accelerated as he made his rounds. "Why in the hell do you wear those stupid religious earrings?" he asked Barbara. "Stop being a clam," he yelled at Bob, "you're letting the rest of us down." When it was over, Carl could not deny that he at last recognized his hostility.

On Sunday, as Marcia was describing an unhappy interlude in her life, Sylvia, noticing the look of concern on my face, asked me why I seemed so involved. "I guess that Marcia's recitation disturbed me," I admitted. "Leon, come out into the middle of the room," said Sylvia. I stood up, and under the encouraging eyes of the group members whom by now I knew so well, stepped forward, with little self-consciousness. I was actually looking forward to an experience that only two days before I would have approached with a sense of dread. The camera swung toward me.

The Self-Actualizing Person in the Fully Functioning Family: A Humanistic Viewpoint

ELLIS G. OLIM

Any discussion of the American family today must take place within the context of what many observers regard as a crisis or, at best, a troublesome time of questioning and transition. We are beset by an unpopular war, social unrest, the repolarization of racial attitudes, the disarray and underfinancing of our public school system and public health services, student revolts, dissent and civil disobedience, the pollution of our air and water supplies, crime in the cities and towns, experimentation with drugs, experimentation with new forms of social structure,[1] and alarm over both birth and abortion rates. This litany of troubles, it seems, adds up to a crisis. The crisis is occurring in the decade we call an "age of affluence." There is a connection between the affluence and the crisis, but not all would agree on what the salient features of that connection are, and even fewer perhaps would agree on the conclusions to be drawn from the connection.

LOOKING BACKWARD

There are some who urge a retreat to an earlier age. They look at the past through gold-colored glasses, forgetting the evils of that past. They have a merciful amnesia about how things really were when they were young. An example of this is the position taken by Dr. Graham B. Blaine, Jr. (1966). He complains that our youth no longer have impulse control; that this comes from the failure of their parents to instill in them clear conceptions of what is right and what is wrong. He states that children should have definite limits firmly set by parents upon their impulsive behavior by clear disapproval, spanking, or deprivation. He says that willingness to punish and firmness of conviction about what is right and wrong are essential qualities of the good parent. It may be granted that there are some victims of overindulgent or negligent parents. Some of our youth have shed the old without having found viable new forms, new patterns, new ways of life. But there are far more victims of the affluent society than the victims of overindul-

---

[1] This refers not merely to the Hippie groups, but what may prove to be more significant, to experiments in intense group experiences and new social arrangements for the family (see Stroller; 1967, pp. 28-33).

gence: the same kinds of victims which we have had in periods of scarcity. Much of the juvenile delinquency and much of the civil disorder occurring today are occurring among the culturally disadvantaged and socially and economically deprived. "Black power" is *not* a response to parental indulgence.

The advice of those who urge a return to the past seems tedious. If anyone could show by any reading of history that man has ever been able to turn back the clock and recreate an earlier age, we should become more receptive to the point of view expressed by Dr. Blaine. Perhaps what the clock turners fail to grasp is that the behavior of individuals at the present time, or indeed at any time in history, is the result of a fantastically complex interaction amongst an incredibly large number of psychosociocultural variables. The recreation of an earlier age is impossible without the most thoroughgoing destruction of the present social structure. Not even those who yearn nostalgically for the past would subscribe to such a program of destruction.

MAN AS BECOMING

The view to which we subscribe, rather, is that man has a rendezvous only with the future. What we need today is a conception of man that is suitable for the world of tomorrow. We cannot accept the conception that parents know what is right and what is wrong, that they know what limits to impose on their children. Parents do not necessarily and automatically know what is good for the child, nor what is the good and what is the bad. And we certainly cannot accept today, in the face of research and clinical observation to the contrary, the idea that punishment and deprivation are good for children. True, if particular types of behavior intrinsically lead to unfortunate consequences for the individual, such punishment probably has some values. However, if punishment or deprivation is perpetrated by an agent, such as a parent or a teacher, there are unfortunate side effects, one of which is resentment and rebelliousness against the punisher. Of course the punishment may work in the short run but the undesirable behavior is merely driven underground, usually ready to reappear when the punisher is absent. If the internalization by the child of his conception of the parents' moral code is *too* effective, so that the child is a life-long victim of a harsh superego (Freud's conscience), the underground, undesirable behavior may never reappear, but in such instances, substitute forms will appear. In such cases, the victim is doomed to live in purgatory all his life, cheating himself of the opportunity to live full and spontaneously.

We do have a new conception of man. It is a conception that enables us to go forward into the future instead of trying to hold back the course of human development. This new conception is that man is constantly becoming. Man need not be a fixed outcome of environmental influences except in the case of the abnormal man who suffers from being fixated at a level of personality development from which he cannot rise, or in the case of men in those preliterate societies which were static, which remained the same over thousands of years. But it is a truism that our society is an evolving one, constantly changing, an open society. Our society challenges its members to develop a flexible stance, a stance that enables them to adapt to changing conditions. What we want, then, is not to encourage a static type of personality based on traditional notions of right and wrong, but the kind of person who is able to go forward into the uncertain future. The man of the future should be self-actualizing. This means that he should ever be moving toward a greater realization of his human protential and, equally important, that he be constantly transcending himself. The idea of self-transcendence has two meanings. In one sense, it means that man should overcome his egocentricity and enlarge his self to include concern with humankind. Its other, more modern, sense is that man is in a constant process of evolving into higher and higher forms of humanness, that his self is constantly going beyond previous selves. Man's human potential is not finite; it is infinite. There are no limits to the process of becoming.

Thus, Maslow (1955) talks of the "self-actualized" person; Rogers (1959) of the "fully functioning" individual; Allport of man as having a "passion for integrity and for a meaningful relation to the whole of Being in his most distinctive capacity" (1955, p. 98); Sullivan (1940) of the basic direction of the organism as forward; Horney of the powerful incentive "to realize given potentialities," "an incentive to grow" (1942, p. 22).

MENTAL HEALTH AND NORMALITY

The question of what kind of people we should be has been argued extensively by those who are concerned with what is mental health, or by a related question — what is the normal personality? One conception of mental health is that it is completely relative to the particular culture in which it occurs, i.e., each society has its own definition of normality. Usually, this conception also assumes that the normal or healthy personality is the modal personality; that the abnormal personalities are at the extremes (see Singer, 1961, pp. 9-90: Mowrer, 1948, pp. 17-46). Wegrocki (1948) argues against both the statistical-normative and the cultural-relativistic points of view. He holds that it is possible to achieve a pan-human definition of normality. He defines the normal person as one who does not react to an inner conflict by unconscious and symptomatic escape from inner conflict but who faces his problems. Mowrer (1948), also seeking a pan-human definition, asserts that all societies, no matter how diverse in form, have some ethical system, and that those members of the society who "play the game" and subscribe to the ethical system are normal. Neither Wegrocki nor Mowrer has refuted the notion of cultural relativity. One can always find commonality among diverse elements if one is willing to utilize a sufficiently high degree of abstraction to the point of lack of content. If we accept the notion that societies differ in the degree of freedom and openness allowed their members and the view that the personality is formed in interaction with the enviroment, then members of different societies will differ in their need to escape from conflict and in the amount of conflict experienced. And the conception of a standard of normality as "playing the game" falls apart when we try to apply it to real people in real societies. For example, were both Dean Rusk and Dr. Martin Luther King playing the same game? Are we to assume that Neville Chamberlin and Albert Schweitzer shared a common definition of "normality?" What is left out of Wegrocki's and Mowrer's definitions is attention to what it means to be *human*.

THE HUMANIST'S CONCEPTION OF THE IDEAL PERSONALITY

The conception of man as becoming, as self-actualizing, as moving toward the fully functioning individual, uses a different criterion, the conception of the "ideal" personality. But like the preceding definition, it, too, is a value judgment. It has no support in traditional scientific methods of verification. Its support comes, in the main, from persons who have become self-actualizing or who have observed others become self-actualizing. Though this is not considered good scientific evidence by those who are addicted to a nineteenth century conception of science, it has been sufficient evidence to motivate some to give up the quest for man as a successful achiever, and to think of him as a process of becoming human. Though the humanistically oriented psychologists and psychiatrists believe that this is the road to self-fulfillment, they can not prove it. But they are willing to take a chance, to encourage people to move from static, fixed, stereotyped personalities to dynamic, ever-changing, variegated personalities.

SELF-ACTUALIZATION AND THE FAMILY

How can we relate this conception of the self-actualizing person to the family? At the strictly sociological level of analysis it is customary nowadays to talk about the functions of the family not in terms of the older kinds of functions, such as that the family provides sustenance for its members, provides clothing and shelter, provides religious or other education and the like, but in terms of the family as an interaction system (Parsons and Bales, 1955). The family is the primary socializing agent in early childhood. Personality development, from a sociological point of view, is a function of this socialization process. In the nuclear family of America, there are two other important functions (Parsons and Bales, 1955) — the instrumental function, which is related to the external aspects of the family, to providing for the maintenance and physical well-being of the family; and the expressive function, which is related to the internal aspects of the family, to providing integrative and socio-emotional support for the family members. But this conception of the functions of the family as system does not demand that the children be socialized to any particular kind of behavior, that they develop any particular kind of personality. Nor does it require that the integrity of the family be maintained and sustained in any particular way.

What needs to be understood about Parsons' approach and that of Wegrocki, and with the approach in general of devising abstract conceptual systems is that these conceptualizations are heuristic devices and not statements about the content that goes into the conceptual system. They do not have the generality of laws in physics, for example, but rather the generality of mathematics. Physical laws can be confirmed by actual instances. However, the statement in mathematics that two plus two equals four cannot be confirmed by actual instances because it is pure abstraction. Although two apples plus two apples equals four apples, the statement that two pieces of white coal plus two pieces of white coal equals four pieces of white coal is not a statement about anything that exists outside the realm of fantasy. The conceptions of man-as-becoming, of man as self-actualizing, are not pure abstractions but deal with demonstrable processes and demonstrable outcomes, processes and outcomes that can be evaluated by some criteria.

What, then, might be some of the implications of the humanist view when applied to the family? What kind of family life would we have if every member of it were on the road to self-actualization? What kind of people would we produce in a fully functioning family? Before undertaking to answer such questions, however, by way of pointing up the contrast, we should like to mention briefly some of the cultural beliefs and values that have contributed to producing persons who are *not* self-actualizing.

It is a truism today that our culture has tended for a long time to promote conformity, triviality, and dehumanization. In the affluent society, things become the measure of man. Unfortunately, the views of Darwin, Weber, and Frued (Maddi, 1967), have been used by many social scientists to reinforce these tendencies.

Because Darwin documented the connection between man and subhuman animals, the characteristics of man that are not present in lower animals have sometimes been dismissed as unimportant or explained in simplistic terms. But man differs markedly from lower animals with respect to those things that make him human. There are internal, psychological processes in man that do not occur in lower animals. Man is aware of himself, he has values, he exercises judgment, he has imagination, he questions his own existence, he sometimes strives to become more human. Actually there is nothing in the concept of a phylogenetic scale that requires that we overlook the importance of characteristics that emerge at higher levels of development (Maddi, 1967). Nor is Darwinism incompatible with the view that man alone among the species undergoes a social evolution so that his personality is ever-evolving into higher forms that are different from those of earlier men.

The sociologist Weber is credited with one so-called sociological view of personality. This view is that the personality is the sum total of the social roles played by a person. We may readily grant that many people have personalities that come close to matching the conception. Nevertheless, persons who are merely the sum of the roles are hollow people. Such people lack an acute sense of personal identity. To them all the world is a stage, and they are actors on it. They are socialized to conformity instead of "creative becoming" (see Allport, 1955, p. 34). Actually though, the sociological role conception of personality can be reconciled with a psychological view of personality (Maddi, 1967). Since man is evolving socially, the social roles that he creates are evolving and changing, too. Social roles can encourage the development of imagination, of aesthetic experience, of creativity, of spontaneity, of the exercise of reason — behavior that leads to growth and self-enhancement. Another type of reconciliation that can be effected is described by Maslow (1967). He points out that in self-actualized individuals their vocational role is not something apart from their identities but that their vocation is an incorporated inextricable aspect of the self.

The humanist view differs from the orthodox Freudian position. In classical libido theory, Freud gives expression to the belief that life represents a compromise between the necessity of playing social roles — the accomplishment of which is done by sublimation of instinctual drives into socially acceptable channels — and the demands of biological, instinctual drives. In Freud, the ego, that part of the personality that is in contact with reality, is essentially defensive in nature. It serves to defend the individual against his anxiety-provoking instinctual drives on the one hand, and the harsh demands of his superego and of society on the other. To the classical Freudian, the wholesome individual is the well-defended one. Abnormality for Frued consists of extremes — on being defenseless or of being overly defended. The normal individual is optimally defended. But, with the exception of sublimation, all the defenses, according to Freud, distort reality to some degree. When the distortion seriously cripples an individual, the defenses are called pathological. There is no denying Freud's monumental contribution to our understanding of man. However, the Neo-Freudians and the ego psychologists have gone beyond Freud's original conception. Some of the ego psychologists reject the notion that the defenses are even necessary. They assume that defenses are always crippling, they deny that sublimation is a defense at all, and assert that it is a coping or adaptive mechanism, and they hold that the road to mental health consists in liquidating the defenses or preventing their origination, substituting adaptive, coping mechanisms in their place. The ego psychological view is extended further by humanists. Maslow (1967) describes self-actualizing people as "expressing" rather than "coping," as spontaneous, "more easily themselves" instead of playing the roles of other people.

THE FULLY FUNCTIONING PERSON

What is the difference between the fully functioning person (at this stage in history, such a person is more an ideal than a fact) and the kind of person here referred to as a conformist, as defensive, as operating at less than his potential, as not being on the road to self-actualization? One critical difference is that the fully functioning person has an acute sense of his own personal identity. As a consequence, he has also an awareness of his own powers to relate effectively to the world. He changes the world. He exercises mastery over it and over himself. The locus of evaluation of himself rests within himself. On the other hand, the normal personality, according to the classical Freudian description, or according to the view of a stimulus-response psychologist, places man in a reactive role. He reacts to environmental influences. He has little or no subjective awareness of his identity as a unique human being, but tends to see himself only as others see him, to see himself as a commodity (Fromm, 1947). He is molded by others: he is programmed as though he were a machine. For him technological progress becomes the automation of dehumanization, to use Kenneth Clark's apt phrase.

Let us now turn to how the fully functioning person might develop. He is not born fully functioning. The development does come about through environmental influences and, in early childhood, this means notably the parent-child relationship. Later it means also the relationship between the child and significant other persons in his environment. Still later his development will be affected by others through what he reads. The most essential ingredient for starting a child on the road to self-actualization is, according to Rogers (1959), the presence of unconditional positive regard. This means that the growing child is appreciated as a human being. He is not punished for being human. He is not taught to become ashamed and guilty about his humanness. Valuing the child for his humanness means that he must be valued for the development of imagination, symbolization, aesthetic awareness, empathy, and reason. When the child is so valued, the initiative for learning and development comes from within the child, not from external rewards or punishments. Obviously the child must be taught some things. Each child cannot discover the whole history of man and man's thought all by himself. Nevertheless, wide latitude must be given to the child to discover and construct reality for himself, to find his own values, his own beliefs, his own moral code, what he wants to do with his life, his own identity. The roles he takes must be selected by him, not foisted upon him. If, as a parent, you wish to cripple your child, value him only when he does the things you want him to, disvalue him when he differs. Emphasize to him that he must assume certain social roles, and that he may not assume others. Concentrate on his roles; neglect his psychology.

To become a self-actualizing individual requires the courage to face the unknown. Therefore, the fully functioning individual is frightening to a conformist, who seeks the security of the known. It can be demonstrated that this is so because we have today in our midst young people who are on the road to self-actualization: the student activists. During the 1950's university students were called the "quiet" generation. They had "buttoned down" minds (Flacks, 1967). Polls, such as the Purdue poll, showed that students were unconcerned with deep values. They were complacent, status-oriented, committed only to exurbanite conformity. They wanted to wear gray flannel suits, become organization men, live in suburbia, and drive station wagons. Then suddenly in the 1960's, there burst upon us a new generation of young people. These people question. They protest. They are indifferent to the opportunity for status and income. These are not youths who were attracted to activism because they were economically deprived, or because their opportunities for upward mobility were blocked (Flacks, 1967). These are highly advantaged youths, whom some call the "victims" of an affluent society. Nor can these young people be explained as a generation in revolt. The youth of the early thirties were, by and large, a generation in revolt. These youths are not. Nor is it entirely a matter of generation gap. The good baby doctor stands shoulder to shoulder with the babies whose rearing he helped to shape. Studies have shown (see Flacks, 1967, p. 20 ff) that the parents of student protestors often share their offsprings' views, that the parents are not conventional conformists. Most activists come from a very special kind of middle or upper-middle class family. Both parents tend to be college educated, the father is a professional, the mother often has a career as well, both parents and children tend to be political liberals. The student activists state that their parents have been permissive and democratic. The parents describe themselves in these terms also. These youths do not want to find meaning in their lives in terms of status and role. Neither are the student activists, by and large, interested in copping out. They are willing to assume some of the dominant values of our culture. They are willing to contribute, but they are not willing to work for things that only have a price tag. They are not willing to make the compromises with their own sense of integrity that the upwardly mobile child from a deprived or non-affluent environment is all too willing to make. To the person willing to compromise and to the conformist, growing up means developing a cynical attitude toward the virtues. Thus, becoming conservative does not often mean desiring to conserve the best in man, but becoming a conformist, a compromiser, a "realist." The student activist rejects this. He has a basic concern with individual development and self-expression, with a spontaneous response to the world. The free expression of emotions and feelings is viewed as essential to the development and integrity of the individual. He is also concerned with self-development and expression in aesthetic and intellectual areas. Moreover, he is concerned with the social condition of others. He has a strong humanitarian outlook. This is what accounts for the popularity of VISTA and the Peace Corps, for the campus revolts, for students joining in civil rights struggles, and for student dissent.

The self-actualizing individual is above all a doubter. Descartes' famous affirmation of his existence, "I think, therefore I am" is well known. What is often overlooked is the context of the statement. It occurs in *Discourse on the Method* and is expounded in his *Meditations on First Philosophy,* in which he describes how he arrived at his insight by starting with a profound doubt about the truth of anything (Haldane and Ross, 1931). The self-actualizing person doubts. He questions the meaning of life, of existence. This is a completely different kind of anxiety from the debilitating feeling with which Freud was concerned. Existential anxiety is the anxiety that one feels as one plunges into an ever-changing, unknown world. Doubt is the mark of man.

There is a serious clash in our society today between a "successful" and "affluent" society, which demands that behavior follow relatively fixed rules of conduct as defined by tradition, and the emerging values and doubts of the new humanists. One of the stated purposes of insisting upon rules is to protect the individual against unpredictable, and possibly destructive, impulses. Some fear that we will create monsters if we permit children to actualize themselves. This is an unfounded fear, a myth. There is nothing in our study of evolution or in our study of man that warrants the conclusion that is allowed to become human, man will be other than humane. Man, humane, is not interested in destroying himself. The humanist therefore rejects fixed rules. He is more flexible. He sees the spontaneous flow of feelings and ideas as intrinsically good, indeed essential, for optimal personal growth. To the child who has grown up in a humanistic environment, pursuit of the status goals encouraged in him by society, by the public school, by college means hypocrisy, the sacrifice of personal integrity.

THE FULLY FUNCTIONING FAMILY

Implicit in the foregoing is the notion that the fully functioning family is one in which all the individuals in it are open to one another, and are open to experience. They do not take stereotypical roles. They do not confuse conservatism with conformity. The fully functioning individual will find his way to traditional values that should be conserved. A person will not find his way to them if they are foisted upon him by moral exhortation, by citation of tradition and authority. The climate in the fully functioning family is thus flexible, highly fluid, in a continuous state of process, of becoming. The members in the family are defenseless before one another. They value one another in toto, not merely for certain aspects of their behavior. Do we not want to create people who are able to work not under coercion, not without any sense of self-fulfillment, but able to work joyously, to work with the thrill and excitement of the artist, the creator? And do we not want to create people who are able to love fully and deeply, to love not only those close to them but to love all mankind?

Humanistic parents raise their children in an environment relatively free of constraints, an environment that is favorable to experimentation, expressiveness, and spontaneity. Humanistic parents stress the significance of autonomous and authentic behavior, freely initiated by the individual and expressing his own true feelings and ideas.

Parents who are afraid of children like this, then, may not have understood the meaning of self-actualization. They have not understood what it means to have a mature mind.

REFERENCES

Allport, G.W. *Becoming: Basic Considerations for a Psychology of Personality.* New Haven: Yale University Press, 1955.

Blaine, G. B., Jr. *Youth and the Hazards of Affluence.* New York: Harper & Row, 1966.

Flacks, R. Student Activists: Result, Not Revolt. *Psychology Today,* 1967, 1, 18-23, 61.

Fromm, E. *Man for Himself.* New York: Rinehardt and Company, Inc., 1947.

Haldane, E. S. and G. R. T. Ross (Trans.) *The Philosophical Works* of *Descartes.* Vol. I, New York: Dover Publication, Inc., 1911.

Horney, K. *Self Analysis.* New York: W. W. Norton & Company, Inc., 1942.

Maddi, S. The Existential Neurosis. *Journal of Abnormal Psychology,* 1967, 72, 311-325.

Maslow, A. Deficiency Motivation and Growth Motivation. In M. R. Jones (Ed.), *Nebraska Symposium on Motivation,* 1955.

Maslow, A. A Theory of Metamotivation: The Biological Rooting of the Value-Life. *Journal of Humanistic Psychology,* 1967, 7, 93-127.

Mowrer, O. H. What is Normal Behavior? In L. A. Pennington and Irwin A. Berg (Eds.), *An Introduction to Clinical Psychology,* New York: The Ronald Press Company, 1948.

Parsons, T. and R. F. Bales, *Family, Socialization and Interaction Process.* Glencoe: The Free Press, 1955.

Rogers, C.R. A Theory of Therapy, Personality, and Interpersonal Relationships, as Developed in the Client-Centered Framework, In S. Koch (Ed.), *Psychology: A Study of a Science.* Vol. 3. New York: McGraw-Hill, 1959.

Singer, M. A Survey of Culture and Personality Theory and Research. In B. Kaplan (Ed.), *Studying Personality Cross-Culturally,* Evanston: Row, Peterson and Company, 1961.

Stroller, F. H. The Long Weekend. *Psychology Today,* 1967, 1, 28-33.

Sullivan, H. S. *Conceptions of Modern Psychiatry.* New York: W. W. Norton & Company, Inc., 1940.

Wegrocki, H. H. A Critique of Cultural and Statistical Concepts of Abnormality. In C. Kluckhohn and H. A. Murray (Eds.), *Personality in Nature, Society, and Culture*. New York: Alfred A. Knopf, 1948.

UNIT STUDY GUIDE

A. *Terms to Review*

Cultural relativity	Instrumental v.	N.O.W.
Conjugal family	expressive	Self-actualization
Ego psychology	Kibbutz	Women's Liberation
Feminine	Masculine stereotype	Zero-sum game
mystique, the	Mass media	

B. *Questions for Discussion and Study*

1. Describe and discuss similarities and differences in the ideologies of the sexual equality and human potentials movements.
2. Identify and discuss some counter-organizational movements designed to negate the sexual equality movement (e.g. the M.O.M. organization and its auxiliary, W.O.W.).
3. Define and illustrate the statistical-normative and culutral-relativistic approaches to the definition of normal, healthy, personality. Compare these with the humanist's conception of ideal personality.
4. Which of the two movements considered do you see as most significant in changing the quality of marital relations in the long-range perspective? Why?
5. Carefully consider your own current family situation. In what ways, if any, do you see your family interaction of marital patterns influenced by the sexual equality and human potentials movements?

C. *Topics-Ideas for Papers and Projects*

1. Research: "The Treatment of the Sexual-Equality Movement in the Confessional Magazines."
2. Locate and interview several persons active in either the sexual equality or human potentials movement in your area. How similar or different are they in their perceptions of movement goals, means, and achievements?
3. "The Nineteenth-century Foundations of the Twentieth-Century Sexual Equality Movement."
4. Research: "Social and Familial Background of Activists in the Human Potentials Movement."
5. It has been suggested by some that unconscious or latent sexism is manifested in the writings of many leaders in the human potentials movement. Design a research project to test this proposition.

PART TWO

PRELUDES TO
MARITAL PARTNERSHIP

Unit 3

Human Sexuality: Potentialities and Realities

... self-actualizing men and women tend on the whole not to seek sex for its own sake, or to be satisfied with it alone when it comes. — *Maslow*

The closer one looks at the various manifestations of human love the more one is conscious of a congruity between spiritual love and sex. — *D'Arcy*

Introduction

The focus of this unit is not on sex in its primarily biological aspects, its features as a basic drive or impulse, but on culturally shaped expression of sexuality as one very important facet of interpersonal relationships. An underlying assumption is that the socio-cultural defining and shaping of biological sexuality holds great potential for defining and shaping, in turn, the quality of interaction in intimate human partnerships.

Historically, of course, the forms of approved sexual expression have been institutionally defined, regulated. Most would probably concede that, in order to survive, any society must have some operating norms; and most would also grant that some constraints on sexual expression are feasible. However, as we have seen in previous readings, American society is characterized by a multiplicity of values. In fact, most of our social and personal problems are to some extent definable in terms of conflicting or confused values. So it is precisely at this point of deciding on the norms for regulating the expression of human sexuality that almost every major institution in our society gets involved in the ambivalence, confusion, and contradictions surrounding this topic in American society. It has been somewhat cynically pointed out by several writers that the U.S. seems to be the only country in the world where love is a national problem. We could add that sex also seems to qualify for this dubious distinction. Some of the problems and issues connected with human sexuality and its expression may be seen in various "trends" which have been proffered by some as evidence of a "sexual revolution."

There is considerable evidence of change in sexual behavior and attitudes over the past few decades. This fact remains regardless of whether or not we choose to take these developments as evidence that a sexual revolution is really occurring. From the viewpoint of this book, most observed trends and changes in matters sexual derive their importance from their being closely tied to issues surrounding the nature or quality of interpersonal, and especially man-woman, relationships in this society. As we have suggested earlier, this emergent reformulating of interpersonal relations patterns has been strongly influenced by the dynamics of the human potentials and sexual equality movements. Problems and issues reflecting the influence of these social movements can be detected as we summarize several observable trends in sexual expression. The trends which are mentioned below should not be taken as a comprehensive listing of the indicators of change in norms, values, and behavior related to sexual expression. Some trends:

1. *The changing uses of sexuality.* A fundamental trend has been from procreative to non-procreative sexuality. In our society this trend has gone hand in hand with the development of contraceptive technology. In value terms, we could describe this trend in part as a movement from *instrumental* toward *expressive* sexuality. The former connotes utilitarian use of sex as a means to an end, as duty or obligation. Typical are the earlier norms legitimizing sexual intercourse only for the purpose of reproduction, or a "bartering" situation in which typically the woman used sex as a means of obtaining from a man those things otherwise denied her. Expressive sexuality connotes intimate and rewarding interpersonal communication, potential for mutual erotic enjoyment, and the perception of erotic behavior as having intrinsic value.

2. *Change in female roles.* In erotic terms, the image of the female as passive, receptive, an object to be "possessed," is giving way to the perception of the woman as active, initiatory, as a true partner in sexual behavior. Bernard has referred to this sub-revolution as "the re-sexualization" of the female body.[1] Speculation suggests a related trend—the decline of the *double standard* of sex morality.

3. *Decline in acceptance of arbitrary sources of sexual morality.* Organized religion has been a potent, though not exclusive, source of proscriptions and prescriptions regarding sexual behavior. A significant trend among Americans, however, is to view sexual behavior in terms of its meaning and impact for the individuals within a particular interpersonal relationship. Sexual morality is thus increasingly defined in flexible situational terms rather than finding its definition in the fixed, relatively absolute dictums of the religious institution. This trend is reflected even in the writ-

ings of chuch leaders. A noted Bishop, John A. T. Robinson, has said, for example, that ". . . nothing can of itself always be labelled 'wrong.' One cannot, for instance, start from the position 'sex relations before marriage' or 'divorce' are wrong or sinful in themselves. . . . the only intrinsic evil is lack of love."[2]

4. *The development of organizations to promote sexual experience.* One of the most unusual, and to some, most shocking, developments in the sexual revolution has been the open organization of groups designed to enhance the "sex is fun" approach. Swinging and swapping clubs with a "recreational" approach to sexuality are scattered throughout the society and it is estimated that as many as eight million couples have at some time participated in the exchanging of partners for sexual purposes.[3] It would be erroneous to conclude that this development *per se* reflects increased promiscuity. Indiscriminate sexual intercourse, contrary to widespread opinion, is not typical behavior among group sex advocates or members of 'sex clubs'. Associated with this development is a decline in the norm of privacy, both in interpersonal relations generally and specifically in the expression of affectional and sexual motives.

5. *Open, candid discussion of sexuality.* This trend has been accompanied by bitter debate over the extent to which it is 'healthy' to discuss sexuality openly. The range of erotically motivated behaviors that should be opened for discussion in schools, and the sources and kinds of information to be used in the process. One person's candor is obscenity to another.

What are some continuing issues in sexuality? In answering this question, we will again be reminded that problems and issues are closely related. In the following listing of "issues," culled from much larger lists provided by many students, there obviously are implications of personal problems. It can be noted also that most of the issues identified by students seem related to ideas central to the concerns of the sexual equality and human potentials movement. Perhaps you could add to this listing. Some issues:

The source of sex morality. Who is to decide: the individual, religion, science, a panel of experts??

Societal needs for control vs. individual needs for expression. How is the balance to be established? Freedom vs. restriction.

Education for sex vs. education against sex. Sex education for whom—the young, the old, the married, the single?? The content of "sex education" and the teaching-learning process—who decides and who implements??

Sexuality and erotic motives as a "natural" component of personality. Can persons accept themselves and their impulses as normal? The question of nudity—interpersonally and in private: can persons accept their own bodies—especially those parts of the body which have a high sexual identity? The problem of shame.

Premarital, non-marital, and extramarital sex. What are the costs, the benefits, the results? Should there be any norms, should commitments be unspoken between mates or should understandings be explicit? Why must all sex prior to marriage be regarded as *premarital?* What are the assumptions each partner has in the sexual relationship before or outside of marriage? The conflict of *de facto* vs. *de jure* norms bearing on sex outside marriage.

The physical attractiveness factor in sexuality. Do current norms of "attractiveness" distort normal sexuality and its expression? *Bona fide* personhood vs. stereotyped images.

The relation of sexuality to sex roles and gender identity. How do prevailing ideas of what men and women are "really like" affect interpersonal relations? How is individual personality shaped by these prevailing images? Can we have sexual expression without sexism?

Sex, love, and commitment. Should sexual intercourse be pursued for its own sake, or should there be evidence of caring for and feeling affection for one another as a basic prerequisite?

Commercialism and exploitation of sexual potential. Sex as a "selling aid." "Sex-appeal toothpaste." What are its effects on values and behavior? Should there be constraints? What about the "porno" movies, "adult" book-shops, etc.??

We have now reviewed a few of the issues and problems associated with human sexuality as it is expressed in this society. In the readings which follow, we could look for some alternatives, implicit and explicit, for dealing with our current situation.

REFERENCES

1. Bernard, Jessie, "The Fourth Revolution," *Journal of Social Issues,* (April 1966), 76-87.

2. Robinson, John A. T. *Honest to God,* (Phila.: Westminister Press, 1963) p. 118.

3. Breedlove, William and Jerrye. *Swap Clubs: A Study in Contemporary Sexual Mores.* (Los Angeles: Sherbourne Press, 1964), p. 44.

4. Margolis, Herbert and Paul M. Rubenstein. *The Groupsex Tapes.* (New York: David McKay Co., 1971), pp. 288-293.

Sexual Adequacy in America

PHILIP E. SLATER

The use of an engineering term like "adequacy" in relation to an act of pleasure exemplifies the American gift for turning everything into a task. Even more curious is that the criteria of adequacy are not the same for men and women. For men, adequacy is usually focused on erection; for women, on orgasm. A man tends to be defined as "adequate" to the degree that he is able to bring a woman to orgasm, preferably through the use of his penis ("Look, Ma, no hands!"). A woman, however, tends to be defined as adequate to the degree to which she is able to "achieve" orgasm rapidly through the same method. A woman gets defined as sexually adequate only insofar as she can make the man feel that *he* is sexually adequate. Note that by these definitions a man is considered adequate when he can delay climax, while a woman is considered adequate when she can accelerate it. Why isn't the same standard of adequacy applied to both sexes?

Some might argue that women have a different timing pattern than men and that the goal of these definitions is to bring men and women into synchrony. We live, after all, in a highly scheduled, clock-oriented society, and it is important that people arrive at the same place at the same time. But who can say whether these much discussed timing differences are biological or cultural. The implicit attitude behind most discussions of female orgasm is that the longer time period preceding it is an unfortunate defect of feminine physiology. Buy why wouldn't it be just as appropriate to say that the shorter time period before the typical male orgasm is due to a defect in men? Don't men say that brevity equals "inadequacy" among men? Then why not say that brevity equals inadequacy for men *in relation to women*? That, in other words, men as a sex are less adequate than women.

Suppose we were to say not that "it takes a woman longer to reach orgasm than a man" but rather that a woman can delay orgasm longer than a man. If we are going to use terms as absurd as "adequacy" in relation to pleasure at all, this seems to me the more reasonable statement. We are talking about the "ability" to tolerate and sustain pleasurable stimulation without release: the simple fact is that women can absorb and tolerate more pleasure than men can and hence are more adequate to the "business" of enjoyment.

I have always been fascinated that women seem to be far more capable of being attracted to a homely male than vice versa. Why is it that a homely woman, or an older one, is so much more likely to be disqualified as a sexual partner? Many men in our society are attracted only to women who are young, thin, long legged, large breasted, made-up, depilated and deodorized. Does the fact that men are so easily turned off—by age, weight and sundry other departures from some narrow *Playboy* ideal—mean that they really don't like women much? Is their heterosexual desire so weak that only some weirdly specialized feminine image can flog it into being? Why is it that women can be turned on by men who are old or ugly? Are they sexier than men? Less squeamish and fastidious? Or do they really like men more than men like women?

Psychiatrists tend to respond to such observations by talking vaguely about latent homosexuality. Yet a large proportion of male homosexuals can be aroused only by *men* who are young or exceptionally good-looking. Reaching the age of 40 can be as great a disaster for a gay male as for a heterosexual woman. In fact, men, whether homosexual or heterosexual, seem far more exacting in their standards of attractiveness than are females of either persuasion. This is another way of saying that women are more easily turned on than men—that they can take their sex with fewer condiments.

This statement flies in the face of the old-fashioned idea that men were "more sexual" than women, but this idea has had a relatively brief history and has been largely limited to the Western world. Historically and cross-culturally it has more often been women who are portrayed as the sexual, earthy beings, with men viewed as more restrained, controlled, spiritual and less susceptible to demands of the flesh. Women, ususally seen as the source of evil, have appeared frequently in folklore and literature as sexually insatiable creatures, undermining the efforts of men to pursue chaste and lofty enterprises.

Men throughout history have devoted a surprising amount of energy to the construction of a Feminine Ideal. These ideals have varied from culture to culture, but they share a large area of agreement. Women should be sexually accessible but not sexually demanding, docile and servile but yet not totally uninteresting. The contradictions are worked out in different ways, usually by emphasizing the passivity of the feminine role (always willing but never asking). The Ideal Woman is sometimes encouraged to develop pleasing little skills that will make her interesting to the male without threatening his vanity. In other instances, it is stated flatly that the Ideal Woman should be an ignorant booby. On one point all writers are in complete agreement: the Ideal Woman exists only for men.

It is difficult to read this literature—whether English, Greek, Chinese, Moslem or American—without sensing the profound pathology that lies beneath them: the obsessional detail; the writer's exhausting struggle to reslove his ambivalence by controlling and constricting another person's behavior; the zealous effort to pretend that the problem lies outside the author's perverse brain; the inability to recognize that a completely accommodating individual can be only a nonperson, a robot. One suspects that these lectures are really misdirected. Intended perhaps for the frantic, seductive, demanding and overpowering mothers of their authors, they are delivered instead to their wives, who, thereby constricted and constrained, transfer all their frantic, seductive and overpowering needs onto their sons, thus continuing the cycle.

Women rarely write such documents, perhaps because fathers, as a rule, are less omnipresent in the life of a small child than are mothers. In any case, women seem to have been able to take men pretty much as they found them. They may have tried to make improvements on a given man, and they may have longed for some perfect Prince Charming, but by and large they have not wasted paper writing treatises on how the Ideal Male should behave in the daily fulfillment of his role.

All this suggests that men feel at a severe sexual disadvantage with women. They want them passive, docile, exciting yet undemanding. They continually argue that if only women could walk this or that psychological tightrope, *then* men would feel safe and be attracted to them. A man, it seems, has difficulty feeling like a man if a woman approaches him as a free, independent, fully sexual being. It is as if he feels handicapped in sexual encounters and needs to create a comparable handicap for the woman.

Perhaps men *have* become sexually handicapped relative to women—not just in the physiological sense of having a more finite capacity for repetition, but culturally, in the sense of having evolved a social role that limits their capacity for physical pleasure. In all civilized societies men have sacrificed a part of their eroticism to the pursuit of wealth, status, power and political dominance over women. They have then harassed their womenfolk in a variety of ways to compensate for the feelings of sexual inferiority that his sacrifice engendered.

Work and sex are natural enemies, and the more personal commitment the work generates, the more inroads it makes into erotic life. For the ambitious careerist, as John Cuber and Peggy Harroff found in their study of successful executives, government officials and professionals (*Sex and the Significant Americans*), eorticism tends to become perfunctory—a release rather than a pastime. Clearly if pleasure is something to be caught on the fly in the interstices of effortful striving, then the quicker it is done with, the better. Men tend to define themselves by their professions—a man is a banker or a lawyer first, a person second, and it is difficult for one who thinks this way to invest himself totally in a love relationship or spend days in leisurely lovemaking.

It is often said that love is only a part of a man's life, the whole of a woman's. Although the intent of this sentiment is to keep women in their place, it expresses a historical reality. Men have invested in professions a part of the energy and interest that women devote to relationships. Eroticism thereby became women's domain, into which men enter as dilettantes in some sense.

The history of sexual mores in civilized societies is a chronicle of the efforts of men to use their political advantage to rectify this sexual disadvantage. The most common form of harassment has been through sexual restrictions, such as premarital virginity and marital fidelity. These restrictions have usually been applied exclusively to women and have succeeded to some extent in warping, crippling and blocking their sexual spontaneity. Nineteenth-century Europe produced a more subtle and insidious form of sexual control. Men began to impose upon women a feminine ideal stripped of sexual impulse. Reversing the usual idea of the spiritual male opposed to the carnal female, they made allowances for the "animal nature" of men and denied that any respectable woman had such a thing. This was a more powerful device since it crippled feminine sexuality at the core. Its transparent absurdity, however, made it vulnerable to social reform.

Ironically, the efforts of psychoanalysis to achieve such reform produced what was by far the most powerful technique yet devised for giving women a sexual handicap comparable to that borne by men. This was the dictum that mature female sexuality should center in the vagina and should de-emphasize the clitoris—a brilliant gambit inasmuch as the clitoris is the center of erotic sensation. Before the researches of Masters and Johnson undermined this dogma, two generations of women had felt guilty and inadequate because of a man's fantasy about how their bodies should function. Thus the psychiatric profession was for some years able to achieve psychically the same goal sought by certain primitive tribes, who limit the sexuality of their women by cutting away the clitoris at puberty.

Whoever makes the labels holds the power, and all these devices have been invented by men. Each has served in one way or another to cause women to doubt their natural sexual impulses, and this limitation on feminine sexuality has in turn served to make men feel more competent in the sexual sphere.

Discussion of sexuality in America has always centered on the orgasm rather than on pleasure in general. This seems to be another example of our tendency to focus on the *product* of any activity at the expense of the *process*. It may seem odd to refer to an orgasm as a product, but this is the tone taken in such discussions. Most sex manuals give the impression that the partners in lovemaking are performing some sort of task; by dint of a great cooperative effort and technical skill (primarily the man's), an orgasm (primarily the woman's, which masculine mystification has made problematic) is ultimately produced. The bigger the orgasm, the more "successful" the task performance.

This thought pattern owes much to the masculine preoccupation with technical mastery. Women in popular sexual literature become manipulable mechanical objects—like pianos ("It's amazing what sounds he can get out of that instrument"). Even more pronounced is the competitive note in writers such as D. H. Lawrence and Norman Mailer, who often make it seem as if lovemaking were a game in which the first person to reach a climax loses.

The emphasis on organsm also reveals, paradoxically, a vestigial puritanism. The term "climax" expresses not only the idea of a peak or zenith but also the idea of termination or completion. Discussion of the sexual act in our society is thus primarily concerned with how it *ends*. Leisurely pleasure-seeking is brushed aside, as all acts and all thoughts are directed toward the creation of a successful finale. The better the orgasm, the more enjoyable the whole encounter is retrospectively defined as having been. This insures against too much pleasure obtained in the here and now, since one is always concentrating on the future goal. In such a system you can find out how much you're enjoying yourself only after it's all over, just as many Americans traveling abroad don't know what they've experienced until they've had their films developed.

Eastern love manuals, although rather mechanical and obsessional in their own ways, direct far more attention to the sensations of the moment. The preoccupation in Western sexual literature with orgasm seems to be a natural extension of the Protestant work ethic in which nothing is to be enjoyed for its own sake except striving.

The antithetical attitude would be to view orgasm as a delightful interruption in an otherwise continuous process of generating pleasurable sensations. This would transform our ways of thinking about sex—we would no longer use the orgasm as a kind of unit for lovemaking, as in "we made love three times that day" (. . . "I have two cars," "I played nine holes of golf," "He's worth five million dollars"). The impulse to quantify sex would be sharply diminished, and along with it the tendency to infuse pleasure-seeking with ideas of achievement and competition. Affectionate caresses exchanged in passing would not be so rigidly differentiated from those interludes culminating in orgasm.

Women already espouse this view to a greater degree than men; witness the complaint of many women that their husbands never caress them except in bed. The reason they assign to this behavior, however—"he's only interested in sex, in my body, not in me"—misses the point. A man who behaves this way is not interested in sex, either—he is interested only in releasing tension. Far from enjoying pleasurable stimulation, he cannot tolerate it beyond a minimum level and wants it to end as rapidly as possible within the limits of sexual etiquette and competent "performance."

This desire for release from tension, for escape from stimulation, lies at the root of our cultural preoccupation with orgasm. In a society like ours, which perpetually bombards its participants with bizarre and dissonant stimuli — both sexual and nonsexual — tension release is at a premium. It is this confused and jangling stimulation, together with the absence of simple and meaningful rhythms in our daily lives, that makes Americans long for orgasmic release and shun any casual pleasure-seeking that does not culminate in rapid tension discharge.

It is men who suffer most from this need for tension release, since it is men who have specialized most acutely in sacrificing feelings in the service of ambition—in postponing gratification, in maintaining a stiff upper lip, in avoiding body contact, in emotional coldness. Women often express the feeling in the midst of intense lovemaking that they want it never to end. I wonder how many men are capable of sustaining such a sentiment—are able to imagine themselves enjoying endless inputs of acute pleasurable stimulation?

The emphasis in popular sexual literature on the ecstatic agony thus caters primarily to men. A favorite theme, for example, is that of the inhibited or resistant woman forced by overwhelming sexual arousal into unexpected and explosive orgasm. This sadomasochistic fantasy has two roots. First, it expresses the common masculine wish for some kind of superpotency—one glance and she falls writhing to the ground; one stroke and she explodes in ecstacy. Second, it involves an identification with the woman herself. For it is *men* who have bottled up feelings and long to burst their controls. But since this yearning endangers the whole edifice of our culture, it cannot be allowed direct expression and is projected onto women. Women are the emotional specialists in our society — they are supposed to do the crying, screaming, clinging and so on, not only for themselves, but for the men as well ("It would break your mother's heart if you went away").

The fantasy of the woman propelled into orgasm against her will is just another expression of the general tendency of men to give women the job of releasing masculine tensions vicariously. Indeed, part of the sexual hang-ups suffered by women spring from having to play out this fantasy for men. Many women feel inadequate when they are not consumed with passion at the first approach of their lover and guilty that they have thereby injured his vanity.

It seems to me that when sexual gratification is plentiful, orgasm is not the goal of every erotic encounter from the start but is a possible outcome arising naturally as the lovemaking proceeds. In a comfortable sexual setting, in other words, some lovemaking is nonorgasmic.

This observation should not be considered some sort of ideal. The last thing I want to do is to add another "should" to our already overburdened sexual mores. The notion of sexual "adequacy" seems to have had a poisonous effect on the American psyche as did simple Puritan probibitions or Victorian restraints, and the contributions of psychiatry, however well intended and often insightful, have merely added to the confusion. Psychoanalysts have demanded "vaginal" orgasms, have ranked orgasms by degree of total bodily involvement, have demanded fantasy-free sex (which has the amusing effect of consigning all sexual intercourse performed with procreation in mind to the realm of perversion). All these efforts to establish medical grading systems for sexual behavior seem to have had the unfortunate effect of increasing the sexual pathology against which they were directed.

From a cold, detached physiological viewpoint, the "goal" of the human orgasm is to maintain some kind of balance in the sphere of pleasurable stimulation. A degree of tension and excitement is prerequisite to life, and a degree of release is necessary for internal order and serenity. The fantasy of complete discharge — of the perfect, ultimate orgasm — is fundamentally a death fantasy. People we view as particularly alive are those capable of sustaining a lot of pleasurable stimulation without discharging it or blunting their senses; but a person *unable* to discharge often seems nervous and jumpy. These styles are sometimes difficult to distinguish in practice, and, by the same token, a person with a low level of tolerance for stimulation may appear either serene or dead. It is most important to recognize that this balance differs for each person, and no one else can decide for that person the appropriate balance to be maintained or the best way of obtaining it.

But this is, as I said, a cold physiological view of the matter. From a merely human viewpoint an orgasm is simply something that happens involuntarily when pleasure peaks, and probably the less cognitive messing about with it we do, the better.

Parent-Child Conflict
in Sexual Values

ROBERT R. BELL

The old cliche that as one grows older he becomes more conservative may be true, if premarital sexual values held by parents are compared with the values they held when they were younger. In this paper, the interest is in the nature of sex value conflict between parents and their unmarried late adolescent and young adult children. Our discussion will focus on values held by parents and by their unmarried children toward premarital sexual intimacy.

Conceptually, our approach focuses upon values related to a specific area of sexual behavior held by individuals from two very different role perspectives. The perspectives differ because parents and children are always at different stages in the life cycle, and while parents are highly significant in the socialization of their children, other social forces increasingly come to influence the child as he grows older. The various social values that influence the child's sexual behavior are often complementary, but they may also be contradictory. Furthermore, various types of influences on the acceptance of a given set of values may operate on the child only during a given age period. For example, the youngster at age fifteen may be influenced by his age peers to a much greater extent than he will be at age twenty.

Given their different stages in the life cycle, parents and children will almost always show differences in how they define appropriate behavior for a given role. Values as to "proper" premarital sexual role behavior from the perspective of the parents are greatly influenced by the strong emotional involvement of the parent with his child. Youth, on the other hand, are going through a life cycle stage in which the actual behavior occurs, and they must relate the parent values to what they are doing or may do. There is a significant difference between defining appropriate role conduct for others to follow and defining proper role conduct to be followed by oneself. Even more important for actual behavior, there is often more than one significant group of role definers to which the young person can turn to as guides for his sex role behavior. Therefore, our discussion will focus more specifically on parent values related to premarital sexual intimacy, the peer group values of youth, and how these two different age groups, as role definers, influence the sexual values and behavior of unmarried youth.

For several reasons, our discussion will center primarily on the middle class. First, this class level has been highly significant in influencing changes in general sexual values and behavior. Second, and on a more pragmatic level, what little research has been done on parent-child conflict over sexual values has been done with middle-class groups. Third, the general values of the middle class are coming to include an increasing proportion of the American population. This also suggests that the values and behavior of college youth are of increasing importance as this group continues to expand in size and influence within the middle class.

A further limit is that our main focus is on the generational conflict between mother and daughter. The history of change in sexual values in the United States has been complexity interwoven with the attainment of greater sex equality and freedom by the female (2). Also, the relationship between the mother and daughter tends to be the closest of the possible parent-child relationships in the family socializing of the child to future adult sex roles. Furthermore, whatever the value system verbalized and/or applied by the girl, she often has more to gain or lose personally than the boy by whatever premarital sexual decisions she makes.

We also believe that any analysis of conflict over premarital sex between generations should center on *value* changes rather than *behaviorial* changes. On the basis of available evidence, it appears that there have been no significant changes in the *frequency* of premarital sexual petting or coitus since the 1920s. Kinsey has pointed out that "there has been little recognition that the premarital petting and coital patterns which were established then (1920s) are still with us" (15, p. 300). Therefore, it is important to recognize that the parents and even some of the grandparents of today were the youth who introduced the new patterns of premarital sexual behavior about forty years ago.

PARENT VALUES ABOUT PREMARITAL SEX

The transmission of sexual values by parents to their children is only a small part of all parent values passed on during the family socialization process. Most parents do a more deliberate and comprehensive job of transmitting values to their children in such areas as educational attainment, career choice, religious beliefs, and so forth than they do with reference to any aspect of sexual values. Often when parents do discuss sex with their children it may be from a "clinical, physiological" perspective with overtones of parental embarrassment and a desire to get a distasteful task over with.

But perhaps more important than the formal confrontation between the parent and child in sexual matters are the informal values transmitted by the parent. In the past girls were often taught that premarital sexual deviancy was dirty and shameful, and that nonconformity to premarital sexual chastity values would mean suffering great personal and social shame. This highly negative view of premarital sex is undoubtedly less common today, but the newer, more "positive" values may also have some negative consequences. Very often today the mother continues to place great value on the daughter's virginity, and stresses to the daughter the great virtues of maintaining her virginity until marriage. But the "romantic" view of the rewards for the girl who waits for coitus until after marriage are often highly unrealistic and may sometimes create problems by leading the girl to expectations that cannot be realistically met in marital sex. Morton Hunt writes with regard to this approach that "if the woman has been assured that she will, that she ought, and she *must* see colored lights, feel like a breaking wave, or helplessly utter inarticulate cries, she is apt to consider herself or her husband at fault when these promised wonders do not appear" (13, 114). Whether or not the "romantic" view of marital sex is presented by her mother the girl often encounters it in the "approved" reading list suggested by the adult world, which tells her about the positive delights of waiting for sex until after marriage. So, though premarital sexual control may be "positive" in that it is based on rewards for waiting, it can be "negative" if the rewards are unrealistic and unobtainable.

For many parents, a major problem as their child moves through adolescence and into early adult years centers around how much independence to allow the child. Because they often recall the child's younger dependency, it may be difficult to assess the independency of the same child who is now older. Also, over the years the growing child has increasingly become involved with reference groups outside — and sometimes competing with — the family. In other words, the self-role definitions by the child and the parents' definitions of the child's role undergo constant change as the child grows older. For example, "The daughter in her younger years has her role as daughter defined to a great degree by her mother. But as she grows older she is influenced by other definitions which she internalizes and applies to herself in her movement toward self-determination. The mother frequently continues to visualize the daughter's role as it was defined in the past and also attaches the same importance to her function as mother in defining her daughter's role. But given the rapid social change associated with family roles the definer, as well as the definitions, may no longer be institutionally appropriate" (5, 388).

Parents may also be biased in their definitions of their child as less mature than they, the parents, were when they were the child's age. One can not recall experiences earlier in the life cycle free from influence by the events that have occurred since. This may result in many parents thinking of their younger selves as being more mature than they actually were. At the same time the parents' view of their child's degree of maturity may be biased by their recall of him when he was younger and less mature. Thus, from the parents' perspective they may recall themselves as youngsters within the context of what has occurred since (more mature) and may see their offspring within the context of their earlier childhood (less mature).

There also may be some symbolic significance for parents who must define their children as having reached the age when something as "adult" as sexual behavior is of relevance. In part, viewing one's children as too young for sexual involvement may contribute to the parents' feeling young, while seeing their children as old enough to be involved in sexual activity may lead to some parents feeling forced to view themselves as aging. For example, the comment about a man seen out with a young woman that "she is young enough to be his daughter" may have implications for his self-role image if the young woman *is* his daughter. We have little research data on how the aging process of parents influences their definitions of appropriate behavior for their young adult children.

In general, it is probable that most parents assume that their children, especially their daughters, accept the traditional restrictive values about premarital sexual behavior unless they are forced to do otherwise. Also, because of the great emotional involvement of parents with their own children, there is a common parental tendency to attribute sexual "immorality" to other youngsters. For many parents to face the possibility that their children do not conform to their values is to suggest some failure on the part of the parents. Often, rather than admit failure, the parents may define their children as having been forced to reject the parent values by other social influences or that their children have willfully let them down.

YOUTH VIEWS ABOUT PREMARITAL SEX

The importance of age peer group influence on the values and behavior of young people has been shown by a number of social scientists (see: 6, 9, 10, 11, 12, 14, 19, 20, 21, 22). Because youth subcultures are to some degree self-developing, they often have conflict points in relation to some dominant adult values. However, the inconsistency and lack of effective adult definitions for adolescent behavior have also contributed to the emergence of youth subcultural values. That adults often view the adolescent with indecision as to appropriate behavior means that sometimes given adolescent behavior is treated one way at one time and in a different way at another time. Since the young person desires some decisiveness and precision in his role definitions, he often develops his own role prescriptions. Often when he creates his own role expectations, he demands a high degree of conformity by other adolescents as "proof" of the rightness of his definitions. It is ironical that the adolescent often thinks of himself as a social deviant. What he fails to realize is that his adolescent group deviates from the adult world, but that the requirements for conformity within his youth subculture are very strong (1, 369-374).

Youth subcultures have developed great influence over many aspects of premarital male-female interaction. The patterns of dating and courtship, appropriate behavior, success and failure are for the most part patterns defined by the youth group and not by the adult world. Yet, heterosexual relationships of youth are often based on adult role patterns, and they are therefore an important part of the youth world because they are seen by the youth as symbolizing adult status. To many young people, who are no longer defined by the adult world as children, but are not yet given full status as adults, their involvement in what they see as adult roles is important to them in seeking for adult status and recognition.

A part of the American youth subculture has been the development of new values related to premarital sexual intimacy. Reiss suggests that "It might well be that, since the 1920s, what has been occurring is a change in attitudes to match the change in behavior of that era" [premarital sexual behavior] (16, 233). The evidence suggests that for at least some college students new sex norms are emerging at the various stages of dating and courtship. One study found that "on the dating level necking is the norm for females and petting for males. During going steady and engagement, petting seems to be acceptable for both sexes. This would suggest that the young people both act and accept a higher level of intimacy than has generally been suggested by courtship norms" (3, 63).

In the past, emhpasis was placed on the girl's virginity at the time of marriage; but today, many young people may only emphasize her being a virgin until she is in love, which may mean at the stage of going steady or engagement (8, Ch. 5 and 16, Ch. 6). If the girls is in love, some premarital sexual relations may be acceptable by peer group standards, although the dominant adult values — that love *and* marriage are basic prerequisites for coitus — continue. In the United States love as a prerequisite for sexual relations has long been a necessary condition for most middle-class females. The condition has not changed; rather, the point in the courtship-marriage process where it may be applied to sexual involvement has shifted. Hence, the major point of parent-child conflict over premarital sex centers around the parent value that one should be in love *and* married before entering coitus and the modified value system of youth that an emotional and interpersonal commitment is important, but that this may occur before marriage.

There are two recent studies that provide some evidence on the nature of generational conflict; one study is of youth and adults in general and the other study is specifically concerned with mothers and their daughters. Reiss, in his extensive study of premarital sexual permissiveness, provides data on values held by adults as contrasted with values in a sample of high school and college students. The respondents were asked to express their beliefs about different combinations of intimacy and degree of interpersonal commitment for both unmarried males and females. Respondents were asked if they believed petting to be acceptable when the male or female is engaged. In the adult sample the belief that petting during engagement was acceptable for the engaged male was the response of 61 per cent, and for the engaged female the response was 56 per cent. Of the student responses 85 per cent approved for the engaged male and 82 per cent for the engaged female (17, 190-191); thus adult attitudes about petting during engagement were more conservative than those of the student population. It may also be noted that for both the adult and student groups there was a single standard — that is, the acceptance rates were essentially the same for both males and females.

Reiss also asked his respondents if they believed full sexual relations to be acceptable if the male or female were engaged. Approval was the response given by 20 per cent of the adult group for males and 17 per cent for females. In the student group acceptance was given by 52 per cent for the male and 44 per cent for the female (17, 190-191). Here, as with petting, there are significant differences between the adult and the student samples, and once again both respondent groups suggest a single standard of acceptance or rejection for both males and females.

A study by Bell and Buerkel compared the attitudes of 217 coeds with those of their mothers. Both mothers and daughters were asked to respond to the question, "How important do you think it is that a girl be a virgin when she marries?" Of the mothers, 88 per cent answered "very important," 12 per cent "generally important," and 0 per cent "not important"; compared to 55 per cent, 34 per cent and 13 per cent of the daughters (4, 391). Both the mothers and daughters were also asked: "Do you think sexual intercourse during engagement is: very wrong; generally wrong; right in many situations?" The percentages for each response category were 83 per cent, 15 per cent and 2 per cent for the mothers; and 35 per cent, 48 per cent, and 17 per cent for the daughters (4, 391).

Both of the questions show sharp differences between the value responses of the mothers and daughters with reference to premarital chastity. Many mothers were undoubtedly influenced in their responses by having a daughter in the age setting where the question had an immediate and highly emotional application. Nevertheless, the differences in mother and daughter responses indicate that the area of premarital sexual behavior is one of potentially great conflict. One means of minimizing conflict is for the daughter not to discuss her sexual values or behavior with her mother. In the Bell and Buerkle study it was found that only 37 per cent of the daughters, in contrast with 83 per cent of the mothers, felt daughters should freely answer question from their mothers in regard to attitudes toward sexual intimacy (4, 392).

The area of sexual values appears to be highly influenced by emotion, especially for the mother with reference to her daughter. Generational conflict with regard to premarital sexual intimacy has a variety of implications. First, the conflict in values clearly suggests that the traditional morality is often not socially effective as a meaningful determinant of behavior. Social values have behavioral influence when they emerge as social norms with significant rewards and punishments. In the case of sexual norms, however, there are rarely clearly articulated rewards, or positive consequences, for the conforming individual. In almost all situations the effectiveness of sexual norms is dependent upon their negative sanctions, or punishments. For example, the traditional norm of female premarital chastity bases its behavioral influence primarily on negative consequences for the girl who fails to conform. This negative means of control is most commonly found as a part of the adult value system. In effect, the major sanctions over premarital chastity are based upon punishments for the girl and for her family if she deviates. Yet, in most cases the girl who has premarital coitus is not discovered by her parents or by the community. The real danger for the girl often centers around premarital pregnancy, because if that occurs and becomes known there can be no denying premarital coitus. Vincent has suggested that an important part of the negative sanction toward premarital pregnancy is not the pregnancy itself, but rather that it symbolizes premarital coitus *and* getting caught (23, Ch. 1).

The available studies indicate that fear of pregnancy is not the major deterrent for most girls (7, 344 and 15, 315). The personal values of the girl appear far more important in restricting her from engaging in premarital coitus. Yet, within the privacy of the youth world, there may operate for some girls certain values positive toward premarital coitus. For example, there may be a strong emotional desire and commitment to the boy and a positive feeling by the girl of wanting to engage in greater sexual intimacy.

There is a tendency by parents, as well as by many who give professional advice, to overlook the pleasurable aspects of sex at all ages, especially for the young who are experiencing sexual pleasure for the first time. Undoubtedly many girls engage in premarital sexual intimacy to "compensate" for some need and many may suffer some negative consequences. But it is foolish to state categorically that the "artificial" setting of premarital sex always makes it negative and unpleasant for the girl. We would be much more honest if we recognized that for many girls premarital coitus is enjoyable and the participants suffer no negative consequences. This was illustrated in the Kinsey research; it was found that "69 percent of the still unmarried females in the sample who had had premarital coitus insisted they did not regret their experiences. Another 13 per cent recorded some minor regrets" (15, 316). Kinsey also found that "77 per cent of the married females, looking back from the vantage point of their more mature experience, saw no reason to regret their premarital coitus" (15, 316).

The Extent of Generational Conflict

With the evidence suggesting strong conflict between generations with regard to premarital sexual values, our final consideration is: how permanent is this generational conflict? We can provide some evidence on this question by examining the values of college-educated females of different ages. This appears justified because higher educated females are generally the most liberal in their views about sexual rights and expectations for women.

The evidence suggests that the premarital sexual liberalism of the college girl may be a temporary phenomenon. The coed's sexual liberalism must be seen as related to the interactional context of her being emotionally involved, and to a future commitment to an on-going paired relationship. The Bell and Buerkle study (4) found that the values of daughters toward the importance of premarital virginity were very similar to those of their mothers, until they had spent some time in college. However, at "around age twenty there emerge sharp differences between mothers and daughters in regard to premarital sexual attitudes. Behavioral studies indicate that it is at this point that sexual activity is greatly intensified, perhaps because it is at this age that college girls are entering engagement. A suggested pattern is that the college girl of twenty or twenty-one years of age, in her junior or senior year and engaged, has a strong 'liberal' pattern toward premarital sexual behavior and attitudes" (4, 392 and 18, 696).

We can get some indication of the persistence of premarital sexual liberalism by comparing the values of mothers by education. In the mothers' views as to the importance of premarital virginity it was found that the college educated mothers were actually as "conservative" as those mothers with lower levels of education (4, 392). It is quite possible that in the future the coeds will become as conservative as the college educated mothers. This may occur when the coed's attitudinal rationales are not related to herself, but as a mother to her own daughter. It is therefore possible that the "sexual emancipation" of the college girl exists only for a short period of time, centering mainly around the engagement years.

Yet, even if the girl becomes more conservative as she grows older, and especially with reference to her own daughter, her temporary "liberalism" probably is contributing to some shift in adult values about premarital sexual intimacy. Certainly, today's parental generation accepts greater sexual intimacy as part of the premarital heterosexual relationship. Probably most parents assume that their adolescent and young adult children are engaging in necking and even some petting. Most parents, as long as they don't actually see the sexual intimacy, don't concern themselves about it. However, to suggest that parents may be more liberal (or tolerant) or premarital sexual intimacy does not necessarily suggest that parents are liberal if the intimacy reaches coitus.

It also appears that there has been some reduction in the severity of negative sanctions by parents if the daughter deviates and is caught. Among middle-class parents today it may be less common to reject the unwed daughter if she becomes pregnant than in the past, and more common for the parents to help her. This is not to suggest that today's parents offer any positive sanctions for premarital pregnancy, but that they may be able to adapt (often painfully) to it, rather than respond with high rejection and anger.

If our suggestion is correct (that parents take a less totally negative view of "discovered" premarital coitus), then this further suggests that traditional sexual values are being altered, since, as we have suggested, in the past the values of premarital chastity were primarily based on the negative consequences for those who deviated and were caught. If these negative consequences have been reduced, then the social force of the traditional values has been reduced as a means utilized by parents to control premarital sexual deviancy.

CONCLUSIONS

Based on the available evidence, there are several general speculations that may be made about future generational conflict over premarital sex. In general we would suggest that conflict between parents and their adolescent-young adult children with regard to premarital sexual intimacy may decrease in the future, because of several trends.

1. The trend in the United States is toward a more liberal view of sexual behavior in general. This is reflected in the generally accepted professional opinion that the woman has a right to sexual satisfaction, and that sexual satisfaction is a desirable end in itself. The trend toward a belief in a single sexual standard for both men and women, even though within the setting of marriage, is bound to influence the beliefs and behavior of the unmarried. For the unmarried, there may be an increasing tendency to attach less importance to the marriage act as the arbitrary dividing line between socially approved and socially disapproved sexual intimacy.

2. Since the evidence suggests that over the past three or four generations the rates of female premarital coital experience have not changed, and since the younger generation has developed some value frameworks for its behavior, modification of traditional values and behavior may increasingly influence the values of parents to be more liberal. That is, it may become increasingly difficult for many parents to hold their children to a set of conservative values which they, the parents, did not hold to when they were younger.

3. Parents seem increasingly unwilling to strongly punish their daughters who sexually deviate and are caught. This parental reduction of punishment may be influenced by the increasing public attention directed at such social problems as illegal abortion. For example, many parents may be more willing to accept and help an unmarried pregnant daughter than take the risk of her seeking out an illegal abortion. The possible negative consequences of abortion may appear more undesirable than the premarital pregnancy.

4. Less generational conflict will occur if parents know less about the sexual activities of their children. A great part of the social activity of young people is carried out in the privacy of their age peer setting;

what they do in the way of sexual intimacy is increasingly less apt to be noted by their parents. With the development and marketing of oral contraceptives, the risks of premarital pregnancy will be greatly reduced. In the future the rates of premarital coitus may remain the same, but with the chances of pregnancy reduced parents may be less aware of their children's premarital coitus.

Over time, then, the values of parents and the adult community in general may become more liberal and the conflict between generations reduced. (There seems little possibility that the opposite will occur; i.e., the younger generation's reducing the conflict by becoming more conservative.) But in the meantime, and certainly in the near future, it appears that parents and their children will continue to live with somewhat different value systems with regard to premarital sexual values. Parents will probably continue to hold to traditional values, and assume that *their* child is conforming to those values unless his actions force them to see otherwise. The youth generation will probably continue to develop their own modified value systems and keep those values to themselves, and implicitly allow their parents to believe they are behaving according to the traditional values of premarital sexual morality. For many parents and their children, the conflict about premarital sex will continue to be characterized by the parent's playing ostrich and burying his head in the sand, and the youth's efforts to keep the sand from blowing away.

REFERENCES

1. Bell, Robert R. *Marriage and Family Interaction,* Homewood, Ill.: The Dorsey Press, 1963.

2. Bell, Robert R. *Premarital Sex in a Changing Society,* Englewood Cliffs, N.J.: Prentice-Hall, (in press).

3. Bell, Robert R. and Leonard Blumbert. "Courtship Stages and Intimacy Attitudes," *Family Life Coordinator,* 1960, 8, 60-63.

4. Bell, Robert R. and Jack V. Buerkle. "Mother and Daughter Attitudes to Premarital Sexual Behavior," *Marriage and Family Living,* 1961, 23, 390-392.

5. Bell, Robert R. and Jack V. Buerkle. "Mother-Daughter Conflict During The 'Launching Stage,' " *Marriage and Family Living,* 1962, 24, 384-388.

6. Bernard, Jessie (Ed.). "Teen-Age Culture," *Annals of the American Academy of Political and Social Science,* November, 1961, 338.

7. Burgess, Ernest and Paul Wallin. *Engagement and Marriage,* Philadelphia: J. B. Lippincott, 1953.

8. Ehrmann, Winston. *Premarital Dating Behavior,* New York: Henry Holt, 1959.

9. Ginsberg, Eli. *Values and Ideals of American Youth,* New York: Columbia University Press, 1962.

10. Gottlieb, David and Charles Ramsey. *The American Adolescent,* Homewood, Ill.: The Dorsey Press, 1964.

11. Grinder, Robert. *Studies in Adolescence,* New York: Macmillan, 1963.

12. Hechinger, Grace and Fred. *Teen-Age Tyranny,* New York: Crest, 1962.

13. Hunt, Morton M. *The Natural History of Love,* New York: Alfred A. Knopf, 1959.

14. Kelley, Earl C. *In Defense of Youth,* Englewood Cliffs, N.J.: Prentice-Hall, 1962.

15. Kinsey, Alfred C., Wardell B. Pomeroy, Clyde E. Martin and Paul H. Gebhard. *Sexual Behavior in the Human Female,* Philadelphia: W. B. Saunders, 1953.

16. Reiss, Ira L. *Premarital Sexual Standards in America,* Glencoe, Ill.: The Free Press, 1960.

17. Reiss, Ira L. "The Scaling of Premarital Sexual Permissiveness," *Journal of Marriage and the Family,* 1964, 26, 188-198.

18. Reiss, Ira L. "Premarital Sexual Permissiveness Among Negroes and Whites," *American Sociological Review,* 1964, 29, 688-698.

19. Remmers, H. H. and D. H. Radler. *The American Teenager,* New York: Charter, 1957.

20. Seidman, Jerome. *The Adolescent,* New York: Holt, 1960.

21. Smith, Ernest A. *American Youth Culture,* New York: The Free Press, 1963.

22. Symonds, P. M. *From Adolescent to Adult,* New York: Columbia University Press, 1961.

23. Vincent, Clark. *Unmarried Mothers,* Glencoe, Ill.: The Free Press, 1961.

Sexual Codes in Teen-Age Culture

IRA L. REISS

Teen-age sexual codes reflect quite clearly the bold outlines of adult sexual codes. The high degree of conformity in teen-age culture increases the observability of teen-age beliefs and adds to our understanding of adult beliefs. The teen-ager exists in a world somewhere between youthful idealism and adult realism, and his sexual codes reflect this state of being. In a very real sense, he is a marginal man with one foot in the world of the child and the other foot in the world of the adult.[1]

The teen-ager is at the stage at which it is vitally important for him to learn how to exist in society independent of his parents. For this reason, he transfers his dependence to his peers and strives to learn from them the secrets of entrance into the adult world. One would think that this vaguely defined status of "almost adult" would lead to confusion and weak statements of belief. To a large extent, this is the case, but nevertheless, it is equally true that it leads to dogmatic statements of belief and a search for conviction through conformity. Teenagers translate and adapt the sexual codes of adults to fit their particular circumstance and state of mind.[2]

GOING STEADY

When unchaperoned dating gained prevalence in the early part of this century, it involved much more rapid change of dating paterns than occurs today. Nevertheless, by the time of World War II, going steady had taken root, and, today, it seems that slightly more than half of the high school students have some going-steady experience. Even among the early teenagers, possibly one quarter go steady.[3]

Class differences are important in examining the going-steady complex. It seems that those high school people who go steady and plan to go to college are not likely to marry their high school steadies, and those who are from lower economic classes and who do not plan to go to college are much more likely to marry their high school steadies.[4] Thus, in looking at the custom of going steady, one must realize that there are different subtypes and that the consequences differ for each type.

Although a psychologist may point to the security of going steady as

Reprinted from "Sexual Codes in Teen-Age Culture" by Ira L. Reiss in volume no. 338 of *The Annals* of The American Academy of Political and Social Science. Reprinted by permission of the publisher and the author.

its chief reason for being, as a sociologist, I would point out how Western society has, for centuries, been developing an association of sexual behavior with mutual affection. This association is hard to achieve in casual dating; but, in steady dating, sex and affection can quite easily be combined, and, in this way, a potential strain in the social system is reduced. Another area of strain which is reduced by going steady is the conflict a girl may feel between her desire for sexual experience and her desire to maintain her reputation. For many, sexual behavior is made respectable by going steady.[5] In these ways, one may say that no other dating custom is quite as central to the understanding of teen-age sexual codes as going steady.

GIRLS' SEXUAL CODES

One of the most popular sexual codes among teen-age girls is petting-with-affection. This code is a modern day subtype of our formal abstinence standard. This subtype of abstinence seems extremely popular among high school couples who are going steady. Such couples feel it is proper to engage in heavy petting if they are going steady, the justification being that they are in love or at least extremely fond of each other. The petting-with-affection sex code probably grew along with the going-steady custom; they both illustrate adaptations of our dating institution to the newer unchaperoned dating circumstances.

What evidence do we have for such petting behavior among teen-agers? Though surely not perfect, the most extensive study of sexual behavior is that done by the Institute for Sex Research, formerly headed by Alfred C. Kinsey and now run by Paul H. Gebhard. It should be noted that the Kinsey studies are most valid for urban, white, northeastern, college-educated people, and, thus, great care must be taken when applying the results to other groups. The reader should keep in mind the tenuousness of any such generalizations made in this paper.

Kinsey's data show that, of the females who were twenty years old or older when interviewed, about one fifth to one fourth admitted they had petted to orgasm while still in their teens. Most of this behavior occurred between the ages of sixteen and twenty. About three-quarters of all the girls twenty years old or more admitted being aroused by some form of petting or kissing in their teens, and approximately 90 per cent stated they had at least been kissed during their teens.[6]

Those girls who marry in their teens start their petting and kissing behavior earlier than those who marry later. In general, the few years previous to marriage are by far the most sexually active for girls. Lower class females marry earlier, and, thus, they are more active in their teens and are more likely to marry their teen-age steadies.

These rates are averages for Kinsey's entire sample of several thousand females; were we to take only the females born in more recent decades, the rates would be considerably higher. For example, of those females born before 1900, only 10 per cent ever petted to orgasm in their teens, whereas, of those girls born in the 1920s, almost 30 per cent, or three times the proportion, petted to orgasm in their teens.[7]

It seems clear that we have developed not only new dating forms such as going steady but also, as we have seen, new sexual codes to go with them. These new codes allow females much more freedom in heavy petting, provided affection is involved. Of course, other girls, particularly in the early teens, adhere to standards which only permit kissing, and a few others adhere to standards which allow full sexual relations, but, by and large, petting-with-affection seems the increasingly popular sex code for high school girls.

The most recent evidence of the nature of teen-age sex codes also supports these contentions. This evidence comes from research which the author is engaged in at present.[8] Some preliminary reports on this study were made in the author's book *Premarital Sexual Standards in America*. The study involves 1,000 high school and college students, most of whom are teen-agers. Although final analysis of the study has not been completed, it is clear that petting-with-affection is an extremely popular code with teen-age girls, particularly with the teen-agers who are high school juniors and seniors.

Finally, one should note that, in my own study and in the Kinsey study, religion was another key factor affecting girls' sexual beliefs and behaviors. Those girls who were devout in their religion were much more conservative in their sexual behavior and belief. Religion was not as strong a factor for boys and did not control their behavior as much. As we shall see, amount of education was the key determinant for male sexual behavior.

BOYS' SEXUAL CODES

Among the teen-age boys, we find a quite different code dominant. Abstinence is given some form of lip service, particularly among the more highly educated classes, but, by and large, it is not an operational code; it is not adhered to in the behavior of the majority of the teen-age boys. Even among the males destined for college, about half have coitus in their teens; among those who stop their education in high school, about three-quarters have coitus in their teens, and, among those whose education stops before high school, about eight-tenths have coitus in their teens. Thus, it is clear that the majority of all males, in this sample of Kinsey's, at least, experienced full sexual relations before reaching twenty years of age.[9]

For teen-age girls, the rate of nonvirginity appears to be considerably lower. Kinsey reports approximately 20 per cent nonvirginity for females by age twenty. Of course, the greater liberality of the boys does not involve a single standard; that is, they are predominantly adherents of the double standard which allows boys to have coitus but condemns girls for the same thing. This is an ancient standard reaching back many thousands of years in Western culture. It is by no means a universal standard, however, for we do find many cultures where the sexes are treated equally.[10]

Although in recent generations, due to our greater equalitarianism and the evolving nature of the dating institution, the double standard seems to have been weakened sharply, it is still quite dominant among teen-age boys. The greater freedom allowed the male child in almost all areas of life constantly buttresses this standard and makes it seem obvious to teen-agers. Teen-agers are not sufficiently objective or sophisticated to be bothered by the contradictions in this or any other sexual code. For example, if all women abided fully by the double standard, then no men could, for the men would have no partners! Thus, this code operates only to the extent that someone violates it.

Some of these double standard teen-age boys will condemn a girl who accepts petting-with-affection, for they believe heavy petting is improper for girls. However, my own data indicate that most of these teen-age males will accept heavy petting in a going-steady relationship. They, of course, allow themselves to go further and may try to have coitus with a steady in order to see if she is a "good" girl. It is not unusual to find a relationship either broken up or its affectionate nature altered if a girl gives in to her double standard steady. Such condemnatory behavior on the part of double standard males keeps many girls from going as far sexually as they might want to. Thus, the double standard male eliminates many potential sex partners because of the attitude he takes toward such sex partners.

Teen-age double standard males are often stricter than their older brothers who accept coitus for a girl when she is in love and/or engaged. These teen-age males are supported in this rigidity by the conformity of their peer group. Double standard males typically view the act of coitus as a conquest, as a source of peer group prestige. Thus, they are quite prone to tell their friends all of the details of any affair. This characteristic tends further to discourage females from yielding to double standard males. Instead, the girl is encouraged to be, in part at least, a tease, that is, to show just enough sexual activity to keep the male interested but not enough to arouse his condemnation. Sexual behavior in this sense involves a great deal of the aspect of a game. Sex comes to be used as a power leverage to control the relationship. Under such circumstances, sexual desire is developed so sharply in the male and so differently in the female that the male wants the female to be both sexually active and sexually pure. Under such conditions, sexual behavior can only with great difficulty relate directly to feelings of affection.[11] This is particularly true for the act of coitus. In fact, one finds very often an inverse relation, in that boys prefer to have coitus with girls they do not care for, because they regard the girls they do care for as "too good" for such behavior. Girls, too, may control their sexual reactions, particularly with someone they care for, until they are sure they will not be condemned for their sexual response.

Thus, in the area of coitus among teen-agers, the double standard does seem to block the association of sex and affection. However, one should quickly add that, on the level of petting, sex and affection can more easily be combined, for this behavior is much more likely to be accepted for both sexes by both males and females.

MINOR STANDARDS

There are minor teen-age standards which are more permissive than petting-with-affection or the double standard. For the older teen-ager, the most popular minor standard is what I shall call permissiveness-with-affection.[12] This standard accepts full sexual intercourse for both boys and girls, provided they are involved in a stable, affectionate relationship. The degree of stability and affection required varies among adherents from feeling strong affection to being in love and engaged. Some teen-age couples who are going steady have coitus in accord with this standard. The situation here is quite different from that of the double standard boy and his girl friend, for, in permissiveness-with-affection, both the boy and girl accept for each other what they are doing. They combine sex with affection and use affection as one of the key justifications of the sexual act.

There is a class difference in sexual standards among boys. My evidence indicates that the lower classes are more likely to be strong supporters of the double standard, while the upper classes, though still mostly double standard, contain a large proportion of boys who are not so dogmatic in their beliefs and a minority who accept permissiveness-with-affection. In general, the upper classes seem to stress equality of the sexes and the importance of affection more than the lower classes. A permissiveness-without-affection code seems more widespread at the lower levels.

Age is a crucial factor among teen-agers. Teen-agers under sixteen are much more likely to accept only kissing than are older teen-agers, who may accept petting or coitus. As noted earlier, religion does not restrict sexual behavior as much among boys as it does among girls. Education is a more important factor, with the more highly educated groups being the most conservative.

PROMISCUITY

The newspapers from time to time pick up stories of high school "sex clubs" and other forms of promiscuous teen-age sexual behavior.[13] The available evidence indicates that promiscuous coitus is common predominantly for double standard males and a few females. Promiscuous coitus is not common on an equalitarian basis, that is, where both male and female accept the behavior as right for each other. Our culture has stressed the association of sex-with-affection to such an extent that it is difficult, at least for many females, to violate this association in coitus. In the case of petting, one finds more likelihood of violation of this norm by both men and women, but, in the case of coitus, it is much more often violated by males. Ehrmann's study of 1,000 college students supports this difference between male and female sexual activity and attitudes.[14] Females, in addition to associating love with sexual behavior more than males, also have more nonsexual motives for sexual behavior, such as the desire to please the boy or to cement a relationship.[15]

During the teens, the sexual outlets of boys and girls differ considerably. The chief outlet for girls seems to be masturbation and petting, whereas for boys the chief outlets include coitus at the fore. In Kinsey's sample, about one third of the girls masturbated to orgasm in their teens, while over 90 per cent of the boys have so masturbated in their teens.[16] Despite their high rate of masturbation, males also have a high rate of coitus. The lower class boys rely less on masturbation and petting and more on coitus for their sexual outlets than do those boys who go to college.

The teen-age girl today is still typically the much more conservative partner and the guardian of sexual limits. However, she appears increasingly to be a half-willing guardian who more and more seeks her self-satisfaction and strives to achieve sexual equality.[17]

There is a general trend in American society toward more equalitarian and more permissive sexual codes in all areas.[18] This is true for teen-age sexual codes, too. The growth within abstinence of petting-with-affection is one sign of this increasing equalitarian and permissive force. Also, within the double standard, one finds increased willingness by males to accept some coitus on the part of females, especially if it occurs when the girl is in love and/or engaged. Finally, in the minor standard of permissiveness-with-affection, one sees this trend in the increased strength of this standard among teen-agers, particularly among older, college teen-agers. And these trends toward equalitarianism and permissiveness seem even stronger among older dating couples in their twenties. The teen-agers are relatively new at sexual behavior, and they, at first, grab the basic outlines of the older couples' codes. With the passage of time, they come to behave in a somewhat more equalitarian and permissive manner.

In my current research, there is evidence that the real change-over in a teen-ager's sexual code is more one of integrating attitudes and changing overt behavior than of changing basic attitudes. In short, it seems that a person holds his basic sexual attitudes in rudimentary form in his teens, but he is not fully ready to act upon them and has not fully learned how to combine these values into a coherent code of living. As he learns to do this, his behavior changes and so does his awareness of his beliefs and their unity, but his basic beliefs may well remain the same. This entire area of how our sexual beliefs are formed and how they change is in need of more careful study. My own research is aimed at probing some aspects of this problem.

Parents are prone to be most aware of what they consider excessive sexual behavior, for they are concerned about the consequences of such behavior as they may affect their children. Thus, parents complain about sexual acts of which they become aware, and they often believe teen-agers are sexually promiscuous. Actually, according to our best estimates, the real increases in teen-age sexual behavior over the last generation are not in the area of sexual intercourse but rather in the area of petting and in the public nature of some petting behavior.[19] Thus, these parents of today have probably had similar rates of coitus but perhaps lower rates of petting. In addition, one should note that the petting behavior today very often is not promiscuous but occurs in a stable affectionate relationship.

YOUTH CULTURE: TAME OR WILD?

About twenty years ago, Kingsley Davis and Talcott Parsons wrote of a youth culture and of a parent-youth conflict and, in doing so, implied in part that youth culture was largely irresponsible, impulsive, and anti-adult.[20] Many people have come to share this view and to expect rather extreme sexual behavior from teen-agers. I myself formerly accepted this view of the teen-ager as valid. However, after examining the evidence in the key areas of teen-age sexual behavior, I must admit that I can no longer accept such a conception of youth culture without serious modification and qualification. I would submit that the vast majority of our approximately twenty million teen-agers are not only not extreme but are quite conservative and restrained in the area of premarital sexual codes and behavior when we compare them to their older brothers and sisters.

There is evidence to show that teen-agers are unsure of how far to go sexually, that they feel ill at ease on dates, and that they are concerned with such "tame" issues as whether one should kiss good night on a first date.[21] A recent study showed that teen-agers rate themselves lower in comparison to adults than adults rate them. Teen-agers in this study rated adults considerably higher than themselves on most all "good" qualities.[22] These are hardly the attitudes of an arrogant or anti-adult youth. They seem more those of a group desirous of becoming like adults and striving toward that goal.

Further, when we look at the rates of female petting to orgasm in the Kinsey studies, we find considerably more of this behavior among girls in their twenties than among girls in their teens. The coitus rate for females doubles between the age of twenty and twenty-five. Masturbation rates also increase considerably after the teens.[23] In all these ways, the teen-agers seem more conservative than those individuals who are in their twenties.

August Hollingshead's excellent study of a midwest community also gives evidence on the conservatism of youth. He found a very close correspondence between social class of parents and social class of teen-ager's dating partners. In this study, too, we are given a picture of youth culture that is very much like adult culture in its status consciousness. Hollingshead and others have also noted the fact that a large proportion of teen-age population is virtually not involved in any dating. A good estimate for the high school age group would be that about one third of the boys and one fifth of the girls are not involved in dating.[24]

Venereal Disease and Pregnancy

Let us now examine two key indices, venereal disease and pregnancy, which should give us additional insights into the behavior of teen-agers. Teen-agers do have significant rates of venereal disease and illegitimacy. However, the press has largely exaggerated such rates. The teen-age rate of venereal disease for ages fifteen to nineteen is only about a third of the rate for the twenty to twenty-four age group and is also lower than that of the twenty-five to twenty-nine age group.[25]

There has been a slight rise in the number of teen-age venereal disease cases in recent years, and this has received much publicity. It is quite likely that the actual rates for teen-agers are not higher and that this slight increase is due to the greater number of teen-agers today. More than 80 per cent of the venereal disease reported is from older groups of people. Finally, the rate of venereal disease among teen-agers is not evenly distributed in the teen-age group. As far as we can tell from reported cases, it is highly concentrated in the lower social classes.[26]

When one examines the national figures for unwed mothers, one finds that 40 per cent are teen-agers. Here, too, several qualifications are needed. First, most of these reported cases are Negro, and class status in general is low. The upper classes, according to Paul Gebhard's recent study, are much more willing to resort to abortion.[27] The upper classes, also, have a greater ability to stay out of public statistics and may, thus, show lower rates. According to Clark Vincent's study, when upper class females become pregnant before marriage, it is more likely to be the result of a love affair, whereas, when lower class females become pregnant, it is more likely to be a result of a casual affair.[28] Thus, there are important class differences here, too.

When we compare teen-age unwed motherhood with that for girls in their twenties, we find that the older girls have about the same proportion of the illegitimate children. We also find that the teen-age rates are not increasing as much as the rates for older groups. For example, in 1940 teen-age mothers were 46 per cent of the total; in 1957 they were 40 per cent.

Thus, from the evidence of national figures, it seems reasonable to conclude that it is a small and specific segment of the teen-age population that becomes involved with venereal disease or premarital pregnancy. Furthermore, the people in their twenties seem somewhat more likely to be involved in such circumstances. Also, these older couples are much more involved in adult culture in terms of their occupations and their nearness to marriage, and yet their sexual behavior is less conservative.

A warning must be added at this point concerning the venereal disease rates and unwed motherhood rates. They are far from perfect indices and, as mentioned, many higher class people manage to be excluded from them because they can afford more private means of coping with their problems. However, to the extent that we use these rates, we fail to find support for the charges made about teen-agers. It is no doubt true that teen-agers are irresponsible in the sense that they seek "to have a good time," but I would suggest that, in the area of sexual codes and behavior, the evidence shows more conservatism and responsibility than one might otherwise suspect. It may be well to avoid the over-all impressions given by a general use of the term "youth culture" as described by Parsons. Here, as elsewhere, qualification and specific research is a step toward better theoretical formulation and better understanding.

A FINAL OVERVIEW

What has occurred in teen-age sexual codes in recent generations is a working out of sexual practices acceptable to teen-agers. Many of these practices are at the level of petting. In short, as unchaperoned dating came into vogue and as adolescence became more prolonged due to our specialized industrial culture, young people worked out additional sexual codes to supplement and modify the older codes of abstinence and the double standard. There always were people who engaged in coitus; today there are more, but, for girls in their teens, it is still a minor activity. When we look at petting, we note something different, for here we see a much more continuous and current change among teen-agers — it is here in this middle ground that teen-agers have come to accept a petting-with-affection standard. The equalitarian and permissive aspects of this standard in many cases lead at later ages to acceptance of the more radical permissiveness-with-affection standard. However, during the teens, petting-with-affection is probably the major standard involved in stable affectionate relationships at middle and upper class levels.

At the present time, it is impossible to predict precise changes in sexual codes. This is especially true because, as we have seen, there are differences according to social class, religion, educational level, and so forth. But one can say that all the signs indicate a continued trend toward equalitarian and permissive codes. The trend seems to be toward that which now obtains in the Scandinavian countries, with the inclusion of sex education in the schools and with permissive attitudes on the formal as well as covert levels. This does not forebode the end of the double standard, for the double standard is still deeply rooted in our male dominant culture, but it does mean a continued weakening of the double standard and more qualifications of its mandates.

Teen-agers are a paradoxical group. They are not as wild as their parents or they themselves sometimes think. Teen-agers do want independence. But, judging by their sexual codes, they want independence from their parents, not from the total adult culture.

REFERENCES

1. Albert J. Reiss, "Sex Offenses: The Marginal Status of the Adolescent," *Law and Contemporary Problems,* Vol. 25 (Spring 1960), pp. 309-334.

2. Of course, there is a biological basis for sexual behavior, but social scientists seem generally agreed that the specific way the sexual drive expresses itself is learned. The wide variety of sexual codes throughout the world testifies to the fact that whatever differences exist biologically between men and women can be compensated for by cultural training. The best brief source for cross-cultural information is Clellan S. Ford and Frank A. Beach, *Patterns of Sexual Behavior* (New York, 1954). For a discussion of this entire issue, see Ira L. Reiss, *Premarital Sexual Standards in America* (Glencoe, Ill., 1960), Chap. 1.

3. For evidence, see Maureen Daly, *Profile of Youth* (Philadelphia, 1951), p. 30. It may be well to note here that the author has conducted a pilot study to test the hypothesis that the advent of the junior high school has spread heterosexual knowledge and behavior to younger age groups and thus encouraged earlier dating. In support of this, one may cite Dr. J. B. Connat's belief that the junior high imitates the high school in its social characteristics. In addition, the anticipatory socialization of sex games like "spin the bottle," "post office," and "flashlight" begin today prior to junior high levels and thus prepare students for dating in junior high. The author's evidence indicates a connection between junior high school and early dating patterns.

4. Robert D. Herman, "The Going Steady Complex: A Re-Examination," *Marriage and Family Living,* Vol. 17 (February 1955), pp. 36-40.

5. For evidence on this point, see Winston W. Ehrmann, *Premarital Dating Behavior* (New York, 1959), p. 141.

6. Alfred C. Kinsey and Others, *Sexual Behavior in the Human Female* (Philadelphia, 1953), Chap. 7.

7. *Ibid.,* p. 244.

8. This investigation is supported by a Public Health Service research grant (M-4045) from the National Institute of Mental Health, Public Health Service.

9. Alfred C. Kinsey, *Sexual Behavior in the Human Male* (Philadelphia, 1948), p. 550.

10. For a full discussion of this standard, its historical sources and reasons for being, see Ira L. Reiss, *Premarital Sexual Standards in America* (Glencoe, Ill., 1960), Chap. 4.

11. Lester Kirkendall has conducted extensive research on the nature of the interaction process in sexual relations, and his evidence to date seems to support my position here. He will soon publish a book on this topic.

12. Ira L. Reiss, *op. cit.*, Chap. 6, for a full discussion of this standard.

13. For a book containing many of these "stories," see Shailer U. Lawton, M.D., and Jules Archer, *Sexual Conduct of the Teen-Ager* (New York, 1951).

14. Ehrmann, *op. cit.*, pp. 263-266.

15. Lester A. Kirkendall and A. E. Gravatt, "Teen-Agers' Sex Attitudes and Behavior," in Evelyn M. and Sylvanus M. Duvall (eds.), *Sexways in Fact and Faith* (New York, 1961), pp. 115-129.

16. Kinsey, *Sexual Behavior . . . Female, op. cit.*, p. 173. See also William R. Reevy, "Adolescent Sexuality," in A. Ellis and A. Abarbanel, *The Encyclopedia of Sexual Behavior* (New York, 1961), pp. 52-67.

17. For an interesting article discussing shifts in male and female attitudes, see J. P. McKee and A. C. Sherriffs, "Men's and Women's Beliefs, Ideals and Self Concepts," in Jerome M. Seidman (ed.), *The Adolescent* (New York, 1960), pp. 282-294.

18. One of the major efforts of my book is to demonstrate the evidence for this trend. See Ira L. Reiss, *op. cit.*, Chap. 10.

19. Kinsey, *Sexual Behavior . . . Female, op. cit.*, pp. 275, 339 *passim.*

20. Kingsley Davis, "The Sociology of Parent-Youth Conflict," *American Sociological Review,* Vol. 5 (October 1940), pp. 523-535; Talcott Parsons, "Age and Sex in the Social Structure of the United States," *American Sociological Review,* Vol. 7 (December 1942), pp. 604-616.

21. H. H. Remmers and D. H. Radley, *The American Teen-Ager* (Indianapolis, 1957), pp. 83, 225-236.

22. R. D. Hess and I. Goldblatt, "The Status of Adolescents in American Society," in Seidman, *op. cit.*, pp. 321-333.

23. Kinsey, *Sexual Behavior . . . Female, op. cit.*, Chaps. 5, 7, 8.

24. August B. Hollingshead, *Elmtown's Youth* (New York, 1949),p. 227. See also Maxine Davis, *Sex and the Adolescent* (New York, 1960),p. 136.

25. T. Lefoy Richman, *Venereal Disease: Old Plague – New Challenge* (Public Affairs Pamphlet No. 292; New York, 1960), p. 7. For more technical data, see T. Lefoy Richman (ed.), *Today's Venereal Disease Control Problem* (New York: American Social Health Association, 1961), especially pp. 36-43.

26. Richman, *Venereal Disease . . . , op. cit.*, pp. 6, 20.

27. Paul H. Gebhard and Others, *Pregnancy, Birth, and Abortion* (New York, 1958), pp. 45, 160.

28. Clark E. Vincent, "Illegitimacy in the United States," in Duvall (eds.), *op. cit.*, p. 143.

Interpersonal Relationships —
Crux of the Sexual Renaissance

LESTER A. KIRKENDALL
ROGER W. LIBBY

A debate over whether sexual morality is declining, or whether we are experiencing a sexual revolution, has broken into the open. The controversy, which has been brewing for over a decade, has been mulled by news media, magazines, books and professional conferences. Varying views have been expressed, but one thing is clear — the very foundations upon which sexual morality has rested, and which have governed the exercise of sexual behavior, are being challenged (16). This, of course, is characteristic of a renaissance.

Many influential people are moving away from the view that sexual morality is defined by abstinence from nonmarital intercourse toward one in which morality is expressed through responsible sexual behavior and a sincere regard for the rights of others. While these people do not advocate nonmarital sexual relations, this possibility is clearly seen as more acceptable if entered in a responsible manner, and contained within a relationship characterized by integrity and mutual concern. In other words, the shift is from emphasis upon an act to emphasis upon the quality of interpersonal relationships.

Liberal religious leaders probably provide the most striking illustration of this change. Selections from their writings and pronouncements could be extended considerably beyond the following quotations, but these three are indicative of the changing emphasis.

Douglas Rhymes, Canon Librarian of Southwark Cathedral, writes:

> We are told that all sexual experience outside marriage is wrong, but we are given no particular rulings about sexual experience within marriage. Yet a person may just as easily be treated as a means to satisfy desire and be exploited for the gratification of another within marriage as outside it. It is strange that we concern ourselves so much with the morality of pre-marital and extra-marital sex, but seldom raise seriously the question of sexual morality within marriage. . . . (21, p. 25)

John A. T. Robinson, Bishop of Woolwich, in his controversial book asserts:

> . . . nothing can of itself always be labelled "wrong." One cannot, for instance, start from the position "sex relations before marriage" or "divorce" are wrong or sinful in themselves They may be in 99 cases or even 100 cases out of 100, but they are not

intrinsically so, for the only instrinsic evil is lack of love (22, p. 118).

Harvey Cox, who is a member of The Divinity School faculty at Harvard University, comments:

> To refuse to deliver a prepared answer whenever the question of premarital intercourse pops up will have a healthy influence on the continuing conversation that is Christian ethics. . . . It gets us off dead-end arguments about virginity and chastity, forces us to think about fidelity to persons. It exposes the . . . subtle exploitation that poisons even the most immaculate Platonic relationships.
>
> By definition premarital refers to people who plan to marry someone some day. Premarital sexual conduct should therefore serve to strengthen the chances of sexual success and fidelity in marriage, and we must face the real question of whether avoidance of intercourse beforehand is always the best preparation (6, p. 215).

What is common to these quotes is readily seen. In each the focus is on what happens to persons within the context of the interpersonal relationship matrix in which they find themselves. Morality does not reside in complete sexual abstinence, nor immorality in having had nonmarital experience. Rather, sex derives its meaning from the extent to which it contributes to or detracts from the quality and meaning of the relationship in which it occurs, and relationships in general.

This changing emphasis is also reflected in marriage manuals — those books purporting to help couples toward an adequate sexual adjustment. One of the earliest to appear in the United States (1926) was *Ideal Marriage* by Theodore van de Velde. The physiological aspect predominates in this 320-page book. Thus 310 pages of the 320 are devoted to detailed descriptions of the genital organs and the reproductive system, their hygiene and care. The last 10 pages (one chapter) are devoted to the psychic, emotional, and mental hygiene of the ideal marriage.

To say that the psychological and emotional aspects are completely ignored except for this chapter is not wholly fair, but the book, written by a physician, carries the vivid imprint of the medical profession with its concentration on physiology. At the time of its publication it was a forward-looking book.

The rising concern for interpersonal relationships, however, can be seen in another book written by a physician, Dr. Mary Calderone, in 1960. Dr. Calderone tries to create for her readers a perception of sexuality which is embedded firmly in the total relationship. At one point she comments:

> Sex responsiveness comes to those who not only view sex as a sacred and cherished factor in living, but who also retain good perspective about it by being sensitive to the needs of their part-

ners and by taking into account the warmth, graciousness and humor inherent in successful marital sex (5, p. 163).

The historical preoccupation with sex as an act has also been reflected in the character of sex research. Until recently it has concentrated on incidences and frequencies of various forms of sexual behavior. Some of the more pretentious studies broke incidences and frequencies of the total research population into smaller groups, e.g., Kinsey (12, 13). He looked for possible differences in sex behavior in sub-groups distinguished by such factors as religious affiliations, socioeconomic levels, rural or urban residence, adequacy of sex education and similar factors. This analysis, of course, took into account situational factors which could and do influence interpersonal relationships. Strictly speaking, however, the research still remained outside the interpersonal relationships framework.

IMPLICATIONS OF THE SHIFT

If an increasing concern for sex as an interpersonal relationship is the trend of the sexual renaissance, and we think it is, then clearly we must know how sex and sexual functioning are affected by relationship and vice versa. An extensive psychological literature has been developed to explain individual functioning; individual differences, individual growth patterns, individual cognitive development have all been explored. But relatively little is known about *relationships as such* — their components, or what precisely causes them to flourish, or to wither and die. A psychology more concerned with interpersonal relationships is now much needed. This also suggests the need to develop a field of research devoted to understanding sex and interpersonal relationships.

Finally, as a psychology and a sociology of relationships is developed, and as research findings provide a tested body of content for teaching, parents and educators may find a new stance. They can become less concerned with interdicting sexual expression of any kind, and more concerned with building an understanding of those factors which facilitate or impede the development of interpersonal relationships.

RESEARCH ASSOCIATING SEX
AND INTERPERSONAL RELATIONSHIPS

It is only within the last few years that some research has come to focus on interpersonal aspects of sexual adjustment.

That this is a fruitful approach is already evident from the results of some of the recent studies. Such research is still meager in scope and its methods and procedures will undoubtedly be much improved with experience. Much still remains in the realm of speculation and conjecture. But a beginning has been made, and the findings are enlightening and exciting.

One generalization growing out of the studies can be advanced at this point. *A sexual relationship is an interpersonal relationship, and as such is subject to the same principles of interaction as are other relationships.* It too is affected by social, psychological, physiological and cultural forces. The effort, so characteristic of our culture, to pull sex óut of the context of ordinary living, obscures this simple but important generalization. Yet research findings constantly remind us of it.

Ehrmann (7) examined the association of premarital sexual behavior and interpersonal relationships. He studied the progression of individuals through increasingly intense stages of intimacy as they moved toward or rejected premarital intercourse. He was interested in understanding the various stages of intimacy behavior in relation to a number of factors. The stages were related to the attitudes with which acquaintances, friends and lovers regarded sexual intimacy, the kinds of controls exercised, and other factors which helped build certain feelings and attitudes in interpersonal relationships.

Two conclusions will illustrate the character of his findings. In discussing the differences in male-female attitudes which are found as affectional ties deepen, Ehrmann writes:

> . . . males are more conservative and the females are more liberal in expressed personal codes of sex conduct and in actual behavior with lovers than with non-lovers. In other words, the degree of physical intimacy actually experienced or considered permissible is among males *inversely* related and among females *directly* related to the intensity of familiarity and affection in the male-female relation. . . .
>
> Female sexual expression is primarily and profoundly related to being in love and going steadily. . . . Male sexuality is more indirectly and less exclusively associated with romanticism and intimacy relationships (7, p. 269).

Ehrmann, then, has educed evidence that maleness and femaleness and affection influence the character of those interpersonal relationships expressed in sexual behavior.

Similarly, Schofield (24) in a study of 1,873 London boys and girls between the ages of 15 and 19 found that

> Girls prefer a more permanent type of relationship in their sexual behavior. Boys seem to want the opposite; they prefer diversity and so have more casual partners. . . . There is a direct association between the type of relationship a girl has achieved and the degree of intimacy she will permit . . . (24, p. 92).

Kirkendall (15) conducted a study which centered upon understanding the association which he believed to exist between interpersonal relationships and premarital intercourse. He posited three components of an interpersonal relationship — motivation, communication and attitudes toward the assumption of responsibility — and studied the impact of premarital intercourse on them. Two hundred college level males reported sexual liaisons with 668 females. These liaisons were arrayed along a continuum of affectional involvement. The continuum was divided into six segments or levels which ranged from the prostitute level, where affection was rejected as a part of the relationship, to fianceés — a level involving deep affection.

The relationship components were then studied to determine their changing character as one moved along the continuum. Thus it was found that communication at the prostitute level has a distinct barter characteristic. At the second (pickup) level there was a testing and teasing type of communication. At the deep affectional and the fiancée level there was much more concern for the development of the kind of communication which would result in understanding and insight.

Similarly, the apparent character of the motivation central to the sexual relationship changed from one end of the continuum to the other. As depth of emotional involvement increased, the motivation changed from a self-centered focus to a relationship-centered one. And, increasing emotional involvement resulted in an increasing readiness to assume the responsibilities involved in the sexual relationship.

The study thus provides clear evidence that considering premarital intercourse in blanket terms — as though intercourse with a prostitute could be equated with intercourse with a fiancée — submerged many nuances and shades of meaning. Until theses interpersonal differentiations are taken into account, there is little chance of any realistic or meaningful understanding of the character of premarital intercourse.

Burgess and Wallin (4) explored the possibility that premarital intercourse might strengthen the relationship of fiancées who engaged in it. They asked those subjects (eighty-one men and seventy-four women) who reported experience in premarital intercourse if they felt the experience strengthened or weakened their relationship. Some 92.6% of the men and 90.6% of the women attributed a strengthening effect to intercourse, and only 1.2% of the men and 5.4% of the women considered intercourse to have a weakening effect. The remainder noted no change either way. Burgess and Wallin comment:

> . . . This finding could be construed as testimony for the beneficial consequences of premarital relations, but with some reservations. First, couples who refrained from having premarital intercourse were not asked whether not doing so strengthened or weakened their relationship. They might have reported unanimously that their relationship had been strengthened by their restraint.
>
> Such a finding could be interpreted as signifying one of two things: (a) that both groups are rationalizing or (b) that given the characteristics, expectations, and standards of those who have intercourse, the experience strengthens their relationships, and, similarly, that given the standards of the continent couples the cooperative effort of couple members to refrain from sex relations strengthens their union (4, pp. 371-372).

Kirkendall (15), after an analysis of his data, reinterpreted the findings of Burgess and Wallin. He envisioned a more complex interplay than simply a reciprocating association between sexual experience and the strengthening or weakening of a relationship. He suggested this interpretation:

> Some deeply affectionate couples have, through the investment of time and mutual devotion, built a relationship which is significant to them, and in which they have developed a mutual respect. Some of these couples are relatively free from the customary inhibitions about sexual participation. Some couples with this kind of relationship and background can, and do, experience intercourse without damage to their total relationship. The expression "without damage" is used in preference to "strengthening," for it seems that in practically all instances "non-damaging" intercourse occurred in relationships which were already so strong in their own right that intercourse did not have much to offer toward strengthening them (15, pp. 199-200).

Kirkendall's study raised a question which the data from his non-randomly selected population could not answer. What proportion of all premarital intercourse occurs at the various levels of his continuum? Of the 668 sexual associations in his survey, 25 (3.2%) involved fiancées and 95 (14.2%) couples with deep affection. Associations involving prostitutes, pickups or partners dated only for intercourse accounted for 432 (64.6%), and those with dating partners where there was little or no affection numbered 116 (17.4%). But would similar proportions be found if a random sampling were used? A study designed to answer this question is needed.

Several studies have linked sexual behavior at the adolescent or young adult level with presumed casual relationships which existed in childhood, particularly those involving some sort of deprivation, usually affectional. This view, of course, will be nothing new to those familiar with psychiatric literature.

An interesting study which demonstrates this linkage is reported by Harold Greenwald (11). Greenwald studied twenty call girls, prostitutes who minister to a well-to-do clientele. He found that ". . . many of the tendencies which lead to the choice of the call girl profession appear early in youth. . ." (11, p. 182). The childhood backgrounds of the call girls appeared to be lacking in genuine love or tenderness. "The fundamental preventive task, then, becomes strengthening the family as a source of love and growth" (11, p. 182).

Ellis and Sagarin (8), in their study of nymphomania, also suggest that its causation has its roots in inadequate childhood relationships.

In studies made at the San Francisco Psychiatric Clinic, Lion (17) and Safir (23) found that promiscuity was related to personality deficiencies, and that these in turn were related to homes characterized by disorganization, weak or broken emotional ties, and lack of loyalties or identification with any person or group.

If a tie of this kind does exist, it would seem logical that changes in the capacity to experience improved personal relationships (arising, for example, through therapy) should result in some change in the sexual pattern. Support of this view comes from Berelson and Steiner (1). In their inventory of scientific findings concerning human behavior, they say that

> Changes toward a more positive attitude regarding sexual activity and toward freer, more enjoyable sexual activity than the patient was previously capable of having, are reported as correlates of psychotherapy from several camps (1, p. 290).

Graham (10) obtained information on the frequency and degree of satisfaction in coitus from 65 married men and women before they began psychotherapy. The data from these couples was compared with similar information from 142 married men and women who had been in treatment for varying periods of time. The results indicated, with certain reservations, that psychotherapy did free individuals for "more frequent and more satisfactory coitus experience" (10, p. 95).

Let us explore this logic from another side. If disorganized and aberrant sexual patterns are more frequent in adolescents or young adults who have experienced some form of emotional deprivation in childhood, it seems reasonable to hypothesize that those who had expereinced normal emotional satisfactions should display more of what is considered conventional in their sexual practices. Since studies are more commonly done with persons who are recognized as problems, this possibility is not so well documented. There is, however, some evidence to support this view.

Loeb (18) in a study involving junior and senior high school youth, attempted to differentiate between boys and girls who do and do not participate in premarital intercourse. He advanced these conditons:

> First, teenagers who trust themselves and their ability to contribute to others and have learned to rely on others socially and emotionally are least likely to be involved in irresponsible sexual activity.
>
> Second, teen-agers who have learned to be comfortable in their appropriate sex roles (boys who like being boys and wish to be men, and girls who like being girls and wish to be women) are least likely to be involved in activities leading to indiscriminate sexuality (18).

Maslow (19) in his study of self-actualized people makes several comments about the character of sexual functioning and sexual satisfaction in people who are considerably above the average so far as emotional health is concerned. He says:

> . . . sex and love can be and most often are very perfectly fused with each other in (emotionally) healthy people . . . (19, p. 241).

. . . self-actualizing men and women tend on the whole not to seek sex for its own sake, or to be satisfied with it alone when it comes . . . (19, p. 242).

. . . sexual pleasures are found in their most intense and ecstatic perfection in self-actualizing people . . . (19, p. 242).

These people do not *need* sensuality; they simply enjoy it when it occurs (19, p. 243).

Maslow feels that the "we don't need it, but we enjoy it when we have it" attitude can be regarded as mature; though the self-actualized person enjoys sex more intensely than the average person, he considers sex less central in his total frame of reference.

Loeb's and Maslow's findings, then, suggest that responsible sexual behavior and satisfying interpersonal relations and personal development are closely related.

Multifarious Associations Between Sex and Interpersonal Relationships

The data which have emerged from various studies also make it clear that a tremendous range of factors can influence the quality of relationships which contain sexual expression; that these factors can and do change from time to time in the course of the relationship; and that almost an unlimited range of consequences can result.

Thus, one of the very important factors influencing the meaning of sex relationship is the degree of fondness which a couple have for one another. As previously noted, Kirkendall (15) in his study utilized a continuum of affectional involvement. He found that the character of motivation and communication, and the readiness of men to assume responsibility for the consequences of intercourse, changed with the degree of emotional involvement. For example, as the length of elapsed time in a dating relationship prior to intercourse increased, there was an increase in the amount of communication devoted to understanding and a decrease in the amount of argumentative-persuasive communication. This finding parallels the findings of Ehrmann (7).

Maturity and developmental level represent still other factors. Broderick (2, 3) has made some interesting studies on the appearance and progressive development of various sexual manifestations with age. In a study of children in a suburban community he found that for many children interest in the opposite sex begins in kindergarten or before. Kissing "which means something special" is found among boys and girls as early as the third and fourth grades. In some communities dating begins for a substantial number of children in the fifth and sixth grades, while "going steady" is common at the junior high school level.

Schofield (24) also found that "those who start dating, kissing and inceptive behavior at an early age are also more likely to have early sexual intercourse" (24, p. 73). In an analysis of family background he also found that

> . . . girls who got on very well with their fathers were far less likely
> to be sexually experienced . . .
> . . . boys who did not get on well with their mothers were more
> likely to be sexually experienced . . .
> . . . girls who got on well with their mothers were less likely to be
> sexually experienced . . . (24, p. 144).

Role concepts, which in turn may be influenced by other factors and conditions, influence the interplay between sexual behavior and interpersonal relationships. This associaton has already been noted in quoting some of Ehrmann's findings.

The interaction becomes extremely complex as role concepts, sexual standards, cultural changes, sheer biology, and still other factors all become involved in a single situation.

Reiss' work (20), especially his discussion of the interplay between role concepts and the double standard, makes this point most vividly. He shows clearly how adherence to the double standard conditions the individual's concept of his own role and the role of his sexual partners. Thus what the individual may conceive of as freely willed and consciously chosen behavior is actually controlled by concepts deeply rooted in a long-existing cultural pattern.

The complexity is further emphasized as the origins of the double standard are studied. Reiss sees the roots of the double standard as possibly existing in "man's mascular strength, muscular coordination and bone structure. . . ." These "may have made him a better hunter than woman; it may have made him more adept at the use of weapons. Couple this hunting skill with the fact that women would often be incapacitated due to pregnancy and childrearing, and we have the beginning of male monopoly to power" (20, p. 92).

Reiss feels that "The core of the double standard seems to involve the notion of female inferiority" (20, p. 92).

Once the double standard became embedded in the mores, however, cultural concepts reinforced it and helped embed it still more deeply. Now, however, cultural developments have begun to weaken the power of the double standard. The declining importance of the physical strength of the male in the modern economy; the ability to make reproduction a voluntary matter; emphasis on freedom, equality, and rationality — these and other forces have been eroding the power of the double standard, and in the process have been altering the association between sexual behavior and interpersonal relationships.

Shuttleworth (25) made an incisive critique of Kinsey's views on masculine-feminine differences in interest in sex as a function and as a physical experience. In the process, he advanced a theoretical position of his own which suggests that much role behavior is inherent in the biological structures of the sexes. He argues that their respective biology disposes male and female to regard their sexual functioning differently. Males, for example, can experience the erotic pleasures of sex more easily and with less likelihood of negative repercussions than can females. This fact, then, has helped to formulate both male and female sex roles, the attitudes of men and women toward sex and themselves, and to condition their sexual behavior. If this theoretical view can be established, it definitely has implications for a better understanding of the kind of interpersonal behavior which can be expected to involve the sexes, and how it may develop.

Vincent's (29) study of unwed mothers helped demonstrate that a wide range of outcomes in interpersonal relationships can arise from the circumstances of premarital pregnancy. The attitudes of unwed mothers ranged from those who found the pregnancy a humiliating and terrifying experience to those who found it maturing and satisfying, from those who rejected their child to those who found great satisfaction in having it, from those who rejected and hated the father to those who accepted him fully. When considering the interpersonal reactions of unwed mothers, no stereotype is possible.

Sexual intercourse in our culture has been invested with so many meanings and such strong emotions have been tied to it that non-participation may have as many consequences for interpersonal relations as participation. Tebor (27) studied 100 virgin college males and found that a large proportion of them felt insecure about their virginity and pressured by their peers to obtain experience. At the same time significant adults — teachers and parents — were quite unaware of what sexual pattern these men were following, and provided them no support in their pattern of chastity.

REQUIREMENTS FOR RESEARCH ON THE RENAISSANCE

The theme of this article has been that a concern for interpersonal relationships as the central issue in the management of sexuality is displacing the traditional emphasis on the avoidance or renunciation of all non-marital sexual experience. Only as a shift of this sort occurs are we in any way justified in speaking of a sexual renaissance.

Some requirements, however, face social scientists who wish to understand this shift. We have four to suggest.

1. *It will be necessary to commit ourselves fully to the study of relationships rather than simply reflecting on them occasionally.* In the area of sex, concern has been over-focused on the physical acts of sex. Thus the senior author, while doing the research for his book, *Premarital Intercourse and Interpersonal Relationships,* became aware that he was giving undue attention to the act of premarital intercourse, even while trying to set it in an interpersonal relationship context. As a consequence, crucial data were ignored. For example, in selecting subjects, if one potential subject had engaged in much caressing and petting, but had renounced the opportunity for intercourse many times, while another possible subject had merely gone through the physical act of copulation a single time, the latter one was defined as a subject for the research and the

first was by-passed as though he had engaged in no sexual nor any interpersonal behavior.

With this realization came a decision to do research on decisions made by individuals concerning sexual behavior, regardless of whether they had had intercourse. The result is a recently completed preliminary study in which 131 non-randomly selected males were interviewed (14). Of this group 72 (55%) had not had intercourse, but apparently only 17 (13%) had not been in a situation which required a decision. Eleven of these had made a firm decision against intercourse, quite apart from any decision-requiring situation, thus leaving only six who had never faced the issue of decision-making. In other words, when one thought of sexual decision-making as an aspect of interpersonal relationships, rather than continuing to focus on whether or not an act had occurred, one greatly increased the number who were potential subjects, and vastly increased the range of interpersonal behavior available for study.

We offer one further illustration of the reorientation in thinking necessary as we come to accept a concern for relationships as the central issue. The view which emphasizes the quality of interpersonal relationships as of foremost concern is often labelled as "very permissive" when sex standards and behavior are under discussion. This conclusion is possible when concern is focused solely on whether the commission of a sexual act is or is not acceptable. Certainly the emphasis on interpersonal relationships diverts attention from the act to the consequences. But having moved into this position, one finds himself in a situation which is anything but permissive. Relationships and their outcome seem to be governed by principles which are unvarying and which cannot be repealed. The fiat of parents or the edicts of deans can be softened, but there is no tempering of the consequences of dishonesty, lack of self-discipline, and lack of respect for the rights of others upon interpersonal relationships. If one wishes warm, accepting interpersonal relationships with others he will be defeated by these practices and no one, regardless of his position of authority, can change this fact. Proclamations and injunctions will be of no avail. There is no permissiveness here!

2. *Conceptual definitions of relationships will have to be developed.* Several social scientists have initiated work on this. For example, Foote and Cottrell (9) have identified six components of interpersonal competence — health, intelligence, sympathy, judgment, creativity and autonomy. Schutz (26) has developed his FIRO test to measure interpersonal behavior around three interpersonal needs — the needs for inclusion, control and affection. As has been noted, Kirkendall (15) centered his study around three components — motivation, communication and readiness to assume responsibility. Communication and motivation have both been frequently recognized aspects of interpersonal relationships.

However, the conceptualization of relationships in a manner which will permit effective research is still at an embryonic level. The numerous (for there are undoubtedly many) components of relationships have still to be determined, and methods and instruments for their measurement must be developed and perfected. Interpersonal relationships as a field of psychological study should be developing concurrently, for only in this way can we gain the needed broadening of our horizons.

3. *Methods and procedures will have to be devised which will enable us to study relationships.* The perceptive reader will have noted that while studies have been cited because, in our estimation, they bore on interpersonal relationships, all of them with the exception of that by Burgess and Wallin (4) obtained their information on interpersonal relationships by using individuals rather than pairs or groups as subjects. This is quite limiting. Would we not get a different view of premarital intercourse if we could interview both partners to the experience rather than one?

Methods of dealing with couples and groups, and research procedures which can zero in on that subtle, intangible, yet real tie which binds two or more people in an association are needed. Some work has already been done in this direction, but it has not been applied to sex and interpersonal relationships.

4. *The isolation of the most important problems for research is a requirement for progress.* Opinions would naturally differ in regard to what these problems are. We would suggest, however, that since sex relationships *are* interpersonal relationships, the whole field of interpersonal relationships with sex as an integral part needs to be attacked.

Kirkendall (15) has suggestions for further research scattered throughout his book. He suggests such problems as an exploration of the importance of time spent and emotional involvement in a relationship as a factor in determining whether a relationship can sustain intercourse, the factors which produce "loss of respect" when sexual involvement occurs, the meaning of sexual non-involvement for a relationship, factors which impede or facilitate sexual communication, and the relation of knowledge of various kinds of success or failure in sexual relationships.

His study poses many questions which merit answering. How do the emotional involvements of male and female engaged in a sexual relationship differ, and how do they change as the relationship becomes more (or less) intense? How nearly alike, or how diverse, are the perceptions which male and female hold of the total relationship and of its sexual component at various stages in its development? How does the rejection of a proffered sexual relationship by either partner affect the one who extended the offer? And what are the reactions and what produced them in the person receiving it? If there are no sexual overtures, how does this affect relationships?

Which value systems make it most (and least) possible for a couple to communicate about sex? To adjust to tensions which may accompany intercourse or its cessation? Which enable a couple to cope most effectively with the possible traumas of having their relationship become public knowledge, or of pregnancy?

In what diverse ways do premarital sexual experiences affect marital adjustments? What enables some couples who have been premarital sexual partners to separate as friends? Why do others separate with bitterness and hostility? What relation has maturity in other aspects of life to maturity in assessing the meaning of and coping with sexual manifestations of various kinds in the premarital period?

The questions could go on endlessly, yet the isolation of important areas for research remains one of the important tasks before us.

REFERENCES

1. Berelson, Bernard and Steiner, Gary A. *Human Behavior.* New York: Harcourt, Brace and World, 1964.

2. Broderick, Carlfred B. *Socio-Sexual Development in a Suburban Community.* University Park: Pennsylvania State University. Unpublished manuscript (mimeographed), 1963.

3. Broderick, Carlfred B. and Fowler, S. E. "New Patterns of Relationships between the Sexes among Preadolescents." *Marriage and Family Living,* 1961, 23, 27-30.

4. Burgess, Ernest W. and Wallin, Paul. *Engagement and Marriage.* Philadelphia: J. B. Lippincott, 1953.

5. Calderone, Mary. *Release from Sexual Tensions.* New York: Random House, 1960.

6. Cox, Harvey. *The Secular City,* New York: Macmillan, 1965.

7. Ehrmann, Winston. *Premarital Dating Behavior.* New York: Henry Holt, 1959.

8. Ellis, Albert and Sagarin, Edward. *Nymphomania.* New York: Julian Messner, 1964.

9. Foote, Nelson and Cottrell, Leonard S., Jr. *Identity and Interpersonal Competence.* Chicago: University of Chicago Press, 1955.

10. Graham, Stanley R. "The Effects of Psychoanalytically Oriented Psychotherapy on Levels of Frequency and Satisfaction in Sexual Activity." *Journal of Clinical Psychology,* 1960, 16, 94-98.

11. Greenwald, Harold. *The Call Girl.* New York: Ballantine Books, 1958.

12. Kinsey, Alfred C., et al. *Sexual Behavior in the Human Female.* Philadelphia: W. B. Saunders, 1953.

13. Kinsey, Alfred C., et al. *Sexual Behavior in the Human Male.* Philadelphia: Saunders, 1948.

14. Kirkendall, Lester A. "Characteristics of Sexual Decision-Making." To be published in *The Journal of Sex Research.*

15. Kirkendall, Lester A. *Premarital Intercourse and Interpersonal Relationships.* New York: Julian Press, 1961.

16. Kirkendall, Lester A. and Ogg, Elizabeth. *Sex and Our Society.* New York: Public Affairs Committee, 1964, No. 366.

17. Lion, Ernest G., et al. *An Experiment in the Psychiatric Treatment of*

Promiscuous Girls. San Francisco: City and County of San Francisco, Department of Public Health, 1945.

18. Loeb, Martin B. "Social Role and Sexual Identity in Adolescent Males," *Casework Papers.* New York: National Association of Social Workers, 1959.

19. Maslow, Abraham. *Motivation and Personality.* New York: Harpers, 1954.

20. Reiss, Ira L. *Premarital Sexual Standards in America.* Glencoe, Illinois: The Free Press, 1960.

21. Rhymes, Douglas. *No New Morality,* Indianapolis: Bobbs-Merrill, 1964, p. 25.

22. Robinson, John A. T. *Honest to God.* Philadelphia: Westminster Press, 1963; p. 118.

23. Safir, Benno, M.D. *A Psychiatric Approach to the Treatment of Promiscuity.* New York: American Social Hygeine Association, 1949.

24. Schofield, Michael. *The Sexual Behavior of Young People.* London: Longmans, Green, 1965.

25. Shuttleworth, Frank. "A Biosocial and Developmental Theory of Male and Female Sexuality." *Marriage and Family Living,* 1960, 21, 163-170.

26. Schutz, William C. *FIRO: A Three-Dimensional Theory of Interpersonal Behavior.* New York: Rinehart, 1958.

27. Tebor, Irving. "Selected Attributes, Interpersonal Relationships and Aspects of Psychosexual Behavior of One Hundred College Freshmen, Virgin Men." Unpublished Ph.D. thesis, Oregon State College, 1957.

28. van de Velde, Theordore H. *Ideal Marriage.* New York: Random House, 1926.

29. Vincent, Clark E. *Unmarried Mothers.* New York: Free Press of Glencoe, 1961.

Transition in Sex Values— Implications for the Education of Adolescents

ISADORE RUBIN

This paper concerns the kind of education which the United States as a pluralistic society can give to adolescents and young adults in its various educational institutions. The concern is *not* with our private set of values either as individuals or parents, but rather with a philosophy of sex education for a democratic society.

THE CONFUSION OF TRANSITION

Family professionals may not agree on the causes of the change, the extent, or the direction, but they do agree that there has been a great transition in sex values in the 20th century. Evelyn Duvall has characterized this transition as "a basic shift from sex denial to sex affirmation throughout our culture."[1]

This transition from sex denial to sex affirmation has not been an easy or smooth one. American culture historically has been rooted in the ideal of asceticism, and only slowly and with a good deal of rearguard opposition is this philosophy being relinquished. Most official attitudes today still constitute what a distinguished British jurist called "a legacy of the ascetic ideal, persisting in the modern world after the ideal has deceased."[2] As values, there exists today an interregnum of sex values which are accepted in theory and in practice by the great majority of Americans.

The confusion is especially great among those who are responsible for the guidance of youth. Last year Teachers' College together with the National Association of Women Deans and Counselors decided to hold a two-week "Work Conference on Current Sex Mores." Esther Lloyd-Jones, Head of the Department of Guidance and Student Personnel Administration at Teachers' College explained why:

"The reason that made me determine to hold that conference was the repeated statement by deans and counselors—as well as by parents—that the kids were certainly confused in the area of sex mores, but that they thought they were just as confused as the kids. They just plain felt they did not know. They were clearly in no position to give valuational leadership."[3]

It is unnecessary to state that this conference—like many others held before it—did not reach agreement on what the sex mores should be.

The Impossibility of Consensus

At the present time, there seems no possiblity for our pluralistic society as a whole to reach a consensus about many aspects of sex values. We cannot do it today even on so comparatively simple a problem as the moral right of persons who are married to have free access to contraceptive information, or the right of married couples to engage in any kind of sex play that they desire in the privacy of the marriage bedroom, or even the right of individuals to engage in the private act of masturbation. Certainly we cannot expect to do so on so emotionally laden a problem as premarital sex relations.

Even in NCFR, made up of the most sophisticated students of this problem, no consensus has been reached after more than 25 years of debate and dialogue, although, as Jessie Bernard pointed out to NCFR last year, there has been a change. "There was a time," she said, "when those arguing for premarital virginity could be assured of a comfortable margin of support in the group. This is no longer always true. Especially the younger members no longer accept this code."[4]

This change in NCFR thinking reflects the great debate that is taking place on a national and an international scale. This debate reflects the fact that—whether we like it or not—we do not today possess a code of sex beliefs about which we can agree. Significantly, it is not only those who refuse to look to religion for their answers who seek a new value framework for sex. A growing body of religous leaders recognize that our modern sex morality can no longer consist of laws which give a flat yes-or-no answer to every problem of sex. These leaders concede that there are many moral decisons which persons must make for themselves.[5]

The Major Competing Value Systems

This writer has found it of value to define six major conflicting value systems of sex existing side by side in this transitional period of morality.[6] These value systems extend along a broad continuum ranging from extreme asceticism to a completely permissive anarchy. The major ones are characterized as follows: (1) traditional repressive asceticism; (2) enlightened asceticism; (3) humanistic liberalism; (4) humanistic radicalism; (5) fun morality, and (6) sexual anarchy. To discuss each of these very briefly:

1. Traditonal repressive asceticism—which is still embodied in most of our official codes and laws—proscribes any kind of sexual activity outside of marriage relationship and accepts sex in marriage grudgingly, insisting upon the linkage of sex with procreation.[7] This value system is intolerant of all deviations from restrictive patterns of heterosexual behavior, it places a taboo on public and scientific discussion and study of sex, and it

conceives of sex morality solely in absolute terms of "Thou shalt" and "Thou shalt not."

2. Enlightened asceticism—as exemplified in views of such spokesmen as David Mace[8]—begins wit a basic acceptance of the ascetic point of view. Mace sees asceticism as a safeguard against the "softness" to which we so easily fall prey in an age when opportunities for self-indulgence are so abundant. He sees youth as the time when invaluable lessons of self-control and discipline must be learned, with sex as one of the supreme areas in which self-mastery may be demonstrated, and he opposes any slackening of the sexual code. However, he takes neither a negative nor a dogmatic attitude toward sex and has been an ardent exponent of the "open forum" in which issues can be stated and weighed.

3. Humanistic liberalism has been best exemplified by the views of Lester Kirkendall.[9] Kirkendall opposes inflexible absolutes and makes his prime concern the concept of interpersonal relationship. He sees the criterion of morality as not the commission or omission of a particular act, but the consequences of the act upon the interrelationships of people, not only the immediate people concerned but broader relationships.

Kirkendall thus is searching for a value system which will help supply internalized controls for the individual in a period when older social and religious controls are collapsing.

4. Humanistic radicalism—exemplified best by the views of Walter Stokes[10]—accepts the humanistic position of Kirkendall and goes further in proposing that society should make it possible for young people to have relatively complex sex freedom. He makes it clear that society must create certain preconditions before this goal may be achieved. He envisions "a cultural engineering project" which may take generations to achieve.

5. Fun morality has as its most consistent spokesman Albert Ellis.[11] Without compromise, he upholds the viewpoint that sex is fun and that the more sex fun a human being has, the better and psychologically sounder he or she is likely to be. He believes that, despite the risk of pregnancy, premarital intercourse should be freely permitted, and at times encouraged, for well-informed and reasonably well-adjusted persons.

6. Sexual anarchy has as its philosopher the late French jurist Rene Guyon.[12] Guyon attacks chastity, virginity, and monogamy and calls for the suppression of all anti-sexual taboos and the disappearance of the notions of sexual immorality and shame. The only restriction he would apply is the general social principle that no one may injure or do violence to his fellows.

Can educators resolve these competing philosophies of sex? Judging by present disagreements, it is hardly conceivable that a consensus will be possible for a long time to come, even by our best social theorists. In fact, it would be dangerous — on the basis of the fragmentary information we now have — to come to a conclusion too quickly.

EDUCATION VERSUS INDOCTRINATION

What then are the educational implications of the confusion and conflict which exist in this transitional period?

The beginning of wisdom for educators is the recognition of the fact that the old absolutes have gone; that there exists a vacuum of many moral beliefs about sex; and that we cannot ignore the conflicting value systems which are openly contending for the mins not only of adults but particularly of youths.

Our key task — if we are to have a dialogue with youths — is to win and hold their trust. This means that we cannot fob them off with easy, ready-made replies; that we cannot give dishonest answers to their honest questions; that we cannot serve up information tainted with our bias.

If we tell them, for example, that there is only one view concerning the need for sexual chastity, they will quickly learn that there are many views. If we give them false information about any area of sex, they will sooner or later learn that we have lied. If we withhold the available data and merely give them moral preachments, they will nod their heads . . . and seek their answers elsewhere.

Our major educational problem is this: How can we help young people (and ourselves) to find some formula for coping with our dilemmas? How can we help them keep their bearings in a period of rapid and unending change, and help them make intelligent choices among the conflicting value systems?

If we indoctrinate young people with an elaborate set of rigid rules and ready-made formulas, we are only insuring the early obsolescence of these tools. If, on the other hand, we give them the skills and attitudes, the knowledge and understanding that enable them to make their own intelligent choice among competing moral codes, we have given them the only possible equipment to face their future. This type of guidance does not deny that a dilemma exists whenever choices must be made. Each choice commands a price to be paid against the advantages to be gained.[13]

There are some adults who would try to hide the obvious from adolescents — that we adults ourselves have no agreement about sex values, that we too are searching. To do this, however, is to forfeit our chance to engage in a dialogue with our youngsters. It is far wiser to admit our own dilemmas and to enlist them frankly in the task of striking a balance in this interim of confusion.

When it comes to sex education, most parents and educators have overlooked a rather simple lesson. The fact of the matter is that we do have a time-tested set of basic principles of democratic guidance that serve us well in many fields, but which are unfortunately laid aside the moment we enter the taboo-laden area of sex.[14]

In teaching politics and government, we do not feel the need to indoctrinate all students into being members of one or another political party. Rather we try to teach them the skills and attitudes which they require to make intelligent choices as adults when faced with a changing world and an array of alternatives.

In science and industry, we do not equip them with a set of tools that will be outmoded in a rapidly evolving technology, but try to equip them with skills which can adjust to a changing field.

Certainly indoctrination of moral values is an ineffective educational procedure in a democratic and pluralistic society where a bewildering array of alternatives and conflicting choices confront the individual — particularly in a period of transition.[15]

A Democratic Value Framework

At this point, the writer hastens to say that he is not advocating that we jettison all the moral values that we have developed over the centuries. He would be very loath to abandon anything that has been tested by time, particularly those institutions that have been found to be almost universal. But there have been virtually no universals in sex values, with only the prohibition of incest coming close to being one.[16] And as the anthropologist Murdock pointed out, as a society we have been deviate — not typical — in our attitudes toward sex and premarital chastity.[17]

We do have need for a value framework for sex guidance. Value commitments are necessary for any person who forms part of a social group, and no society can survive without a set of core values which the majority of its members really believe in and act upon.[18] However, it is clear that most of the values represented in the official sex code have left the core of our culture and entered the arena of competing alternatives.

We must then seek our values for sex education in the core values of a democratic society. These values have been defined as (1) faith in the free play of critical intelligence and respect for truth as a definable moral value; (2) respect for the basic worth, equality, and dignity of each individual; (3) the right of self-determination of each human being; and (4) the recognition of the need for cooperative effort for common good.[19]

The acceptance of a scientific point of view in our thinking about sex ethics would be of inestimable importance in the education of youth. Since a great deal of thinking about sex has been based either on religious values, prejudice, or irrational fears, the consistent application of this point of view would be of tremendous significance in bringing about a re-evaluation of our thinking about sex.

It would imply, first of all, that the effect of practices which are not sanctioned in our official codes would be described objectively and scientifically rather than in terms of special pleading for the official code. Reiss has shown that treatment by leading marriage and family texts of the consequences of premarital intercourse "neglects or misinterprets much of the available empirical evidence."[20] Studies by Gebhard *et al.*[21] (on abortion), Kirkendall[9] (on premarital intercourse), Vincent[22] (on unwed mothers), and other investigators, for example, have shown that behavior contrary to the accepted codes cannot be described solely in terms of negative consequences for individuals engaging in it, even in our present culture.

The application of critical intelligence also implies that moral behavior would be viewed not in terms of obedience to fixed laws, but on the basis of insights from various disciplines "that add to the picture of the world in which man lives and acts, that throw light upon the nature of man and his capacities, social relations, and experiences." It would also mean that adolescent sex activities would be limited for the actual protection of their health and well-being rather than for the protection of adult moral prejudice.[23]

There is no doubt that there is an extremely difficult problem for social control when the individual is allowed a choice in moral behavior. Landis asserts: "In moral codes taboo acts must be condemned regardless of advantages gained by certain individuals or groups who violate them. . . When acts are no longer forbidden to all, when the individual is authorized to decide whether or not violation will be advantageous, the moral code vanishes."[24]

This is indeed a dilemma for society. Unfortunately, at the present time many of the taboos still present in our official codes are no longer accepted either in precept or in practice by the vast majority of our people. We can take as an obvious example the proscription against birth control. A great debate has been opened on many other aspects of our sexual codes. If we do not equip our adolescents to participate intelligently in this debate, we do not ensure the protection of our moral codes. What we do ensure is that youngsters will have no rationale to enable them to make intelligent decisions.

To advocate autonomy is not necessarily to encourage the flouting of conventional mores or to encourage libertarian behavior. In the absence of fixed and rigorously enforced codes, a great deal of adolescent sexual behavior is determined by the mores of the teenage subculture. The advocacy of self-determination, therefore, may foster resistance to teenage pressures rather than to conventional norms.[25]

In short, what the educator must do is not provide ready-made formulas and prepackaged values, but provide knowledge, insight, and values on the basis of which the adolescent may choose for himself with some measure of rationality among competing codes of conduct.[26] In a changing world, we must develop "a frame of mind which can bear the burden of skepticism and does not panic when many of the habits are doomed to vanish."[27]

SEX EDUCATION AND SOCIAL POLICY

In our thinking about sex education and the adolescent, we almost always think solely in functional terms of helping the adolescent cope with his problems and of preparing him for courtship and marriage. We tend to overlook completely the aspect of social policy — the fact that increasing knowledge of all areas of sex is being required of all individuals as citizens.

Issues dealing with all aspects of sex are more and more entering the arena of national and international debate and decision. On an international scale, problems of birth control, venereal disease, and prostitution have been subject to wide-scale discussion and decision. In legislative and legal arenas, with the concomitant aspects of public discussion, there have been sharp conflicts about public policy concerning censorship, pornography, birth control, abortion, illegitimacy, changes in sex laws, homosexuality, and emergent problems like artificial insemination.

All of these require for their solution an informed citizenry sufficiently open-minded to make required decisions on the basis of rational consideration rather than prejudice and irrationality.

SUMMARY

In summarizing the major tasks of sex guidance of the adolescent, the writer would like to repeat the proposals which he made to the Deans' Workshop on Changing Sexual Mores at Teachers' College last year:

1. Create the "open forum" that Mace has emphasized in the family life field. Do not attempt to hide the obvious from college students — that major value conflicts exist in our society and that no consensus exists among adults. Enlist students to take responsibility for helping resolve the confusion inherent in the transition of values. Re-evaluate texts and curricula so that in this field, as in others, the principles of scientific objectivity will hold.

2. Apply the time-tested and traditionally accepted principles of education in a democracy — give guidance by education rather than indoctrination; deal with the known facts and results of research; teach critical judgment in dealing with ethical controversy.

3. Adopt as the main goal in regulating adolescent conduct measures that will equip students for intelligent self-determination rather than conformity to procedures which will have no educative effect on their real choices of conduct.

4. Help identify and destroy those outmoded aspects of the ascetic ideal which no longer represent the ideals of the vast majority of American ethical leaders or of the American people, and which no longer contribute either to individual happiness and growth or to family and social welfare.

All of this in no way denies that teachers should have strong ethical convictions of their own, or that they should feel it necessary to conceal these convictions from the adolescents with whom they deal. What they should *not* do is play the role of the apologist for the status quo, devising a "new rationale for an established policy when it has become clear that the old arguments in its favor are no longer adequate."[28]

1. *Sex Ways – In Fact and Faith: Bases for Christian Family Policy*, ed. by E. M. Duvall and S. M. Duvall (New York: Association Press, 1961).

2. G. Williams, *The Sanctity of Life and the Criminal Law* (New York: Alfred A. Knopf, 1957).

3. E. Lloyd-Jones, "The New Morality," unpublished paper presented at the New York State Deans and Guidance Counselors Conference, November 3, 1963.

4. J. Bernard, "Developmental Tasks of the NCFR, 1963-1988," address delivered at the annual meeting of the National Council on Family Relations, Denver, August 1963, published in *Journal of Marraiage and the Family*, 26:1 (February 1964), pp. 29-38.

5. See, for example, A. T. Robinson, *Christian Morals Today*, Philadelphia: Westminster Press, 1964; and J. M. Krumm, "The Heart and the Mind and the New Morality," unpublished baccalaureate sermon, Columbia University, June 2, 1963.

6. I. Rubin, *Conflict of Sex Values, in Theory and Research*, unpublished paper, Workshop on Changing Sexual Mores, Teachers' College, August 2, 1963.

7. See A. C. Kinsey et al., *Sexual Behavior in the Human Male*, (Philadelphia: W.B. Saunders, 1948), and A. Ellis, *The American Sexual Tragedy* (New York: Grove Press, 1963).

8. D. A. Mace and R. Guyon, "Chastity and Virginity: The Case For and the Case Against," in *The Encyclopedia of Sexual Behavior*, ed. by A. Ellis and A. Abarbanel (New York: Hawthorn Books, 1961), pp. 247-57; D. A. Mace and W. R. Stokes, "Sex Ethics, Sex Acts and Human Needs — A Dialogue," *Pastoral Psychology*, 12 (October-November 1961), pp. 34-43, 15-22; and W. R. Stokes and D. A. Mace, "Premartial Sexual Behavior, "*Marriage and Family Living*, 15 (August 1953), pp. 235-49.

9. L. A. Kirkendall, *Premaritial Intercourse and Interpersonal Relations* (New York: Julian Press, 1961); L. A. Kirkendall, "A Suggested Approach to the Teaching of Sexual Morality," *Journal of Family Welfare* (Bombay, India), 5 (June 1959), pp. 26-30; and T. Poffenberger et al., "Premarital Sexual Behavior: A Symposium," *Marriage and Family Living*, 24 (August 1962), pp. 254-78.

10. W. R. Stokes, "Guilt and Conflict in Relation to Sex," *The Encyclopedia of Sexual Behavior*, pp. 466-71; W. R. Stokes, "Sex Education of Children," in *Recent Advances in Sex Research*, ed. by H. G. Beigel (New York: Hoeber-Harper, 1963), pp. 48-60; Mace and Stokes, "Sex Ethics"; and Stokes and Mace, "Premarital Sexual Behavior."

11. A. Ellis, *If This Be Sexual Heresy* (New York: Lyle Stuart, 1963).

12. R. Guyon, *The Ethics of Sexual Acts* (New York: Alfred A. Knopf, 1934); and Mace and Guyon, "Chastity and Virginity."

13. C. Kirkpatrick, *The Family: As Process and Institution* (New York: Ronald Press, 1954).

14. W. H. Kilpatrick, *Philosophy of Education* (New York: Macmillan, 1951).

15. J. F. Cuber, R. A. Harper, and W. F. Kenkel, *Problems of American Society: Values in Conflict* (New York: Henry Holt, 1956).

16. M. Edela nd A. Edel, *Anthropology and Ethics* (Springfield, Ill.; Charles C. Thomas, 1959).

17. G. P. Murdock, *Social Structure* (New York: Macmillan, 1949).

18. A. Kardiner, *Sex and Morality* (New York: Bobbs-Merrill, 1954).

19. Kilpatrick, *Philosophy of Education;* and E. Nagel, "Liberalism and Intelligence," Fourth John Dewey Memorial Lecture, Bennington, Vt.; Bennington College, 1957.

20. I. L. Reiss, "The Treatment of Pre-Marital Coitus in 'Marriage and the Family' Texts," *Social Problems,* 4 (April 1957), pp. 334-38.

21. P. H. Gebhard et al., *Pregnancy, Birth, and Abortion* (New York; Hoeber-Harper, 1958).

22. C. E. Vincent, *Unwed Mothers* (Glencoe, Ill.; Free Press, 1961).

23. R. A. Harper, "Marriage Counseling and Mores: A Critique," *Marriage and Family Living,* 21 (February 1959), pp. 13-9.

24. P. H. Landis, book review in *Marriage and Family Living,* 24 (February 1962), pp. 96-7.

25. D. Riesman, "Permissiveness and Sex Roles, *Marriage and Family Living,* 21 (August 1959), pp. 211-17.

26. D. P. Ausubel, "Problems of Adolescent Adjustment," *The Bulletin of the National Association of Secondary-School Principals,* 34 (January 1950), pp. 1-84, and I. Rubin, *A Critical Evaluation of Certain Selected Operational Principles of Sex Education for the Adolescent,* unpublished Ph.D. dissertation, New York University School of Education, 1962.

27. K. Mannheim, *Diagnosis of Our Time* (New York: Oxford U. Press, 1944).

28. D. Callahan, "Authority and The Theologian," *The Commonweal,* 80 (June 5, 1964), pp. 319-23.

UNIT STUDY GUIDE

A. *Terms to Review*

Asceticism	Generation gap	Reiss permissiveness
Castration fear	Humanistic liberalism	scale
Coitus	Humanistic radicalism	Sexual anarchy
Double standard	Latent homosexuality	Sexual deconditioning
Fun morality	Permissiveness with	ing
	affection	Sexual revolution
		"Swinging"

B. *Questions for Discussion and Study*

1. For each of the articles in the unit, identify and list: a) problems and issues addressed, and b) alternative posed — both implicit and explicit.

2. Discuss the possible long-range implications of the alleged sex revolution in this society from the perspective of values central in the human potentials and sexual equality movements.

3. Discuss the role and functions of language in shaping human values and responses to the sex impulse or drive.

4. Place yourself in the hypothetical role of a parent who has been asked by a sixteen-year-old daughter: "What's wrong with my 'going all the way' with my boyfriend, since I really love him?" What sociological, ethical, or other factors would you cite in your answer? Write a parent-child dialogue, showing the response you would anticipate and how you would answer . . .

5. Many scientific sex studies and much discussion in the mass media is addressed to topic of *orgasm*. Discuss cultural, psychological, and sociological factors which may be associated with this observed emphasis on orgasm.

6. Debate: "Sex pursued without mutual commitment and caring is animalistic and inherently degrading to the participants."

C. *Ideas-Topics for Papers and Projects*

1. Do a survey and synopsis of all laws in your state which pertain to human sexuality in any way.

2. Research: "Male-Female Initiatory Patterns in Sexual Expression Among College Students."

3. "The Family as a Source of Sex Education for Adolescents — Ideal Vs. Actual."

4. "Contributions of the Human Potentials Movement to the Improvement of Human Sexual Expression."

5. Interfiew educators in your community to determine the content and scope of curricula bearing on human sexuality.

Unit 4
Getting Together:
The Partner-Selection Process

*Love is an activity, not a passive effect; it
is a "standing in," not a "falling for."* – *Fromm*

Introduction

In American society, formalization of marital partnership is typically
preceded by socially-approved heterosexual interaction generally recognized as tentative, exploratory, and affectionally oriented; such interaction varies in its duration for each pairing, in the number of such
relationships formed, and in the depth of emotional involvement
which develops among the partners. Obviously, not all such relationships developed in the course of males and females' initial "getting
together" are distinctly oriented toward formation of a marital partnership. It is apparent, of course, that virtually all marriages are
preceded by a conscious partner-selection process. Furthermore, although it may not be recognized as such, the partner-selection process
is implied in behaviors traditionally associated with dating, going
steady, pinning, engagement, and variations on these patterns. In
recognition of the interrelationship of factors in dating and conscious
partner-selection processes, articles dealing with both are included in
your readings for this unit. An underlying assumption in organizing
the materials for this unit was that the nature of the partner-selection
process (*and* the learning associated with non-marriage-oriented dating experience) is important in shaping, at least initially, the nature and
quality of married-pair relationships.

Thus, judging by our present rates of marital disruption and unhappiness, contemporary modes of exploratory heterosexual interaction and the conscious partner-selection process as well, appear to be
faulty. Some contend that the basic structure of traditional marriage
itself is entirely to blame for most distresses experienced in today's
marriage. There may be much truth in this. However, our position
would be that many of the difficulties experienced in the marital

partnership could be traced to features of the partners' preliminary interpersonal relationships, existing even in early dating, which predispose individuals to difficulties in their later marital partnership. A glaring example is found in the accounts by many persons of the facades, the social and personal camouflages maintained by partners in the dating process. Disfunctional insincerity and "masking" during the dating and partner-selection process is hardly a good foundation or preparation for functional honesty or authentic personal functioning in a marriage partnership. As we shall see, the readings in this unit raise some basic questions about the contemporary "getting together" process in terms of its implications for personal growth and identity within a context of valued, but relatively tentative, man-woman relationships.

Since dating is recognized in this society as a basic form for exploratory male-female interaction and virtually always is involved to some degree in the partner-selection process, some comment on its study seems appropriate. Rather than review the history of dating as a social phenomenon, which you can in several sources,[1] we will simply comment on the work of social scientists. For many years, sociologists concentrated on "family pathologies": attention was focused, for example, on divorce as a threat to the family system. Not much attention was paid to the possible significance of male-female interaction in dating as an integral component of family-related experience, despite the tacit acknowledgement that norms regarding male-female interaction generally constituted one function of the familial institution. Serious sociological study of dating behavior was barely under way in the nineteen-forties. In terms of its focus, the social scientist's analysis and discussion of dating behavior has tended to emphasize its "functions." Thus, from a conceptual point of view, dating is said to provide: practice in heterosexual relations — it could be construed as an entry point for the individual's assumption of adult socio-sexual roles, reduction of tensions between the sexes — tensions which are assumed to have arisen from negativistic aspects of earlier sex-role typing, a setting for the exploratory testing of heterosexual love and affectional impulses, a setting for anticipatory socialization toward later marital-familial roles, security and "belongingness," erotic experience, and a succession of potential marriage partners. The materials under this topic in the Selective Bibliography will be of help should you decide to do further study in this area.

Much of what has been said about dating functions could, of course, also be said about the relatively conscious process of mate or partner-selection. Interestingly, mate-selection process, which has traditionally been called "courtship," has been pithily described in recent sociological analysis as "training in bargaining." According to this view, the central focus of the bargaining process is on the conditions of the courtship association. Two changes in belief systems surrounding marriage have strongly influenced the interpersonal quality of partner-selection, according to this argument. One such change is the decline of the belief in inevitablility, that there is a "one and only" mate ("you were meant for me"). The other is reflected in the decline of the belief that even a satisfactory mating is for one's lifetime (". . . 'til death do us part"). In essence, as McCall has pointed out, contemporary courtship functions to teach the individual ". . . how to form, maintain, and leave relationships."[2]

It is apparent then, just as it is in other aspects of family life and marriage, that significant change is taking place in values and behavior connected with the dating and partner-selection processes. We have seen previously that change is accompanied by problems and issues which have consequences for individual and societal functioning. Change thus generates debate. Part of this debate, as we shall see in our readings, involves various alternatives which have emerged as tentative answers to serious problems of ambiguity, conflict, and self-concept confronting persons in the traditional dating and partner-selection processes.

What are some of the issues and problems connected with dating and partner-selection in contemporary American society? Some fairly general ones are examined below; perhaps you could add to this list.

Pressures to endogamy. Social forces are at work in every phase of the individual's socialization which tend to channel heterosexual love, erotic, and marital choices toward approved, ordinarily in-group, individuals. Such pressures range from subtle hints to clearcut warnings; their disregard may lead to reactions ranging from embarrassment or hurt feelings in significant others to outright, literal rejection. Coercion to endogamy in a society which purports to value the freedom of individual choice, and in an era where increasing value is given to the idea that persons should be regarded as inherently worthy — apart from their ascribed status — is likely to engender much confusion and conflict. Few viable alternatives have been discussed — and fewer implemented! — to facilitate development of human potentials in interfaith and interracial dating and mate-selection processes.

Inputs in the partner-selection decision. Although it is usually conceded that ours is a participant-run dating and partner-selection process, there remain persisting questions and issues about the extent to which various persons other than the potential partners ought to contribute to the decision forming a marriage. Economic dependency on parents, physical and mental health conditions, intelligence levels, relative emotional maturity, and other factors lurk in the background of the partnership-formation process. Arranged marriage as an alternative is likely to be rejected out of hand. But it has been said that any mate-choice made solely by the participants without regard to meaningful others is likely to contain the seeds of its own destruction. Should parents, kin, confidants, "experts," or community representatives have a decisive input to the mate-selection process?

Sex-role typing effects. Strongly internalized traditional concepts of "maleness-femaleness" may lead to difficulties in every level of heterosexual interaction, since many more women are cognizant of the sexual equality movement's theme that females are victimized by traditional concepts. Thus, a persisting question concerns the existence of double standards in dating behavior. A twenty-two-year-old female asks, "Why is it that I'm 'acting like a tramp' if I show my date that I'm sexually aroused while it's 'normal' for him to come after me?" A young male says, "She works. Why should I have to pick up the check every time?"

The love factor. Most long-run dating relationships are likely to evince an element of love impulse. Also, as theory and research suggest, mate-choices in this society are made predominantly on the basis of love feelings.[3] Some contend that the euphoria associated with love, especially in the early stages of a heterosexual relationship, impairs rational consideration of important factors and thus leads to serious misunderstandings in marriages which are formalized too soon. A problem may consist in purposive rejection of the differentiation between physical-attraction-based love and love emerging from shared commitments. Recognizing that any particular relationship may contain a blend of both tendencies, one alternative here consists in attempting rational examination of the bases of love feelings in the partnership.

Personal identity problems. Can one maintain one's own identity in the context of an affectionally-charged dating or love relationship? Such a relationship obviously rules out isolation and genuine separateness; can it at the same time permit one to be truly a whole person, to retain one's integrity? A neighborhood sage once said, "The strongest chains in the world, but the lightest ones, are the bonds of love."

Authenticity in relationships. Citing the pressures to dishonesty, the facades, and the general fakiness of it, many persons have rejected the traditional "dating game." Increasingly, heterosexual premarital relationships are coming to be valued in terms of their capacity for engendering close friendship, mutual caring, and genuine respect. In cohabitation, as an alternative to traditional patterns of getting together, authenticity, openness, and honesty may be valued even more highly than love — especially romantic love.

These, then, are some of the more general problems and issues. Obviously, the list could be extended; for example, the question of sexual versus social maturity, conflicting motives in forming pair-relationships, and so forth. One theme seems to run through many of the problems and issues in contemporary dating and partner-selection process, as we shall see in our readings: this is the growing concern that the individual personhood does not get extinguished by the pairing process, valued though it may be.

REFERENCES

1. Cf. Turner, E. S. *A History of Courting* (New York: Ballantine Books, 1954); Burchinal, Lee G. "The Premarital Dyad and Love Involvement," in Harold T. Christensen (ed.), *Handbook of Marriage and the Family* (Chicago: Rand-McNally, 1964).

2. McCall, Michael M. "Courtship as Social Exchange: Some Historical Comparisons," in Bernard Farber (Ed.) *Kinship and Family Organization* (New York: John Wiley & Sons, 1966), pp. 190-200.

3. Cf. Goode, Wm. "The Theoretical Importance of Love." *American Sociological Review* 24 (1959), 38-47. Also, Greenfield, Sidney M. "Love and Marriage in Modern America: A Functional Analysis." *The Sociological Quarterly* 6 (Autumn, 1965), 361-377.

The Romantic Love Complex in American Culture

CHARLES B. SPAULDING

Romantic love has been a constant theme in the songs and stories of the American people. Recently a growing body of research has begun to explore the incidence of these ideals among various categories of people.[2] The present article expends this enterprise by exploring the proposition that the acceptance of the Romantic Love Complex is more strongly associated with conservative culture values than with selected personality dispositions.

In order not to fall into confusion it is necessary to distinguish carefully between the Romantic Love Complex and other forms of love. Such a distinction is particularly important because serious American writers on marriage have generally perceived the Romantic Love Complex and other forms of love. Such a distinction is particularly important because serious American writers on marriage have generally perceived the Romantic Love Complex to be an unfortunate basis for marriage, while at the same time they have often explained its peculiar role in the society and have praised some kinds of love. The basic nature of the required distinction has been well stated by William Goode who has differentiated the "romantic love complex" from the "love pattern." He said in part.

> "... we can separate a love pattern from the romantic love complex. Under the former, love is a permissible, expected prelude to marriage, and a usual element of courtship — thus, at about the center of the continuum, but toward the pole of institutionalization. The romantic love complex (one pole of the continuum) includes, in addition, an ideological prescription that falling in love is a highly desirable basis of courtship and marriage; love is strongly institutionalized ...
>
> But this complex is rare. Perhaps only the following cultures possess the romantic love value complex: modern urban United States, Northwestern Europe, Polynesia, and the European nobility of the eleventh and twelfth centuries. Certainly it is to be found in no other major civilization ..."[2]

While this statement does not elaborate the content of our Romantic Love Complex, it does indicate that it is an extreme (one pole of a continuum) and rare ideological prescription.

That the Romantic Love Complex constitutes an obvious and important element in American culture seems to be beyond serious question.

Many observers both foreign and domestic have remarked upon the peculiarly virulent development of the complex in this land.[3] In spite of the fact that many serious writers and current dissenters decry its impact, romantic ideas are all around us in such places as movies, popular songs, books, magazine stories, advertisements, television shows, and the delighted tittle tattle of high school girls.

When sociological scholars have turned to such materials in efforts to identify some of the elements of this ideal type, they have not come away empty handed. A number of years ago Llewellyn Gross[4] developed a list of some forty key elements embedded in the romantic love ideal, and more recently Dwight Dean has developed a new index by examining the same kinds of materials.[5]

PROFESSIONAL DISAPPROVAL

Efforts to characterize romantic love do not necessarily indicate approval. As a matter of fact, a whole generation of writers on marriage has tended to decry its effects.[6] At least a generation ago Ernest W. Burgess[7] wrote an article in *Survey* indicating romantic love as a basis for marriage, and not much later Ralph Linton published in *The Study of Man* that famous quote in which he compared the lover who fits the ideal type to the rare person who can produce an ideal epileptic fit — an ideal type also among some Arabic peoples.[8]

Since that time, at least, the general position taken by writers of marriage texts has been to advocate something called "real," "true," "conjugal," or "mature" love, and to contrast this good thing with romantic love or infatuation.[9] In this context infatuation seems usually to encompass many of the elements usually associated with the romantic love ideal. In the quotes displayed by Reiss in his article on the sociology of the heterosexual love relationship, the good love is contrasted with that which is fallen into, comes at "first sight," delibitates, and is untested.[10]

These inferior forms of love are often said to be associated with immaturity, neuroticism, ineffectiveness, or other less than ideal behaviors.[11] In a book entitled *The Adjusted American* the Putneys have maintained that typical American forms of love are simply the result of the projection of frustrated personal aspirations onto the prospective mate.[12]

Writers who want to weigh and balance judiciously sometimes point out that certain sociological scholars have had kind words to say about romantic love.[13] In a sense, so they have; but the discussion has not been a real debate, for the two groups of writers have really been talking about different things. Those with favorable comments have usually been analyzing the role of romantic love in the social system and explaining why it should be so popular in a society structured as ours is. No one really seems to think that the archetype of romantic love is a desirable basis for satisfactory marriage.

Among the most widely known of those with favorable comments are

William Kolb, Talcott Parsons, Hugo Beigel, and Waller and Hill. Kolb's approach is really a counter offensive against many of the writers on marriage.[14] His position is that, in their enthusiasm to denegrate the romantic love ideal, they are actually attacking democratic individualism. But he seems to be in favor of freedom and equality and not to be advocating the actual practice of the Romantic Love Complex as perceived in the present study.

Parsons has attempted to explain the popularity of romantic love in the United States in terms of the needs of young people in this highly differentiated society and of its role as a motivating force for marriage.[15] But he does not seem to advocate the Romantic Love Complex in its extreme form. In an early essay he concluded that the most desirable pattern of adjustment for "able, intelligent, and emotionally mature women" was the "good companion pattern" as opposed to the glamour or the domestic pattern.[16] Of course, it is the glamour pattern which seems most to typify extreme romanticism. In a later work, he looks with question upon the "going steady" pattern, although he explains the reasons for its popularity. He suggests that the romantic complex seeks unrealistically simple goals.[17] In an ingenious article Theodorson attempts to support Parson's idea that romantic love constitutes a motivating force for marriage, by means of cross cultural statistical comparisons.[18] But Theodorson's index of romantic love seems to be aimed at a companionship ideal as much as at the romantic complex, and his analysis does not prove that individual people who are more romantic tend to regard marriage as more desirable.

A famous article by Hugo Beigel[19] is sometimes sighted as looking favorably upon the role of romantic love in the modern world. But a very careful reading of this article suggests that Beigel has done what the marriage counselors so often do. He has reinterpreted the love he favors (and he does favor it) so that it is not the Romantic Love Complex. He says toward the end of his article: ". . . it is also a fact that in a sexually gratifying relationship that has been built on love, that is, on understanding and mutual assistance in emotional conflicts, on moral support and common interest, on mutual confirmation and emotional security — unavailable anywhere else — the chance of creating an atmosphere of loyalty and friendship, tolerance and confidence are greater than in any other. . . . It (love) must be judged in its true form and not in poor falsification." (p. 333). Earlier in the same article he states that ". . . the modern love concept is not identical with romantic love, but is a derivative, modified in concord with the conditions of our age . . ." (p. 331). He goes on to say that under modern conditions this "true form" of love "has saved monogamous marriage from complete disorganization" (p. 333).

Waller and Hill also explain the reasons for the popularity of the romantic love idea in American culture.[20] They explain how social blocking of the consummation of love and personal internal conflict over it generate a great emotion, the cultural channeling of which sweeps the hesitant prospect into marriage. But they still do not seem to regard this device for ensuring mating to be a very good one. For no sooner have they finished the summary of their explanation, on pages 127 and 128, than they say: ". . . Love is blind, but only for a season, and passionate kindness does not last forever. . . ." And, ". . . it is possibly very unfortunate that people must make one of their most important decisions on the basis of certain delusive emotions of adolescence . . . and persons who have the power to excite this madness in others are by no means always the persons with whom it is possible to live happily after the knot is tied."

BACKGROUND AND PERSISTENCE OF THE CONCEPT

If scholars do not look with favor upon the Romantic Love Complex, why does it persist, and why should it be regarded as an element in conservative (rather than liberal) American culture? Whatever the explanation, history seems to indicate that the complex has in truth been a part of our traditional, Christian, democratic culture; and at least certain sociological theorists, including several of those already mentioned, suggest that good reasons for its persistence are to be found in the very nature of our society. Hunt's analysis of the historical vicissitudes of the love ideal in Western culture suggests that the idea of romantic love as an essential part of marriage came to us at the hands of those same Puritans whose ideals have left such a mark on American life,[21] and Beigel tends to support this view also.[22] There seems little doubt that romantic love has been an important ideal in America since the advent of our status as an independent nation.[23] And the history of the development of the ideology undoubtedly explains some of the specific elements in the complex.

That our type of society might well be expected to put a heavy emphasis on love in the mating and marriage process has, of course, been a theme of the functionalists. As already noted, this has been the tenor of the works of Goode, Parsons, Beigel, and Waller and Hill. While their theories do not seem adequate to explain fully the rather extreme form of our Romantic Love Complex, they do suggest that there is a fundamental "elective affinity" between the major institutional structure of our society and the idea that love should have a fundamental role in the creation and perpetuation of marriages. The gist of these ideas is, of course, that urban and industrial society destroys the basis for arranged marriages and emotional support by kin and community. In this situation persons must seek their own mates and hope for satisfying emotional support in marriage. In this context the love ideal has relevance.

If the structure of the society favors the practice of love, and the love model made readily available by the established institutions is that of the romantic complex, the adoption of that complex as a standard by considerable segments of the population seems logical enough. Much of the learning of human beings seems to be at least partially explained in terms of the models available to persons at those points in their lives when such models appear to provide means for achieving goals or relieving the pressures of needs.

Assuming that adequate reasons exist for the perpetuation of the Romantic Love Complex as an ideal of the society, why should it be associated with a conservative way of life? If the popularity of the complex and the results from it fit with modern society, why should it not be most popular with those who have departed most from the norms of bygone days? The answers to these questions appear to lie in part in the clear distinction (made earlier) between the Love Pattern and the Romantic Love Complex. It may be that the denizens of the new left emphasize love to a greater degree than do conservatives, but they may be talking more of what was once called "free love" or of human brotherhood than of the Romantic Love Complex. If this complex with its fairly unusual rules was established here by the same ancestors who gave us the basic formulations of our more traditional value structures, it might logically be expected to be found in association with other traditional patterns. That romanticism is in truth a conservative element in American culture has been suggested by Reiss.[24]

Note should be taken of the fact that this expectation concerning romanticism rests upon the assumption that the association is with cultural beliefs which are widespread and related to the basic institutions of the society rather than on the sheer fact that culture is involved. For in truth there are cultural guides to deviant behavior, as Scheff has argued in the case of mental aberrations. There seem to be cultural guides to being crazy, just as there are cultural guides to being normal.[25]

VARIED INCIDENCE

There is much evidence to show that the incidence of even traditional values tends to be somewhat different in various segments of the population. Much of the research in the areas of stratification, deviance, and political sociology deals with these distributions. Furthermore, the Romantic Love Complex itself is a kind of ideal type, and probably not many persons would be expected fully to accept and live up to all aspects of it. After all, saints are not very common among us, and businessmen notoriously depart from the ideal of perfect competition. That young Americans tend to grow into love rather than to fall into it in true romantic fashion has, of course, been documented by Burgess and Wallin.[26]

But the fact that most people fail to live up to the ideal types of their culture does not mean that these ideal concepts are not of importance in understanding any given society. Will anyone really argue that a knowledge of cultural ideals does not help to understand Americans as compared to Russians, Japanese, Igorots, or even Swedes?

The view here expressed suggests that within the American population the degree to which the ideal type is approxmiated will be better explained by its association with traditional cultural elements than by its association with psychological variables. In other words, beliefs in romantic love will be more associated with orthodox religion and a conservative politicoeconomic position than with measures of submissiveness, immaturity, neuroticism, or psychiatric impairment. The generally negative results of Dean's efforts to find an association between acceptance of the romantic love ideology and maladjustment or immaturity tend to support this proposition.[27]

But the fact that persons are or are not bearers of the traditional culture would not be expected to account for all possible variations in the incidence of the Romantic Love Complex among the various elements of the American population. For a person may select for emphasis at any time those elements of his cultural equipment which seem to serve his current needs. When looked at from the viewpoint of the individual, culture may be seen in part as a series of devices for solving individual problems. Of course, it precedes the individual's needs in time, and his choices are not unlimited, but when he is hungry he is shown how to use a fork, chopsticks, a horn spoon, or his fingers. And when he wants a mate he is advised to go to see his father, his uncle, his mother, or to go courting. He may be told that he should marry for love, for wealth, for children, for the survival of the tribe, or more likely for some combination of these things.

The whole development of the sociology of knowledge suggests that a person, a group, or a category of persons will tend to choose from among the techniques or ideas available those which are perceived to cater to its basic needs and interests. This is again the matter of "elective affinity." And so it seems likely that persons in different roles might well tend to show differences in romantic tendency. It seems probable that differences in such things as socioeconomic status, age, race, phase of mating process, and sex might be associated with differences in acceptance of the Romantic Love Complex, even among traditionalists.

Research by others has in part suggested that the romantic tendency may be associated in some degree with emotional adjustment, race, level of school attended, sex, courtship stage, physical presence or absence of the object of one's attention, and with various subcultures. In spite of its generally negative results, Dean's research did reveal a significant correlation (.19) among college women between emotional maladjustment as measured by the Bell Adjustment inventory and romanticism as measured by his index.[28] Reiss reported modest associations between romanticism and being Negro rather than white, a high school student rather than a college student, and a female rather than a male.[29]

But Hobart's data seem to indicate that the male exhibits greater romanticism in both the college and post-college situations.[30] His data also suggest that the college male is more romantic when going steady or engaged (than when inexperienced in heterosexual relationships) and also when separated from his steady date or fiancee. The same variables affect women, but in somewhat different ways and degrees, and prolonged marriage seems to produce some declines in romanticism, relative to the courtship period, for both sexes. The college male also appears to exhibit more change in relation to changing conditions than does the female, but the reverse is true for the post-college group.

In addition to personal relationships, membership in particular subcultures seems to affect degree of romanticism. Hobart tries to explain some of his results by ascribing to the college culture (as compared to the post-college culture) a particularly romantic orientation,[31] while Reiss has pointed out that the students of the New York college were less romantic than those attending colleges in Virginia.[32]

PROCEDURES

In the face of the ideas already outlined, the availability of a series of student questionnaires with relevant information impelled the writer to explore the thesis that the romanticism of individuals is primarily related to the relative acceptance of traditional cultural values and is not greatly influenced by personal or interpersonal dispositions. The questionnaires here analyzed were collected from students in the required beginning English sections at the University of California, Santa Barbara, during the winter and spring quarters of 1967, and are part of a much larger aggregate of questionnaires collected primarily for a panel study. Nevertheless, the present study was from the first a subsidiary objective of the whole enterprise. The first 500 questionnaires returned by men and by women were used.[33]

In order to concentrate upon the relationships of romanticism (the Romantic Love Complex) with values and with dispositions, an effort was made to control as many other variables as possible. The fact that the particular student body is well known to have consisted in 1966-67 largely of white, middle-class young people, most of whom live during the school year either on campus or in the immediate environment made the task relatively easy. Because the writer distributed the questionnaires to all the classes personally, he is sure that very few of the respondents are from obvious minority groups such as Blacks or Mexican-Americans. On the basis of preliminary analyses of the relationships between romanticism and a number of variables, the sample was limited to never-married, citizen, freshmen. There were 461 women and 443 men who may be properly described as being white, generally middle-class, single, citizen, freshman students. Because men and women are known to react differently to indices of romanticism, the two sexes were analyzed separately. The factor of dating experience was not controlled, in part to avoid further reduction of the sizes of the samples and in part because its impact on these particular samples appeared to be minimal. The association of romanticism with a dichotomy dividing the men into those who were going steady, pinned, or engaged and others proved not to be statistically significant. For women the difference in romanticism between those pinned or engaged and others was significant at the .05 level, but only 22 women were either pinned or engaged.

The questionnaire provided a basis for the creation of some fifty variables which seemed possibly relevant to the present analysis. Forty-five of these are accounted for by 23 scales and by 22 statements concerning relative values. The scales were created by a modified Likert technique in which items were selected which correlated positively with the sum of all proposed scale items and did not correlate negatively with any other item in the scale. The relative value statements were contained in two lists: one on general values and one on values in family life.[34] In each of the lists of values eleven statements (e.g., "being successful in financial arrangements") were provided, and respondents were asked to number them in order of "their importance to you." A few other items on the questionnaire could be distributed to form what could be regarded as scales of some sort. For variables not used in the table see footnote.[35]

In most of the analyses the scale of the Romantic Love Complex was regarded as the dependent variable. The nature of that scale is, therefore, of fundamental importance to the investigation. The scale utilized eleven questions which met the indicated criteria.[36]

After the final samples had been established, the relationships between romanticism and all of the other variables for both men and women were analyzed by means of contingency tables.[37] In addition, a correlation matrix involving 47 variables was created for each sex separately. Unless otherwise noted, all statements of relationships in this analysis are based on the contingency tables. The correlation matrix did, however, show much the same pattern of relationships as that derived from the contingency tables.

Table I was created by first recording in columns 3 and 5 all the Gammas from the contingency tables for the total samples which were significant at the .10 level or better according to the size of X^2 (except for three statistically significant Gammas of less than .03). Then all of the comparably significant Gammas from the tables for the religiously orthodox men and women were recorded in columns 4 and 6. When a factor showed a significant (.10 or better) association with romanticism for a sex in either analysis, the Gamma for the other group (total sample, or religiously orthodox) was added in the appropriate column.

In column two of Table I is a classification of the variables into several categories as follows:

V stands for value
GV for general value
FV for family value
P for personality attribute or disposition
Pi for an interactional personality disposition

TABLE I

ASSOCIATION OF THE ROMANTIC LOVE COMPLEX WITH SELECTED VARIABLES FOR SINGLE, CITIZEN, FRESHMAN STUDENTS

		Males		Females		
Variable	Variable Type	Total Sample	Religiously Orthodox	Total Sample	Religiously Orthodox	
1	2	3	4	5	6	7
Religious Orthodoxy	V	+.25***	—	+.30***	—	
Successful Family Life[a]	GV	+.24***	+.21			
Restriction of Speech	V	+.23***	+.10	+.32***	+.22	
Live by Religious Principles	GV	+.21***	+.07	+.15*	+.23	
Love and Affection	FV	+.21***	+.30**			
Traditional Religion[b]	V	+.20**	—	+.10**	—	
Achievement	V	+.20***	+.28**	+.18**	+.24*	
Pol-Economic Conservatism	V	+.19***	+.04			
Submissiveness	Pi	+.14*	+.05			
Abasement	Pi	+.14**	+.02			
Unhappiness	P	+.09**	-.004			
Succorance	Pi			+.15**	+.12	
Nurturance	Pi	+.09	+.25*	+.13***	+.09	
Inclusiveness	Pi			+.18***	+.14	
Home Maintenance	FV			+.07	+.29**	
Energy	P			+.02	+.32**	

Alienation	V	−.21***	−.10	−.24***	+.02
Sexual Permissiveness	V	−.19**	−.25*	−.23***	−.05
Religiousness^c	V	−.19***	+.08		
Intellectual Capability	GV	−.18***	−.36	−.22**	−.03
Artistic Appreciation	GV	−.18**	−.24*		
Personality Development	FV	−.16*	−.10		
Common Interests	FV	−.15*	−.11		
Hang-Loose Ethic^d	FV	−.13*	−.14	−.10*	+.10
Intellectual Self-Concept^e	V	−.13**	−.04		
Psychiatric Impairment	P			−.17*	
Emotional Security	FV	−.10	−.24*		−.24*

Positive Amounts   * P≤.10;   ** P≤.05;   *** P≤.01

Negative Amounts

a For general values and family values the signs of the Gammas have been reversed to show the true direction. In the original analysis a positive sign for these values showed a negative association, but this situation created difficulty in reading the table.

b This item was based on a division of religious preference into "No preference" versus Catholic or Protestant, ignoring other choices.

c Based on a four-choice division: (1) not religious; (2) affiliated with religion primarily because of parental or other influences, for the sake of children, for social contacts, etc., and do not consider it a major force in my life; (3) moderately religious; (4) very religious.

d This scale was developed as a measure of a tendency toward a Hippie philosophy and was based in part on ideas found in J. L. Simmons and Barry Winograd, *It's Happening.* (Santa Barbara: Marc-Laird, 1967).

e Based on one question with a five point range.

This classification is essentially arbitrary and has been created for this analysis, but it does make some sense. The nature of the GV and FV categories has already been explained. Those scales which have been marked V generally indicate the acceptance of some body of ideas or behaviors as true, good, or desirable. The scales classified as P or Pi concern self perceptions of tendencies to act or react; and in addition, the subset classified Pi measure tendencies to act or react in face-to-face relationships with other people. The items marked V, P, and Pi were measured by scales and not by ranking of value statements in relation to other items.[38]

<h2 align="center">FINDINGS</h2>

The answers to the individual questions in the romanticism scale certainly do not suggest that the students were especially enthusiastic about the Romantic Love Complex. The original sample of 500 men distributed their answers to the eleven questions as follows: strongly agree, 6.1 per cent; agree, 19.0 per cent; neutral, 19.8 per cent; disagree, 42.8 per cent; and strongly disagree, 12.2 per cent. There were slight variations between the distributions for men and women. The mean for men was a little higher than that for women — 29.06 to 27.26, in essentially bell-shaped distributions.

Columns 3 and 5 of Table I give strong support to the idea that acceptance of the Romantic Love Complex tends to be associated with a conservative value structure for both men and women. For the men (Column 3) the highest positive associations are obviously between romanticism and values, and high romanticism is universally associated with the conservative pole of the value ranges.

The negative associations for men are all with values, and these values may generally be described as opposed to the conservative culture, but the picture is not as clear as with the positive associations. One surprise is the fact that those who claim to be very religious are not inclined to accept the Romantic Love Complex. The explanation seems to be that those who declare themselves to be very religious tend to be the liberals rather than the conservatives. When this relationship was first noted in the preliminary runs on all 500 men, an analysis was undertaken to determine what sorts of persons perceived themselves to be very religious. Those who so viewed themselves were particularly numerous among persons professing no particular religion, conceiving themselves to be intellectuals, and rating high on acceptance of the Hang-Loose Ethic, and also high on Alienation.

Another question arises over the negative association of romanticism with the family values of Personality Development and Common Interests. But analysis of the whole pattern of reaction suggests that this simply means that the partisans of romanticism tend to rate more highly than their opposites such family values as Love and Affection, Happy Children, and Economic Security. Since high rating of some values necessarily means low rating of others (in certain sections of the questionnaire), the negative associations of "Personality Development" and "Common Interests" seems to be understandable.

Column 3 of Table 1 indicates that, contrary to expectation, the romantic men do seem to display certain personality dispositions to a greater degree than their opposites. While the positive associations with the personality variables are less strong than the positive associations with values and than several of the negative associations, they do seem to make a sensible package. That package suggests that the romantic men are a relatively mild lot. It suggests that the more aggressive and independent men tend to be less likely to accept the tenets of the Romantic Love Complex.

In fact some exploration of the matrix of correlation coefficients suggests that romantic men may be not only mild, but may display some tendency toward psychological disturbance. There may be a factor composed of eight personality variables and having a positive associa- tion with romanticism in the group of 443 men. The elements in this factor would be three of those shown as applying to the total sample of men in Table I (Submissiveness, Abasement, and Unhappiness) plus Succorance, Misanthropy, Sensitivity, Neuroticism, and Psychiatric Impairment. Of the 28 correlation coefficients among these items all are positive and all but 2 are statistically significant at or above the .05 level. Each of these eight items is also positively associated with roman- ticism in the contingency tables, although only the three associations shown in Table I are statistically significant at the .10 level or better.

Column 5 of Table I shows that for the total sample of women also values tend to be more often and on the whole more strongly associated with romanticism than are personality variables. These associations (both positive and negative) also indicate that the more romantic per- sons tend to be conservative in terms of other values. But the personal- ity variables in column 5 of Table I which show statistically significant relationship with romanticism for women suggest a rather different picture for women than for men. The overall impression is one of strength and stability rather than of weakness and disturbance. The romantic women tend to be nurturant, inclusive, and energetic and to be without psychiatric impairment. The only suggestion of weakness is the positive association of Succorance with romanticism for women. But exploration of the correlation coefficients suggests no general factor like that noted above for men. Perhaps the succorant tendency in women results essentially from a cultural prescription.

In so far as they showed an association between conservative cultural values and romanticism the findings supported the original proposi- tions underlying the investigation. But a nagging question arose, which asked whether all that had been accomplished was to discover that the members of the presently protesting groups (New Left, Hippies, etc.) had become alienated and had rejected the standard values of the "hypocritical establishment." The original proposition had been that romanticism would vary among the general student population in relation to the degree of acceptance of traditional values. That Hippies and the members of the New Left would not be inclined to accept the Romantic Love Complex had been assumed. In order to explore the possible effects of recent protest movements, the analysis reported in columns 4 and 6 of Table I was undertaken. The samples of men and of women were dichotomized into groups high and low on Religious Orthodoxy, and a new set of (2 × 2) contingency tables was prepared for the more orthodox groups in which the associations between romanticism and other variables were assessed.[39]

The more religiously orthodox halves of the samples are regarded as being composed of "squares," of young people largely untainted by the "Hang-Loose Ethic" of the Hippies and varying essentially on value axes longer established in the society. The justifications for this assumption are essentially two: in the first place, when both men and women are considered, Religious Orthodoxy is as strongly associated with romanticism as is any other variable and more strongly than all save Restriction of Speech. It also shows a negative correlation with Alienation (−.58 for men and −.20 for women) which has the highest negative association with romanticism. It seems logical to assume, therefore, that removing the persons who are low on Religious Orthodoxy and high on Alienation would essentially remove the protest groups. Secondly, the author's observation is that persons enamored of protest were in the spring of 1967 a very small part of the student body involved. The fifty percent of those freshmen who were high on Religious Orthodoxy and relatively low on Alienation could almost surely be regarded as "squares."

In any case, the new analysis revealed the associations recorded in columns 4 and 6 of Table I. The general trend of the attributes of the males revealed to be significantly associated with romanticism seems to be generally in line with that suggested by column 3 of Table I. The man who believes in the romantic complex tends to approve of the good old traditional value of Achievement, to be relatively less interested in Artistic Appreciation, and to be less sexually permissive. In addition, he has a relatively high interest in the family value of Love and Affection. The fact that he is high on Nurturance suggests that he is concerned about human relations of some warmth and is not likely, therefore, to be the most autonomous and aggressive.

The few significant associations in column 6 of Table I depict a relatively traditional type of girl concerned with Achievement and Home Maintenance, full of energy, and with no signs of Psychiatric Impairment.

While the general trend of the significant associations for the religiously orthodox seems to support the findings for the total samples, these associations are disappointingly few. The conclusion that they do indeed confirm the general trends established for the total sample is, however, supported by the fact that the data seem to display a certain stability of pattern. This persistence of pattern impressed itself upon the writer as he worked with the materials of the study, and may be demonstrated by considering the nonsignificant associations reported in the columns of Table I. For every significant item in either column for males, the Gamma for the same item was listed in the opposite column. The same was done for the females. Since two items associated with romanticism in the total samples were not run for the religiously orthodox groups, a total of 33 comparisons between the total samples (male or female) and the religiously orthodox samples is created. In these 33 comparisons only four produce Gammas which are not in the same direction. Of these three seem unimportant. One is a change for male unhappiness from $+.09$ for the total sample to $-.004$. Another is a change for males in religiousness which seems to result from an artifact inherent in the nature of the question asked. The third is a change from $-.24$ to $+.02$ in Alienation for women. In any case, the fact that 29 of the 33 associations should be in the same direction when the religiously orthodox are compared to the total samples does demonstrate the stability of the general trend of the findings.

Summary and Discussion

Although male, single, citizen, white, middle-class, college freshmen tend to be somewhat more inclined to accept the Romantic Love Complex than do their female counterparts, the modal position of each sex is to disagree with or be neutral toward the affirmative elements in a scale designed to measure this value.

For both men and women the factors showing the strongest positive association with romanticism tend to be conservative values, like Religious Orthodoxy; and those most strongly associated in a negative direction tend to be opposed to the acceptance of the traditional culture, such as Alienation. The essential character of these associations remains when the analysis is confined to male and female groups high on Religious Orthodoxy.

While less impressive than the associations with traditional values or their opposites, personality dispositions do seem to be related to the acceptance of the complex more strongly than was contemplated in the statements of the propositions underlying the investigation. Also an unanticipated difference between men and women was discovered. Romantic men seem to show a moderate tendency toward weakness and disturbance. Romantic women, quite to the contrary, appear to be peculiarly stable, energetic, outgoing, and kindly.

In addition to the differences between the sexes in dispositions, there are unanticipated differences between them in the particular values which are significantly associated with romanticism. For the total samples, there are no values showing significant associations for women and not for men, but the following additional eight values display significant positive or negative associations for men: Successful

Family Life, Love and Affection, Political-Economic Conservatism, Religiousness, Artistic Appreciation, Personality Development, Common Interests, and Intellectual Self Concept.

While differences between the sexes were anticipated, the particular differences discovered were not predicted. Some speculation about their meaning seems, therefore, to be in order. The romantic man seems to be less strong than his opposite, to be oriented to domestic values and conservative politicoeconomic ideas, and yet to be adverse to a number of things interpreted by American culture to be nonmasculine, such as art and intellectualism, and to be not very enthusiastic about psychological ideas like personality development or common interests. He seems to this writer to be a perfectly understandable American male type.

That similar tendencies in women should not be associated with romanticism also seems comprehensible. Most writers assume that women generally are oriented to the family, including love and affection, and they may in all likelihood more properly be artistic, intellectual, and psychological (in the middle class of our society) than men would be, who must be oriented to occupations. It seems logical enough, therefore, that these tendencies might be more important in determining men's than women's acceptance of romanticism.

REFERENCES

The author wishes to express appreciation to the following: David Gold for comments on an earlier draft; Jack Bryan, Dan Primont, Tony Shih, and Brad Smith for assistance with computer operations; the Computer Center at the University of California, Santa Barbara; the Research Committee and the Chancellor of UCSB for financial assistance. The data were collected from students by means of questionnaires during the winter and spring of 1967.

1. Much of the relevant research will be cited in subsequent sections of this paper.

2. William J. Goode, "The Theoretical Importance of Love," *American Sociological Review, 24,* (February, 1959), 38-47, 42.

3. William J. Goode, *op. cit.;* Morton M. Hunt, *The Natural History of Love* (New York: Alfred A. Knopf, 1959), 342; Ralph Linton, *The Study of Man* (New York: D. Appleton-Century, 1936), 175.

4. Lleyellyn Gross, "A Belief Pattern Scale for Measuring Attitudes Toward Romanticism," *American Sociological Review, 9* (October, 1944), 463-72.

5. Dwight G. Dean, "Romanticism and Emotional Maturity: A Preliminary Study," *Marriage and Family Living, 23,* (February, 1961), 44-45

6. Ira L. Reiss, "Toward a Sociology of the Heterosexual Love Relationship," *Marriage and Family Living, 22,* (May, 1960), 139-45.

7. Ernest W. Burgess, "The Romantic Impulse and Family Disorganization," *Survey, 57* (December 1, 1926), 290-94.

8. Ralph Linton, *op. cit.;* 175.

9. William J. Goode, *op. cit.;* Ira L. Reiss, *op. cit.*

10. Ira L. Reiss, *ibid.*

11. Dwight G. Dean, *op. cit.,* 44; William J. Goode, *op. cit.,* 38-39; Judson T. Landis and Mary G. Landis, *Building a Successful Marriage* (Englewood Cliffs, New Jersey; Prentice Hall 1968, Fifth Edition, 114 and 132).

12. Snell Putney and Gail J. Putney, *The Adjusted American: Normal Neuroses in the Individual and Society* (New York: Harper Colophon Books, 1964), Chapter 10.

13. J. Richard Udry, *The Social Context of Marriage* (Philadelphia: J.B. Lippincott Co., 1966), especially 193-97.

14. William L. Kolb, "Family Sociology, Marriage Education, and the Romantic Complex," *Social Forces, 29* (October, 1950), 65-72.

15. Talcott Parsons, *Essays in Sociological Theory, Pure and Applied* (New York: The Free Press, a Division of The Macmillan Co., 1949), 240-42; on differentiation, "An Outline of the Social System," in Talcott Parsons, *et al.* (eds.), *Theories of Society* (New York: The Free Press, a Division of The Macmillan Co., 1961), 47ff.

16. Talcott Parsons, *op. cit.,* 227.

17. Talcott Parsons, *Social Structure and Personality* (New York: The Free Press, a Division of The Macmillian Co., 1964), 175 and 177.

18. George A. Theodorson, "Romanticism and Motivation to Marry in the United States, Singapore, Burma and India," *Social Forces, 44* (September 1965), 17-27.

19. Hugo G. Beigel, "Romantic Love," *American Sociological Review, 16* (June, 1951), 326-34.

20. Willard Waller and Reuben Hill, *The Family: A Dynamic Interpretation* (New York: The Dryden Press, Inc., 1951).

21. Morton M. Hunt, *op. cit.,* especially Chap. VII.

22. Hugo G. Beigel, *op. cit.*

23. Herman R. Lantz, *et al,* "Pre-Industrial Patterns in the Colonial Family in America: A Content Analysis of Colonial Magazines," *American Sociological Review, 33* (June 1968), 413-26.

24. Iral L. Reiss, "Pre-marital Sexual Permissiveness Among Negroes and Whites," *American Sociological Review, 29* (October, 1964), 688-98, 694.

25. Thomas J. Scheff, *Being Mentally Ill* (Chicago: Aldine Publishing Co., 1966).

26. Ernest W. Burgess and Paul Wallin, *Engagement and Marriage* (Chicago: J. B. Lippincott Co., 1953), 172.

27. Dwight G. Dean, "Romanticism and Emotional Maturity: A Further Exploration," *Social Forces, 42* (March, 1964), 298-303.

28. Dwight G. Dean, *op. cit.,* 44-45.

29. Ira L. Reiss, *The Social Context of Pre-marital Sexual Permissiveness* (New York: Holt, Rinehart and Winston, 1967), 80.

30. Charles W. Hobart, "The Incidence of Romanticism During Courtship," *Social Forces, 36* (May, 1958), 362-67; "Attitude Changes

During Courtship and Marriage," *Marriage and Family Living, 22* (November, 1960), 352-59.

31. Charles W. Hobart, *op. cit.*
32. Ira L. Reiss, *op. cit.*, 80.
33. In 1967, during the winter and spring quarters 2,009 questionnaires were distributed and 1,355 (67 percent) were returned.
34. The general values were an adaptation of a list used in Theodore M. Newcomb, *The Acquaintance Process* (New York: Holt, Rinehart, and Winston, 1961), 39. The family values were an adaptation of a list of family "standards" found in Bernard Farber, "An Index of Marital Integration," *Sociometry, 20* (June, 1957), 117-134, especially p. 120.
35. The items used in the analysis but not appearing in either table or the body of the paper were: (1) formal scales: aggression, autonomy, communication, dominance; (2) general values: well-adjusted person, financial success, being well-liked, cooperating with others, power, occupational status, helping others; (3) family values: sex relations, community respect, happy children, economic security, emotional security, moral and religious unity, companionship; (4) other items: urban vs. suburban community, ethnicity vs. none.
36. The items used in the index of the Romantic Love Complex were: (1) As long as they at least love each other, two people should have no trouble getting along together in marriage. (2) A girl should expect her sweetheart to be chivalrous on all occasions. (3) A person can't help falling in love if he (she) meets the right person. (4) Lovers should freely confess everything of personal significance to each other. (5) Happiness is inevitable in true love. (6) True love leads to almost perfect happiness. (7) To be truly in love is to be in love forever. (8) Love is an "all-or-nothing" feeling; there is no in-between. (9) When one is in love, the person whom he loves becomes the only goal of his life. One lives almost solely for the other. (10) There is only one real love for a person. (11) True love is known at once by the people involved.
37. The contingency tables were created after inspection of the frequency distributions of the variables. The dependent variable (romanticism) was divided into varying numbers of segments depending on the lengths of arrays and the shapes of the distributions, with an effort being made to create segments roughly equal in size. Sixteen-cell and twenty-cell tables were most frequent.
38. The scales were developed by using questions from many sources and selecting items for retention as noted in the text. Many of the scales bear considerable resemblance to scales or sets of questions developed in well-known works, because many of the questions were selected from or molded after those developed by such writers as Henry A. Murray, Ira L. Reiss, Rose Goldsen, Bernard Farber, Dwight G. Dean, William C. Schultz, Gweynn Nettler, Thomas S. Langner, Lewis M. Terman. Because of the number of scales involved, the

questions used will not be listed—except for the romanticism scale, and the notes on Table 1 concerning scales of divergent nature. A copy of the questionnaire showing the questions used in the various scales may be obtained by writing the author.

39. The Gammas for the group high on Religious Orthodoxy were compared to the Gammas for the total samples (male and female) rather than to those of the group low on Religious Orthodoxy because the intent was to show that the tendencies found in the total samples could be considered to be associated with differences in the degree to which traditional American culture patterns were accepted by individuals, even though these individuals had not adopted sets of radically different values, as might be the case for the protest groups.

Campus Values in Mate Selection:
A Replication

JOHN W. HUDSON
LURA F. HENZE

Past research indicates the influence of social class and family in the mate selection process which, in large part, accounts for the endogamous quality of mate selection.[1]

It has long been recognized that the family is the major agency of socialization. While the process of socialization never ends, it does decelerate with most learning taking place when the person is young.[2] The choice of a mate is limited by the individual's formation of generalized-value systems before maturation.[3] Values learned early in life tend to persist.

In the mass media, college students are often depicted as having departed from the traditional values of the society.[4] Thus, the youth of today are frequently charged with being less serious in mate selection than were young people a generation ago. Is this mass media image valid?

Since societal values regarding the family tend to change slowly, it is to be expected that values expressed in mate selection would vary little from one generation to the next. Parents play highly significant roles in the courtship of their children in that they have much to do with the kind of person the child will choose as a mate.[5] Whether consciously or unconsciously, the person's value system serves as criteria for mate selection.

The thesis of this paper is that the value system of the current college population regarding mate selection is not as different from the college population of a generation ago as thought by parents and portrayed by the mass media.

To compare values in mate selection held by college students today with those of earlier years, the literature was reviewed for relevant research. This review indicated that among the studies cited most often were the "Campus Values in Mate Selection" done by Hill and McGinnis.[6] These studies were selected for replication as they focused on personal characteristics related to mate selection and because the students who were the respondents in 1939 are the parental generation of today.

The earlier studies of "Campus Values in Mate Selection" were done at the University of Wisconsin in 1939 by Reuben Hill and in 1956 by Robert McGinnis. In the initial study by Hill, participants were enrolled in a noncredit marriage course. In the 1956 study McGinnis drew a one-percent systematic sample from the university student directory.

To broaden the base of this study, an investigation was conducted on four campuses located in widely separated geographic regions — three in the United States and one in Canada. The American colleges selected were Arizona State University, the University of Nebraska at Omaha, and the State University of New York at Stony Brook. The Canadian college chosen was the University of Alberta at Edmonton.

A copy of the "Campus Values" questionnaire, together with a cover letter explaining the nature of the study and a postage-paid return envelope, was mailed to each student in the sample. The original questionnaire had been prepared by Reuben Hill and Harold T. Christensen.

Description of the Questionnaire. Included in the questionnaire were the usual background items of age, sex, marital status, education, and family data. The evaluative section included preferences on age at time of marriage, age difference between husband and wife, number of children, and personal characteristics. The personal characteristics were 18 traits to be evaluated according to their degree of importance in choosing a mate. Provision was made for the respondent to add any further personal characteristics which he felt should be included.

Students were asked to assign a numerical weight of "three" to characteristics which they believed were indispensable, "two" to traits important but not indispensable, "one" to those desirable but not important, and "zero" to factors irrelevant in mate selection. Thus, respondents evaluated each trait and assigned an appropriate numerical weight to each; the investigators then ranked the traits on the basis of mean values computed from the numerical weights. For the purposes of this paper, the terms "ranked" and "evaluated" are used synonymously.

Description of the Sample. A one-percent random sample of full-time students at each of the four universities was drawn by the registrars' offices. Questionnaires were mailed to a total of 826 students; 566 (68.5 percent) were returned and usable.

The sample included 337 males and 229 females. The median age was 21.6 years for men and 20.4 years for women. Seventy-six percent of the men and 82 percent of the women were single.

Age Factors in Mate Selection. College men and women in the 1967 sample indicated a preference for marriage at an earlier age than had been indicated in the previous studies. (See Table 1). The median preferred age at marriage for men in 1939 was 25.1 years and was 24.9 years for the 1956 sample. The age preference dropped to 24.5 years in 1967. The median age preference for women in 1939 was 24.0 years, and in 1956 and 1967, it declined to 22.9 and 22.5 years, respectively.

In all three studies, males and females agreed that the husband should be older than the wife but did not agree on the preferred age difference. Women preferred a greater age gap between spouses than did men.

TABLE 1

MEDIAN PREFERENCES (BY SEX
AND YEAR) REGARDING AGE AT MARRIAGE,
DIFFERENCE IN AGE BETWEEN HUSBAND
AND WIFE, AND NUMBER OF CHILDREN

Year	Preferred age at marriage		Preferred age difference between husband and wife		Preferred number of children	
	M	F	M	F	M	F
1939	25.1	24.0	2.3	3.4	3.3	3.5
1956	24.9	22.9	1.2	2.1	3.6	3.9
1967	24.5	22m5	1.5	2.0	2.9	3.3

Number of Children Preferred. In all three time periods investigated, women preferred more children than did men. The trend was toward more children wanted by men and women in 1956 (3.6 and 3.9) than in 1939 (3.3 and 3.5), and fewer children in 1967 (2.9 and 3.3) than in either of the earlier periods.

Personal Factors in Mate Selection. The data indicate that from one time period to the next, three of the 18 items, as evaluated by men, maintained the same rank and 11 did not vary by more than one place. (See Table 2.) Males, in all three studies, evaluated dependable character as the most indispensable personal characteristic in a mate. Sociability and favorable social status consistently held their rank of twelfth and sixteenth place, respectively, in 1939, 1956, and 1967.

Chastity, as evaluated by men, declined to a greater degree than did any other characteristic. This was indicated by mean scores as well as by rank. In 1939 the mean score for chastity was 2.06, and in 1967 it was 1.28. In rank, the decline was from tenth place to fifteenth.

Greater emphasis was placed on good looks by males in 1967 than in either of the earlier studies. During the time period under study, health declined in importance from fifth to ninth place. The traits which moved consistently upward from 1939 to 1967 were mutual attraction, good cook-housekeeper, and similar educational background — each moved up two positions. The characteristic which fluctuated the most was similar religious background, which changed from thirteenth place in 1939 to tenth in 1956 and declined to fourteenth in 1967.

TABLE 2

RANK OF 18 PERSONAL CHARACTERISTICS IN MATE
SELECTION BASED ON MEAN VALUE, BY YEAR AND SEX

	Male			Female		
	1939	1956	1967	1939	1956	1967
1. Dependable character	1	1	1	2	1	2
2. Emotional stability	2	2	3	1	2	1
3. Pleasing disposition	3	4	4	4	5	4
4. Mutual attraction	4	3	2	5	6	3
5. Good health	5	6	9	6	9	10
6. Desire for home-children	6	5	5	7	3	5
7. Refinement	7	8	7	8	7	8
8. Good cook-housekeeper	8	7	6	16	16	16
9. Ambition-industriousness	9	9	8	3	4	6
10. Chastity	10	13	15	10	15	15
11. Education-intelligence	11	11	10	9	14	7
12. Sociability	12	12	12	11	11	13
13. Similar religious background	13	10	14	14	10	11
14. Good looks	14	15	11	17	18	17
15. Similar educational background	15	14	13	12	8	9
16. Favorable social status	16	16	16	15	13	14
17. Good financial prospect	17	17	18	13	12	12
18. Similar political background	18	18	17	18	17	18

In the responses by women, no trait was consistently evaluated as more important in 1956 and 1967 than it had been in 1939. One of the 18 traits — good cook-housekeeper — ranked sixteenth in all three studies; the rank of eight other traits did not vary by more than one place. Emotional stability and dependable character ranked first or second in each time period studied. Women gave the least weight to good looks and similar political background.

For women, the evaluation of chastity declined to a greater extent than for any other characteristic. This was indicated by mean scores and by rank. The mean score for chastity was 2.0 in 1939 and .93 in 1967, while the rank in 1939 was tenth and in 1956 and 1967 it was fifteenth. Ambition, good health, and sociability moved downward with consistency. Fluctuation was greatest for education-intelligence which ranked ninth in 1939, fourteenth in 1956, and seventh in 1967.

Male and female responses to the additional question asking for further characteristics felt to be important in mate selection were insufficient to warrant analysis.

Preliminary analysis of data from the four colleges indicates no significant differences in student responses from one campus to the others. Analysis of data from each of the campuses will be reported in a subsequent paper.

CONCLUSIONS

Preference in Age Factors. This study has indicated that the preferred age at first marriage has continued to show a decline since the 1939 study. A sidelight of the younger age at first marriage in the United States has been an increase in the proportion of college students who marry and remain in school.[7] It has been noted by other writers that, while student marriage was not unknown during the 1930s, it was not widespread.[8] Prior to World War II married students were rare and frequently prohibited from enrollment. Today they are an accepted fact.

From discussions with college students, the investigators have concluded that there has been increased emphasis on dating at the pre-teen level and that this pattern has been initiated largely by parents and school systems. According to students, a further parental influence in the early stages of dating has been the insistence that dating partners be drawn from the same age and social group. This early requirement of dating a person from the same age group structures the subsequent dating pattern. Since mate selection is a function of whom one dates, the age gap between husband and wife has narrowed in terms of preferences stated by college students and according to Parke and Glick.[9]

The overall decline in preferred age at first marriage is probably a reflection of both economic conditions and the current high value placed on marriage. The convergence in agreement on age differential is probably the result, in part, of changes in dating and mate selection patterns as well as changes in female status.

Preference in Number of Children. The findings do not constitute an adequate basis for predictions of future birth rates. Birth rates and desired number of children are very sensitive to social and cultural conditions. Thus, little significance can be attached to changes in the number of children wanted by students in 1939, 1956, and 1967 since factors which influence preferences are closely linked to cycles and fashions of the time.

Personal Characteristics. When the 18 characteristics were ranked and a comparison was made between the findings of the three studies, it became apparent that over the years there has been a striking consistency in student evaluation of desired traits in a mate. For example, college students today assign the same importance to dependable character as did college students a generation ago.

Good health, as evaluated by both men and women, has become less important in mate selection. This is probably a reflection of the general improvement in overall health which has, in part, resulted from the increased availability of comprehensive medical services and health insurance.

The personal characteristic which evidences the greatest decline in rank was chastity. Although chastity ranked in fifteenth place for both sexes in 1967, this does not indicate that the same importance is placed on this factor by men and by women. When the mean values are examined, it is evident that the double standard is still operating. Men continue to evaluate virginity as a more important characteristic for a wife than women do for a husband, as evidenced by the mean scores. It should be noted that the lowered evaluation of chastity may not indicate that it is less important; the change in rank may simply indicate that other attributes have become more meaningful since the time of the Hill study.

SUMMARY

While this study does not clearly and precisely add to theory construction, it does add substantive material which suggests generational stability in criteria used in mate selection. For although a child may rebel against domination, he cannot escape the ideas conditioned in him from his childhood.[10]

In 1967, compared to 1939, there have been changes in the behavior patterns of the college populations studied in terms of age factors in mate selection and in marrying while in college. However, this change is compatible with the high value placed on marriage by the parental generation — who were the college students of 1939 — and the younger generation who are the students today.

The charge that young people have departed from traditional values and are less serious about mate selection is not given support by the present study. Indeed, the findings suggest that youth's values regarding the importance of personal characteristics in mate selection are much the same today as they were a generation ago.

It might be said in conclusion that social change in the area of mate selection has not been as great as indicated by the press, feared by the parent, and perhaps hoped by the youth.

REFERENCES

1. Ira L. Reiss, "Social Class and Campus Dating," *Social Problems,* 13:2 (Fall, 1965), p. 195. August B. Hollingshead, "Cultural Factors in the Selection of Marriage Mates," *American Sociological Review,* 15 (October, 1960), p. 627.

2. Kingsley Davis, "The Sociology of Parent-Youth Conflict," *American Sociological Review*, 5 (August, 1940), p. 524.

3. Marvin B. Sussman, *Sourcebook in Marriage and the Family*, Boston: Houghton Mifflin Company, 2nd ed., 1963, p. 63.

4. Stephen Birmingham, "American Youth: A Generation Under the Gun," *Holiday*, 37 (March 1, 1965), p. 44.

5. Alan Bates, "Parental Roles in Courtship," *Social Forces*, 20 (May, 1942), p. 483.

6. Reuben Hill, "Campus Values in Mate Selection," *Journal of Home Economics*, 37 (November, 1945). Robert McGinnis, "Campus Values in Mate Selection: A Repeat Study," *Social Forces*, 36 (May, 1959).

7. Paul C. Glick, *American Families*, New York: John Wiley and Sons, Inc., 1957, p. 57.

8. Jessie Bernard, *Dating, Mating and Marriage*, Cleveland: Howard Allen, Inc., 1958, pp. 217-218. Victor A. Christopherson and Joseph S. Vandiver, "The Married College Student, 1959." *Marriage and Family Living*, 22 (May, 1960), p. 122. Ernest Haveman, "To Love, Honor, Obey and Study," *Life*, 38:21 (May 23, 1955), p. 152.

9. Robert Parke, Jr. and Paul C. Glick, "Prospective Changes in Marriage and the Family," *Journal of Marriage and the Family*, 29:2 (May, 1967), p. 249.

10. Robert H. Coombs, "Reinforcement of Values in the Parental Home as a Factor in Mate Selection," *Marriage and Family Living*, 24 (May, 1962), p. 155.

Should Parents or Cupid Arrange Marriages?

ELEANOR STOKER BOLL

After spending the past five years in India, Dr. Marie Finger Bale of the Methodist Board of Missions recently remarked that there might be fewer divorces in the United States if we borrowed a little from Indian customs. Divorce is almost unknown in India, she said, because parents select their children's mates and continue to control their sons' and daughters' lives after marriage.

It would be impossible, even if it were desirable, to adopt outright a major feature of a culture so different from our own. Yet there is no denying that we have become conspicuous for our marital failures. Our annual divorce rate today is about one for every four marriages. We might, therefore, take a look at India's system of arranged marriages. What features of it — if any — might we adopt?

The Hindu joint-family system is designed to achieve continuation of the family line, including its reputation, status and property. Families confer in an attempt to mate young people of similar religion and status, of good health and good character — a responsibility considered too grave for the immature. In making the decision, the parents sometimes "engage" a very young child to another from an acceptable family.

After marriage, family control is maintained by having the young couple live permanently with the bridegroom's parents. His mother strictly supervises their personal lives, social relations and the rearing of their children. She also holds the purse strings; whatever they earn is put into a family kitty, along with other family earnings, and dispensed by the mother for the group as a whole. As the family ages and the parents die, the eldest son and his wife are in a position to assume control over the younger members of the family. Thus there is a continuous process of education for and control of marriage and family living.

Arranged marriages and continued control are not unique in India but have been customary for centuries in various places, including China, Japan and the Arab world. Even though the law today in most areas permits free choice, the old tradition dies slowly because it worked well in accomplishing its purpose — family stability, family protection, family survival.

The case for "arranged marriages" in the United States — or at least more parental control — is based, first, upon the fact that the marriage

age is low here. One out of every three girls in this country who marries for the first time is 18 or under. Our most frequent ages of first marriage today are 18 and 19 for girls and 21 and 22 for boys.

The results do not speak well for the judgment of young people who insist on early marriage and on living as they please. Dr. Judson Landis of the University of California, in a selected sample, found divorce rates six times higher in marriages where both spouses were under 21 when they married than in marriages in which both were 31 or over at the time of marriage. In selected United States states, according to the 1958 United Nations Demographic Yearbook, 22.5 per cent of divorced women were 24 or under and 24 per cent of those divorced had been married less than two years. In fact, one out of every twenty divorced women now remarrying is a teen-ager.

Another argument for more parental say-so about marrying is the inexperience of our young people — a factor related to our standards of education. More and more young people stay in high school until 18, college until 22 — and then go on to professional schools. During this time many want to marry and more of them are doing so every year. Yet what preparation have they had for marriage and parenthood? One is reminded of the 19-year-old girl who knew her boy friend was the right mate for her because they were "mentally compatible" — i.e., they could spend a whole evening discussing Plato's philosophy.

In addition, more than one out of every five Americans change residence every year and many a child moves from neighborhood to neighborhood and school to school five or more times before finishing high school. How can such young people learn the qualities about their associates that are most essential to stable marriage? Do they not, in these circumstances, need all possible parental wisdom and guidance?

A further point in favor of arranged marriages is that our children today live with others from a variety of religious, racial, social and economic backgrounds. The new or different is always appealing, especially during the adolescent's rebellion against traditional family values — precisely at the time when so many Americans choose their mates. Yet a growing number of studies indicate that marriages which cross racial, religious and economic lines yield more broken families than those where the backgrounds are similar.

And when a child's marriage breaks, it is the family that has to bind up the fracture. A case in point is Martha, who at 16 fell in love with a boy of whom her whole family and most of her friends heartily disapproved. The day she turned 18 — the age of consent in her state — she eloped with the young man. Three years and two babies later she was back, financially dependent, and in need not only of a divorce but of physical protection as well. For the boy, just as her parents had pointed out, had a violent temper and was threatening to take the children away.

Is it so unreasonable that parents — who have to mend the damage they have warned against — should wish to exercise some control?

A wedding is a ceremony with notably long-lasting consequences. It produces children who have to be reared, children who become the society's future. Dr. Carle C. Zimmerman of Harvard, in a study of the family throughout history, concludes that the strength of a nation closely parallels the solidarity of its family system. Must the "right" of young people to marry whom and when they please take precedence over the interests of society?

But there is another side of the picture. The arguments against arranged marriage are based on its unsuitability to our type of society and on the damage it can do to the individual. When marriage is completely dictated by the family, human values are often the last thing to be considered.

In India, for example, young girls have been married to princes and wealthy men regardless of suitability — witness the 14-year-old girl who was wed to a 70-year-old man, bore him three children before his death, and remained a widow from age 19 for the rest of her life. The arranged marriage, going hand in hand with a low status for women, bears most heavily upon the female, who can be and often is miserably exploited. The male has always been harder to control.

Such Indian misadventures could well occur in different form here, even though parents hew less rigorously to the family line. Consider the kind of marriages that might be arranged by Old World parents resentful of New World ways and anxious to keep their children within their own cultural patterns; by status-seeking parents who would gladly sacrifice any child for improved social position; by parents who consider marriage itself such a mark of accomplishment that they' shame their children into early wedlock; or by parents who for their own purposes seek to keep their young people from marrying. Such parental pressures occur frequently enough even under our presnt system of free choice.

Furthermore, if our young people know their prospective mates only superficially — as the supporters of arranged marriage point out — do the parents know them any better? The casualness of our relationships, and the restless moving about from which it stems, both in turn derive from a pace of cultural change that is something new in history.

In these circumstances, it is at least questionable whether one generation's way of dealing with its problems will work for the next. Many an American teen-ager today has already achieved, through better education and choice of friends, a social level higher than that of his parents; could his parents make a wise marriage choice for him? Another aspect of this same social mobility makes it well-nigh impossible to impose a system of arranged marriages on our society. When our young people can get jobs of their own and support themsleves, they can marry whether their parents like it or not.

Among the major curses of our society is the thinness of family emotional relationships. Indeed, this is what drives many of our chil-

202 Getting Together: The Partner-Selection Process

dren into early marriage. One wonders if parents who have done poorly in their own marriages are likely to be more successful in guiding those of their children.

Moreover, as the opponents of arranged marriage point out, there is the all-important question of love. The lack of love has obvious and unhealthy effects on human beings — there is even an affliction called marasmus, which causes infants who do not experience love simply to waste away. Quite apart from its own enchantment, the experience of loving and being loved is probably essential to good mental hygiene.

Love is a minor consideration in countries given to arranged marriage, where mates often do not even see one another before the wedding, and where any spontaneous romance between young people is looked upon with suspicion.

Americans, in contrast, have developed a kind of marriage based on romantic affection between two people. This may indeed be an uncertain foundation for marriage. Nevertheless, when matched with congeniality and common values, it can produce the finest type of family life and the healthiest atmosphere for rearing children. And happy families, so the studies say, create more happy families in the next generation.

What, then, is an intelligent balance between these two views of marriage? After years spent in studying modern American marriage at the William T. Carter Foundation, we have come to believe that more control over the marriage of young people should be exerted by law, by parents, by the general public and by educators.

First, we could, and probably should, make it more difficult for the very young to marry in the face of family protest. Most states demand that a boy be 21 before he can marry without parental consent, but in five states he can do so at 18. For girls, the age of consent is 18 in thirty-three states, and 16 in two. While laws alone will never solve the problem of hasty marriages, our laws seem intent on encouraging them.

Parents themselves could become a major controlling force, were they to begin consciously conditioning their children toward good marriages at a very early age. Though they may not formally "engage" young children as the Hindus do, they can effect similar results in several ways.

One is to teach children attitudes toward marriage as a responsibility to the family line, past and future, and not as an orgy of romantic satisfaction between two individuals. Parents can also instill feelings of such pride in the basic values inherent in their own race, religion and social class that their offspring will not be intrigued by other values which, in marriage, will cause conflict.

Parents should seek to select almost from a child's birth, and particularly during adolescence, the companions with whom he associates in neighborhood, in school and in recreation. Children *can* learn to prefer mates approved by parents if other possibilities are kept to a minimum. Furthermore, parents should discuss their own marriage sincerely and realistically with their children, who are sure to take the reasons for its relative success or failure very much to heart.

Parents who try to guide their children into good marriages need, and deserve, the support of public opinion. At present, they get too little of it. For one reason, we are devoted to the ideal that all people are created equal and that there should be no discrimination in association. But we neglect to point out to young people that in marriage, the most intimate and important relationship in life, discordance of values has been seen to lead to failure. Agin, as a romatic-minded people, we tend to look askance at any parental interference with young love. We side with the starry-eyed. Even in school courses on marriage and family living, many teachers tend to undercut parents by discussing marriage as a union between two people who should learn to be personally compatible.

According to Dr. A. H. Hobbes, the most popular textbooks for such courses emphasize romance and individuality, playing down marriage's crucial role in creating the next generation. When parents oppose a marriage, children often seek advice from others. Apparently, they do not have to look far.

Control over mate selection *alone* is no answer to the problem of divorce. Along with control, young people must receive from early childhood an attitude toward marriage so thoughtful and serious that they will *seek* their parents' counsel. True, some parents are selfish and some are unwise. But by and large, no one knows us better — or wishes us so well.

Trial Marriage:
Harnessing the Trend
Constructively

MIRIAM E. BERGER

ANTHROPOLOGICAL AND
HISTORICAL SURVEY

Trial marriage has been practiced among the Peruvian Indians of Vicos in the Andes for more than four centuries. (Price, 1965; MacLean, 1941) Arranged by the parents in the earlier form, the purpose was to test the girl's work abilities and the couple's general compatibility. In modern Vicos there is a free choice of marriage partners with romantic love playing an important role, but men still seek responsible, hardworking girls who have mastered household skills and can help in the fields. Study of couples who entered a trial marriage for the first time indicated that the average duration of such trials was less than fifteen months and that 83 percent of the relationships were finalized with marriage. There was no stigma if the couple had children, but did not marry. Permanent separations after marriage were rare, occurring in two to three percent of the cases. One of the advantages of these trial marriages noted by Price was the ease of transition from adolescence to adulthood. The couple acquired certain social and sexual advantages of adulthood without assuming full responsibility.

The Trobrainders had a "bachelor's house" in which courting couples slept together and had exclusive sex prior to marriage. In contrast to Western civilization, before marriage Trobraind couples were not permitted to eat together or share any interest, except sex. (Malinowski, 1929)

In the eighteenth century, Maurice of Saxony, illegitimate son of the Elector Augustus the Strong and Countess Aurora of Konigsmark, sought a solution to the marriage problem. He recommended temporary marriages, contracted for a limited time. If the partners agreed, the contract could be prolonged, but marriage for life was a "betrayal of the self, an unnatural compulsion." (Lewinsohn, 1956)

"Bundling" orginated in Europe and was brought to the New World in the eighteenth century. In New England, where it was too cold to sit up late, courting couples were permitted, with parental approval, to get into bed with their clothes on. Some bundling experiences were probably innocent, especially when they included a center-board for the bed (Marriage Museum), but "certainly many got sexually involved and married when conception occurred." (Scott, 1960; Fielding, 1961)

"Trial nights," an old Teutonic custom (Marriage Museum), is still practiced today in Staphorst, Holland, an insular, inbred town whose customs have for centuries sealed them off from contemporary life. The swain spends three nights a week with his girl friend, with the knowledge of her parents who hope she will prove fertile. Until she becomes pregnant, there can be no marriage. If she is barren, the community regards her with primitive suspicion and contempt. Once she is pregnant, however, the marriage must take place. (Gibney, 1948)

TWENTIETH CENTURY AMERICA

The first American to propose trial marriages as a concept was Judge Ben B. Lindsay. (1927) Bertrand Russell who was then teaching in New York, approved of Lindsay's Companionate Marriage, but felt it did not go far enough. Russell favored trial marriage for university students and believed that work and sex were more easily combined "in a quasi-permanent relationship, than in the scramble and excitement of parties and drunken orgies" that were prevalent during the Prohibition Era. Russell felt that if a man and woman chose to live together without having children, it was no one's business but their own. He believed it undesirable for a couple to marry for the purpose of raising a family without first having had sexual experience. (Russell, 1929)

Lindsay and Russell were ostracized, and the concept of trial marriage lay dormant until an evolving sexual morality led anthropoligst Margaret Mead to revive it. (Mead, 1966) Building on Lindsay's Companionate Marriage, she recommended a two-step marriage: *individual,* in which there would be a simple ceremony, limited economic responsibilities, easy divorce, if desired, and no children; and *parental marriage,* which would be entered into as a second step by couples who were ready to undertake the lifetime obligations of parenthood, would be more difficult to enter into and break off, and would entail mutual continuing responsibility for any children. Her rationale was that sex, now considered a normal need in youth, often drove them into premature and early marriage, frequently leading to unhappiness and divorce. She made the plea that divorce be granted before children are conceived, so that only wanted children of stable marriages are brought into the world. Responses to Dr. Mead's proposal (Mead, 1968) ranged from disapproval for tampering with tradition (instead of helping couples adjust to traditional marriage) to complaints from students for setting up too much structure. A typical student response was: "Why get married? Why can't we live together, with a full sex life, with no pregnancy, until we're ready to get married and have children?"

Margaret Mead's two-step marriage was elaborated on by Michael Scriven, a philosophy professor, who proposed a three-step plan:

> We try to make one institution achieve three aims, which all too often lie in perpendicular dimensions. The aims are sexual satisfaction, social security and sensible spawning. The solution would be to create three types of marriage arranged so that any combination is possible: preliminary, personal and parental marriage. The first would simply be legitimized cohabitation, contractually insulated against escalation into "de facto" commitment. It would be a prerequisite for other kinds and would impose a period of a year's trial relationship before the possibility of conversion to personal marriage . . . (Scriven, 1967)

In *The Sexual Wilderness,* Vance Packard (1968) concluded that the first two years of marriage are the most difficult. He recommended a two-year confirmation period, after which the marriage would become final or would be dissolved. Packard felt that this proposal differed from trial marriage because the couple would marry in earnest and with the hope that the marriage would be permanent. He saw trial marriage as highly tentative and little more than unstructured cohabitation. Packard's concept is based on his conviction that the expectation of permanency contributes to success in that it motivates a couple to work hard to adapting, and is, in fact, a strong stabilizing and reinforcing factor.

In "Marriage as a Statutory Five Year Renewable Contract," Virginia Satir, family therapist, said:

> Maybe there needs to be something like an apprentice period . . . in which potential partners have a chance to explore deeply and experiment with their relationship, experience the other and find out whether his fantasy matched the reality. Was it really possible through daily living to have a process in which each was able to enhance the growth of the other, while at the same time enhancing his own? What is it like to have to undertake joint ventures and to be with each other every day? It would seem that in this socially approved context, the chances of greater realness and authenticity continuing would be increased, and the relationship would deepen, since it started on a reality base. (1967)

Another variation of the renewable contract concept was proposed by Mervyn Cadwallader, a sociology professor, in "Marriage as a Wretched Institution:"

Marriage was not designed to bear the burdens now being asked
of it by the urban American middle class. It was an institution that
evolved over centuries to meet some very specific needs of a
non-industrial society ... Marriage was not designed as a
mechanism for providing friendship, erotic experience, romantic
love, personal fulfillment, continuous lay psychotherapy, or recreation. It's purposes ... have changed radically, yet we cling
desperately to the outmoded structures of the past ... The basic
structure of Western marriage is never questioned, alternatives
are not proposed or discussed ... Why not permit a flexible
contract, for one or more years, with periodic options to renew? If
a couple grew disenchanted with their life together, they would
not feel trapped for life ... They would not have to go through
the destructive agonies of divorce, and carry about the stigma of
marital failure, like the mark of Cain on their foreheads. Instead
of a declaration of war, they could simply let their contracts lapse
and while still friendly, be free to continue their romantic quest
... What of the children in a society that *is* moving inexorably
toward consecutive, plural marriages? ... If the bitter and
poisonous denouement of divorce could be avoided by a frank
acceptance of short-term marriages, both adults and children
would benefit. Any time spouses treat each other decently,
generously, and respectfully, their children will benefit. (Cadwallader, 1966)

Today many young people have carried the concept of trial marriage
a step further, as Bertrand Russell advocated, by living with a roommate of the opposite sex. Sociologist Robert N. Whitehurst coined a
word to describe them, "unmalias," a condensation of unmarried
liaisons. (1969) Whitehurst mentions some of the problems encountered by students who have an "experimental semester of living together, such as when a male senior must leave the campus for graduate
school, job, or military service. (1969)

The Harrad Experiment (Rimmer, 1966) incorporated some of the
above mentioned ideas on trial marriage and added some new dimensions. In Rimmer's novel, college students lived with computer-
selected roommates of the opposite sex. Unlike the informal arrangements now made by college students on their own (Karlen, 1969; Life,
1968), the Harrad Experiment was controlled and guided by the
Tenhausens, a husband-and-wife team of sociologist and marriage
counselor. The novel focused on several couples who married after
four years of living together. The students attended vrious neighbor-
ing colleges, but roomed at Harrad during the four years, and were
required to take a course in human values at Harrad taught by the
Tenhausens and to do required reading in the subjects of marriage,
love, sex, contraception, moral values, philosophy, etc. Whenever the
students were troubled about their relationships, the Tenhausens were
available for consultation. There was also considerable peer support

through endless discussions of common problems. Rimmer favored a structured, socially approved form of premarital experimentation that would give the male, and female an opportunity to realize themselves fully, without guilt, and to adjust to their new marital roles without legal entanglement, recognizing marriage as the commitment a couple makes to society when they decide to have children. (1969) Accused of trying to undermine America's family structure Rimmer asserted that, on the contrary, he believed a strong family to be a *sine qua non* of social existence and that his proposals would strengthen and preserve that structure.

In an article in *The Humanist* (1970) Rustum and Della Roy discussed alternatives to traditional marriage in view of the increasing divorce rate:

> By one simple swish of tradition, we can incorporate all the recent suggestions for trial marriage . . . and cover them all under the decent rug of the "engagement" — engagements with minor differences—that in today's society, they entitle a couple to live together, but not to have children . . . By no means need this become universal norm.

NCFR Workshop

A workshop led by the author was conducted at the annual meeting of the National Council on Family Relations in 1969. The participants were primarily college instructors of marriage and family courses, but included a social worker, a clergyman, a sociologist, and a college counselor of students. The following is a summary of the highlights of the workshop:

It was agreed that there ought to be alternative methods of courtship, approved by society, that would serve as a better preparation for marriage than dating. Those opposed to trial marriage as one such alternative felt it was not the same as a real marriage and therefore not a valid preparation for marriage. It was also subject to exploitation and abuse, as was any method of courtship, and was more to the interest of the male than the female, who is likely to be more concerned about security. Opponents also pointed out that it takes a great deal of maturity to make a relationship work, and if a couple are not mature enough to marry, they may not be mature enough to end a relationship when indicated, nor to cope with the attendant rejection, not to mention accidental pregnancy, or a partner who flits from one relationship to another.

Those who favored trial marriage felt it should be morally sanctioned by society as an optional alternative.

Clerical Attitudes

Although many clergymen disapprove of trial marriage, there have been some notable exceptions. Typical of the negative opinion is that of Dean John Coburn of the Episcopal Theological School, Massachusetts:

> How can two people trust one another on a temporary basis? Marriage is a total commitment, and trial marriage is a contradiction in terms. (Eddy, 1968)

On the other hand, a Unitarian minister, Robert M. Eddy (1968), regarding the casual promiscuity and resulting unwanted children as tragic developments of the "new morality," offered the following alternatives:

> (1) that parents continue the financial support of their college-attending children who are having companionate marriages;
> (2) that it be illegal for youngsters under the age of seventeen to conceive; that seventeen to nineteen year olds, after obtaining parental consent, might live together with the privileges and responsibilities of the relationship defined by a contract as detailed or loose as the parents would desire. Such a relationship could be solemnized by a rite similar to the wedding ceremony and could be ended by mutual consent, as long as the couple did not have children. The next type of cohabitation agreement essentially would be identical to the present marriage relationship, but under the new system, would be limited to adults and would be, in effect, a license to raise children.

HARNESSING THE TREND CONSTRUCTIVELY

Whether one's professional or religious beliefs lead to a view of trial marriage as conservative or radical, acceptable or sinful, a valid or non-valid preparation for marriage, there may be a need to recognize that trial marriage and its variations are being practiced by some young people. (Eddy 1968; Karlen, 1969; Life, 1969; Whitehurst, 1969) As a marriage counselor and emotional health consultant, the author proposes a service that would guide and serve young people who do venture into trial marriage, legal or otherwise, so that they learn from their experiences, rather than stumble blindly from one relationship to another. It is recommended that they assess the experience with a consultant, exploring, individually or in a group, some of the following:

What did I learn about myself from this experience? How did I adjust to living with a peer, as distinguished from living with parents and siblings, or alone? What have the problems of adjustment been? Would I have the same problems with another roommate or spouse? How much did I contribute to these problems and how much was the responsibility of the partner? What neurotic games did we play? What hangups did I bring to the relationship that were reinforced by our interaction? What kind of person do I need to live with, dominant, submissive, detached, involved, affectionate, etc? What was our style of communication, constructive (Gordon, 1968), silent treatment, hitting below the belt? (Bach, 1968) How effectively do I communicate my needs and feelings? How did our communication problems affect our sexual adjustment? On the assumption that personal happiness is achieved through satisfying closeness to another human being, what problems did I have in achieving and maintaining that closeness?

The author would like to see colleges take the leadership by providing emotional health consultants for the preventive service described above, in addition to the usual counseling services. To encourage college students to avail themselves of the service, its use is recommended as a preventive mental health measure, e.g., at the end of each year when living arrangements are likely to be changed, when students finish the first year in a dormitory, whether single-sex or co-ed dorm, the second and third years with a roommate of the same sex, and whatever the arrangement is for the fourth year. Once accustomed to using the service and finding the consultant understanding, nonjudgmental, and helpful in developing insight, the student is more likely to use the service to discuss any relationships with the opposite sex. Periodic check-ups would give the consultant a chance to know a student and to provide direction and guidance. When a student is ready to marry his current partner or someone else, his selection of a mate will have greater sophistication and insight, or he may be motivated if he had repeated adjustment problems with successive roommates, to obtain counseling. (Kardiner, 1970) If colleges initiated such a preventive service, it would, in time, become acceptable for noncollegians. In urban centers where many young people live away from their families, the service is available through the facilities of "Check-Up for Emotional Health"; it could also be available in community settings, such as family agencies, premarital counseling services, Y's, community mental health centers, and religious organizations.

RESEARCH INDICATIONS

One critical issue is whether trial marriage is a valid test and preparation for marriage. Some probably know of couples for whom trial marriage culminated in a satisfactory legal marriage. Nevertheless, the following case studies raise questions about the validity of trial marriage as a test:

> Sue, age 24, was referred for psychotherapy because of severe anxiety symptoms that had their onset immediately after marriage. She had lived with her husband six months prior to marriage, during which phase she had been relaxed, her real self, and not unduly concerned over the success of the relationship. Exploration revealed that Sue was so anxious for the marriage to succeed that she was repressing all negative feelings, and denying

her identity in an effort to fulfill her image of a good wife. Now she was afraid of becoming as aggressive, argumentative, and opinionated as she had been as a teenager.

Ada, age 22, came for psychotherapy because of severe obsessional symptoms. Since her marriage two years earlier, she had been frigid. She had lived with her husband weekends for one year prior to marriage, during which phase she had experienced orgasm. The source of conflict revealed in the exploration was that after marriage she felt her husband was too demanding sexually, that he valued her only for sex, which made it demeaning to her, and that she found it difficult to limit him. She had transferred her excessive need to have her parents' approval to having her husband's approval, resolving the conflict by denying her resentment and thereby becoming frigid and obsessional.

Sue's and Ada's trial marriages were not deliberate tests; both had drifted into their living-together experiences. Perhaps, when the trial marriage is deliberate, similar anxieties would occur before, rather than after the permanent marriage. Was it just that trial marriage was not a valid test for these women with neurotic personalities? It is only the troubled who come to the attention of the professional. Study of the marriages of a large sample of couples who first had trial marriages might provide more reliable information upon which to base a conclusion. In planning the research design, it would be necessary: (1) to distinguish between deliberate trials and unstructured cohabitation that happened to result in permanency; and (2) to explore whether motivation to adapt (Packard, 1968; Lederer and Jackson, 1968) differed during the trial and in permanency.

REFERENCES

Bach, George and Peter Wyden. *Intimate Enemy*. New York: W. Morrow and Company, 1968.

Cadwallader, Mervyn. "Marriage as a Wretched Institution," *Atlantic Monthly*, 1966, 218 (5), 62-66.

Eddy, Robert M. "Should We Change Our Sex Laws?," *The Register-Leader*, March 1966, Detroit, Michigan.

Eddy, Robert M. "Why We Must Allow Sexual Freedom for Teens," *Pageant*, September, 1968, 118-129.

Fielding, Wm. J. *Strange Customs of Courtship and Marriage*. London: Souvenir Press, 1961.

Gibney, Frank. "The Strange Ways of Staphorst," *Life*, September 27, 1948, 2-8.

Gordon, Thomas. *Parent Effectiveness Training*. 110 South Euclid Avenue, Pasadena, California.

Kardiner, Sheldon H. "Convergent Internal Security Systems — A Rationale for Marital Therapy," *Family Process*, 1970, 9 (1), 83-91.

Karlen, Arno. "The Unmarried Marrieds on Campus," *New York Times Magazine*, January 26, 1969, 29-30.

Lederer, Wm. J. and Don D. Jackson. *The Mirages of Marriage.* New York: W. W. Norton and Company, 1968, Ch. 21-23.

Lindsey, Ben B. "The Companionate Marriage," *Redbook,* October 1926; March 1927.

Lewinsohn, Richard. *The History of Sexual Customs.* New York: Harper Brothers, 1958. Original edition in German, 1956, translated by Alexander Mayce.

MacLean, R. "Trail Marriage Among the Peruvian Aborigines," *Mexican Sociology,* 1941, 1, 25-33, in Spanish.

Malinowski, Bronislaw. *The Sexual Life of Savages.* London: Geo. Routledge and Sons, 1929.

Marriage Museum, formerly located at 1991 Broadway, New York, N. Y.

Mead, Margaret. "Marriage in Two Steps." *Redbook,* 1966, 127, 48-49.

Mead, Margaret. "A Continuing Dialogue on Marriage," *Redbook,* 1968, 130, 44.

Packard, Vance. *The Sexual Wilderness.* New York: David McKay Company, 1968, 466-468.

Price, Richard. "Trial Marriage in the Andes," *Ethnology,* 1965, 4, 310-322.

Rimmer, Robert H. *The Harrad Experiment.* Los Angeles: Sherbourne Press, 1966.

Rimmer, Robert H. *The Harrad Letters.* New York: New American Library, Signet Book No. 4037.

Rustum, Roy and Della Rustum. "Is Monogamy Outdated?" *The Humanist,* 1970, 30 (2), 24.

Russell, Bertrand. *Marriage and Morals.* New York: Liveright Publishing Company, 1929.

Satir, Virginia. "Marriage as a Statutory Five Year Renewable Contract." Paper presented at the American Psychological Association 75th Annual Convention, Washington, D.C., September 1, 1967. Copy available from author, P.O. Box 15248, San Francisco, Calif. 94115.

Scott, George Ryley. *Marriage – An Inquiry Relating to all Races and Nations from Antiquity to Present Day.* New York: Key Publishing Company, 1960.

Scriven, Michael. "Putting the Sex Back into Sex Education," *Phi Delta* 1968, 49 (9), based on a paper given at a Notre Dame University Conference on "The Role of Women," Fall, 1967.

Whitehurst, Robert. "The Unmalias on Campus," presented at NCFR Annual Meeting, 1969. Copy available from author, University of Windsor, Windsor, Ontario, Canada.

Whitehurst, Robert. "The Double Standard and Male Dominance in Non-Marital Living Arrangements: A Preliminary Statement," paper presented at the American Orthopsychiatric Association Meeting, New York, 1969. Copy available from author, University of Windsor, Windsor, Ontario, Canada.

Couples Believe A Few Punches Make a Marriage

JURATE KAZICKAS

The punch cards shuffled through the machine. Patricia's Absolute Factors sought out Don's Psychological Valences. Don's Physical Inventory nestled with Patricia's Interests and Attitudes. Click. Deep in the heart of the computer, love blossomed.

Patricia, 31, was a divorcee with two children. She had tried finding suitable dates every other way when she heard about computer dating, and figured she had nothing to lose.

Don, 40, a bachelor, admitted he was lonely and shy and wasn't having the best of luck in finding the kind of woman he wanted. Operation Match, a computer date finder in Great Neck, N.Y., got them together.

The computer people got $5 for their service. Don and Patricia got each other. Four months after they were matched, they married.

What started as a whimsical idea for arranging a Harvard mixer in 1964 has become the Space Age alternative to the blind date and the marriage broker. Today, more than 250,000 couples can thank their lucky cards for their mates.

Trusting the electronic Cupid, Patricia and Don Brisson of Belair Bluff, Fla., found each other by answering 110 true-false and multiple-choice questions divided into categories like Psychological Valences — "Once I make up my mind, I seldom change it. True or false? — and Specific Interests: Agriculture and gardening? Community service? Bridge?

"Don had just about everything I was looking for," said Patricia. "We both liked classical music, fishing and reading. And I do think that similar interests help keep a good marriage."

Married now for 2½ years, Pat adds: "As you do things together you become more and more companionable and that's really a large part of a successful marriage."

Bernard and Victoria Teeman, a New York couple in their late 20's tried the computer as a big joke when they were in college.

"Neither of us was in a dating slump," recalls Victoria, "but it just seemed like an interesting way of meeting new people."

"I had a lot in common with almost everyone the computer matched me up with," said Bernard, "but I must say I liked Victoria best of all. I think what really got us together was not so much our mutual interests but that unknown quality. There was real chemistry between us."

They married exactly one year after the computer introduced them.

Couples who have married their computer dates insist that the computer was merely an aid in bringing them together. As the founder of Operation Match, Stephen Milgrim, likes to say: "We create the relationship and the rest is up to you."

Milgrim, 45, agrees that common interests are a large part of ideal mating. But, he adds: "People have certain wants and needs that are much more important than compatible interests in sports or music. And that's what the computer tries to match up." As to exactly how the matching works, he declines to elaborate.

Anyway, it does. Milgrim, who advertises nationally, is one of the few survivors of the many who went into the electronic dating game in the '60s. He has since sold stock in his firm to the public.

Mitchell Mamber, 26, an urban planner in New York, felt that the computer didn't do a very good job in matching him up with Barbara, a loan correspondent in a bank. "She liked the opera and the ballet to an extreme, and really I couldn't care less."

But eight months after their first meeting, Mitchell and Barbara got married. "So I guess the computer must have done something right," he admits.

Certain questions on the Operation Match test have greater significance, depending on geographical area. In the South's Bible Belt, for example, women tend to want men who don't drink or smoke and who are churchgoers. In the big Eastern cities, romantic love seems to be more important.

The questionnaire also has been updated more than 25 times since 1964, to keep pace with changing social attitudes. Whereas once the question was simply "Democrat or Republican?" it now asks if clients are left or right of center.

New questions will be phased in soon to include Women's Liberation for those men who don't want an overly independent woman and for those women who don't want to get stuck with a male chauvinist.

"We don't want to match you up with someone who will make you unhappy," says Milgrim.

Who uses the computer dating and mating system? By now, nearly five million Americans have programmed their wants and needs and interests and let the cards fall where they will.

It was a big college fad in the '60s, but now less than 1 per cent of undergraduates use the computer to find a Saturday night date, perhaps because the cost has gone from $2 to $20. But more than 77 per cent of computer daters have college degrees and another 21 per cent have gone on to graduate work.

Today, more than 35 per cent who enroll in Operation Match are divorced and the majority of marriages have taken place between those in the 30 to 40 age bracket.

Milgrim says, "Those who use the computer might be shy, but they don't have any real dating problems. Socially inept people who can't make it on their own don't make it through the computer, either."

But like any new-fangled appliance in this machine age, the computer can and does make mistakes. One boy was matched up with his sister, and it is not unusual for divorced partners to be recommended to each other.

One woman wanted to sue Operation Match for giving her the name of someone totally objectionable and contrary to what she had specified. The threatening letters continued for several months until finally one arrived saying she and that "disastrous" match were getting married.

"I get thousands of letters each week thanking me for Operation Match," says Milgrim. "And just last week I got $2 in the mail with a note that the money was for cigars to celebrate the birth of a first baby."

Heterosexual Cohabitation Among Unmarried College Students

ELEANOR D. MACKLIN

During the past five or six years there have been periodic allusions in the popular press to a developing pattern of cohabitation among unmarried youth (*Newsweek*, 1966; *Esquire,* 1967; Grant, 1968; McWhirter, 1968; Schrag, 1968; *Time,* 1968; Bloch, 1969; Karlen, 1969; Rollin, 1969; Shehy, 1969; *Life,* 1970; Coffin, 1971), but little attempt has been made to explore this phenomenon in the professional literature. The majority of research has continued to dwell on questions regarding the sexual values and attitudes of college students, documenting their increased willingness to engage in and to approve of premarital sexual relations (Bell and Chaskes, 1970; Cannon and Long, 1971; Christensen and Gregg, 1970; Herr, 1970; Kaats and Davis, 1970; Mosher and Cross, 1971; Luckey and Nass, 1972), but providing little information about the changes in living patterns which are simultaneously occurring. Exceptions include a series of published interviews with cohabiting college couples (Ald, 1969), an unpublished master's thesis based on interviews with cohabiting 28 student couples at the University of Iowa (Johnson, 1968), the unpublished work on "unmarried college liaisons" ("unmalias") by sociologist Robert N. Whitehurst (1969), a study of student and parental attitudes with respect to the university's responsibility in the area of off campus cohabitation at Michigan State University (Smith and Kimmel, 1970), and a call for further research and counseling facilities by emotional health consultant Miriam Berger (1971).

It was because so little was known about the current patterns of cohabitation among college youth that the present study was undertaken. This report summarizes the initial pilot phase of this research. In order to obtain a more complete picture of the various forms which living together might assume, a fairly inclusive definition of cohabitation was adopted: To share a bedroom for at least four nights per week for at least three consecutive months with someone of the opposite sex. Throughout this paper, this definition of cohabitation will be used.

The objectives of this phase of the research were to gain an estimate of the prevalence of this experience, and an understanding of the nature of the relationship, the reasons for involvement, and the problems and benefits experienced. A series of four-hour semistructured interviews was conducted in April, 1971, with fifteen junior and senior female students at Cornell University, Ithaca, N.Y., who had experienced heterosexual cohabitation. In September, 1971, a questionnaire based on the interview schedule was given to 104 junior and senior women in a course on adolescent development at Cornell. Of the 86 who responded, 29 had experienced cohabitation. The fifteen interviewees had been involved in a total of 20 such relationships (eleven had experienced one such relationship, three had had two, and one, three). The 29 questionnaire respondents had experienced a total of 35 cohabitation relationships (24 had had one, four had had two, and one had had three).

The following discussion will be based on the information obtained from the combined group of 44 cohabitants. Questionnaire data will serve as the basis for all quantitative reporting, but it should be understood that interview data were generally corroborative.

PREVALENCE

From the present data one can only surmise the frequency with which cohabitation currently occurs at Cornell. Of the 86 junior and senior women who completed the questionnaire,[1] 34 percent had already had such an experience by the beginning of the 1971 fall term. When these 86 students were asked to predict what percentage of Cornell undergraduates probably experience cohabitation prior to graduation, almost three-quarters predicted that 40 percent or more would do so. When asked how many of their close friends had experienced or were experiencing cohabitation, only seven percent said "none," and over 40 percent said "many" or "most."

Of the 57 respondents who had not experienced cohabitation as defined, almost two-thirds checked that they had stayed with someone but not for as long as indicated in the definition. When asked why they had not cohabited, the large majority indicated that it was because they had not yet found an appropriate person. A few checked that it would be unwise for them at present due to the stage of their relationship, their immaturity, the possibility of discovery, or physical impracticality. Only one person said she had not because it would be wrong to do so outside of marriage.

Further clues to the frequency of cohabitation come from the questionnaire pretest which was given to two undergraduate classes in April 1971. Of 150 underclassmen responding, 28 percent indicated having experienced cohabitation. From an upper-class seminar on delinquency taught by the author, twelve of the 20 students volunteered to be interviewed regarding their cohabitation experience. One is led to conclude from all available evidence that cohabitation is a common experience for students on this particular campus and is accepted by many as a "to-be-expected" occurrence.

[1] Of the 104 junior and senior women in the class, 86 completed the questionnaire. Of these, 58 handed it in on the due date and 28 after a follow-up request. Since the percentage of cohabitants was the same for the initial and the follow-up respondents, it is assumed that the percentage would be similar for the eighteen non-returnees.

Description of the Cohabitation Experience

A wide variety of types of cohabitation experiences were revealed: among them, living with a male roommate in a co-op (with no sexual involvement and with both roommates having other romantic attachments), living in a tent while traveling in Europe, sharing a dormitory or a fraternity room, or sharing a room with another cohabiting couple. However, the most common pattern was for the girl to move into the boy's room (or vice versa) in an apartment or house which he was sharing with several other males (one of whom might also have a girl living in). Graduate student pairs are more likely to live alone in an apartment or a house; freshman couples are more likely to share a dormitory room. Very few couples shared their bedroom with a third person.

In the majority of cases, living quarters had not been obtained initially with living together in mind (although many men arrange to have a single room in order to allow privacy for any potential entertaining). Living arrangements were not usually jointly arranged until the second year of a relationship. However, even then, couples were hesitant to arrange for a single joint living situation, and planning simply involved ensuring that the potential apartment-mates were willing to have a girl share the premises. Practically all girls also maintained a room in the dormitory or sorority or in an apartment with other girls. Most went back once a day for a few hours to visit, get messages or mail, exchange clothes, shower, or study. Maintaining a separate residence precludes having to explain to parents, ensures a place to live if the relationship is not working well, helps maintain contact with female friends, serves as a convenient place to study, and provides often necessary storage space (the boy's room being too small to hold both sets of belongings).

In about half of the relationships, the couple spent seven nights a week together. In the remaining half, the girl returned to her own room one or two nights a week in order to ee her friends and to allow him time with his friends. It should be noted at this point that spending the night together, even in the same bed, need not imply a full sexual relationship. Aside from the instance of the non-emotionally involved coed roommates, there were couples who had lived together for more than three months without intercourse because they did not yet feel ready for this experience (these were usually virgin women). The irony of this is the frequency with which the older generation refuses to accept that this could be true, or if it is, insists that the male must be a "queer."

There was a wide range in amount of time spent together. The majority reported being together about 16-17 hours a day on weekdays (5 p.m. to 8 a.m. plus lunch). Most couples shared at least two meals a day, although occasionally dinner was eaten separately because of the inconvenience involved in having an extra person at dinner or because her parents had already paid for her meals on campus and funds were tight. There was practically no instance of total pooling of finances in these relationships, although the couple normally shared food and entertainment expenses. Usually the girl paid her way and maintained her own separate finances, either because the couple could not afford otherwise or as a matter of principle. When there were chores involved, the couple generally did them together (e.g., shopping or laundry), although there was a tendency for the girl to assume responsibility for cooking and cleaning. There was a wide range in the degree to which they shared activities (e.g., classes, study, or hobbies) or spent time with others. The tendency was to share the majority of activities, to have many mutual friends, and to spend much of their time with others as opposed to time only with one another.

WHY STUDENTS LIVE TOGETHER

There are three aspects to the question of why students are now living together: the circumstances existing at the particular institution, the broader societal reasons, and the personal motivations of the specific students.

Changes in dormitory regulations and the slow demise of *in loco parentis* have greatly facilitated the development of the new pattern. If one goes back to earlier issues of the campus newspaper (*Cornell Daily Sun*, 1962, 1963, 1964), one notes that in 1962, a graduate student was indefinitely suspended from the University for living with a woman in his apartment, and in 1964, a male student was reprimanded for staying overnight at a local hotel with a non-University female. Sexual morality was considered a legitimate concern of the University faculty and "overnight unchaperoned mixed company" was considered by the Faculty Council on Student Conduct to be a violation of sexual morality (*Cornell Daily Sun*, 1962, 2).

Today, Cornell students are free to live in much the same way that nonstudents who are living and working in the outside world are free to live: they are likely to be residing in a structure which also houses pesons of the opposite sex (many of the dorms are now coed, with men and women segregated by floors, wings or suites, although there is experimentation with men and women living on the same corridor); if they are sophomores or beyond, they are free to elect to live off campus; and they may entertain someone of the opposite sex in their room at any time during the 24-hour day. Official policy still prohibits "continuous residence" with someone of the opposite sex in the dormitory setting, but this is difficult to police.

These changes in curfew and dormitory policy must be seen as a reflection of broader social changes: a change in the status of women which makes it difficult to justify different regulations for men and for women, youth's increasing demand that they no longer be treated as children, a questioning of the rigid sexual mores which have traditionally governed people's lives, a greater willingness to grant individuals the right to select their own life style, and the increasing availability of contraception and abortion services.

When students are asked to hypothesize why cohabitation has become more common and more open, they mention youth's search for meaningful relations with others and the consequent rejection of the superficial "dating game;" the loneliness of a large university and the emotional satisfaction that comes from having someone to sleep with who cares about you; the widespread questioning of the institution of marriage and the desire to try out a relationship before there is any, if ever, consideration of permanency; the desire on the part of many to postpone commitment until there is some certainty that individual growth will be compatible with growth of the relationship; the fact that young people mature earlier and yet must wait so long until marriage is feasible; and the fact that the university community provides both sanction and feasibility for such a relationship to develop. Given peer group support, ample opportunity, a human need to love and be loved, and a disposition to question the traditional way, it seems only natural that couples should wish to live together if they enjoy being together. One might almost better ask: Why do students choose *not* to live together?

When one asks students why they personally become involved in a cohabitation relationship, one finds a mixture of enjoying being together and expediency (e.g., too far to drive her home at night, easier to stay than to get up and go back at midnight, less expensive, someone else living with one's roommate, or partner was sick and needed someone to care for him). On occasion, curiosity about what it would be like to live with the opposite sex was involved, and sometimes "to test out the relationship" was mentioned, but it was rarely such a purposeful act.

In fact, living together was seldom the result of a considered decision, at least initially (cf., Ryder, Kafka and Olson's concept of "unquestioned beginnings" which they suggest characterize much of courtship in our society). Most relationships involved a gradual (and sometimes not so gradual) drifting into staying together. The general pattern was to stay over one night; in several weeks, if all was well, to stay for the weekend; in another few weeks to add a week night; in another few weeks, a second week night, and so forth. In half the relationships the couple had begun staying together four or more nights a week by the end of four months of dating.

If and when a decision with conscious deliberation was made, it was usually precipitated by some external force (e.g., need to make plans for the summer or next fall, graduation, unexpected pregnancy, or a necessary housing or room change). Until this time, there was only a mutual, often unspoken, recognition of the desire to be together — a natural progression of the relationship.

NATURE OF THE RELATIONSHIP

When asked to indicate the nature of the relationship at the time they began living together four or more nights per week, about half checked that they "had a strong, affectionate relationship but were also open to other relationships." Only a few indicated tentative engagement; even fewer stated that they were just "friends." See Table 1.

TABLE 1

NATURE OF RELATIONSHIP WHEN COUPLE FIRST STARTED LIVING TOGETHER FOR AT LEAST FOUR NIGHTS PER WEEK, AS REPORTED BY 29 UPPERCLASS FEMALE STUDENTS FOR 35 COHABITATION RELATIONSHIPS

Nature of Relationship	Number of Relationships
1. Formally engaged	1
2. Tentatively engaged (contemplating marriage)	3
3. Strong, affectionate relationship; not dating others ("going steady")	17
4. Strong, affectionate relationship; open to other dating relationships	12
5. Friends	1
6. Other ("met and immediately started living together")	1
Total	35

It is interesting to note that the above is very similar to answers given by all 86 questionnaire respondents when asked what kind of relationship they felt should exist before college-aged students cohabit. (See Table 2.) One is impressed by the fact that cohabitation is more frequently associated with the "going steady" stage of a relationship than with engagement, even tentative engagement.

The initial commitment to the relationship varied greatly. Some saw it strictly as temporary (e.g., "while traveling," "he was planning to leave Ithaca," or "he was already committed to someone else") and a few, at the other extreme, definitely planned "marriage in the future when it was more convenient." But the vast majority entered it either with a "let's see" attitude (i.e., to test the relationship — to stay together as long as it was mutually satisfying), or — a somewhat more definite commitment — planned to do all they "could to develop a lasting relationship, but future marriage was not definite."

This raises some question about the label "unmarried marrieds" which has often been applied in the popular literature to unmarried cohabitation. Most of the undergraduate couples did not consider themselves married in any sense of the word. Not only did they not consider themselves married, they rarely considered marriage as a viable alternative to their present cohabitation. When asked, "Did you consider the possibility of getting married instead?", a frequent response was "Heavens no!" Marriage might be seen as a possibility for

TABLE 2

RESPONSES OF 86 UPPERCLASS FEMALE STUDENTS TO "WHAT KIND OF
RELATIONSHIP DO YOU FEEL *SHOULD* PREVAIL BEFORE COLLEGE-AGED
STUDENTS COHABIT?"

Nature of Relationship	Percent of Respondents
1. Married	4
2. Formally engaged	—
3. Tentatively engaged (contemplating marriage)	8
4. Strong, affectionate relationship; not dating others ("going steady")	60
5. Strong, affectionate relationship; open to other dating relationships	15
6. Friends	8
7. Other (e.g., "anything acceptable to both parties")	5
Total	100%

the future, but the distant future. The future seemed too indefinite to
plan that far ahead, they needed more time to grow and develop before
considering marriage, and it was financially impractical. Moreover,
marriage appeared to have some negative connotations for many of
these students — it was seen as limiting their freedom and their growth
(cf., the period of youth as discussed Keniston in *Young Radicals*), and
they feared falling into the traditional roles they associated with being
wives, even though over two-thirds of those interviewed said their
parents would consider their own marriage "very successful."

PROBLEMS ENCOUNTERED

As with any real relationship, these were not always blissful. It was
encouraging that those interviewed seemed very aware of the problem
areas and were able to verbalize about them easily.

Problems could be divided into four major categories: emotional
problems, sexual problems, problems with parents, and problems related to the living situation. (In the interviews, no one had experienced
problems with the community; thus the question was not included in
the questionnaire.)

The major emotional problem (see Table 3) was the tendency to
become overinvolved and to feel a subsequent loss of identity, lack of
opportunity to participate in other activities or be with friends, and an
over-dependency on the relationship. On the basis of the available
data, one is tempted to hypothesize that how this issue is dealt with and
the success with which it is handled are major determinants of the
outcome of the relationship. The problem of how to achieve security
without giving up the freedom to be oneself, and how to grow together
and yet leave enough space so the individuals can grow also, appears
central.

Other problems in this category were feelings of being trapped (should break up but afraid to do so), feelings of being used, jealousy of partner's involvement in other activities or relationships, and lack of feeling of belonging (e.g., "When I expect that he will share his money with me now that my parents have cut me off, he reminds me that we are not married"). It should be recognized, however, that although there were a few who indicated that these problems caused them a great deal of trouble, the majority indicated little or no problem. It is also important to note that more than two-thirds indicated no feelings of guilt, and the remainder indicated only a minimal amount. In the interviews, when guilt was stated to be present, it was usually related to having to conceal the relationship from parents or it occurred in those instances where they knew that the relationship could not last.

Sexual problems were common. (See Table 3.) Only a few indicated "no problem" in this area. Differing degrees or periods of sexual interest, lack of orgasm, fear of pregnancy, vaginal irritations, feelings of sexual inhibition, and less satisfaction with sex as the relationship deteriorated were the more frequently mentioned problems. However, in spite of problems, over three-fourths of the respondents rated the relationship as sexually satisfying. Practically all used contraception (over 80 percent used either the pill or the diaphragm), with about two-thirds of these having started contraception before or at the time of the first intercourse in the cohabitation relationship.

A major problem area was parents. More than one-fourth indicated that parents had caused "some" or "many" problems: parental disapproval of the boy, fear of discovery, guilt because they were deceiving or hurting their parents, rejection by or ultimatums from parents, and most frequently, sadness at not being able to share this important part of their lives with their parents. Because of fear of disapproval or unpleasant repercussions, more than two-thirds had tried to conceal the relationship from their parents — by not telling them the whole story, by distorting the truth, and by developing often elaborate schemes to prevent discovery. Almost half of the respondents believed their parents to be unaware of their cohabitation, with the remainder divided equally between those who felt they definitely knew, those who thought they probably knew, and those who were unsure. The boy's parents were much more likely to be aware.

Problems related to the living situation were considered minimal. Lack of privacy, lack of adequate space, lack of sufficient funds or disagreement over money, and friction with apartment mates were all mentioned, with lack of space or privacy and tension with others in the living situation the most common. It should be noted that there was practically no problem experienced as a result of the external community, i.e., landlords, local employers, school administration, neighbors, or contemporaries. In fact, the great majority felt their friends strongly approved of and supported their relationship. In cases where this was not true, it was because friends considered the particular relationship rather than the cohabitation *per se* undesirable.

TABLE 3

EXTENT TO WHICH EMOTIONAL, SEXUAL, AND LIVING SITUATION PROB-
LEMS WERE EXPERIENCED IN 35 COHABITATION RELATIONSHIPS AS RE-
PORTED BY 29 UPPERCLASS FEMALE STUDENTS (CATEGORIES ARE OR-
DERED BY NUMBER OF PERSONS REPORTING THE PROBLEM)

Problem Area	Number Indicating		Average rating given by those indicating some problem*
	No Problem	Some Problem	
Emotional Problems			
1. Overinvolvement (loss of identity, lack of opportunity to participate in other activities or with friends, overdependency)	14	21	2.7
2. Jealousy of partner's involvement in other activities or relationships	14	15	3.1
3. Feeling of being trapped	18	15	2.9
4. Feeling of being used	19	13	2.6
5. Guilt			
—at beginning of relationship	20	9	3.7
—during relationship	25	5	3.8
—at end of relationship	15	2	4.0
6. Lack of feeling of "belonging" or of being "at home"	22	9	3.4
7. Other "will have to separate for a while after his graduation"	—	1	3.0
Sexual Problems			
1. Differing degrees or periods of sexual interest	10	23	3.4
2. Lack of orgasm	11	21	3.6
3. Fear of pregnancy	15	15	3.1
4. Vaginal irritation or discharge after intercourse	17	15	3.4
5. Discomfort of partner during intercourse	18	10	3.7
6. Impotence of partner	23	6	3.0
Problems Related to Living Situation			
1. Lack of privacy	15	17	3.4
2. Lack of adequate space	19	13	3.0
3. Did not get along with apartment or housemates	20	6	2.2
4. Lack of sufficient money	26	6	3.3
5. Disagreement over use of money, sharing of money, etc.	27	4	3.5

*Respondents were asked to rate each problem from 1 to 5, with 1: great deal of problem, 5: no problem (no other points defined). The last category (5: no problem) has been separated because it may be qualitatively different from the other rating categories. Average ratings are therefore based on ratings from 1 to 4; thus, the lower the average rating the greater the problem for those experiencing it.

Benefits

It is important that the problems not be seen as outweighing the values of such relationships. More than half rated their relationship as "very successful," and more than 80 percent checked that it was "both maturing and pleasant." Even in those few cases where the relationship was said to be "painful," they emphasized the personal growth which had occurred, e.g., "I question whether I'd understand myself as well without the hard times." In no case was the experience rated "very unpleasant" or "not at all maturing," and in no case was it considered primarily detrimental to the person involved. In more than 60 percent of the cases, they would do it over again with the same person, even in those relationships which had broken up at the time of the report.

The benefits seen by the participants included a deeper understanding of themselves and of their needs, expectations, and inadequacies; increased knowledge of what is involved in a relationship and of the complexities of living with someone else; clarification of what they wanted in a marriage; increase in emotional maturity and in self-confidence, e.g., "learned not to commit myself too soon," "learned through breaking up how much strength I have," increased ability to understand and relate to others; emotional seucrity and companionship; and confidence in the possibility for success of the particular relationship, e.g., "because we have coped with problems and come out top side, I have more faith that we will be able to do so again." The main undercurrent in the data was the many ways in which the experience had fostered growth and maturity. All persons interviewed indicated that they would not consider marriage without having lived with the person first, and all — while hesitant to say what others should do — felt the move toward cohabitation could only be seen as a healthy trend.

Outcome of the Relationship

At the time of the questionnaire, one-third of the relationships had dissolved (having lasted an average of four and one-half months from the time they began staying together four or more nights a week), one-third were married or planning to be married, and another third were still in the process of defining the relationship (either were still living together but not yet contemplating marriage, or were still "going together" but not living together — either because the partner was away or they sought more freedom than they had when living together). A somewhat larger portion of those interviewed had broken their relationship, but this may be due to the fact that the interview was later in the academic year. The 23 relationships which were still in process had existed an average of 13 months, with five having continued for two or two and one-half years.

Implications

1. It appears that cohabitation has become an increasingly common

aspect of courtship on the campus studied and one could predict that the trend will proliferate.

Although the phenomenon of unmarried persons living together is obviously not a new one, either in this society or others (Berger, 1971), it has certainly not been a common phenomenon among unmarried middle class youth in the United States until quite recently. Some pass it off by saying it is merely a more open expression of what students have been doing sexually on the sly for years, but this suggests a very narrow interpretation of the present situation. The pattern which is currently evolving appears to be primarily concerned with total relationships and only incidentally with the sexual aspects. It is this concern with getting to know another as a whole person and the emphasis on sharing as openly and as completely as possible with that person, which is probably the major new dimension being added to old courtship patterns.

2. There is some question whether cohabitation as now practiced on the college campus fits the concepts of trial marriage, premarital marriage, companionate marriage, or two-stage marriage which some have sought to apply to it. (Berger, 1971; Grant, 1968; Karlen, 1969; LeShan, 1971; Mead, 1966) Trial marriage, for instance, tends to imply a level of commitment usually associated with the engagement portion of the courtship continuum which is not characteristic of the campus relationships studied. These students do not in general see themselves as consciously testing or even contemplating a potential marriage, at least not initally. Instead, in most cases, living together seems to be a natural component of a strong, affectionate "dating" relationship — a living out of "going steady" — which may grow in time to be something more, but which in the meantime is to be enjoyed and experienced because it is pleasurable in and of itself.

3. In addition to the question of whether it does in fact lead to healthier marriages or more "fully functioning" persons, there are other intriguing issues. For instance, what is the relationship between commitment to a relationship and identity formation? To what extent must one have developed a strong identity before one can achieve a strong intimate relationship (in Erikson's sense)? What chance is there for a mature, mutual relationship when the individual is still so necessarily focused on his own development? How much commitment to a relationship is necessary for it to have a strong chance of success? Alternately, does early commitment to a relationship hinder identity development? When a person should be at a point of maximum identity development, is it healthy for him to be devoting so much of his energy to the development of a relationship or will this simply accelerate the process? These become very real problems as cohabitation inevitably occurs early and becomes increasingly common as a freshman experience.

4. There is a great need to help society adjust to the evolving courtship patterns. Parents in particular tend to see cohabitation as antithetical to all that they consider healthy or moral. They need help if they are to understand and to react without alarm, recrimination, and

rejection. Consideration will have to be given to legal implications of the new patterns — some present laws conflict and maybe should be changed, and some new protections of the rights of unmarried participants may be necessary. The professions touched by the new trends are myriad. Bankers, for instance, as they seek to help parents write wills and set up trust funds, and as they themselves seek to administer these trusts, find themselves confronted with having to understand and interpret the new patterns. Students in particular need more realistic preparation, both at home and in school, and more opportunity for relationship and sex counseling, if they are to cope as responsibly and effectively as possible with the increased freedom and the new pressures. The first step, which most of the adult population has not yet taken, is to acknowledge that the changes are actually occurring and to be willing to entertain the hypothesis that they may indeed be an improvement on the traditional patterns.

REFERENCES

Ald, Roy. *Sex Off Campus.* New York: Grosset and Dunlap, 1969.

Bauman, Karl E. Selected Aspects of the Contraceptive Practices of Unmarried University Students. *Medical Aspects of Human Sexuality,* August 1971, 5, 76-89.

Bell, Robert R. and Jay B. Chaskes. Premarital Sexual Experience among Coeds, 1958 and 1968. *Journal of Marriage and the Family,* 1970, 32, 81-84.

Berger, Miriam E. Trial Marriage: Harnessing the Trend Constructively. *The Family Coordinator,* 1971, 20, 38-43.

Bloch, Donald. Unwed Couples: Do They Live Happily Ever After? *Redbook,* April 1969, 90+.

Cannon, Kenneth L. and Richard Long. Premarital Sexual Behavior in the Sixties. *Journal of Marriage and the Family,* 1971, 33, 36-49.

Christensen, Harold T. and Christina F. Gregg. Changing Sex Norms in America and Scandinavia. *Journal of Marriage and the Family,* 1970, 32, 616-627.

Coffin, Patricia. Young Unmarrieds: Theresa Pommett and Charles Wals, College Grads Living Together. *Look,* January 26, 1971, 634+.

College and University Business. Parents OK Strict Rules, December, 1968, 16.

Cornell Daily Sun, October 9, 1962; October 8, 1963; March 6, 1964.

Crist, Takey. *The Coed as a Gynecological Patient.* University of North Carolina, Chapel Hill, North Carolina, 1970. (mimeo)

Davids, Leo. North American Marriage: 1990. *The Futurist,* October 1971, 190-194.

Esquire. Room-Mates, September 1967, 94-98.

Fell, Joseph P. A Psychosocial Analysis of Sex-Policing on Campus, *School and Society,* 1970, 98, 351-354.

Fleming, Thomas and Alice Fleming, What Kids Still Don't Know About Sex. *Look,* July 28, 1970, 59+.

Grant, A. No Rings Attached: A Look at Premarital Marriage on Campus. *Mademoiselle,* April 1968, 66, 208+.

Hall, Elizabeth and Robert A. Poteete. A Conservation with Robert Robert H. Rimmer about Harrad, Group Marriage, and Other Loving Arrangements. *Psychology Today,* 1972, 5, 57-82.

Herr, Sylvia. Research Study on Behavioral Patterns in Sex and Drug Use on College Campus. *Adolescence,* Spring, 1970, 5, 1-16.

Hunt, Morton. The Future of Marriage. *Playboy,* August 1971, 117+.

Johnson, Michael P. *Courtship and Commitment: A Study of Cohabitation on a University Campus.* Master's thesis. University of Iowa, Iowa City, 1969.

Kaats, Gilbert R. and Keith E. Davis. The Dynamics of Sexual Behavior of College Students. *Journal of Marriage and the Family,* 1970, 32, 390-399.

Karlen, Arno. The Unmarried Marrieds on Campus. *New York Times Magazine,* January 26, 1969, 29+.

Keniston, Kenneth. *Young Radicals.* New York: Harcourt, Brace and World, 1968.

LeShan, Eda J. *Mates and Roommates: New Styles in Young Marriages.* Public Affairs Pamphlets, No. 468, 1971. Public Affairs Pamphlets, 381 Park Ave. So., New York 10016.

Lever, Janet and Pepper Schwartz. Men and Woman at Yale. *Sexual Behavior,* October 1971.

Life. Coed Dorms: An Intimate Campus Revolution, November 20, 1970, 32+.

Luckey, Eleanore B. and Gilbert D. Nass. Comparison of Sexual Attitudes in an International Sample of College Students. *Medical Aspects of Human Sexuality,* 1972, 6, 66-107.

Malcolm, Andrew H. Sex Goes to College. *Today's Health,* April 1971, 27-29.

McWhirter, William A. The Arrangement at College. *Life,* May 31, 1968, 56+.

Mead, Margaret. A Continuing Dialogue on Marriage: Why Just Living Together Won't Work. *Redbook,* April 1968, 130, 44+.

Mead, Margaret. Marriage in Two Steps. *Redbook,* July 1966, 127, 48+.

Mosher, Donald L. and Herbert F. Cross. Sex-Guilt and Premarital Sexual Experiences of College Students. *Journal of Consulting and Clinical Psychology,* February 1971, 36, 27+.

Moss, J. Joel, Frank Apolonio, and Margaret Jensen. The Premarital Dyad During the Sixties. *Journal of Marriage and the Family,* 1971, 33, 50-69.

Newsweek. Unstructured Relationships: Students Living Together. July 4, 1966, 68-78.

Packard, Vance. *The Sexual Wilderness.* New York: David McKay, 1968.

Peters, Muriel and William Peters. How College Students Feel About

Love, Sex, and Marriage. *Good Housekeeping Magazine,* June 1970, 85+.

Reiss, Ira L. The Sexual Rennaissance in America: Summary and Analysis. *Journal of Social Issues,* April 1966, 22, 123-137.

Rimmer, Robert H. *The Harrad Experiement.* Los Angeles: Sherbourne Press, 1966.

Rockefeller, John D. III. Youth, Love and Sex: The New Chivalry. *Look,* October 7, 1969, 32+.

Rollin, Betty. New Hang-up for Parents: Coed Living. *Look,* September 23, 1969, 22+.

Ryder, Robert G., John S. Kafka, and David H. Olson. Separating and Joining Influences in Courtship and Early Marriage. *American Journal of Orthopsychiatry,* April 1971, 41, 450-464.

Sarrel, Philip M. and Lorna J. Sarrel. How We Counsel Students on Sex Problems at Yale. *The Osteopathic Physician,* June 1971.

Schrag, Peter. Posse at Generation Gap: Implications of the Linda LeClair Affair. *Saturday Review,* May 18, 1968, 51, 81.

Sheehy, Gail. Living Together: The Stories of Four Young Couples Who Risk the Strains of Non-marriage and Why. *Glamour,* February 1, 1969, 136+.

Smith, Patrick B. and Ko Kimmel. Student-Parent Reactions to Off-Campus Cohabitation. *Journal of College Student Personnel,* May 1970, 188-193.

Time. Linda, the Light Housekeeper. April 26, 1968, 51.

Whitehurst, Robert. The Unmalias on Campus. Presented at NCFR Annual Meeting, 1969. Copy available from author, University of Windsor, Windsor, Ontario, Canada.

Whitehurst Robert. The Double Standard and Male Dominance in Non-Marital Living Arrangements: A Preliminary Statement. Paper presented at the American Orthopsychiatric Association Meeting, New York, 1969. Copy available from author, University of Windsor, Windsor, Ontario, Canada.

UNIT STUDY GUIDE

A. *Terms to Review*

Arranged marriage	*In loco parentis*	Role-reversal
Bundling	Joint-family system	Self-esteem (Maslow)
Cohabitation	New Morality	Sexism
Endogamy, mating	Operation Match	Trial nights

B. *Questions for Discussion and Study*

1. In American society, which factors seem strongly related to endogamy in partner-selection? Explain the origins and significance of these factors from a socio-cultural point of view.

2. Identify and discuss at least three alternatives to current dating and partner-selection practices in this society.

3. Explore and discuss the proposition that the Platonic relationships of one's childhood influence later heterosexual love impulses and the partner-selection process.

4. Summarize and discuss salient problems and issues associated with the partner-selection process as presented in the readings for this unit.

5. Discuss some likely ways in which the partner-selection process and dating behavior may be influenced or altered by the growing acceptance of ideas promoted by the sexual equality movement.

6. Keeping in mind that some have claimed that "too much honesty and openness is harmful," discuss the factors of honesty, openness, and trust as they may affect the quality of the dating and partner-selection process.

C. *Topics-Ideas for Papers and Projects*

1. Using the questionnaire employed by Hudson and Henze, conduct a survey among the students at your school to determine their preferences in mate-selection. Compare your findings with those discovered in 1939 and 1967 as discussed in the Hudson and Henze article.

2. Research: "Ethnic-group Variation in the Relationship Between Self-esteem and Dating Practices."

3. "The Influence of Mass Media on Dating and Partner-Selection Processes in Contemporary Society."

4. Using a standardized personality test, plan a study of the relationship between personality factors and dating behavior in first-year students at your school.

5. Do a content analysis of "advice to teens" columns in your local newspaper or those found in magazines like *Seventeen.* Examine trends in advice regarding dating and partner-selection over the past five years.

PART THREE

ENCOUNTERS
IN MARRIAGE

Unit 5
Marriage Today: Challenge and Choice

All tragedies are finish'd by a death,
All comedies are ended by a marriage. — *Byron*

Clearly it is not reason that has failed.
What has failed — as it has always failed, in
all of its thousand forms — is the attempt to
achieve certainty, to reach an absolute, to
bind the course of human events to a final end. — *Wheelis*

Introduction

It is apparent to even the most casual observer of the familial scene in this society that marriage today is confronted by challenges and choices having unprecedented potentials for change, change in the behaviors typical of conventional marital partnership and in the very norms and values imbedded in marriage as an institution. For those who assume that alteration of the traditional forms of marriage must also imply its devaluation, the currents of change in today's marriage scene may appear threatening. Indeed, some concerned people seemingly conclude that drastic change in marriage must inevitably lead to its extinction a few years hence.

But it is possible, and perhaps a bit closer to the facts, to take a considerably more optimistic stance; especially is this true in regard to the survival of the traditional pairing of a woman and a man in a marital partnership. In familial matters, as in most others, the past is still the best predictor of the future. On these grounds, it seems highly unlikely that the basic monogamous form will suddenly disappear. After all, the familiar dyadic model has been in existence, though not exclusively, for more than twenty centuries. Despite its ills, marriage as a formalized relationship continues to be the vital core of family life. Furthermore, as other writers have pointed out, many of the signs of grave disorder surrounding contemporary marriage reflect attempts, not to destroy it, but to improve it, to develop meaningful and workable variations on the traditional form.

In preceding units we have seen a remarkably similar set of problems and issues running through the discussion of each aspect of familial-marital experience. One component of this set reflects a quest for the personal dignity and positive self-image that comes only with equality in human relationships; it carries a corollary value which rejects personal identity based on ascribed status such as sex or race. The other component, just as important, concerns the quest for authentic, genuine personhood; along with it goes a rejection of the idea that pairing, even ultimately satisfactory pairing, must entail a submerging of one's own identity, one's own integrity as an individual. The growing thrust of these basic issues into every aspect of American familial experience is virtually obvious to all who pursue a serious analysis of it. The significance of these basic problems will again emerge in this unit's consideration of formalized marriage.

It seems clear that the challenges and choices confronting marriage today do not derive their major importance from what they may imply about the structure or *forms* of marriage — that is, its size, whether dyadic, triadic or otherwise or yet what is implied about the marital sex ratio, whether it is a monogamous, polygynous, or polyandrous marriage. On the contrary, the crucial questions emerging from the social maelstrom surrounding contemporary marriage are concentrated mainly on the nature and quality of the marital *relationship*, on interpersonal functioning. This is not too surprising, since it is mainly the malfunctioning of relationships within the framework of long-established and valued-but-troublesome models that has led to such widespread personal unhappiness in this society's current family experience. The major challenge facing marriage today may actually consist in the opportunity to develop unprecedented capacities for satisfying, vital relationships mainly within our existing monogamous form. It could be argued, of course, that the quest for improvement should not exclude drastic variations in form. Conceivably, a polygynous or polyandrous form might work well for some. Our present society has sufficient resources and sufficient range in values to permit wide and possibly effective choice in the task of building satisfactory marital partnerships, regardless of the particular form.

Since the readings in this unit will explore some problems typically associated with seriously troubled marriages, some comment on their empirical study seems pertinent. The sociologist typically approaches the study of marital problems by developing a list of problem-categories within which reported difficulties are classified. One such study of major problems revealed by seriously troubled marital partners grouped their reported difficulties or unhappiness into eight categories:[1]

1. *Affectional relations* (implied loss or lack of affectionate love relationship with the partner).

2. *Sexual relations* (erotic interaction-centered difficulty between the partners).

3. *Personality relations* (interaction focused on attributed personality traits or characteristics of mate or self).

4. *Role-tasks* (interaction around traditional sex-based distribution of family-group responsibilities).

5. *Parental-role relations* (parent-child interaction and mate interaction regarding matters of child-rearing).

6. *Inter-cultural relations* (interaction of the partnership with directive institutional sectors in its environment, such as religion, kinship structure, etc.).

7. *Deviant behavior* (interaction regarding the definition within the marriage of individual behaviors which deviate from approved norms of personal behavior, e.g. gambling, illicit sex, compulsive drinking, etc.).

8. *Situational conditions* (partner interaction and perceptions regarding objective conditions under which the marriage functions, the "givens" at any particular time, e.g. financial status, housing, health status, etc.).

On the basis of objective findings issuing from the use of such a category system, it may be feasible for the researcher to suggest more generic problems or problem-sources. For example, in the study cited, the researcher observed a strong clustering of problems in categories 1, 2, and 3; speculation suggested that the implied ". . . pervasive cultural emphasis on marriage as an emotionally gratifying pair-relationship" is a significant source of potential marital unhappiness. It was further speculated that while the situational conditions under which the group functions may be important, they are probably of much lesser significance for problem-experiencing than the quality of interpersonal relationships between the partners.

Let us now turn to some of the interconnected *problems and issues* which confront modern marriage. Below we will cite several, some of which are general while some are more specific.

Task-differentiation. American marriage, and family experience generally, have been traditionally characterized by a sex-based division of labor. Due to a male superiority history, this has almost always meant that work performed by the female is viewed as being less important, having less intrinsic worth. Housework has never rated as high as most lower-level office tasks. There are fundmental questions: Should there be a familial-marital division of labor based on anything but ability? Is there a rational base for a sex-based differentiation? Sexual equality leaders have suggested that an immense loss in human resources results from training women for, and forcing them into, tasks that are frequently not much more than "idiot-level," *simply because they are women.* Functionalist thinking in the social sciences, on the other hand, has led to statements such as this: ". . . as long as the wife stuck to her cooking and the husband to his hunting, some of the advantages of specialization accrued. Such advantages would be lost if husband and wife were to merge their work completely."[2] Does traditional sex-based differentiation of tasks lead to unfair advantages, rewards, and benefits for one partner?

The Ownership syndrome. Given the emphasis, in this society, on private property, it is not too surprising that the material, property-related values — exemplified in private ownership — get translated into social relationships. The stronger the extent to which such possessives as "my husband," "my wife," etc. truly reflect security needs of the marital partners, the greater is the potential for corrosive jealousy, aggressive maintenance of personal and social boundaries, and the tendency to regard all who come near as threatening to one's territory and "possessions." How much, if any, boundary-maintenance is needed in a marital partnership? Can a marriage have a pair-identity without developing the ownership syndrome?

Individual needs vs. group goals. When people form a stable social relationship such as marriage they face some basic dilemmas which may take on the character of issues in interpersonal functioning. Some of these are: freedom vs. restriction, choice vs. coercion, and instrumental vs. expressive relationships. The impact of the sexual equality and human potentials movements on contemporary marriage is such that certain vital questions must be dealt with by the partners. Here are some: To what extent should the desires and needs of the individual be subjugated to the demands of the partnership per se? Is the marriage more inportant than the individuals comprising it? Should individual happiness in the relationship constitute the major criterion of a "successful" marriage? Do the individual needs for growth and self-expression take precedence over the tendencies toward a "pair-identity"?

The permanence ethic. The Judeo-Christian background of marriage in this society gives persisting credence to the notion of a life-long commitment to marriage, despite a strong counter-trend toward tentativeness. Questions and issues persist. Does subscription to the ethic of permanence guarantee greater depths of commitment in the marital relationship? Does conscious tentativenss in formation of a marriage necessarily imply a shallowness of commitment? Does an emphasis on "here and now" (as contrasted to "now and forever") in marital communication weaken the relationship?

Expectation levels. Other things being equal, it has been said, the higher the levels of aspiration the greater is the potential for disillusionment in human relations. While this may sound cynical, it raises a serious question; namely, is too much expected of marriage? Can a marriage partner truly be "all things" to one? It has been observed that the high divorce rate in American society is probably not an indicator of lessening regard for marriage but of much greater expectations for it.[3] Can one expect too little as well as too much from marriage?

Marriage and the law. Numerous questions arise concerning the role of law; these are focused mainly on the question of legitimation processes. Why, for example, is it necessary to require registration and solemnization of marriage? Whose purposes are served by existing laws? Is there sex discrimination in laws which permit marriage of females at a younger age than males? What should be the minimum age for marriage? Do we need uniform national laws on marriage?

It is apparent that a probe into almost any aspect of marriage will likely lead to a variety of issues, sub-issues, and questions. Having reviewed at least a few of these, we can now turn to a topic which, in itself, constitutes a much-discussed issue: the proposing of alternatives to our current forms and processes of marriage.

In our brief review of some proposed alternatives, it ought to be noted that the ones we will consider here (as is true of most that have appeared from time to time) place value on some type of marriage per se. Strictly speaking, they are not alternatives *to* marriage such as would be true for the proposal that people live together rather than forming a marriage.[4] The fundamental implication of most alternatives is for the modification of relationships within the marital framework. As we consider the alternatives listed below, some of which are discussed in more detail in our readings, it may prove helpful to keep in mind the question of feasibility: Could this work, and with what level of probable success?

1. *Two-tier marriage.* Briefly, this proposal is that young couples should marry now, but live together later. It would make engagement unnecessary. Its proponents hold that this system would engender a greater sense of responsibility and that it would give the couple greater financial security for entering into the second tier of their marriage.

2. *Renewable contract marriage.* In this alternative, the partners would make a contract which might expire every five years, for example, with a six-month notice required for termination. Proponents claim that the implied contract (as in traditional marriage) is unrealistic, does not recognize that persons may change, and consequently may be unfair to the partners. It is claimed that in the future most marriages will involve a legal contract drawn to individual needs.

3. *Trial marriage.* In this alternative, the participants would enter into an intimate relationship with the avowed purpose of

238 *Marriage Today: Challenge and Choice*

ascertaining, over some stated time period, whether they were sufficiently compatible to enter into a permanent marriage. Recent newspaper accounts have described a minister in Florida who offered one-year, spiritually-sanctioned trial marriage ceremonies to those who vow to love, honor, and practice contraception. No rings were to be used, and no reference would be made to "husband" or "wife." This is congruent with Satir's proposal that "There ought to be something like an apprentice period which would be socially approved, that precedes an actual marriage, in which potential partners have a chance to explore deeply and experiment with their relationship."[5] ·

4. *Marriage in Two Steps.* As proposed by Margaret Mead, this proposal reflects a concern for the needs of the two partners and any future children. "Individual" marriage is followed by a "parental" marriage in this plan. Individual marriage recognizes the human needs for close relationship (sexual, emotional, and intellectual — not economic) and would begin with individuals of college age. Those who wanted to take the second step into parental marriage would be required to show proof of their maturity through a stable individual marriage and evidence of economic ability to support a child.

5. *Group Marriage.* Ellis has defined group marriage as consisting in two or more couples living together as a family, sharing economically, emotionally, intellectually, and sexually. While it is acknowledged by its proponents that it is a difficult model to implement, there are presumably certain advantages. These would include: a high degree of sexual variety, widening and enhancing of love relationships for many people, economic advantages of pooled incomes, resources, etc., provision of an exhilarating experimental aspect to life in a family, and its possibilities for building a true sense and awareness of intimate community. Numerous proposals fall into this general category. One such is Kassel's idea of polygyny among older persons as a viable solution to the loneliness and isolation suffered by the elderly. Triadic, multilateral, and communal marriage would also fall in this grouping, as would Rimmer's notions of corporate marriage as discussed in *Proposition 31.*[6]

6. *Marriage as Approved Voluntary Association.* This proposal is that couples be allowed to live together legally without a State certificate of marriage. As proposed by Greenwald, this is not seen as a temporary union, since it considers the effects on children born to the couple. Property rights and child-care responsibilities would be worked out on an individual case basis where the marriage was dissolved. Presumably, voluntary association would eliminate or drastically reduce the economic problems connected with divorce, reduce the emotional problems tied to divorce and

illegitimacy (as currently defined), and allow for greater experimentation with variable forms of family living.

7. *Reinvention of marriage (within marriage).* Psychologist Sidney Jourard has proposed a novel approach, essentially a form of psuedo-serial polygamy which is defined as a series of relations with the same partner. This could be contrasted to serial monogamy where one changes partners through divorce. Jourard's notion is based on the assumption that there are numerous combinations of relationships within a partnership, and a potentially fantastic variety of options open to persons within an existing marriage.

8. *Open Marriage.* Proposed by the O'Neills, this proposal is built on the fundamental ideas central to the human potentials movement. As opposed to "closed" characteristics of conventional marriage, open marriage is oriented toward maximizing the growth of each partner in the relationship as a person. Its guidelines are: living for now, realistic expectations, privacy, role flexibility, open and honest communication, open companionship, equality, identity, and trust. Such a marriage may call for drastic interpersonal change and a clear departure from rigid conformity to established partner roles which exist in contemporary marriage.

As we turn from this brief overview of problems, issues, and alternatives, we may recall from our earlier discussion of social movements that dissatisfaction on a broad scale within society tends to elicit a wide variety of problem-solving responses. Judging from the variety of alternatives to conventional marriage currently under discussion in American society, one strong inference we could make is that there is a growing segment of the population which is unwilling merely to "suffer in silence" within the confines of the contemporary and mainly traditional marital structure.

REFERENCES

1. De Burger, James E. "Marital Problems, Help-Seeking, and Emotional Orientation as Revealed in Help-Request Letters, *Journal of Marriage and the Family* 29 (November 1967): 712-721.

2. Blood, Robert O. and Wolfe, Donald M. *Husbands and Wives: The Dynamics of Married Living* (New York: The Free Press of Glencoe, 1960).

3. Parsons, Talcott and Bales, Robert F. *Family, Socialization and Interaction Process* (New York: The Free Press of Glencoe, 1955), 24-25.

4. Lyness, Judith, Milton E. Lipetz, and Keith E. Davis, "Living Together: An Alternative to Marriage," *Journal of Marriage and the Family* 34 (May 1972): 305-311; Wells, T. and Christie, L. "Living

Together: An Alternative to Marriage," *The Futurist* 5 (May 1970): 50-57.

5. Most of the alternatives listed here, including Satir's comments, are discussed in Herbert A. Otto (ed.), *The Family in Search of A Future* (New York: Appleton-Century-Crofts, 1970.)

6. Rimmer, Robert. *Proposition 31* (New York: The New American Library, 1968).

New Orientations on
Marital Maladjustment

VINCENT D. MATHEWS
CLEMENT S. MIHANOVICH

Through the years, marital research, modeling itself on the original studies by Burgess-Cottrell, Terman, and Locke, has been concerned mainly with the factors coducive to marital success. Studies of the divorced or separated by Goode, Thomas, Kephart, and Monahan more directly investigated marital failure. While valuable insights have been gained by both approaches, relatively little attention has been directed to the study of marital maladjustment itself, especially in marriages still in existence.

What are the problems of married people? To what factors, sociological and psychological, are such problems related? Do the happily married have the same problems as the unhappily married? Do people solve their problems? Is it possible to construct a general theory of marital unhappiness? To answer these and like questions, some twenty-eight hypotheses, for which little or conflicting evidence existed, were tested on marriages still in existence. This paper reports our findings on one of the hypotheses tested and also some exploratory findings which suggest new orientations for future research.

A persistent theme running through the literature is that the happily married are not people without problems but those who solve their problems, that the happy have the same problems as the unhappy. As far back as 1930, Ernest Groves wrote of: "The belief I have long held that there is no difference in the character of the problems that the successful and unsuccessful families have to meet, but that the difference is in the resources the families have. . . ."[1] Nimkoff raises an objection to this view, but even in his dissent he seems to imply that the Groves' hypothesis is generally valid but not in all cases.[2] Quite recently, Goode echoed the same theme as Groves:

> However, even if we assume that respondents are able to tell us the "real" reasons for their divorce, our research plan would not give us the causes of divorce generally. After all, we have questioned only those who did get divorces. We do not have any way of comparing the kinds of answers non-divorcees would have given to similarly phrased questions. Perhaps a systematic probe would inform us that those who stay married have the *same kind of complaints* as those who do not, although divorcees perhaps experience them with a deeper intensity, or were unhappier about them.[3]

To test this hypothesis that the happy have the same problems as the unhappy, a problem check list of four hundred items was devised from a review of the literature (mainly case-study material) on marital conflict. Ten general areas of tension were selected for study: basic human needs, financial problems, conflicts involving home life and children, job problems, family and in-law problems, religious difficulties, sexual conflicts, problems of interaction especially decision making, personality problems, and problems in the area of social life. Each area contains forty problems, twenty on the self and twenty on the mate. Following the example of the Mooney problem check list, we arranged the problems of each area horizontally across the page, so that subjects would respond successively to five items from each of ten different areas rather than to all forty problems in any one area. Subjects were instructed that there are no right answers, and that they should merely go through the list underlining the particular problems of concern to them in their married life. A data sheet requested information on age, sex, duration of marriage, education, income, occupation, number of children, employment of husband and wife, fact of and attitude toward living with in-laws. To distinguish the happily married from the unhappy, we used the schedule developed by Burgess and Wallin which in some 21 questions measure the marital happiness of the self and also the respondent's conception of the mate's marital happiness.[4]

Since there was good reason to believe that couples would be reluctant to reveal their problems, especially in the intimate detail the check list required, the respondents were volunteers with their anonymity completely protected. Questionnaires were distributed in a middle-class and two working-class parishes after a talk on marriage which stressed the social utility of the survey. Four copies of the instrument were sent to ninety-six priests across the country, and they were asked to administer the check list to married people coming to the rectory with problems. Approximately two hundred seminarians were asked to send check lists, with safeguards for anonymity, and an explanatory letter to two couples, one happy and the other unhappy in their estimation. Check lists were distributed at a retreat house and also through a marriage counselor. In all cases, the completed questionnaire was returned to the author directly in the business-reply envelope.

Of the 3,800 questionnaires distributed in the manner described, 1,004, or 26.4 per cent, were returned. The length and intimate nature of the instrument undoubtedly increased the rate of non-response. Our sample was composed of 984 respondents (58.73 per cent women) from Catholic marriages still in existence. Some degree of bias, known and unknown, evidently exists, but our sample in such social characteristics as income, number of children, duration of marriage, and education is more representative than the major marriage studies with the possible exception of Locke.[5] Although there is a lack of randomization and correlated biases have not been controlled, our interest was in discovering, disproving, or confirming whether an observed difference does or does not exist. Uncontrolled variables or biases do not vitiate the legitimacy of a test of significance for the existence of a difference.

Using the Burgess-Wallin schedule, we found 64.02 per cent of our subjects were happy and 35.98 per cent unhappy. To test whether the happy and unhappy had the same problems, we contrasted the two groups on all of the 400 problems. Thirty-six problems had a theoretical frequency of less than five in one of the cells, but the 364 remaining problems were subjected to chi-square analysis. Our results revealed a statistically significant difference between the happy and unhappy groups at the five per cent level for 334 of the 364 problems. Of the 334 problems, only one problem was associated with being happily married. In all, 333 problems were associated with marital unhappiness. Some thirty problems of the 364 tested bore no statistical relationship at the five percent level to either happiness or unhappiness, verifying at least partially the hypothesis that the happy have the same problems as the unhappy. However, the major weight of the evidence would argue that, for the most part, the unhappy have more and different problems. Further evidence on this hypothesis is available. The median number of problems in our study was 19.1 problems per married person. Using the test of significance for the median, we find that unhappy people are much more likely than the happy to have more than nineteen problems, 84.74 per cent versus 27.61 per cent.

The rejected hypothesis appears to be a biased overgeneralization of the adjustment school and of the authors of manuals with their easy and mechanical recipes for marital happiness. Thomas once complained of the adjustment school:

> Adaptability is the key word in their vocabulary. The underlying premise is that human nature is almost infinitely malleable. Hence you can educate and train people to adjust themselves to any kind of sexual relationships and family roles. . . .[6]

Whether the extensive maladjustment of the unhappy is a result of the circular reaction, or that the unhappy are problem people, or that they lack the ability to adapt themselves, further research must determine. A clue to the kind of adjustment that actually takes place in marriage was revealed by our research. In the course of testing formulations of Goode and Thomas on the relationship of certain problems to duration, we found that relatively few problems declined significantly in frequency as the years roll by. Of 190 problems tested on the duration dimension, only thirty-six show a statistically significant decrease with an increase in marital duration. The fact that 150 out of 190 problems were as likely to occur at any period of married life, suggests that problems generally do not disappear, are not solved, but continue as irritants, with which, in one way or another, people must learn to live.[7] Our findings might be explained by the composition of our sample which embraced only Catholic marriages since it may legitimately be expected that Catholics suppress divorce.[8] The cost of stressing the institutional ends of marriage may well involve learning to accept and live with problems. On the other hand, this mode of adjustment may be the normal response of most spouses. The limited plasticity of personality, the existence of situational, cultural, and personality constants, the continued use of role repertoires developed through long years of living and in the marriage itself, should lead us to expect that problems perdure, that problems are not usually solved but are reluctantly accepted in a "for better, for worse" spirit.[9]

General Theory of Marital Maladjustment

Although the overriding purpose of our study was the testing of hypotheses, some tentative conclusions on the nature of the maladjustment were also suggested by our research. Analysis of the kinds of problems which *most* distinguish the happy and unhappy produced a rather striking pattern of difference. Using the magnitude of percentage differences, we found that of the first *fifty* problems discriminating the happy from the unhappy, twenty-one are from the area of basic human needs, eighteen from the area of interaction (mainly decision-making), seven from the area of personality complaints, three from the social area, and one from the area of sex. Of the first *hundred* problems, in rank order of percentage differences, thirty-four are needs problems, twenty-eight are interaction (decision-making), thirteen personality, eight social, five sexual, five home and children, three income, two religion, and two others are in-law problems. Although problems classified roughly as needs or interaction (decision-making) constituted 20 per cent of the items in the check list, they accounted for 78 per cent of the first *fifty* items and 62 per cent of the first *hundred* problems distinguishing the happy and the unhappy.

Examination of the first 50 items that most distinguish the happy and unhappy (Table 1) shows that neglect, lack of affection, understanding, appreciation, and companionship are the lot of the unhappy. Worse, their self respect is attacked, for their mate magnifies their faults, makes them feel worthless, belittles their efforts, and makes false accusations. Conflict, lack of communication, withdrawal characterize their interaction. No one item is determining of marital unhappiness, as the relatively small percentages indicate, but the pattern and trend of our data seem clear.

Admittedly, this is not rigorous evidence. However, we present it only as a point of theoretical interest to be tested by further research. The categorization itself of problems into neat pigeonholes does violence to behavior. All behavior, one might argue if he accepts such constructs, involves needs and personality traits. Further, the check list in on the conscious level and the problems may be only indices of deeper conflicts.

However, it would seem a mark of wisdon to begin a study of

maladjustment in marriages still in existence by discovering reality as married people view it. It is to this reality that they must adjust. No doubt, long-term neurotic needs and reaction patterns underlie our findings. A woman who says, "Mate makes me feel worthless" very likely has felt worthless all her life. But considering the relatively undeveloped status of personality theory, it is much too early to theorize that what we found is basically nothing more than the brawling and bawling of two neurotic personalities, emotionally clad in diapers, seeking to resolve childhood conflicts. Rather, it seems more of truth to hold that much of the above behavior is also generated by the conflict process itself; that even non-neurotic people usually react to you the way you act towards them; that conflicts and quarrels all too often roll on like huge snowballs, gathering momentum and carrying everything in their path; that what happens between people is often as much a determinant of future me-you action-patterns as existing personality structures of the individuals involved. Our finding, emphasizing the importance of the level of need satisfaction and interaction, appears to us to be of some value because it harmonizes with the most recent theorizing and also makes possible a rapprochement between clinical and non-clinical studies. In fact, clinician Nathan Ackerman gives a rather good statement of our finding in his own descriptive analysis of marital maladjustment.

> Disturbances of marital relationships are characterized by two salient elements: (1) failure of reciprocity of satisfactions and (2) conflict. These central features are influenced by several processes: disturbance of empathic union and identification; defective communication; the failure of devices of restitution following an upset in the balance of the relationship; and a failure of complimentarity in which the one partner no longer derives from the other satisfaction of needs, support of personal identity and buttressing of necessary defenses against anxiety."[10]

Richard Hey and Emily Mudd, also on the basis of counseling experience, believe that basic human problems underlying difficulties such as budget, finances, sex, infidelity, in-laws, religious differences, constant arguments, job dissatisfactions are loneliness, rejection, and breakdown of meaningful communication.[11]

Beginning with Burgess' concept of companionship, family sociologists, especially Winch, have also stressed the role of need satisfactions in marriage over institutional ends. Recently, Parsons has broadened and deepened the concept to include mental health. He argues that tension management is a system goal of the sub-system marriage and that the American family rather than task-oriented is aimed primarily at such emotional social values as companionship, personality development, a home, emotional security and satisfaction with affection shown: "We have argued above that in American society the nuclear family is specialized far over in the 'expressive' tension-

TABLE 1

First Fifty Items Distinguishing Happy And Uhappy In Rank Order Of Percentage Difference

Problem and Category ( )a	Happy N=630 No.b	%	Unhappy N=354 No.	%	X^2	c̄
1. Don't think alike on many things (D)	69	10.95	178	50.28	186.47 c	.56
2. Mate has little insight into my feelings (D) .	38	6.03	143	40.39	178.29	.55
3. Say things that hurt each other (D)	78	12.38	160	45.19	133.11	.48
4. Often feel unloved (N)	21	3.33	125	35.31	183.41	.56
5. Mate takes me for granted (N)	54	8.57	137	38.70	131.52	.48
6. Need someone to confide in (N)	35	5.55	120	33.89	137.19	.49
7. Mate rarely compliments me (N)	84	13.33	147	41.52	100.27	.43
8. Have to give in more than mate (D)	66	10.47	135	38.13	106.67	.44
9. Desire more affection (N)	72	11.92	136	38.41	99.03	.42
10. Can't talk to mate (D)	29	4.60	109	30.79	128.91	.48
11. Mate does not enjoy many things I enjoy (So)	37	5.87	113	31.92	119.02	.46
12. Often feel neglected (N)	20	3.17	100	28.24	133.07	.48
13. Keep things to myself (P)	90	14.28	139	39.26	79.20	.38
14. Can't please mate (D)	19	3.01	99	27.96	133.68	.48
15. Don't confide in each other (D)	23	3.65	101	28.53	127.38	.47
16. Mate is not open to suggestion (D)	16	2.53	97	27.40	137.81	.49
17. Can't discuss anything with mate (D)	18	2.85	97	27.40	132.28	.48
18. Mate is stubborn (P)	49	7.77	114	32.20	97.83	.42
19. Mate can't accept criticism (D)	59	9.36	119	33.61	89.95	.40
20. Mate magnifies my faults (N)	19	3.01	94	26.55	123.53	.47
21. Mate believes what he (she) wants to believe (D)	21	3.33	94	26.55	118.40	.46
22. Lack of companionship (N)	14	2.22	90	25.42	129.07	.48
23. Mate has frequent temper outbursts (D)	32	5.07	99	27.96	102.86	.43
24. Mate is often moody (P)	55	8.73	102	31.48	80.55	.38
25. Mate does not show his love (N)	15	2.38	88	24.85	122.18	.47
26. Mate has not grown up (P)	11	1.74	84	23.72	124.56	.47
27. Don't feel I am appreciated (N)	35	5.55	97	27.40	93.12	.41
28. Mate is too critical and faultfinding (P) ...	22	3.49	88	24.85	104.21	.43
29. Mate is inconsiderate and insensitive to my needs	8	1.26	80	22.59	126.61	.47
30. Not the center of mate's life (N)	16	2.53	83	23.44	109.47	.44
31. Decline in affection for mate (N)	6	.95	73	20.62	118.74	.46
32. Mate often nags me (D)	19	3.01	78	22.03	92.25	.41
33. Mate does not share experiences (N)	23	3.65	80	22.59	86.82	.40
34. Often refuse to speak to each other for hours (D)	23	3.65	80	22.59	86.82	.40
35. Mate does not like to do the same things (So).	26	4.12	81	22.88	82.25	.39
36. Have to cater to mate's wishes (D)	19	3.01	77	21.75	90.36	.41
37. Unhappy, too much of the time (P)	12	1.90	73	20.62	100.62	.43
38. Mate is emotionally immature (P)	17	2.69	72	20.33	85.73	.40
39. Mate makes me feel worthless (N)	5	.79	65	18.36	105.86	.44
40. Mate criticizes me too much (N)	16	2.53	70	19.77	84.40	.39

41.	Doubt mate's love for me (N)	10	1.58	66	18.64	92.51	.41
42.	Mate sulks or holds grudges (D)	20	3.17	71	20.05	76.96	.38
43.	Mate thinks only of his or (her) own pleasure (Sx)	10	1.58	65	18.36	90.57	.41
44.	Mate does not understand me (N)	13	2.06	66	18.64	84.38	.39
45.	Mate won't listen to my opinions (D)	15	2.38	65	18.36	77.49	.38
46.	Mate likes to argue (D)	13	2.06	62	17.51	76.84	.38
47.	Mate does not try to please me (N)	4	.63	55	15.53	89.29	.40
48.	Mate tries to hurt my feelings (N)	5	.79	53	14.79	82.13	.39
49.	Mate is too bossy and acts superior (D)	6	.95	52	14.68	77.10	.38
50.	Mate does not care for me as before marriage (N)	4	.63	49	13.84	17.57	.38

a Symbol in parentheses designates type of problem. Thus: N = Needs problem; D = Decision making or interaction; P = Personality problem, So = Social; Sx = Sex problem.

b Number and Percentage of those who said they *had* problem from the happy group (630 respondents) and unhappy (354 repondents).

c One degree of freedom. P is less than .001 for all problems Listed.

management and socialization directions." [12] Blood and Wolfe remark that the mental-hygiene function of marriage seldom appears in the standardized list of family functions, but they consider it to be of ever growing importance with the passing of the patriarchal family.[13]Their conception of the mental hygience function seems quite narrow, for in their own research they studied only understanding. Nevertheless, they did find that Detroit wives ranked understanding as a more valuable component of marriage than love.[14]

Recent thinking in the family field, stimulated by small group theory, has also turned to interaction analysis for an understanding of marriages at work. For years, of course, it has been understood that "marriage tends to move at a rate and in a direction that is a function of the interactions that have gone before." [15] Frustration, failure, conflict, for instance, can give rise to emotions of anger, hate, disappointment which may change present motive patterns including perception, performance and thought, and thus influence future actions or reactions. But so little research has been done on the role of cumulative circular responses that Buerkle and Badgley could write in 1959: "We believe that at present actually very little is known about the exact interactive patterns conducive to marital 'happiness' or 'stability.'" [16]

Parsons and Bales have laid down the general theoretical lines of this new approach. They suggest that each marriage through interaction develops a kind of emotional culture.[17]

Some sociologists and psychiatrists have held that open conflict in marriage is beneficial in that it results in problem-solving and in the release of tensions and frustrations.[18] F. Ivan Nye and Evelyn Mac-Dougall, however, have shown that marital happiness correlates with the absence of conflict.[19] Our findings lend support to this latter view.

CONCLUSION

The basic findings of this study of marital maladjustment failed to confirm the oft-repeated speculation that the happy have the same problems as the unhappy. Unhappy marriages have many more and different problems. An exploratory excursion also revealed that most problems are not solved but perdure through the life cycle. Further, empirical trends in our data strongly suggest that the two most important areas of disturbance in unhappy marriages concern the fulfillment of each other's needs and the kind of interaction which prevails between the spouses if basic needs are not satisfied. What are the specific interactive patterns involved, future research must determine. The necessity and fruitfulness of a sociological rather than a psychological approach to marital happiness seems indicated by our data. By the constructs of need-satisfaction and the conflict process, attention can be focused on interaction, on a dynamic and changing relationship, on a dialectical process of responding negatively and positvely to what happens during marriage rather than on the static personality traits of individuals.

REFERENCES

1. Ernest R. Groves, "Are Successful Families Different," *Social Forces,* VII (June, 1930), p. 536.

2. Meyer F. Nimkoff, *Marriage and the Family,* Boston: Houghton Mifflin Company, 1947, p. 488.

3. William J. Goode, *After Divorce,* Glencoe, Ill.: The Free Press, 1956, p. 115.

4. Ernest W. Burgess and Paul Wallin, *Engagement and Marriage,* Chicago: J. B. Lippincott Company, 1953, pp. 486-87.

5. Median duration of marriage = 12.1 years; median number of children, 3.25; median income: $5,914; the average respondent was a high school graduate.

6. John L. Thomas, "The Changing Family," *Social Order,* II (February, 1952), 57.

7. Since our results were a by-product, no attempt, unfortunately, was made to discover if problems are more likely to decline with duration in happy rather than unhappy marriages.

8. Roswell H. Johnson, "Suppressed, Delayed, Damaging, and Avoided Divorces," *Law and Contemporary Problems,* 18 (Winter, 1953), 72.

9. For the role of these factors in remarriage see Jessie Bernard, *Remarriage,* New York: Dryden Press, 1956, pp. 335-42.

10. Nathan W. Ackerman, *The Psychodynamics of Family Life,* New York: Basic Books, Inc., 1958, p. 154.

11. Richard Hey and Emily Mudd, "Recurring Problems in Marriage Counseling," *Marriage and Family Living,* XXI (May, 1959), 127-28.

12. Talcott Parsons and Robert Bales, *Family, Socialization, and Interaction Process,* Giencoe, Ill.: The Free Press, 1955, pp. 162-63, 123.

13. Robert O. Blood and Donald M. Wolfe, *Husbands and Wives,* Glencoe, Ill. The Free Press, 1960, pp. 176-78.

14. *Ibib.,* p. 181.

15. Clifford Kirkpatrick, "Techniques of Marital Adjustment," *Annals of American Academy of Political and Social Sciences,* CLX (Marcy, 1932), p. 180.

16. Jack V. Buerkle and Robin F. Badgley, "Couple Role Taking: The Yale Marital Interaction Battery," *Marriage and Family Living,* XXI (February, 1959), p. 58.

17. Parsons and Bales, *op. cit.,* p. 364.

18. Ackerman, op. cit., p. 152; Robert M. Hunington, "The Personality Interaction Approach to Study of Marital Relationship," *Marriage and Family Living,* XX (February, 1958), pp. 43-46.

19. F. Ivan Nye, "Employment Status of Mother and Marital Conflict, Permanence and Happiness," *Social Problems,* VI (Winter, 1958-59), pp. 260-67.

Why Good Marriages Fail

RICHARD FARSON

As impossible as it may sound, good marriages probably fail more often than bad ones. What's more, they fail precisely because they are good.

Human experience is full of such paradoxes. People often do just the opposite of what one would expect. For example, researchers have found that revolutions do not break out when conditions are at their worst, but when the situation has begun to get better. Once reforms have started, people gain strength and, more importantly, a vision of what their lives might be like — both of which are necessary to energize a revolution. Historians call this the problem of rising expectations.

The same kind of analysis can help us understand why so many good marriages fail. Perhaps if couples could incorporate such paradoxical thinking into their lives, their chances of maintaining a good marriage might improve. At least they might eliminate some of the ugliness of divorce by not deprecating what was, all things considered, a good relationship.

How can a good marriage fail? The easy explanation is that it wasn't basically good. It may have looked good on the outside, but it must have been flawed on the inside. That's the way we usually try to rationalize divorce. But what about marriages that by every conceivable criterion compare favorably with most other marriages? They can fail, too. And because of the heightened expectations present in good marriages, they are often in greater jeopardy than bad ones.

It is not easy to find support for this point of view, because we tend to look at divorces for things that went wrong, not for things that went right. In fact, the best evidence for this argument will have to come from marriages and divorces you know about, perhaps even from your own marriage.

Take, for example, the most recent divorce among your friends. Try to remember what the marriage was like. Chances are you thought of it as being as good as most. You knew of nothing seriously wrong. On the contrary, the couple seemed to enjoy family life, had adequate finances, physical attractiveness, common interests. Even more, they may have had a good deal of respect for each other, perhaps even deep affection.

Yet, they decided to separate. You try to imagine what could have happened. You look for some basic incompatibility, some distinct flaw, some terrible incident. But when you ask them why they are divorcing, they are apt to say something like, "Well, we've simply grown apart," or "I feel trapped in this relationship," or "We just can't communicate," or

"He won't let me be me," or "We just felt that surely there must be more to life than we are getting from this marriage."

In all probability, there is no awful hidden truth. Probably there is nothing in their marriage that makes it different from, or worse than, most others.

The common element in all their answers is that they are expressing high-order discontent. Their complaints have nothing to do with the rather low-order justifications for divorce recognized by law — brutality, desertion, adultery, etc. Instead, their complaints reflect an awareness of what the good life should be. Their discontent comes from the difference between what they are actually experiencing in their marriage and what they have come to believe is possible.

The couples who get in the most trouble are those who know enough to see the things that are wrong with their marriage. And, ironically, it takes quite a bit of success in a marriage to make that understanding possible.

So good marriages fail because, by the very fact of being good, they generate discontent. The discontent may come from many sources, some rather unexpected. Here are eight of them:

1. *Discontent arises because the basic needs of the marriage have been satisfied.* Yet, people are never entirely satisfied. Once they have met one set of needs, they simply move on to develop higher-order needs, in an ever-accelerating pattern of demand.

Marriage, after all, was never meant to be as good as it is. It was instituted in the beginning to insure survival, then security, then convenience. Now we take for granted that it will not only meet all those basic needs but much higher needs as well. Marriage is now burdened with the expectations that husbands and wives should enjoy intellectual companionship, warm intimate moments, shared values, deep romantic love, great sexual pleasures. Couples expect to assist and enhance each other in ways never thought of as being part of the marriage contract.

The trouble is that these higher-order needs are more complex, and therefore less easy to satisfy on a continuing basis, than are, say, financial needs. For that reason, they give rise to more frustration and discontent when they are not met.

2. *Discontent arises because mass education and mass media have taught people to expect too much from marriage.* Today almost no one is ignorant of the marvelous possibilities of human relationships. Time was when people modeled their own marriage after their parents' marriage; it was the only model they knew. Now, with much of our population college-educated, saturated with books, recordings, films, and television, just about everyone has some new ideals for his marriage to live up to — and has, consequently, some new sources of dissatisfaction.

The problem is made even worse by the mass media: The romantic vision has been oversimplified, translated into a smoothly functioning, syrupy sweet "nuclear" family and sold to the American public. The perpetuation of this stereotype (two married adults and their own minor children) as the only acceptable marriage model, and the implication that a constant state of affection and unity in family life is actually achievable, give cause to rising dissatisfaction in one's own marriage.

Television is totally devoted to the nuclear family; the only variation ever shown is when one parent is widowed (rarely divorced) and is seeking a return to "normal" family life. Not only is the nuclear family a relatively new invention (never before in history were families formed along these lines), but many authorities now regard this arrangement as entirely too burdensome and difficult to remain workable. Two parents having to serve as all-purpose adults, accomplishing everything by themselves, is anything but easy. TV just makes it look easy.

The simple fact is that more than 60 percent of Americans now do not live in nuclear-family arrangements. They live in some other form of domestic unit — as single adults, for example, or divorced adults with children. But their constant instructions from the mass media are that to be genuinely fulfilled, they must be part of a nuclear family.

3. *Discontent arises because couples succeed in filling their masculine and feminine roles.* One would think that success in meeting society's expectations as men and women should make marriage work better. Shouldn't the woman who is feminine, gentle, tender, aesthetic, childlike, emotional, understanding, and yielding be a perfect companion for a man who is masculine, firm, strong, aggressive, rugged, decisive, rational, and dominant?

The odds are that it works just the other way. These roles are so limiting, and at the same time so demanding, that the result can be truly monstrous. As we are now beginning to see, the oppressive concept of "woman's role" and "woman's place" has led to great rage on the part of many women, rage that has only recently been openly expressed. Similarly, the man's role leads to such strong feelings of pressure, guilt, impotence, and artificiality that he, too, is now demanding relief.

One would think that the strain of such role-demands could be alleviated in the intimacy and protection of the family unit, but for the most part, it is not. Unfortunately, the marriage relationship is not usually a place one can let down. Too often it serves not as a buffer against the impositions of society, but as a reinforcer. Husbands and wives are notorious in forcing these stereotyped roles on one another. The frustration that comes from an inability to deliver on such expectations only makes matters worse, and instead of blaming society for demanding that they perform these roles, they blame themselves and each other.

The various liberation efforts for men and women that are currently under way may eventually offer relief, but in the short run they simply deepen the problem. The stress on marriage that has resulted from women's liberation, for example, has already taken its toll in separation and divorce. No one can say why. It could be because the husband and wife are not being liberated at the same rate, or because they have come to see their marriage as symbolizing their slavery to these oppressive roles, or because their new understandings show their marriage to be so limiting that they can no longer live with the incongruity between what they have and what they feel they *must* have.

4. *Discontent arises because marriage now embraces a new concept of sexual fulfillment.* The deluge of words and images giving us a totally new idea of what human sexuality could be has become inescapable. We are no longer willing to settle for the sexuality of past generations. Married couples now expect sex to be playful, experimental, and greatly permissive. They expect a wide range of sexual performance and are seriously disappointed when the experiments don't succeed. Not only is there a desperate search for orgasm, but more — superorgasm, ecstasy, peak experiences. Not sometimes, but every time; so here again, while the sexual relationship in a marriage may have been quite adequate, it is now expected to be a good deal more than adequate. The better it is, the better it must become.

No one wants to turn back the clock, to deny the new understandings of human sexual potential and return to Victorian prudery. We should be pleased that individuals now demand the right to full sexuality. But we can't ignore the fact that in previous generations these high expectations were not a recognized source of discontent.

5. *Discontent arises because marriage counseling, psychotherapy, and other efforts to improve marriage actually make it more difficult.* It may be that marriage counseling and psychotherapy with married couples tend to create more discontent than they cure. Not because counseling isn't any good, but partly because it *is* good; by helping, it has made the problem worse.

First of all, any effort to improve life, whether by education or religion or philosophy or therapy — seldom makes life simpler. In fact, it makes it more complex. Just as labor-saving devices have caused us more labor and complicated our lives, so counseling has further burdened our marriages by asking us to live up to what we know to be our best. That always turns out to be difficult and painful.

Secondly, counseling provides an example of an intimate relationship that is achievable only under the special circumstances of the psychotherapeutic hour; nevertheless, it makes the client wonder why that level of intimacy and understanding can't exist at home. In comparison to an expert counselor, most marriage partners must seem obtuse indeed.

Third, most psychotherapists continue to endorse, even promote, narrow and outdated ideas, based largely on Freudian concepts of sexuality, male-female roles, and family relationships. They describe a model of marriage that is all but impossible to live up to, and is, in the light of newer understanding, not very desirable anyway. In this area, the psychotherapist is, for the most part, the unwitting enemy of the liberation movements for both men and women. This is especially tragic when you realize that human liberation, the chance to live up to one's potential, is what counseling and psychotherapy are all about.

Fourth, and perhaps most serious, counseling gives a person the feeling — much more than is probably true — that he is in charge of his own life, that his problems are basically of his own making, and that their solutions are within his control. People constantly live with the idea that they are beset with unique and *personal* problems — problems that stem from their own neurotic disorders or from mistakes they have made, conditions that are solvable and correctable by individual action. But more likely, for most people, it is the *situation* in which they find themselves that is the problem. And it is not always a situation that individual initiative can do much about.

Constant attention to our problems as personal rather than as universal (which happens in counseling) has given us a highly distorted picture of what we can do about the problems we find in marriage. We actually have very little control over the major conditions that affect our marriages, and, consequently, marriages change very little as a result of counseling.

Finally, it is rather well known that psychotherapists and marriage counselors themselves have a high incidence of separation and divorce. This is not cited to suggest that, as a way of justifying their own actions, they subconsciously welcome their clients' decisions to separate. Rather, it points out yet another example of how constant attention to marriage, and the consequent high-order expectations about the marriage relationship, can produce casualties in those one would think best able to avoid them.

6. *Discontent arises because marriages suffer from the gains made in the consciousness revolution.* This revolution, thought by some to be the only revolution that is actually changing behavior, stems from the hippie movement — drug culture, new-left politics, rock music, Eastern philosophy, occult phenomena, encounter groups, etc. — all combining to paint pictures of what life might be if we were to reach the human potential.

The alternate life-styles that have grown out of this revolution are now affecting the values of all of us, and, most certainly, they have reshaped our concepts of married life. Consider, for example, the impact of the encounter group and other group efforts to develop awareness and sensitivity to one's self and others. More than 6 million Americans have now participated in encounter groups of one form or another. As is the case with psychotherapy, the encounter group has given its participants moments with other people that are remarkably beautiful, intimate, and fulfilling. These experiences can't help making a person think that he is going to be able to bring this new awareness and strength into his own marriage. But it seldom works that way. More likely, it has furnished him with a reference point indicating what a relationship *might* be, but which his marriage can never achieve. Not because his marriage isn't good, but because it can't match the freedom of a temporary relationship.

The consciousness revolution works in other ways to make marriage more difficult. For example, the value placed on honest relationships, on complete truthfulness in dealing with others, puts such an excessive strain on marriages that some cannot survive. The idea is, the more honesty the better. Following the teachings of the new-consciousness gurus, husbands and wives have regaled each other with all manner of honest statements in what appear to be efforts to enrich marriage, but in fact make it almost impossible to endure. Most marriages can't take such honesty as sharing fantasies about other people during sexual intercourse, detailing extramarital affairs, etc. Jean Kerr wrote a good line for a wife who has just been told by her husband that he has been cheating, "If you had the decency of a truck driver, you'd keep your lousy affair secret!"

The values of the new consciousness emphasize honesty over loyalty and kindness. Honesty is rarely unadulterated, however, and all too often is used to alleviate guilt and transfer responsibility. It may help to remember that marriage, like any other important institution, needs some myth and mystique to keep it vital.

Above all, the new consciousness has created the expectation of high-level intimacy in marriage, something that is very rare indeed. There is little question that the intimacy of shared feelings that occurs between teen-age friends, for example, far and away transcends that which is possible in most marriages. Perhaps marriage is too important to be burdened with such intimacies. People simply cannot take such risks with a relationship that matters so much to them.

7. *Discontent arises because of fantasies about what other marriages are like.* Just as individuals find it necessary to present a facade in life, married people feel that they must create an image of their marriage that shows only its best side. The truth is that we live in almost total ignorance of what other people's marriages are like. Everyone recognizes that no marriage is perfect, that everyone has fights and difficulties and disillusionments. Yet, many times we undermine our marriages by assuming that other marriages must somehow be better. This fantasy, like a casual flirtation, doesn't have to pass any real tests of real life. And, if we really could know more about other people's marriages, we would see that they are much more similar than different — painfully, hilariously, reassuringly alike.

8. *Discontent arises from comparing the marriage relationship with itself in its better moments.* The memories couples carry of their premarital or early marriage experiences inevitably make their current situation seem less romantic and exciting.

This is particularly true for couples with children. For most people, the major change in life comes not with marriage, but with the birth of the first child. It is at that point that real commitment is required, that major limitations set in, and it is then that the affection and attention of the wife moves from husband to child. A decrease in sexual activity, and an increase in the complications of family life, as treasured and as beautiful as they may be, are sources of discontent when compared with what went before.

But probably the most important source of discontent is the comparison of the marriage with its own good moments in the present. Not too many marriages have great moments; but the best ones do. These peaks, however, are inevitably followed by valleys. Couples lucky enough to have these moments find themselves unable to sustain them, and, at the same time, unable to settle for ordinary moments. They want life to be a constantly satisfying state. But to be a constant state, to avoid the valleys, it is necessary to eliminate the peaks, which puts the marriage on a narrow band of emotionality and involvement. Good marriages are not like that, but the price they exact in depression and pain is high.

The constant talk today about marriage, whether it's positive or negative, has only led to greater hopes for it, making it more popular and desirable than ever. As someone once remarked, "Marriage is like a beseiged city. Everybody that's out wants in, and everybody that's in wants out."

What's difficult to remember is that marriages of all kinds, bad and good, are very fragile, easily wrecked. They can withstand some kinds of difficulty and trauma, but they cannot stand the abuse of unmet expectations. They particularly can't stand comparisons between what they are and what they might be. It is that kind of comparison that leads to separation and divorce. That is why maintaining a good marriage is more difficult than maintaining a bad one.

The calamity of divorce is not in the failure of the relationship; the relationship has probably succeeded fairly well, right to the end. Instead, the calamity comes from the problems of child custody, property, finances, social stigma, unsolved feelings of dependency, responsibility, guilt, and failure — the feelings of having let everyone down.

It's a pity that we must regard the end of a marriage as proof of its failure. In order to justify a separation, we must somehow put down the marriage, negate it, make it less worthy than it has been.

Society won't allow us to celebrate separations, but perhaps that's not such a bad idea. There is some reason to believe that people leave one rich relationship to find a richer one. Sociologist Jessie Bernard's classic study of divorce and remarriage suggests that couples move on to seek and find high-order marriages, sometimes several in a series. Clearly a new concept of evaluating marriage must be brought into being, one that assesses not longevity or satisfaction but the quality and level of the discontent it engenders.

Somehow we have the idea that we can only leave a marriage if it's bad. We simply can't bring ourselves to see that the reason for leaving a marriage may be because of the new vision it permitted us to have of what life could be like. Too bad we can't live with this paradox.

If we could realize that the better the marriage is, the worse we will sometimes feel, then we might prevent the incidents that occur in any marriage from leading to separation and divorce. Such an understanding could give us the insight we need to make one good marriage last a lifetime.

Marriage: His and Hers

JESSIE BERNARD

For centuries men have been told — by other men — that marriage is: no bed of roses, a necessary evil, a noose, a desperate thing, a field of battle, a curse, a school of sincere pretense. Supposedly, Oscar Wilde proclaimed marriage a wonderful institution: every woman should be married, but no man. H. L. Mencken is credited with the observation that since it was to man's interest to avoid marriage as long as possible and to woman's to marry as favorably as possible, the sexes were pursuing diametrically antagonistic ends.

These male cliches could hardly have been more wrong. For, contrary to all the charges leveled against it, the husband's marriage, whether he likes it or not (and he does) is awfully good for him. The findings are consistent, unequivocal, and convincing. The superiority of married men over never-married men is impressive on almost every index — demographic, psychological, or social.

After middle age the physical health of married men is better than that of never-married men. But regardless of age, married men enjoy better mental health and fewer serious symptoms of psychological distress. To take an extreme example, in the United States, the suicide rate for single men is almost twice as high as for married men.

And the actions of men with respect to marriage speak far louder than words — or statistics. Once men have known marriage, they can hardly live without it. Most divorced and widowed men remarry. At every age, the marriage rate for both divorced and widowed men is higher than the rate for single men. Half of all divorced men who remarry do so within three years after divorce.

Could it be that the gentlemen protest too much? Are their verbal assaults on marriage a kind of compensatory reaction to their dependence on it?

Some men do not marry because they do not want to, for whatever reason, and some because no one wants to marry them. In either case, we are faced with the inevitable, and insoluble chicken-and-egg, cause-and-effect question. This selectivity factor is undoubtedly part of the explanation of the superiority married men show over the unmarried, and cannot therefore be ignored in evaluating the impact of marriage. But the weight of the evidence explaining differences by marital status seems to me to be overwhelmingly on the side of the beneficent effects which marriage has on men rather than on the initial superiority of the married men. Are married men so much better off than the never-married because marriage is good for them or because the less good prospects were selected out of the married population in the first place?

By comparing the married with the widowed, we minimize the selective factor, for the widowed did once choose marriage or were chosen by someone. Such comparisons give us an indication of the value of marriage by showing what happens to men who are deprived of it by death. They are miserable. Widowers show more than expected frequencies of psychological distress, and their death rate is very high.

One would expect the unmarried to be the "easy riders," the men who cannot tolerate the restrictions of conventionality, but seek to satisfy a wide gamut of desires. One study did, indeed, find that the unmarried more than the married felt marriage to be restrictive. It was, however, a more negative kind of reaction — a passive avoidance of the difficulties of marriage — rather than a postitive commitment to unlimited wants, desires, or aspirations. Other studies have shown that more single than married men suffer from inertia, passivity, antisocial tendencies, greater moral conflict, and a history of stressful child-hoods.

I have emphasized only the documentable, research-based evidence of the benefits of marriage. But every happily married man will be able to add a dozen more: marriage is more comfortable than bachelor-hood; sex is always available; responsibility is a rewarding experience. It is reassuring to have a confidante. And then there is love, friendship, and personal service. . . .

The benefits of marriage for men do not come without costs. Some freedom must be surrendered. To be sure, the bachelor party that used to be popular the night before the marriage was a recognition that hereafter there would indeed be sacrifices — no more carousing, no more irresponsible fun.

Economic responsibilities and sexual restrictiveness are the two major costs men feel they pay to maintain a haven. Many husbands therefore name two areas of potential improvement of the state of matrimony. One would be to relieve them from the responsibility for the entire support of wives and children, and the other to make sexual varietism more feasible. Both seem to be in the process of realization.

What will happen to "the husband's marriage" as the wife's economic contribution increases and the couple's fidelity expectations decrease, is a matter of sociology in the making.

But at the present time, there is no better guarantor of long life, health, and happiness for men than a wife well socialized to perform the "duties of a wife," willing to devote her life to taking care of him, providing, even enforcing, the regularity and security of a well-ordered home.

The story of the husband's marrige can be short and simple; not so, however, the story of the wife's.

In summarizing the research of a generation, the indicators add up to a sorry betrayal of the bride's ideal. It appears conclusive that more wives than husbands report marital frustration and dissatisfaction. More wives than husbands consider their marriages unhappy, have considered separation or divorce, and have regretted their marriages. Fewer married women than married men report positive companionship. Understandably, therefore, it is mostly the wives who seek marriage counseling and initiate divorce proceedings.

Even among happily married couples, issues such as finances, religion, sex, friends, and life goals show the wives reporting problems in more than twice as many areas as husbands.

Although the physical health of married women is as good as, or even better than that of married men, the women suffer far greater mental-health hazards.

One disheartening study found that more married women than married men have felt they were about to have a nervous breakdown; more have feelings of inadequacy in their marriages and blame themselves for their own lack of general adjustment. Other studies report that more wives than husbands show phobic reactions, depression, and passivity; greater than expected frequency of psychological distress; and mental-health impairment.

If the mental and emotional health of wives — anxious, depressed, psychologically distressed — is so dismal, perhaps we are dealing with a sex difference quite unrelated to marriage. Perhaps the mental and emotional health of wives shows up so poorly simply because they are females — who are "naturally" weak, vulnerable, emotional, moody, and unable to cope.

This interpretation is one version of the perennial charge against women: it's their own fault. When a woman takes her problems to a psychiatrist, the response of the therapist has all too often suggested that her misery was self-generated and could be relieved only by learning to come to terms with her position. (The buck stops with the wife, even though, as several clinicians have reported, both husbands and wives believe that the husband is usually the source of problems in the marriage.)

However, this "it's-merely-a-sex-difference" interpretation cannot account for an intrasex discrepancy: the mental-health picture of wives shows up just as unfavorably when compared with unmarried women. Thus, we are impressed by a study reported in 1938 when marriage was the only alternative lifestyle, and single women were less often glamorized and more often pitied than today. This study nonetheless found that more *married* than single women had their feelings easily hurt, were happy and sad by turns without apparent reason, cried easily, felt hurt by criticism, sometimes felt miserable, found it hard to make up their minds, were burdened by a sense of remorse, worried over possible misfortune, would cross the street to avoid meeting people, and were self-conscious about their appearance. Recent studies tend to confirm such differences, adding such testimony about wives' feelings as: unhappy most of the time, disliking their present jobs, sometimes feeling they are about to go to pieces, afraid of death, worried about contracting diseases, and bothered by pains and ailments. Many other symptoms of psychological distress, such as nervousness, inertia, insomnia, trembling hands, nightmares, fainting, headaches, dizziness, and heart palpitations, show up *less* frequently than expected among unmarried women and *more* frequently than expected among wives.

All the statistics lead to the inescapable conclusion that single women have it over everyone. The bachelor women report less discomfort and greater happiness. They are more active about working through their problems. They're less often neurotic, antisocial, depressed, or passive. And these differences hold true regardless of age, education, occupation, and income.

Why do married women reveal so many more distress symptoms than both married men and single women? Is is because only distress-prone women prefer to marry? Or because men prefer to marry that type of woman? Or could it be that women start out with an initial advantage which marriage reverses?

Until the resurgence of feminism, very few women remained single because they *did not want* to marry, as in the case of some men. Because of powerful role-conditioning, practically all young women want to marry for lack of other inviting options or available alternatives. And so the root of a woman's single state (in a society in which men traditionally do the proposing) is likely to lie in the behavior of men. The women that men select in marriage reflect what men want in wives.

By and large, research has shown that both men and women tend to marry mates with the same general class and cultural background. But within that common background, men tend to marry women slightly below them in such measurable items as age, education, and occupation.

What men do *not* want in wives may be deduced from evidence gathered in a study of never-married women; the profile reads like an impressive résumé rather than a portrait of a reject. Single women tend to be upwardly mobile, they, more than married women, had started life in lower socioeconomic levels and pulled themselves up educationally and professionally. The implication is that they were "aggressive" and had stronger "achievement motivation" than most women. The talents it takes (for women or men) to achieve the best-paying jobs — competitiveness, aggressiveness, drive, and will to succeed — seem to be precisely those qualities most men fear, suspect, or reject as inconsistent with wifehood.

The second type of woman men do not choose is the too-conventional one. The cliche claims that while men may play around with the freewheeling swinger, they marry the "good girl." Not so, reports a key study. It's the married women who have more often engaged in unconventional heterosexual activities; and it's their single sisters who are more frequently morally strict, conscientious, and scrupulous about family obligations.

An analysis of those women whom men select *out* of the marriage market does little to explain the grim mental-health picture of wives. Sooner or later, practically everyone marries. What, then, is it about marriage itself that can explain the situation?

Years ago, I propounded "a shock theory" of marriage. It was my idea that marriage introduced such profound discontinuities into the lives of women as to constitute a genuine emotional health hazard.

There are some standardized "shocks" that are almost taken for granted. For example, one analyst cites the conflict the bride experiences between her attachment to her parental family and her attachment to her new husband. Another shock marks the end of the romantic idealization when the honeymoon is over and disenchantment sets in. The transition from the best-behavior presentation of the self during courtship to the daily lack of privacy in marriage (hair curlers, the unshaven face) presents its own kind of shock. So does the change that occurs when the wife ceases to be the catered-to and becomes the caterer. Discontinuities such as these demand a redefinition of the self, with the assumption of new role obligations.

When another type of shock registers on every woman's scale of myths and misconceptions, there is a sense of betrayal: girls are reared to see themselves as naturally dependent creatures entitled to lean on the greater strength of men. They enter marriage fully confident that these expectations will be fulfilled. They are therefore shaken and dismayed when their husbands turn out to be human. The "strong, protective, superior man" cannot solve his own problems, let alone his helpless wife's. Like everyone else, she was fooled by the stereotypes and by the structural imperatives.

Some of the shocks that marriage may produce have to do with the lowering of status that it brings to women. For, despite the possibilities of a woman's "marrying up," becoming a wife is a step down in the eyes of society. In many states the legal status of wives is lower not only than that of husbands but also than that of unmarried women. But that is relatively minor compared to other forms of status loss, as William Congreve's Mrs. Millamant in *The Way of the World* so well knew when she spoke of "dwindling" into a wife. Even after she had bargained with her husband Mirabel to preserve at least some of her prerogatives in marriage, she said, "These articles subscribed, if I continue to endure you a little longer, I may by degrees dwindle into a wife." And Mirabel recognized that his status would be enhanced: "Well, have I liberty to offer conditions, that when you are dwindled into a wife I may not be beyond measure enlarged into a husband?"

This dwindling takes time — time for a woman to redefine herself and reshape her personality to conform to the wishes or needs or demands of her husbands. Roland G. Tharp, a psychologist, concludes from a summary of the research literature that wives "conform more to husbands' expectations than husbands do to wives'." Women who are quite able to take care of themselves before marriage may become helpless after 15 or 20 years of marriage. No wonder sociologist Alice Rossi warns us that "the possibility must be faced . . . that women lose ground in personal development and self-esteem during the early and middle years of adulthood, whereas men gain ground in these respects during the same years." For it is the husbands's *role* — not necessarily his own wishes, desires, or demands — that proves to be the key to the marriage and requires the wife to be accommodating.

This in turn tallies with the common finding that wives make more of the adjustments called for in marriage than do husbands. The psychological and emotional costs of these adjustments show up in the increasing unhappiness of wives with the passage of time and in their increasingly negative and passive outlook on life.

One of the basic differences in the wife's and the husband's marriages results from lifestyle — namely, the almost complete change in occupation that marriage brings in her life but not in his. For most women today there are certain years in a marriage when a wife becomes a *housewife*. Even those women who work outside the home are still, in traditional marriages, housewives too. After a nine-to-five day on the job these women tackle the cleaning, cooking, and laundry with the blind obedience of an ordained domestic. Few deny the economic and sociological importance of housework and homemaking. But housewives are not in the labor force. They are not paid for the services that they perform.

The low status of the wife's work has ramifications all through her marriage. Since the husband's work is higher than hers in status, earnings, and degree of competition, his needs have to be catered to first.

Eventually the difference in the work of wives and husbands has alienating effects on the relationship. They may not share the same kinds of problems. The couple who began their marriage at the same early stage of their development may find that they and their interests have grown apart in later years. Most often the husband's horizons expand and the wife's contract. "The idea of imprisoning each woman alone in a small, self-contained, and architecturally isolating dwelling is a modern invention," Philip Slater reminds us. "In our society the housewife may move about freely, but since she has nowhere in particular to go and is not part of anything, her prison needs no walls."

Isolation has negative psychological effects on people. It encourages brooding; it leads to erratic judgments, untempered by the leavening effect of contact with others. It renders one more susceptible to psychoses, and heightens one's sense of powerlessness.

We have a ready-made life experiment to demonstrate that it is the role of housewife rather than the fact of being married which contributes heavily to the poor mental and emotional health of wives. By comparing married housewives with married working women, we find that wives who are rescued from the isolation of the household by outside employment show up very well. They may be neurotic, but they are less likely than full-time housewives to be psychotic. In nearly all symptoms of psychological distress — from headaches to heart palpitations — the working women are overwhelmingly better off. In terms of the number of people involved, the housewife syndrome might well be viewed as Public Health Problem Number One. Ironically, the woman suffering from it is not likely to elicit much sympathy. Her symptoms of psychological distress are not worth anyone's attention. Only advertisers take the housewife seriously, and to them she seems only a laughable idiot with a full wallet and an insatiable need for approval. But it's even simpler than that. In truth, being a housewife makes a woman sick.

If we were, in fact, epidemiologists and we saw bright, promising young people enter a certain occupation and little by little begin to droop and finally succumb, we would be alerted at once and bend all our research efforts to locate the hazards and remove them. But we are complacent when we see what happens to women in marriage. We put an enormous premium on their getting married, but make them pay an unconscionable price for falling in with our expectations.

If the wife's marriage is really so pathogenic, why do women marry at all? There is a wide variety of reasons: emancipation from the parental home; babies; pressure of social expectations; the absence of any better alternatives.

The real question is not why do young women marry, but why, in the face of all the evidence, so many more married than unmarried women report themselves as happy? As, in fact, they do.

The anomaly may be explained by the fact that happiness is interpreted in terms of conformity. Those who do not marry are made to feel failures. Escape from being "an old maid" is one definition of happiness.

Such conformity to the norm of marriage is not merely imposed from the outside. Women have internalized the norms prescribing marriage. And since marriage is set up as the *summum bonum* of life for women, they interpret their achievement of marriage as happiness, no matter how unhappy the marriage itself may be. "I am married, am I not? Therefore I must be happy."

Another way to explain the anomaly of depressed, phobic, and psychologically distressed women reporting themselves as happy may be that they are interpreting happiness in terms of adjustment. The married woman has supposedly adjusted to the demands of marriage; she is reconciled to them. She interprets her reconciliation as happiness, no matter how much she is paying for it in terms of psychological distress.

Another way to solve the paradox of depressed wives reporting their marriages as happy is to view the socialization process as one which "deforms" women in order to fit them for marriage. We cut the motivational wings of young women or bind their intellectual feet, all the time reassuring them that it is their natural destiny and all for their own good.

Women accustomed to expressing themselves freely could not be happy in such a relationship; it would be too confining and too punitive. We therefore "deform" the minds of girls in order to shape them for happiness in marriage. It may therefore be that married women say they are happy because they have been made sick.

"But what about love? Isn't that what marriage is all about?" the young bride cries. "None of what you say has even included the word!" True, love has been what marriage has been partially if not all about at least since the 17th century. Love is, in fact, so important to women that they are willing to pay an exorbitant price for it.

But the basic question is, does the satisfaction of these needs for love and companionship have to extort such excessive costs? Can marriage — for women — ever become more often for better than for worse?

REFERENCES

Broverman, Inge K., et al, "Sex-Role Stereotypes and Clinical Judgments of Mental Health." *Journal of Counseling and Clinical Psychology* 34 (February 1970).

Burr, Wesley R., "Satisfaction with Various Aspects of Marriage over the Life Cycle." *Journal of Marriage and the Family* 32 (February 1970).

Durkheim, Emile, *Suicide*. Trans. by J. A. Spaulding and George Simpson. New York: Free Press, 1951.

Glick, Paul C., "First Marriages and Remarriages." *American Sociological Review* 14 (December 1949).

Johnson, Winifred Burt, and Terman, Lewis M., "Personality Characteristics of Happily Married, Unhappily Married, and Divorced Persons." *Character and Personality* 3 (June 1935).

Klemer, Richard H., "Factors of Personality and Experience Which Differentiate Single from Married Women." *Marriage and Family Living* 16 (February 1954).

Knupfer, Genevieve; Clark, Walter; and Room, Robin, "The Mental Health of the Unmarried." *American Journal of Psychiatry* 122 (February 1966).

Locke, Harvey J., *Predicting Adjustment in Marriage: A Comparison of a Dovorced and Happily Married Group*. New York: Holt, 1951.

Maddison, David, "The Relevance of Conjugal Bereavement for Preventive Psychiatry." *British Journal of Medical Psychiatry* 41 (June 1968).

Martinson, Floyd M., "Ego Deficiency as a Factor in Marriage." *American Sociological Review* 20 (April 1955).

Marx, John, and Spray, S. Lee, "Marital Status and Occupational Success among Mental Health Professionals." *Journal of Marriage and the Family 32* (February 1970).

Odin, Melita H. "The Fulfillment of Promise: 40-Year Follow-up of the Terman Gifted Group." *General Psychology Monographs* 77 (1968).

Veroff, Joseph, and Feld, Sheila, *Marriage and Work in America*. New York: Van Nostrand-Reinhold, 1970.

Marriage
(Today's Choices)

JOAN COOK

Three decades ago, sociologist Pitirim Sorokin predicted glumly: "Divorces and separations will increase until any profound difference between socially sanctioned marriages and illicit sex-relationship disappears . . .The main sociocultural functions of the family will further decrease until the family becomes a mere incidental cohabitation of male and female, while the home will become an overnight parking place mainly for sex-relationship."

While the statistical picture is far from reassuring, there is considerable evidence that Sorokin's gloomy forecast is yet to be realized. Today, one in every four U.S. marriages ends in divorce. The rate is rising rapidly for marriages made in the past several years, and in some densely populated West Coast communities, it is running as high as 70 percent. At the same time, the birth rate has declined from 30.1 births per thousand in 1910 to 17.7 in 1969.

The question would seem to be less whether marriage will survive than whether it will survive in its present form. But whatever the eventual form, there is evidence that marriage and the family as a whole need help, ranging from sex education and universal day-care and health services to a less cumbersome judiciary system.

That modern love is less than perfect is attested to by the strictures of a seemingly endless stream of critics from Philip Wylie, the writer, to R.D. Laing, the Scottish psychiatrist. But there is much to suggest that its present situation is the result of a number of forces deeply rooted in the history of mankind.

Perhaps the most basic conflict, and one that affects both men and women, is the cultural norm that requires children to be sexless during their formative years, yet to become sexual in adult life. For society's sake, the child is taught to prohibit sexual feelings for the parents in favor of love and affection.

The Greeks approached the problem with a layer-cake solution. They had concubines for sex, companions for love and wives for housekeeping. With the advent of Christianity, a wave of asceticism broadened the gap between love and sex, and the distance was widened during the Victorian era. Today, puritan ideals of sex are still influential despite efforts to temper them.

As author Morton Hunt puts it in *The History of Love,* "In the first decade of life the boy and girl learn that love is good and sex is evil; in the second decade that love is still better, while sex has been slightly upgraded to the status of a forbidden fruit; and in the third decade that love is better than ever, while sex has suddenly become normal and healthful."

As a result, many people marry only to find that a genuinely satisfactory sexual adjustment eludes them — a fact that accounts for the plethora of psychiatrists, psychologists, marriage counselors and fortune tellers in a country that puts a premium on sex appeal and prides itself on sexual frankness. Although modern marriage is supposed to be an equal partnership, boys and girls still have considerably different social experiences. For most girls, the old notion of being both sexually desirable and discreet with favors before marriage still prevails, while the sexual adventures of boys are regarded with tolerance bordering on admiration. This contradiction, combined with inadequate sex education, can lead to astonishing ignorance on the part of women of how other women feel about sex.

Marriage counselors' files are replete with cases like the following: Sara N., 19, an attractive girl from Vermont, was concerned about her husband's desire for sex. "I think my husband must be oversexed," she told the counselor. "He wants to make love three, even four times a week."

The counselor reassured her that this was completely normal for a man her husband's age, adding that many women would be disappointed if their husbands didn't feel this way. Her reaction was one of complete incredulity.

"You mean there are actually women who want sex that often?" she asked in disbelief.

Female frigidity for physiological reasons is rare, but according to the records of the Margaret Sanger Research Bureau, findings that are supported by other investigators, about one out of four women is sexually unresponsive, with feelings ranging from disinterest to violent disgust.

Sex is not the only factor that affects the success of marriage today. Throughout most of Western history, which derived its values from the Church, from philosophers and from social traditions, society as a whole strongly supported marriage and the family. With the removal of traditional values in the 20th century, it is not surprising that modern marriage is subject to a number of new influences.

Sociologist Reuben Hill, among others, has chronicled the seven traditional functions of marriage (that is, the family): reproduction, protection and care of children, economic production of family goods and services, socialization of children, education of children, recreation, and affection-giving.

During the past century, Hill says, the economic, educational, recreational and socializing functions have been lost in varying degrees to industry, schools and government.

As a source of affection and reproduction, the family remains a social institution, but with the removal of the traditional supporting structure, the "marriage rests in the family and not the family in marriage," according to sociologist Edward Westermarck. The removal of all practical purposes beyond love leaves the family stability under severe strain.

Another factor that figures in current divorce rates is longevity. As man's life-span increases, so does the life of his marriage. Today's grandmother, freed from household chores by modern conveniences, is young and vigorous; she can look forward to 25 or 30 years of life.

"You know why my first marriage broke up?" a recently remarried woman in her forties candidly said. "We'd just been married too long. We knew each other so well we got bored."

Other marriages go to opposite extremes: some couples become so immersed in one another that their personalities are seemingly fused. As one observer commented. "People who have been married a long time begin to look alike. It isn't a matter of physical characteristics so much as mannerisms and habit patterns."

While such a relationship can be a rich one, it can also boomerang. A couple can become so dependent on one another that the death — or even prolonged absence — of one causes irrational panic and anxiety in the other.

In its isolation from traditional family patterns, marriage in the nuclear age is in danger of becoming ingrown, of romanticizing itself and its function.

According to the Scottish psycholoanalyst R. D. Laing, the "initial act of brutality against the average child is the mother's first kiss." Taking one step further Laing's objection to the helpless dependency of children on their parents — "even to having to accept affection" — Dr. David Cooper, a South African psychoanalyst, calls the nuclear family the "ultimately perfected form of nonmeeting." In his recent book *The Death of the Family,* Dr. Cooper demands its abolition.

Dr. Cooper, who is divorced, prefers communal living. By no means a new concept, the commune has an almost mystical attraction for those who are dissatisfied with the existing structure of the family or who are simply unable to cope with its multiple pressures.

Five years ago there were about 100 communes in the U.S. founded in the main by religious groups, Utopian socialists or conscientious objectors. Today there are about 3,000, a third of which are in rural settings. Most of the latter-day recruits to communal life are opting out of what they consider the crass materialism and hypocrisy of modern marriage, as well as its loneliness and confinement.

Life-styles within a commune range from the most primitive and naive grouping of young people attempting to wrest a living from the earth and to flee the urban-suburban sprawl, to sophisticated outposts such as the one at Lama, 18 miles north of Taos, New Mexico.

"We work together — we collectively grow and distribute the crops — but we go back to our individual nests at night." says 28-year-old

Satya De La Manitov, who recently moved from a tepee into a still unfinished A-frame house that cost him $1,500 and took him 12 months to build.

Like De La Manitov, most couples at the Lama commune are married, are in their late twenties, have children and own their own homes. They respect property rights and deeply believe in honest toil. Although the concept of sexual freedom has a few followers at Lama, it plays a minor role. "Were it not for their long hair, predilection for 'grass' and rejection of the American political system, Lama residents could pass for solid, middle-class citizens," said a news reporter.

The City Commune

Although most people tend to identify communes with young people and a country setting, the majority of them in fact are in cities and attract more than a few middle-class adults.

A 30-year-old New York lawyer and his wife, a sculptress, found the answer to their frustrations in a city commune.

"Neither of us have any relatives within 3,000 miles," the lawyer explains. "Between my work and my wife's sculpting, we were spending a fortune on baby-sitters and spending all our spare time doing the laundry and cleaning."

The lawyer, his wife and their three children moved into an old brownstone with five other families in a similar position. They converted the house into a comfortable city commune with private apartments that open in on one another and a communal nursery, playroom and library. Work is pooled, with a different couple taking on cooking each week and all the residents sharing the child care.

"Since we've been living here my husband sees more of the children," one wife observed. "We both have more time to do the things we want to do."

Not all such arrangements work out so smoothly. One young dropout from a middle-class background found, to his astonishment, that living in a commune did not, of itself, breed love and concern for others.

"I met people who didn't have the first notion of what consideration means," he said wryly. "It taught me that you can't judge a man by the length of his hair — short or long."

Disillusionment with current lifestyles has led some to seek still other alternatives. They range from *ménage à trois* (a set-up more likely to include two women and a man than the other way round) to four-person marriages.

In Chicago, Shirley, 26, an accountant, lives with Michael, 29, a divorced salesman, and Laura, 30, a commercial artist, in a small but comfortable apartment. Their "arrangement" has excited no interest in the neighborhood.

"We get along just fine," Shirley says comfortably. "We are all three independent and still interdependent. There may be a better way, but so far that is the best there is."

"Look, it's an experiment," Michael explains. "So far, everything's great. I don't want to be tied down, but I don't want to be alone either, and Laura and Shirley feel the same way."

FOUR-PERSON MARRIAGES

In Pegram, Tennessee, a "family" of 270 persons established its own commune; the family includes 14 four-person marriages. Family members talk enthusiastically of the sharing of problems and the greater stability in a four-way relationship, an arrangement that sufficiently aroused the interest of the local Methodist Women's Club to move them to request a speaker from the group.

"They were very friendly and interested and even intuitive into the possibilities of larger marriages," said Ina May, who forms a four-person marriage with Stephen, Michael and Margaret (the group does not use last names).

Members of the family, many of them former professionals and most of them college educated, have pooled their resources — $40 here, $900 there, all apparently given freely and according to the individual's resources — and amassed about $50,000, with which they plan to buy property that will provide them with a permanent home.

In the last six months 10 children have been born. Each was assisted into the world by Margaret, with the help of a Mexican Rural Midwives' Handbook. This brings the total number of youngsters 12 years old or younger in the family to 42. Men and women share responsibility for the children's welfare in the community. On a recent workday, for example, women taught the children to make bread, while the men cleared rocks and built a wooden bridge over a rushing stream.

Most members of the Pegram family come from East and West Coast cities, but a few have farm backgrounds. Some have picked up a knowledge of camping and farming. There is no medical experience among them — except for Margaret's midwifing — but they say they are in fine health because they eat vegetables and nuts and avoid meat.

Despite the fact that money is pooled and labor shared, the bulk of the decision-making is done by men, less because the women do not have a voice than because they seldom use it. The women seem content to let the men handle the major responsibilities.

As one of the male members bluntly put it, "We make the decisions during the day; the girls make the decisions when the lights go out."

Working on another front to change the present structure of marriage is Women's Liberation. In the U.S., women account for 40 percent of the country's entire working force.

Margaret Benston, a Women's Liberation theoretician, places the blame for the "exploitation" of women directly on the family. Since women's work in the home is not paid for, she asserts, society looks on it as valueless. Under existing conditions, women who work outside the home have two jobs, not one. Ms. Benston believes that women will not be free until all the housework is bought, like any other service. That way, any woman can earn a salary — either for housework or for her work away from home. Innovations such as communal kitchens and child-care centers will make it easier for women to work away from home.

Homosexuals, men and women, have developed a new militancy and are increasingly acknowledging their status without apology. In recent months hundreds of homosexuals have banded together to form at least a dozen predominantly homosexual church congregations in major American cities — and many homosexuals who have chosen to stay within "Establishment" churches have escalated their demands.

"The church has been glad to benefit from the labors of gay hymn writers, gay saints, gay artisans and gay contributors," said the Reverend Robert W. Wood, a United Church of Christ pastor from Newark, N.J., at the National Conference on Religion and the Homosexual in New York. "Now let it recognize their participation with thanksgiving and equal treatment."

Elsewhere, independent groups have started their own homosexual churches to serve clear-cut needs, including that for a place where homosexuals can relate to each other in social situations without the high pressure that prevails in traditional meeting spots such as gay bars.

THE NEW MARRIAGES

In the new churches, homosexual "marriages" are solemnized. Many clergymen shy away from such words as "marrying," preferring terms like "blessing a relationship." Most agree with the Reverend Robert Clement, founder of the Church of the Beloved Disciple in Manhattan, that "it is important to give sacramental acknowledgement of the pledge and covenant between two people who love each other."

Active in both the Gay Liberation and the Women's Liberation movement are lesbian groups and their supporters, such as the National Organization for Women, Radicalesbians, Daughters of Bilitis, Columbia Women's Liberation and New York Radical Feminists.

Not all lesbians agree. According to a report in *The New York Times Magazine,* Mrs. Betty J. of suburban Larchmont, N.Y., a nurse of 45 with two adolescent sons ("They both like girls"), has been a lesbian since she was a teenager.

"I really don't care for the women's lib business," she said recently before a Daughters of Bilitis meeting. "I think they should stay on their side and take care of their day care centers. I mean, either you're a lesbian or you're not."

Mrs. J. was divorced from her husband 10 years ago, she said, "because I was never completely happy — I just kept thinking of women." Whenever she attends D.O.B. meetings, she tells her sons she is going to the theater or shopping at Bloomingdale's.

Some sociologists feel that this reshaping of the Garden of Eden is all to the good. Monogamy is not a natural pattern for man or any other mammal, they maintain.

Of 185 societies analyzed in the Human Relations Area Files at Yale University, only about five percent were monogamous to the extent of disallowing or disapproving all outside sexual activity for males.

Monogamy, some scholars feel, is unnatural, difficult and much too costly. A society that insists on it fosters hypocrisy, guilt, unhappiness and divorce, they believe.

Similarly, there are two schools of thought *vis á vis* infidelity. One is that infidelity sets up hostile barriers, even if the other partner is unaware of it, and closes off a part of the person to his mate. Dr. Abraham Stone reported that in 30 years of marriage counseling he found infidelity to be almost never innocuous, but practically always a cause of concealment, guilt and impairment of the marriage relationship.

The other side of the coin is that, despite its obvious risks, infidelity may keep a shaky marriage going, assuming that such a marriage is, for some reason, desirable.

Contrary to popular opinion, men in the lower economic and education groups are less apt to link sex to tender and affectionate relationships and are far more likely to indulge in extramarital affairs than men of higher education and economic status, according to the Kinsey studies. The divorce rate is correspondingly higher among the lower economic classes than among the neurotic, success-flayed middle class, according to national census data. This makes marriage difficult for minority groups in general, and for the black community in particular.

RENEWABLE CONTRACTS

Some experts openly predict a greater emphasis on a renewable marriage contract instead of one that is binding for life. Listen to psychiatrist Thomas P. Malone:

"A lot of people nowadays — and not just women's lib people — think it is idiotic to put two people together at the age of twenty and expect them to be happy for fifty years. What we may be talking about is a three-year contract. Or you may contract with somebody to have children and raise them till they're, say, sixteen."

Dr. Malone thinks "we'll see a greater acceptance of trial marriage in some form; that is to say, where there are limited responsibilities incurred between two people if they begin living together."

Last March, two Maryland state legislators — both women — attempted to introduce a bill that would make marriage a three-year contract, with an option to renew by the mutual consent of both partners. Their attempt was defeated, but they say they will try again.

Despite the many problems plaguing it and the prophets of doom gainsaying it, marriage is still in style. With all its tensions and inner conflicts, it is more popular than ever: there were 2,146,000 marriages in America in 1969, almost equaling the all-time high of 1946.

A larger proportion of adults marry today than did at the turn of the century, and even the young — for all that is said about sexual freedom and experimentation — are marrying in numbers comparable to those of a generation ago. Even those who subsequently divorce are in favor of marriage, for nearly six out of seven remarry. And even the demands of homosexuals for legal marriages can be viewed as a desire for an enduring love relationship.

Different people seek and find different ways of coping with an environment that is increasingly hostile. That so many continue to do so within the framework of marriage clearly demonstrates that this institution, at least, is here to stay.

Communes, Group Marriage, and the Upper-Middle Class

JAMES W. RAMEY

Most current articles and discussions about communes and group marriage begin with the assumption that these phenomena are generally associated with youthful dropouts from society, or religious fanatics. There would appear to be, however, a much more significant group, larely made up of upper-middle class, thoughtful, successful, committed individuals, that is also involved in or exploring the possibility of setting up communes or group marriages. There are at least three reasons why this movement is relatively unknown. First, sensational reporting sells newspapers, and "dropouts" in colorful clothing and unwashed beards tilling the soil are sensational. Second, most of us would prefer to think of such unusual life styles as aberrant or deviate practices that would only be associated with inexperienced disaffected youth, or religious "kooks." Finally, the people who set up communes or group marriages *without* dropping out of society take great care to remain unnoticed by their neighbors and associates.

In this report on almost three years' of activity among a sample of eighty couples, *both* husbands and wives are from the two top occupational classifications, that is, they are almost all in academic, professional, or managerial positions, if they are employed at all. These individuals believe that a commune or group marriage might provide a framework in which they could do better what they are already doing well. In order to function optimally within the present social and economic structure, they seek to organize family units on a more complex basis than the nuclear family structure can accommodate.

What is a commune? Structure and modus operandi among communes can differ to such a degree that the following working definition is suggested:

> When individuals agree to make life commitments as members of one particular group, rather than through many different groups, they *may* constitute a commune. The number of common commitments will vary from commune to commune, the critical number having been reached at the point at which the group sees itself as a commune, rather than at some absolute number.

What, then, is a group marriage? The critical factor in group marriage is that *each* of the three or more participants considers himself to be married to at least two other members of the group. Actually, in today's world we should say "pair-bonded" instead of married since some pair-bonded couples may not be legally married. Constantine (1971) has coined the term "multilateral marriage" as a substitute for group marriage since, according to him, group marriage has traditionally involved two pairs, and thus the term would not accommodate a triad group. I prefer to retain the more familiar term, which I believe is self-explanatory, whereas multilateral marriage is not.

This paper concerns both group marriage *and* "evolutionary" communes because the eighty couples in the study were curious about both forms of complex living. Although only eighteen of these couples had any previous experience with group marriage or communal living, they were all initally attracted to the group by advertisements in *Saturday Review, New York Review of Books,* and similar places, inviting couples interested in exploring the pros and cons of various forms of expanded family to meet with the group. The few couples who initiated this activity were open-minded as to the degree of complexity they were willing to consider, ranging from intimate friendship to group marriage, but they were not willing to accept everyone who answered their ad.

They devised a questionnaire as a preliminary screening device which was to be answered by respondents, along with a short essay indicating why they wanted to join the group. The avowed purpose of this screening was to eliminate "swingers" and others whose interest was considered "not serious." Upon receipt of the questionnaire and essay, couples deemed tentatively acceptable were interviewed by telephone and a decision was made to either suggest that they forget about this group or invite them to an orientation session. In our three-year follow-up study, we hope to interview the fifty-five couples who were not invited to join the group as well as the eighty couples who "passed" to see if we can find any real differences between the "accepted" and "rejected."

We have reported elsewhere (Ramey, 1972) the logarithmic increase in the degree of complexity in relationships as one moves from monogamous dyadic marriage through open marriage, intimate friendship, and communal living, to group marriage. It should be recognized that the degree of intensity also increases as one moves up this scale in the complexity of marriage alternatives. Intensity might be called one of the distinguishing characteristics of the subjects of this report. In addition to ability to deal with more complex relationships there must be willingness to take on such a task.

In dyadic marriage the commitment is to the individual. Kanter (1968) calls this cathectic commitment. I would call it "willingness to accept unlimited liability for." A commune is held together by a different kind of commitment, a group commitment rather than commitment to an individual. A group marriage combines these different types of commitment. In Kanter's terms, the addition of cognitive and evaluative commitment to cathectic commitment.

The subjects of this study saw these differences in concrete terms. They were aware that dyadic marriage has become institutionalized in our society and internalized by each of us as we grow up, so that the decisions facing a newly married couple are relatively minor ones (how many children?) within a well-defined formal structure. No such formal structure exists for intimate friendship, communes, or group marriage, however. The participants must evolve their own structure.

This group, then, expended considerable energies on working through cognitive commitment (was the group making sufficient progress to justify continuing to invest energy that could be directed elsewhere?) and evaluative commitment (were the perceived goals and aims of the group worthy of continued support?). These two types of commitment have long since been institutionalized for dyadic marriage.

It was not necessarily the intent of these eighty couples to form communes or group marriages, although several did result from their activities. They seemed more intent on "hashing out" the actual ground rules and decision structure required for setting up alternatives to marriage at varying levels of complexity. Some couples were content to stop at the level of developing intimate friendships. Others were willing to take the additional step of adding propinquity to this relationship and forming some kind of "commune," while a few found other couples with whom they were willing to take the final step of cathectic commitment, *i.e.,* actually establishing multiple pair-bonds. Many couples found that they were either uncomfortable with the level of complexity required or "were still looking for the right people" with whom to become involved in some type of relationship more complex than dyadic marriage.

This paper indicates the kind of people involved in this activity, explicates the concerns that led them to this action, and reports the kinds of problems they discussed and the various activities in which they engaged as a part of the exploration process. Both communes and group marriages have emerged from this group and it is expected that others will emerge. This paper is based on the initial questionnaires, anecdotal information, correspondence files, and observation of group activities.

A few portions of the demographic data will be presented in comparative fashion, contrasting the eighteen couples who have actually lived or are living in communes or group marriages with the sixty-two couples who have expressed active interest in doing so, although it should be understood that the samples are so small that statistical significance cannot be attached to the numbers. For the sake of brevity, the 18 experienced couples will be called Doers and the 62 inexperienced couples will be called Talkers.

TABLE 1
AGE OF PARTICIPANTS

	Talkers		Doers	
	Male	Female	Male	Female
Youngest	21	21	24	23
First Quartile	28	26	29	26
Median	33	28.5	33.5	28
Third Quartile	42	38	38	37.5
Oldest	56	55	52	47
Mean	35.2	30.7	34.7	29.8
SD	8.66	6.48	3.89	3.87

Only six couples in the total sample live *outside* a major metropolitan area. New York City, Boston, and Philadelphia metropolitan areas together account for 63 per cent of the Talkers and 79 per cent of the Doers. The age range in the two groups is indicated in Table 1.

Most of these couples have at least one child, and the age ranges of the children in the two groups are comparable. Over two-thirds of each group have at least one child and 50 per cent have at least two, with comparable figures for three, four, and five, and insignificantly small numbers above five.

Standard Census Bureau Occupational Classification categories were collapsed together to arrive at the distribution shown in Table 2. The national percentage distribution is included for comparative purposes. An additional category has been added to account for students, retired individuals, and housewives. The only statistically significant difference between the two groups shows up in this Table, *i. e.*, the

TABLE 2

OCCUPATIONAL CLASSIFICATION

	Males			Females		
Classification	U.S.	Talkers	Doers	U.S.	Talkers	Doers
	%	%	%	%	%	%
Professional, Scientific, and kindred workers	11.9	72.4	81.3	13.0	44.1	61.1
Managers, Officials, Proprietors, etc.	13.2	19.0	18.7	4.4	6.8	22.2
Clerical, Sales, and kindred workers	13.0	1.7	——	38.7	6.8	——
Craftsmen, Foremen, and Skilled workers	19.0	1.7	——	1.1	——	——
Operatives, Services, Farmers, and Laborers	42.9	——	——	42.8	——	——
Graduate Students, Retired, and Housewives.	——	5.2	——	——	42.3	16.7

percentage of housewives in the two groups is significant at the .05 level.

Academic level is in line with occupational classification. About 90 per cent of the men and 42 per cent of the women have completed four or more years of college and 22 per cent of the men and 9 per cent of the women hold the Ph.D.

The original impetus for this group came from several couples who were curious to see if there were others who shared their interest in complex marriage. They decided to run the aforementioned ad in *Saturday Review* and to install an unlisted phone for receiving calls from prospective members. The couple who agreed to answer the phone also accepted the responsibility for maintaining correspondence files and doing much of the "secretarial" work. At first the entire group screened prospects, but once general criteria had been established, this task was turned over to a volunteer committee. The questionnaire used for initial screening is reproduced in Table 3, with the composite answers of the eighty couples. The original intent of these questions was said to be to indicate the degree of "openness" in the marriages of applicants to the group. The answers to questions two and twelve suggest that this group was unusual along the sexual dimension as well as in other ways previously indicated.

TABLE 3

GROUP-DESIGNED QUESTIONNAIRE FOR APPLICANTS*

	Talkers		Doers	
Question	YES	NO	YES	NO
	%	%	%	%
We have formed close emotional ties with other families in the past.	69	31	83	17
We have formed close ties with other families that involved sexual intimacy.	47	53	72	28
Our ideal is to link up closely with other families, each retaining its own home & privacy but with much emotional sharing.	90	10	81	19
Our ideal is to form a commune.	43	57	53	47
Our ideal is to form a group marriage.	44	56	53	47
We've had experience in a commune or group marriage.	—	100	100	—
We have a professional background in the behavioral science.	50	50	67	33
We have participated in therapy, group therapy, sensitivity training, or encounter groups.	69	31	83	17
Children require firmness and consistency to guide them until they can determine their own attitudes.	71	29	81	19
Children should be given as much freedom as possible so long as they don't harm themselves or inconvenience others.	100	—	100	—
We take care that our children don't observe us in a sexual situation.	50	50	43	57
We would expect to be sexually free with any couple with whom we related really well.	76	24	88	12
We can enjoy sex with others without requiring an emotional involvement.	37	63	28	72

*Composite answers for the eighty couples in the study.

What concerns led these couples to spend as many as three nights a week in the various activities of this group? Predictably, certain problems weighed more heavily for the women, others for their husbands, while a few seemed to be of equal concern to both. I have distilled these basic issues from many hours of interviews, discussions, and reading anecdotal records and correspondence.

Wives seemed more concerned about (1) the sense of isolation that comes with raising children, (2) overdependence on the husband for adult contact, and (3) less than optimal development and use of their talents and training.

The first problem occurs over a surprisingly large age span. Many wives feel it even more severely because they waited until their late twenties to start families. Leaving budding careers made them feel even more isolated by the children. These families move more often than the general population. They seldom have a group of ready-made relatives and friends to fall back on. Many who live in the city are afraid to venture out at all unless absolutely necessary. Those who live in the suburbs complain of a lack of any real community of interest with their neighbors, apart from the children, and even this is lacking unless the children are in the same age group.

Interwoven with the first problem is the tendency toward overdependence on the husband for adult contact. Without support from kinship, friendship, and neighbor groups, husband and wife share isolation in the home, and, as Slater (1968) has put it, they must be lovers, friends, and mutual therapists. What with moving every couple of years, these couples do not have time to develop many friends. The husband satisfies his need for outside contact at the office, but the wife who is not employed outside the home faces a barren prospect indeed. Not that she has no neighbors. She may have many acquaintances but one looks for one's friends among peers, and neighbors frequently seem not to provide peers from whom to choose.

Most of the women in this sample are college educated and trained in a career specialty, but a substantial minority have not had the opportunity to develop a career that optimally utilizes this training. Either they have dropped out of the job market while the children are small or they have been forced to make willy-nilly job changes when their husband's career moves the family to a new location. Others have been unable to make *any* use of their training and ability because their families have been so large as to require their full-time presence in the home.

The men are particularly concerned about two problems that are probably universal among men in our society. They seek a means of freeing themselves from financial insecurity and the rat-race. They also would like to achieve higher living standards.

The first of these concerns is often linked to the need of the wife to pursue her career goals. What do you do when a career opportunity for the husband necessitates a move to Oshkosh, Wisconsin, which will blast the wife's career? Family financial security may be an overwhelming factor in the decision, as when the husband's current job is being phased out. Will the family's financial resources permit them to stay put while he tries to match the Oshkosh offer locally? For many upper-middle-class families the answer is "Not for very long!" Aside from this kind of bind, most males must constantly evaluate and re-evaluate the nature of "opportunity." Is it fair to themselves and to their families to turn down an opportunity to move up the career ladder? Will the career be blighted if the "opportunity" is turned down? How many pounds of flesh does one owe to Mammon (or to increasing family income) anyway?

The second male concern is related to the first. Although they explore the idea cautiously, the notion of sharing at least some capital expenditures, perhaps a summer home or a houseboat or hobby equipment, is an appealing partial solution to the problem of raising the family standard of living — one that men are as eager to explore as the problem of increasing financial security. Not only is it economically sound, if done with the proper safeguards, it is even ecologically desirable to conserve natural resources (this sounds "tongue-in-cheek" but has been a matter of serious discussion in the framework of having to start somewhere, so why not where it is more personally rewarding). While initially concerned about stretching family resources, many of these men have gone on to realize that an enlarged family with multiple incomes and reduced expenses would be very advantageous insofar as all family economic functions in our quasi-capitalistic society are concerned.

As long as the basic economic unit is a nuclear family that must survive on one or at the most two adult incomes, the family is hard put just to stay even with the ever-mounting cost of living. More and more families are tempting bankruptcy just putting their children through college, now that the cost of a year of college is ranging as high as $5,000 with no end in sight. Setting aside money for investment seems far removed from the reality of trying to break even. The opportunities to share in the joys of capitalism are real enough — they abound at every turn — but without a stake they are unattainable. Conversations about pooling resources to buy big ticket or luxury items almost invariably shift to consideration of the competitive advantages, within our societal structure, of a commune or group marriage. Setting up a rainy day fund to weather a period of unemployment or a Clifford trust for educating the kids are exciting possibilities, but they pale in the wake of the tax and income-producing advantages of, for example, incorporating a group marriage or a small commune as a subchapter S corporation, or using the condominium approach in order to swing the financing of an apartment building.

Childrearing and training are a major concern for both parents and nonparents among our sample. There is common concern for providing the growing child with a variety of adult relationships. Both the commune and group marriage seem to promise the kind of flexibility that would not only provide more adult models, but provide a better male/female mix since there would presumably be more frequent male presence in the home. There is also an expressed need to raise children among adults with compatible life styles so that the children will feel more secure with respect to differences in the life style of their own family and their friends' families, especially after they reach school age. Many respondents are vitally interested in the training of the new generation, whether they have children of their own or not. They hope to establish free schools or to at least explore the possibility of supplementary training.

A major concern of these couples is freedom to include sexual intimacy among the joys of friendship when appropriate. Forty-one couples have formed ties with other families that included sexual intimacy and indicate that they would expect to be sexually free with any couple with whom they related really well. Although the other 39 couples in the sample have not yet had such experience, only 14 of these couples indicated that they would *not* expect to be sexually free with any couple with whom they related really well. One out of three couples in the first group indicated that they also could enjoy casual sexual contacts. Only one out of five couples in the second group so indicated.

This desire to be free to establish intimate friendships appears to reflect both the need to broaden and deepen adult contact outside the dyadic marriage and the belief that such activity measurably strengthens the couple's own marriage. As noted above, there can be little doubt that the stress here is on person-to-person rather than genital-to-genital relationships. These individuals simply do not want to exclude the possibility of intimacy as a part of friendship where and when appropriate. They deny emphatically that intimate friendship is another term for swinging and this distinction would seem to be substantiated by their responses with regard to casual sexual contacts. As I have noted elsewhere (Ramey, 1972), there is a well-developed transitional pattern between swinging with minimal emotional involvement and "matured swinging groups," which Stoller (1970) calls "intimate family networks." I believe the term "intimate friendship" delineates this type of group or network in a more meaningful way, because it applies equally well to friendship with a single individual or couple and such a friendship should not be excluded by terminology from our understanding of the kind of relationship we are discussing, *i.e.*, one in which the emphasis is on the friendship rather than on the intimacy.

The final major theme that brings these couples together is a shared concern for what is happening. In every age there are a few individuals, often academic or professional people, at the growing edge of society, questioning, examining new social issues before most people know they are issues, looking for new ways to maximize their potential, opportunities, and pleasure within current social structures. Many people seem to believe that youth has a corner on the market of challenging the accepted responses to problems of living and that the older generation simply follows where youth leads. History tells us otherwise. The couples in this sample are among the "life style leaders" of today. By way of example, while social scientists are just now discussing seriously the possibilities inherent in consensual extramarital and comarital relationships, a preponderance of these eighty couples have already been involved in intimate friendships, some of them for over two decades, or since the new generation was in rompers!

How are these couples approaching the task of seriously considering group marriage or communal living? The array of interaction has covered a wide range of activities. Nearly every day at least one group was meeting and on weekends there were usually several, such as regular Saturday afternoon children's activities, a music group, an ongoing encounter group, or the meeting for newcomers.

This latter activity is especially noteworthy because it set the tone for newcomer participation in other activities. Although there was no formal structure or organization among these couples (individuals simply initiated activities that interested them), several individuals volunteered to screen newcomers for the group. First the new couple sent in the questionnaire form on which the screening committee passed judgment. Assuming the new family was found acceptable, they were invited to an orientation meeting, where the emphasis was on drawing out the newcomers, ascertaining their interests more specifically, and telling them about the various study groups, experimental groups, discussion groups and other activities currently under way, so that they might find their way into the various activities that interested them most. These initial sessions with newcomers achieved a level of candor seldom encountered in any but old established friendships. When asked about this, newcomers cited both their anticipation, based on the screening they had survived, and the emphasis at the meeting on openness, feedback, acceptance of differences in perception and opinion, and willingness to dispense with taboo subjects. This atmosphere of permissiveness and understanding in which feelings and attitudes could be freely and nonjudgmentally expressed and in which males and females tended to be treated as peers appeared to be characteristic of all of the activities of these eighty couples.

Some of their activities involved only a few intensely interested people while a few, such as family day outings, involved almost the entire group. A few activities were almost exclusively female while a few attracted no wives, but most tended to be couple projects. Some discussions or activities were short-lived, for example, putting together a complete listing of all families in the group, with addresses, phone numbers, and a 100-word statement of their interests. The first time this was attempted it took six weeks or so and two or three people were involved in the project. When it was attempted a second time, after the first listing was out of date, there wasn't enough interest among the group as a whole to get the project off the ground, even though several people were willing to do the work.

Some activities were longer-term in nature. Study groups tackled a number of potential projects, for example, setting up a free school, converting a brownstone, running encounter groups, discussing the ins and outs of a subchapter S corporation, setting up a babysitting co-op, building a boat, food co-ops, investment pools, condominiums, building co-ops, buying co-ops, nonprofit corporation and foundation structure, art and drama groups for the kids, or setting up a home-exchange program.

One of several experimental projects centered around a three-couple group marriage that was the focus of a discussion group that provided a sounding board for the problems of the group marriage, which in turn was the guinea pig for the group. This group met as often as the group marriage felt the need, and the discussion group survived the group marriage, which broke up after six months. The feedback was invaluable for all members of the group as well as for the six participants in the group marriage, who at this writing still maintain an intimate friendship circle, but do not feel ready to make a second attempt at establishing a group marriage.

While it is clearly understood by all members of the sample that their involvement in discussions and activities associated with determining just what their interest might be in group marriage and communes is *not* a commitment to actually undertake living in a commune or group marriage, it is nevertheless of interest to those investigating this area that three group marriages and several communes have developed as off-shoots from this group of eighty families so far, and others may reasonably be expected to develop.

Other experimental projects have included joint vacations, renting summer property together, and weekend living together. Another experimental activity was the partial exchange of predominantly male and female family roles between husband and wife or between several adults during periods of experimental living together.

One of the important ongoing discussion themes was the working through of expectations that each couple brings to any consideration of communal living or group marriage, going through the give-and-take process of shaping the nature of the commitments involved and determining the kinds of decision making and ground rules that would be acceptable. This is a difficult but rewarding task and one that inevitably gives rise to splinter groups as like-minded couples find each other.

A representative list of typical problem areas discussed will indicate the complexity of this undertaking. This list is *not* definitive, nor are the decision areas listed in order of importance, since rank order depended on who was involved in the discussion. Those primarily interested in group marriage had to consider many more personal issues dealing with the nature of marital interaction, in addition to these more general questions. Most groups were concerned about decision-making procedures, group goals, ground rules, prohibitions, intra- and extra-group sexual relationships, privacy, division of labor, role relationships, careers, relationship with outsiders, degree of visibility, legal jeopardy, dissolution of the group, personal responsibilities outside the group (such as parental support), geographic location, type of shelter, children, childrearing practices, education of children, group member career education, taxes, pooling assets, income, legal structure, trial period, investment policy, sequential steps in establishing the group, and prerequisites for membership.

One of the impressive aspects of this group is its lack of formal organization. In the beginning a decision was apparently made to charge a $3.00 minimum application fee (a larger donation was acceptable) and to charge a $3.00 refreshment and financing fee to each couple attending any meeting of the group. This custom was very informally observed. Sometimes the host at a particular meeting would waive the fee and at other times some couples might throw an extra twenty-dollar bill in the pot. In this manner the group was able to finance an occasional newsletter, a membership register which involved a 100-word description of each member family, frequent mailings of the "calendar" of coming meetings, and extensive correspondence with individuals, groups, organizations, and publishers interested in communes and group marriage.

The typical meeting would be hosted by a couple interested in a particular group activity or discussion topic on a rotating basis, although some activities were always associated with a particular couple and place. The convention was to notify the hostess at least 48 hours ahead of time of intent to attend. Several different couples acted as clearinghouses for certain activities. They could always be called for the next dates, times, and locations of a particular activity. Except for family activities, there were few times when the entire group was involved in a specific meeting. Groups tended to limit themselves to a number small enough to involve all those who wished to become involved, generally about four to ten couples. Larger groups soon split up in order to achieve greater participation. Each group acted autonomously and sometimes it was impossible to decide who was the leader of a given group. Some groups operated by consensus, others voted, and a few appeared to simply acquiesce to the decisions of one or two individuals within the group. Consensus was far and away the most common means of reaching decisions when decisions were required. The second most frequent pattern was delegation to one couple who were trusted to understand the "sense" of the group and act accordingly.

One of the anomalies of the group was its inability to handle single-parent families or single adults. Since the avowed purpose of the group was to explore the possibilities for building complex family relationships with deliberately chosen members to "replace" the extended family few, if any, of these couples had personally experienced, one could reasonably expect that single-parent families and selected single adults would have been welcomed. To the contrary, such individuals were systematically and almost invariably turned down by the screening committee. The weeding out was not 100 per cent however. Occasionally a single female or a female single-parent family was admitted to the group. No single males or single-parent (male) families were ever admitted. The reasons for the exceptions could not be satisfactorily ascertained, but the reason for the exclusions appeared to be fear of their "unsettling" influence.

In some cases extensive correspondence and/or phone conversation with one of these applicants would transpire before the decision was finally reached. Discussion with both the screening committee and the accepted singles failed to elicit the reasons why some were accepted and others rejected. This remains an area in which the group has not reached consensus, and as long as a large minority feel threatened by the possibility that singles pose some sort of "take-over" or "free-loader" threat, the policy is unlikely to change.

The implementation of decisions by various activity groups within the total sample depended on both the level of interest and the ingenuity of the individuals involved. The same individuals could be observed behaving very differently depending on the group one was observing. One group becoming concerned about the personal qualities regarded as essential for self and others in a group marriage or commune, decided to take a poll. They circulated a questionnaire to all members who wished to participate (about forty couples), with the profile shown in Figure 1.

FIGURE 1.

GROUP PROFILE: QUALITIES VALUED IN SELF AND OTHERS

N=40

PERSONAL QUALITIES	NOT IMPORTANT	SLIGHTLY IMPORTANT	FAIRLY IMPORTANT	EXTREMELY IMPORTANT	ESSENTIAL
Financially secure					
Neat appearance					
Good looks					
Good Education					
"Grooviness"					
Artistic appreciation					
Happily married					
Good conversationalist					
Sense of humor					
Intelligence					
Capacity for feeling					
Frankness in relationships					

Solid line = Others   Dashed line = Self

This figure suggests value differences as well as differences in standards set for Self and Others. In the main, the highest values are placed on internal, or "feeling" qualities rather than on such external factors as education or appearance. The fact that in every instance these couples set higher standards for Self than for Others is consistent with Self-Other reports in a number of other studies, *e.g.,* Ramey (1958). There appears to be a consistent tendency to set "ideal" standards for Self while appraising Others in more realistic terms. Birkman, Ward, and the present author, working with executives in 1952, found that under stress, the individual was likely to revert to the type of behavior he predicted for Others, even though under normal circumstances he made every effort to maintain his "ideal" pattern. We believe "Other" to be an expression of minimum role norms and expectations, whereas standards for "Self" represent optimum behavior.

One other example of group decision leading to action should suffice. A small splinter group consisting of three couples, two with small children and one with grown children, and a single female with teenage children, were intensely interested in pooling resources and setting up a commune in an urban setting for the purpose of owning and operating a free school. As the nucleus of an action group, they took the initial step of jointly renting a summer residence together, so that they could actually share living quarters on an experimental basis. Next they began a systematic survey of private schools in the metropolitan area that might be available for purchase, since they reasoned that it was more realistic and simpler to start with an existing school than to start from scratch. They located several schools that could be purchased for approximately $250,000 and began preparing budget projections and studies of the relationship of type of curriculum to expense, enrollment projections, etc. They also began expanding the group on a carefully selective basis, taking into account the skills that would be needed as well as the simple desire of other couples to become involved. At each step of this process the group acted as a committee of the whole with respect to major decisions but delegated many decision functions to individuals within the group who had special competencies in the relevant decision area.

A major asset of the transactional process among these eighty couples was the fluidity of the group. The fact that it was loose-knit led to an ebb and flow of interaction patterns that was definitely enhanced by input from outside contacts of the member couples. Some were involved in various activities of the group for the entire three-year period. Some moved in and out depending on their interests, and what was happening at a given time. Others were involved only long enough to find like-minded people with whom they then entered into a communal or group marriage arrangement at a distant location, so that their further interaction became spasmodic.

The planned follow-up study should provide some interesting insights with respect to changes in attitude, interest, and life style among these seekers of more complex forms of interrelationship than are possible within the confines of monogamous dyadic marriage.

REFERENCES

Constantine, Larry and Joan Constantine. 1971, "Multilateral marriage: alternate family structure in practice." In Robert H. Rimmer, (ed.), *You and I Searching for Tommorow.* New York: New American Library.

Kanter, Rosabeth M. 1968, "Commitment and social organization: a study of commitment mechanisms in utopian communities." *American Sociological Review* 33 (August).

Ramey, James W. 1958, "The relationship of peer group rating to certain individual perceptions of personality." *Journal of Experimental Education* 27 (Spring). 1972, "Emerging patterns of behavior in marriage: deviations or innovations? *Journal OEEAX Research* 8 (February).

Slater, Philip E. 1968, "Some social consequences of temporary systems." In W.G. Bennis and P.E. Slager, *The Temporary Society.* New York: Harper and Row.

Stroller, Frederick H. 1970, "The intimate network of families as a new structure." In Herbert Otto (ed.), *The Family in Search of a Future.* New York: Appleton-Century-Crofts.

Open Marriage:
A Synergic Model

NENA O'NEILL
GEORGE O'NEILL

In the wake of increasing dissatisfaction with the prevailing pattern of traditional monogamous marriage, a number of alternative marriage styles have begun to emerge. These experimentations vary from those involving more than three persons in the basic pattern and include group marriage, communal life styles, and polygamous patterns (more often triadic, and more often polygynous rather than polyandrous) to modifications in the basic one-to-one monogamous configuration. This last group may be divided into those which are nonmarriage relationships (still monogamous but extra-legal) and those which represent innovations, changes, deletions, and additions to the standard expectations for those legally married. These modifications may include such various items as separate domiciles, extramarital sexual relations in group or partner-exchange contexts, or reversal of traditional role patterns; i.e., woman provides, man housekeeps. None of these patterns are particularly new in transcultural contexts since all have occurred elsewhere in other societies at one time or another. However, their proliferation and the motives which have impelled men and women in our society to increasingly seek innovations in our marriage style deserve closer scrutiny.

It is not enough to say that society is pluralistic and that these alternate patterns for marriage have appeared in response to the changes in our society and the development of different life styles. Even though one can foresee a future in which there is a range of marriage patterns to choose from, the questions still remain: Why have so many experimental forms appeared? And more important, what are the personal motivations for seeking these innovative styles? Compendiums of sociological explanations seemed somehow to pass over the personal dimensions involved. Yet these questions are exceedingly important for the future especially since that future will affect our styles of child-rearing and thus the perpetuation of those values we deem most humanistic and worthy of saving. Even excluding experimental family forms, Sussman (1971) has pointed out that even today some children may live in numerous variant forms of the traditional nuclear family during their formative stages. Under these conditions some changes in our value system are to be expected. The questions are which values and how many?

With the above questions in mind we began to explore contemporary marriage in 1967.[1] The authors' interviews began first with those who were involved in experimental structures and in the greatest variations from the norm in traditional marriage. It was felt that these innovators would have greater insight because they had already opted for change, and that they would perhaps be more articulate and perceptive about why they had chosen change. The interviewers then moved on the the divorced, the nonmarrieds,[2] the singles, the young, and to those who were either disillusioned or contented with traditional monogamous marriage. As research was carried out in a primarily middle class setting, Cuber and Harroff's (1965) delineations of types of marriage relationships (i.e., conflict-habituated, devitalized, passive-congenial, the vital, and the total) gained increasing validity. During the research in the anthropological literature it was found that little attention had been given to the interpersonal dimension of marriage or to the interrelation of the intrapsychic and ideological aspects of marriage. However, it was felt that the anthropological perspective gave a holistic approach to the problems of contemporary marriage that was considered valuable. While cultural ideologies and prescriptions for marriage behavior persisted, value orientations and actual behavior were changing, thus creating confusion for many.

The Problem

As exploratory insights to the problems evolved, the authors became increasingly convinced that the central problem in contemporary marriage was relationship. The attempt to solve the problem by moving

1. In developing the concept of open marriage, the authors interviewed approximately 400 persons from 1967 to 1971. Informant-respondents were 17 to 75 years of age, urban and suburban middle class in orientation and occupation, and approximately 75 percent were married or had been married. Thirty interviews, both formal and informal, with professional therapists and marriage counselors supplemented this data. The interviews included individual and couple in-depth sessions (frequently tape recorded), discussion in group settings, and short mini-interviews in a variety of social settings. While some topical and background questions were used (i.e., age, occupation, marital status, etc.: "What do you think the ingredients of a good marriage are?"), the interviews were primarily open-ended and exploratory in nature, focusing on eliciting information through face to face encounter, about values, feelings and attitudes toward marriage and changes they perceived as necessary for improvement.

2. The term nonmarrieds applies to those relationships in which there is some commitment but which are not legalized. They can range in time from a few months to a life time. Premarital is an accurate term for only a portion of these relationships since some never intend to marry the nonmarriage partner, or the relationship is frequently considered only a temporary plateau before each has the sustaining personal resources to move on to another level, or another person. Formerly marrieds would probably comprise a separate category. The word cohabitation is also misleading as a coverall term for these relationships. Since cohabitation implies both a shared domicile and sex without legal marriage, it did not apply to some relationships encountered, e.g., a couple who did not share a domicile but did form a cohesive unit insofar as they shared all their spare time, vacations, and sex, and presented themselves as a couple in social situations. Therefore, the term nonmarriage relationship is suggested.

into group and communal situations did not seem to mitigate the problems we discovered in interpersonal relationships. With the breakdown of many external supports for traditional marriage, the pressures on the interpersonal husband-and-wife relationship became intensified. There was a need for that relationship to provide more fulfillment and benefits both on a personal and interpersonal level. Problems in marriage were manifested by the inability of the majority of individuals to find in the marital relationship both intimacy and opportunity for developing their personal potential. Understanding of the problem concluded in addition that:

1) Marital partners and those contemplating marriage expressed a need for intimacy and growth in a relationship where they could actualize their individual potential without destroying the relationship.

2) Most people did not have the skills in relating and in communication which would allow for growth in a noncritical atmosphere. The typical dyadic marital role relationships had already been precut for them. They were locked into a negative involuted feedback system. This was their perception of their situation as well, although not with the same terminology.

3) Many of the innovations and experimental forms, although not all of them or all of the people involved in them, were a reflection and indication of this lack of skills in interpersonal relations.

4) Other important impediments to growth were the unrealistic expectations and myths stemming from the traditional marriage format of the past, in particular, overriding emotional dependencies, and possessive jealousy.

This left us as the observers and researchers with the options of reporting the alternate styles with their attendant disillusionments and problems, or of choosing another path in utilizing the research. While one can catalogue all the sociological and technological forces that are contributing factors to the breakdown of marriage and the family, it offers little in the way of ameliorating the problems each individual faces when he comes to grips on an interpersonal basis with the old mores and patterns of institutions that have not changed, while his needs and the external socio-cultural conditions affecting his behavior *have* changed. Therefore, the authors chose to present a model for personal change and value reorientation that individuals could utilize on an interpersonal basis within their own marital situation.

THE ACTION MODEL

The concept of open marriage, which is outlined elsewhere in detail (O'Neill & O'Neill, 1972), is primarily based on the expression of desires for change and the perceived routes to change drawn from the interviews conducted over a period of four years and upon the actual changes already made in many relationships that were observed. The research conducted was utilized to create a model for change. In so

290 Marriage Today: Challenge and Choice

doing the authors have stepped beyond the role of objective researcher reporting the data and findings into the realm of what can be termed action anthropology: that is, delineating a model for change by placing the problem areas in their cultural context. An attempt has been made to present the traditional marital configuration in its societal setting and to delineate the cultural imperatives and values implicit in these imperatives for examination by those involved in marriage relationships. The purpose, then, is to make it possible for individuals to become aware of the idealized precepts of the institution of marriage and the forces influencing their attitude toward, and their behavior in, marriage. Without an awareness of the present conditions, they cannot perceive the pathways to change. It is to be fully understood that some will choose to remain within traditional marriage where the perimeters and dimensions are defined for them by the norms. But for those who feel a need for change, awareness and insight are a necessary first step to determining or discovering what pathways are available.

Action anthropoligy is a variation on the theme of action research. In the past, action research (Festinger, 1953; Selltiz, 1963) has been associated with institutional or organizational change directed toward finding solutions to organizational or social problems. The flow has been from the institutional level down to the individual in effecting change. More recently it has been recognized that individuals can initiate measures for change and reverse the flow to effect change on the institutional level. Weinberg (1965) has noted that this is a problem-solving, action-oriented society, and continues:

> On this action level, society and the person are both symbolic systems with varying capacities for solving problems. Both society and the person can respond to problems in terms of their knowledge and their capacity for decision making and executive knowledge. Both can communicate, plan, and implement programs to solve problems. . . . The individual deliberates about alternatives before selecting a problem-solving response. (4)

Today, the orientation toward methods of change must begin with the individual. The need for a measure of self-determination is paramount. Yet the individual is frequently overlooked as a primary force for change, the assumption being that his behavior is shaped by impinging social forces in the environment and that he has neither sufficient knowledge and perspective to perceive these forces, nor is adequately equipped to institute directive and self-motivated change. This attitude underestimates the individual. The sample encompassed a broad range of middle class informant-respondents. The majority expressed a desire for some feeling of self-determination and autonomy in their lives and marriage behavior. Many had already instituted it. Furthermore, most had a knowledge of what the problem areas were in marriage.

One quote is offered from an interview with a 23-year-old single woman, who was at this time in a nonmarriage relationship with a young man and seriously contemplating marriage:

> I don't want to say yes, yes we are going to be in love forever. It's like saying, yes, yes you know the ocean — and the next wave is going to look like this one, but I *can* say it is worth the risk *if* I feel I can do something about it. I want to be understanding, and start out with the attitude of, well it ain't going to be bliss but if I do my homework I stand a very good chance, and knowing what the chances are and stepping into it with your eyes open, you got a chance of making your marriage work . . . and there is a lot more homework to do today because people have to make decisions they never had to make before in marriage, but those marriages will be better for it . . . it's not I'm doing this because I've got to do it, it's doing this because I *chose* to do it, and that's what it is, man is a thinking animal, therefore I am. Once you get down to this kind of foundation and you can build, you know, 'well begun is half done.'

THE OPEN MARRIAGE MODEL

Open marriage is presented as a model with a two-fold purpose:

1) To provide insights for individuals concerning the past patterns of traditional marriage, which has been termed closed marriage. Based on a closed systems model, traditional marriage was perceived as presenting few options for choice or change.

2) To provide guidelines, through an open systems model, for developing an intimate marital relationship that would provide for growth for both partners in the context of a one-to-one relationship. This does imply some degree of mutuality. It does not imply that growth will always be bilateral, but rather that there will be supportive assistance and tolerance during unilateral growth. Shostrom and Kavanaugh (1971) have delineated the rhythmic relationship which best exemplifies this pattern. These guidelines have been designed in answer to the needs expressed by the majority of our informant-respondents for a relationship which could offer them more dimensions for growth together than either could attain singly. The principle through which this mutually augmenting growth occurs is synergy. Many couples found that this synergistic self-actualizing mode of relating became possible only through the revision and deletion of some of the expectations of closed marriage.

Open marriage can then be defined as a relationship in which the partners are committed to their own and to each other's growth. Supportive caring and increasing security in individual identities makes possible the sharing of self-growth with a meaningful other who encourages and anticipates his own and his mate's growth. It is a relationship which is flexible enough to allow for change, which is constantly being renegotiated in the light of changing needs, consensus in decision making, in tolerance of individual growth, and in openness to new possibilities *for* growth. Obviously, following this model often involves a departure, sometimes radical, from rigid conformity to the established husband-wife roles and is not easy to effect.

In brief, the guidelines are: living for now, realistic expectations, privacy, role flexibility, open and honest communication, open companionship, equality, identity, and trust. The first step is for partners to reassess the marriage relationship they are in, or anticipate, in order to reevaluate expectations for themselves and for their partner. Couples in today's society are not educated for marriage or the requisites of a good human relationship, nor are they aware of the psychological and myriad other commitments that the typical marriage contract implies. The expectations of closed marriage — the major one being that the partner will be able to fulfill all of the other's needs (emotional, social, sexual, economic, intellectual, and otherwise) — present obstacles to growth and attitudes that foster conflict between partners. Awareness of these expectations and a realignment more in accord with a realistic appraisal of their capabilities are fundamental to instituting change and to solving their problems in relationship.

Living for now involves relating in the present rather than in terms of the past or in terms of the future goals which are frequently materialistic and concrete rather than emotional and intellectual in nature. The granting of time off, or privacy, can be used for examination of the self and for psychic regeneration. A way out of what many marital partners conceive as the role-bind involves working toward a greater role flexibility both in terms of switching roles temporarily or on a part-time basis, and as a therapeutic device for understanding the self and the position of the other partner. Open and honest communication is perhaps the most important element in an open relationship. The lack of communication skills creates a formidable barrier between husband and wife, yet these skills are the most important in sustaining a vital relationship, promoting understanding, and in increasing knowledge of self. Open companionship involves relating to others, including the opposite sex, outside the primary unit of husband and wife, as an auxiliary avenue for growth. Equality involves relating to the mate as a peer in terms of ways to achieve stature rather than through the status attached to husband and wife roles. Identity involves the development of the individual through interaction with mate and others and through actualizing his own potentials. Trust, growing through the utilization of these other guidelines and based on mutuality and respect, creates a climate for growth. Liking, respect, sexual intimacy, and love grow through the exercise of these elements.

Each progressive guideline becomes increasingly abstract. The system can be seen as an expanding spiral of evolving steps in complexity and depth in the marital relationship. The system operates through the principle of synergy, a concept drawn from medicine and chemistry, first utilized by Benedict (Maslow and Honigmann, 1970) in cultural, and later by Maslow (1965, 1968) in interpersonal contexts. In open marriage, the concept of *synergic build-up* is defined as a mutually augmenting growth system. Synergy means that two partners in marriage can accomplish more personal and interpersonal growth together than they could separately without the loss of their individual identities. Synergic build-up defines the positive augmenting feedback that can enhance mutual growth.

While only a limited few may be able to utilize all these guidelines in their totality and simultaneously, open marriage would best be considered a resource mosaic from which couples can draw according to their needs and their readiness for change in any one area.

The majority of the sample had already explored the possibilities for change in some of the areas covered by the guidelines. Many of these reflected only a change in attitude, while behaviorial changes were acknowledged as difficult. The two areas of greatest difficulty were the conflicts arising from changing man-woman and husband-wife roles and the problems encountered in self-development.

The question of marital and extramarital sexual behavior, while ever-present, did not seem to be the central problem with which they were coping. While marital sex sometimes presented problems, many felt that the emphasis on sexual adjustment, in terms of manuals and the media, was exaggerated. Although many felt that they could not cope with sexual jealousy in terms of extramarital sex, they were on the verge of deciding that sex *per se* was not their central problem in the marriage. Numerous couples had already effected some degree of sexual latitude in their own relationships. Some had done so with tacit knowledge but without verbalized agreement. Others had done so in various types of consensual arrangements, including group sex and partner exchange. While some benefits were noted, it was observed that by and large these experiences did not occur in a context where the marital partners were developing their primary marriage relationship sufficiently for this activity to count as a growth experience. Frequently it obscured relationship problems, became an avenue of escape, and intensified conflicts. For some, however, it did become a means of revealing other problem areas in the marriage.

Underlying the marital couple's explorations into any area of nonconformity, whether it was extramarital sex or the equally important area of changes in typical role behavior (i.e., male-female, man-woman, husband-wife), was the central problem of relationship.[3] That

3. Concerning these two areas of change, the authors are least optimistic about the movement into group marriage and communal living situations which involve random or even structured sexual intimacy among many. No true group marriage, as it is being explored in our society, with equal sexual sharing among all partners has existed according to the anthropological literature. Among all societies where larger family structures exist, they are maintained by elaborate kinship ties and other supportive structures interwoven with the institutional framework of the society, thus goals are integrated for the group or extended family. Certainly communal or community situations where the goals are banding together to share economic, child care, or recreational activities have many advantages and hopefully will increase. But when couples and individuals in groups are pressed into situations of total intimacy — including the sexual dimension — for which they have not been prepared either emotionally by training or by

is, how could the marital partners relate in terms of their changing needs and those of society in a mutually beneficial fashion? Open marriage presents some of the elements in interpersonal relationships that would allow for change, for increasing responsibility for the self and for others, and for increased understanding between husband and wife.

The open marriage model offers insights and learning guides for developing more intimate and understanding marital relationships. An open relationship in marriage, as well as in any interpersonal matrix, involves becoming a more open person. Since the open-minded personality is one which can perceive options and alternatives and make decisions about the paths to change (Rokeach, 1960), efforts to help the marital couple in perception and skills should increase their ability to solve many problems in marriage. However, it will not be easy for most couples. Emotional maturity, and the development of responsibility and confident identity cannot emerge overnight. But standing still, or merely exploring experimental structural forms without attention to the interpersonal factors only seems to be increasing the number of problems in marriage and decreasing the benefits to be gained from it. Open marriage is not intended to solve marital problems, but by using the open marriage model, the couple will at least be substituting problems which promote growth and learning for problems which are currently insoluable.

IMPLICATIONS

It is in the arena of interpersonal relations that marriage and the family will have to find new meaning and gain greater strength, no matter what the structural framework may be. Children cannot be taught the value of supportive love and caring, responsibility, problem-solving, or decision-making skills unless the parents have first developed these qualities in their own relationship. The inadequacy of organized institutions to instill these values and skills is only too apparent. Therefore, intimate, long-term relationships such as those of marriage and the family must provide them, and in order to do this they must be more rewarding and fulfilling for their members and there must be feedback and caring for each other's welfare.

Focusing on the methods for achieving a rewarding one-to-one relationship provides something that individuals can deal with and work with on a self-determining level. By encouraging personal responsibility, self-growth and bonding through the synergic relationship, the basic unit of husband and wife should become more rewarding and offer more avenues for fulfillment.

---

conditioning, the strain of the multistranded relationships tends to fragment the group. The goals of cooperation and support are difficult to maintain under the pressure of emotional conflicts which are intensified by prescriptions for sexual intimacy.

Building from within strengthens the individual, the couple, and then the family unit, and thus the entire social structure, since the fundamental unit of society is the family. Whatever form the family unit may be, its strength will still depend upon the rewards gained from interpersonal relationships. It is in this sense that the individual, and the married couple, can become not only a fulcrum for change but also a key factor leading to the strengthening of the social structure. Thus both family and society can be better equipped to cope with accelerating technological and cultural change. Hopefully, open families can evolve to an open society and eventually to an open world.

REFERENCES

Cuber, John F. and Peggy B. Harroff. *Sex and the Significant Americans*. Baltimore: Penguin Books, 1965.

Festinger, Leon and Daniel Katz. *Research Methods in the Behavioral Sciences*. New York: Holt, Rinehart and Winston, 1953.

Maslow, Abraham H. *Eupsychian Management*. Homewood, Illinois: Richard D. Irwin, Inc., 1965.

Maslow, Abraham H. Human Potentialities and the Healthy Society. In Herbert A. Otto, (ed.). *Human Potentialities*. St. Louis: Warren H. Green, Inc., 1968.

Maslow, Abraham H. and John J. Honigmann (Eds.). Synergy: Some Notes of Ruth Benedict. *American Anthropoligist,* April 1970, 72.

O'Neill, Nena and George O'Neill. *Open Marriage: A New Life Style for Couples*. New York: M. Evans and Company, Inc., 1972.

Rokeach, Milton. *The Open and Closed Mind*. New York: Basic Books, Inc., 1960.

Selltiz, Claire, Marie Jahoda, Morton Deutch, and Stuart W. Cook. *Research Methods in Social Relations*. New York: Holt, Rinehart and Winston, 1963.

Shostrom, Everett and James Kavanaugh. *Between Man and Woman*. Los Angeles: Nash Publishing, 1971.

Sussman, Marvin B. Family Systems in the 1970's: Analysis, Politics, and Programs. *The Annals of the American Academy of Political and Social Science*. July 1971, 396.

Thomlinson, Ralph. *Sociological Concepts and Research*. New York: Random House, 1965.

Weinberg, S. Kirson. *Social Problems in Modern Urban Society*. Englewood Cliffs, New Jersey: Prentice-Hall, Inc., 1970.

UNIT STUDY GUIDE

A. *Terms to Review*

Contract marriage	Multilateral Marriage	Two-tier
Dyadic marital model	Open Marriage	marriage
High-order discontent	Standardized shocks	Synergy

B. *Questions for Discussion and Study*

1. "Marriage consists in an interpersonal relationship, not in a ritual of legitimation approved by the state." Discuss.
2. Locate and read the laws bearing on marriage in your state. Discuss the social-cultural factors which may have influenced their provisions regarding age, residence, parental approval, and any other controls.
3. Of the alternatives to conventional monogamous marriage discussed in this unit, which one do you see as: a) most feasible, b) most attractive, and c) most acceptable to prevailing norms?
4. Distinguish between *trial marriage* and *living together*. Would one expect differences in communication, commitment, honesty, openness, and potential for personal growth in each? Discuss.
5. Illustrate and discuss the extent to which husbands and wives differ in their perception of problems in contemporary marriage. In troubled marriages is there a sex difference in perceived problems? What changes in problem-perception may be expected to occur with increasing diffusion of ideas from the sexual equality and human potentials movements?
6. Beginning with the issues listed in the introduction to this unit, see how many additional ones — both general and specific — you can identify.

C. *Topics-Ideas for Papers and Projects*

1. Invite a couple who are "living together" to discuss with your group the adjustments, satisfactions, and difficulties they have experienced. Compare these with similar aspects of interaction in a formalized marriage partnership.
2. Research: "Marital Problems as Revealed in Letters to Advice Columnists."
3. "Social Class Differences in the Impact of Sexual Equality Movement Ideology on Women's Roles in Marriage."
4. Using records available in your county clerk's office, do a study of the frequency of teen-age marriage in your area; take into account any related social variables or vital data included in the records.

Unit 6

Situational Stresses

---

*There is no cure for birth and death save
to enjoy the interval. — Santayana*

*We learn looking backward. We live looking
forward. — Anonymous*

Introduction

In the preceding unit we first considered some categories of problems typically occurring in troubled marriages and we then sought to trace out some of the related issues. It was proposed that malfunctioning relationships with consequent individual distress are the core of the major difficulties typically experienced in American marriage today. Thus, we saw that most alternatives which have been proposed, both the prosaic as well as the more sensational ones, tend to focus on the challenging task of profound modification of the interpersonal relations in marriage. A central aim of such proposals is to optimize the potentials for building simultaneously in marriage a vital pair-relationship and processes or structures which would maximize growth and self-realization for the partners as individuals.

Sociological research supports the claim that it is the quality of the interpersonal functioning in the marital partnership that will "make or break" the marriage.[1] However, while we have mainly focused on relationships thus far, the readings in this unit give ample reason to believe that the day-to-day, situational conditions within which the marriage functions may constitute a potent source of stresses for the marital partnership.

Even in marriages where there are initially few or no overt difficulties in the relationship, the situational conditions of existence may effectively induce great stress for the partnership. These situational stresses and their impact on marriage will be the focus of this unit. By *situational stresses* we mean distressing or unhappiness-inducing forces emerging from the objective conditions under which the group functions. The objective conditions consist in the existential "givens" at any particular time for the marriage. As distinguished from relationships, they comprise fairly constant factors either within the participants (such as chronic illness or disability) or in the material background (such as socio-economic status), over which the partnership has little or no direct control. For example, the married pair per se would have little control over the objective fact of one partner's paraplegia; this would simply constitute a condition of existence for the pair. Nor would the partnership effectively have any direct control over its status as a "poverty-level" family, its minority or ethnic status, and its community environment. Yet, these conditions of existence over which little control can be gained may constitute a significant source of stresses for the marriage, both in the interaction of the partnership with its environing society and patterns of relations between the partners.

While considerable research has been conducted on the effects of crises on families and the relative ability of family members to adapt to them, comparatively little serious research has explored the relationship of marital interaction quality to situational conditions or stresses. The readings in this unit imply a need for serious study, for example, of ways in which physiological changes in individuals or somatic illness may induce stress in interpersonal relationships. Research could also profitably be directed toward measuring the extent to which particular interpersonal patterns may contribute to the perpetuation of economic or cultural deprivation.

As we turn now to a discussion of problems and issues, we can briefly note two related factors which have strong influence on the experiencing of situational stresses by the marital partnership. These are *subcultural forces* and *the affluence problem.*

Every marriage is, to some degree, continuously answerable to subcultural forces implied in norms which issue from kin, peers, and associates. By definition, a subculture implies not only prescriptions for living (norms) but usually entails also a life-style, patterned ways of coping with the environment. A major source of stress from subcultural forces lies in their diversity. Thus, a marriage transplanted from rural to urban settings, from central city to suburb, or from one region to another may encounter rejection and disapproval of its attempts to maintain patterns of behavior which were approved and even rewarded in the prior situation. For that matter, even within familiar surroundings, the subcultural norms may induce stress because of their divergence from norms impinging on the marriage from overarching institutional sources such as religion, law, work, etc. An example of this is found in the anxiety experienced by some married couples who entertain euphoric drug-using friends in their homes.

Subcultural forces can, of course, be supportive and stabilizing as well as stress-inducing. For example, subcultural norms favorable to "getting ahead" tend to converge with and reinforce the more general societal norms imbedded in what has been termed "the achievement syndrome" in American society. Perhaps some of the most potentially important subcultural forces pertain to economic motives or norms; this is implied in the following discussion of a problem that is difficult to conceptualize: affluence.

Although it seems foreign to American thought to think of material abundance in "trouble" terms, there are good grounds for arguing that marital problems may significantly reflect the effects of this society's emphasis on economic and material achievement. But first let us define our terms. Essentially, *affluence* presupposes the acquisition or possession of a level of economic capacity which will permit: (1) considerable choice in expenditures, both in types and amounts, (2) discernible pleasure in consumption behavior per se, and (3) relative freedom from a "hand-to-mouth" existence. Those who live at a subsistence level are not affluent.

Two related norms may be cited which possibly account for most of the troublesome aspects of affluence. While these two sources of stress may not be solely responsible for problems related to affluence within marriage, they are very important ones. First, contemporary American culture, reinforced by tradition and the organization of society, places high value on a maximization of creature comforts. Secondly, cultural norms conveyed in the earliest stages of the socialization process condition and train the individual to seek maximum physical-material evidences of achievement or success. Thus, no matter what the particular occupation or endeavor one engages in, one must produce *material* evidence of success or achievement. An artist who sells no paintings is unsuccessful; and the same could be said for the clergyman who dines on bologna and beans, drives a dilapidated auto, and wears frayed collars.

Affluence, or the American compulsion to attain it, may thus pose problems for marriage due to the strong cultural expectations regarding the material aspects of the marital situation. It thus becomes difficult for Americans to judge a marriage or family as "successful" where the husband is penniless and unemployed, the residence shabby, and the children in worn-out clothing. And, it is probably no less difficult for those within such a situation. Due to persisting tendencies to socialize females for dependent roles, wives may be strongly predisposed to expect and anticipate material success from their husbands. Thus, the "successful" husband or father is one who has achieved affluence and its material evidences. The potential for disillusionment is evident. Some further comment on this topic seems pertinent.

In an abstract statistical sense, the current median family income of slightly more than $12,000 would seem to imply a rather affluent state of affairs. But there are subterranean rumblings of unemployment, bankruptcy, foreclosures, and an ever-increasing cost of living index. Sadly, among America's five-figure-income families, the pressures of impulse-buying, the emulation of visible "success" traits of significant others, and the persistence of Veblenian patterns of conspicuous consumption have probably all contributed to the marital stresses experienced in those families.

It could justifiably be claimed that Americans are victimized by the very culture to which they so avidly subscribe. An example of this is found in traditional American family norms which include a sex-role differentiation in regard to economic responsibilities, specifically the production of income. This differentiation is reinforced by law, industry, socialization practices, and subcultural norms. Due to the persisting influence of sexism on the occupational structures, most family income is likely to be produced by the husband. In some marriages, this disproportionate earning situation may be a constant reminder of unequal status for the female; in such a scene, it is unlikely that the hard-working husband will be viewed with a mixture of praise and sympathy. Indeed, aside from the potential stresses on the marital relationship in this situation, there are subtle indices, possible shreds of evidence accumulating, which suggest that the American male pays dearly for his adherence to the myths and norms of male superiority and to the creeds of materialism. Evidence suggests a higher incidence among males of heart failure, coronaries, etc. which may be related to stresses in the "rat race" of upward-mobility striving.[2] Our tendency in this society, as Fromm put it, "to love things and use people" is obviously a strong deterrent to the emergence of a healthy, growth-oriented system of marriage.

Let us now review a few of the more general issues bearing on the topic of the situational conditions of existence. With those that are cited below, some mention is made of alternatives.

> *Economic inequities.* Complaints about the functioning of the economic system in this society are not new; concentration of great wealth among a relative few has given rise to expressions such as "the rich get richer and the poor get poorer." In view of the regressive taxation policy effective in American society, there may be much substance to this claim. Belying the American image of universal economic well-being, the truth is that we have poverty in the midst of affluence. It is striking, for example, that ten percent of the family groups in this country in 1971 were below the poverty level for family income.[3] From the perspective of the human potentials movement, this condition implies a fundamental problem. Namely, the process of maximizing one's growth and the progress toward self-actualization are dependent on the relative conditions of existence. It would seem that the basic needs of shelter, food, clothing and the like must be met adequately before the individual can take fullest advantage of the inherent capacities for spiritual, intellectual growth. How much creative potential within American families is blocked by economic constraints? How much stress in marital-familial relationships is induced by the conflict of high aspirations for material goods with low levels of opportunity to achieve them? Some alternatives

proposed in recent years include: a guaranteed minimum income for families, family allowances to help defray the costs of raising minor children, and guaranteed full employment for all.[4]

Inadequacies in health-maintenance. Inadequate health maintenance in a partnership can often be seen as an outcome of particular subcultural influences, lack of education and basic knowledge, and a history of negative health-related experiences within the family itself. However, another source of inadequacy is implied in the foregoing discussion of economic distress; namely, economically deprived families and neighborhoods have more than their share of health problems. There is still another side of the picture; despite all the claims that America has the best health care in the world, there seem to be serious deficiencies in the functioning of health care organizations and in the social role of medicine in this society. In the area of chronic and disabling illnesses and conditions, those having especially significant implications for family and marital functioning, there are glaring deficiencies in the provision of treatment, personnel, and facilities. It seems incredible that a society which has the technology and funds to land men on the moon would have a shortage of available dialysis equipment for the seriously ill. Of the many alternatives and proposals to alleviate this situation, a few can be listed: upgrading and promotion of health education for all, training of paraprofessionals in medicine, neighborhood health centers, national health-insurance plans, training of physicians for family practice, and propagation of the belief that optimum health and its maintenance is the right of every citizen.[5]

The long arm of the job. Conflict between job and marital-familial roles is a familiar theme in this society. We need merely cite some persisting questions. Which should come first — family or job? Should industry bear equally the costs of career-disruption and family disruption? Should there be enforceable limits on the amount of time an employer could expect an employee to spend away from home? Proposals to create a more humane relation between familial groups and the world of work include: joint training and employment of husband-wife teams, shortened work week, paternity leaves with pay, integration of the job's mobility requirements with the growth and change cycles in the family group, and rotation of outside-the-home employment between wife and husband.

The functions of the state. Assuming that the state has a legitimate interest in the functioning of the family system, certain issues can be identified. A basic issue concerns the divergence between the possible value of a national policy on marriage or family life, and their conditions of existence and the entrenched individualism and material competitiveness of this society. Issues are implicit in questions such as these: To what extent should the processes of family life and the family's interaction with its environment be subject to state guidance and control? Can the state guarantee family rights as well as individual rights? Is the state to be held responsible for the quality of situational, objective conditions within which the family functions? If so, can the state assume such responsibility without taking control of internal marital-familial processes? Obviously, basic issues revolve around the degree of independence of the marriage or family group from its social and material setting.

In addition to those cited above, there are doubtless various other problems, issues, and stresses with roots in the situational conditions within which marriage exists. In the larger culture or in the immediate subculture of most marriages, for example, there are persisting norms which foster interaction in terms of dominant stereotypes or ascribed statuses rather than in terms of individual personality integrity. There are thus possibilities for stress and conflict associated with sexism, since the attitudes and behaviors comprising it are likely to pervade all of one's relationships, including marriage. And the development of truly humane, loving and caring relationships in the marriage or family is not likely to be enhanced by attitudes and values which subordinate the personhood of one's intimates to their social or biological status. Still another source of stress may lie in chronic illness or physical-mental disability, since these may affect not only the intimate patterns of interaction between partners, but also the ongoing daily transactions between the partnership and its social environment.

In all our foregoing discussion and, as we shall see, in our readings for this unit, there is one recurrent theme: no marriage or familial group can be truly independent of its society. The significance of this theme·will become apparent as we get into the readings.

REFERENCES

1. DeBurger, James E., *Husband-Wife Differences in the Revelation of Marital Problems: A Content Analysis* (Ann Arbor: University Microfilms, Inc., 1966), pp. 81-100; Gurin, Gerald *et al, Americans View Their Mental Health* (New York: Basic Books, 1960), pp. 95-100.

2. Syme, S. Leonard and Leo G. Reeder (eds.), *Social Class and Cardio-vascular Disease* (New York: Millbank Memorial Fund, 1967).

3. U.S. Dept. of Commerce, *USA Statistics in Brief–1972* (Washington: Government Printing Office, 1972).

4. Green, Christopher. "Guaranteed Income Plans — Which One Is Best?" *Transaction* 5 (Jan.-Feb., 1968): 49-53; Scott Briar, "Why Children's Allowances?" *Social Work* 14 (Jan. 1969): 5-12; Robert Theobald, "The Goal of Full Employment," *The New Republic* (March 11, 1967): 15-18.

5. Relevant sources could include these: Bert E. Swanson, "The Politics of Health," in Howard E. Freeman *et al, Handbook of Medical Sociology* (Englewood: Prentice-Hall, 1972), pp. 435-455; William C. Richardson, "Poverty, Illness, and the Use of Health Services in the United States," *Hospitals* 43 (July 1969): 34-40; "Toward A Public Policy for Health Care: Some Current Issues," in E. Gartly Jaco (ed.), *Patients, Physicians and Illness* (New York: Free Press, 1972), pp. 364-396: "Medical Care: Individual or Organizational Problem," in Russell Dynes *et al, Social Problems: Dissensus and Deviation in An Industrial Society* (New York: Oxford Univ. Press, 1964), pp. 224-254.

Health and Marital Experience in an Urban Population

KAREN S. RENNE

American families — small, monogamous, housed in separate, self-contained "nuclear" units — are so structured that relations with the spouse are vital to the average adult's social and emotional well-being. Each spouse is expected not only to provide emotional support, sexual gratification, companionship and economic support or assistance for the other, but also to complement the other's roles as parent, friends, colleague, kinsman and so on. An unhappy marriage deprives both partners of support in some or all of these areas, so that each is handicapped in performing his own roles. And to the extent that each spouse devotes time and emotional energy to frustrating or destructive exchanges with the other, he is handicapped in his relations with his children and others outside the family, just as a person suffering from a chronic heart condition is handicapped in his physical activities. In short, an unhappy marriage can be regarded as a social disability, because it tends to impair all the relationships in which the partners are involved.[1]

My purpose here is to show that unhappily married persons are more susceptible than other married persons or divorced persons (of the same race, sex, and approximate age) to physical and psychological health problems, not primarily because they bring these problems to the marriage but also because the marriage itself affects health. To this end I shall compare happily and unhappily married persons who had never been divorced with those who had remarried after divorce, and with persons who were still divorced at the time of our survey.

Previous studies have indicated that divorced persons are *less* healthy than married persons generally. LaHorgue (1960) published direct evidence on this point from the 1954-55 California Health Survey, and others have analyzed vital statistics for the U.S. as a whole to show that the *mortality* of married people is lower (from most major causes) than that of divorced, widowed, or single persons of the same age and sex (Zalokar, 1960; Sheps, 1961; Berkson, 1962).

---

1. This conception of marriage owes most to Willard Waller (1930; 1951); it represents an "interactional" rather than a "structural-functional" approach to the family (see Christensen, 1964; Ch. 3-4, for a detailed summary of each type of theory and the kind of research it generates). The definition of marital satisfaction in terms of functional areas follows Blood and Wolfe (1960). Bott (1957) established an empirical association between marital patterns and relations with outsiders for a small number of English couples studied in depth.

Our data would support the same conclusion if they were handled the same way — that is, divorced people in our sample are sicker than married people. In the present analysis, however, I have compared divorced persons not simply with married persons, but with those who were unhappy in their marriages, separately from those who were not unhappy.

Unhappy marriage is correlated, in our sample, with poor health, social isolation, low morale, and emotional problems (Renne, 1970). But unlike such disabilities as minority race, chronic disease or physical impairment, a disabling marriage can be terminated. If unhappy marriage is an illness, divorce is a remedy, perhaps the only effective one, and the evidence I am about to present shows that divorced persons were healthier physically and psychologically, enjoyed higher morale and were less isolated socially than those who had, at the time of our survey, chosen to remain with an unsatisfactory mate.

SAMPLE AND QUESTIONNAIRE

Unlike most studies of marriage and divorce, this one is based on a large area probability sample, drawn in 1965 for a comprehensive investigation of the relation between health and way of life. Marital status and marital happiness are, of course, important dimensions of "way of life."

The sample consisted originally of 4,452 households in Alameda County, California, a highly urbanized area with a population of 1,056,000 in 1965.[2] These households were enumerated in 1965, yielding 8,267 adults (ages 20 and older, or 16-19 and ever married). The enumerator left a questionnaire for each adult in the household, with instructions to fill it out and mail it back. Reluctant respondents received a reminder letter and later a telegram, and approximately 30 days after the initial contact an interviewer visited everyone who had not responded and attempted to retrieve the questionnaires. (Respondents who were unable to complete the questionnaire because of illness or language difficulty were interviewed at this time.) Of the total enumerated, 6,928 (84 percent) mailed in their questionnaires or supplied the information in interviews. The majority (81 percent) of those who completed questionnaires returned them by mail.

About three-quarters of the respondents were married, and most of the 5,163 married persons were couples. All married people were asked nine questions about their marriages; six were used to construct an index of marital satisfaction (see Renne (1970) for a description of the questionnaire and details of the index). The 4,924 married persons who answered all six questions were classified "happy" or "unhappy"

2. For a complete description of the sample as well as extensive data on Alameda County, see California Department of Public Health (1966a). The study was supported by research grant CH 00076 from the Division of Community Health Services, U.S. Public Health Service.

according to their responses. Approximately one marriage in five was "unhappy," on the basis of this index.

Black people were more likely than white to be unhappily married (35 percent compared with 19 percent of whites), probably for reasons associated with poverty, discrimination in employment, and other aspects of the poor quality of life for black people in America. They were also more likely to be separated or divorced (Table 1): almost a third of black women 45 and older, for example, were separated or divorced, compared with 10 percent of white women and 11 percent of black men in the same age group.

TABLE 1
MARITAL STATUS BY AGE, SEX AND RACE[a] (Percentages)

| | Under 45 | | | | 45 and Over | | | |
| | White | | Black | | White | | Black | |
	Men	Women	Men	Women	Men	Women	Men	Women
Married [b]	80	79	70	62	84	61	79	53
Happily	63	62	42	35	68	44	54	31
Unhappily	14	15	24	24	11	13	18	18
Separated	1	2	5	16	1	2	4	12
Divorced	2	6	5	10	6	8	7	19
Never Married	16	12	19	11	4	6	3	1
Widowed	+	1	+	1	6	24	6	14
All Persons	100	100	100	100	100	100	100	100

a N's are shown in Appendix A.214 Japanese, Chinese and other Orientals, and 233 people of "other" races were excluded from this and all subsequent tables because when subdivided by age, sex and race there were too few to analyze. (Only 7 Orientals and 17 "others" were separated or divorced.)

b In this and all subsequent tables, "Married" includes persons who did not answer all of the index questions on marriage and therefore could not be rated "happy" or "unhappy."

+ Less than 0.5 percent.

The following analysis is confined to that portion (83 percent) of the sample that was married, divorced or separated at the time of the survey. "Separated" and divorced women were analyzed separately, but separated and divorced men had to be combined because only 40 men checked "separated" as their marital status — too few to permit controls for age or race. (Separated and divorced women far outnumbered separated and divorced men in our sample, partly because unmarried men were probably undernumerated in this survey, as in all such surveys, and partly because men are more likely to remarry after divorce (U.S. Public Health Service, 1968:8).)

Widowed and single people are shown in Table 1 to indicate their relative weight in each subgroup, but they were excluded from the analysis. Widows and widowers are socially and psychologically distinct from other formerly married people (Hunt, 1966: 21), less likely to remarry (U.S. Public Health Service, 1968:8), and, because they are much older than either married or divorced people, they tend to be less healthy physically and to have inferior socioeconomic resources and prospects.

Single people were excluded for similar reasons. Not only do they lack the marital experience and continuing family responsibilities of the divorced, but also they are younger.

The analysis is presented in two parts: first, unhappily and happily married persons are compared with each other and with separated and divorced people, with respect to physical, social and psychological health. Comparisons are made within subgroups formed by age, sex and race — three variables associated with marital status and marital happiness, as well as with most aspects of health.[3] In the second part of the presentation, essentially the same "dependent" variables are examined again, but this time marital history — the prior experience of divorce — is also taken into account.

In this two-part presentation I shall first establish that health is associated with marital happiness more strongly than with marital status or marital history. Subsequently I will show that the good health of happily remarried divorceś, relative to that of current divorceś, and unhappily married people in first marriages, suggests a temporal sequence structured by at least two processes: (1) healthy people are "selected" by the divorce and remarriage process, and (2) at the same time, the quality of the marriage itself contributes to the health and morale of each spouse.

HEALTH AND MARITAL HAPPINESS

Although married women in our sample were healthier than separated or divorced women, the largest and most consistent differences were between happily and unhappily married men and women. Those who complained about their marriages were far more likely than those who didn't to report a physical disability or chronic illness, or both, and these unhappily married people also tended to be less healthy than the separated and divorced (Table 2, part A).

"Separated" women and divorced black men and women over 45 had very high rates of illness, in some cases higher than those of the unhappily married. As the following analysis shows, separated women were generally demoralized, depressed and deprived. Some of them, undoubtedly, were unmarried mothers; others, deserted by their hus-

---

3. I did not use tests of statistical significance in this analysis because (1) replications of the same pattern in a number of subgroups (in this case defined by sex, race and age) is, in my opinion, at least as persuasive as the size of particular differences, and (2) most significance tests are unsatisfactory for one reason or another, e.g., parametric assumptions are required, or significance is partly a function of sample size. In general too, the "level" of significance is arbitrary and, no matter what level is chosen, the test tends to focus attention on particular differences rather than the trend or pattern in an entire series.

TABLE 2

PHYSICAL HEALTH BY MARITAL STATUS AND MARITAL HAPPINESS[a]

| | Under 45 | | | | 45 and Over | | | |
| | White | | Black | | White | | Black | |
	Men	Women	Men	Women	Men	Women	Men	Women
(A) Percent Reporting Disabilty or Chronic Illness[b]								
Married	30	26	30	36	56	59	57	64
Happily	27	24	26	34	53	55	55	61
Unhappily	41	36	40	41	70	72	63	62
Separated		45		40		60		81
Divorced[d]	29	37	(22)	22	55	67	86	75
(B) Percent Describing Own Health as "Fair" or "Poor"[c]								
Married	8	11	19	24	20	24	38	41
Happily	7	8	14	14	19	21	35	30
Unhappily	17	19	29	41	28	36	47	56
Separated		18		45		39		52
Divorced[d]	22	14	(32)	18	24	29	48	27

[a]Minor reductions due to missing data will not be noted unless the percentage base falls below 20, in which case the percentage will be shown in parentheses when the base is 10-19 and not shown when the base is less than 10.

[b]Respondents were asked to check which (if any) disabilities, conditions and symptoms they had had in the past year. *Disabilities* are functional: trouble feeding or dressing oneself or moving around; inability to work or to work a normal schedule; trouble climbing stairs, etc. *Chronic Illness* includes high blood pressure, heart trouble, bronchitis, rheumatism, diabetes, cancer, etc. and impairments (a missing limb, trouble seeing even with glasses or hearing even with a hearing aid). ("Symptoms" include pain in the heart or chest, leg cramps, back pains, stomach pains, headaches, paralysis, trouble breathing, constant coughing, etc.) Of the 1024 "disabled" people in the total sample, 98 percent also reported a chronic illness or a "symptom" or both.

[c]The question, concluding a six-page series on health and illness, was "All in all, would you say that your health is generally excellent, good, fair or poor?"

[d]Includes separated men.

bands, were also subject to more severe stress than divorced women normally experience.

Divorced white men and divorced blacks under 45 were relatively free of serious health problems. Rates for divorced men were comparable to those of happily married men in the same age group, and divorced black women under 45 were less likely than even the happily married to be ill.

Asked to evaluate their health generally, however, divorced men were about as likely as unhappily married men to say "fair" or "poor," and the precentages saying fair or poor were also very similar for separated and unhappily married women (Table 2, part B). But divorced women were less likely to indicate poor health than unhappily married women of the same age.

These "subjective" evaluations of general health probably reflect morale as well as objective physical condition, and answers to direct questions about morale were also related to marital happiness.[4] But persons who reported a disabilty *were* more likely to say their health was "fair" or "poor" than those who reported a chronic condition, symptoms, or none of these (57 percent vs. 23, 11 and 3 percent, respectively).

On the basis of either of these health indices, then, marriage was associated with better health only when the relationship was unsatisfactory to the respondent. People who complained about their marriages were most likely to report poor health; those who had divorced were, on the whole, healthier than those who had remained in an unhappy marriage.

This finding does not establish a causal sequence, of course: it does not tell us whether poor health makes a marriage unhappy or an unhappy marriage damages health. But in either case, the divorced seem to represent the healthiest among those who had been unhappily married in the past. If it is the healthier people who dissolve their unhappy marriages, then those remaining in the "unhappily married" status would be more likely to report a disability or chronic illness. In other words, a disabled or chronically ill person might well prefer an unhappy marriage to life without a partner; another, not himself disabled or ill, might be reluctant to abandon a sick spouse.

NEUROSIS, DEPRESSION AND ISOLATION

Separation and divorce involve radical changes in social role, emotional balance and general life style, yet the separated and divorced in our sample apparently were little, if any, more neurotic, depressed or isolated than the unhappily married people. Differences between the unhappily married and the happily married exceed those between the unhappily married and the divorced by a substantial amount, in most comparisons in the next two tables.[5]

Table 3, part A, presents an index designed to rank people according to their "ego resiliency." It consists of 19 true-false items dealing largely with difficulties in interpersonal relations: a low score indicated inordinate sensitivity to the reactions of others. Unhappily married people were on the whole more likely than the separated and divorced to display low ego strength.

So far as this index reflects neurotic tendencies that existed prior to the marriage, the low (more neurotic) scores of the unhappily married suggest that failure to terminate an unhappy marriage may itself be an

4. For example, when asked, "All in all, how happy are you these days?", about a quarter of the unhappily married and similar proportions of separated women and divorced men said they were "not too happy", while almost none of the happily married chose this response (data not shown). Divorced women displayed relatively high morale on this and other similar questions.

5. For simplicity of presentation, these tables omit the age control used in Tables 1-3. In general, the relation between each independent variable and marital status was the

TABLE 3.

PSYCHOLOGICAL HEALTH BY MARITAL
STATUS AND MARITAL HAPPINESS

	White		Black	
	Men	Women	Men	Women
(A) Percent Low on Ego Resiliency[a]				
Married	13	21	12	24
Happily	11	18	9	15
Unhappily	22	36	19	38
Separated		35		30
Divorced[c]	15	21	25	22
(B) Percent Depressed[b]				
Married	8	12	8	12
Happily	5	7	2	4
Unhappily	23	32	19	22
Separated		27		19
Divorced[c]	20	18	18	10

[a]"Low" means that the respondent gave an answer indicating ego strength or "resiliency" to no more than seven of the 19 itmes in this scale. Examples of the items are: "I usually don't like to talk much unless I am with people I know very well"; "Sometimes I cross the street just to avoid meeting someone"; "I get pretty discouraged sometimes"; "I sometimes feel that I am a burden to others." (There are true-false items; in these examples but not in all 19 items, this answer "true" indicates low ego resiliency.)

[b]"Depressed" means that the respondent answered at least four of the nine items in the scale in a way indicating depression or isolation. The nine items refer to loneliness, depression, general dissatisfaction, uneasiness,and meaninglessness of life. The two most closely related to marital happiness were: "It often seems that my life has no meaning (True/False)" and "How often do you feel very lonely or remote from other people (Never/Sometimes/Often)?"

[c]Includes separated men.

indicator of low ego strength. The relatively high (less neurotic) scores of divorced women and most divorced men may mean that people with "stronger" or more resilient egos were more willing than others to break up their marriages.

At the same time, relations with the spouse affect one's relations with others and therefore one's self-respect, so that low ego strength may be partly a *consequence* of unhappy marriage. At least, bad relations with the spouse are likely to aggravate any neurotic tendencies an individual had prior to his marriage. Cut off from others, and at the same time made anxious or angry by his partner's antagonism or indifference, an unhappily married person is necessarily more prone to low morale, depression, and isolation than one who finds his marriage satisfactory.

Our index of isolation and depression shows that unhappily married people were indeed more likely than others to feel lonely and depre-

same for both age groups, except that divorced black men 45 and older had higher rates of neurosis, depression and isolation than unhappily married men in the same subgroup. (Among younger black men, the unhappily married had the highest rates).

ssed. Very few happily married people gave a depressed response to as many as four of the nine items in this index, and divorced women again were relatively healthy (Table 3, part B).

REFERENCES

Berkman, Paul. "Spouseless motherhood, psychological stress and physical morbidity." *Journal of Health and Social Behavior* 10, December 1969, 323-334.

Berkson, Joseph. "Mortality and marital status." *American Journal of Public Health* 52, August 1962, 1318-1329.

Bernard, Jessie. *Remarriage.* New York: Dryden, 1956.

Blood, Robert O., Jr. and Donald M. Wolfe. *Husbands and Wives.* New York: Free Press, 1960.

Bott, Elizabeth. *Family and Social Network.* London: Tavistock, 1957.

California Department of Public Health. Alameda County Population 1965, Human Population Laboratory Series A, No. 7, 1966.

————. Divorce in California. Berkeley: Bureau of Vital Statistics, 1966.

Christensen, Harold T., Ed. *Handbook of Marriage and the Family.* Chicago: Rand McNally, 1964.

Goode, William J. *Women in Divorce.* New York: Free Press, 1956.

Hunt, Morton. *The World of the Formerly Married.* New York: McGraw-Hill, 1966.

Jacobson, Paul H. *American Marriage and Divorce.* New York: Rhinehart, 1959.

LaHorgue, Zeva. "Morbidity and marital status." *Journal of Diseases* 12, October 1960, 476-498.

Monahan, Thomas P. "The changing nature and instability of remarriages." *Eugenics Quarterly* 5, February 1958, 73-85.

Renne, Karen S. "Correlates of dissatisfaction in marriage." *Journal of Marriage and the Family* 31, February 1970, 54-67.

Sheps, Mindel C. "Marriage and mortality." *American Journal of Public Health* 51, April 1961, 547-555.

U.S. Public Health Service. Marriage Statistics Analysis, 1963 National Center for Health Statistics, Series 21, No. 16, 1968.

Waller, Willard. *The Old Love and the New.* New York: Liveright, 1930.

————. *The Family* (revised by Reuben Hill). New York: Dryden, 1954.

Zalocar, Julia R. "Marital status and major causes of death in women." *Journal of Chronic Diseases* II, January 1960, 50-60.

Our index of isolation and depression shows that unhappily married people were indeed more likely than others to feel lonely and depressed. Very few happily married people gave a depressed response to as many as four of the nine items in this index, and divorced women again were relatively healthy (Table 3, part B).

Public Policy and the Changing Status of Black Families

ROBERT STAPLES

According to Bell and Vogel (1968), the family contributes its loyalty to the government in exchange for leadership which will provide direct and indirect benefits for the nuclear family. While there is little doubt that Black families have been loyal to the political state in America, it appears that they have derived few reciprocal benefits in return. Although the political system has the power to affect many of the conditions influencing Black family life, it has failed to intervene in the service of the Black population and, in fact, has been more of a negative force in shaping the conditions under which Black families must live. As Billingsley (1968, 177) has stated, "no subsystem has been more oppressive of the Negro people or holds greater promise for their development."

Historically, we find that state, local, and federal governmental bodies have pursued policies that have contributed to the victimization of Black families. Under slavery, marriages between slaves were not legal since the slave could make no contract. The government did nothing to insure stable marriages among the slave population or to prevent the arbitrary separation of slave couples by their owners. Moreover, the national government was committed to the institution of slavery, a practice which was most inimical to Black family life (Frazier, 1939).

Although this fact may not seem relevant today, it illustrates the federal government's default in protecting the integrity of the slave family. This failure to intervene and its impact is most clearly demonstrated when compared to the laws passed in many South American countries that possessed slaves. While the slave states in North America had slave codes that required slaves to submit to their masters and other white men at all times, the South American governments passed laws that provided for the physical protection and integrity of the slaves, as it did for free citizens (Elkins, 1968). Because the United States government was not as benign, slavery was a more oppressive institution which has left us with a legacy of racial inequality in all spheres of American life — a past that had significant repercussions in the area of Black family life.

In more recent years, some state governments have passed laws which impose middle-class values on lower-income families, many of which are Black. Various state legislatures have passed laws designed to reduce or eliminate welfare benefits to women who have given birth to a child out-of-wedlock. A few states have even attempted to pass laws sterilizing women on welfare who have had more than one "illegitimate" child. All these attempts have failed, as the laws were subsequently invalidated by the courts.

While the welfare system may be viewed as a positive governmental action in assisting families who are economically deprived, it has often served to tear low-income families asunder. The Aid to Families with Dependent Children (AFDC) program was designed to economically maintain children whose father was absent from the home. Hence, it was available, until recently, only to those families where the husband/father was not present in the home. A family in need of assistance due to the male breadwinner's unemployment could not receive help unless he "deserted" the family. Many lower-class Black males have been forced to abandon their wives and children in order to satisfy this restrictive governmental welfare policy.

When the federal government finally decided to develop a program to strenghten Black family life, the attempt was made in a very curious way. It began with a report by Daniel Moynihan (1965) who was then an Assistant Secretary of Labor. According to Rainwater and Yancey (1967), Moynihan wanted to have the Black problem redefined by focusing on the instability of the Black family. As an index of Black family deterioration, he used the census reports which revealed that Blacks had more female-headed households, illegitimate children, and divorces than white families. While these characteristics were applicable to only a minority of Black families, Moynihan generalized their effect and influence to the entire Black population.

Since the validity of the Moynihan Report has been dealt with extensively elsewhere (Staples, 1971), our concern here is with the role of the government in formulating a policy for strengthening Black family life. First, we might question the political strategy involved in issuing such a report on the Black family at that particular time or at any time. The Moynihan Study was published at a time when Blacks had defined their problem as deriving from institutionalized white racism. The effect of the Moynihan Report was to redefine the problem as emanating from weaknesses in the Black family, which was the main factor in the alleged deterioration of Black society. In other words, Blacks were largely responsible for their conditions, not the legacy of slavery or subsequent racist practices in American life.

Moreover, the national action that Moynihan spoke of was not delineated in the report. At a later time, he did recommend social services and noted that a policy of benign neglect had not been too detrimental. Moreover, he is generally credited with being the creator of one government policy designed to affect the family life of low-income Americans. This policy proposed the creation of a Family Assistance Program, which was designed to correct the inadequacies of the AFDC system by substituting workfare for welfare. At this time the proposal has not yet been acted on by Congress.

The Family Assistance Program ostensibly was designed to aid families who are not eligible for welfare benefits under the present welfare system. However, the additional benefits seem to be secondary to the strong work requirements contained in the present bill. In fact, the purpose of the plan is to force several million Black welfare mothers to work — mostly at wretchedly paid, menial jobs. This purpose is unmasked by the fact that economic benefits under the proposed plan would actually be lower than those presently given in most state controlled AFDC programs (Axinn and Levin, 1972).

In a recent study of welfare families, Goodwin (1972) noted that the results of the FAP may be just the opposite of those intended. The past history of work programs have conclusively demonstrated that few of the welfare mothers will find work at all, and those who do are in jobs no better than domestic service. These low-paying jobs will not provide a sufficient income for women to support their families without continued governmental aid. Moreover, being confined to ill-paid jobs that do not enable them to support their families may reinforce the same psychological orientation which presently characterize low-income families and discourage them from further work activity.

This emphasis on mandatory work requirements is based on the false stereotypes of the poor as lacking the incentive to work because of the economic security provided them by public assistance programs. Yet, Goodwin (1972) found that the poor have just as strong a work ethic as the middle-class. In fact, poor Black youth who have grown up in welfare families have a more positive attitude toward the desirability and necessity of work than the children of the white middle-class. Furthermore, Black women on welfare see getting a job as far more important than middle-class white women for whom work has little relevance to their upward mobility. However, securing employment for these Black women really depends on the availability of meaningful, decent-paying jobs, not on a training program.

It can reasonably be stated that the federal government's efforts to promote Black family solidarity have been misguided and ineffective. The purpose of this article is to review the changing status of Black families and its implications for a meaningful public policy to strengthen Black family life. In describing the contemporary condition of Black familes, we will not attempt to deal with the larger sociological factors responsible for current Black family patterns. Our intent is to point out the changes that are taking place and the public policy that would be relevant to future trends among Black families.

EDUCATION, EMPLOYMENT, AND INCOME

Among the principal variables that undergird family life are education, employment, and income. Looking at the 1970 census, we find some absolute progress in certain areas for Black families, little change in their status *vis-a-vis* white families, and the general problems of poverty and unemployment unchanged overall for many Black families. In education, for example, the proportion of Blacks graduating from high school increased slightly. Nevertheless, Blacks were still more likely than whites to be high school dropouts. The median number of school years completed by Black Americans over 24 years of age was 10.0 in contrast to 12.1 for white Americans (U.S. Bureau of Census, 1971).

There are two important aspects of the education situation to consider in assessing its relevance to Blacks. First, Black women tend to be slightly more educated than Black men at all levels. In the past decade, the educational level of the white men increased to reach the average of white women, while Black men continued to lag behind Black women (U.S. Bureau of the Census, 1971). Hence, an increase in the educational level of the Black population will not automatically mean a rise in income or employment opportunities. The fact that much of that increase in education belongs to Black women reduces the mobility level for Blacks because Black women, even educated ones, tend to be concentrated in lower-paying jobs than Black men. Another significant factor is the sexual discrimination that women in our society face in the labor force (Pressman, 1970).

The second important aspect of education is that it does not have the same utility for Blacks as it does for whites. While the yearly incomes of Black college graduates and whites who have completed only elementary school are no longer the same, the equal educational achievements of Blacks and whites still are not reflected in income levels. The 1970 census reveals that Blacks are still paid less for comparable work than whites. While white male professional, managerial, and kindred workers earned $11,108, Blacks in the same occupational category only earned $7,659. Among craftsmen, foremen, and kindred workers the white median was $8,305, the Black median was $5,921. Similar, but smaller, Black-white descrepancies appear on other occupational categories (U.S. Bureau of the Census, 1971). These figures lend substance to the Jencks, et al. (1972) argument that education alone will not equalize the income distribution of Blacks and whites. In fact, the relative income gap between Blacks and whites increases with education. While both Blacks and whites incur difficulties due to a low level of education, college educated whites face fewer barries to their career aspirations. In computing the estimated lifetime income of Blacks as a percentage of white estimate lifetime income at three educational levels, Siegel (1965) found that the Black elementary school graduate would earn 64 percent of his white counterpart's lifetime income, but the Black college graduate's lifetime earnings would be only 50 percent of his white peer's lifetime income. Hence, highly educated Blacks suffer the brunt of income discrimination more intensely than those with less education.

During the past decade, the median family income for Blacks increased at a faster rate than the median for the population as a whole.

Yet, Black family income is still only 60 percent of white family income. The median income for white families in 1970 was $9,961, for Black families only $6,067. Even these figures are misleading because they do not show that Black family incomes must be used to support more family members and that their family income is more often derived from the employment of both the husband and wife. Also, according to the Labor Department, the majority of Black families do not earn the $7,000 a year needed to maintain themselves at a non-poor intermediate standard of living (U.S. Bureau of the Census, 1971).

Furthermore, about a third of the nation's Black population is still living in official poverty. About a fourth of them are receiving public assistance. The comparable figures for whites were ten and four per cent. Almost half of these Black families living in poverty are headed by females. About 41 percent of all Black children are members of these families, who exist on an income of less than $3,700 a year. Only ten percent of white children live in households that are officially defined as poor (U.S. Bureau of the Census, 1971).

The unemployment rate for Blacks in 1971 was at its highest level since 1961. Overall, 9.9 percent of Blacks were officially unemployed compared to 5.4 percent for whites. In the years 1969-1971, Black unemployment increased from 5.8 to 8.7. Furthermore, this increase in unemployment during that three year period was highest among married Black men who were the primary breadwinners in their household. Just as significant is the unemployment rate of Black women who were heads of families and in the labor force. About ten percent of that group was unemployed as compared to six percent of white women. The highest unemployment rates in the country are among Black female teenagers in low-income areas of central cities. Their unemployment rate is about 36.1 percent and has risen as high as 50 percent (U.S. Bureau of the Census, 1971).

What the recent census figures indicate is that the decade of the sixties saw little significant change in the socioeconomic status of Black families. An increase in educational achievements has produced little in economic benefits for most Blacks. Based on the rate of progress in integrating Blacks in the labor force in the past decade, it will take 9.3 years to equalize the participation of Blacks in low-paying office and clerical jobs and a period of 90 years before Black professionals approximate the proportion of Blacks in the population (Purcell and Cavanagh, 1972).

CHANGING PATTERNS OF BLACK FAMILY LIFE

Recent years have brought about significant changes in the marital and family patterns of many Americans. We have witnessed an era of greater sexual permissiveness, alternate family life styles, increased divorce rates, and reductions in the fertility rate. Some of these changes have also occurred among Black families and have implications for any public policy developed to strengthen Black family life.

The sexual revolution has arrived, and Blacks are very much a part of it (Staples, 1972). By the age of 19, over half of the Black females in a recent study had engaged in intercourse. While the proportion of comparable white females was only 23.4 percent, they were engaging in premarital coitus more often and with a larger number of sexual partners. However, a larger number of sexually active Black females were not using reliable contraceptives, and 41 percent had been, or were, pregnant (Zelnik and Kantner, 1972).

One result of this increased premarital sexual activity among Blacks is the large number of Black children born out-of-wedlock. Almost 184 of every 1,000 Black births were illegitimate in the year 1968. However, this rate was lower for Blacks than in the most recent earlier periods. The racial differences in illegitimacy rates also narrowed in the last 20 years (U.S. Bureau of the Census, 1971). One reason for the decline is the easier accessibility to safe, low-cost abortions. Nationwide, Black women received 24 percent of all legal abortions performed in hospitals (Population Council, 1971). In all probability, the Black birth rate will continue to decrease as contraception and abortion readily become available.

When Blacks choose to get married, the same economic and cultural forces that are undermining marital stability in the general population are operative. In the last decade, the annual divorce rate has risen 75 percent. For white women under the age of 30, the chances are nearly one in three that their marriage will end in divorce. Among Black women, their chances are one in two. In 1971, 20 percent of every married Black women were separated or divorced compared to six percent of similar white women. The divorce rate of middle-class Blacks is lower, since the more money that a family makes and the higher their educational achievements, the greater are their chances for a "stable" marriage (U.S. Bureau of the Census, 1971).

A combination of the aforementioned factors has increased the proportion of Black households headed by females. The percentage of female-headed families among Blacks increased eight percent in the last decade, from 22 percent to 30 percent. A third of these female household heads worked and had a median income of only $4,396 in 1971. The proportion of Black children living with both parents declined in the last decade, and currently only 64 percent of children in Black families are residing with both parents. It is apparently the increasing pressures of discrimination, urban living, and poverty that cause Black fathers to leave their homes or never marry. At the upper-income level of $15,000 and over, the percentage of Black families headed by a man is similar to that for white families (U.S. Bureau of the Census, 1971).

The fertility rate of Black women is hardly a factor in the increase of female-headed households among Blacks. Between 1961 and 1968, the total birth rate for Black women decreased sharply. The fertility rate of Black women (3.13 child per Black woman) is still higher than the 2.37 birth rate for white women. However, the average number of total births expected by young Black wives (2.6) and young white wives (2.4) are very similar. As more Black women acquire middle-class status or access to birth control and abortion, we can expect racial differentials in fertility to narrow (U.S. Bureau of the Census, 1971). The birth rate of college educated Black women is actually lower than their white counterparts (Kiser and Frank, 1967).

This statistical picture of marital and family patterns among Blacks indicates a continued trend toward attenuated nuclear families caused by the general changes in the society and the effects of the disadvantaged economic position of large numbers of Black people. An enlightened public policy will address itself to the needs of those families, rather than attempting to mold Black families into idealized middle-class models, which no longer mean much, even for the white middle-class. What is needed is a government policy that is devoid of middle-class puritanism, the protestant ethic, and male-chauvinist concepts about family leadership. In the concluding section, we will spell out the elements of such a public policy.

A PUBLIC POLICY FOR BLACK FAMILIES

The following elements of a public policy for Black families is a combination of the author's ideas and other recommendations by various Black groups concerned with certain problems of the Black family.

In most proposals to strengthen Black family life, it is common to assert that providing meaningful, gainful employment to Black males is necessary in order to ensure that they will remain with, and support, their families. While this is of concern here, it will not be accorded the highest priority. Although unemployment and low income are key factors in Black family disorganization, there are other cultural and social forces which threaten the continued existence of the Black nuclear family. Among them are weaknesses in the institution of marriage itself, which make it less than a viable solidarity medium for either Blacks or whites. The demographic nature of the Black community will also insure the existence of large numbers of female-headed households among them. Since there are approximately one million more Black females than males, there is less opportunity for many Black women to establish a monogamic nuclear family. Although part of this sex-role differential is due to underenumeration of Black males in the census, there is a shortage of more than a million Black males available to Black women for marriage because of the higher male rates of mortality, incarceration, homosexuality, and intermarriage.

Our focus will be on efforts needed to assist families which may be headed by women. These should include decisive and speedy government action to remove all arbitrary sex-role barriers in obtaining employment and providing opportunities for job mobility for women. Those women in low-income categories should be given subsidized training for jobs which pay decent salaries and are not restricted only to men. Since the economy is not really geared to provide jobs to prepared and willing workers, we would recommend a guaranteed income of $6,000 to a family with at least one parent and three children.

While the above figure has been criticized as being too high and not politically feasible, it seems a reasonable amount in light of the Labor Department's admission that an annual income of $7,000 is required to maintain a family of four at the non-poor but low standard of living in urban areas. This will also free women of their dependency on men to maintain a decent standard of living. Women will be able to enter marriage out of desire, rather than economic need. Although this may not slow down the rising tide of dissolved marriages, it does give women a greater life choice.

To facilitate the entrance of women into the labor force, we also recommend community-controlled 24-hour child care centers. The Bureau of Labor Statistics shows that a larger proportion of Black women are employed fulltime than white women. This is particularly true of the 16-24 year age group, who are most likely to have very young children with no child care facilities they can afford in which to leave them. These child care services should be provided on a sliding fee scale, based on income by the government. They will serve a dual function by freeing working women from the responsibilities of child care and providing employment for women and men who work in the child care centers.

Closely related to the concept of child care centers is the need for the government's commitment to a national comprehensive program of child development. This would provide for the establishment of a national system of child development centers and programs which would provide comprehensive health services, education, recreation, and cultural enrichment for preschool children (Billingsley, 1972).

To further protect Black children, we need to reconsider the traditional methods of child placement. Since caring for other's children on a temporary basis is a time-honored practice in the Black community, there is no reason why the family who accepts a child on a permanent basis should not be subsidized by the government to do so. The idea of subsidized adoption should become a part of public policy and would deal with the paradoxical situation of mothers who do not want to rear their children and families who want them, but cannot afford them. We should also get some community input into foster care arrangements.

For Black women who do not wish to bear children, there should be available safe, free contraceptives or abortion. However, these services should be organized into a community-controlled comprehensive health program and center. This will demonstrate that white society is not only concerned about preventing Black children from entering the world, but wants to safeguard the health of the mothers and provide decent health care to those Black children that are born.

Also, any governmental policy to help Black families should recognize the desire of Blacks to control their own community and destiny. Thus, the initial formulation of such a public policy should include a major input from the Black community. Programs imposed by white people on Black families are no longer acceptable or desirable if we wish to establish a policy which will begin to promote the conditions necessary for a strong Black family structure.

In concluding, we might note that public policy has not favored any family which is poor or uneducated, but the Black family has been singled out and discriminated against in employment, housing, education, health, and other services which require special remediation. Although public policy was not designed to disadvantage any particular group, its ineffectiveness has been felt most significantly in the area of lower-income Black family life. This special need of Black families, however, should not distract from the necessity of a major governmental effort on behalf of all families. Work training means nothing unless there is a commitment to provide jobs for all willing to work. And, the provision of jobs will mean little to Black families unless there is a concomitant elimination of racial discrimination in employment and promotional opportunities.

REFERENCES

Axinn, June and Herman Levin. Optimizing Social Policy for Families. *The Family Coordinator,* 1972, 21, 163-170.

Berry, Mary. *Black Resistance—White Law: A History of Constitutional Racism in America.* New York: Appleton-Century-Crofts, 1971.

Billingsley, Andrew. *Black Families in White America.* Englewood Cliffs, New Jersey: Prentice-Hall, 1968.

Billingley, Andrew. *Children of the Storm.* New York: Harcourt Brace Jovanovich, 1972.

Elkins, Stanley. *Slavery: A Problem in American Institutional and Intellectual Life.* Chicago: University of Chicago Press, 1968.

Frazier, E. Franklin. *The Negro Family in the United States.* Chicago: University of Chicago Press, 1939.

Goodwin, Leonard. *Do the Poor Want to Work? A Social-Psychological Study of Work Orientations.* Washington: Brookins, 1972.

Jencks, Christopher, et al. *Inequality: A Re-Assessment of the Effect of Family and Schooling in America.* New York: Basic Books, 1972.

Kiser, Clyde and Myrna Frank. Factors Associated with the Low Fertility of Non-white Women of College Attainment. *Milbank Memorial Fund Quarterly,* October 1967, 425-429.

Population Council Report on Abortions by Age and Race. Washington: U.S. Government Printing Office, 1972.

Pressman, Sonia. Job Discrimination and the Black Woman. *The Crisis*, March 1970, 103-108.

Purcell, Theodore and Gerald Cavanagh. *Blacks in the Industrial World*. New York: The Free Press, 1972.

Rainwater, Lee and William Yancy. *The Moynihan Report and the Politics of Controversy*. Cambridge, Massachusetts: The M.I.T. Press, 1967.

Siegel, Paul M. On the Cost of Being Negro. *Sociological Inquiry*, 1965, 35, 52-55.

Staples, Robert. Towards a Sociology of the Black Family: A Theoretical and Methodological Assessment. *Journal of Marriage and the Family*, 1971, 33, 19-38.

Staples, Robert. The Sexuality of Black Women. *Sexual Behavior*, 1972, 2, 4-14.

United States Bureau of the Census, Department of Commerce. *The Social and Economic Status of the Black Population in the United States*, Series P. 23, No. 42. 1971.

Zelnik, Melvin and John Kantner. Sexuality, Contraception, and Pregnancy Among Young Unwed Females in the United States. A paper prepared for the Commission on Population Growth and the American Future, May 1972.

Alcoholism and the Family

JOAN K. JACKSON

Until recently it was possible to think of alcoholism as if it involved the alcoholic only. Most of the alcoholics studied were inmates of publicly supported institutions: jails, mental hospitals, and public general hospitals. These ill people appeared to be homeless and tieless. As the public became more aware of the extent and nature of alcoholism and that treatment possibilities existed, alcoholics who were still integral parts of the community appeared at clinics. The definition of "the problems of alcoholism" has had to be broadened to include all those with whom the alcoholic is or has been in close and continuing contact.

At present we do not know how many nonalcoholics are affected directly by alcoholism. However, an estimate can be derived from the available statistics on the marital histories of alcoholics. The recurrently arrested alcoholic seems to affect the fewest nonalcoholics. Reports range from 19 per cent to 51 per cent who have never married[1] — that is, from slightly more than the expected number of single men to three to four times the expected rate. The vast majority who had married are now separated from their families. Alcoholics who voluntarily seek treatment at clinics affect the lives of more people than jailed alcoholics. While the number of broken marriages is still excessive, approximately the expected number of voluntary patients have been married.[2] Any estimate of nonalcoholics affected must take into consideration not only the present marital status of alcoholics, but also the past marital history. About one-third of the alcoholics have been married more than once. Jailed alcoholics had multiple marriages less frequently than clinic alcoholics.

There has been no enumeration of the children and other relatives influenced by alcoholism. From the author's studies it can be estimated that for each alcoholic there are at least two people in the immediate family who are affected. Approximately two-thirds of the married alcoholics have children, thus averaging two apiece. Family studies indicate that a minimum of one other relative is also directly involved. The importance of understanding the problems faced by the families of alcoholics is obvious from these figures. To date, little is known about the nature of the effects of living with or having lived with an alcoholic. However, there is considerable evidence that it has disturbing effects on the personalities of family members.

Reprinted from "Alcoholism and the Family" by Joan K. Jackson in volume no. 315 of *The Annals* of the American Academy of Political and Social Science. Reprinted by permission of the publisher and the author.

Once attention had been focused on the families of alcoholics, it became obvious that the relationship between the alcoholic and his family is not a one-way relationship. The family also affects the alcoholic and his illness. The very existence of family ties appears to be related to recovery from alcoholism. Some families are successful in helping their alcoholic member to recognize his need for help and are supportive of treatment efforts. Yet other types of families may discourage the patient from seeking treatment and may actually encourage the persistence of alcoholism. It is now believed that the most successful treatment of alcoholism involves helping both the alcoholic and those members of his family who are directly involved in his drinking behavior.[3]

THE ALCOHOLIC AND HIS CHILDREN

The children are affected by living with an alcoholic more than any other family member. Personalities are formed in a social milieu which is markedly unstable, torn with dissension, culturally deviant, and socially disapproved. The children must model themselves on adults who play their roles in a distorted fashion. The alcoholic shows little adequate adult behavior. The nonalcoholic parent attempts to play the roles of both father and mother, often failing to do either well.

The child of an alcoholic is bound to have problems in learning who he is, what is expected of him, and what he can expect from others. Almost inevitably his parents behave inconsistently towards him. His self-conception evolves in a situation in which the way others act towards him has more to do with the current events in the family than with the child's nature. His alcoholic parent feels one way about him when he is sober, another when drunk, and yet another during the hangover stage.

What the child can expect from his parents will also depend on the phase of the drinking cycle as well as on where he stands in relation to each parent at any given time. Only too frequently he is used in the battle between them. The wives of alcoholics find themselves disliking, punishing, or depriving the children preferred by the father and those who resemble him. Similarly, the child who is preferred by, or resembles, the mother is often hurt by the father. If the child tries to stay close to both parents he is caught in an impossible situation. Each parent resents the affection the other receives while demanding that the child show affection to both.

The children do not understand what is happening. The very young ones do not know that their families are different from other families. When they become aware of the differences, the children are torn between their own loyalty and the views of their parents that others hold. When neighbors ostracize them, the children are bewildered about what *they* did to bring about this result. Even those who are not ostracized become isolated. They hesitate to bring their friends to a home where their parent is likely to be drunk.

The behavior of the alcoholic parent is unpredictable and unintelligible to the child. The tendency of the child to look for the reasons in his own behavior very often is reinforced inadvertently by his mother. When father is leading up to a drinking episode, the children are put on their best behavior. When the drinking episode occurs, it is not surprising that the children feel that they have somehow done something to precipitate it.

Newell[4] states that the children of alcoholics are placed in a situation very similar to that of the experimental animals who are tempted towards rewards and then continually frustrated, whose environment changes constantly in a manner over which they have no control. Under such circumstances experimental animals have convulsions or "nervous breakdowns." Unfortunately, we still know very little about what happens to the children or about the duration of the effects.

Yet some of the children appear undisturbed. The personality damage appears to be least when the nonalcoholic parent is aware of the problems they face, gives them emotional support, keeps from using them against the alcoholic, tries to be consistent, and has insight into her own problems with the alcoholic. It also appears to mitigate some of the child's confusion if alcoholism is explained to him by a parent who accepts alcoholism as an illness.

THE ALCOHOLIC AND HIS WIFE

The wives of alcoholics have received considerably more attention than the children. The focus tends to be on how they affect the alcoholic and his alcoholism, rather than on how alcoholism and the alcoholic affect them. Most writers seem to feel that the wives of alcoholics are drawn from the ranks of emotionally disturbed women who seek out spouses who are not threatening to them, spouses who can be manipulated to meet their own personality needs. According to this theory, the wife has a vested interest in the persistence of the alcoholism of her spouse. Her own emotional stability depends upon it. Should the husband become sober, the wives are in danger of decompensating and showing marked neurotic disturbances.[5]

A complementary theory suggests that pre-alcoholic or alcoholic males tend to select certain types of women as wives. The most commonly reported type is a dominating, maternal woman who uses her maternal role as a defense against inadequate femininity.

Any attempt to assess the general applicability of this theory to *all* the wives of alcoholics runs into difficulties. First, the only wives who can be studied by researchers are those who have stayed with their husbands until alcoholism was well under way. The high divorce rate among alcoholics suggests that these wives are the exception rather than the rule. The majority of women who find themselves married to alcoholics appear to divorce them. Second, if a high rate of emotional disturbance is found among women still living with alcoholics, it is difficult to determine whether the personality difficulties antedated or postdated the alcoholism, whether they were partly causal or whether they emerged during the recurrent crises and the cumulative stresses of living with an alcoholic. Third, the wives who were studied were women who were actively blocking the treatment of their husbands, who had entered mental hospitals after their husbands' sobriety, who were themselves seeking psychiatric care, or who were in the process of manipulating social agencies to provide services. It is of interest that neither of the studies which deal with women who were taking an active part in their husbands' recovery process comment upon any similarities in the personality structures of the wives.[6]

It is likely that the final test of the hypotheses about the role of the wives' personalities in their husbands' alcoholism will have to await the accumulation of considerably more information. No alcoholic personality type has been found on psychological tests; no tests have been given to the wives of alcoholics. Until we know more about the etiology of alcoholism and its remedy, the role of the wives' personalities in its onset, in its persistence, and in its alleviation will remain in the realm of speculation.

No one denies that the wives of active alcoholics are emotionally disturbed. In nonthreatening situations, the wives are the first to admit their own concerns about "their sanity." Of over one hundred women who attended a discussion group at one time or another during the past six years, there was not one who failed to talk about her concerns about her own emotional health. All of the women worry about the part which their attitudes and behavior play in the persistence of the drinking and in their families' disturbances. Although no uniform personality types are discernible, they do share feelings of confusion and anxiety. Most feel ambivalent about their husbands. However, this group is composed of women who are oriented towards changing themselves and the situation rather than escaping from it.

THE IMPACT OF ALCOHOLISM ON THE FAMILY

When two or more persons live together over a period of time, patterns of relating to one another evolve. In a family, a division of functions occurs and roles interlock. For the family to function smoothly, each person must play his roles in a predictable manner and according to the expectations of others in the family. When the family as a whole is functioning smoothly, individual members of the family also tend to function well. Everyone is aware of where he fits, what he is expected to do, and what he can expect from others in the family. When this organization is disrupted, repercussions are felt by each family member. A crisis is under way.

Family crises tend to follow a similar pattern, regardless of the nature of the precipitant. Usually there is an initial denial that a problem exists. The family tries to continue in its usual behavior patterns until it is obvious that these patterns are no longer effective. At this point there is a downward slump in organization. Roles are played with less enthusiasm and there is an increase in tensions and strained relationships. Finally an improvement occurs as some adjustive technique is successful. Family organization becomes stabilized at a new level. At each stage of the crisis there is a reshuffling of roles among family members, changes in status and prestige, changes in "self" and "other" images, shifts in family solidarity and self-sufficiency and in the visibility of the crisis to outsiders. In the process of the crisis, considerable mental conflict is engendered in all family members, and personality distortion occurs.[7] These are the elements which are uniform regardless of the type of family crisis. The phases vary in length and intensity depending on the nature of the crisis and the nature of the individuals involved in it.

When one of the adults in a family becomes an alcoholic, the over-all pattern of the crisis takes a form similar to that of other family crises. However, there are usually recurrent subsidiary crises which complicate the over-all situation and the attempts at its resolution. Shame, unemployment, impoverishment, desertion and return, nonsupport, infidelity, imprisonment, illness and progressive dissension also occur. For other types of family crises, there are cultural prescriptions for socially appropriate behavior and for procedures which will terminate the crisis. But this is not so in the case of alcoholism. The cultural view is that alcoholism is shameful and should not occur. Thus, when facing alcoholism, the family is in a socially unstructured situation and must find the techniques for handling the crisis through trial and error behavior and without social support. In many respects, there are marked similarities between the type of crisis precipitated by alcoholism and those precipitated by mental illness.

ATTEMPTS TO DENY THE PROBLEM

Alcoholism rarely emerges full-blown overnight. It is usually heralded by widely spaced incidents of excessive drinking, each of which sets off a small family crisis. Both spouses try to account for the episode and then to avoid the family situations which appear to have caused the drinking. In their search for explanations, they try to define the situation as controllable, understandable, and "perfectly normal." Between drinking episodes, both feel guilty about their behavior and about their impact on each other. Each tries to be an "ideal spouse" to the other. Gradually not only the drinking problem, but also the other problems in the marriage, are denied or sidestepped.

It takes some time before the wife realizes that the drinking is neither normal nor controllable behavior. It takes the alcoholic considerably longer to come to the same conclusion. The cultural view that alcoholics are Skid Row bums who are constantly inebriated also serves to keep the situation clouded. Friends compound the confusion. If the wife compares her husband with them, some show parallels to his behavior and others are in marked contrast. She wavers between defining his behavior as "normal" and "not normal." If she consults friends, they tend to discount her concern, thus, facilitating her tendency to deny that a problem exists and adding to her guilt about thinking disloyal thoughts about her husband.

During this stage the family is very concerned about the social visibility of the drinking behavior. They feel that they would surely be ostracized if the extent of the drinking were known. To protect themselves against discovery, the family begins to cut down on their social activities and to withdraw into the home.

ATTEMPTS TO ELIMINATE THE PROBLEM

The second stage begins when the family defines the alcoholic's drinking behavior as "not normal." At this point frantic efforts are made to eliminate the problem. Lacking clear-cut cultural prescriptions for what to do in a situation like this, the efforts are of the trial and error variety. In rapid succession, the wife threatens to leave the husband, babies him during hangovers, drinks with him, hides or empties his bottles, curtails money, tries to understand his problem, keeps his liquor handy for him, and nags at him. However, all efforts to change the situation fail. Gradually the family becomes so preoccupied with the problem of discovering how to keep father sober that all long-term family goals recede into the background.

At the same time isolation of the family reaches its peak intensity. The extreme isolation magnifies the importance of all intrafamily interactions and events. Almost all thought becomes drinking-centered. Drinking comes to symbolize all conflicts between the spouses, and even mother-child conflicts are regarded as indirect derivatives of the drinking behavior. Attempts to keep the social visibility of the behavior at the lowest possible level increase.

The husband-wife alienation also accelerates. Each feels resentful of the other. Each feels misunderstood and unable to understand. Both search frantically for the reasons for the drinking, believing that if the reason could be discovered, all family members could gear their behavior in a way to make drinking unnecessary.

The wife feels increasingly inadequate as a wife, mother, woman, and person. She feels she has failed to make a happy and united home for her husband and children. Her husband's frequent comments to the effect that her behavior causes his drinking and her own concerns that this may be true intensify the process of self-devaluation.

DISORGANIZATION

This is a stage which could also be entitled "What's the use?" Nothing seems effective in stabilizing the alcoholic. Efforts to change the situation become, at best, sporadic. Behavior is geared to relieve tensions rather than to achieve goals. The family gives up trying to understand the alcoholic. They do not care if the neighbors know about the drinking. The children are told that their father is a drunk. They are no longer required to show him affection or respect. The myth that father still has an important status in the family is dropped when he no longer supports them, is imprisoned, caught in infidelity, or disappears for long periods of time. The family ceases to care about its self-sufficiency and begins to resort to public agencies for help thereby losing self-respect.

The wife becomes very concerned about her sanity. She finds herself engaging in tension-relieving behavior which she knows is goalless. She is aware that she feels tense, anxious, and hostile. She regards her pre-crisis self as "the real me" and becomes very frightened at how she has changed.

ATTEMPTS TO REORGANIZE IN SPITE OF THE PROBLEM

When some major or minor subsidiary crisis occurs, the family is forced to take survival action. At this point many wives leave their husbands.

The major characteristic of this stage is that the wife takes over. The alcoholic is ignored or is assigned the status of the most recalcitrant child. When the wife's obligations to her husband conflict with those to her children, she decides in favor of the children. Family ranks are closed progressively and the father excluded.

As a result of the changed family organization, father's behavior constitutes less of a problem. Hostility towards him diminishes as the family no longer expects him to change. Feelings of pity, exasperation, and protectiveness arise.

The reorganization has a stabilizing effect on the children. They find their environment and their mother more consistent. Their relationship to their father is more clearly defined. Guilt and anxiety diminish as they come to accept their mother's view that drinking is not caused by any behavior of family members.

Long-term family goals and planning begin again. Help from public agencies is accepted as necessary and no longer impairs family self-respect. With the taking over of family control, the wife gradually regains her sense of worth. Her concerns about her emotional health decrease.

Despite the greater stabilization, subsidiary crises multiply. The alcoholic is violent or withdraws more often; income becomes more uncertain; imprisonments and hospitalizations occur more frequently. Each crisis is temporarily disruptive to the new family organization. The symbolization of these events as being caused by alcoholism, however, prevents the complete disruption of the family.

The most disruptive type of crisis occurs if the husband recognizes that he has a drinking problem and makes an effort to get help. Hope is mobilized. The family attempts to open its ranks again in order to give him the maximum chance for recovery. Roles are partially reshuffled and attempts at attitude change are made, only to be disrupted again if treatment is unsuccessful.

EFFORTS TO ESCAPE THE PROBLEM

The problems involved in separating from the alcoholic are similar to the problems involved in separation for any other reason. However, some of the problems are more intense. The wife, who could count on some support from her husband in earlier stages, even though it was a manipulative move on his part, can no longer be sure of any support. The mental conflict about deserting a sick man must be resolved as well as the wife's feelings of responsibility for his alcoholism. The family which has experienced violence from the alcoholic is concerned that separation may intensify the violence. When the decision is made to separate because of the drinking, the alcoholic often gives up drinking for a while, thereby removing what is apparently the major reason for the separation.

Some other events, however, have made separation possible. The wife has learned that the family can run smoothly without her husband. Taking over control has bolstered her self-confidence. Her orientation has shifted from inaction to action. The wife also has familiarity with public agencies which can provide help, and she has overcome her shame about using them.

REORGANIZATION OF THE FAMILY

Without the father, the family tends to reorganize rather smoothly. They have already closed ranks against him and now they feel free of the minor disruptions he still created in the family. Reorganization is impeded if the alcoholic continues to attempt reconciliation or feels he must "get even" with the family for deserting him.

The whole family becomes united when the husband achieves sobriety, whether or not separation has preceded. For the wife and husband facing a sober marriage after many years of an alcoholic marriage, the expectations for marriage without alcoholism are unrealistic and idealistic.

Many problems arise. The wife has managed the family for years. Now her husband wishes to be reinstated as head of the house. Usually the first role he re-establishes is that of breadwinner. With the resumption of this role, he feels that the family should reinstate him immediately in all his former roles. Difficulties inevitably follow. For example, the children are often unable to accept his resumption of the father role. Their mother has been mother and father to them for so long that it takes time to get used to consulting their father. Often the father tries to manage this change overnight, and the very pressure he puts on the children towards this end defeats him.

The wife, who finds it difficult to believe that her husband is sober permanently, is often unwilling to relinquish her control of family affairs even though she knows that this is necessary to her husband's sobriety. She remembers when his failures to handle responsibility were catastrophic to the family. Used to avoiding any issues which might upset him, the wife often has difficulty discussing problems openly. If she permits him to resume his father role, she often feels resentful of his intrusion into territory she has come to regard as her own. If he makes any decisions which are detrimental to the family, her former feelings of superiority may be mobilized and affect her relationship with him.

Gradually the difficulties related to alcoholism recede into the past and family adjustment at some level is achieved. The drinking problem shows up only sporadically — when the time comes for a decision about permitting the children to drink or when pressure is put on the husband to drink at a party.

PERSONALITY DISTURBANCES IN FAMILY MEMBERS

Each stage in the crisis of alcoholism has distinctive characteristics. The types of problems faced, the extent to which the situation is structured, the amount of emotional support received by individual family members, and the rewards vary as to the stage of the crisis. Some stages "fit" the personalities of the individuals involved better than others.

Although each stage of the crisis appears to give rise to some similar patterns of response, there is considerable variation from family to family. The wife whose original personality fits comfortably into denying the existence of the problem will probably take longer to get past this phase of the crisis than the wife who finds dominating more congenial. The latter will probably prolong the stage of attempting to eliminate the problem. Some families make an adjustment at one level of the crisis and never seem to go on to the next phase.

With the transition from one stage to another, there is the danger of marked personality disturbance in family members. Some become their most disturbed when drinking first becomes a problem; others become most disturbed when the alcoholic becomes sober. In the experience of the author, there has been little uniformity within families or between families in this respect. However, after two or three years of sobriety, the alcoholics' family members appear to resemble a cross section of people anywhere. Any uniformities which were obvious earlier seem to have disappeared.

THERAPY AND THE FAMILY

The major goal of the families of most alcoholics is to find some way of bringing about a change in father's drinking. When the alcoholic seeks treatment, the family members usually have very mixed feelings towards the treatment agency. Hope that father may recover is remobilized and if sobriety ensues for any length of time, they are grateful. At the same time, they often feel resentment that an outside agency can accomplish what they have tried to do for years. They may also resent the emotional support which the alcoholic receives from the treatment agency, while they are left to cope with still another change in their relationship to him without support.

Most families have little awareness of what treatment involves and are forced to rely on the alcoholic patient for their information. The patient frequently passes on a distorted picture in order to manipulate the family situation for his own ends. What information is given is perceived by the family against a background of their attitudes towards the alcoholic at that point in time. The actions they take are also influenced by their estimate of the probability that treatment will be successful. The result is often a family which works at cross purposes with therapy.

Recently there has been a growing recognition that the family of the alcoholic also requires help if the alcoholic is to be treated successfully. An experiment was tried at the Henry Phipps Psychiatric Clinic of Johns Hopkins Hospital. Alcoholics and their wives were treated in concurrent group therapy sessions. The Al-Anon Family Groups provide the same type of situation for the families of AA members and have the additional asset of helping the families of alcoholics who are still not interested in receiving help for themselves. Joint treatment of alcoholis and the members of their family aims at getting a better understanding of the underlying emotional disturbance, of the relationship between the alcoholic and the person who is most frequently the object and stimulus of the drinking behavior, and of the treatment process.[8]

Joint treatment of the alcoholic and his family has other assets, as Gliedman and his co-workers point out.[9] Joint therapy emphasizes the marriage. In addition, with both spouses coming for help, there is less likelihood that undertaking treatment will be construed as an admission of guilt or that therapy will be used as a weapon by one against the other. The wife's entrance into therapy is a tacit admission of her need to change too. It represents a hopeful attitude on the part of both the alcoholic and his wife that recovery is possible and creates an orientation towards working things out together as a family unit.

The members of an Al-Anon group with which the author is familiar receive understanding of their problems and their feelings from one another, emotional support which facilitates change in attitudes and behavior, basic information about solutions to common problems, and information about the treatment process and about the nature of alcoholism as an illness. Shame is alleviated and hope engendered. The nonalcoholic spouses gain perspective on what has happened to their families and on the possibilities of changing towards greater stability. Anxiety diminishes in an almost visible fashion. As they gain perspective on the situation, behavior tends to become more realistic and rewarding. By no means the least important effect derived from membership in the group is a structuring of what has seemed to be a completely unstructured situation and the feelings of security which this engenders.

REFERENCES

1. J. K. Jackson, "The Problem of the Alcoholic Tuberculous Patient," in P. J. Sparer (Ed.), *Personality, Stress and Tuberculosis* (New York: International Universities Press, 1956), pp. 504-38; R. Straus and S. D. Bacon, "Alcoholism and Social Stability: A Study of Occupational Integration in 2,023 Male Clinic Patients," *Quarterly Journal of Studies on Alcohol,* Vol. 12, June 1951, pp. 231-60.

2. *Ibid.;* E. P. Walcott and R. Straus, "Use of a Hospital Facility in Conjunction with Outpatient Treatment of Alcoholics," *Quarterly Journal of Studies on Alcohol,* Vol. 13, March 1952, pp. 60-77; F. E. Feeny, D. F. Mindlen, V. H. Minear, E. E. Short, "The Challenge of the Skid Row Alcoholic: A Social, Psychological and Psychiatric Comparison of Chronically Jailed Alcoholics and Cooperative Clinic Patients," *Quarterly Journal of Studies on Alcohol,* Vol. 16, December 1955, pp. 645-67.

3. D. J. Myerson, "An Active Therapeutic Method of Interrupting the Dependency Relationship of Certain Male Alcoholics," *Quarterly Journal of Studies on Alcohol,* Vol. 14, September 1953, pp. 419-26; L. H. Gliedman, D. Rosenthal, J. Frank, H. T. Nash, "Group Therapy of Alcoholics with Concurrent Group Meetings of Their Wives," *Quarterly Journal of Studies on Alcohol,* Vol. 17, December 1956, pp. 655-70.

4. N. Newell, "Alcoholism and the Father Image," *Quarterly Journal of Studies on Alcohol,* Vol. 11, March 1950, pp. 92-96.

5. D. E. MacDonald, "Mental Disorders in Wives of Alcoholics," *Quarterly Journal of Studies on Alcohol,* Vol. 17, June 1956, pp. 282-87; M. Wellman, "Toward an Etiology of Alcoholism: Why Young Men Drink Too Much," *Canadian Medical Association Journal,* Vol. 73, November 1, 1955, pp. 717-25; S. Futterman, "Personality Trends in Wives of Alcoholics," *Journal of Psychiatric Social Work,* Vol. 23, 1953, pp. 37-41.

6. J. K. Jackson, "The Adjustment of the Family to the Crisis of Alcoholism," *Quarterly Journal of Studies on Alcohol,* Vol. 15, December 1954, pp. 562-86; Gliedman, Rosenthal, Frank, and Nash, *op. cit.* (note 3 *supra*).

7. W. Waller (revised by Reuben Hill), *The Family: A Dynamic Interpretation* (New York: Dryden Press, 1951), pp. 453-61.

8. Gliedman, Rosentha, Frank, and Nash, *op. cit.* (note 3 *supra*).

9. *Ibid.*

The Effects Of
Poverty Upon Marriage

MIRRA KOMAROVSKY

It seems to the author that society played a greater part in their unsatisfactory occupational status than the workers themselves were able to perceive. Their work histories tell the story of frequent shifts from one unskilled or semi-skilled job to another. They ran elevators, drove taxis, handled freight and worked in a variety of factory jobs. Sometimes they were laid off, but more often they changed jobs to improve working conditions or pay. Granted that those who had dropped out of school contain a certain proportion of incompetent or unmotivated persons, but whatever their personal limitations, their schools and communities did not provide adequate guidance, training and information.[1] The men attempted to improve their position but lacked the resources for doing so. They relied upon chance remarks and help of associates: "I heard good jobs are opening up in the West"; "I told everybody to be on the lookout for a good job for me." Their chief sources were the union, for those who were members, and relatives. Only two men capitalized upon the occupational training they received in military service.

Lack of education and isolation from many institutions of the larger society limit utilization even of such assistance as the community provides through the printed word and existing social agencies. In the case of an economic or moral breakdown, existing institutional help does reach working-class families, but the more stable families appear to be at a disadvantage in this respect.

Certain dilemmas of occupational choice are peculiar to some positions in the occupational structure. Conflict between the desire for status and for money is such a dilemma. When the monetary and the prestige rewards attached to jobs are not closely associated, the worker is confronted with a difficult choice between them. For example, a 27-year-old high school graduate, a truck driver's helper earning $5900 a year who had a chance to become a driver with an income of $7500, described his conflict:

> "I don't know what I want to be. I am trying to get something that will raise me and my family in society. I don't want my child to grow up hearing 'Your father is a truck driver.' I know that the

average person thinks truck drivers and teamsters are hard-driving, lower-class in society. I am thinking of becoming a policeman. But when you're used to living at a certain pay level, think of dropping to one-half of it. I have come to believe that money means a lot in this world."

A semi-skilled factory worker reports that his wife wants him to take a desk job: "Something that is important and that she can talk about." As for him, "I don't care what they call me as long as I make a lot of money." Another man made a similar choice. He was a stock boy in Woolworth's, but found that he could make more money as a laborer. The opposite decision was made by a high school graduate who earned over $100 a week but did not like working with colored people. He changed to a job with lower pay because "I wanted to raise my social status." But he is very anxious to make more money again and is still looking for a job which will combine status with adequate pay.

The men caught in this conflict between status and economic drives are, with one exception, high school graduates, who understandably tend to have higher status aspirations than the less educated husbands.

The Shape of the Future

As we have seen, only one-fifth of these workers hope to get out of their blue-collar jobs, but this does not mean that the rest have no hope of improvement. Quite the contrary, the vast majority appear to feel that the future will be brighter than the present. This optimism may in part be explained by the fact that about one-half of the men are still in their twenties. The hopes of the future include higher wages, steadier jobs without the threat of seasonal layoffs, pleasanter conditions of work and more convenient work shifts.

A universal ambition is to own a home, a goal which one-fifth of the families have already achieved. An additional fifth live in parental homes, which in some cases the couple expect to inherit. Something akin to moral disapproval was occasionally expressed towards a man who still "rents" despite good earnings. Other economic aspirations include a car, modern appliances, better furniture and, infrequently, the luxury of a summer cottage. Only one person referred to "travel," though several mentioned vacations in Florida. "My sister has it good," said one woman with ten years of schooling, "a great big refrigerator, nice house, two irons, a regular and a steam iron, three radios, a beautiful T.V. set. She's got everything you could want."

Few would be so naive in a post-Veblenian era as to assume that these economic strivings are free from status overtones. But more explicit forms of status-seeking are also expressed. The most frequent of these is the desire to move to a "better-class" neighborhood, usually for the children's sake. And there is the wish of the men to join a lodge and other organizations. Club membership for women is not regarded as a channel of upward mobility, even though it actually had such effects in two cases. The high school women belong to the P.T.A. and church groups and are Girl Scout leaders more frequently than is the case for less-educated women, but there is nothing resembling the middle-class housewife who joins the prestigeful clubs in the community to gain entry into the next higher social stratum. In general, social life, in the sense of cultivation of the "right" people, plays a very minor role in the efforts to improve status. Nor do the upwardly mobile men expect any help from their wives through social contacts.

"Keeping up with the Joneses" is disapproved of by these families and in fact there appears to be little conpetitive consumption among them. In the restricted social life of Glenton's families, apart from relatives, few couples ever visit each others' homes. There is, consequently, less incentive for competitive consumption and there are fewer models to inspire emulation. As one women put it: "You wouldn't want the things that your aunts and uncles have because they are probably old-fashioned, and there aren't that many people your own age among the relatives." Mass media provide models and stimulate desires for possessions, but the limited social contacts reduce competitive display in comparison with the middle classes.[2]

The few who express the wish for cultural self-improvement through correspondence courses or hobbies consider this either as a means of upward mobility or a compensation for lack of economic success. A 28-year-old grammar school graduate said: "If I can't make my success in the world of material things perhaps I could become something like a poet."

Aspirations for the future find their fullest expression in parental hopes for children. Among themes mentioned repeatedly in reference to children are good character ("We hope they'll turn out all right and be nice people") and improvement in the life situation ("We'd like to give them the chances we didn't get"). When asked, "Would you like you son to follow in your line of work?" the great majority of fathers replied, "Oh no, I'd like him to go much farther." These fathers certainly do not see themselves as occupational models for their sons. Nearly all fathers want their sons to go to college, although some doubt their ability to help them: "Perhaps if he has the ability he can get some scholarship." A number of young couples have taken out insurance policies to send their sons through college.

If college education is valued in Glenton for other than vocational purposes, there is no inkling of it. Only one person, a woman high school graduate, suggested another value: "College offers an experience which one should have if one can afford it." The others agreed with the view that "by the time he is ready to go to work a good job will require a college degree." Partly because college is regarded as an avenue towards occupational mobility, college education for the daughters of the families is considered to be a dispensable luxury —

"She'll get married"; "Let her husband support her"; "We can't afford giving a college education to both the boys and the girls and it is more important for the boys." The few exceptions are not the mothers, but several fathers who want their favorite daughter to attend college. One such couple quarreled because the husband wished to take out an insurance policy for the education of their little girl and the wife thought it an unnecessary expense.

With a regularity that suggests a strongly held value, mothers and fathers disclaim any preferences for a particular occupation for their children. "It is up to the children to pick their own occupations." At times the futility of planning is also stressed: "It don't do any good—children have ideas of their own and the times change." Only rarely do parents express the hope that a daughter might become a nurse or a musician; business, engineering, and other professions are mentioned for the sons. Incidentally, not a single parent expressed regret that he could not afford to send his children to a summer camp. Only in one family each wished they could afford dancing and music lessons for their children.

Men and women in general share similar aspirations. Among the young couples in their twenties, one wife of every four wishes that her husband were more ambitious, and only one of ten thinks that her husband drives himself too hard. Thus one-fourth of the young husbands have to contend with an unfavorable evaluation of their performance on the part of their wives. It was noted that, among the less-educated, the wives tended to explain poor earnings of their husbands by his "bad luck" or lack of education, whereas the high school graduate married to a poor provider spoke more frequently about her husband's lack of drive or lack of ambition.[3]

THE EFFECTS OF POVERTY UPON MARRIAGE

Poverty may be a relative matter, but one-fourth of these families are poor by any American standard. The annual income of the poorest one-fourth of these families varies from the low of $2000 to the high (in only two cases) of $3500. Some of these poor couples are young and hopeful; others, in their thirties, are deeply discouraged. Daily life is a constant struggle to meet the bills for rent, groceries, a pair of shoes, a winter coat, and the T.V. set and the washing machine. The oppressive, almost palpable burden of bills seldom lifts. "What sort of things make you happy?" asked the interviewer and a 25-year-old woman answered: "I had myself a ball once when I came out two dollars over the budget that we didn't have to pay out all at once. I know it sounds goofy that a couple of lousy bucks make you feel good, but it sure does." A 31-year-old woman, the mother of three children, remarked: "There ain't much call to get set up about much when you're so broke."

Dread of illness is ever present because serious sickness means getting into debt or losing furniture or the house. "We had no money, the children were sick and he was half out of his mind," said a mother of five children, whose 28-year-old husband earned $3400 a year as a freight handler. Speaking of her husband's desire to find a better job, this woman explained that if he lost a week or two of pay they would "really starve"—he cannot take any chances.

Possessions are few and the hold on them is precarious.

> A 23-year-old wife of a street cleaner was describing the helpfulness of her older sister. "She even got socks for my husband once when he was out of them. He was wearing a pair with the front half of one of them missing. I had it fixed up with a piece of yarn to hold it over the toes. We were having it rocky and I don't know how she saw it, but she got him some army surplus socks so I didn't have to wash those out every night and iron them dry."

Another incident was described by a 26-year-old woman, mother of two children.

> "We'd made a down payment on this bedroom set. It was secondhand anyhow. Something happened, we couldn't keep up the payments and the guy said he was going to take it away. We slept on the floor before, but I got used to the bed now. I was so down about this I couldn't see straight. The men came to take the bed away. When I heard them coming, I took the kids out and locked the door and hid in my neighbor's place. She came out to talk to them and said that I was out and wouldn't be back till the next day. When my husband got home and saw how I felt about it, he went out and borrowed the money. I don't know where he got it, but he got it somehow. He went around to that bastard's shop in the morning and gave him a piece of his mind. We weren't troubled no more after that even though we were slow on some payments. I sometimes wonder if he [the husband] said he'd smash his windows if he didn't lay off."

> The same woman describes the pleasures of her life: "I got a deal with a hock shop downstairs. He is a real sweet guy. I got a little player in hock down there. Sometimes I scrape together enough money to get it out of hock for a couple of hours and maybe over a week end we all listen to records and then I take it back to him the next day. He don't charge me much more than a quarter for taking it out over the week end."

> A father with eight years of schooling talked of his difficulties in supporting a family of five children. At one time he had to let most of his furniture go, but kept the bed, chairs and T.V. set. He had to sell some books which, he felt, he should have kept for his children, but he decided that it was more important for them to have the T.V.

This is one of many illustrations of the view that a T.V. set is a necessity. As another man put it, "I guess everybody knows you gotta have a place to live, something to eat, clothes. Just about everybody gotta have a T.V. now, too." One woman said: "I had to make up my mind if I wanted the T.V. or the phone the most. You can count on T.V. any old time but if you want to talk to somebody on the phone he's got to be there."

Unhappy marriages are somewhat more frequent among the poorest families than in the rest of the group. Of 15 couples with incomes of $3500 or less, 7 are unhappily married, whereas among the remaining 44 there are 15 unhappy couples. But these facts understate the effects of poverty. The good marriages among the poor also manifest the corrosion of poverty even when the destructive effects are not so marked as to place a marriage in the "unhappy" category.

Economic deprivations, anxiety about the future, the sense of defeat, concern about the failure to give one's children a good start in life, the bleak existence — these and other features of poverty are found to affect marriage in a variety of ways. These features tend to produce tensions in the personalities of family members, with inimical consequences for the marital relationship. They also create dislocations in institutional roles. For example, the relative failure of the husband as a provider disturbs the reciprocities inherent in conjugal roles. Poverty is found at times to hamper marital communication. All of these effects tend to be interdependent, and the task of unraveling them may begin at any point.

The adverse effects of poverty include the loss of self-esteem on the part of the poor providers. The men in their early twenties are still hopeful, but those over 30, with one or two exceptions, reveal a deep loss of self-esteem. A Southern couple who had migrated North some ten years prior to our interview had failed to "make good":

> "The reason he drinks so much here," remarked his wife, "is that he cannot stand to think he'd been a flop. He thought he was going to get himself a fine job. He said we'd shake the dust out of our shoes and we'd show them all. Well, we haven't showed them much. His wages sound good down South and I wrote my folks that we're doing just fine, but they live better down home than we do."

These disappointed men tend to blame themselves even more than their wives blame them. Many wives restrain their criticism out of pity, or expediency, or because they do not hold their husbands completely responsible for the plight of the family. After all, slack seasons, low pay, even being on relief had been familiar experiences for a few of these women in their parental families. But even the wives who do not voice any criticism could not conceal their disappointment—a worried face can be enough of a reproach. Eventually, however, all but the most compassionate and restrained wives are provoked into some criticism.

The women's deprivations and anxieties lead to a more critical scrutiny of their husbands' personalities. A barely perceptible weakness, one which might be tolerated in a good provider, tends to be seized upon as a possible cause of the husband's failure. This excessive sensitivity to the husband's faults unhappily feeds into another typical tendency: fault-finding is easy because economic failure is likely to magnify shortcomings. The poor providers are, themselves, frustrated and anxious. Not many men can handle these destructive emotions without further painful consequences, such as drinking, violence, irritability, increased sensitivity to criticism, and withdrawal. Whatever temporary relief some of these reactions may provide for the men, their long-range effects are to deepen the husband's sense of guilt and to antagonize his wife.

There is another reason why even the more considerate wives are drawn occasionally into disparagement of their husbands. The poor providers offer their wives too obvious a weapon not to be used in a fit of anger. Thus, a wife insisted that her child finish the food on her plate and her husband took the daughter's part, saying that he sympathizes with his daughter's dislike of this particular dish. The wife "hollered at me at the table and said if I'd make enough money she could get the food they liked."

The extreme shortage of money might be thought to rule out quarrels over expenditures because every dollar must be spent on necessities. But this is not the case. The couples quarrel over the order in which bills are to be paid — the milk bills first, so that the children can be fed properly — or the electric bill, so that the light is not turned off. They quarrel over the few discretionary expenditures that do remain — beer, cigarettes or clothes. Every minor difference in economic preferences may cause a conflict because the shortage of money necessitates choices.

Conflict is intensified also because lack of money deprives some husbands of the use of certain rapport devices to decrease marital tensions. When money is available, an apology often takes the form of a gift to break the ice after a quarrel, even if it is only a coffee ring and "Let's have some java to go with it." Thus husbands lack the resources to alleviate marital strain at a time when the strain is exacerbated by poverty.

Some common means of coping with the problems of poverty often provide temporary relief only at the cost of long-range losses. A certain remoteness in marriage and a loss of spontaneity are a case in point. To talk about what matters most — the bills, the fear of sickness and of the uncertain future — is only to intensify the anxiety, and by suppressing these topics one hopes to find some relief. But avoidance of one's uppermost concern blocks other sharing as well. A slightly dishonest tinge to the whole relationship is given by still other suppressions. For example, the wife curbs her irritation out of pity and, more frequently, out of fear of driving her husband to drink or intensifying some other defensive reaction. Again, among the economically more secure and aspiring couples, common aspirations for the children, the purchase of a house and other plans constitute one of the strong ties of marriage.

But for these poor couples the future is not an enticing prospect to be relished in repeated discussions; it is uncertain and threatening. Asked whether she and her husband ever discussed their dreams for the children, a 29-year-old woman said: "Nah, that's too sore." The avoidance of painful subjects in turn increases the loneliness of each partner, at the time when each is most in need of emotional support.

Some poor couples continue to have a very full sex life, but even these reported some adverse effects of poverty. Worry about having more children is one problem. The effect of anxiety and of drink upon the husband's potency is another.

> Speaking of her husband, a 29-year-old woman remarked: "Things have been going hard for him and the soul takes it out on the body. Sometimes he's so down in the mouth he just hasn't got his heart in it." She confessed another difficulty. When her husband is very drunk he wets his bed, so that when he comes in drunk, he sleeps on the iron cot in the front room and she lies in bed "just like a wild cat raging in the woods." She might not have wanted him in the first place when he returns in this state, but somehow she "gets raging inside" anyhow and feeling disappointed.

The strain of doubling up with relatives for the sake of economy is another problem of the poor.

Not every poor couple experiences each or all of these problems with equal intensity. For one thing, the poverty of a young couple hopeful of a better future is not the same experience as poverty ten years later. Of six poor husbands who are 25 years old or younger, only one is unhappily married; out of nine older poor men, six have unhappy marriages. There are many other factors affecting the reaction of the family to poverty even within the same age category. To explore these differences we shall compare three marriages in some detail. None of the three is immune from the adverse effects of poverty, but each exemplifies a variety of sustaining forces which keep the marriage from complete breakdown. It was to be expected that psychological resiliency of individuals and their stability in the face of adversity would safeguard a marriage. So would, clearly, the presence of assets in the relationship itself which might offset external deprivations. But the following cases were selected to illustrate the more unusual situations. We shall see, for example, that psychological resiliency may actually weaken the marital bond and conversely, that the bond may remain strong despite considerable deterioration in the husband's behavior.

THE RELATIVE VULNERABILITY OF MARRIAGES TO THE STRESSES OF POVERTY

Of the two couples to be described first, the Parkers and the Roberts, the latter are happier. The major difference between the two couples lies in the quality of the marital relationship. For the Roberts their marriage is in itself so supportive and rewarding that in the face of adversity the couple turn to each other for emotional aid. The Parkers, apart from their strong sexual tie, are unable to help one another. They seek escape in drink and in other relationships. But the Roberts also show the disturbing effects of poverty. As deprivations continue and anxieties mount, the demands for emotional support become excessive and neither can dispel the worries of the other.

The Parkers have four children, aged 7, 6, 4, and 2. Mr. P. is 33 years old and his wife is 28. Both are grammar school graduates. Mrs. P. said that she did not like school and was "put back a couple of times." This was also true of her husband, she reported. The fathers of both parental families had been on relief in the 1930's.

> "I don't remember it so good," said Mrs. P., "but he does. He was only a little boy but he said it was awful. He said they could never have any fun, they just sat around and nobody played or did anything. His folks were real mad about everything and they'd yell at him and he said it was hell."

Mr. P.'s morale is low. He cannot get full-time work and his earnings for the past year were about $3500. He said:

> "I was born five or ten years too late. I'd have done all right during the last war, but now I am in a jam. I have learned all I can about metal work without working. Now I have to have experience in work and seniority and that's something I never get. I go from one place to another, and I don't get union rights because of it. Oh, sure, they'll help me look for another job, but when there ain't no jobs, what are you going to do? Who could have been more sure about being right than I was in metal work? And look at me now.
>
> "We have gone down-hill ever since we've been married eight and one half years ago. We had one good year and we thought we had the world by the tail. But then with the layoffs and the babies coming we was wised up."

Asked about his wife's attitude towards their economic plight, Mr. P. expressed some appreciation of her:

> "I can't say my wife stands by me or don't complain, but she don't make you feel bad like my mom. Mom's a good woman, a wonderful woman, but even if she don't say nothing or don't ride me, she makes me feel I don't do good enough. But my wife was the one to tell me it was just bad luck when I got mad at myself and thought I was no good. She don't ask me for nothing she shouldn't." He did complain that she was lazy about housework and that she drank too much beer. "I wouldn't drink at home so much, but I hate to see her starting down to the tavern. I wouldn't even mind it so much if she would just quietly have a drink and go

out, but I hate to have her talking down there and have people tell me what she had said. I told the bartender to throw her out and not to serve her," and the bartender had chided him for this. "Beer's good stuff to help you get along in life but it can ruin you. I wouldn't want the kids to be ashamed if I got in trouble with the cops if I got drunk. That's one reason we lay off."

Speaking of his children. Mr. P. said: "Maybe one reason that I like them so much is that I can't do enough for them, and I cannot do what I want to. I would like to see them go to college." He then said very sadly that he didn't think he'd be able to help them, but he had "heard that some boys were smart enough to work their way through." When asked if his wife knew about his wanting the children to go to college, he said rather bitterly, "She'd think I'd gone nuts if I told her."

Mrs. P. was resting on the davenport in a dirty pink quilted wrapper when the interviewer first visited her, unexpectedly. The two older children were in school, the two younger ones were napping and her girl friend was visiting her. This friend and Mrs. P. exchange baby-sitting services to enable each to pick up an odd job now and then. Mrs. P. works at the diner and babysits. Asked whether her husband helped her with the shopping, Mrs. P. gave a picture of their life:

"He gets paid Friday and shops is open Thursday nights. By Thursday night we ain't got no money left. If he does a full day's work on Friday, he don't get home in time. Friday night he goes to the tavern and he usually can't get up in time to help me Saturday morning. Friday and Saturday nights is a big deal with him." Saturday night is also spent at the tavern "having a hand of cards over beer. . . . So it winds up with me doing most of the shopping in the afternoon and about a dollar's worth just about every day. The milk and the bakery come here, but I usually spend four or five dollars on Saturday while he is sleeping it off."

Mrs. P., at the end of the interivew, summed up her husband in these words: "Like I told you, he is kind of good looking and he can still have awful good manners. He is poor, he ain't got much ambition and sex is a big deal with him." "Isn't he smart enough to get a better job?" she was asked. "He is much smarter than he needs to be for the job he is in now. A lot of men that knows less than he and isn't as good workers have better jobs. He's just unlucky. I know he's tried; sometimes when he ain't got a full day's work he goes and tries other places around." "Well then, he really is ambitious," said the interviewer. Mrs. P. explained: "What I mean, he ain't set on buying any Cadillacs and we ain't figuring on buying a house. We'd just like to get all our bills paid off and we'd like to know for sure we weren't going on relief."

As to marriage, here again is Mrs. P.'s summary: "You have fun and then you have babies and then you get scared of having more babies. He worries about the same kind of things I worry about, mostly about bills and how everything is going to turn out, what will happen if we have more kids. No, we don't talk about that. We worry too much about it if we talk about it — it's bad enough as it is." Their sexual relations are very satisfactory, but are beginning to be disturbed by Mr. P.'s anxiety. "Do you think," she was asked, "that this [sex] is one of the most important things in marriage?" She replied: "For us it is. We were lucky that way. It turned out right. But he can't do much when he is lit. When he's a sourpuss he'd practically knock you down if you touched him."

Despite all the sympathy they have for one another, the Parkers turn outward for emotional support, Mr. P. to drink and male companionship at the tavern: Mrs. P. to drink and to her family and girl friends. She derives much pleasure out of earning an occasional $5 to $10 baby-sitting or waiting on tables. The communication between the pair is inadequate and the signs of this inadequacy are numerous:

> Asked what usually arouses his wife's anger, Mr. P. said: "God knows what's going to set her off next — when the children are disobedient or when she thinks I am holding out too much money on her. She talks too much, but I guess she has to let off steam somehow." When the interviewer asked him whether he did not think it would help if he stayed home and let her talk to him to let off steam, he said, "That would be all very nice, if I could take it, but I can't take it." He, in turn, is unfulfilled in marriage, because it is difficult to talk to her: "It ain't that she couldn't understand, but she's busy with the babies or something else most of the time. I go my way and she has a right to go hers." Can he discuss his job with his wife? "About the best news that I could tell her was that I landed a good job." When the interviewer tried to pin him down about his wife's interest in his daily work, asking whether she was perhaps "too interested" or not interested enough, he replied, "She's not interested enough."

Mrs. P. presented her side of the story in her interview, explaining why she tends to "go my way and let him go his":

> "I don't like him to talk about the bills, nothing you can do but pay them and I wish he'd shut his trap. No good talking about it." "If you both gave up drinking," tried the interviewer, "and both worked, couldn't you get a house one day?" The wife answered, "About the time we was sixty when we'd already killed ourselves with work, maybe we could get a place." She was questioned further, "And you think it's all right that he goes to the tavern with the fellows?" She said hopelessly, "What can you do? You'd go nutty if you couldn't do something. Anything that's fun costs money. You can't take a drive, you can't go to a movie, you can't go anywhere without spending two or three bucks."

Asked about her husband's moods, Mrs. P. said: "Sometimes everything is going all right and suddenly he's a sourpuss. He'll just sit there with his sourpuss sticking out a mile. He's more likely to go sourpuss than to blow his top. He gets the slow burn on about things and I don't know exactly what it is that sets him off. He stalks around and he mumbles along and sometimes he'll go out and get a drink, that is, if it isn't the wrong time of the day like early in the morning when he is real sourpuss sometimes." "Can you help him when he is like that?" asked the interviewer. "Not me," she answered. "I'm too busy over the babies the time that he is going off, they're yelling around making an awful racket. Sometimes I wish I could stomp out to work myself. . . . When he feels good, there's no need for him to go out to the tavern. He goes out to see the fellows on the week end and in the evening sometimes. He'll go out earlier, but that's only when he is a sourpuss. When he feels good, he'll play with the girls and even with the boys. He'll do something like wind up their toys, or sometimes he'll feel so good he'll come home and bring a present of some kind, maybe a little bit of candy or a ballpoint pen for the girls.

"Sure — we fight sometimes. I ride him and he rides me too; I don't know what gets into us but those things just happen. One word leads to another and sometimes he will hold out his hand like he is going to hit me but he don't. Then he'll go out and get a drink."

Illustrating the things that hurt her husband's feelings, Mrs. P. described the time when their oldest girl wanted to go on a picnic and her husband "had to help out somehow but didn't want to be bothered. The big girl just said, 'You're not like the other dads with their kids, what kind of dad are you?' Honestly you would've thought she had hit him in the mouth with a truck. He looked like he was going to cry. He went out and got a couple under his belt and then he came and he fixed the kids up like they wanted." Does he cheer her up when she feels blue? "No, I'm the one who has to cheer him up. He comes home and tells me about what's going on and I tell you, he is lower than I am and I have to tell him, 'Have a drink and get over it.' "

Mrs. P. enumerated some of the things that made her feel happy: "Well, they say I am the cheerful sort. I'm happy if I get a big tip down in the diner or if I pick up a nice piece of change from work or can get a new dress cheap. I guess everybody knows it if I have enough beer to feel happy." She does not usually tell her husband when she makes this extra money: "It isn't always a good idea to tell him." She feels that when she earns the money, she has a right to spend it the way she wants to "because as long as I keep the house clean it is up to him to support us. He likes to drink beer a lot more than I do and it is only fair that I can keep what I can pick up." She thinks her husband doesn't approve of that. She gets "awful mad with him because he won't tell me things he should. People will tell him to tell me about a job and he'll forget — at least he says he forgets. The other day a neighbor of ours had a job for me and I lost maybe five or ten bucks. Wouldn't it make you mad? I suppose he thinks because I don't toss it in the kitty and let him drink it all up, he is not going to let me make anything. He hurt his foot once and I got a case of beer for him from money out of my table-waiting and he sure appreciated that. Golly, he laughed and carried on. I told him he wasn't to give none of it to the fellows. This was just for him and me, and that time, he made a grab for me and he squeezed me and he really got all sloppy about that."

Although her secrecy about her own earnings is acknowledged to be a source of friction, Mr. and Mrs. P. have never talked about this directly. This lack of communication tends to spiral marital tension. Mr. P. (at least in part because he cannot talk out his problems with his wife) seeks escape in drink. His wife sympathizes with this reaction because she also drinks, but at the same time she resents his expenditures at the tavern, especially when she suspects that he "holds out" on her on payday. She makes a little money on her own, but does not "put it into the kitty." With her, it is partly a matter of principle — a wife who meets her role obligations is entitled to her husband's support, while her own earnings are none of his affair. Moreover, his "holding out" on her gives her a further excuse to keep her earnings. But her secrecy leads Mr. P. to exaggerate the amount of her earnings and he uses this to justify his own behavior. Mrs. P.'s pattern of avoiding talk about the painful subject of bills leads to lack of communication about money in general. This, in turn, deprives the couple of a chance to iron out their different principles: she *thinks* he doesn't approve of her withholding her earnings, but they have not discussed these differences.

The marriage of the Parkers has some strong assets. One is their sexual tie and the other is the wife's attitude towards her husband, which is relatively free of nagging or belittling. Nevertheless, this marriage is vulnerable because, sex and mutual sympathy notwithstanding, neither can offer the other enough understanding and support in the face of economic hardships. "I go my way and he goes his," said Mrs. P., and Mr. P. described their relationship in almost identical words.

Whatever the psychological forces at work here, some social conditions contribute to this centrifugal tendency. The Parkers view the sharp separation of masculine and feminine interests as the natural pattern. "But they are girls," Mrs. P. exclaimed when the interviewer noted that she apparently talked more freely to her girl friends than to her husband. Admittedly, the couple does share many instrumental domestic concerns. But these sooner or later lead to the painful subject of money. The kinds of interests they do share, then, are tinged with the gloom of their poverty and hopelessness.

This case also illuminates the role of the wife's personal adjustment in the marriages of the economically deprived families. Understandably, the wife's discouragement and too-close identification with her husband may intensify his stress, but so occasionally does her relatively good adjustment. Mrs. P.'s personal adjustment, which is superior to that of her husband, is based upon a variety of supports which do not involve her husband. These are the job at the diner, kidding with the customers, beer, her girl friends, her family, and her relationship with her oldest daughter. But her good cheer makes Mr. P. feel all the more lonely.

The Roberts present a contrasting case. Mr. R. is 27 years old, had seven years of schooling, and is now a fish cleaner in a fish market, earning about $50 a week. His family consists of his 25-year-old wife (who had ten years of schooling) and their three children, aged 4, 3 and 1. They share an apartment with Mr. R.'s brother and his family. The R.'s have little privacy: in their bedroom two screens and some cardboard partitions separate the half of the room in which they sleep from the other half, which is actually a hall opening into the common bathroom and the kitchen.

The relative resiliency of this marriage in the face of economic hardships derives in part from certain features of the marital relationship. Mrs. R. is deeply dependent upon her husband's emotional support and homage to her. Moreover, the exceptional personality of the husband, unimpaired by his economic difficulties, plays a role in the stability of the relationship.

"My mother," Mrs. R. told us, "didn't want me to marry John because he had trouble with his eyes and was poor. 'You had to go and fall for a big hunk like that,' she said. But I'm not sorry I married him. He don't make much dough and I sure hope things will get better, but he is an easy guy to have around and he is a good husband and a good father." The children like him better than they like her, but she thinks this is natural because when he comes home at night, he plays with them. She has to work at home, and is always having to "shoo the children out of the way." He can make a formula and feed the baby its bottle, and he has helped out a lot in giving them baths. She said, "He gets a kick out of it." He also almost always helps her with the dishes. And sometimes when she has heavy marketing to do, he helps to carry things up the stairs to their third-floor flat.

Her husband appears to be helpful to Mrs. R. in other ways. She is an insecure woman and he reassures her. For example, she often wishes she weren't so tall, and he says, "I like big women." At other times, when she is depressed, he advises her to stop housework and watch T.V. for a while or to go out with the children and see her girl friends or her mother.

Perhaps the best clue to the relationship is given by her remark that she feels better when her husband is around. "He enjoys life, likes food, T.V., bright colors, and he is real popular with the crowd."

The emotional dependence of the wife upon her husband characterizes not only the Roberts but three other "poor but happy" couples. The emotional security of these women is so bound up with their husbands that they are ambivalent about week-end and evening jobs which take husbands out of the home, despite the chance of some needed additonal earnings.

In three cases, including the Roberts, membership in a clique serves to offset to some extent the adverse effects of poverty. Clique membership has this salutary influence because in these cases the husband is the acknowledged social leader of the pairs. "They ask us because of him," admitted one wife, "mind you, it's not just that he's my husband. Women I meet in the afternoon often tell me how nicely he sang or tell me they liked some story or joke he told." The popularity of the husbands raised their own self-esteen and their status in the eyes of their wives. Mr. R. remarked: "I tell my wife those stories but she ain't interested but when we are in a crowd and everybody laughs, she laughs too."

The clique, also, provides some shared pleasures when pleasures are scarce. "Life is no good," said Mrs. R. "if you can't have a good time sometimes. All the good time we got is watching T.V. and going around with the crowd."

The clique serves as a form of group therapy. The interviews of the two men were punctuated with such comments as: "We talked about it with the crowd" or "The crowd kidded us that time." Relatives, also, offer such support, but an advantage of the clique lies in the similar ages and stages of the family cycle, not always present in the kinship group. Moreover, clique relationships lack the intense and sometimes ambivalent character of kinship ties.

But the ability to use the support of such a clique is not a matter of accident. It presupposes the existence of joint social life which is not universal even among the gregarious families. It may also require an exceptional social talent for the husband to obtain a reward from "the crowd" great enough to offset the humiliation of economic failure.

Despite the sustaining forces, the economic deprivations of the Roberts have begun to affect their marital relationship.

"We ain't fixed so good," said Mrs. R. "He got no education and he has trouble with his eyes. When we got married it looked like things were going to be good, but things ain't so good now . . . gee, I'd like to have a different house, this place is a pig-pen." The fish market offers no chance for promotion. Their only hope is that he and his brother can one day open a fish market of their own; Mr. R. told us it would take, at best, many years to accumulate the needed capital, and neither side of the family can help them.

Apart from worry about subsistence, Mrs. R. is very unhappy about living together with her sister and brother-in-law. Her nerves are frequently on edge.

> "It's all right for a little while to be doubled up like this, but when it goes on and on, you can't stand each other," Mr. R. told us. "Much as my brother and I like living together, we got our family to think of. Our wives would like to live apart. It would be nice if we could live beside each other, but in different apartments." They heard of a place in a neighboring town, where there were two flats, "sort of run-down," but convenient. "The girls," he said, "will have to make up their minds whether they want to move so far away from their mothers and their folks." (It would be about a fifteen-minute bus ride.)

Another source of anxiety is the fear of pregnancy. The couple would have liked to have six children but "We ain't got enough dough. We want to give the children good food. Food is real important to him, too. Vitamins cost an awful lot of money." The R.'s have been married for six years. Much as she appreciates her exceptionally kind and supportive husband, Mrs. R. has expressed some disappointment with his economic performance, and there are no prospects for improvement. Furthermore, her depressions are already beginning to strain the marriage.

> Mrs. R. expressed the regret that neither of them had much education. "But I guess he couldn't help it with his eyes. He gets tired if he tries to read. Funny thing," she added, musingly, "it don't seem to bother him when he cleans fish or watches T.V." She described her husband as "more ambitious than able." Speaking about herself, she said she wished she could be a more cheerful person. "Yes, I get moody, any little old thing can set me off, maybe coming out behind with the budget, maybe the kids not feeling well and squabbling. The baby got sick a couple of months ago and we were scared for a while. The doctor thought maybe we should send her to the hospital and we didn't have no plans for it [insurance]. The downer you get, the downer you go; you have to get some breaks or you might wind up jumping in the river."

And now from Mr. R.'s interview:

> "When she feels good, she kind of skips. She kind of jumps and dances around. I like to see that. It makes me feel good too. I tell her I like her to be cheerful. But she gets cranky, she says she's nervous, I don't know what it is. I sent her to the doctor, and he said it wasn't nothing but her imagination. I asked him and he told me, and I told her as long as she is moody, she had better have good moods."

Unlike Mr. P., whose personality remains intact and who compensates his wife for economic privations by the good natured homage he pays her, Mr. Smith, the husband in our third case, is far from being a model husband. He drinks and squanders money required for the daily necessities of life. He spends three to five evenings away from home, usually in the tavern, leaving his wife alone and completely isolated, since she has no relatives or friends in the community. If he has not actually been unfaithful there is enough gossip to give his wife uneasy suspicions, but with all that, the marriage is an exceptionally stable one. What enables this marriage to withstand such adversities?

The S.'s, born in South Carolina, left the South soon after their marriage because Mrs. S.'s family was "uppity" towards Mr. S. and his own people, according to his wife, "weren't very nice and certainly weren't good to him." Mr. S. is 33, had nine years of schooling, and earns $3000 to $3500 a year operating a handtruck for an express company.

> "I haven't got any skills. Just push a truck around. This damn thing called automation is not something I can do much about. Sure, I'd like to have more education. I'd like to have it shoved at me. I'm not energetic enough to go out and get it. . . . Well, I work all day. I'm tired when I get home."

His job is steady, but he cannot always count on a full week's work. He picks up odd jobs and he once got into trouble with the union because he was doing unlicensed porter's work.

Mrs. S. is 29 years old, and had nine years of schooling. The couple lost two children in infancy and they still mourn their loss. Their love for their only child, a 9-year-old girl, is intense.

The S.'s have moved around a great deal during their stay in Glenton. Their furniture was made by the husband, who salvaged some second-hand chairs, a table and an iron cot and remodeled these pieces. Mrs. S. made attractive pillows for the chairs and the sofa. Complimented on their handmade furniture, Mrs. S. drew herself up with a certain pride and said that her husband was very good with his hands. With all the pride in their handiwork, she looked around at the two-room apartment and said rather bitterly: "If you can call this a home." Mrs. S. would have liked to have returned to her home in the South. She longs to be back with her large family, but Mr. S. is still bitter about her folks so that she tries to "keep her mouth shut" about her homesickness. Mr. S. does want news from home when she gets letters, but she has to be careful as to what she can tell him. During the fourth visit to the family, the interviewer saw Mr. and Mrs. S. together. Mr. S. has admitted his defeat in the East and has begun talking about trying his luck in some other part of the country. This is the conversation that took place in the presence of the interviewer:

> Mrs. S. said: "I had a hankerin' to get back home ever since we got here. I didn't say nothing because he thought he was making better wages. But if he can get as good wages down there I think we'd better get up and git." Did they ever talk this over, asked the

interviewer. "No! I didn't say nothing because I didn't want to make him uneasy." Mr. S. broke in and said: "I knew it anyhow." In his own interview Mr. S. said: "It would be a lot easier back home because she would have somebody to talk to. She ain't got any friends up here and it gets real lonesome."

The direct and indirect effects of poverty strain this marriage and we shall trace the vicious circle of influences. Mr. S.'s disappointment in himself leads to his drinking. His excessive drinking, as well as his discouragement, is destroying their sex life.

Mrs. S. said with some pity: "He drinks because he can't stand to think he'd been a flop." He leaves after dinner, usually for the bar, but he doesn't always tell his wife where he is bound for or when he will be home. In the joint interview Mr. S. was talking about his drinking and he turned to his wife to ask belligerently whether she thought he was a drunk. No, she said, but he did drink too much for his health. Mr. S. suddenly became all smiles and said he knew he drank too much for the health of his budget, but what does a working man have outside of his wife and the bar. "Yup, I can get a lot out of my system talking to people at work and in the tavern. If she'd come to the bar she'd feel a lot better. I try to get her to come out to have a beer but she thinks it's wrong."

"A bar is no place for a woman to be," commented his wife. "Drinking is bad enough but drinking in a bar is terrible." When the interviewer turned to Mrs. S. and asked whether it might not be harmless to keep her husband company in the bar, Mr. S. at once came to his wife's defense, smiling benignly, "She's kinda religious." Mrs. S., like her folks in the South, thinks that drinking and even smoking is wrong.

The sex life of the S.'s is now rarely satisfactory. The remark, cited earlier in this chapter, that "the soul takes it out of the body" was made by Mrs. S. in describing how his discouragement affected her husband's sex life. She described a spat they had had the night before the interview:

"He came home drunk and was mushing it around kissing me. . . . I would not have minded it if he could stand straight and if he didn't stink so much. After he has some coffee and a bath I don't mind him by me in bed and I'd be awfully disappointed if he didn't kiss me goodnight."

Whether because his wife is a witness to his economic defeat or for other reasons Mr. S. is, in all probability, occasionally unfaithful to his wife. The suspicion of unfaithfulness was aroused by Mrs. S.'s staunch defense of her husband against the gossip of their neighbors.

"I get furious," said Mrs. S. "because the neighbors' children tell my daughter nasty things about her father's drinking and maybe flirting with somebody. One time a man came in boiling mad, because one of the neighbors had said that my husband was going with this man's wife. He came to the house a little tipsy to look for his wife. I almost took a stick to him and pushed him out of the door and told him if he ever came to our house and said anything like that in front of our daughter I'd take a knife to him. He wanted to search the house and I told him he would do it over my dead body. He came around and apologized the next day, quiet, when the girl was in school. He stayed off from work to do it." She said she would not dream of discussing anything like this with the neighbors as she would not want her daughter to find out. When her daughter grew older she said she would have to explain some things to her and try to keep her loving both of them.

When Mr. S. was asked about sources of happy moods, he included "seeing pretty women walking along the street with nice airy dresses, nice limbs and all that sort of thing."

The husband's status in the marriage is still high, but it has been adversely affected by his failure. Lack of money has created for Mrs. S. a conflict between her conjugal and parental roles.

"Down home," said Mrs. S., "they say your first duty is to your husband. They say a child can die and your husband has the power for a new one, and he is your lord. When you marry him you say you are going to obey him." The question of the conflicting demands of her husband and her daughter admittedly troubles Mrs. S. a great deal. She apparently feels guilty because she occasionally makes a decision in favor of her daughter's interests, concerning food preferences, for example.

Speaking about conjugal roles, Mr. S. said in the presence of his wife, "A poor man ain't a king nowhere, not even in his own family." His wife looked hurt and said that she knew it was a woman's duty to look after her husband but that they just hadn't enough money for him to get the kind of food and service that he expected. She had after all to look out for the health of their daughter and to make their own clothes.

Marital communication between the Smiths has deteriorated in the sense that an increasing number of topics are "too sore to discuss. He is touchy," said Mrs. S., "because he can't do things better for me so he grouches and sulks and I had to learn to keep my mouth shut." Throughout the interview Mrs. S. repeatedly explained that she was unable to share this or that worry with her husband because she feared that he would become moody and leave for the bar.

This reserve in marriage draws the wife closer to her nine-year-old daughter who is becoming her confidante. This is not to suggest that there is a coalition of mother and daughter against the father. The daughter adores her father and is in turn deeply loved by him. Mrs. S.

cautions her daughter against repeating the gossip of the church women for fear of disturbing her husband.

Mrs. S. has no friends in the community. She feels herself superior in morals and manners to her neighbors, but her complete isolation is also an indirect result of their situation. She cuts herself off from the women in her church as well as in the housing development in order to guard her daughter from what she describes as the mean gossip about her husband. She gives a picture of a sad and very lonely work-driven woman, anxious about the future of the family. Asked about sources of happy moods, she said that making a pretty dress for her daughter, so that she would not ask for one in the store, made her feel lighthearted. She feels pleased with herself when she can get all her work done. Once in a while when her husband is in a good mood then everybody is happy. He'd shuffle around, half-dancing, singing and "talking sweet" to her. And once she had a wonderful day when a family from her home town came to Glenton and visited them.

When, at the conclusion of the interview, Mrs. S. was asked what, if anything, she would like to change about her marriage, she laughed loudly for the first time in the interview: "If I wasn't so crazy about him I'd change the whole thing from A to Z." She'd start off all over again by falling in love with another man, a rich man who would buy them a big house and a car and she'd have a lot of kids. Then in a more serious and sad voice she added that the only thing she'd change about her husband would be to make him luckier.

Among the sustaining forces of this marriage are the firm patriarchal convictions of the wife. Mr. S. may say that a poor man is not the king of his family, but he enjoys high status in his own marriage. Mrs. S.'s patriarchal attitudes blunt her resentment against her husband. She takes upon herself the burden of adjustment to her bleak and lonely life. She explained her loneliness not by his neglect of her but by her separation from her family. To the extent that these attitudes help maintain Mr. S.'s status in the family, they also bolster his self-esteem and safeguard his personality from more serious disintegration.

Mr. S. explained that his wife does not expect him to help with housework: "She is old-fashioned that way." However, he does help on his own initiative and is always rewarded by her gratitude. Where another wife may demand help with housework precisely because the poor provider does not fulfill his own role obligations, Mrs. S. is grateful for his aid. Such aid, offered as a voluntary gift, does not lower his status. Mrs. S.'s patriarchal attitudes are revealed in other ways. Asked whether he is an easy man to talk to, she said: "Yes, when he is not troubled but he usually wants to talk about himself more than about me, and men are supposed to talk more."

The common values shared by this couple are all the more binding because they still feel themselves alien in the East; even Mr. S. with his wider contacts and his gregarious personality finds the Eastern attitudes on race and other issues different from his own. This isolation in an alien environment makes Mrs. S. all the more dependent upon whatever attention and support her husband is willing to give her. In the discussion of T.V. preferences, she said that she feels so much better when her husband is home that she is only too glad to let him watch whatever he likes on T.V. irrespective of her own preferences.

Another sustaining force is the deep mutual empathy and affection characterizing their marriage.

> Mrs. S. describes their mourning after the death of the two infants. "We was grieving together without saying a word." She felt they were very close to each other then. Sometimes, she said, he can be very comforting, he can understand her "real spooky, but, of course, if he has other things on his mind you might as well talk to yourself." Her pity for him is shown in her attitude towards his drinking: "He takes an awful lot of money for his beer, but he has had it awfully hard and it is one of his few pleasures." Asked whether he ever shows any appreciation of her, she answered: "He acts as though I was the most marvelous movie star in the world and he is a great kisser." When he is happy he waltzes around with her and just before they go to sleep he often tells her how much he loves her. Once in a while he even brings her a little present, such as a handkerchief. "Once or twice he got some flowers for me free from a florist. He brought the flowers home, cute and bashful like a high school kid . . . kind of like he is trying to say he is sorry for what he is, but I don't mind what he is, although I get awfully griped with things the way they are." Mr. S. in turn expressed great satisfaction with his wife as a mate, as a mother and as a housekeeper.
>
> Mrs. S. is not as subservient to her husband as it might appear. She gave several illustrations of their arguments — once they had planned to do some errands together and instead he got cross and went to the bar. "I was fit to be tied. I went and did some of the errands myself, not the ones he wanted done, and then he came in and hollered at me about it and I bawled him out real good, and told him to go and do the errands himself, that it serves him right if he was going to run off to the bar in the morning. We had a real bust-up but it was all right in a little because I was so tired and he too."

The Smiths illustrate that the wife's tenderness and pity for the husband can survive not only economic privation, but excessive drinking, marital neglect and, perhaps, unfaithfulness. As we have seen, her patriarchal attitudes, the common values she shares with her husband in an alien environment, his empathy and romanticism are among the other sustaining forces.

To sum up, none of Glenton's poor families is immune from the destructive effects of poverty and economic failure, but the effects vary in degree and in kind. The cases illustrated the variety of factors that made some families more vulnerable to these stresses than others. A cluster of such factors centers around the marital relationship itself — for example, the interpersonal relations, as seen in the compatibility of emotional and sexual roles. The Parkers turn outward for emotional support with progressive estrangement in marriage, whereas for the Roberts and the Smiths the spouse is often a shield against external hardships. The norms of marriage also play a role in the outcome. Mrs. Smith's patriarchal norms, for example, provide some immunity to the effects of poverty. Interpersonal competence is still another feature of a marriage which was traced in the foregoing case studies. The lack of communication between the Parkers tends to increase mutual suspicion and Mr. P.'s loneliness.

In addition to the marital relationship, the interplay between the pair and their social environment comprises another category of relevant forces. The isolation of the Smiths among neighbors of whom they are critical deepens their sense of mutual respect and dependence. Mr. Robert's high position in his "crowd" buttresses his self-esteem and in part compensates his wife for his lack of achievement.

It is to be expected that psychological resiliency of the husband and of the wife in the face of economic hardships will benefit marriage, and indeed this is amply borne out. The more surprising finding, however, is that under certain conditions personal integration actually undermines the solidarity of the couple. Mrs. Parker's cheerfulness makes her husband feel all the gloomier. The cohesion of the pair requires something more than the stability of the two personalities.

The cases also document the circular processes of marital interaction — the vicious circles which undermine the solidarity of the couple and the "virtuous" circles sustaining the marriage despite external stresses. An act having an unfavorable effect all too often starts a chain reaction. But so also does a salutary act, and seemingly small initial differences therefore may lead to increasingly divergent marital patterns.[4]

REFERENCES

1. See Bernard Barber, 1961, pp. 110-112, for proposed social measures to improve educational life chances for children of lower socio-economic classes.

2. In a study of grades of residences in an urban area, clerical workers were found to have higher mean dwelling ratings that blue-collar workers at the same income level. Charles Tilly, 1961.

3. For guides to the extensive literature on mobility aspirations, see textbooks such as Bernard Barber, 1957, and Joseph A. Kahl, 1957.

4. For a discussion of and bibliography on family adjustment to crises see Reuben Hill, 1963, and Howard J. Parad and Gerald Caplan, 1963.

The Double Standard of Aging

SUSAN SONTAG

"How old are you?" The person asking the question is anybody. The respondent is a woman, a woman "of a certain age," as the French say discreetly. That age might be anywhere from her early twenties to her late fifties. If the question is impersonal — routine information requested when she applies for a driver's license, a credit card, a passport — she will probably force herself to answer truthfully. Filling out a marriage-license application, if her future husband is even slightly her junior, she may long to subtract a few years; probably she won't. Competing for a job, her chances often partly depend on being the "right age," and if hers isn't right, she will lie if she thinks she can get away with it. Making her first visit to a new doctor, perhaps feeling particularly vulnerable at the moment she's asked, she will probably hurry through the correct answer. But if the question is only what people call personal — if she's asked by a new friend, a casual acquaintance, a neighbor's child, a co-worker in an office, store, factory — her response is harder to predict. She may sidestep the question with a joke, or refuse it with playful indignation: "Don't you know you're not supposed to ask a woman her age?" Or, hesitating a moment, embarrassed but defiant, she may tell the truth. Or she may lie. But neither truth, evasion, nor lie relieves the unpleasantness of that question. For a woman to be obliged to state her age after "a certain age" is always a miniature ordeal.

If the question comes from a woman, she will feel less threatened than if it comes from a man. Other women are, after all, comrades in sharing the same potential for humiliation. She will be less arch, less coy. But she probably still dislikes answering and may not tell the truth. Bureaucratic formalities excepted, whoever asks a woman this question — after "a certain age" — is ignoring a taboo and possibly being impolite or downright hostile. Almost everyone acknowledges that once a woman passes an age that is actually quite young, her exact age ceases to be a legitimate target of curiosity. After childhood the year of a woman's birth becomes her secret, her private property. It is something of a dirty secret. To answer truthfully is always indiscreet.

The discomfort a woman feels each time she tells her age is quite independent of the anxious awareness of human mortality that everyone has from time to time. There is a normal sense in which nobody, men and women alike, relishes growing older. After thirty-five any mention of one's age carries with it the reminder that one is probably closer to the end of one's life than to the beginning. There is nothing unreasonable in that anxiety. Nor is there any abnormality in the anguish and anger that people who are really old, in their seventies and eighties, feel about the implacable waning of their powers, physical and mental. Advanced age is undeniably a trial, however stoically it may be endured. It is a shipwreck, no matter with what courage elderly people insist on continuing the voyage. But the objective, sacred pain of old age is of another order than the subjective, profane pain of aging. Old age is a genuine ordeal, one that men and women undergo in a similar way. Growing older is mainly an ordeal of the imagination — a moral disease, a social pathology — intrinsic to which is the fact that it afflicts women much more than men. It is particularly women who experience growing older (everything that comes *before* one is actually old) with such distaste and even shame.

The emotional privileges this society confers upon youth stir up some anxiety about getting older in everybody. All modern, urbanized societies — unlike tribal, rural societies — condescend to the values of maturity and heap honors on the joys of youth. This revaluation of the life cycle in favor of the young brilliantly serves a secular society whose idols are ever increasing industrial productivity and the unlimited cannibalization of nature. Such a society must create a new sense of the rhythms of life in order to incite people to buy more, to consume and throw away faster. People let the direct awareness they have of their needs, of what really gives them pleasure, be overruled by commercialized *images* of happiness and personal well-being; and, in this imagery designed to stimulate ever more avid levels of consumption, the most popular metaphor for happiness is "youth." (I would insist that it is a metaphor, not a literal description. Youth is a metaphor for energy, restless mobility, appetite: for the state of "wanting.") This equating of well being with youth makes everyone naggingly aware of exact age — one's own and that of other people. In primitive and pre-modern societies people attach much less importance to dates. When lives are divided into long periods with stable responsibilities and steady ideals (and hypocrisies), the exact number of years someone has lived becomes a trivial fact; there is hardly any reason to mention, even to know, the year in which one was born. Most people in nonindustrial societies are not sure exactly how old they are. People in industrial societies are haunted by numbers. They take an almost obsessional interest in keeping the scorecard of aging, convinced that anything above a low total is some kind of bad news. In an era in which people actually live longer and longer, what now amounts to the latter *two thirds* of everyone's life is shadowed by a poignant apprehension of unremitting loss.

The prestige of youth afflicts everyone in this society to some degree. Men, too, are prone to periodic bouts of depression about aging — for instance, when feeling insecure or unfulfilled or insufficiently rewarded in their jobs. But men rarely panic about aging in the way women often do. Getting older is less profoundly wounding for a man, for in addition to the propaganda for youth that puts both men and women on the defensive as they age, there is a double standard about aging that denounces women with special severity. Society is much more permissive about aging in men, as it is more tolerant of the sexual infidelities of husbands. Men are "allowed" to age, without penalty, in several ways that women are not.

This society offers even fewer rewards for aging women than it does to men. Being physically attractive counts much more in a woman's life than in a man's, but beauty, identified, as it is for women, with youthfulness, does not stand up well to age. Exceptional mental powers can increase with age, but women are rarely encouraged to develop their minds above dilettant standards. Because the wisdom considered the special province of women is "eternal," an age-old, intuitive knowledge about the emotions to which a repertoire of facts, wordly experience, and the methods of rational analysis have nothing to contribute, living a long time does not promise women an increase in wisdom either. The private skills expected of women are exercised early and, with the exception of a talent for making love, are not the kind that enlarge with experience. "Masculinity" is identified with competence, autonomy, self-control — qualities that the disappearance of youth does not threaten. Competence in most of the activities expected from men, physical sports excepted, increases with age. "Femininity" is identified with incompetence, helplessness, passivity, noncompetitiveness, being nice. Age does not improve these qualities.

Middle-class men feel diminished by aging, even while still young, if they have not yet shown distinction in their careers or made a lot of money. (And any tendencies they have toward hypochondria will get worse in middle age, focusing with particular nervousness on the specter of heart attacks and the loss of virility.) Their aging crisis is linked to that terrible pressure on men to be "successful" that precisely defines their membership in the middle class. Women rarely feel anxious about their age because they haven't succeeded at something. The work that women do outside the home rarely counts as a form of achievement, only as a way of earning money; most employment available to women mainly exploits the training they have been receiving since early childhood to be servile, to be both supportive and parasitical, to be unadventurous. They can have menial, low-skilled jobs in light industries, which offer as feeble a criterion of success as housekeeping. They can be secretaries, clerks, sales personnel, maids, research assistants, waitresses, social workers, prostitutes, nurses, teachers, telephone operators — public transcriptions of the servicing and nurturing roles that women have in family life. Women fill very few executive posts, are rarely found suitable for large corporate or political responsibilities, and form only a tiny contingent in the liberal professions (apart from teaching). They are virtually barred from jobs that involve an expert, intimate relation with machines or an aggressive use of the body, or that carry any physical risk or sense of adventure. The jobs this society deems appropriate to women are auxiliary, "calm" activities that do not compete with, but aid, what men do. Besides being less well paid, most work women do has a lower ceiling of advancement and gives meager outlet to normal wishes to be powerful. All outstanding work by women in this society is voluntary; most women are too inhibited by the social disapproval attached to their being ambitious and aggressive. Inevitably, women are exempted from the dreary panic of middle-aged men whose "achievements" seem paltry, who feel stuck on the job ladder or fear being pushed off it by someone younger. But they are also denied most of the real satisfactions that men derive from work — satisfactions that often do increase with age.

The double standard about aging shows up most brutally in the conventions of sexual feeling, which presuppose a disparity between men and women that operates permanently to women's disadvantage. In the accepted course of events a woman anywhere from her late teens through her middle twenties can expect to attract a man more or less her own age. (Ideally, he should be at least slightly older.) They marry and raise a family. But if her husband starts an affair after some years of marriage, he customarily does so with a woman much younger than his wife. Suppose, when both husband and wife are already in their late forties or early fifties, they divorce. The husband has an excellent chance of getting married again, probably to a younger woman. His ex-wife finds it difficult to remarry. Attracting a second husband younger than herself is improbable; even to find someone her own age she has to be lucky, and she will probably have to settle for a man considerably older than herself, in his sixties or seventies. Women become sexually ineligible much earlier than men do. A man, even an ugly man, can remain eligible well into old age. He is an acceptable mate for a young, attractive woman. Women, even good-looking women, become ineligible (except as partners of very old men) at a much younger age.

Thus, for most women, aging means a humiliating process of gradual sexual disqualification. Since women are considered maximally eligible in early youth, after which their sexual value drops steadily, even young women feel themselves in a desperate race against the calendar. They are old as soon as they are no longer very young. In late adolescence some girls are already worrying about getting married. Boys and young men have little reason to anticipate trouble because of aging. What makes men desirable to women is by no means tied to youth. On the contrary, getting older tends (for several decades) to operate in men's favor, since their value as lovers and husbands is set more by what they do than how they look. Many men have more success romantically at forty than they did at twenty-five; fame, money, and above all, power are sexually enhancing. (A woman who has won power in a competitive profession or business career is considered less, rather than more, desirable. Most men confess themselves intimidated or turned off sexually by such a woman, obviously because she is harder to treat as just a sexual "object.") As they age, men may start feeling anxious about actual sexual performance, worrying about a loss of sexual vigor or even impotence, but their sexual eligibility is not abridged simply by getting older. Men stay sexually possible as long as they can make love. Women are at a disadvantage because their sexual candidacy depends on meeting certain much stricter "conditions" related to looks and age.

Since women are imagined to have much more limited sexual lives than men do, a woman who has never married is pitied. She was not found acceptable, and it is assumed that her life continues to confirm her unacceptability. Her presumed lack of sexual opportunity is embarrassing. A man who remains a bachelor is judged much less crudely. It is assumed that he, at any age, still has a sexual life — or the chance of one. For men there is no destiny equivalent to the humiliating condition of being an old maid, a spinster. "Mr.," a cover from infancy to senility, precisely exempts men from the stigma that attaches to any woman, no longer young, who is still "Miss." (That women are divided into "Miss" and "Mrs.," which calls unrelenting attention to the situation of each woman with respect to marriage, reflects the belief that being single or married is much more decisive for a woman than it is for a man.)

For a woman who is no longer very young, there is certainly some relief when she has finally been able to marry. Marriage soothes the sharpest pain she feels about the passing years. But her anxiety never subsides completely, for she knows that should she re-enter the sexual market at a later date—because of divorce, or the death of her husband, or the need for erotic adventure—she must do so under a handicap far greater than any man of her age (*whatever* her age may be) and regardless of how good-looking she is. Her achievements, if she has a career, are no asset. The calendar is the final arbiter.

To be sure, the calendar is subject to some variations from country to country. In Spain, Portugal, and the Latin American countries, the age at which most women are ruled physically undesirable comes earlier than in the United States. In France it is somewhat later. French conventions of sexual feeling make a quasi-official place for the woman between thirty-five and forty-five. Her role is to initiate an inexperienced or timid young man, after which she is, of course, replaced by a young girl. (Colette's novella *Chéri* is the best known account in fiction of such a love affair; biographies of Balzac relate a well-documented example from real life.) This sexual myth does make turning forty somewhat easier for French women. But there is no difference in any of these countries in the basic attitudes that disqualify women sexually much earlier than men.

Aging also varies according to social class. Poor people look old much earlier in their lives than do rich people. But anxiety about aging is certainly more common, and more acute, among middle-class and rich women than among working-class women. Economically disadvantaged women in this society are more fatalistic about aging; they can't afford to fight the cosmetic battle as long or as tenaciously. Indeed, nothing so clearly indicates the fictional nature of this crisis than the fact that women who keep their youthful appearance the longest —

women who lead unstrenuous, physically sheltered lives, who eat balanced meals, who can afford good medical care, who have few or no children — are those who feel the defeat of age most keenly. Aging is much more a social judgment than a biological eventuality. Far more extensive than the hard sense of loss suffered during menopause (which, with increased longevity, tends to arrive later and later) is the depression about aging, which may not be set off by any real event in a woman's life, but is a recurrent state of "possession" of her imagination, ordained by society—that is, ordained by the way this society limits how women feel free to imagine themselves.

There is a model account of the aging crisis in Richard Strauss's sentimental-ironic opera *Der Rosenkavalier,* whose heroine is a wealthy and glamorous married woman who decides to renounce romance. After a night with her adoring young lover, the Marschallin has a sudden, unexpected confrontation with herself. It is toward the end of Act I; Octavian has just left. Alone in her bedroom she sits at her dressing table, as she does every morning. It is the daily ritual of self-appraisal practiced by every woman. She looks at herself and, appalled, begins to weep. Her youth is over. Note that the Marschallin does not discover, looking in the mirror, that she is ugly. She is as beautiful as ever. The Marschallin's discovery is moral—that is, it is a discovery of her imagination; it is nothing she actually *sees.* Nevertheless, her discovery is no less devastating. Bravely, she makes her painful, gallant decision. She will arrange for her beloved Octavian to fall in love with a girl his own age. She must be realistic. She is no longer eligible. She is now "the old Marschallin."

Strauss wrote the opera in 1911. Contemporary opera-goers are rather shocked when they discover that the libretto indicates that the Marschallin is all of thirty-four years old; today the role is generally sung by a soprano well into her forties or in her fifties. Acted by an attractive singer of thirty-four, the Marschallin's sorrow would seem merely neurotic, or even ridiculous. Few women today think of themselves as old, wholly disqualified from romance, at thirty-four. The age of retirement has moved up, in line with the sharp rise in life expectancy for everybody in the last few generations. The *form* in which women experience their lives remains unchanged. A moment approaches inexorably when they must resign themselves to being "too old." And that moment is invariably — objectively — premature.

In earlier generations the renunciation came even sooner. Fifty years ago a woman of forty was not just aging but old, finished. No struggle was even possible. Today, the surrender to aging no longer has a fixed date. The aging crisis (I am speaking only of women in affluent countries) starts earlier but lasts longer; it is diffused over most of a woman's life. A woman hardly has to be anything like what would reasonably be considered old to worry about her age, to start lying (or being tempted to lie). The crisis can come at any time. Their schedule depends on a blend of personal ("neurotic") vulnerability and the swing of social mores. Some women don't have their first crisis until thirty. No one escapes a sickening shock upon turning forty. Each birthday, but especially those ushering in a new decade—for round numbers have a special authority—sounds a new defeat. There is almost as much pain in the anticipation as in the reality. Twenty-nine has become a queasy age ever since the official end of youth crept forward, about a generation ago, to thirty. Being thirty-nine is also hard; a whole year in which to meditate in glum astonishment that one stands on the threshhold of middle age. The frontiers are arbitrary, but not any less vivid for that. Although a woman on her fortieth birthday is hardly different from what she was when she was still thirty-nine, the day seems like a turning point. But long before actually becoming a woman of forty, she has been steeling herself against the depression she will feel. One of the greatest tragedies of each woman's life is simply getting older, it is certainly the *longest* tragedy.

Aging is a movable doom. It is a crisis that never exhausts itself, because the anxiety is never really used up. Being a crisis of the imagination rather than of "real life," it has the habit of repeating itself again and again. The territory of aging (as opposed to actual old age) has no fixed boundaries. Up to a point it can be defined as one wants. Entering each decade — after the initial shock is absorbed — an endearing, desperate impulse of survival helps many women to stretch the boundaries to the decade following. In late adolescence, thirty seems the end of life. At thirty, one pushes the sentence forward to forty. At forty, one still gives oneself ten more years.

I remember my closest friend in college sobbing on the day she turned twenty-one. "The best part of my life is over. I'm not young any more." She was a senior, nearing graduation. I was a precocious freshman, just sixteen. Mystified, I tried lamely to comfort her, saying that I didn't think twenty-one was *so* old. Actually, I didn't understand at all what could be demoralizing about turning twenty-one. To me, it meant only something good: being in charge of oneself, being free. At sixteen, I was too young to have noticed, and become confused by, the peculiarly loose, ambivalent way in which this society demands that one stop thinking of oneself as a girl and start thinking of oneself as a woman. (In America that demand can now be put off to the age of thirty, even beyond.) But even if I thought her distress was absurd, I must have been aware that it would be not simply absurd but quite unthinkable in a *boy* turning twenty-one. Only women worry about age with that degree of inanity and pathos. And, of course, as with all crises that are inauthentic and therefore repeat themselves compulsively (because the danger is largely fictive, a poison in the imagination), this friend of mine went on having the same crisis over and over, each time as if for the first time.

I also came to her thirtieth birthday party. A veteran of many love affairs, she had spent most of her twenties living abroad and had just returned to the United States. She had been good-looking when I first knew her; now she was beautiful. I teased her about the tears she had shed over being twenty-one. She laughed and claimed not to remember. But thirty, she said ruefully, that really is the end. Soon after, she married. My friend is now forty-four. While no longer what people call beautiful, she is striking-looking, charming, and vital. She teaches elementary school; her husband, who is twenty years older than she, is a part-time merchant seaman. They have one child, now nine years old. Sometimes, when her husband is away, she takes a lover. She told me recently that forty was the most upsetting birthday of all (I wasn't at that one), and although she has only a few years left, she means to enjoy them while they last. She has become one of those women who seize every excuse offered in any conversation for mentioning how old they really are, in a spirit of bravado compounded with self-pity that is not too different from the mood of women who regularly lie about their age. But she is actually fretting much less about aging than she was two decades ago. Having a child, and having one rather late, past the age of thirty, has certainly helped to reconcile her to her age. At fifty, I suspect, she will be ever more valiantly postponing the age of resignation.

My friend is one of the more fortunate, sturdier casualties of the aging crisis. Most women are not as spirited, nor as innocently comic, in their suffering. But almost all women endure some version of this suffering: A recurrent seizure of the imagination that usually begins quite young, in which they project themselves into a calculation of loss. The rules of this society are cruel to women. Brought up to be never fully adult, women are deemed obsolete earlier than men. In fact, most women don't become relatively free and expressive sexually until their thirties. (Women mature sexually this late, certainly much later than men, not for innate biological reasons but because this culture retards women. Denied most outlets for sexual energy permitted to men, it takes many women *that* long to wear out some of their inhibitions.) The time at which they start being disqualified as sexually attractive persons is just when they have grown up sexually. The double standard about aging cheats women of those years, between thirty-five and fifty, likely to be the best of their sexual life.

That women expect to be flattered often by men, and the extent to which their self-confidence depends on this flattery, reflects how deeply women are psychologically weakened by this double standard. Added on to the pressure felt by everybody in this society to look young as long as possible are the values of "femininity," which specifically identify sexual attractiveness in women with youth. The desire to be the "right age" has a special urgency for a woman it never has for a man. A much greater part of her self-esteem and pleasure in life is threatened when she ceases to be young. Most men experience getting older with regret, apprehension. But most women experience it even more painfully: with shame. Aging is a man's destiny, something that must happen because he is a human being. For a woman, aging is not only her destiny. It is also her vulnerability.

To be a woman is to be an actress. Being feminine is a kind of theatre, with its appropriate costumes, decor, lighting, and stylized gestures. From early childhood on, girls are trained to care in a pathologically exaggerated way about their appearance, and are profoundly mutilated (to the extent of being unfitted for first-class adulthood) by the extent of the stress put on presenting themselves as physically attractive objects.

Women look in the mirror more frequently than men do. It is, virtually, their duty to look at themselves—to look often. Indeed, a woman who is not narcissistic is considered unfeminine. And a woman who spends literally *most* of her time caring for, and making purchases to flatter, her physical appearance is not regarded in this society as what she is: a kind of moral idiot. She is thought to be quite normal and is envied by other women whose time is mostly used up at jobs of caring for large families. The display of narcissism goes on all the time. It is expected that women will disappear several times in an evening—at a restaurant, at a party, during a theater intermission, in the course of a social visit—simply to check their appearance, to see that nothing has gone wrong with their makeup and hairstyling, to make sure that their clothes are not spotted or too wrinkled or not hanging properly. It is even acceptable to perform this activity in public. At the table in a restaurant, over coffee, a woman opens a compact mirror and touches up her make-up and hair without embarrassment in front of her husband or her friends.

All this behavior, which is written off as normal "vanity" in women, would seem ludicrous in a man. Women are more vain than men because of the relentless pressure on women to maintain their appearance at a certain high standard. What makes the pressure even more burdensome is that there are actually several standards. Men present themselves as face-and-body, a physical whole. Women are split, as men are not, into a body and a face—each judged by somewhat different standards. What is important for a face is that it be beautiful. What is important for a body is two things, which may even be (depending on fashion and taste) somewhat imcompatible: first, that it be desirable and, second, that it be beautiful. Men usually feel sexually attracted to women much more because of their bodies than their faces. The traits that arouse desire—such as fleshiness—don't always match those that fashion decrees as beautiful. (For instance, the ideal woman's body promoted in advertising in recent years is extremely thin; the kind of body that looks more desirable clothed than naked.) But women's concern with their appearance is not simply geared to arousing desire in men. It also aims at fabricating a certain image by which, as a more indirect way of arousing desire, women state their value. A woman's value lies in the way she *represents* herself, which is much more by her face than her body. In defiance of the laws of simple sexual attraction, women do not devote most of their attention to their bodies. The well-known "normal" narcissism that women display—the amount of time they spend before the mirror—is used primarily in caring for the face and hair.

Women do not simply have faces, as men do; they are identified with their faces. Men have a naturalistic relation to their faces. Certainly they care whether they are good-looking or not. They suffer over acne, protruding ears, tiny eyes; they hate getting bald. But there is a much wider latitude in what is esthetically acceptable in a man's face than what is in a woman's. A man's face is defined as something he basically doesn't need to tamper with; all he has to do is keep it clean. He can avail himself of the options for ornament supplied by nature: a beard, a moustache, longer or shorter hair. But he is not supposed to disguise himself. What he is "really" like is supposed to show. A man lives through his face; it records the progressive stages of his life. And since he doesn't tamper with his face, it is not separate from but is completed by his body — which is judged attractive by the impression it gives of virility and energy. By contrast, a woman's face is potentially separate from her body. She does not treat it naturalistically. A woman's face is the canvas upon which she paints a revised, corrected portrait of herself. One of the rules of this creation is that the face *not* show what she doesn't want it to show. Her face is an emblem, an icon, a flag. How she arranges her hair, the type of makeup she uses, the quality of her complexion — all these are signs not of what she is "really" like but of how she asks to be treated by others, especially men. They establish her status as an "object."

For the normal changes that age inscribes on every human face, women are much more heavily penalized than men. Even in early adolescence, girls are cautioned to protect their faces against wear and tear. Mothers tell their daughters (but never their sons): You look ugly when you cry. Stop worrying. Don't read too much. Crying, frowning, squinting, even laughing — all these human activities make "lines." The same usage of the face in men is judged quite positively. In a man's face, lines are taken to be signs of "character." They indicate emotional strength, maturity — qualities far more esteemed in men than in women. (They show he has "lived.") Even scars are often not felt to be unattractive; they too can add "character" to a man's face. But lines of aging, any scar, even a small birthmark, on a woman's face are always regarded as unfortunate blemishes. In effect, people take character in men to be different from what constitutes character in women. A woman's character is thought to be innate, static — not the product of her experience, her years, her actions. A woman's face is prized so far as it remains unchanged by (or conceals the traces of) her emotions, her physical risk-taking. Ideally, it is supposed to be a mask — immutable, unmarked. The model woman's face is Garbo's. Because women are identified with their faces much more than men are, and the ideal woman's face is one that is "perfect," it seems a calamity when a woman has a disfiguring accident. A broken nose or a scar or a burn mark, no more than regrettable for a man, is a terrible psychological wound to a woman; objectively, it diminishes her value. (As is well known, most clients for plastic surgery are women.)

Both sexes aspire to a physical ideal, but what is expected of boys and what is expected of girls involves a very different moral relation to the self. Boys are encouraged to *develop* their bodies, to regard the body as an instrument to be improved. They invent their masculine selves largely through exercise and sport, which harden the body and strengthen competitive feelings; clothes are of only secondary help in making their bodies attractive. Girls are not particularly encouraged to develop their bodies through any activity, strenuous or not; and physical strength and endurance are hardly valued at all. The invention of the feminine self proceeds mainly through clothes and other signs that testify to the very effort of girls to look attractive, to their commitment to please. When boys become men, they may go on (especially if they have sedentary jobs) practicing a sport or doing exercises for a while. Mostly they leave their appearance alone, having been trained to accept more or less what nature has handed out to them. (Men may start doing exercises again in their forties to lose weight, but for reasons of health — there is an epidemic fear of heart attacks among the middle-aged in rich countries — not for cosmetic reasons.) As one of the norms of "femininity" in this society is being preoccupied with one's physical appearance, so "masculinity" means *not* caring very much about one's looks.

This society allows men to have a much more affirmative relation to their bodies than women have. Men are more "at home" in their bodies, whether they treat them casually or use them aggressively. A man's body is defined as a strong body. It contains no contradiction between what is felt to be attractive and what is practical. A woman's body, so far as it is considered attractive, is defined as a fragile, light body. (Thus, women worry more than men do about being overweight.) When they do exercises, women avoid the ones that develop the muscles, particularly those in the upper arms. Being "feminine" means looking physically weak, frail. Thus, the ideal woman's body is one that is not of much practical use in the hard work of this world, and one that must continually be "defended." Women do not develop their bodies, as men do. After a woman's body has reached its sexually acceptable form by late adolescence, most futher development is viewed as negative. And it is thought irresponsible for women to do what is normal for men: simply leave their appearance alone. During early youth they are likely to come as close as they ever will to ideal image—slim figure, smooth firm skin, light musculature, graceful movements. Their task is to try to maintain that image, unchanged, as long as possible. Improvement as such is not the task. Women care for the bodies—against toughening, coarsening, getting fat. They *conserve* them. (Perhaps the fact that women in modern societies tend to have a more conservative political outlook than men originates in their profoundly conservative relation to their bodies.)

In the life of women in this society the period of pride, of natural honesty, of unself-conscious flourishing is brief. Once past youth, they are condemned to inventing (and maintaining) themselves against the inroads of age. Most of the physical qualities regarded as attractive in women deteriorate much earlier in life than those defined as "male." Indeed, they perish fairly soon in the normal sequence of body transformation. The "feminine" is smooth, rounded, hairless, unlined, soft, unmuscled — the look of the very young; characteristics of the weak, of the vulnerable; eunuch traits, as Germaine Greer has pointed out. Actually, there are only a few years — late adolescence, early twenties — in which this look is physiologically natural, in which it can be had without touching up and covering up. After that, women enlist in a quixotic enterprise, trying to close the gap between the imagery put forth by society (concerning what is attractive in a woman) and the evolving facts of nature.

Women have a more intimate relation to aging than men do, simply because one of the accepted "women's" occupations is taking pains to keep one's face and body from showing the signs of growing older. Women's sexual validity depends, up to a certain point, on how well they stand off these natural changes. After late adolescence women become the caretakers of their bodies and faces, pursuing an essentially defensive strategy, a holding operation. A vast array of products in jars and tubes, a branch of surgery, and armies of hairdressers, masseuses, diet counselors, and other professionals, exist to stave off, or mask, developments that are entirely normal biologically. Large amounts of women's energies are diverted into this passionate, corrupting effort to defeat nature: to maintain an ideal, static appearance against the progress of age. The collapse of the project is only a matter of time. Inevitably, a woman's physical appearance develops beyond its youthful form. No matter how exotic the creams or how strict the diets, one cannot indefinitely keep the face unlined, the waist slim. Bearing children takes its toll: the torso becomes thicker; the skin is stretched. There is no way to keep certain lines from appearing, in one's mid-twenties, around the eyes and mouth. From about thrity on, the skin gradually loses its tonus. In women this perfectly natural process is regarded as a humiliating defeat, while nobody finds anything remarkably unattractive in the equivalent physical changes in men. Men are "allowed" to look older without sexual penalty.

Thus, the reason that women experience aging with more pain than men is not simply that they care more than men about how they look. Men also care about their looks and want to be attractive, but since the business of men is mainly being and doing, rather than appearing, the standards for appearance are much less exacting. The standards for what is attractive in a man are permissive; they conform to what is possible or "natural" to most men throughout most of their lives. The standards for women's appearance go against nature, and to come anywhere near approximating them takes considerable effort and time. Women must try to be beautiful. At the least, they are under heavy social pressure not to be ugly. A woman's fortunes depend, far more than a man's, on being at least "acceptable" looking. Men are not subject to this pressure. Good looks in a man is a bonus, not a psychological necessity for maintaining normal self-esteem.

Behind the fact that women are more severely penalized than men are for aging is the fact that people, in this culture at least, are simply less tolerant of ugliness in women than in men. An ugly woman is never merely repulsive. Ugliness in a women is felt by everyone, men as well as women, to be faintly embarrassing. And many features or blemishes that count as ugly in a woman's face would be quite tolerable on the face of a man. This is not, I would insist, just because the esthetic standards for men and women are different. It is rather because the esthetic standards for women are much higher, and narrower, than those proposed for men.

Beauty, women's business in this society, is the theatre of their enslavement. Only one standard of female beauty is sanctioned: the *girl*. The great advantage men have is that our culture allows two standards of male beauty: the *boy* and the *man*. The beauty of a boy resembles the beauty of a girl. In both sexes it is a fragile kind of beauty and flourishes naturally only in the early part of the life cycle. Happily, however, men are able to accept themselves under another standard of good looks — heavier, rougher, more thickly built. A man does not grieve when he loses the smooth, unlined, hairless skin of a boy. For he has only exchanged one form of attractiveness for another: the darker skin of a man's face, roughened by daily shaving, showing the marks of emotion and the normal lines of age. There is no equivalent of this second standard for women. The single standard of beauty for women dictates that they must go on having clear skin. Every wrinkle, every line, every gray hair, is a defeat. No wonder that no boy minds becoming a man, while even the passage from girlhood to early womanhood is experienced by many women as their downfall, for all women are trained to want to continue looking like girls.

This is not to say there are no beautiful older women. But the standard of beauty in a woman of any age is how far she retains, or how she manages to simulate, the appearance of youth. The exceptional woman in her sixties who is beautiful certainly owes a large debt to her genes. Delayed aging, like good looks, tends to run in families. But nature rarely offers enough to meet this culture's standards. Most of the women who successfully delay the appearance of age are rich, with unlimited leisure to devote to nurturing along nature's gifts. Often they are actresses. (That is, highly paid professionals at doing what all women are taught to practice as amateurs.) Such women as Mae West, Dietrich, Stella Adler, Dolores Del Rio, do not challenge the rule about the relation between beauty and age in women. They are admired precisely because they *are* exceptions, because they have managed (at least so it seems in photographs) to outwit nature. Such miracles, exceptions made by naure (with the help of art and social privilege), only confirm the rule, because what makes these women seem beautiful to us is precisely that they do not look their age. Society allows no place in our imagination for a beautiful old woman who does look like an old woman — a woman who might be like Picasso at the age of ninety, being photographed outdoors on his estate in the South of France, wearing only shorts and sandals. No one imagines such a woman exists. Even the special exceptions — Mae West & Co. — are always photographed indoors, cleverly lit, from the most flattering angle and fully, artfully clothed. The implication is they would not stand a closer scrutiny. The idea of an old woman in a bathing suit being attractive, or even just acceptable-looking, is inconceivable. An older woman is, by definition, sexually repulsive — unless, in fact, she doesn't look old at all. The body, of an old woman, unlike that of an old man, is always understood as a body that can no longer be shown, offered, unveiled. At best, it may appear in costume. People still feel uneasy, thinking about what they might see if here mask dropped, if she took off her clothes.

Thus, the point for women of dressing up, applying make-up, dyeing their hair, going on crash diets, and getting face-lifts is not just to be attractive. They are ways of defending themselves against a profound level of disapproval directed toward women, a disapproval that can take the form of aversion. The double standard about aging converts the life of women into an inexorable march toward a condition in which they are not just unattractive, but disgusting.

The profoundest terror of a woman's life is the moment represented in a statue by Rodin called *Old Age:* a naked old woman, seated, pathetically contemplates her flat, pendulous, ruined body. Aging in women is a process of becoming obscene sexually, for the flabby bosom, wrinkled neck, spotted hands, thinning white hair, waistless torso, and veined legs of an old woman, are felt to be obscene. In our direst moments of the imagination, this transformation can take place with dismaying speed — as in the end of *Lost Horizon,* when the beautiful young girl is carried by her lover out of Shangri-La and, within minutes, turns into a withered, repulsive crone. There is no equivalent nightmare about men. This is why, however much a man may care about his appearance, that caring can never acquire the same desperateness it often does for women. When men dress according to fashion or now even use cosmetics, they do not expect from clothes and make-up what women do. A face-lotion or perfume or deodorant or hairspray, used by a man, is not part of a disguise. Men, as men, do not feel they need to disguise themselves to fend off morally disapproved signs of aging, to outwit premature sexual obsolescence, to cover up aging as obscenity. Men are not subject to the barely concealed revulsion expressed in this culture against the female body—except in its smooth, youthful, firm, odorless, blemish-free form.

One of the attitudes that punish women most severely is the visceral horror felt at aging female flesh. It reveals a radical fear of women installed deep in this culture, a demonology of women that has crystallized in such mythic caricatures as the vixen, the virago, the vamp, and the witch. Several centuries of witch-phobia, during which one of the cruelest extermination programs in Western history was carried out, suggest something of the extremity of this fear. That old women are repulsive is one of the most profound esthetic and erotic feelings in our culture. Women share it as much as men do. (Oppressors, as a rule, deny oppressed people their own "native" standards of beauty. And the oppressed end up being convinced that they *are* ugly.) How women are psychologically damaged by this misogynistic idea of what is beautiful parallels the way in which blacks have been deformed in a society that has up to now defined beautiful as white. Psychological tests made on young black children in the United States some years ago showed how early and how thoroughly they incorporate the white standard of good looks. Virtually all the children expressed fantasies that indicated they considered black people to be ugly, funny-looking, dirty, brutish. A similar kind of self-hatred infects most women. Like men, they find old age in women "uglier" than old age in men.

This esthetic taboo functions, in sexual attitudes, as a racial taboo. In this society most people feel an involuntary recoil of the flesh when imagining a middle-aged woman making love with a young man—exactly as many whites flinch viscerally at the thought of a white woman in bed with a black man. The banal drama of a man of fifty who leaves a wife of forty-five for a girl friend of twenty-eight contains no strictly sexual outrage, whatever sympathy people may have for the abandoned wife. On the contrary. Everyone "understands." Everyone knows that men like girls, that young women often want middle-aged men. But no one "understands" the reverse situation. A woman of forty-five who leaves a husband of fifty for a lover of twenty-eight is the makings of a social and sexual scandal at a deep level of feeling. No one takes exception to a romantic couple in which the man is twenty years or more the woman's senior. The movies pair Joanne Dru and John Wayne, Marilyn Monroe and Joseph Cotten, Audrey Hepburn and Cary Grant, Jane Fonda and Yves Montand, Catherine Deneuve and Marcello Mastroianni; as in actual life, these are perfectly plausible, appealing couples. When the age difference runs the other way, people are puzzled and embarrassed and simply shocked. (Remember Joan Crawford and Cliff Robertson in *Autumn Leaves*? But so troubling is this kind of love story that it rarely figures in the movies, and then only as the melancholy history of a failure.) The usual view of why a woman of forty and a boy of twenty, or a woman of fifty and a man of thirty, marry is that the man is seeking a mother, not a wife; no one believes the marriage will last. For a woman to respond erotically and romantically to a man who in terms of his age could be her father is considered normal. A man who falls in love with a woman who, however attractive she may be, is old enough to be his mother is thought to be extremely neurotic (victim of an "Oedipal fixation" is the fashionable tag), if not mildly contemptible.

The wider the gap in age between partners in a couple, the more obvious is the prejudice against women. When old men, such as Justice

Douglas, Picasso, Strom Thurmond, Onassis, Chaplin, and Pablo Casals, take brides thirty, forty, fifty years younger than themselves, it strikes people as remarkable, perhaps an exaggeration — but still plausible. To explain such a match, people enviously attribute some special virility and charm to the man. Though he can't be handsome, he is famous; and his fame is understood as having boosted his attractiveness to women. People imagine that his young wife, respectful of her elderly husband's attainments, is happy to become his helper. For the man a late marriage is always good public relations. It adds to the impression that, despite his advanced age, he is still to be reckoned with; it is the sign of a continuing vitality presumed to be available as well to his art, business activity, or political career. But an elderly woman who married a young man would be greeted quite differently. She would have broken a fierce taboo, and she would get no credit for her courage. Far from being admired for her vitality, she would probably be condemned as predatory, willful, selfish, exhibitionistic. At the same time she would be pitied, since such a marriage would be taken as evidence that she was in her dotage. If she had a conventional career or were in business or held public office, she would quickly suffer from the current of disapproval. Her very credibility as a professional would decline, since people would suspect that her young husband might have an undue influence on her. Her "respectability" would certainly be compromised. Indeed, the well-known old women I can think of who dared such unions, if only at the end of their lives — George Eliot, Colette, Edith Piaf — have all belonged to that category of people, creative artists and entertainers, who have special license from society to behave scandalously. It is thought to be scandal for a woman to ignore that she is old and therefore too ugly for a young man. Her looks and a certain physical condition determine a woman's desirability, not her talents or her needs. Women are not supposed to be "potent." A marriage between an old woman and a young man subverts the very ground rule of relations between the two sexes; that is, whatever the variety of appearances, men remain dominant. Their claims come first. Women are supposed to be the associates and companions of men, not their full equals — and never their superiors. Women are to remain in the state of pemanent "minority."

The convention that wives should be younger than their husbands powerfully enforces the "minority" status of women, since being senior in age always carries with it, in any relationship, a certain amount of power and authority. There are no laws on the matter, of course. The convention is obeyed because to do otherwise makes one feel as if one is doing something ugly or in bad taste. Everyone feels intuitively the esthetic rightness of marriage in which the man is older than the woman, which means that any marriage in which the woman is older creates a dubious or less gratifying mental picture. Everyone is addicted to the visual pleasure that women give by meeting certain esthetic requirements from which men are exempted, which keeps women working at staying youthful-looking while men are left free to age. On a deeper level everyone finds the signs of old age in women esthetically offensive which conditions one to feel automatically repelled by the prospect of an elderly woman marrying a much younger man. The situation in which women are kept minors for life is largely organized by such conformist, unreflective preferences. But taste is not free, and its judgments are never merely "natural." Rules of taste enforce structures of power. The revulsion against aging in women is the cutting edge of a whole set of oppressive structures (often masked as gallantries) that keep women in their place.

The ideal state proposed for women is docility, which means not being fully grown up. Most of what is cherished as typically "feminine" is simply behavior that is childish, immature, weak. To offer so low and demeaning a standard of fulfillment in itself constitutes oppression in an acute form — a sort of moral neocolonialism. But women are not simply condescended to by the values that secure the dominance of men. They are repudiated. Perhaps because of having been their oppressors for so long, few men really *like* women (though they love individual women), and few men ever feel really comfortable or at ease in women's company. This malaise arises because relations between the two sexes are rife with hypocrisy, as men manage to love those they dominate and therefore don't respect. Oppressors always try to justify their privileges and brutalities by imagining that those they oppress belong to a lower order of civilization or are less than fully "human." Deprived of part of their ordinary human dignity, the oppressed take on certain "demonic" traits. The oppressions of large groups have to be anchored deep in the psyche, continually renewed by partly unconscious fears and taboos, by a sense of the obscene. Thus, women arouse not only desire and affection in men but aversion as well. Women are thoroughly domesticated familiars. But, at certain times and in certain situations, they become alien, untouchable. The aversion men feel, so much of which is covered over, is felt most frankly, with least inhibition, toward the type of woman who is most taboo "esthetically," a woman who has become — with the natural changes brought about by aging — obscene.

Nothing more clearly demonstrates the vulnerability of women than the special pain, confusion, and bad faith with which they experience getting older. And in the struggle that some women are waging on behalf of all women to be treated (and treat themselves) as full human beings — not "only'" as women — one of the earliest results to be hoped for is that women become aware, indignantly aware, of the double standard about aging from which they suffer so harshly.

It is understandable that women often succumb to the temptation to lie about their age. Given society's double standard, to question a woman about her age is indeed often an aggressive act, a trap. Lying is an elementary means of self-defense, a way of scrambling out of the trap, at least temporarily. To expect a woman, after "a certain age," to tell exactly how old she is — when she has a chance, either through the generosity of nature or the cleverness of art, to pass for being somewhat younger than she actually is — is like expecting a landowner to admit that the estate he has put up for sale is actually worth less than the buyer is prepared to pay. The double standard about aging sets women up as property, as objects whose value depreciates rapidly with the march of the calendar.

The prejudices that mount against women as they grow older are an important arm of male privilege. It is the present unequal distribution of adult roles between the two sexes that gives men a freedom to age denied to women. Men actively administer the double standard about aging because the "masculine" role awards them the initiative in courtship. Men choose; women are chosen. So men choose younger women. But although this system of inequality is operated by men, it could not work if women themselves did not acquiesce in it. Women reinforce it powerfully with their complacency, with their anguish, with their lies.

Not only do women lie more than men do about their age but men forgive them for it, thereby confirming their own superiority. A man who lies about his age is thought to be weak, "unmanly." A woman who lies about her age is behaving in a quite acceptable, "feminine" way. Petty lying is viewed by men with indulgence, one of a number of patronizing allowances made for women. It has the same moral unimportance as the fact that women are often late for appointments. Women are not expected to be truthful, or punctual, or expert in handling and repairing machines, or frugal, or physically brave.

Most women share the contempt for women expressed in the double standard about aging — to such a degree that they take their lack of self-respect for granted. Women have been accustomed so long to the protection of their masks, their smiles, their endearing lies. Without this protection, they know, they would be more vulnerable. But in protecting themselves as women, they betray themselves as adults. The model corruption in a woman's life is denying her age. She symbolically accedes to all those myths that furnish women with their imprisoning securities and privileges, that create their genuine oppression, that inspire their real discontent. Each time a woman lies about her age she becomes an accomplice in her own underdevelopment as a human being.

Women have another option. They can aspire to be wise, not merely nice; to be competent, not merely helpful; to be strong, not merely graceful; to be ambitious for themselves, not merely for themselves in relation to men and children. They can let themselves age naturally and without embarrassment, actively protesting and disobeying the conventions that stem from this society's double standard about aging. Instead of being girls, girls as long as possible, who then age humiliatingly into middle-aged women and then obscenely into old women, they can become women much earlier — and remain active adults, enjoying the long, erotic career of which women are capable, far longer. Women should allow their faces to show the lives they have lived. Women should tell the truth.

Business Technology and the
American Family:
An Impressionistic Analysis

EUGENE J. KOPROWSKI

The relationship among business, technology, and the family is intimate, complex, and currently troublesome. This has serious implications for our society. Even the most casual observer is aware that something is wrong. Fortunately or unfortunately, people in this country are becoming anesthetized by the dulling repetitiveness of unpleasant news. They are learning to live with high divorce and suicide rates, drugs, alcohol, crime, violence, poor workmanship, high industrial turnover and absenteeism, and various forms of strikes and work stoppages. This casual adjustment to these danger signs may be the predictable outcome Alvin Toffler calls "future shock," but is certainly not an appropriate reaction for a society concerned with its well-being and self-renewal.

People concerned with improving the current state of affairs have, for the most part, focused on specific societal units rather than on interaction patterns among such units. For example, business leaders and public administrators have been seeking answers to the problems of worker apathy, alienation, militancy, and withdrawal primarily within their organizations. Typically they attempt to solve these problems with "improved" employee selection procedures, tightened control systems, and management training aimed at arming managers with increasingly sophisticated methods for manipulating human behavior. At the same time, sociologists, psychologists, clergymen, social welfare workers, and family counselors are seeking answers to delinquency, crime, mental illness, and the drug, alcohol, and suicide problems with various group therapy models where the family unit is the focal point for "treatment."

THE FAMILY AND THE TECHNOSTRUCTURE

Neither of these response patterns is adequate since both fail to take into account the nature of the relationship between the family and what many observers refer to as the technostructure — or the organized means by which our society produces the goods and services it needs to sustain itself.

Looking at this relationship in terms of the past and present, the technostructure has played the role of the consumer and the family the role of producer of human talent and energy. When Paleolithic hunters roamed the outer fringes of the great ice masses in search of food, they required individuals who were brave, self-sacrificing, resourceful, adaptive, and cooperative. As the glaciers receded, Neolithic food-gatherers demanded different qualities of their labor. Planting, tending, and harvesting crops required individuals who were obedient, long-suffering, hard-working, loyal, and predictable. These same qualities served the technostructure's needs through the Industrial Revolution and well into the first half of this century. While it is difficult to pin-point exactly when the family emerged as a social unit, it is reasonably clear that one of its primary roles has been the transmission of the values, skills, and discipline required to fuel the technostructure and make it run effectively. In return for their contribution to the technostructure, the individual family members could expect certain payoffs in the form of food, clothing, shelter, protection, comradeship, and recognition for talent or a job well done.

Until recent times, this arrangement seemed to work quite well and to the mutual benefit of both social institutions. But there is growing evidence that this is no longer the case — something seems to be out of balance. The family is no longer producing the type of people who readily adjust to the demands of the world of work. There are a number of possible explanations of why this situation has developed. A lion's share of the credit must go to the leaders of the technostructure and not to the family. This indictment requires explanation.

America has become a consumer society. This means that the health of our economy depends to a large degree upon creating new needs. Yet the American family has traditionally developed people primarily to serve the technostructure as producers of labor, and not as consumers of an endless array of new goods and services. To make the economy function smoothly, this state of affairs obviously had to be changed. This metamorphosis was probably accomplished through a sequence of events that went something like this: Phase I involved finding new powerful instruments for changing attitudes and values on a mass scale. The traditional vehicle for value transmission in our society, the family, was too slow and too difficult to control. Besides, most parents born before World War II held the value systems of producers and not consumers. Television proved to be the ideal tool. Through its hypnotic beam, it was capable of transmitting instant values. Phase II involved creating through advertising new life styles that required the support of new products and services.

Unfortunately what remains is an increasingly schizophrenic society where citizens are expected to play two incompatible roles-the impulsive, style-conscious, dissatisfied consumer, and the long-suffering, predictable, hard-working producer.[1]

This is not to suggest a conspiracy on the part of the business and governmental leaders to consciously create this state of affairs. To do so would call for a more coordinated effort than our polymorphous democracy could presently deliver. Instead, what is being suggested is that we are in a situation that is not particularly healthy for our society, and one which we must do something about. This will call for new roles for both the family and the technostructure.

Planned change implies some sense of direction or purpose. It implies some vision of what man is and what man is becoming. Implicit in the decision of every leader within the technostructure or every parent are these types of value positions. The problem with implicit assumptions is that they are not common knowledge. They cannot be openly discussed and debated for these reasons. If these social institutions are to be effectively changed, we must know what purposes are served by these changes and we must make these purposes explicit.

Within this context, there are at least four major purposes that must concern every social institution.[2] The first and primary purpose is to better serve human needs. Whether an organization is producing automobiles or human beings, it is serving this primary purpose. The second purpose has to do with resources. Both technostructure and the family must have certain human, financial, and physical resources to do their jobs. Since there is a limited supply of most resources, a second purpose of every social institution is to learn how to optimize their use. The third purpose involves survival. Unless one lives to fight another day, the first two purposes have little meaning. Surviving means learning how to anticipate and solve problems before they become so large and so complex that they are impossible to handle. Finally, every social institution must concern itself with self-renewal. It must learn to continually regenerate its vital juices and to heighten its level of creative response to the environment.

SERVING HUMAN NEEDS

With these broad purposes in mind, it is now possible to discuss new directions for the family and the technostructure. A good place to begin is by asking how well these two social institutions fulfill their primary purpose of serving human needs. If the mounting human problems they face are any indication, neither the family nor the technostructure score very high when we apply this measuring stick. But it is not enough to know that they are not doing a very good job of satisfying human needs; it is also important to know why. A significant clue can be found in the concepts about human motivation that were formulated by the late Abraham Maslow. Maslow contended that human needs exist in a hierarchy and that once needs at a lower level are satisfied, new higher-level needs become more important to the individual. At the lowest level of Maslow's hierarchy is the need for survival. Once survival needs are met, the individual seeks to consolidate his position, and safety needs become primary. When safety is assured, the individual seeks companionship and love. Next, ego needs or the desire to be recognized for one's worth becomes most important. At the top of the hierarchy is the need for self-actualization or the need to grow and develop as a human being.

Within Maslow's framework, both the family and the technostructure might be concentrating on the wrong level of the hierarchy in dealing with their members. For example, in some families children are controlled or motivated by parents through various types of reward and punishment. Rewards generally take the form of protection and love in return for obedience and respect. Punishment is simply the opposite side of the same coin. Here the parent says "Obey and respect me or I will withhold protection or love." There are many reasons why some families spend little or no time beyond the first four levels of Maslow's hierarchy and give attention to the self-actualization needs of the child. To assist another person in self-actualization means that eventually that person will seek to free himself from your control. He will begin thinking and acting on his own. This is obviously threatening and unfulfilling to some parents. A dependent child means the parent has a legitimate opportunity to play the role of the dominant, omnipotent parent.

In similar fashion it appears that many business and governmental bureaucracies may be appealing to the inappropriate levels of needs in their employees. Promises of salary increases or promotions have little to do with self-actualization. Neither do service awards, benefit programs, or modern working conditions. Beyond appealing to inappropriate need levels, the technostructure has another type of problem relating to the satisfaction of human needs. Any large bureaucracy must not only be concerned with the needs of its workers, but also with the needs of its managerial groups, its stockholders, and its consumers. Devoting too much energy to satisfying the needs of any one of these groups is often done at the expense of others.

Many business organizations have done a remarkably good job of optimizing the use of limited resources. Managerial technologies for the efficient control of financial and physical resources have mushroomed in recent years, thanks to a new emerging discipline called management science which uses mathematical modeling along with computers to sharpen rational decision making. Unfortunately, these same organizations do not always pay similar attention to the optimization of human resources.

Beyond the family budget, the house, the car, and the television set, households do not concern themselves with abstract notions like optimizing limited resources. This is unfortunate because this is a subject that must concern all social systems. Within the family, perhaps the most important resource is the parents' time. Both husband and wife serve as models for behavior for their children. Parents who have no time or no energy left for this important role must abdicate it to less desirable models.

A third purpose shared by the family and the technostructure is survival. No social institution can achieve any of the other purposes mentioned unless it can develop effective mechanisms for continuous reality testing and adaptation to the rapidly changing environment. If the primary purpose of both the family and the technostructure is to meet human needs, what can we reasonably predict about the future that will be helpful in providing a framework for change? The following are submitted as examples of rather high probability "hunches" about the future.[3] First, the rate of technological and social change is likely to continue to accelerate through the year 2000. Second, people will be required to be highly mobile and will spend a good deal of their time in small, temporary problem-solving or recreational groups. Third, people will tend to cluster into large urban areas. Fourth, human effort is likely to be organized around collecting, processing, and interpreting data, and around various new forms of creative recreation. Fifth, the world will tend to become "smaller" through increased international and space travel, electric technology, and other forms of mass communications. Sixth, the amount of knowledge will greatly increase, requiring lifelong learning and regeneration on the part of individuals and social institutions.

The final common purpose shared by the family and the techno-structure is self-renewal. Assuming that both the family and the tech-nostructure are interested in self-renewal, there are a number of possibilities that should be considered. To begin with, those leaders who control the technostructure must be made to realize that they directly and indirectly have a major impact on what happens inside the family. They influence in varying degrees the working parents' time, space, energy level, and self concept.

Time control is a two-edged sword since the employer frequently not only determines how many hours an individual will be spending with the family, but also the quality of those hours. The quality of hours spent at home is affected when fathers or mothers are forced to work on weekends or on special shifts that are incompatible with the daily routines of their children.

Space control has several important dimensions. The employer to some degree controls the physical environment of the parent during working hours, the neighborhood where the family lives, and the number of relocations the family must make to sustain the parent's career movement with the organization. A parent who works all day in an uncomfortable or hazardous environment cannot be expected to come home and play the role of the model parent. Nor can a child who is forced to live in a company neighborhood expect to become cultur-ally enriched by being exposed to a wide range of people.

Related to time and space control is energy control. To perform the new roles suggested in this paper requires not only a thoughtful sensi-tive parent, it also requires a parent with considerable creative energy to devote to his family. A parent who comes home physically exhausted or mentally drained each night has little left for his family. Exhaustion, however, does not come only from overwork. Connecting six bolts every twelve seconds on an assembly line might not take much physical energy, but it may drain considerably psychic energy by forcing the man to do work that he hates or that he feels is demeaning.

Finally, much of a person's self image is formed by the type of work he is given to do. The way society views an individual tends to be tied to whether he works with his hands or with his brain, whether he is a leader or a follower, and whether he is in a "masculine" or a "feminine" occupation. Implicit societal norms state that it is better to do brain work than to work with your hands, that it is better to be a leader than a follower, and that a man must do "manly" work. If one does not comply, both the individual and his family feel the subtle sanctions of society.

New Directions: Technostructure

Since the technostructure plays such a major role in family life, what can be done by private and public employers who are interested in strengthening the role of the family in our society? Here are some specific suggestions for exploration:

Shorten the work week to allow parents more time with their children.

Change work schedules to allow parents more time at home when children are there.

In planning new plant or office locations, consider the family. Whenever possible, help design new communities or towns such as Columbia or Reston where work is an integral part of the organic life system.

Minimize the number of major geographic moves required of employees. When such moves are necessary, plan them around certain natural growth cycles in the family's life. For example, if the employee to be transferred has a child who is a senior in high school, wait until the child graduates before requiring the move.

Eliminate whenever possible working conditions that create unnecessary frustration or tension. Excessive noise, smoke, heat, cold are a few examples of environmental conditions that are undesirable.

Allow employees to take some of their creative energies home with them at night. Try to eliminate the concept of overtime. Use part-time or temporary replacements to do overload work. Rotate the tough, energy consuming jobs among all the staff.

Remember the work given a person has much to do with his self-image and his self-esteem. It is unrealistic to spend five minutes telling an employee what a good person he is and then send him back to a boring demeaning job that tells him for eight hours a day that he is little better than a trained monkey. Find ways to enrich jobs and make work more challenging. Include employees whenever possible in problem identification and problem solving. Rotate the leadership role whenever possible, and rotate men and women in jobs.

Review more closely the types of programs and advertisements sponsored on television. What value systems and problem solving techniques are implicitly endorsed by the typical western or spy thriller? Or what tensions and conflicts are transmitted to an assembly line worker who suddenly finds that his new racy sports car doesn't make him handsome, intelligent, independent, or sexy. A new brand of social responsibility is badly needed in this critical area.

New Directions: Family

While the technostructure plays an important role in the lives of family members, it is equally true that what happens inside the family has a dramatic impact on the technostructure. Impulse control, attitudes toward authority, attitudes toward others, and basic attitudes toward work are formulated early in the life of an individual within the family setting. When these are at odds with the requirements of the world of work, they tend to produce frustration, hostility, and withdrawal. In some American families children learn that by raising a little fuss they can receive immediate need gratification. In later life this gives rise to weak impulse control. As a result many young people who enter government and business do so with built-in expectancies that their needs will be immediately satisfied — that they will be given interesting work to do on their first assignment, that they will quickly move up the promotional ladder, and that their uniqueness as an individual will be immediately recognized and rewarded. Ambivalent feeling toward authority seems to be a trademark of some American families. Of primary importance is the fact that our current technostructure is based on the principle that power and authority come from formal position in the hierarchy. This notion is contradicted in the family where the father holds the formal position of authority, but the mother generally exerts the greatest amount of influence. While cooperation and mutual respect are stressed in the relationships among brothers and sisters in some families, competition is still stressed in many business and governmental organizations. This is especially true in our educational system where students must compete for grades, awards, and the professor's favor.

Probably the most critical difference between what children learn in the family and the way they are expected to perform in the technostructure has to do with attitudes toward work. While many families still attempt to transmit the Protestant Work Ethic to their children, economic conditions have so changed over the past generation that young people in increasing numbers are beginning to question the notion that work is *the* central theme of life. They have observed that the Protestant Work Ethic has failed to provide meaning to their parents' lives, and they are determined not to make the same type of mistake. To these young people work has become instrumental to the "good life," rather than an end in itself. This feeling is reinforced by mass media advertising that stresses leisure activities in what is perceived by the advertisers to be a growing leisure market.

This discussion of the impact the family has on the work-related attitudes is not meant to imply that child-rearing practices should be changed to fit the current needs of the technostructure. Instead, what is suggested is that both the technostructure and the family alter their roles to fit better the needs of a self-actualizing population. Some specific recommendations were made for the technostructure. Here are some possibilities that should seriously be considered by the American family.

Rotate the various roles that must be played in the family. Let the husband keep house during certain time blocks while the wife plays the breadwinner role. Allow children to assume leadership roles in planning certain activities like a family outing or vacation.

Involve all members of the family in task-force problem solving. When a major problem faces the family, decide together what additional information is necessary to solve the problem, where that information is located, who will generate it, what criteria should be used in arriving at a decision, and how that decision will be implemented.

Try "Family by Objectives." Together decide what the major objectives of the family should be, and how these should tie in to the specific objectives of each family member. Periodically review progress toward these objectives.

Set up specific developmental goals for the family, and determine the necessary strategies to reach those goals. Among these goals might be becoming aware of options in life, and learning how to learn, how to make choices, how to interact efficiently with other people, how to appreciate beauty and feeling as well as logic and reason, and how to validate knowledge.

Either burn all television sets in the home or learn how to use them more judiciously. This is one of the most powerful learning/teaching technologies man has invented. Parents must play an active role in determining what reaches the family through this miraculous tube. At a minimum they should determine how many hours of the day the child is exposed to the set and what types of programs are beneficial to the child's development.

Organize efforts to influence appropriate change in other social institutions that affect family life. If families unite their efforts, perhaps something can be done to change the technostructure in the directions suggested.

Take appropriate steps to gain a greater say in what is presented to the family through the mass media.

CONCLUSION

Implicit in this entire discussion is the assumption that there is some value in salvaging the nuclear family and that leaders in business and government play a key role in moving us beyond consumerism to a self-actualizing society. There are alternatives. In his book, *Future Shock,* Alvin Toffler refers to professional parents, corporate families, and homosexual daddies. He also discusses the odds against love in our post-industrial society and suggests marriage trajectories where different mates are selected and discarded at different stages in one's life cycle. All of these new forms of social organization are possible — some even probable. But before disposing of the bathwater, it may be time to take a careful look at the baby.

REFERENCES

1. For an elaboration of this theme see Charles A. Reich, *The Greening of America,* Random House, 1970, 189-216.
2. The notion of a matrix of purposes common to all social institutions is discussed in great detail in Bertram M. Gross, *Organizations and Their Managing,* Free Press, 1968, 263-297.
3. Similar predictions can be found in Herman Kahn and Anthony J. Wiener, *The Year 2000,* Macmillan, 1967, 1-64; Toward the Year 2000, *Daedalus,* Summer, 1967, 711-716; and Bert Nanus, The World of Work in 1980, *The Futurist,* December, 1971, 248-250.

UNIT STUDY GUIDE

A. *Terms to Review*

Alcoholism	Etiology	Mortality rate
Depression	Marital health	Normalization
(psychological)	Median income	Poverty, poverty-level
Ego-resiliency		

B. *Questions for Discussion and Study*

1. Read and prepare for discussion, *Grapes of Wrath.* Does poverty have the same implications for families today that it did in the Great Depression years? If not, illustrate and show what has changed.
2. In terms of their possible disorganizing effects on marriage, compare and contrast alcoholism and drug addiction.
3. In what ways does economic deprivation affect the interaction of mates? Examine affectional, sexual and other aspects of interpersonal relations and develop a list of possible effects in these and other areas.
4. Sexual equality leaders have contended that much of the situational stress borne by marriage and family groups stems directly

from entrenched sexism in society's economic and legal institutions. Trace out and discuss the logic and validity of this claim.

5. Research shows a correlation between health status and quality of marital interaction. Describe and discuss the interrelation of these variables, dealing especially with the question of "causes."

C. *Topics-Ideas for Papers and Projects*

1. Arrange for a representative of the public assistance office in your city to speak to your class. Discuss typical problems and crises confronting families where the father is absent or disabled.

2. Consulting the 1970 Census data, determine the number of families in your area with incomes below the poverty level. How many children are involved?

3. "Sexism, Racism, and Ageism as Sources of Stress for Interpersonal Relations in Contemporary Marriage."

4. Research: "The Effect of Socioeconomic Levels on the Perception of Situational Stresses by Marital Partners."

5. Assume that you are age 25, married, and parents of one four-year-old child. Assuming that you have a total family income of six thousand dollars per year (both partners working), construct a complete annual budget showing where you would live and the rent you would pay, and show your projected expenditures for recreation, medical care, clothing, car, insurance, etc. Evaluate your probable lifestyle.

Unit 7
Intimate Interaction

In love, the paradox occurs that two beings become one and yet remain two. – *Fromm*

Unless you are willing to risk caring and possibly being hurt, you cannot experience the joys of love. – *Rollo May*

Introduction

In American society, most expectations and beliefs about marriage reflect its perception as a "special" kind of relationship between two persons. These values are bound up with the concept of *intimacy*. And much the same could be said of allusions to "good" marriages. Since they are founded on the principle of a love relationship, marriages today which do not provide a sufficient level and range of closeness or intimacy between the partners are likely to be perceived as deficient, as seriously lacking the prime ingredients necessary for sustaining a vital, satisfying marriage.

For purposes of definition, intimacy can be regarded as an interpersonal situation where there is spontaneous and relatively complete absorption in the experiential reality of one's relation with another. Within the marital partnership, possible examples of intimacy would include shared activity of several kinds — erotic play, touching, conversation, and affectional behavior either verbal or otherwise. Psychologists suggest that intimacy could thus be characteristic of almost any shared activity ". . . that is engaged in with a totality of unselfconscious involvement, attention, and participation."[1] Intimacy experiences in the partnership may be relatively continuous or sporadic, frequent or infrequent. Since sexual and affectional behavior have been shown to be extremely important in defining the quality of a marital relationship, this unit's materials will focus mainly on intimacy in these two areas of interaction.

Marriage, as a relationship founded on choice and love, would indeed seem to be an ideal setting for the development of deep and satisfying intimacy. Viewed from the human potentials movement perspective, marriage has the potential for providing an interpersonal scene where basic individual needs for human contact, understanding, and emotional support can be met. The idea that individuals basically tend to strive toward the establishment of close relationships with other humans is gaining in validity. As Fromm has pointed out, among humans probably the most power striving is ". . . the desire for interpersonal fusion."[2] Marriage today, therefore, assumes great importance as a setting for the exploration and potential satisfaction of physical, spiritual, emotional, and communicative needs. In this connection, Desmond Morris has pointed out the close relation of physical intimacy and understanding between persons, implying the fundamental need of every person for communication authenticated by intimacy. Thus:

> It is a matter of being understood emotionally, and in that respect a single intimate body contact will do more than all the beautiful words in the dictionary. Physical feelings can transmit emotional feelings in a truly astonishing way.[3]

In the areas of sexuality and affectional behavior, then, marriage may be especially important since it provides not merely sex and affection but a potential for making these aspects of marriage a significant part of the human growth experience.

Thus, the quality of the intimacy between partners may largely define the quality of their over-all relationship; where the intimate relations are frequent and satisfying (e.g. valid), the pair relation is likely to be primary and to be perceived as intrinsically valuable and fulfilling for the partners. Such conditions, however, do not come automatically to all who marry. As we have observed previously, the pressures of modern society tend to impel individuals — even in relations with those they love — toward an instrumental, goal-achieving kind of behavior. As many marriage counselors could testify, a couple may live in a common residence and share the same bedroom and bed but seldom experience valid intimacy. For example, emphasizing the valid and core function of sexual intercourse as communication between partners, Masters and Johnson point out that too often intimate communication in the sex act is not experienced because of two "spectators" in the bedroom. One of these is the man worrying whether he will be successful in the act and the other is the woman concerned whether she has any chance of getting pleasure in so uncertain a situation.[4] The instrumental, goal-achieving nature of this kind of pseudo-intimate interaction is an effective deterrent to valid, satisfying sexual intimacy in the partnership.

From the position of the human potentials movement, several comments could be made. First, the development of valid intimacy in love relationships, even among the married, would be seen as depending largely on the extent to which both partners have begun to nurture their capacities for caring, loving, and understanding — both toward themselves and toward the other. Thus, in authentic intimacy one cannot be instrumental or manipulative of the other; for the truly intimate relationship is characterized by trust, a lowering or casting away of defenses around the self, and honest, open communication between the partners.[5] In its most satisfying form, then, intimacy is accompanied by spontaneity, by an ever-growing awareness of feelings in self and the other and an acceptance of those feelings as a valuable component of the relationship.[6]

In view of what we have said, then, authentic intimacy in a partnership seems contingent on certain other aspects of the relationship. Perhaps the three most important ones could be listed as: (1) *Communication* — open, honest, spontaneous; (2) *Mutuality* — involving two-way commitment, caring, and trust; and, (3) *Positive self-concept* — entailing personal awareness of one's intrinsic worth and the perception that one experiences intimacy as an expression of genuine communication and not merely as a culturally-shaped role-performance related to one's status (e.g. the woman expected to be passive and the man to be aggressive in sexual matters). In short, the development and maintenance of valid intimacy goes hand in hand with the nurturing of a growth-oriented marriage in terms which were discussed in earlier materials.

It is a bit more difficult to isolate specific issues on this topic than on some others we have examined previously. However, in preparation for the readings, those cited below will perhaps generate questions and discussion.

Priority of intimacy in marriage. The issue here revolves around the concept of marital roles which is held. Some contend that intimacy between partners is fine but that one should not expect much in this regard; thus some hold that successful coping with everyday problems of living is the main business of marriage. Does a meaningful intimate relationship have less priority than, say child-rearing, household maintenance, or the partners' civic responsibilities? Is the expectation of valid intimacy in a marital partnership too great a burden for marriage to bear?

Knowledge levels. Marriage counselors suggest that many difficulties in the erotic aspects of the pair relationship arise from inadequate understanding of basic sexual anatomy, physiology, and psychology. Frequently, movement by partners toward the acquisition of appropriate knowledge is hindered by culturally engendered shame, guilt, and embarrassment. Furthermore, much learning occurring in the growth toward valid intimacy must be accompanied by sometimes-traumatic unlearning of misinformation acquired earlier. A basic issue here goes back to the questions surrounding education for human sexuality as discussed earlier.

Maintaining valid intimacy. The frequently-repeated folk wisdom invoked to help explain extramarital sex in conventional marriages is that "familiarity breeds contempt." Is this a statement of objective fact or in the nature of a "self-fulfilling prophecy?"

Practical issues revolve around the question of how a satisfying and highly-valued sexual-affectional relationship can be kept viable. Or, should it be assumed at the outset that eventual boredom is inevitable?

Technology and marital intimacy. Some argue that, living as we do in the height of the technological era, we should make use of any means at our command to enhance the sexual and affectional aspects of marriage. Included in the possible aids to intimacy would be techniques and preparations oriented toward all five senses: e.g. aphrodisia, erotic music, vibrators and massage instruments, perfumes, etc. An opposing view is that authentic intimacy should be built and developed as a pattern of interpersonal responses between mates and should therefore be independent of "crutches."

These are probably but a few of the issues and problems connected with intimacy in marriage today. It seems likely, of course, that many of the fundamental issues discussed in the unit on Human Sexuality would also be pertinent here.

REFERENCES

1. Saxton, Lloyd, *The Individual, Marriage, and the Family* (Belmont, Cal.: Wadsworth Publishing Co., 1968), p. 249.

2. Fromm, Erich. *The Art of Loving* (New York: Harper and Row, 1956), p. 22.

3. Morris, Desmond. "The Disguises of Intimacy," *McCall's* (March 1972): 90. Cf. also by the same author: *Intimate Behavior* (New York: Random House, 1972).

4. *Time*, "Repairing the Conjugal Bed," (May 25, 1970): 49-52.

5. Rogers, Carl R. *On Becoming A Person* (Boston: Houghton-Mifflin, 1961).

6. Maslow, Abraham. *Motivation and Personality* (New York: Harper, 1954).

Jealousy and Sexual Property

KINGSLEY DAVIS

ONE

Descartes defined jealousy as "a kind of fear related to a desire to preserve possession." He was, if we look at what is customarily called jealous behavior, eminently correct. In every case it is apparently a fear or rage reaction to a threatened appropriation of one's own, or what is desired as one's own, property.

Conflicts over property involve four major elements: Owner, Object, Public, and Rival (or Trespasser). These have a slightly different nature and a slightly different relation according to whether the conflict situation is one of regulated and legitimate competition or of illegitimate trespass. In the former case Ego is a *would-be* owner and his enemy a rival. A popular fallacy has been to conceive the jealous situation as a triangle. Actually it is a quadrangle, and the failure to include the public or community element has led to a failure to grasp the social character of jealousy. The relationships between the four elements are institutionally defined. They constitute the fixed traditional constellation of rights, obligations, and neutralities called property, and are sustained by interacting attitudes.

Since property, however, is not always actually in the hands of the owner, ownership must be distinguished from possession, the one being a matter of law and mores, the other a matter of fact. Possession by a person other than the owner may either be licit or illicit. Illicit possession shows that institutions of property are susceptible of evasion; licit possession by one not the owner, as with a borrowed or rented piece of property, emphasizes their strength.

Acquisition of property proceeds usually according to socially established rules of competition, and, in many cases, by stages. In the initial stage the field is generally open to a class of persons, anybody in this class being free to put in a claim. The qualifying rounds of an amateur golf tournament or the sudden entrance of a strange but attractive young woman are cases in point. Gradually a few competitors take the lead. Social order then requires that others recognize the superiority of these, quit struggling, and turn their attention elsewhere. Finally, after continued competition among the favored few, one competitor wins. This is the signal for everyone who was initially interested to drop all pretense of a claim and take his defeat in good spirit. Competition for this particular piece of property is now, by social edict, either temporarily or permanently over. It is owned by one man, behind whose title stands the authority of the community.

Values, however, do not invariably change hands in any such orderly fashion. The unscrupulous stand always ready to take possession in defiance of the rules, to replace the orderliness of rivalry with the disarrangement of trespass. They may at any stage, under peril of organized retaliation, upset the procedure and seize physical possession of the property.

There are thus two dangers which beset any person with regard to property. The first is that somebody will win out over him in legitimate competition. This is the danger of superior rivalry. The second is that somebody will illegitimately take from him property already acquired. This is the danger of trespass.

Most malignant emotions are concerned with these two dangers, being directed either at a rival or trespasser or at someone who is helping a rival or trespasser. Such emotions may be suppressed by the group culture or utilized for maintaining the organized distribution of property. In general fear and hatred of rivals is institutionally suppressed; fear and hatred of trespassers encouraged.

In the initial stages of acquisition fear of rivals is frequently paramount. Such fear is merely the obverse side of strong desire to win. In so far as society fosters the desire to win and builds up an emotional drive in the individual to that end, it inevitably fosters the fear of losing. By the same token, when defeat actually occurs it implies a frustration of strong desire, hence an inevitable emotion. This emotion, since most competitors cannot win, occurs frequently. Yet social organization requires that such emotions, once the property is in the winner's hands, be curbed. Society tends necessarily to suppress them, and to encourage one-time rivals to be "good sports," "graceful losers."

The successful rival, however, need not suppress these emotions. Once established as owner, he is encouraged by the culture to express them toward any trespasser. Free expression of malevolent emotion against a trespasser protects the established distribution of property and maintains the fixed rules for its competitive acquisition.

Two

Can the relationship of affection between two persons be conceived as a property relationship? This is a question not to be answered too glibly. The affectional relationship is certainly not identical with *economic* property, although sheer sexual gratification, as in prostitution, may be. Affection assumes that the object is desired in and for itself. It therefore cannot be bought and sold; it is not a means to something else, not an economic thing. Yet the affectional relationship has features that are characteristic of property in general. It is regulated, highly institutionalized; and involves some sort of institutionalized exclusiveness, hedged about with rights and obligations. There is competition for possession, a feeling of ownership on the part of the successful competitor, a "hands-off" attitude on the part of the public, and a general resentment against anyone who endeavors to break up the relationship by "stealing" the object. In view of these considerations I feel justified in applying the term property to the institutionalized possession of affection. There exists no other term, apparently, which will describe those types of sanctioned possession which are not economic. Nevertheless the distinction between economic and non-economic property must be made clear. This can be accomplished by a more detailed consideration of types and sub-types of property.

Economic property is that type in which the object possessed is a means to an ulterior end. Non-economic property is that type in which the object is an end in itself. Several sub-types can be distinguished under each head, but I shall rest content with distinguishing three kinds of economic and one kind of non-economic property, calling them by the attitude which Ego has in each case towards the object—respectively, *need, vanity, pride,* and *love.*

1. *Need.* Some objects of property satisfy organic needs. Food, shelter, prostitute, or servant may fall into this category. The object is not valued for itself, but simply as a means of satisfying the need; it may be bought, sold, and substituted. The attitude of the public is subsidiary. A person desires the public to regard the object as his property, but solely because he needs it.

2. *Vanity.* When an object is valued not for the satisfaction of a need but for the response it elicits in one's neighbors, and when the only connection between owner and object is mere possession, a new property situation is apparent. The attitude of the public is no longer subsidiary but paramount. An expensive diamond, a top-hat, a long automobile are useless except as tokens and instruments of the owner's social status. The ulterior end is the envious approval of the community.

Whereas in the need situation a rival or trespasser could proceed only by gaining possession of the actual object, he may in the vanity situation employ an additional procedure. He may gain the ulterior end by possession of a different but superior object.

Vanity is often condemned on moral grounds because there is no necessary relationship between merit and possession of an enviable object. A fool may inherit a crown; an ignorant farmer acquire riches in oil; a silly girl possess incomparable beauty. When such people attribute merit to themselves for such possessions, they are vain, and such vanity, for the public, is thin and unlovely.[1]

---

1. This type, like the others, is of course an abstraction—an ideal-type. Motives and attitudes in actual life situations are nearly always mixed. Need, vanity, pride and love will be present in practically every concrete situation. Rarely, for example, is sheer possession the reason for the public's envy and respect. Usually the secret of such envy and respect is that possession conveys power. Such power may be valued merely for the envy it commands, in which case the relationship remains within the vanity type. Or it may be valued because it enables one to satisfy needs, to succeed in love, or to acquire skills, in which case it falls by implication into one of the other three types. In actual life, however, several or all of these attitudes are present in the same situation.

3. *Pride.* This type is characterized by an intrinsic relation between owner and object. The object is some form of accomplishment, and reflects professional ability. There is thus a necessary connection, recognized by the public, between the qualities of the owner and the nature of his possession. The ownership is indeed more a matter of accomplishment than of legal technicality. All that law or the public can do is to recognize and protect it when it comes; it cannot create it.

4. *Love.* In the three previous cases the object, while not necessarily inanimate or completely passive, takes no dynamic part in the equilibrium. In the present case, however, the object consists in a personal attitude—an attitude of affection. Since affection is a phenomenon of will, the question of possession is thereby placed largely in the hands of the object.

Out of this pecularity grow the other idiosyncrasies of love-property. We find, for instance, that a jealous lover often attacks the love object herself, seeking to restrain or retaliate. Having control of the vital element in the situation—affection—she is in a position to decide the issue. She can bestow affection either on Ego or on his rival, as she chooses. A man might destroy his food in order to keep another from getting it; he might destroy his jewels or other emblems of prestige; he might even renounce and forsake his profession—but unless indulging in an anthropomorphic extravaganza he would not do this out of resentment toward the object itself. Yet in the case of sexual jealousy the resentment may be more against the object of love than against the rival.

In the situations both of vanity and of pride we noted that the thing really desired was the envy or admiration of the public—in other words, an attitude. The same is true of the love situation, where an attitude of affection is desired. To this extent the three property situations are similar, and we do find that jealousy has been applied to all of them—especially to the pride situation as "professional jealously." (Only to the need situation does jealousy seem totally inapplicable.) Yet in spite of similarities we have to separate the love-property situation from the others, because the object possessed in this situation is purely an end in itself. This is a peculiarity which it shares with other forms of property. Moreover, the affectional relationship implies a reciprocal, mutual interchange between owner and object which is not true of the other forms. Thus the relationship, in addition to being an end in itself, gives the object a dynamic role in determining the direction of the conflict situation. It may be, too, that conflicts over love generate more emotion than other kinds. When the object possessed is another person the universal process by which the owner identifies himself with the thing possessed (transmuting "mine" into "I") is perhaps more complete than when the object is not a person. Still this identification, simply because the object is not inert but willful, is probably most tenuous of all. The relationship thus being usually close and at the same time unusually tenuous, becomes doubly intense.

THREE

In depicting the four types of property relationship we have stopped four processes in mid-air. They are not static but dynamic—instable conflict situations tending inevitably toward their own solution. Fidelity to fact would require that some notion be given of their processual sequence from *debut* to *deñouement*.

A complete sequence in love-property conflict would begin with the rivalry phase. It would depict the changing attitudes of the rivals, and of the object and the public, as some are eliminated and one finally wins. The next phase would show the winner in secure possession at some level of ownership such as the "sweetheart," the "fiancee," or the "spouse" level. He is no longer jealous because rivalry is finished and no trespasser is in sight, and the public has an attitude of "don't disturb." The third phase, trespass, would describe the attitude of Ego as he becomes aware of an enemy—his attitudes toward the trespasser, the love object, and the public. It would describe also the attitudes of the trespasser; and since the direction of the sequence hinges largely upon the woman, her attitudes toward lover, rival, and public. If she favors the trespasser and is willing to risk Ego's and the community's wrath, Ego may lose. On the other hand if she does not favor the trespasser, or if he, himself, is not willing to take the risk, or if Ego or the public uses irresistable force, Ego may win. The complexity of attitudes between the four interacting agencies grows amazingly complex. Innumerable combinations are possible. To describe them all, though a fascinating adventure into the anatomy of dramatic reality, would require a tome.[2]

FOUR

Since in love-property the object of possession is the affection of another person we may expect jealousy to have direct bearing upon the sociology of intimacy. Only when there is a presumption of *gemeinschaft* or *primary* association in past, present, or future can jealousy, apparently, appear.

Yet jealousy signifies at least a partial negation of that rapport

---

2. One attitude that seems dependent upon the stage of conflict is envy. Envy is the attitude not of the owner but of either the public or a potential rival. It implies that a person would like to have a possession that another owns but that he is at the time making no effort to wrest it away from the owner. It can hardly be present in one's mind at the same time as jealousy, because the latter implies some claim to possession or at least a right to compete. Envy is the obverse side of the desire for the valuables of a community, and since it usually cuts across the institutional distribution it is frowned upon by the group culture.

between persons which we commonly ascribe to intimacy. It admits that affection has strayed in the direction of a rival. Even where affection has not strayed jealousy shows on the lover's part a mistrust inimical to the harmony of perfect intimacy.

What, then, is the function of jealousy with regard to intimate association? As a fear reaction in the initial stages of rivalry it is simply the obverse side of the desire to win the object. The desire to win being institutionally cultivated, the fear of losing is unavoidably stimulated also, though its expression is publicly frowned upon. But after ownership has been attained, jealousy is a fear and rage reaction fitted to protect, maintain, and prolong the intimate association of love. It shelters this personal relationship from outside intrusion. This is not to say that it never defeats its own purpose by overshooting the mark. So deeply emotional is jealousy that it appears in the midst of modern social relationships, which are most profitably manipulated by self-composed shrewdness, as a bull in a china shop. Nonetheless its intention is protective. It is a denial of gemeinschaft only in so far as its presence admits a breach; and is destructive of it only in so far as it muddles its own purpose.

Jealousy stresses two characteristics of gemeinschaft relationship: its ultimate and its personal qualities. The relationship is for the jealous person an ultimate end in itself, all other considerations coming secondary. This explains the bizarre crimes so frequently connected with jealousy — crimes understandable only upon the assumption that for the criminal the affection of a particular person is the supreme value in life. It also explains the connection between extreme jealousy and romantic love. The "personal" quality of the relationship is manifested by the unwillingness of the jealous person to conceive any substitute for the "one and only." He insists upon the uniqueness of personality. Were the particular person removed, the whole relationship and its accompanying emotion of jealousy would disappear.

An old debate poses the question whether or not affection is divisible. Is it possible to love two people sincerely at the same time? Most sexologists answer that it is possible, and cite cases as proof. Iwan Bloch, for example, asserts that simultaneous passion for several persons happens repeatedly.[3] He adds that the extensive psychic differentiation between individuals in modern civilization increases its likelihood, for it is difficult to find in a single person one's complement. He gives numerous examples from history and literature, particularly cases where one aspect of a person's nature is satisfied by one lover, another aspect (usually the sensual) by a different lover.

3. *Sexual Life of Our Time*, pp. 206-207. Havelock Ellis, *Studies in Psych. of Sex*, VI, 568-69, agrees. Also Joseph K. Folsom, in his *Social Psychology*, pp. 154-55.

The conclusion invariably deduced from this is that jealousy is harmful and unjustified. But to end the discussion with this ethical argument is to miss the point. Even though love, like any other distributive value, is divisible, institutions dictate the manner and extent of the division. Where exclusive possession of an individual's entire love is customary, jealousy will demand that exclusiveness. Where love is divided it will be divided according to some scheme, and jealousy will reinforce the division.

FIVE

While the love-property situation contains a relationship of intimacy and throws light upon the sociology of gemeinschaft association, it also contains a diametrically opposite kind of relation—namely, that of power—which concerns the sociology of dominance and subordination. This relationship, which obtains between the lover and his rival or trespasser, is not a value in itself but a means to an ulterior end; and it connotes an absolute opposition of purpose, in the sense that if one succeeds the other fails. The rival or trespasser may be a stranger or a close friend; in either event, so far as the common object is concerned, he is an enemy.

Here, as elsewhere in the discussion, it makes a difference whether the enemy is a trespasser or a rival. Rivalry is most acute in the early stages of acquisition, and jealousy is at this point a fear of not winning the desired object. Toward one's rival one is supposed to show good sport and courtesy, which is to say that society requires the suppression, in this context, of jealous animosity. Regulated competition constitutes the *sine qua non* of property distribution and hence of stable social organization. But as one person gets ahead and demonstrates a superior claim, his rivals, hiding their feelings of jealous disappointment, must drop away. If any rival persists after the victor has with institutional ritual fortified his claim he is no longer a rival but a trespasser.

Jealousy toward the trespasser is encouraged rather than suppressed, for it tends to preserve the fundamental institutions of property. Uncles in our society are never jealous of the affection of nephews for their father. But uncles in matrilineal societies frequently are, because there is a close tie socially prescribed between uncle and nephew. The nephew's respect is the property of the uncle; if it is given to the father (as sometimes happens because of the close association between father and son), the uncle is jealous. Jealousy does not occur in the natural situations—and the "natural situations" are simply those defined in terms of the established institutions. Our malignant emotions, fear, anger, hate, and jealousy, greet any illicit attempt to gain property that we hold. They do not manifest themselves when a licit attempt is made, partly because we do not then have the subjective feeling of "being wronged," and partly because their expression would receive the disapprobation of the community. The social function of jealousy against a trespasser is the extirpation of any obstacle to the smooth running of the institutional machinery.

Discussions of jealousy usually overlook the difference between rivalry and trespass. A case in point is the old problem of whether one can be jealous of a person not one's equal. If the person is a trespasser the answer is that he can be at any social distance away. But if he is a rival he cannot be too far distant. Rivalry implies a certain degree of equality at the start. Each society designates which of its members are eligible to compete for certain properties. While there are some properties for which members of different classes may compete, there are others for which they may not compete. In such cases the thought of competition is inconceivable, the emotions reserved for a rival fail to appear, and the act is regarded not as rivalry but as a detestable thrust at the class structure. Thus it happens that for a given lover some people cannot arouse jealousy as of a rival. If the love-object yields to a member of a distinctly inferior social class, jealousy will turn into moral outrage, no matter if the lover himself has no claim on the love-object. It is inconceivable, for this reason, that a Negro could be the rival of a southern white man for the hand of a white girl. The white man would have him lynched. Southern society does not permit Negroes as a class to compete for the affection of white girls. It is almost equally inconceivable that a white man could be a Negro's rival for the hand of a colored girl. The Negro has either too much advantage in the likelihood of social ostracism for the white man, or too little advantage in that the white man, if immune to ostracism, can take the property by force.

But jealousy against a trespasser is another matter. A trespasser being by definition a breaker of customary rules, the more he breaks, including the rules of class structure, the more of a trespasser he is. A violator of property rights may for this reason occupy any position on the social scale.

The fact that men of native races sometimes prostitute their wives to civilized men without any feeling of jealousy, while they are extremely jealous of men of their own race,[4] is sometimes pointed out as showing that men are jealous only of their equals. This is true only in so far as jealousy of rivals is meant. The civilized man is not conceived by the natives as a rival, nor as a trespasser. He may be conceived as a trespasser—if, for example, he attempts to retain the wife without paying anything. Yet in the case mentioned he is not a trespasser, but merely one who has legitimately paid for the temporary use of property. His very payment recognizes the property rights of the husband. The following case is much more illustrative: "A Frenchman of position picks for his mistress a girl who is not his social equal. You can see for yourself that his wife is not jealous. But let him choose a woman of his own social rank — then you'd see the fur fly . . . "[5] Among some

4. Malinowski, *Sexual Life of Savages*, p. 271.
5. Reported by Ben. B. Lindsey, *Companionate Marriage*, p. 88.

social spheres in France, if we are to believe what we hear, women of different classes customarily exercise proprietary rights in the same man, and no jealousy is felt. But since it is not customary for members of the same rank to share a man, such a condition is either rivalry or trespass, and arouses intense jealousy.

One may argue that the nearer two people are in every plane, the more intense will be the jealousy of rivalry; while the further apart they are, the greater the jealousy of trespass.

But between the lover and the object of his love the relationship is not one of power. If a woman is regarded simply as a pawn in a game for prestige the pattern is No. 2 in our typology, not No. 4. It is a question of vanity rather than jealousy. In the love situation the jealous person values the affection for itself. It is his fear of losing this intrisically valuable affection to a rival or a trespasser, rather than his fear of losing prestige in the eyes of his public and his rival, that paralyzes him.

SIX

Into every affair of love and battle for power steps society. It has an inherent interest in love not only because future generations depend upon it but because social cohesion rests upon the peaceful distribution of major values.

A question that all authorities feel compelled to settle concerns the social or antisocial character of jealousy. Forel declares that jealousy "is only the brutal stupidity of an atavistic heritage, or a pathological symptom,"[6] while Havelock Ellis calls it "an anti-social emotion."[7] The chief arguments are that it is an inheritance from animal ancestors, a hindrance to the emancipation of women, and an obstacle to rational social intercourse.

The hasty readiness to praise or condemn prevents a clear understanding of the relation of jealousy to institutional structure. Careful analysis is cut short by the quick conclusion that jealousy is instinctive, the assumption being that certain stimuli call forth a stereotyped, biologically ingrained response. Jealousy is therefore regarded as an animal urge, and since biological nature and sociological nature are assumed to be eternally at odds, jealousy is denounced as anti-social.[8]

This view fails to analyze jealous behavior into its different components—to distinguish between the stimulus (with its physical

6. *The Sexual Question,* pp. 118-119.
7. *Studies in Psychology of Sex,* VI, 564.
8. The logic of social ethicists at times becomes badly scrambled. Frequently it is clear that what they call "instinctive" is merely the institutions to which they are habituated and to which they lend their approval. The biological basis of the institutions is thus assumed to justify them, for, if a thing is instinctive, like love, it should be given free expression, not suppressed. On the other hand the inverterate propensity to derive all social phenomena from the genetic qualities of the individual leads the ethicists to infer that certain disapproved behavior, like criminally, war, or jealousy, is also instinctive. In this case the assumption that it is biological becomes, not a justification, but a reason for condemnation. It is "atavistic," "barbaric," "animal-like."

and meaningful aspects) and the physical mechanism of response. It puts all constituents into the undifferentiated category of instinct.

Doubtless the physiological mechanism is inherited. But the striking thing about this mechanism is that it is not specific for jealousy, but operates in precisely the same manner in fear and rage. The sympathetic nervous system plays, apparently, the usual role: increased adrenal activity speeding the heart, increasing the sugar content of the blood, toning up the striated and staying the smooth muscles.

If we are to differentiate jealousy from the other strong emotions we must speak not in terms of inherited physiology but in terms of the type of situation which provokes it. The conflict situation always contains a particular content, and the content varies from one culture to the next. The usual mistake in conceiving jealousy is to erect a concrete situation found somewhere (often in the culture of the author) into the universal and inherent stimulus to that emotion. This ignores the fact that each culture distributes its sexual property and defines its conflict situations in its own way, and that, therefore, the concrete content cannot be regarded as an inherited stimulus to an inherited response.

This mistake is made, I think, by those theorists who seek to explain certain human institutions on the basis of instinctive emotions. In the field of sexual institutions Westermarck is the outstanding theorist who has relied upon this type of explanation. He disproves the hypothesis of primeval promiscuity and proves the primacy of pair marriage largely on the basis of allegedly innate jealousy.[9] He assumes, indeed, that all types of sexual relationship other than monogamy, as he knows it in his own culture, are native stimuli to instinctive jealous retaliation.

As soon, however, as we admit that other forms of sexual property exist, and that they do not arouse but instead are protected by jealousy, the explanation of monogamy breaks down. Whether as the obverse side of the desire to obtain sexual property by legitimate competition, or as the anger at having rightful property trespassed upon, jealousy would seem to bolster the institutions where it is found. If these institutions are of an opposite character to monogamy, it bolsters them nonetheless. Whereas Westermarck would say that adultery arouses jealousy and that, therefore, jealousy causes monogamy, one could maintain that our institution of monogamy causes adultery to be resented and, therefore, creates jealousy.

Had he confined himself to disproving promiscutiy instead of going on to prove monogamy, Westermarck would have remained on surer ground. Promiscuity implies the absence of any sexual property-pattern. Yet sexual affection is, unlike divine grace, a distributive value. To let it go undistributed would introduce anarchy into the group and destroy the social "system." Promiscuity can take place only in so far as society has broken down and reached a state of anomie.

The stimulus to jealousy, moreover, is not so much a physical situation as a meaningful one. The same physical act will in one place denote ownership, in another place robbery. Westermarck appears to believe

9. *History of Human Marriage*, Ch. 9.

that it is the physical act of sexual intercourse between another man and one's wife that instinctively arouses jealousy. But there are cultures where such intercourse merely emphasizes the husband's status as owner, just as lending an automobile presumes and emphasizes one's ownership of it.

We may cite, for example, the whole range of institutions whereby, in some manner, the wife is given over to a man other than her husband. These run from those highly ritualized single acts in which a priest or a relative deflowers the wife, to the repeated and more promiscuous acts of sexual hospitality and the more permanent and thorough-going agreements of wife-exchange; not to mention the fixed division of sexual function represented by polyandric marriage. In societies where any institution in this range prevails, the behavior implied does not arouse the feeling of jealousy that similar behavior would arouse in our culture. Jealousy does not respond inherently to any particular situation; it responds to all those situations, no matter how diverse, which signify a violation of accustomed sexual rights.

SEVEN

Possession of a thing of value without any right to it is a prevalent condition in sexual behavior, affection being evidently difficult to govern. The converse—ownership without custody—appears equally prevalent. At least in our culture the instances are countless in which there is no overt trangression of convention and yet affection has strayed. Wives and husbands abound who have little or no affection for their mates, but who would not actually sully the marriage tie. Their affections is owned by their mates, but not possessed.

Our discussion seems to have associated jealousy exclusively with ownership, with outward conformity, rather than with actual possession. This has not been due to ignorance of possible discrepancy between the two, or to ignorance of the fact that many lovers, especially the romantic variety, profess to care only for the possession of affection, and nothing at all for conformity to senseless tradition. It has been due, rather, to a conviction that so-called outward conformity, either through speech or overt behavior, is always the symbol of the inward state. If a woman never, by word or deed, let the fact appear that she did not love her husband, he would never have cause to feel jealous. She must say or do something contrary to a wife's institutionally sanctioned role before jealousy will be justified. If she says she loves her husband and yet does things contrary to the mores, such as have intercourse with a prohibited man, actions will be presumed to speak louder than words, and jealousy will be in order.

To us who conform outwardly to many meaningless and secretly detested conventions, and perform an even greater number of routine technological acts which try our patience, a close correspondence between inner feeling and external act seems questionable. Yet if we analyze the less conspicuous because less conscious aspects of our behavior, we find the correspondence frequently quite close. In situations where we are supposed to feel ashamed, we feel ashamed—and prove it by our outward embarrassment. In situations where we are supposed to show respect, we usually feel respect. In only a few civilizations is the distinction between external act and internal feeling sharply realized, and even then they are not far apart. In any case action which conforms to the institutions of property is the symbol of genuine possession, and contrary action the symbol of lack of possession.

It is true that conformity at any particular time may be a deception, but the deception is hardly significant unless it manifests itself at some time in non-conformist outward behavior. Whether or not it is a deception depends, of course, upon the internal stae, which is the motivating factor. So the aim of the lover is always to control the inner state of affection, not simply to enforce a present conformity which guarantees nothing concerning future behavior. This in spite of the fact that his only clue is the loved one's outward conformity or non-conformity.

Unless through each stage of progressive ownership actual possession also progresses, inconvenience will result. A girl who becomes engaged to a man without caring for him and without intending to marry him is in an uncomfortable position. She cannot complain if her finance's legitimate jealousy and the public's interest in morality restrict her actions.. She knows that when she breaks her engagement she must have a good excuse wherewith to avoid social censure. At all times she is constrained to feign an affection she does not feel. On the whole the inconvenience of a hiatus between real feeling and institutional status is in this case greater than the advantage. Moreover, most girls are trained to think of such a thing as not only unwise but also unfair and immoral. In this way ownership tends to approximate genuine possession.

EIGHT

Unfortunately our treatment has been couched entirely in terms of the stable and integrated culture, and there is not space to treat the complications arising when society has reached a state of anomie. As the institutions of property in general disintegrate, sexual property follows suit. In extreme cases, apparently, ownership may disappear and be replaced entirely by sheer possession.

Juxtaposition of contrary mores and rapid change have given our culture a certain amount of anomie, which is reflected in the emotions surrounding the distribution of sexual favor. None of our sexual institutions is sanctioned by all groups. Consequently, no matter how customary the sexual behavior, somebody can be found who is made jealous by it. For example, those who are not used to dancing and who disapprove of it are apt to grow extremely jealous if a wife or sweetheart indulges. This, coupled with other traits such as our individualism and romanticism, has tended, in the eyes of our intelligentsia, to give jealousy a negative value. Yet among the juries of the land the "unwritten law" is still a sanctioned reality.

Sex Games Married People Play

MORTON HUNT

To look at Arthur Tully, you'd never think he was the kind to play sexual games with his wife. He himself would be the last to recognize that that's what he has been doing lately. "Sexual games?" he'd snort, if you asked him about it, "—I hardly have the time or even the energy for sex these days." For Arthur Tully — that's not his real name, of course — is a pale, tense, driven young man of 35 who puts in long hours as the junior partner in an accounting firm, moonlights three evenings a week as an assistant professor of accounting at a junior college, and is active in half a dozen clubs and organizations for the sake of the business contracts that they offer.

Most nights, by the time he gets home, he's too tired for sex; even when he does come home early, he nearly always brings along a fat briefcase full of work that keeps him up until all hours. He and his wife, Muriel, had a passionate relationship when they married 10 years ago, but nowadays they make love only two or three times a month. Muriel sometimes drops hints or makes tentative approaches, but nearly always Arthur wearily and apologetically explains that he's exhausted, and sometimes he simply doesn't seem to notice.

This is a sexual game?

Absolutely. Not a game of the kind portrayed in contemporary sex-liberation literature — blindfolded Guess Who at big parties, key-swap clubs, group sex — but one of the kind dealt with by the late Dr. Eric Berne in his celebrated book, *Games People Play*. By that term, Dr. Berne meant not a form of sport or play, but a common type of fraudulent interaction between persons in which the first offers a "come-on" or "bait," the second eagerly responds to it, and the first then "pulls a switch" on the second, frustrating the latter and getting a "payoff"—the gratification of some hidden and, generally, neurotic need of his own.

In Arthur Tully's case, sex is the bait, fatigue is the switch, and revenge is the payoff. Like many a traditionalist, Arthur wanted to be the sole money earner and have his pretty, young wife stay at home. She liked the idea fine, and at first all went well. Indeed, as Arthur began to earn more money, he and she built a lovely home, furnished it well, took vacation trips, and luxuriated in their life and their love. But the gradual accumulation of children, insurance policies and financial burdens began to weigh heavily upon him. He worked harder than ever to keep improving their way of life, but unconsciously he began to resent her total dependence on him and his total responsibility for the family upkeep. He could hardly upbraid her for this because he had wanted it that way, and still did, consciously. Unconsciously, however, he wanted to get even — and these hidden feelings took the form of a declining interest in lovemaking, excused as the result of fatigue.

Thus Arthur is playing a game: He seemingly offers Muriel sex by his status as her husband, then denies it to her because he is so worn out from earning money for her and the children, thus punishes her and, wins his revenge. He plays what one might call "Money-earner's Trump," a game that one can outline (following Dr. Berne's style) in three simple steps:

He: I bring home the money, and you give me love.

She: Gladly. How about tonight?

He: Sorry. I had a tough day. (*Trump!*)

So he wins; but she, in losing, wins something too, or she would not continue to play it again and again—she wins a little punishment, which relieves her guilt feelings for letting him bear the whole burden of financial responsibility. As long as both of them get these neurotic gratifications, they will keep on playing.

Sexual games, indeed, become a way of life—a chronic, crippling, self-depriving method of dealing with one's problems.

Somewhat analogous to "Money-earner's Trump" is a game popular with some wives influenced by the more aggressive spokeswomen for Women's Liberation. The wife, if she works, resents the advantages men have in the career world; if she stays at home, she resents her "enslavement" to unpaid, unhonored domestic labor. To get even, she plays "Women's Lib Trump": She gives her husband cues and hints he has always associated with sexual interest on her part — the perfumed bath, the lacy negligee, the draperies drawn back to let in the moonlight — but when he reaches out for her, she is surprised and sarcastic, or even hostile ("Not tonight, Harold". . . "Why not?" "Because I don't happen to feel like it, even if you do. It's a two-way thing these days — haven't you heard? . . .Oh, you *thought* — well, don't think. I'll let you know when.")   Or, again using a shorthand analysis of the three moves involved:

She: Come get me . . .

He: Here I come!

She: Male chauvinist pig! (*Trump!*)

This game, too, may be played repeatedly, if both players get payoffs of their unconscious needs. But if the husband has no secret sense of guilt at being an overprivileged male, he will not find the punishment acceptable. Instead of responding again and again with "Here I come," he may begin to ignore his wife — saying, in effect, "*You* come get *me*" — or may even quietly find himself a non-game-playing mistress.

Almost all husbands and wives play sexual games — most of them now and the, some of them for a lifetime — for nearly everyone is prey at times to unconscious needs of an immature or neurotic nature, and seeks to satisfy them by misusing conscious and healthy needs as bait. Of the various forms of bait, including money, fame and power, almost none has so powerful an appeal or is as universally available as sex:

hence the prevalence of sexual games. And that is a pity; in such games, a priceless treasure is traded away for cheap and shoddy goods.

Games of revenge, such as the two we have just seen, are probably the most common. The underlying cause of resentment may involve money, domination, nagging, thoughtlessness or any one of many other problems that could be dealt with openly by an adult, inwardly secure person. But the immature or insecure person may be afraid to do so, or may feel guilty about being resentful, or may fail altogether to recognize his or her own feelings. Instead, he or she expresses the resentment by involuntarily losing interest in the spouse, or by making love in a detached and bored fashion, or by "helpfully" criticizing the other's sexual technique or by begging off for any of various reasons ("I have a headache tonight," "I have to get up terribly early tomorrow," "Let's wait until the weekend.").

A particularly malicious game of revenge is one we might call "By the Way." Herbie Soster, a sweet, long-suffering druggist, has a wife who is a whiz at it. Time and again, she kids or teases him about sex during the evening until he is eager and certain — and then, at bedtime, she brings up some pressing problem — money, vacation plans, the children's misbehavior — which leads to a nasty discussion, wrecks the mood and cancels his plans for sex. Other people who play the same game suddenly remember just before retiring that some urgent chore must be done at once, even though it will last until too late for lovemaking. Even TV may provide the excuse — psychiatrist Alfred Auerback of the University of California School of Medicine, San Francisco, says that the *Late, Late Show* is now commonly used to avoid sex. (One can imagine the "switch": "Darling, look what's on! I've been wanting to see the rerun of it for years. You don't mind, do you?—I'll make it up to you tomorrow night.")

By far the most hurtful game of revenge is the one played by those who express their unconscious anger by developing sexual anesthesia. Many cases of gradually developing impotence or frigidity in marriage, says New York marriage counselor Dr. Rebecca Liswood, have nothing to do with sexual conflicts at all, but are the sexual expression of other kinds of discord. For sexual non-responsiveness is a powerful weapon of retribution: There is almost no way of humiliating one's husband so effective as remaining unaroused by his lovemaking, and almost no way of crushing one's wife so effectively as becoming impotent with her.

Marital infidelity is yet another way of taking revenge. To be sure, many unfaithful husbands and wives are not playing games but seeking reassurance, sex or affection missing in their marriage. But a substantial minority of the unfaithful, as I found in a survey of my own, are primarily seeking to get even with their mates; their infidelities are games, for the goal is something other than that which it seems to be.

Many of them, indeed, maximize their revenge by seeing to it that their mates find out, and suffer. Some accidentally drop clues, others become increasingly obvious about their absences and strange hours, and still others burst out with tortured confessions. But the most abject and penitent confessor may be the most sadistic of all. One woman I recently interviewed told me that her ex-husband insisted on confessing his infidelities at length in order to abuse and humiliate himself — and so managed to tell her every physical detail of his extramarital lovemaking, although hearing these details was excruciatingly painful for her. (But she, in passively listening, may have been playing her own neurotic game — she may have been accepting suffering from having failed, as she thought, to be an adequate wife.)

Suffering is, in fact, almost as important a motive in sexual games as revenge. Many people who feel themselves to be unworthy, undesirable or unlovable play games designed to prove their fears correct. A woman may suggest sex to her husband just when she is likeliest to be refused — when he is upset by business problems, for instance, or when it is too late at night or right after an unresolved quarrel. His lack of interest wounds her, but in a curious way gratifies her by confirming her suspicions. In effect, her untimely suggestion is a way of saying, "I don't suppose you'd be interested . . ." and when he agrees that at this moment he wouldn't be, she takes it as a rejection, saying to herself, "I knew it! — He doesn't love me."

In another version of "I Knew It!" the sufferer suspects her innocent mate of infidelity, and manages to make her fears come true. One woman, overweight and prone to feelings of intellectual inferiority, began after some years of marriage to fear that her husband was having extramarital affairs with more attractive and brighter women. She badgered him about it increasingly, began to go through his wallet at night, started phoning frequently to check up on him at work, and was tearful and accusing by turns, until he became so resentful that at last he cheated on her to get even — and thus made her unconscious wish come true. Which is why her reaction consisted not only of hurt and rage, but of triumphant suffering ("I knew it! I was right all along!")

Another group of sexual games consists of those in which the hidden goal is the obtaining of control over one's mate. The most familiar form of the game seems to be a simple swap — sex for money, money for sex. The gold digger is the best-known practitioner, chilly to her husband when he isn't buying her what she wants or giving her a generous allowance, but sexy when he is. Externally, it seems as though sex and money are merely being exchanged in such games, but when one looks more closely, it is clear that the transaction concerns power: The gold digger gets her money, but her real victory consists of having *made* her husband pay for sex.

A somewhat subtler game of control can be called, "You Owe Me." Described (in another context) by Dr. George Bach and Ronald Deutsch in their book, *Pairing,* this is a stratagem in which one partner accedes to the other's wishes — but afterwards reveals that he or she had not wanted to, or found it unpleasant, or now feels ill as a result, and thus makes the other feel guilty and eager to make restitution. An example: A wife makes love when her husband approaches her in the middle of the night, but the next day she lets him know that she is fatigued because she could not get back to sleep afterwards. A far more ambitious version: A wife agrees to "take a chance" when her husband is in the mood and she is unprepared; a pregnancy results that puts him permanently in her debt.

Games of control can become very complex. In *The Strategy of Sex*, psychiatrist A. H. Chapman describes one that involves many steps. A domineering wife belittles her husband and often refuses him sex; he becomes impotent with her; he seeks to regain his potency with another woman, and does so; he lets his wife know about it; she, fearful that she is about to lose him, becomes submissive and seductive — and he regains his potency with her. And more than that: He has now learned how to keep the upper hand — and either continues his affair, or holds the threat of renewed infidelity over her to keep her in line.

Still another group of sex games includes those whose hidden goal is the avoidance of intimacy — a goal which seemingly is the very antithesis of sexual union. Many adults cannot tolerate deep intimacy with any one person of the opposite sex; it makes them feel "hemmed in," suffocated and invaded, and so they construct married life so as to set limits to it. Sometimes they use what sociologists call "avoidance devices" — excessive hours of work, long business trips, continual company, separate bedrooms — but even sex can be made to serve as emotional insulation. A fair number of men and women, for instance, indulge in fantasies during lovemaking, imagining themselves in the arms of persons other than their mates. Psychiatrists who have studied this phenomenon say that it generally is a way of maintaining some psychological distance from the real person one is making love to.

Another use of sex to maintain emotional distance is a concentration upon technical expertise, and the diligent perfecting of the physical acts and variations described in sex manuals. For as the distinguished psychoanalyst and author, Dr. Rollo May, has pointed out, an overemphasis on technique makes for a mechanistic attitude toward lovemaking, and promotes alienation and depersonalization rather than intimacy. As one tearful young woman said to her psychologist, "My husband thinks he's a great lover, but he has no idea how lonely I feel in the midst of it all!"

Even those sexual activities that first come to mind when one hears the term "sexual games" — the contemporary experiments in sanctioned extramarital acts — are often games in the psychological sense as well, their hidden purpose being to maintain distance from one's marital partner. Mate-swapping, group sex and the like can all be used to "segmentalize" one's love relationships: So much for the mate; so much for other persons. But such games succeed only at considerable cost. Many of the researchers who have studied these practices report that there is a high incidence of jealousy, competitiveness, marital conflict and divorce among the practitioners.

Indeed, all sexual games yield certain benefits, but always at great cost. For game playing is a faulty adaptation to one's emotional problems rather than a genuine solution to them; a make-do way of living and loving; an indirect, dishonest and generally hurtful way of getting along with one's self and one's mate. Sexual game players gain something by their maneuvers and deceits, but pay for it with much of the joy, love and fulfilment that could be theirs if they dealt with themselves and each other directly and straightforwardly.

The Most Common Sex Problems in New Marriages

WENDA WARDELL MORRONE

It's as if there were a myth that the first few years of marriage are a period with no sexual problems. Before marriage, we can admit to them — the tensions of *should I? will he respect me? do I know him well enough?* and *does he want it too often? did I or didn't I have orgasm?* Afterward, problems can be acknowledged, too, but the myth of the flawless honeymoon remains because it is firmly stated, in every gauzy Doris Day fadeout and happily ever after, that a normal man and woman with all glands functioning properly have only to see the nuptial sheets before plunging into instant orgasms. As Erich Segal has so clearly pointed out, the only thing that can come between married lovers is leukemia. Dr. Natalie Shainess, a New York psychiatrist, would no doubt disagree. "A really good sex life just is not going to come at once," she says. "It takes about two years to evolve." Just because sex problems, especially early in marriage, are not talked about uninhibitedly doesn't mean they don't exist. Common sense says that if marriage beds were so untroubled, the sales figures of Masters and Johnson, Reuben, J, and Mr. and Mrs. K would dwindle substantially — no one would have time to read them.

Dr. Sallie Schumacher, who worked with Masters and Johnson at their clinic in St. Louis and has now opened a similar one in the Long Island Jewish Medical Center, says that the sexual problems that bring couples to therapy begin the first year of marriage and before marriage. One part of her program has in fact been set up particularly to deal with adjustment difficulties in new marriages. Immediately upon meeting this attractive woman you have the feeling that anything you say — tragic, selfish, grotesque — would be heard with a comforting lack of surprise, an ideal atmosphere for the counseling of sex problems.

Dr. Shainess, however, works with her patients on a definitely more traditional counseling basis, but she, too, feels sexual problems early in marriage are far more common than is generally acknowledged. A good-looking woman with beautiful eyes and almost compelling sense of calm, Dr. Shainess lectures in psychiatry at Columbia College of Physicians and Surgeons and is a member of the faculty of the William Alanson White Institute of Psychiatry, Psychoanalysis and Psychology. "Very few people have a mature sense of what they have to expect from marriage," she says, "and that's why things fall apart so quickly."

Just what sex problems are the most common in new marriages? They fall into four general groups. The largest is problems of adjustment (one partner's sex drive might be more intense than the other's). Others are sexual inhibitions and preferences, problems with contraceptives, and minor physical problems. Dr. Schumacher feels that such problems may not even be recognized as problems because the couple may not realize that any solutions are possible.

Dr. Shainess sets forward three other groups of problems. In one, the pattern is of good premarital sex that reverses after marriage — the extent ranges all the way from a marked lessening of enjoyment to temporary frigidity or impotence. Another group of problems has the pattern of sex beginning very well immediately after marriage, then deteriorating. Then there are women who find little satisfaction in sex before marriage but assume that it will improve once sex is legal, and it doesn't.

Part of the solution to these problems is quite directly related to the trouble. The problems of adjustment, for example, can be attributed to youth and inexperience. Most new husbands and wives are young, with limited experience; this means not recognizing subtle signs of displeasure, not realizing how wounding a rejection might be and how long-lasting its effects — not realizing, then, the complexity of the adjustment they are trying to make. Whether such problems do smooth over with time or become more serious depends on how the couple handles them.

Some of the problems may relate to the circumstances of the marriage. Dr. Shainess explains that if a man felt pressured into the marriage, the role of sex can suddenly change for him from the cool image of a swinging affair to something that he must perform, a duty; sex immediately begins to go downhill. The same feeling could easily be experienced by a woman who feels that, before marriage, sex was up to her to give — freely, perhaps, but nevertheless from choice. After marriage it becomes an obligation which doesn't sound or seem the least bit sexy. If people come from homes where parents pressured them to perform, and they taught themselves to dig in their heels for self-protection, when they feel in the marriage a return to a "duty" situation, the same reflex begins even though it is interfering with their own enjoyment.

The couples whose marriages begin with great sex which then deteriorates are often those who didn't know each other well before marriage — which may be the result of a short courtship or can still be true after a couple has lived together. As husband and wife, they become involved with the sticky intricacies of living together and surviving; the areas of unsuspected and serious disagreement also carry over into sex.

The women who have had little interest or enjoyment in sex and discover no change after marriage are often those who had thought of marriage as an alchemic process that would provide a cure-all, then discover that it doesn't.

These solutions are quite closely related to specific situations, but there are other influences which lie deeper and which apply more loosely to us all. These fall into two groups, although there is some crossing over. Together they shape the sexual image we have of ourselves. As Dr. Shainess points out, "Sexual expression and experience is what I call a distillate of the total person, because whatever capacities a person has in terms of vitality and constitution and whatever his essence as a person is, is expressed sexually too."

The first influences shaping this sexual image differ for each person and relate to one's individual experiences. "Human beings live in a civilized world and are very different from a lower animal in its native habitat," says Dr. Shainess. "All kinds of attitudes from early life and experience and relationships are bound up with sex." Looming large among all these experiences are what Dr. Shainess refers to as *transference reactions:* "distorted attitudes toward new people in one's life carried over from experience with significant adults in one's early life. These reactions are always going on. They are the irrational in human relationships. There is something about being married—that very intensive relationship—that tends to elicit transference reactions. Husband and wife begin to experience some things that are done more and more in the irrational mode. And as these transference reactions occur, they also tend to defeat or interfere with the sexual relationships."

There are other events that Dr. Shainess feels contribute to your image of yourself sexually, whether you like it or not. Some reach far back into childhood: Crushes you had on boys, girls, teachers: how you acted them out and how you were treated. The kinds of fantasies you had as a child. Whether beginning to menstruate was pleasant or painful, how it was treated by your mother and friends. What your early sex education was. Your history of dating, petting, first intercourse. The courtship leading to your marriage. Your honeymoon.

Dr. Schumacher feels that there is one basic problem in early life: that ours is "a society which says on Day 1 that if you're a male, you have a right to be sexual, you not only have a right but everybody expects it; while on the other hand it says to a baby girl she doesn't really need to be sexual, she's not encouraged to feel sexual. It wasn't too long ago when it used to be thought that females *never* felt sexual, especially little girls. That's not true. They masturbate just as much as little boys."

But no doubt without admitting that they do. Because this negative emphasis toward all the sexual milestones of a girl's life tends to produce a woman who is uncomfortable living in her own body, who fails to come to terms with her own sexuality.

Dr. Schumacher mentioned that "a lot of people can't even examine their own genitalia with any degree of confidence. A lot of females, for example, have never taken a mirror and looked at themselves to know what they look like."

There are, then, individual experiences each of us has had, perhaps no longer remembered, but nevertheless playing a part in our every response. The culture we live in influences the ways in which we were repulsed or encouraged or shamed, so some of the responsiblity for how we feel about ourselves goes there. But society gets at us in more ways than that; there are many opinions and attitudes and hang-ups about sex that can't be pinned down to explicit experience. They operate almost mythically; they are really hang-ups of the culture rather than the person, and because we live within it, we can't wholly avoid their pressure. These are the second group of influences on our sexual image.

One of these damaging myths, says Dr. Schumacker, is the idea that sex is something one person does to another. Someone has to be the aggressor and somebody the aggress*ee*. A man asks, a woman gives permission; a woman "saves herself" for marriage; a man seduces her; she "puts out," he "screws."

A significant part of this particular myth is the idea that a woman can't feel pleasure without a man. "Many females cannot masturbate, for example." says Dr. Schumacher. "Oh I couldn't have any sexual feelings myself, he must arouse them. He must give me permission to be sexual.'" *He must give me permission to be sexual!* The same idea of permission crops up again when it comes to sex practice—anything that veers from the norm (at night, lights off, woman beneath man, penis in vagina until orgasm) makes people uneasy, as if some authority were standing behind the bed taking notes for blackmail later on. "The idea of being sexual just because it feels good, to experience pleasure, is difficult for many people."

This myth is damaging to both the man and the woman. For the man it extends into marriage the pressure he feels in every other part of life—to perform. For the woman the idea that she is supposed to be passive may at once lock up any real emotions with resentment and give her a copout. Both husband and wife have to realize that the woman has a right to sexual pleasure and that she also bears part of the responsibility for it. "A man needs a vital partner, not a dead fish," says Dr. Shainess.

A second cultural hang-up is the so-called sexual revolution. This is really a vague umbrella of a term which can mean anything from the unending *Playboy* philosophy to Kate Millett, and it does in fact cover several almost unrelated problems. Let us accept Dr. Shainess's definition of the sexual revolution as "a marked change in goals and attitudes sexually and in actual sexual behavior in the last few years."

One bad effect comes simply from the omnipresence of sex: sex studies under laboratory conditions, vaginal sprays, "The Stewardesses" with twenty-foot, three-D breasts. Because of all this, says Dr. Shainess, "there are norms of sexual achievement in terms of orgastic success that lead to unrealistic expectations—something to be lived up to as in other areas of life. It has tended to render sex something to be judged so much in terms of accomplishment and achievement that the true sexual expression of the person in terms of whatever thay are and whatever can give pleasure and whatever comes from them is no longer acceptable." One has, instead, to try to lead as sex-oriented a life as the video-culture puts forth as normal.

With the revolution has come a plethora of literature, most concentrating on technique and little if any on how to tune into one's own most meaningful expressions. Masters and Johnson mention the sex flush in which the woman's breasts redden as she approaches orgasm (Dr. Shainess speculates that it may in fact have been prickly heat from the laboratory lights). David Reuben has the mammary lie detector in which a woman's nipples become erect following orgasm (not true for all women, says Dr. Schumacher, and inverted nipples never will become erect). I began to imagine a mad conversation:

"Oh, the earth really moved for me that time, Sidney."

"What do you mean, moved? Your breasts aren't even pink, Jane, let alone flushed."

"Maybe I was holding my breath or something."

"Jane, your nipples didn't even start getting erect."

"How can you tell? You were *lying* on them!"

Poor Jane, besides knowing when to put bluing in collars and remembering his fathers birthday, now has to have the biggest orgasm on the block.

Dr. Schumacher feels that it is up to the individual to keep any sex studies in perspective, that since sex has only begun to be seriously studied and comparatively little is proved beyond question, any information that seems accurate today may be proved wrong tomorrow. While this is undoubtedly true, I think it runs counter to that unadmitted need of people for permission to enjoy sex: there is the feeling, however unreasonable and unacknowledged, that the books make it permissible to think about sex by reducing it to data—what could be salacious about data?—thus making people disproportionately dependent on the information, or misinformation, as the case may be.

Then there is the matter of contraceptives—a relatively new thing, culturally speaking. Sex, for women, has for so long been tied in with making babies, or fearing to make babies, that it is still difficult to separate pregnancy from sex, even if the conflict may by now be much in the subconscious. Dr. Schumacher feels that this, too, is tied in with the idea that sex is something that requires permission. Wanting a baby automatically gives you permission; wanting pleasure doesn't.

Beyond the mere presence of contraceptives is the question of the kind, which Dr. Shainess has studied in depth. "Each carries a freight of physical and psychological hazards with it that may interfere with love-making." These differ from unmarried to married and from couple to couple. The physical consequences would presumably be caught by a doctor and need not be mentioned here, but the psychological consequences might not be considered by a doctor. The Pill, while requiring a woman to anticipate sex in a general way, still allows her to be swept off her feet by each separate act in the sense that she acts not so much deliberately on her own desire as that she is carried along by circumstances. The Pill can interfere with the hard-to-define sex drives of women, their libido. Sometimes this is so marked that women are taken off the Pill, but it may be more common than we are generally aware of. Both of these factors tend to make the Pill more appealing to a woman who thinks of sex as something done to her, and desire as something that resides not in her but in the man who arouses it. If she thinks of herself as an active sexual participant she might be more bothered.

The intrauterine devises share with the Pill the advantage of long-distance preparation with no specific act in mind. Their psychological disadvantages are different, however. If a woman has fantasies and anxieties about being mutilated or injured, her sex life may be complicated by the awareness of a foreign body inside of her which might move or hurt her during intercourse. Or she may subconsciously be afraid of hurting the man. The man may have corresponding fears of hurting the woman, and of being hurt.

Since the condom cuts down on physical enjoyment by both parties it isn't often used within marriage (except for men who feel that it helps with the problem of premature ejaculation). That leaves the diaphragm, which Dr. Shainees feels is presently the best contraceptive — partly for the very inconveniences for which many people condemn it: it requires "anticipation, preparation, responsibility for the individual act and the specific partner," requires, in fact, that a woman take an active, positive role in preparing to make love.

This isn't intended to imply that all people harbor all fears of contraceptives. But some people may have such fears, unaware of them and unable to explain a limiting of sexual enjoyment.

Dr. Schumacher feels, on the other hand, that the choice of contraceptive isn't as important as how the couple approaches the idea of contraception. A diaphragm will be hard to use if a woman "does it in the way that the physician has taught her, fumbling it around, putting it in at the last minute or even jumping out of bed and running into the bathroom." It should be an automatic routine, done far enough ahead, say an hour or so, to avert a break in spontaneity (but of course not so far ahead as to run the risk of losing the spermicide's effectiveness). Other contraceptives can be made a part of the loveplay. "If the female is using foam, the male can learn to insert it. They can make it a mutual thing and have fun and enjoy even that aspect of it. If he's using a condom, she can even learn how to put it on. I don't know of a case where the hang-up on contraception was the one problem, but helping people to become comfortable with contraception is a vital part of therapy."

Then there is the clitoral orgasm. The idea that the clitoral orgasm is just as, or more, intense than the vaginal orgasm was originally stated in Masters and Johnson and picked up by many people in Women's Lib. Ever since I saw the copious writings on this topic summarized as *clit. lit.*, I have been unable to take it seriously, but it has been so publicized, criticized and counter-criticized in so many quarters that it has become a bona fide component of the sexual revolution. Dr. Shainess considers this idea to be very damaging to a sound mutual sex life (and I must say, if I were a man it would make me feel a bit defensive approaching a bed). "Fixating on the clitoral is like push-button sex. In other words, it's an attempt to wrest sensation from the body in the most obvious way, which is not necessarily the best, most complete, or most fulfilling way."

Another aspect of the sexual revolution which has been damaging to women has been a misinterpretation of sexual freedom as meaning any number of affairs. "Oddly enough this furthers something very old-fashioned," says Dr. Shaines. "It furthers women's use of their bodies for something other than a true expression of themselves. Having a man around, being in, being with it — all the old things for which women in a sense sold themselves before." This encourages women to confuse being *desirable* with being *sexual*. The biggest tease at the party may not know how to take pleasure for herself in bed.

Premarital affairs may seem far away from sex in marriage, but in fact the constant presentation of sex as something free, unthinking, uncomplicated, is damaging to any kind of durable sexual relationship because it fosters the idea that sex is something instant, that sex has exactly the same importance regardless of the people or the circumstances, that the kick is in the number of conquests or orgasms or doing it in threes or watching or whatever is this month's fad. Whereas, says Dr. Shainess, "the ultimate of fulfillment in sex is within the capacities of the person engaging in it."

For the young wife, the sexual revolution has one last bad aspect (one begins to wish it had never taken place): it does not include a role for her. Most of the girls selling men's cologne or cars or toothpaste with a come-on are not wives talking to their husbands. National Airlines is urging us all to fly Barbara and Linda but never Mrs. Jones or Mrs. Berman. The image is of a long-haired, long-legged girl swinging in a blur of flickering strobe lights from one man to another. Whether or not she wants her private life to follow suit, the image is alway there for the unmarried girl to preen herself on and ally with publicly.

When she marries the image changes — or rather, ceases to exist. Unless she needs cough medicine, she won't have a place in the video-culture again until she is pregnant enough for disposable diapers or has changed her focus to washing machines and paper towels. There is no pattern for her to follow. If she has followed the old cultural rule of no-sexual emphasis until marriage, suddenly after marriage that doctrine of a lifetime seems wrong. If she broke away to follow the sexual revolution, suddenly after marriage that, too, is wrong — she isn't supposed to appeal to every man in sight and virtue is no longer to be flouted. There seems no way for her to present herself as sexy *and* wifely — yet privately she is supposed to be sexy as hell.

Apart from the sexual revolution, one of the problems of any society as far as sex is concerned is simply the physical setup of it superimposed on one's natural impulses — it interferes with one's timing. Dr. Shainess feels that people fail to recognize the significance of this. There is

the obvious interference in that we really only have evenings to ourselves (unless both husband and wife like to wake up before the alarm),
and the end of the day is not logically the prime time for physically
demanding activity. But there is something further: "Women experience much more fulfilling sex if it comes at a time of libidinal urge
through endocrinal stimulation," says Dr. Shainess. "But very few
women are aware of this drive in themselves." A woman's drive is not so
easily determined as a man's physical demand of a backing up of fluid
in the seminal vesicles and "it's a rather evanescent thing — if you've
been having a sexual drive in the afternoon and you have to wait till
night it's not likely to be as gratifying." This is not to say that you cannot
have fulfilling sex at any time, but if it is timed when your endocrine
structure is pushing you, there is a further, deeper drive. And between
nine-to-five jobs, long hours of commuting and Sunday football, civilization pretty effectively interferes with this libidinal drive; little wonder so few of us are aware of it.

That's a capsule history of how personal experiences plus the pressures of society have combined to hammer out the way each person sees
herself sexually. Imagining the man's equally complicated background, one begins to think that a good sex relationship must be
practically impossible to achieve. Not true — although that attitude is
more promising than the expectation of instant orgasm.

First let's consider what a good sexual relationship would include for
a woman. Dr. Shainess describes this as "the culmination of a sexual act
participated in out of pleasurable anticipation, relatively free of anxiety, and in which awareness of time is of little concern and gradually
recedes. It implies a kind of communication between partners, often
quite subtle, which permits each to contribute to the arousal of the
other, without, however, a controlling, manipulative, push-button
'stimulus must yield response' kind of orientation in either partner,
especially the woman." She must feel that her sexual activity is something she chooses for herself, and the framework of an ongoing relationship such as marriage enhances her pleasure since her responses
are to an extent learned in relation to her partner.

Notice I said "good sexual relationship" rather than "orgasm" because they are not the same, and while a good sexual relationship most
probably will include orgasm, the reverse isn't true — searching for
orgasm may undercut the whole relationship. Both Dr. Shainess and
Dr. Schumacher emphasis the point that most people expect the wrong
things of sex—or rather, expect only one thing. Our fantasies have
been shaped by Harold Robbins and Jacqueline Susann; we think that
if we do everthing "correctly," orgasm will happen gong! like a strong
man ringing the bell at the circus. Accurately, predictably, repeatedly.
Whereas every sexual experience is in fact different from every other
even with the same partner, a woman's tenuous libidinal drive will
affect it as will the mood-setting events of the day. "The male learns at
one time how to stimulate his wife in a very pleasurable way," says Dr.
Schumacher, "and the next time it might be a different spot that feels
good for her. You really must avoid getting caught in a rut."

Dr. Schumacher goes on to say we must learn that sexual activity doesn't invariably mean penis-in-vagina. "Suppose the female just out of curiosity wanted to fondle the male penis and lift up the scrotum and take note of everything that was happening, like to watch the wrinkles of the skin disappear as the penis became erect and liked just to hold the penis in her hand. That doesn't mean she has to want intercourse. This may be all she wants to do that night. Or suppose the male wants really to examine his wife and reach in and feel the cervix. Maybe he's not trying to get interested in any specific sexual activity, maybe his penis isn't even erect. That doesn't mean he's not male. He might want intercourse later on, he might not. People should learn to expect different things from sex."

Knowing what a good relationship could be in the abstract and knowing what your particular relationship could become are two different things — in sex as in other parts of your marriage you have to find the common denominators between you, whether that means different times of the day or trying it under (or on) the grand piano.

But even with that as a realistic goal, there is an obstacle — and this circles right back to where we began: the difficulty young couples have in discussing sex. In marriage or out. Young wives have told psychiatrists with pride that they don't mention their husbands' premature ejaculation or the fact that they simulate orgasm to please him; they keep it to themselves because it would supposedly belittle his manhood. Dr. Schumacher calls this killing with kindness: "She doesn't want to hurt him. Well, which is the greater hurt? With all that is written about sex today, he is aware of the problem. The fact that she doesn't mention it means that she thinks he can't take it. That is really putting the partner down — he is too weak. Or the female who pretends to be orgasmic — she is also building up an enormous store of resentment because of the pretense."

The lack of discussion most probably also extends to other areas of the marriage. "We are taught not to show our feelings," says Dr. Schumacher; her therapy is in large part directed to helping people feel vulnerable to each other. Only about 10 percent of the time is spent specifically on a couple's sexual problems; if the rest of the relationship can be made open, then the honesty can be spread to the sexual.

The timing of discussions can be important, because calm, objective talk and the romantic tension of sex seem mutually destructive. There are subtle cues of likes and dislikes that come by instinct and are an essential part of love-making, but more involved problems are difficult to discuss in bed. Right after the fact is untactful, to say the least. "Post-mortems," says Dr. Shainess, "can be devastating." The important thing to remember is that a problem unresolved can only become worse, and that it is really harbored grievances that drain the passion out of love-making, not talking about a problem, however awkward the conversation may be. It's also important to guard one's tongue so that talk dosen't become attack, that the tone is "You know, honey, I was just thinking about last night and I was kind of unhappy about thus-and-so" and doesn't move on to "You did this and you'd better stop it." Discussion mustn't be punitive. And one should never, *never* apply difficulties in bed to other areas: "Oh, you have trouble being a man in the office too." That spells death to the relationship.

Another thing to avoid is arguing about *styles* of sex. Dr. Shainess sees this problem on the increase. If you want different things, then you must find peaceable ways of compromising. This does not mean one person giving in, as this makes the act an aggression and puts you a step back. "Mutually consenting adults" is what we consider general legal terminology. If fellatio or cunnilingus or sex during menstuation or manual play to clitoral orgasm are mutually pleasurable, fine. If those or any other practices are seriously displeasing to either partner, then, says Dr. Shainess, "the compromise has to be in the direction of the partner who finds something really unpleasant. If you want something but the other person cannot satisfy it, I think it's incumbent upon you both to explore why not. And if it's impossible to resolve, then it's something that has to be by-passed. You cannot demand in sex something that is repugnant to the partner."

You have the best chance at a sound relationship sexually as in other areas if the marriage begins on a realistic footing. This means working out mutual expectations, without pressuring, and with real knowledge of each other. People can come at these expectations in their own individual ways. One is by working out one's own wedding ceremony. "At first, when I found out people were rewriting marriage ceremonies it seemed amusing," says Dr. Shainess. "But then I realized what an important and valuable thing it is, because it says that this couple has really thought about the premises of marriage, and the expectations and goals of marriage, which have been ritualized into getting a marriage license or having a marriage ceremony."

The traditional engagement period is another way of clarifying one's expectations of marriage and shouldn't be skimped. Planning the details of the wedding, deciding where to live and how to live, which role each will have in the marriage — if the engagement is used in this way and not drowned in material details of bridal gowns and banquet seating, it can be a very creative time for the couple's relationship.

Sex cannot play a direct part in working out these expectations, because you cannot discuss your sex life until you have one, and as we have seen, sex after marriage dosen't necessarily parallel any previous experience. Sexually the ideal at marriage would be an openness to talk, to constructive criticism and to change, and a willingness to suspend judgement. And to be patient, because the long-range goal is a demanding one: a sexual relationship as fulfilling and as particular and as personal as every other aspect of your marriage.

Sex in Troubled Marriages

JAMES E. DeBURGER

There are two schools of thought about the significance of sexual problems revealed by persons seeking help for a disrupted marriage. One holds that sexual and affectional relations between mates are especially vulnerable to deterioration under such crisis situations as unemployment and that sexual complaints usually represent a convenient focus of personal attack on the mate's deficiencies. In other words, the sexual problem is not the primary one. The point of view I subscribe to holds that sexual problems should be recognized as central and fundamentally related to the level of happiness in marital relations. Given the emerging and critically important role of the marital relationship as possibly the last bastion of primary person-to-person relationships in a mass society, it seems that revealed marital problems (and especially sexual problems) may increasingly tend to reflect concern with the attainment of happiness in the intimate relations between mates.

One thing has become apparent to me over several years of counseling experience: among seriously troubled married persons seeking professional help, major marital problems connected with the intimate patterns of interaction between mates far outweigh other types of problems. This conclusion is supported by a research project I conducted recently.

THE RESEARCH AND THE SUBJECTS

I analyzed letters requesting help from the national office of the American Association of Marriage Counselors written by 252 husbands and 1160 wives from various parts of the United States. These letters constituted a sample from a much larger collection of over 14,000 received by the Association over a ten-year period.

Each was carefully analyzed and coded to indicate major and secondary problems revealed by the writer — a problem was considered major if it appeared to be considered by the help-seeker as the chief cause of marital unhappiness; secondary problems included any other complaints or concerns discussed in the letter.

Among the 1412 help-seekers represented in this study, the average age was 39 for husbands and 36 for wives. Most were Protestant and all were Caucasian. The average length of marriage for all subjects was approximately 12 years.

Several kinds of major problems were revealed: Sexual, Affectional, Role Tasks, Parental-Role, Intercultural and Situational Conditions,

Deviant Behavior, and Personality Conflict. Of all the findings which grew out of the entire research project,[1] my emphasis here on sexual problems was impelled both by their prominence and recurrence and by my conviction that successful sexual interaction will emerge as the expressive behavioral core of meaningful and satisfactory marital relations. In addition to analysis of its problem content, each help request was inspected and coded for various aspects of the help-seeking process itself and for the emotional tone or orientation associated with the marital difficulties.

AFFECTIONAL PROBLEMS ARE BLAMED BY MANY

Sexual relations problems ranked second only to the closely related category of affectional relations. Nearly one fourth of the 1412 help-seekers saw their marital trouble as due to some form of maladjustment in sexual relations. Specific complaints reported included in order of frequency (1) serious overall dissatisfaction in sexual relations, (2) difficulties connected with orgasm dysfunction, frigidity or impotence, (3) feelings of sex deprivation or insufficient coital frequency, and (4) "unnatural" sex desires on the part of the mate. Most problems were encompassed by the first three items; the few cited under the fourth category consisted almost entirely of repugnance toward the mate's insistence on oral sex. The large proportion of those who traced their marital disruption to some sexual problem is dramatically compounded when both major and secondary problems were combined. Forty-one percent of those who had not revealed a sex-related major problem were discovered under further analysis, to be complaining nevertheless of some sexual difficulty in their marriage!

It is remarkable that so few major problems involving parental role relations were disclosed by these help-seekers. Since so many of them (nearly 80%) were parents, it was expected that a fairly large proportion would indicate parental problems as a major source of difficulty for their troubled marriage. This was not borne out by the analysis. This lack of parental problems may be implicit support for the argument that the crucially determining forces at work in a seriously troubled marriage should be sought in the network of intimate (sexual and affectional) relations between mates. We cannot suggest that everything will be "just great" in a familial situation if only the intimate interaction of the married pair is satisfying. However, given the increasing significance of emotional sustenance needs and functions in the American scheme of marriage, it seems unlikely that a couple will consider their marriage satisfactory if sexual and affectional interaction does not provide these gratifications.

HUSBANDS AND WIVES SEE DIFFERENT PROBLEMS

In accordance with prior research that pointed to sex differences in the disclosure of problems, our analysis showed that husbands and wives did indeed differ significantly in regard to the kinds of major problems, particularly sexual ones, revealed in their help-request letters.

The proportion of husbands citing a sexual relations problem as the major cause of their marital difficulties (42.1%) was more than double that of wives (20.6%). The pattern was reversed in the closely related area of affectional relations, with wives accounting for many more (31%) of the affectional relations problems than the husbands (11.5%). When we take the two kinds of problems together — sexual and affectional — it becomes clear that these two problem types constitute more than 50 percent of all major problems revealed by these help-seekers.

It could be argued, of course, that affectional and sexual components are very similar and are perhaps overlapping. In an attempt to distinguish between them, problems were recorded as sexual only if there was a clear erotic element present in the description. Affectional relations problems struck two themes: a lack of affectional gestures, contact, or verbalization; and the presence or threat of lowered commitment to the marriage by the mate. Undoubtedly there may be sexual undertones in these complaints but for our purposes it seemed feasible to make a distinction between the two kinds of problems, a distinction which supports Ehrmann's conclusion that ". . . females seem more directly and overtly concerned with romanticism and males with eroticism." [2]

If, as Ehrmann has suggested, females are brought up with an affectional rather than a sexual orientation to marriage, wives probably are more sensitive than husbands to any change in their spouse's display of affection. It seems to me that the possession impulse in marriage — the need for security based on ownership — also operates more strongly among women than men. Among our subjects the need for maintaining feelings of exclusiveness in affectional relations was much stronger among wives. Speaking as a counselor, it seems that exclusiveness and the possessive attitude are very often a prelude to "taking the other for granted." This process may lead to strong male disenchantment and a vicious cycle of male behavior ("I'll show her!") calculated to maintain a sense of unique personal worth and attractiveness. At the risk of appearing chauvinistic, I must note that many husbands resort to the pursuit of extra marital sex objects as an outgrowth of their feelings of no longer being sexually desired within marriage. Predictably, in our subjects, husbands much more often than wives appeared as role-deviant due to their extramarital sexual activities.

In general, then, husbands and wives differ in their disclosure of problems perceived to be central to marital disruption. The specific complaints cited predominantly by wives are: (1) "mate is in love with another," (2) "mate wants sex too often," (3) sex relations per se are disgusting, (4) mate's "crudeness in sex behavior," (5) orgasm dysfunction, and (6) "mate's extramarital sex relations." Those cited more often by husbands are: (1) general serious dissatisfaction with quality of marital sex relations, (2) "sex frustration — inadequate frequency of coitus," (3) "affectional approach spurned by mate," (4) "mate is cold . . . unloving," and (5) worries about effect of low sex drive on marriage. Conflict and arguments with the mate showed the same sex-differentiated pattern. Most husbands reported conflicts over sexual relations while most wives reported conflicts associated with exclusive-possessive aspects of affectional relations. Overall, it appears when a marriage is in serious trouble that the wife is most likely to define the problem in affectional terms and the husband in sexual. At the risk of appearing simplistic, I must suggest that such a dichotomy (one which I believe to be widespread in marital disruptions in this society) can be resolved if our primary agencies of socialization adopt realistic procedures for education in sexuality and affectional behavior for both males and females.

Major marital problems involving sexual relations were much more frequently revealed by blue-collar than white-collar husbands. On the other hand, while more than one fifth of the white-collar husbands disclosed major problems in the affectional relations category, none of the blue-collar husbands did. We must note here that within either social class the husband-wife differences discussed earlier persisted for both problems types. When blue-collar and white-collar wives were compared, no drastic differences were seen in the extent to which sexual and affectional problems were revealed.

Analysis of those help-requests in which length of marriage had been identified (758) revealed some association between length of marriage and the disclosure of problems in the areas of sexuality and affection. Since most of the data in this study pertain to marriages of somewhat less than ten years duration, the findings on this point are quite tentative. However, two trends seem to emerge. First, for both husbands and wives problems connected with affectional relations tend to increase significantly with length of marriage. Secondly, for husbands, sexual problems show considerable decrease over time. Among wives, however, while sexual relations problems are appreciably less than for husbands, they tend to persist and even increase slightly in the later years of marriage.

Emotional Factors

Negative feelings were much more frequently reported by persons experiencing sexual problems than by those who disclosed other kinds of problems. There was also some indication of sex differences. A much larger proportion of wives than husbands (20% to 8%) reported feeling that they were degraded by their mate. About the same proportionate differences between husbands and wives were found in regard to expressions of anger, resentment toward the mate, depression, nervous exhaustion, and disillusionment in marriage. This sex difference was somewhat weaker for the white-collar than for the blue-collar class. Data collected by Gurin[3] showed that women report greater stress and more problems in marriage than do husbands. There is also some evidence to suggest that women to a geater extent than men consciously experience tension and dwell on their marital problems and that more wives than husbands feel inadequate in their familial roles.

A much larger proportion of wives than husbands (50% to 25%) blamed the mate for the sexual relations problem and the consequent marital disruption. Also, more husbands than wives attribute blame to themselves. These differences were somewhat stronger in the blue-collar than in the white-collar class. This prominence in self-blaming may be related to the male's somewhat greater initiative in certain forms of deviant sexual behavior. Again, assuming a persisting tendency in this culture to portray marital failure in terms of wrongdoer and the wronged, it may be that blame would more likely be attached to the more initiatory, aggressive role of the husband than to the relatively more passive role of wife.

Among those who were seeking help for sexual relations problems, husbands more often expressed optimism and less often experienced pessimism regarding possibility of resolving the difficulties. This difference was more pronounced in the blue-collar class. One could speculate that these differences stem from integral sex-role differences which begin early in life and persist in marriage. Thus, the centrality of the wife's role in modern marriage probably ensures that she will have more immediate and persisting contact with the everyday dynamics and content of a troubled marriage. These conditions may account in part for the observed sex differences in revealed feelings of despair, depression, degradation, and disappointment.

THE HELP-SEEKING PROCESS

Females are much more frequent seekers of help than males. There is almost a five-to-one ratio of wives to husbands among the persons represented in our data. This concurs with other studies of persons utilizing professional help-sources. It may be that wives are relatively more involved in and committed to their marital roles than are husbands, and therefore more highly motivated than husbands to seek professional help as a means of preserving a marriage.

For about 80 percent of all 1412 cases, the help-request letter was the first step toward contact with a formal helping agency. In this respect there was very little difference between persons with sexual relations problems and those having other kinds of problems. Among persons with sexual relations problems husbands more often than wives (33% to 12%) had sought help elsewhere.

Of those who had sought help elsewhere for sexual problems, most (66%) had talked with a physician, but were still unable to deal with their problems. The remaining third had consulted with clergymen, psychiatrists, or psychologists, and miscellaneous other persons and agencies. A social class difference was found in only one instance: more white-collar than blue-collar persons consulted psychiatrists or psychologists. Numerous complaints emerged concerning the quasi-counselor role of physicians. Many help-seekers felt that the physician ". . . was too brusque, really not concerned about my problem," or that ". . . he gave me pills but no guidance about our sexual problem."

The help-request letter was, of course, a response to information about sources of help for sexual and marital problems. But what were the sources of this information? Approximately two thirds of both husbands and wives reported magazines as their source of information. Very few, indeed less than 2 percent, had learned about the referral role of the American Association of Marriage Counselors from professionals (such as physicians and clergymen) in their local community. Miscellaneous reported sources of information included newspapers, lectures, radio or TV programs, books, and the advice of friends. In view of the increasing significance of sexuality for the conjugal family system, it seems remarkable that so few resources exist for the systematic referral, processing, and treatment of problems related to marital sexual relations.

One interesting implication of these data is that some forms of the mass media may serve significant functions in linking problems and troubled marriages with suitable sources of help. In this connection, most of the prominent women's and family magazines have in recent years frequently carried "case record" articles dealing with problems of sexuality in marriage. Such articles are sometimes accompanied by an offer to refer troubled persons to competent counselors or therapists. Articles dealing with sexual problems (especially "case histories") conceivably afford a means by which a sexually troubled marriage or a specific sexual problem may be identified. Furthermore, models of appropriate help-seeking and problem-solving behavior may be provided in such materials.

This speculation raises a rather broad but pertinent question which is not adequately treated in the literature of sex research: namely, the impact of culture on the patterns and dynamics of the help-seeking process. For the question of how Americans actually do try to solve their sex-related marital problems cannot be separated from the related question of how they *ought* to solve them in the light of relevant cultural norms. In this respect the role of mass media is probably crucial in the transmission of socially approved models of help-seeking and in providing channels of information and communication between troubled persons and the professional sources of help.

A striking characteristic of all these requests for help was their lack of mutuality and lack of urgency. Less than 19 percent of the documents revealed a joint effort in the problem-solving; few expressed desire on the part of both husband and wife to work out the sexual difficulties troubling the marriage. In spite of the massive problem content of the help-requests only about 10 percent expressed urgency or pressed for an immediate answer to their plea. One last and intriguing observation: most help-requests from husbands were written during colder weather while those from wives during warmer seasons. I leave interpretation of this phenomenon to those who wish to speculate on the effect of climate on behavior.

As for the kinds of information sought, the most frequent request was for the title of a book or manual which might help solve the sexual relations problem at hand. This kind of request, reflective perhaps of the "do-it-yourself" tendency in American culture, came from over 95 percent of both husbands and wives. There are implications here of a cookbook approach to marital problems which assumes the notion of ready-made "self-help" formulas, comparable to the phenomena of self-diagnosis and self-treatment in physical illness. Other requests were for information on sex techniques, aphrodisiacs (husbands 44%, wives 27%), and sexual anatomy and physiology (husbands 44%, wives 27%).

Conclusion

Generally speaking the patterns which are seen in the help-seeking behavior of persons experiencing sexual problems in marriage seem little different from those observed in marriages experiencing other kinds of problems. This is probably due in part to the fact that problem-solving resources for troubled marriages in this society give little special emphasis to the problems connected with sexuality per se. Marriages beset with parental role problems can often obtain help from "child guidance" centers, for example, but where does one find a sexual guidance center in this society?

These data support our original proposition that in seriously troubled marriages, the unhappiness is closely related to unsatisfactory patterns of intimate relations between mates. Rather than euphemizing — talking about "communication," "transaction," etc. — we should recognize the specifically sexual and affectional character of these intimate relations. A close look at the changes occurring in contemporary society suggests that the quality of intimate relations between mates may become crucial to criteria of marital happiness or unhappiness as the family group becomes more isolated from kin networks.

REFERENCES

1. DeBurger, J.E.: Husband-Wife Differences in the Revelation of Marital Problems: A Content Analysis. Unpublished Ph.D. thesis, 1966, Indiana University.

2. Ehrmann, W.: *Premarital Dating Behavior* (New York: Bantam Books, 1960).

3. Gurin, G., et al.: *Americans View Their Mental Health* (New York: Basic Books, 1960).

Sex as Work:
A Study of Avocational Counseling

LIONEL S. LEWIS
DENNIS BRISSETT

It is commonly accepted that America is a society of leisure. The society is said to have shifted from one of production to one of consumption.[1] The American of today spends little time working; he has a great deal of time to play.

With this surfeit of leisure, Americans have been called upon to engage in forms of consumption quite unknown to their inner-directed predecessors. There exist extensive opportunities for play, but little knowledge of how to conduct oneself in this play. As Riesman has remarked, "To bring the individual into unfrightening contact with the new range of opportunities in consumption often requires some guides and signposts."[2] Knowing how to play has become problematic; it is something the individual must learn. He must, in a word, be socialized into the art of play.

Faced with this necessary socialization, the consuming American seeks out persons to teach him how to play. Very often this involves engaging the services of avocational counselors. The term avocational counseling ". . . describe[s] the activities undertaken by a number of relatively rapidly growing professions in the United States, including travel agents, hotel men, resort directors, sports teachers and coaches, teachers of the arts, including dancing teachers, and so on."[3] Each of the various counselors supplies the American public with advice on play and leisure. The advice of one such group of counselors is the subject matter of this paper.

Quite recently, Nelson Foote has observed that sex, since it is becoming increasingly dissociated from procreation, is becoming more and more a kind of play activity. He states that "the view that sex is fun can . . . hardly be called the invention of immoralists; it is every man's discovery."[4] The arena of consumption is extended to include the realm of man's sexual activity, and the avocational counselor finds himself a place advising people on the vicissitudes of sex as play.

1. Leo Lowenthal, "The Triumph of Mass Idols," in *Literature, Popular Culture, and Society*, Englewood Cliffs, New Jersey: Prentice-Hall, 1961, pp.109-140.
2. David Riesman (with Nathan Glazer and Reuel Denney), *The Lonely Crowd*, Garden City, New York: Doubleday Anchor Books, 1953, p. 341.
3. Riesman, *loc. cit.*
4. Nelson Foote, "Sex as Play," in Eric Larrabee and Rolf Meyersohn, editors, *Mass Leisure*, Glencoe, Illinois: Free Press, 1958, p. 335.

Concomitant with this increasing amount of leisure time, and the attendant problem of learning how to play, it has been observed that the play of most Americans has become a laborious kind of play. "Fun, in its rather unique American form, is grim resolve. . . . We are as determined about the pursuit of fun as a desert-wandering traveler is about the search for water. . . ."[5] Consumption, to most Americans, has become a job. Like work, play has become a duty to be performed. This interpretation is supported by the emergence of what Wolfenstein has labeled a "fun morality." Here "play tends to be measured by standards of achievement previously applicable only to work . . . at play, no less than at work, one asks: 'Am I doing as well as I should?' "[6] Consumption very definitely has become production.

It is the purpose of this paper to examine the products of the avocational counselors of marital sex and to inquire as to their depiction of man's sexual behavior. If it is true that play is becoming work in the mass society, it might be necessary to amend Foote's notion of the character of sexual play. In focusing on how marital sex is handled by these avocational counselors, we will show how sex, an area of behavior usually not thought of as involving work, has been treated as such. We will emphasize how general work themes are presented as an essential part of sexual relations, and how the public is advised to prepare for sex just as they are advised to prepare for a job.

MARRIAGE MANUALS

The avocational counselors of sex with the widest audience are those who write what are frequently referred to as marriage manuals. These manuals are designed to explain all aspects of the sexual side of marriage. Their distribution is wide: many are in paperback and are readily available in drug stores; many can be found in multiple copies in public and university libraries; and some are distributed by facilities which offer services in sex, fertility, and contraception, such as Planned Parenthood clinics.

Fifteen manuals were selected from a listing of almost 50 for analysis in this study. They are listed under References. The first criterion for using a manual was wide circulation. This was determined by number of printings and number of copies sold. For example, one volume (15) in 1965 was in its forty-fifth printing and had sold more than one-half million copies in the United States; a second (13) was in its forty-eighth printing and had sold almost six hundred thousand; a third (3) was in its thirtith printing[7] and has "been read by " two million eight hundred thousand[8]; and a fourth (5) advertises on its cover "over a million and a

5. Jules Henry, *Culture Against Man,* New York: Random House, 1963, p. 43.
6. Martha Worlfenstein, "The Emergence of Fun Morality," in Eric Larrabee and Rolf Meyersohn, *op. cit.,* p. 93.
7. We were unable to obtain this most recent printing, and our copy was the twenty-ninth printing.
8. These figures were published in *Newsweek,* October 18, 1965, p. 100.

half copies in print." Other criteria were that the book be still read and available. The fifteen volumes ranged from 14 page pamphlets to full sized, indexed, hard-bound books.

Each manual was read by both authors, and principal themes were recorded. Notes were taken, compared, and classified. Only material about whose meaning both authors agreed was utilized in drawing conclusions about the themes in a book.

WORKING AT SEX

Marital sex, as depicted by the marriage manuals, is an activity permeated with qualities of work. One need not even read these books, but need only look at the titles or the chapter headings to draw this conclusion. Thus, we have books titled *The Sex Technique in Marriage* (10), *Modern Sex Techniques* (14), *Ideal Marriage: Its Physiology and Technique* (15). There are also chapters titled "How to Manage the Sex Act (3)," "Principles and Techniques of Intercourse (7)," "The Fourth Key to Soundly Satisfying Sex: A Controlled Sexual Crescendo (5)."

From the outset, as we begin to read the books, we are warned not to treat sex frivolously, indeed not to play at sex:

> An ardent spur-of-the-moment tumble sounds very romantic. . . . However, ineptly arranged intercourse leaves the clothes you had no chance to shed in a shambles, your plans for the evening shot, your birth control program incomplete, and your future sex play under considerable better-be-careful-or-we'll-wind-up-in-bed-again restraint (5, pp. 34-35).

In other words, marital sex should not be an impromptu performance.

Moreover, sex should not be approached with a casual mien. Rather, we are counseled, sexual relations, at least good sexual relations, are a goal to be laboriously achieved. It is agreed that "satisfactory intercourse is the basis for happy marriage." However, it is added, "It does not occur automatically but must be striven for (12, p. 39)." In the plain talk of the avocational counselor, "Sexual relations are something to be worked at and developed (7, p. 6)."

This work and its development are portrayed as a taxing kind of endeavor; as behavior involving, indeed requiring, a good deal of effort. That sex involves effort is a pervasive theme in the 15 manuals. From the start one is advised to direct his effort to satisfying his or her mate so that mutual climax is achieved, sexual activity is continual, and one's partner is not ignored after climax. Thus, we are told:

> Remember, *couple* effort for *couple* satisfaction! That's the key to well-paced, harmonious sex play (5, p. 62).

Certain positions of intercourse are also seen as particularly taxing, in fact so taxing that certain categories of people are advised not to use them. One author, in discussing a particularly laborious position, remarks that "This is no position for a couple of grandparents, no matter how healthy and vigorous they are for their age, for it takes both effort and determination (4, p. 201)." Quite obviously, certain kinds of marital sex are reserved only for those persons who are "in condition."

The female is particularly cautioned to work at sex, for being naturally sexual seems a trait ascribed only to the male. The affinity of sex to her other work activities is here made clear: "Sex is too important for any wife to give it less call upon her energy than cooking, laundry, and a dozen other activities (5, p. 36)." To the housewife's burden is added yet another chore.

Even the one manual that takes great pains to depict sex as sport, injects the work theme. It is pointed out that

> You certainly can [strive and strain at having a climax] — just as you can . . . help yourself to focus on a complex musical symphony. . . . Just as you strive to enjoy a party, when you begin by having a dull time at it. Sex is often something to be worked and strained at — as an artist works and strains at his painting or sculpture (6, p. 122).

Sex, then, is considered a kind of work; moreover, a very essential form of labor. Regular sexual activity is said, for instance, to contribute to "physical and mental health (7, p. 27)," and to lead to "*spiritual unity* (14, frontpiece)." In the majestic functionalist tradition, "A happy, healthy sex life is vital to wholesome family life, which in turn is fundamental to the welfare of the community and of society (1, XIII)." Marital sex, most assuredly, is the cornerstone of humanity, but not any kind of marital sex — only that which leads to orgasm. "It is the orgasm that is so essential to the health and happiness of the couple . . . (10, p. 80)."

Indeed it is the orgasm which may be said to be the *product* of marital sexual relations. It is the *raison d'etre* for sexual contact, and this orgasm is no mean achievement. In fact,

> Orgasm occasionally may be the movement of esctasy when two people together soar along a Milky Way among stars all their own. This moment is the high mountaintop of love of which the poets sing, on which the two together become a full orchestra playing a fortissimo of a glorious symphony (4, pp. 182-183).

In masculine, and somewhat more antiseptic terms, "ejaculation is the aim, the summit and the end of the sexual act (15, 133)." Woe be to the couple who fail to produce this state as there are dire consequences for the unsuccessful, particularly for the woman.

> When the wife does not secure an orgasm, she is left at a high peak of sexual tension. If this failure to release tension becomes a regular thing, she may develop an aversion to starting any sex play that might lead to such frustrations. . . . Repeated disappointments may lead to headaches, nervousness, sleeplessness, and other unhappy symptions of maladjustment (1, p. 65).

So important is it to reach orgasm, to have a product, that all the other sexual activities of marriage are seen as merely prosaic ingredients or decorative packaging of the product.

In fact, orgasm as a product is so essential that its occasion is not necessarily confined to the actual act of intercourse, at least for the woman. Numerous counselors indicate that it may be necessary for the man to induce orgasm in the woman during afterplay. "A woman who has built up a head of passion which her husband was unable to requite deserves a further push to climax through intensive genital caress . . . (5, p. 111)." Particularly in the early years of marriage, before the husband has learned to pace his orgasm, he may have to rely on the knack of digital manipulation. In one author's imagery, "Sometimes it may be necessary for the husband to withdraw and continue the stimulation of his wife by a rhythmic fondling of clitoris and vulva until orgasm is attained (1, p. 66)."

The central importance of experiencing orgasm has led many of the authors to de-emphasize the traditional organs of intercourse. The male penis (member) is particularly belittled. It is considered "only one of the instruments creating sensation in the female, and its greatest value lies as a mental stimulant and organ of reproduction, not as a necessary medium of her sexual pleasure." The same author adds, ". . . the disillusioning fact remains that the forefinger is a most useful asset in man's contact with the opposite sex . . . (14, p. 71)." Furthermore, this useful phallic symbol should be directed primarily to the woman's seat of sensation, the clitoris. Only a man who is ignorant of his job directs his digital attention to the vulva, the female organ that permits conventional union.

One must often deny himself immediate pleasure when manufacturing the orgasm. One author, in referring to an efficient technique to attain orgasm, states that: "Unfortunately, some men do not care for this position. This, however, should be of little importance to an adequate lover, since his emotions are the less important of the two (14, p. 122)." Likewise, the woman may have to force herself in order to reach orgasm, even though she may not desire the activity which precedes it. It is specified that "If you conscientiously work at being available, you may ultimately find the feminine role quite satisfying even in the absence of ardor or desire (5, p. 38)." The work ethic of the sexual side of marriage, then, is one resting quite elaborately on what has been referred to as the "cult of the orgasm."

Still, one cannot easily perform one's job; its intricacies must first be mastered. After all, ". . . there is considerably more in the sexual relationship than . . . at first thought (8, p. 136)." "Remember that complete development of couple skills and adaptations takes literally years (5, p. 206)." There is a great deal to be learned. One author talks of eight steps "in order to facilitate sexual arousal and lead, finally, to satisfactory orgasm" and of seven "techniques which she and her mate may employ to help her attain full climax (6, pp. 124-126)."

All of this requires a good deal of mastery, a mastery that is necessary if the sex relationship is not to undergo "job turnover." Firstly, in the face of incompetence, the marriage partner may, at times, turn to auto-eroticism. One author stipulates that "There cannot be a shadow of a doubt that faulty technique, or a total lack of it on the man's part, drives thousands of wives to masturbation as their sole means of gratification (3, p. 140)." Moreover, if sexual skills are not acquired, the husband or wife may seek out new partners for sexual activity. The woman is admonished that adequate sexual relations will keep a man from "The Other Woman . . . (4, pp. 264-265)." The male also must be proficient in sexual encounters for "it is the male's habit of treating . . . [sexual relationships] as such [mechanically] which causes much dissatisfaction and may ultimately drive the wife to someone who takes it more seriously (14, p. 77)."

LEARNING SEX: PASSIVE AND ACTIVE

Marital sex is said to necessitate a good deal of preparation if it is to be efficiently performed. In one author's words: "This [complete satisfaction] cannot be achieved without study, practice, frank and open discussion . . . (12, p. 45)." This overall preparation seems to involve both a passive and an active phase. The passive phase seems most related to an acquisition of information previous to engaging in sexual, at least marital sexu~l, relations. The active phase best refers to the training, one might say on-the-job training, that the married couple receive in the sexual conduct of wedlock.

The matter of passive preparation receives a great deal of attention from the avocational counselors. Thirteen of the fifteen books call attention to the necessity of reading, studying and discussion the various facets of sexual relationships. After listing a number of these activities, one author advises that "If the two of them have through reading acquired a decent vocabulary and a general understanding of the fundamental facts listed above, they will in all likelihood be able to find their way to happiness (1, p. 20)." Another counselor cites the extreme importance of reciprocal communication by noting that " . . . the vital problem . . . must be solved through intelligent, practical, codified and instructive discussion . . . (14, p. 7)." The general purpose of all this learning is, of course, to dispel ignorance, as ignorance is said to lead to "mistakes at work," and such cannot be tolerated. The learning of the other partner's physiology is particularly emphasized, most counselors devoting at least one chapter and a profusion of illustrations to relieve the ignorance of the marriage partners. One author, however, quite obviously feels that words and pictures are insufficient. Presenting a sketch of the woman's genitals, he asserts that "It should be studied; on the bridal night . . . the husband should compare the diagram with his wife's genital region . . . (14, p. 18)."

Together with learning physiology, the various manuals also stress the critical importance of learning the methodology of marital sex. Sexual compatibility seems not a matter of following one's natural proclivities, but rather "The technique of the sexual relation has to be learned in order to develop a satisfactory sex life (13, p. 172)." One must know one's job if one is to be successful at it. Not surprisingly, to like one's job also requires a learning experience, particularly for the woman. As one book scientifically asserts:

> There is a striking consensus of opinion among serious specialists (both men and women) that the average woman of our time and clime must *learn* to develop specific sexual enjoyment, and only gradually attains to the orgasm in coitus . . . they [women] have to *learn how* to feel both voluptuous pleasure and actual orgasm (15, p. 262).

In summary, then, passive learning involves the mastering of physiology and techniques. By the desexualized female of the marriage manuals, the fine art of emotional experience and expression is also acquired. And the naturally inept male must learn, for

> If the husband understands in even a general way the sexual nature and equipment of his wife, he need not give the slightest offense to her through ignorant blundering (1, p. 20).

This learning process, according to most of the manuals, eventually becomes subject to the actual experience of matrimonial sex. The marriage bed here becomes a "training" and "proving" ground. Again, wives seem particularly disadvantaged: "Their husbands have to be their guides (3, p. 108)." However, generally the training experience is a mutual activity. As one author suggests in his discussion of the various positions for coitus,

> In brief, the position to be used is not dictated by a code of behavior but should be selected as the one most acceptable to you and your mate. To find this you will examine your own tastes and physical conformations. By deliberate application of the trial and error method you will discover for yourselves which is most desirable for you both (11, p. 11).

In training, rigorous testing and practice is a must. In the words of one manual "experimentation will be required to learn the various responses within one's own body as well as those to be expected from one's beloved . . . (9, p. 7)," and also, "After a variable time of practice, husband and wife may both reach climax, and may do so at the same time (11, p. 10)."

Both the husband and wife must engage in a kind of "muscular control" training if the sex act is to be efficiently performed. The woman's plight during intercourse is picturesquely portrayed with the following advice. "You can generally contract these muscles by trying to squeeze with the vagina itself . . . perhaps by pretending that you are trying to pick up marbles with it (5, p. 97)." Fortunately, the man is able to practice muscular control at times other than during intercourse. Indeed, the man, unlike the woman, is permitted to engage in activities not normally related to sexual behavior while he is training. It is advised that "You can snap the muscles [at the base of the penile shaft] a few times while you are driving your car or sitting in an office or any place you happen to thnk of it . . . (5, p. 96)." The practice field, at least for the male, is enlarged.

In general, then, careful learning and a studied training program are necessary conditions for the proper performance of marital sex. As seems abundantly true of all sectors of work, "Nature is not enough. . . . Man must pay for a higher and more complex nervous system by study, training, and conscious effort . . . (7, p. 34)."

THE JOB SCHEDULE

As in most work activities, the activity of marital sex is a highly scheduled kind of performance. There is first of all a specification of phases or stages in the actual conduct of the sex act. Although there is disagreement here, some authors indicating four or five distinct phases (15, p. 1), the consensus of the counselors seems to be that "Sexual intercourse, when satisfactorily performed, consists of three stages, only one of which is the sex act proper (11, p. 7)."

The sexual act therefore is a scheduled act and the participants are instructed to follow this schedule. "All three stages have to be fitted into this time. None of them must be missed and none prolonged to the exclusion of others (8, p. 155)." Practice and study is said to insure the proper passage from one phase to another (12, p. 42). Moreover, to guarantee that none of the phases will be excluded, it is necessary to engage in relations only when the sexual partners have a sizeable amount of time during which they will not be distracted: ". . . husbands and wives should rarely presume to begin love-play that may lead to coitus unless they can have an hour free from interruptions (1, p. 51)." Even then, however, the couple must be careful, for there is an optimal time to spend on each particular phase. For instance, "Foreplay should never last less than fifteen minutes even though a woman may be sufficiently aroused in five (14, p. 43)." Likewise, the epilogue to orgasm should be of sufficient duration to permit the proper recession of passion.

Given this schedule of activity, the marriage manuals take great pains to describe the various activities required at each particular phase. It is cautioned, for instance, that "all contact with the female genital region . . . should be kept an absolute minimum (14, pp. 42-43)" during foreplay. The man is warned furthermore to "refrain from any excessive activity involving the penis (14, p. 77)" if he wishes to sustain foreplay. Regarding afterplay the advice is the same; the partners must not permit themselves "any further genital stimulation (15, p. 25)."

The "job specification" is most explicit, however, when describing the actual act of intercourse. It is particularly during this stage that the sexual partners must strain to maintain control over their emotions. Innumerable lists of "necessary activities" are found in the various manuals. The adequate lovers should not permit themselves to deviate from these activities. Sometimes, in fact, the male is instructed to pause in midaction, in order to ascertain his relative progress:

> After the penis has been inserted to its full length into the vagina, it is usually best for the husband to rest a bit before allowing himself to make the instinctive in-and-out movements which usually follow. He needs first to make sure that his wife is comfortable, that the penis is not pushing too hard against the rear wall of the vagina, and that she is ready as he to proceed with these movements (1, p. 61).

TECHNIQUES

The "labor of love" espoused by the avocational counselors is one whose culmination is importantly based on the proper use of sexual technique. In fact, " . . . *miserable failure results from ignorance of technique* (3, p. 49)." Indeed "no sex relationship will have permanent value unless technique is mastered . . . (8, p. 1773)." Thirteen of the fifteen books devote considerable space to familiarizing the reader with the techniques of sexual activity. These discussions for the most part involve enumerating the various positions of intercourse, but also include techniques to induce, to prolong, to elevate, and to minimize passion. Many times the depiction of particular coital positions takes on a bizzare, almost geomteric aura. In one such position, "The woman lies on her back, lifts her legs at right angles to her body from the hips, and rests them on the man's shoulders; thus she is, so to speak, doubly cleft by the man who lies upon her and inserts his phallus; she enfolds both his genital member and his neck and head. At the same time the woman's spine is flexed at a sharp angle . . . (15, p. 218)." Often however, the mastery of sexual technique seems to involve little more than being able to keep one's leg untangled ". . . when the woman straightens her right leg the man, leaving his right leg between both of hers, puts his left one outside her right, and rolls over onto his left side facing her (1, 58)."

At times, in order to make love adequately, it is required of the participants that they supplement their technique with special equipment. Some of this equipment, such as lubricating jellies, pillows, and birth control paraphernalia, is simple and commonplace. Others are as simple but not as common, such as chairs, foot-high stools, and beds with footboards or footrails. Some, like aphrodisiacs, hot cushions, medicated (carbonic acid) baths, and sitz baths, border on the exotic. Still others actually seem to detract from the pleasure of intercourse. In this vein would be the rings of sponge rubber which are slipped over the penis to control depth of penetration and the various devices which make the male less sensitive, such as condoms and a local anesthetic applied to the glans.

This equipment that minimizes stimulation, while not particularly inviting, might be said to give greater pleasure than still other techniques that are suggested to add variety to the sex life. The latter, in fact, seem cruelly painful. For instance,

> ... both partners tend to use their teeth, and in so doing there is naught abnormal, morbid or perverse. Can the same be said of the real love-bite that breaks the skin and draws blood? Up to a certain degree—yes (15, p. 157).

Indeed, a certain amount of aggression should be commonplace.

> ... both of them can and do exult in a certain degree of male aggression and dominance. .... Hence, the sharp gripping and pinching of the woman's arms and nates (15, p. 159).

At times, the authors seem to go so far as to indicate that the proper performance of the sex act almost requires the use of techniques that create discomfort. The element of irksomeness becomes an almost necessary ingredient of the conduct of marital sex.

Concluding Remarks

The kinds of impressions assembled here seem to support the notion that play, at least sexual play in marriage, has indeed been permeated with dimensions of a work ethic. The play of marital sex is presented by the counselors quite definitely as work.

This paradox, play as work, may be said to be an almost logical outcome of the peculiar conditon of American society. First of all, it seems that in America, most individuals are faced with the problems of justifiying and dignifying their play. In times past, leisure was something earned, a prize that was achieved through work. In the present era, it might be said that leisure is something ascribed or assumed. Indeed, as Riesman and Bloomberg have noted, "leisure, which was once a residual compensation of the tribulations of work, may become what workers recover from at work." [9]

The American must justify his play. It is our thesis that he has done this by transforming his play into work. This is not to say that he has disguised his play as work; it is instead to propose that his play has become work. [10] To consume is, in most cases, to produce. Through this transformation of play, the dignity of consumption is seemingly established; it is now work, and work is felt to carry with it a certain inherent dignity. The individual now is morally free to consume, and

---

9. David Reisman and Warner Bloomberg, Jr., "Work and Leisure: Tension or Polarity," in Sigmund Nosow and William H. Form, editors, *Man, Work and Society*, New York: Basic Books, Inc., 1962, p. 39.

10. Many investigators have observed the intertwining of work and play. We are here only interested in one aspect of admixture, the labor of play.

moreover free to seek out persons to teach him how to consume, for leaning how to play is simply learning how to do one's job in society.

This transformation of play into work has been attended by another phenomenon that is also quite unique to contemporary American society. Given the fact that work has always been valued in American society, a cult of efficiency has developed. As a consequence, the productive forces in America have become very efficient, and an abundance of consumer goods have been created. So that such goods will be consumed, Americans have been socialized into being extremely consumption oriented. As Jules Henry[11] has noted, the impulse controls of most Americans have been destroyed. The achievement of a state of general satisfaction has become a societal goal. To experience pleasure is almost a societal dictum.

Thus there seem to be two antagonistic forces operating in American society. On the one hand, there is an emphasis on work and, on the other hand, there is an emphasis on attaining maximum pleasure. These two themes were recurrent in the fifteen manuals which we read, and as one writer put it:

> ... it may well be that the whole level of sexual enjoyment for both partners can be stepped up and greatly enriched if the man is able to exercise a greater degree of deliberation and management (1, p. 33).

It was as if the avocational counselors were trying to solve a dilemma for their audience by reminding them to both "let themselves go" while cautioning them that they should "work at this." If sex be play, it most assuredly is a peculiar kind of play.

REFERENCES

1. Oliver M. Butterfield, Ph.D., *Sexual Harmony in Marriage*, New York: Emerson Books, 1964 (sixth printing).

2. Mary Steichen Calderone, M.D., M.S.P.H., and Phyllis and Robert P. Goldman, *Release from Sexual Tensions*, New York: Random House, 1960.

3. Eustace Chesser, M.D., *Love Without Fear*, New York: The New American Library, 1947 (twenty-ninth printing).

4. Maxine Davis, *Sexual Responsibility in Marriage*, New York: Dial Press, 1963.

5. John E. Eichenlaub, M.D., *The Marriage Art*, New York: Dell Publishing Co., 1961 (fourteenth printing).

6. Albert Ellis, Ph.D. and Robert A. Harper, Ph.D., *The Marriage Bed*, New York: Tower Publications, 1961.

7. Bernard R. Greenblat, B.S., M.D., *A Doctor's Marital Guide for Patients*, Chicago: Budlong Press, 1964.

11. Henry, *op. cit.*, pp. 20-21.

8. Edward F. Griffith, *A Sex Guide to Happy Marriage,* New York: Emercon Books, 1956.

9. Robert E. Hall, M.D., *Sex and Marriage,* New York: Planned Parenthood-World Population, 1965.

10. Isabel Emslie Hutton, M.D., *The Sex Technique in Marriage,* New York: Emerson Books, 1961 (revised, enlarged and reset edition following thirty-fifth printing in 1959).

11. Lena Levine, M.D., *The Doctor Talks with the Bride and Groom,* New York: Planned Parenthood Federation, 1959 (reprinted, February 1964).

12. S. A. Lewin, M.D., and John Gilmore, Ph.D., *Sex Without Fear,* New York: Medical Research Press, 1957 (fifteenth printing).

13. Hannah M. Stone, M.D., and Abraham Stone, M.D., *A Marriage Manual,* New York: Simon and Schuster, 1953.

14. Robert Street, *Modern Sex Techniques,* New York: Lancer Books, 1959.

15. Th. H. Van de Velde, M.D., *Ideal Marriage: Its Physiology and Technique,* New York: Random House, 1961.

The Liberated Orgasm

BARBARA SEAMAN

Years ago Margaret Mead suggested that, "the human female's capacity for orgasm is to be viewed . . . as a potentiality that may or may not be developed by a given culture."

We don't need to be anthropologists to realize that our Western culture has not only failed to develop that potentiality, but it has stifled and repressed it.

As a result, we women have been afraid to think for ourselves about our own sexual tastes and pleasures. We have tried to model our own preferences after the prevailing views of normality. We have been shy about telling our lovers what we want. We have feared it would be unwomanly to do other than let the male take the lead, however ineptly.

The modern sex manuals are filled with misinformation — for instance, the standard advice to men that they should flail away at the sensitive clitoris. But even when their suggestions are applicable to some women in some moods, they are rarely applicable to all women in all moods, and they foster a certain technical rigidity that is antithetical to really good sex.

Female sexuality is so easily bruised and buried in the myths and medical models of the prevailing culture that the self-awareness needed for liberation will be difficult to achieve unless women explore their own true sexual feelings and needs.

We know that all orgasms are similar on a motor level, and that all orgasms are different on a sensory level.

We know also that there is no ideal or norm, except in our own imaginations. The truth is that the liberated orgasm is an orgasm *you* like, under any circumstances *you* find comfortable. (The only qualification is that liberated persons don't exploit each other — that's just for masters and slaves.)

In the spring of 1971, my research assistant Carol Milano and I completed an informal but we think rather enlightening sex survey of 103 women. They were career women or students: models of the new woman who enjoys more than average sexual awareness and freedom.

In our survey all but six regularly achieved some sort of orgasm with relative ease. This is substantially higher than the figure for women in general in our society, especially when you consider that perhaps one-third of the women in our survey were under 25. (From the Kinsey report and more recent investigations, we know that while the majority of women do achieve orgasms sooner or later, for many it is later. It often takes years or even decades for adult women to achieve sexual satisfaction.)

There was a group in our survey who could not comment on the clitoral *versus* the vaginal orgasm at all and said that to them the whole debate seemed meaningless. These women simply did not experience their orgasms in one place more than the other. But with this group left out, there were the two extremes of women who stated a preference for, or more frequent experience of, one type or the other. That is to say, regardless of the actual physiology of the event, they *felt* most of their orgasms in either the vagina or the clitoris.

Women are so varied in their sexuality that even those who seem alike are different. Let us contrast two, whom I shall call Marie and Antoinette.

Both women are sexually informed and active, and both have given considerable thought to their sexual needs. To achieve orgasms, both require direct clitoral stimulation.

They are not militant clitorists, for neither doubts that some women obtain orgasms via vaginal stimulation, but it doesn't work for them. Marie says, "I know that lots of girls do *not* need as much direct stimulation as I do — but I think this is because they have larger and better placed clitorises." Antoinette says, "I don't think anyone really knows what percentage of women have orgasms during intercourse. It would seem to depend on individual anatomy and placement of the clitoris."

Although clitorises are highly variable in size as well as placement, Masters and Johnson say that in eleven years of research they found no evidence to support the belief that differences in clitoral anatomy can influence sexual response. This, however, must be viewed as a highly tentative finding since they were unable to observe any clitorises during orgasms. Masters and Johnson think that in certain women the thrusting penis does not exercise the traction on the labia and clitoral hood, that it does for others. So perhaps idiosyncrasies of the vagina, rather than the clitoris, better explain the anatomical need for direct stimulation. Direct clitoral stimulation bones of the man and woman are touching.

What, in the experience of Marie and Antoinette, is the most common lovemaking error that men make?

Marie: "Not enough direct manipulation of the clitoris."

Antoinette: "Many men don't realize that the clitoris is the source of orgasms."

Two peas in a pod. Of all the women in my survey, there were no two who were more similar . . . and yet Marie loves sexual intercourse, while Antoinette finds it dull.

Marie: "Intercourse to me is very exciting! I get depressed if sexual contact doesn't include penetration, and a man doesn't come inside me."

Antoinette: "How a man performs intercourse is unimportant to me; I've never achieved and never expect to achieve orgasm during coitus."

Marie isn't the only woman who swears that for a first-rate orgasm she requires a penis or other object within the vagina. Nor is Antoinette the only one who indifferent. No doubt there are many psychological as well as anatomical variations that might influence a woman's perceived degree of vaginal sensitivity.

Analysts are undoubtedly telling us the truth when they report that they have "converted" thousands of women to vaginally experienced orgasms. The point is merely that, for some women at least, the strong desire to notice vaginal sensations makes these more noticeable. If Masters and Johnson are correct, all orgasms are essentially the same and quite sensibly involve all the pertinent parts God gave us.

But if all orgasms are the same, why do women not recognize the fact? Are we hopelessly stupid or recalcitrant?

Or are we complex human organisms whose responses are as varied and individual as we are ourselves? Some women noted a difference in their response to vaginal stimulation after childbirth. Several other women noted that they first experienced "vaginal" orgasm — that is, orgasm without direct clitoral stimulation — during intercourse with men who could either sustain vaginal thrusting for an exceptionally long period of time (compared to other lovers) or who had organs that seemed exceptionally large and "filling." One woman also noted a difference in male "sex rhythms": ". . . with some of my lovers I need my clitoris fondled to reach orgasm, and with others I don't. I find that every man has his own individual sex rhythm and way of thrusting. This is something a man cannot control, no matter how much he may wish to. Some men make short, rapid, jerky thrusts, and other men make longer, deeper thrusts, which I like better. With a man who takes the longer thrusts, I can have orgasms without clitoral manipulation, and with a man who takes jerky thrusts I can't. This is oversimplifying of course, because every one of my fourteen lovers had his own unique sex rhythm, and I more or less enjoyed them all, even though some required that the man use his finger in supplementation. I believe that I could recognize most of my lovers blindfolded, just on the basis of their own unique sex rhythms. This, to me, is one of the most fascinating differences in men."

Several of the women who need direct clitoral stimulation gave what appeared to be very sound anatomical explanations of their preference. Here is one example: "Before the birth of my son, who weighed over nine pounds and had an inordinately large head, I used to reach orgasm without needing to have my clitoris massaged. I don't believe that my vagina was repaired properly after childbirth. I think it must have gotten stretched out of shape because my same husband, with the same penis (and to whom I feel closer than ever), cannot bring me to orgasm so easily by his thrusting alone. I enjoy sex more than ever. My desire, if anything, has increased. But something is different about me, and if my understanding of Masters and Johnson is correct, I believe that the difference is that my vagina was slightly damaged, so that my husband's thrusting no longer provides as much traction on my clitoris."

So, allowing for the probability that there are anatomical differences that may have a strong bearing, what were the other differences between "vaginal" and "clitoral" women?

From the evidence gathered in our survey, there were more women in the vaginal group whose early experience with men had been favorable and who had not had to struggle to learn to enjoy sex. These women, perhaps because they were more "trusting" or perhaps, more simply, because their earliest lovers were better controlled and had stimulated them vaginally for long enough periods to bring them to orgasm by that route, had somehow learned to experience "feeling" in their vaginas and to let themselves come to orgasms through vaginal stimulation alone.

The "clitoral" types generally had been exposed to more selfish or fumbling lovers, particularly in their early experiences. Some, of course, had themselves insisted on the practice of merely "petting to climax" in order to preserve a token virginity during their premarital years.

Outside or in, clitoral or vaginal, we are in no way as standardized as Hugh Hefner's airbrushed and siliconed playmates. For example, while fourteen women in our survey complained that their lovers did not engage in enough physical foreplay, and eight others complained that their lovers did not engage in enough verbal foreplay, pillow talk, or converstation, two respondents took the opposite position. They like to get down to the main business of sex more swiftly than their lovers. One observed: "I find foreplay detrimental. When I really get into rubbing up against him, the feelings become sensuous, not sensual. Sex is more direct — from the inside out." So that is how one woman feels, and she is sexually active and well realized. The second woman asks wryly: "I have very little interest in foreplay. Is that an inhibition or a total lack of it?"

Or consider the question of the handsome stranger, an alleged apparition in the dreams of younger females. Most of the women in my survey dislike sex with strangers. Over and over they emphasized the importance (to them) of warmth, intimacy, trust, tenderness. For example, "I appreciate kindliness in a man — and one who appreciates and loves women (*i.e.*, me). Too many people use sex as an outlet — it should be a mutual experience of lovingness. . . ."

Yet, undeniably, for some women intimacy breeds boredom or contempt. One girl admitted, "I can only be uninhibited in sex with men I do not know very well."

Some women even deem it best to withdraw entirely from men. A prominent feminist confided: "I think it's wonderful that women have discovered masturbation, because it will enable us to keep apart from men as long as necessary. When you have work to do, you can't allow yourself to be diverted by sexual relationships. Masturbation is what male revolutionaries have always used to relieve themselves. Some of the women I know are so pathetic. They run around looking for a man, any man at all."

A 55-year-old woman admits: "I was born too early and too late. Unlike my mother, I realized that I too had sexual desires, but unlike my daughter, I considered it unthinkable to vocalize them. In the early years of my marriage I suffered unbearable frustration because I couldn't bring myself to tell my husband what he was doing wrong. By the time I worked up the courage he had lost most of his interest in sex. I've learned how to satisfy myself with an electric massager, but it's lonely. Some women are very sexy, and it's cruel to all concerned that delicacy prevents them from expressing it."

But what precisely is the female orgasm (which may or may not be developed by a given culture) and where does it take place? A woman knows when she's had one (if she doubts it, she hasn't), but since her orgasm is not punctuated by the sure sign of ejaculation, men have felt free to develop lunatic theories about it, and women have not learned to trust their own bodies.

A woman's external sex organs consist of labia majora, or outer lips; labia minora, or inner lips; and the highly eroticized clitoris, the only organ known to man or woman whose sole purpose is to receive and transmit sexual pleasure. The hood of the clitoris is attached to the labia minora, which are directly affected by penile thrushing. Thus, intercourses causes the labia to exert traction on the clitoral hood, producing rhythmic friction between it and the clitoris itself.

Masters and Johnson have proved — or believe that they have proved; their work has not yet been replicated — that virtually all feminine orgasms, however vaginal some of them may seem, do include indirect clitoral stimulation, the labia minora being the agent of mediation. Some Freudian analysts have long maintained that vaginal orgasms are entirely distinct from clitoral orgasms and are, indeed, the hallmark of sexually mature woman. If clitoral stimulation, whether direct or transmitted through the labia, occurs in all orgasms, then distinguishing them is invalid. So is the complicated mystique attached to the distinction. Vaginal women have been said to be mature, feminine, loving and happy, while clitoral women have had all the opposite traits attributed to them.

However, if I read Masters and Johnson correctly, they are saying that clitoral stimulation may occur in orgasm, but orgasm does not chiefly occur in the clitoris.

To the contrary, orgasm, which is a total body response, is always marked by vaginal contractions. No specific physiologic response in the clitoris has yet been recorded.

Let us review the physiology of the female sex cycle:

Stage One: Excitement. Within ten to thirty seconds after erotic stimulation starts, the vaginal lining is moistened with a lubricating fluid.

Nipples erect, and the breasts begin to swell, increasing in size by one-fifth to one-quarter in women who have not nursed a baby. (Breasts that have been suckled do not enlarge as much.) Other changes start to occur in the clitoris, labia, and vagina as vasocongestion (the engorgement of vessels and organs with blood) and muscular tension start to build. Late in the excitement phase, some women may start to develop a measleslike rash, or sex flush, across their bodies. (Seventy-five percent of the women evaluated by Masters and Johnson showed this response on some occasions.)

Stage Two: Plateau. The tissue surrounding the outer third of the vagina engorges and swells, creating an "orgasmic platform." The deeper portion of the vagina balloons out to form a cavity. The uterus enlarges. The swelling of the outer third of the vagina reduces its diameter, allowing it to grip the penis better. The clitoris retracts, and it becomes harder to locate.

Just prior to the orgasmic phase, the labia minora undergo a marked color change called the sex skin reaction. In the woman who has not had children, the labia minor turn pink or bright red. In the mother, they turn bright red or deep wine (presumably because she has a greater number of varicosities). This coloration remains throughout orgasm, but disappears ten to fifteen seconds afterward. When a woman develops sex skin, she is almost certain to go on to orgasm. Women who are aroused to plateau levels but not brought to orgasm experience a prolonged and sometimes uncomfortable ebbing away of vasocongestion and muscular tension.

State Three: Orgasm. The typical orgasm lasts only ten or fifteen seconds, if that long. Changes occur throughout the body. Muscles of the abdomen, buttocks, neck, arms and legs may contract; pulse and breathing are more rapid; and blood pressure climbs. The woman experiences a series of the rhythmic muscular contractions in the outer third of the vagina and the tissues surrounding it and in the uterus. These contractions, each taking about four-fifths of a second, serve to discharge the accumulated vasocongestion and tension that have been brought on by sexual stimulation. A mild orgasm usually involves three to five contractions; an intense one, as many as fifteen.

From time to time a woman may experience what some Samoan Islanders call the "knockout" orgasm, and what Masters and Johnson term the "status orgasmus." Masters and Johnson suspect, but are not certain, that the woman is probably having rapidly connected multiple orgasms, over a time period of sixty seconds or so.

In prolonged intercourse a woman may have three, four, or five separate orgasms, and in a few primitive cultures, where men have good control of themselves, multiple female orgasms are apparently the norm. Some masturbating women can have up to fifty successive orgasms according to clinical observation.

Multiple orgasms are most apt to occur when intercourse is prolonged. Thus, while the much vaunted "mutual orgasm" has some very nice features, it also has some drawbacks from the woman's point of view. Or to put it another way, there is no need for a woman to hold back deliberately, for if the male can maintain effective thrusting for a long enough period, the woman will have several preliminary orgasms and, quite possibly, another when he reaches his.

Women who don't have multiple orgasms may fear that they are missing something, but women who do have them often report that these are not their most pleasurable experiences. "If I've had a great orgasm, I can't bear to go on," one such woman explained.

This mysterious thing called orgasmic intensity is measured, principally, in the number of contractions. Masters and Johnson maintain that females have the most intense orgasms when they are free to please themselves only—"without the distraction of a partner." But they do qualify it. "A woman might tell me that she had a delightful experience with the machine," Dr. Masters commented at the New York Academy of Medicine in 1968, "but the next night with her husband might have been even better, in her opinion, although we registered fewer orgasmic contractions."

Stage Four: Resolution. Blood vessels emptied and muscular tensions relieved, the various parts and organs return to their normal condition, some rapidly and some slowly. One woman in three develops a film of perspiration across her body.

According to Masters and Johnson, the clitoris contributes crucially to the buildup of sexual tensions, but orgasm itself is more correctly described as centering in the vagina. Tensions established, it is vaginal contractions that bring relief by emptying engorged organs and vessels. Masters and Johnson call these vaginal contractions "the visible manifestations of female orgasmic experience."

Yet, even for those lucky women who can fantasy to orgasm, the clitoris serves as receptor and transformer of sexual stimuli, while vaginal contractions punctuate the orgasm itself.

However, it is important to note that some women who do not possess a clitoris seem to be capable of orgasm. Dr. Michael Daly, a Philadelphia gynecologist, reports that he has studied in depth two patients in whom the total clitoris was removed because of cancer. Both continued to have orgasms, and both said that their sexual responsiveness after surgery was a great as it was before.

There also are established cases of women in whom an artificial vagina had to be created, because they were born without one. These women also are capable of reaching orgasm.

Apparently, it is lucky for us that most of our sex tissue is internal and can be stimulated by an almost infinite variety of methods.

It is clearly false to say "vaginal orgasm is a myth." But does the vagina contribute to sexual arousal? Or (as some sex researchers, most notably Kinsey, and some women have thought) does it have no feeling?

Yes, it does, Vaginal sensations are believed to be proprioceptive, which means that they are sensations resulting from a stimulus within our own bodies, not imposed from outside.

Close your eyes; extend an arm and bend it. If you can describe the position of your arm, if you know whether it is bent or straight, you are receiving and using proprioceptive information. Ordinarily, we do not pay much conscious attention to our proprioceptive intelligence, but without it we would not even be able to walk.

The vagina is most apt to develop proprioceptive abilities during states of sexual arousal and distention. In unaroused states, as, for example, when a gynecologist inserts a speculum, it may be quite unresponsive.

Obviously, there is a crucial distinction between motor experience (what's happening) and sensory experience (what we're aware of). Masters and Johnson do not always draw this distinction as sharply as many psychologists (and women) might wish.

Some orgasms seem to be experienced vaginally or deep in the vagina, while others seem to be in the clitoris. Some orgasms occur while direct clitoral stimulation is taking place, while others occur only with vaginal stimulation. The experts who have been discussing us have never even defined the terms "vaginal" and "clitoral" orgasm, and women could hardly be sure whether a clitoral orgasm meant an orgasm that was induced by clitoral stimulation, an orgasm that seemed to be experienced in the clitoris, or both.

The same woman may, at different times, experience orgasms in different locations or from different types of stimulation. Women know this, but as a rule men appear to have difficulty comprehending it. In 1968, Drs. Jules Glenn and Eugene Kaplan accused psychoanalysts of assuming, incorrectly, that clitorally stimulated orgasms are necessarily experienced clitorally. They described a patient who, following a fleeting touch to the clitoris, experienced intense orgasms localized deep within the vagina which did not involve any conscious clitoral sensations at all. Glenn and Kaplan classify such orgasms as "clitorally stimulated, but vaginally experienced."

They go on to say that their patients have reported a great variation in the location of the experienced orgasm. Occasionally, sites other than the vagina and clitoris (the abdomen, the anus) seem to be the focus of feeling. The area in which the orgasm is experienced need not be the area of stimulation, and there is great variation in the area or areas stimulated, as well as the area or areas where orgasm is felt. The terms "vaginal orgasm" and "clitoral orgasm," according to Glenn and Kaplan have been "widely used but ill-defined."

The charge of technical rigidity is frequently leveled against not only writers of certain types of sex manuals, but also sex researchers, such as Kinsey, and Masters and Johnson.

There is a great deal that can be said against Masters and Johnson, and some of it has been said very well and very publicly. Among the many eloquent critics, Yale psychologist Kenneth Keniston has observed that Masters and Johnson are, although unintentionally, "helping to perpetuate rather than to remedy some of the more prevalent ills of our time — the confusion of human sexuality with the physiology of sexual excitement, naïveté with regard to the psychological meaning of the sexual act, and an inability to confront the ethical implications of sex." He also points out how little has been told of actual laboratory procedures and adds, "Masters and Johnson repeatedly reduce human sexuality to physical responses."

Dr. Natalie Shainess considers the Masters and Johnson view one in which "sex seems little more than a stimulus-response reflex cycle, devoid of intra-psychic or interpersonal meaning. . . . What is the attitude toward sex in a researcher who says, 'Masturbating women concentrate on their own sexual demand without the distraction of a coital partner'? Distraction! Is that the meaning of a partner in sex? This points to the dehumanizing view."

But with all this, the fact remains that Masters and Johnson have recorded some sexual response cycles in women, and have done it in a way that helps clarify many issues for us. If we use their findings in a self-destructive way, it is we who are choosing to do so. It is probably too much to ask that they be humanitarians and love advisers, as well as intrepid researchers.

Some of the anatomical details Masters and Johnson unearthed are interesting and useful to know, certainly for gynecologists and perhaps for women. And yet the interest we express in their work is, above all, a testament to the abysmal limits put on us by our own timidity.

Certain marriage counselors have long maintained that a loving wife is content merely to satisfy her husband, for instance, and that it need be of no consequence if she fails to achieve satisfaction. We have Masters and Johnson to thank for convincing them that sexual frustration can even give a woman cramps and headache. But how sad it is that we had to wait for sex researchers to demonstrate it. Didn't we know it all the time?

If there is going to be a breakthrough in human sexuality—and I think that such a breakthrough may be in the wind—it is going to occur because women will start taking charge of their own sex lives. It is going to occur because women will stop believing that sex is for men and that men (their fathers, their doctors, their lovers and husbands, their popes and kings and scientists) are the authorities. We need only study a little anthropology or history to understand that sexuality is incredibly plastic and easily repressed.

Women must discover and express their own sexuality, without shame or inhibition. And instead of following sex manuals or trusting the lockerroom sexpertise of their fellows, men must learn to seek and receive signals from the women they love.

Do We Need to Know More About Sex
or
Is It Knowledge of Love
We Really Lack?

BARBARA SEAMAN

AN INTERVIEW WITH DR. ROLLO MAY

One night last spring, psychologist Rollo May and publisher Hugh Hefner appeared together on the Dick Cavett program. Susan Brownmiller and Sally Kempton of the Women's Liberation Movement were also present. To dramatize her objections to *Playboy* magazine, her belief that the magazine demeans women, Miss Brownmiller asked Hef tartly, "Would you like to walk around with a cottontail taped to your rear end?" Dr. May joined in the laughter with the audience and then surprised everyone by adding that he thinks *Playboy* demeans *men* as well. Here are his reasons:

"You discover naked girls with silicated breasts and you conclude on first blush that the magazine is firmly on the side of the new enlightment. But as you look more closely, you see a strange expression in these photographed girls—detached, mechanical, uninviting, vacuous. You discover that they are not sexy at all, that *Playboy* has only shifted the fig leaf from the genitals to the face. No involvement, playing it 'cool,' is elevated in the ideal. One gets the impression that women are '*Playboy* accessories.' One gets the impression that men are training to be sexual athletes. But what is the great prize of the game? Excessive concern with sexual performance leads to *reduction* of feeling. The man makes himself *feel less* to *perform* better. We psychoanalysts are getting used to the complaint from the couch, "We made love but I didn't feel anything.' Where is the zest, the adventure, the self-discovery of authentic love? There are no statistics but it is my impression that impotence is increasing these days despite—or is it because of?—unrestricted sexual freedom. *Playboy* stands for a new puritanism which, like the old, separates sex and love. It encourages men to avoid real women and real relationships.

"It is an old and ironic habit of human beings to run faster when we have lost our way; and we grasp more fiercely at research, statistics and technical aids in sex when we have lost the values and meaning of love."

Rollo May is one of the commanding figures in world psychology. Parents of rebellious teenagers may be comforted to learn that as a young man, he was expelled from his first college, Michigan State, for editing a liberal magazine on education. In time he earned not only his

Ph.D. in clinical psychology, but a degree in theology as well. ("To ask questions, ultimate questions about human beings—not to be a preacher.") He has written eight books (his latest *Love and Will,* was a best seller and is likely to become a classic) and has taught at as many universities.

I visited Dr. May at his office in a skyscraper on New York City's West Side. All our interviews took place there, 25 stories above the Hudson River. His office is spare, blue-gray and has an aura much like the prow of a great ship. By day it is filled with sun; at night it is dominated by wind sounds and river lights.

Rollo May is a tall man with expressive brown eyes, a lover of painting, poetry and nature. ("Sometimes I think that if the world gets too . . . I might go to Montego Bay and paint. But I actually won't do it, because I'm very much a fighter. Well, fighter's not the right word, but I'm *involved* and I couldn't detach myself in that way. I've done a great deal of landscaping at my country house—planting trees, cutting the hedges so they slant and accent the valleys and mountains. I get a great kick out of it.")

Dr. May maintains that his patients are his most important teachers. "Therapy," he says, "isn't curing somebody of something; it's a means of helping a person explore himself, his life, his consciousness. My purpose as a therapist is to find out what it means to be a human. Every human being must have a point at which he stands against the culture, where he says, 'This is me and the world be damned!' Leaders have always been the ones to stand against the society—Socrates, Christ, Freud, all the way down the line."

Naturally, during our interviews, we explored the thinking, the philosophy that he poured into his masterpiece, *Love and Will.* One reviewer called it "the kind of book I've been waiting for; the kind I am tempted to say our troubled age has been waiting for—without knowing that it was waiting." It is the kind of book to read if you are troubled by the state of love and morality today, if you feel that your own family relations are less than they could be.

I remarked to Dr. May, *"Everyone knows they need love—yet they're not really sure what love is. How would you define it?"*

He replied, "Love is a blend of four components. First, obviously, there is sexual desire, or lust. I do not believe there is anything wrong or sinful about sex for its own sake, but, in the long run, it is not very satisfying. After sex, we want to sleep. After a more profound love experience, we want to stay awake thinking of the other person.

"What people need and want is intimacy and authentic love. Anyone who has experienced true intimacy with another person will tell you that this is what he or she really treasures, not sheer sexual excitement or bigger and better orgasms. Authentic love between a man and a woman has three components in addition to lust.

"The second component is *eros,* or passion. Eros takes wings from the human imagination and forever transcends technique—making love rather than manipulating organs. Eros transforms us. It is through eros that we become poets and inventors and achieve ethical goodness. Eros is the power that binds all things and all men together. St. Augustine said that eros is the power that drives men toward God.

"The third component is friendship, or brotherly love. I think it's important to like to be with the other person, like to do things with him or her, like to go places together. Couples who do not share common interests soon get bored with each other. Patients have said to me, "I love him but I don't like him.' That is no basis for a sound marriage.

"The fourth component is selfless love devoted to the welfare of the other. The prototype of this is the love of God for man. It's the love that's illustrated by the way a mother can feel for her child. It's esteem for other people that goes beyond what you yourself get out of it.

"Now, all four of these forms of love—lust, eros, friendship and selfless love—ought to be part of an ideal marriage. I think in various ways and to some degree they're all part of any genuine or authentic love."

Asked whether he would wear a button reading *Make Love, Not Sex,* Dr. May remarked: "I don't know. Making love and making sex *are* actually different activities. Some people are afraid to use the term 'making love' even when they're doing it, because they think it sounds too sentimental. But what is far worse, many people are afraid to make love at all because they don't want to lose their cool.

"Keeping cool is a way of staying sufficiently detached so that you can preserve your own center. To some extent keeping cool is desirable and good; otherwise we might be overwhelmed by the tremendous stimuli that come from every direction—radio, TV, newspapers. If we don't protect ourselves, we could become a mere echo of the last opinion we heard.

"But there is another way of preserving our cool—we don't listen at all. We don't feel. We protect ourselves so much that we cannot get involved with other people. Soon we grow detached and apathetic. If you are cool, you cannot be passionate. As radio and TV and telephone extensions proliferate, we become more and more lonely. Real communication between persons is all but destroyed."

"What has happened to make us afraid?" I inquired.

"Everything," Dr. May answered. "The progress of science without sufficient progress in human values. The fear of the bomb. The fear of having our lives managed by computers. The lack of honorable, shared values to give us a sense of identity and purpose.

"We have become preoccupied with sexual technique because we can follow certain rules and apparently succeed while experiencing practically no emotion. This fits in with keeping cool, almost too cool! Technologies and techniques are made for this too-cool person. You can learn how to do something superbly and you don't have to put yourself into it. Now the cool person can learn sexual techniques and can live with them as a way of avoiding the involvement of love."

"Surely there are still many people who are ignorant about sex, or inhibited?" I wondered.

"I think 'Victorianism' is becoming a dead horse, at least among younger people," Dr. May replied. "Today I rarely see patients with sex repression. There is lots of talk and activity. But feeling and passion are lacking. There is so little meaning in sex, or even fun. 'Enlightenment' has not solved our sex problems. In fact, the new emphasis on technique has backfired. Beyond a certain point, mechanistic attitudes lead to greater loneliness and frustration. In our society, people are more afraid of psychological nakedness—sharing their hopes and dreams—than they are of physical nakedness. Our highly vaunted sexual freedom is just a new form of puritanism. The body is still separated from the emotions. The body is used as a machine. People don't want to lose themselves in passion or in an unseemly commitment that might be interpreted as placing unhealthy demands on their partner. The new puritanism grossly limits feeling and it tells you it's immoral *not* to express your libido. Victorians wanted to have love without falling into sex and we want to have sex without falling into love."

"But isn't it hard to stay in love if a couple is incompatible? Masters and Johnson believe they have saved hundreds of marriages by teaching the couples better sexual techniques."

"Masters and Johnson's work represents the application of technology to sexual relationships and, on the simplest level, nobody could have any objection. The more we learn about sex the better. But that's only one small part of it and the really important thing is that they represent the thrust of our technological society already now taking over the person's sexual relationship. Masters and Johnson's research represents the incursion of technology into that most personal thing of all—sexual relations between a man and a woman. Such research leads people to assume that sex is related to how much they practice, how much they've done, what they have learned. Actually, that's not the way it is at all. Sex depends on the relationship between the man and the woman. A man can be as practiced as Don Giovanni and still be impotent with one woman and not with another.

"Even sexologists are starting to raise the eyebrows about our overemphasis on orgasm. Women don't want to be asked if they made it. Intimacy is what they remember. Every man and woman at some time wants to enjoy sheer lust, but if this is all that ever happens in one's personal life, loneliness and alienation lie around the corner. The distinguishing characteristic of a machine is that it can go through all the motions but it never feels. Unless you are willing to risk caring and possibly being hurt, you cannot experience the joys of love. The more sex becomes mechanical the more pleasure decreases.

"Rules and techniques may be useful up to a point, but then they start to defeat themselves. Technique becomes the end in itself. Love and passion fall by the wayside. Remember, too, everyone is different in terms of sexual response. True lovers explore each other. They do not follow sex manuals. I think it really boils down to how much each cares about what the other is experiencing."

"What about modern marriage today?" I asked.

"Marriage today is a crossing of our fingers and hoping. We cling to each other and persuade ourselves that what we feel is love.

"Wives are right to feel insulted if their husbands read girly magazines. This means that the man is searching for kicks of some sort, and it may be a symptom that the wife is failing to provide him with enough kicks or to join with him in finding them.

"I couldn't have an authentic relationship with more than one person. The more I'm committed to a relationship, the more it becomes its own reason for being, and it absorbs me. I don't find myself yearning for someone else. I don't think it's possible to feel strong sexual attraction for more than one person at a time. I think, in most cases, an unfaithful husband or wife doesn't feel much sexual passion for his spouse.

"A play by Ionesco called *The Bald Soprano* describes the true state of many modern marriages. A man and a woman happen to meet and engage in polite, mannered conversation. As they talk, they discover that they both came to New York on the 10 A.M. train from New Haven and, surprisingly, they have the same address on Fifth Avenue. They live in the same apartment and both have a seven-year-old daughter. Finally they discover that they are man and wife."

"Can women do anything to bring the romance back into their marriages. Is it too late after, say, 20 years?"

"No! No! No!" he replied emphatically. "It's never too late! Often long-married couples have their most fruitful sexual relationships in their 40s and sometimes later. Let me say a few things about the how-to. I'd advise women, I think, that the best way to refurbish a sexual relationship that is losing its kick is simply playing. Sexual relationships can be compared to great music. If music is only playful, it soon becomes superficial. If it's only sensual, it soon becomes cloying. If it's only serious, it soon becomes heavy. In the same way, sexual relationships ought to have all three elements — play, sensuality and even some element of the tragic or demonic.

"Remember that every person longs for union with another, a relationship that stretches him to be greater than himself. We are created in two sexes, each yearning for the other for completion. Sexual love is the most powerful act of relatedness.

"A total response requires intensity, discipline, openness and courage. These are not easy to attain but they can be cultivated. It takes courage to submit oneself to another being, to let oneself be carried away, to let oneself respond to the feeling of the other person. The rewards are well worth the risks. Spontaneity is a relief after assembly-line sex.

"Caring is a state in which something matters. Caring for your beloved must be a conscious psychological fact."

"Doesn't every woman want to care for her lover?"

"Objectively, yes. But she may be fearful. If you care, really care, you also develop a sense of tragedy, a personal realization that love may bring both joy and destruction. It lifts the lover in a whirlwind that destroys rational control. A famous psychologist once said that Romeo and Juliet wouldn't have committed suicide if only they'd had a little counseling. He may be right, but to me the most tragic thing is the attitude that love and passion don't matter, that it's better to be cool."

"Refusing to feel is worse than suicide?"

"Refusing to feel is living death. The woman who wants to love fully should also cultivate her own talents and creativity. It may be that original ideas and feelings are reserved for the few. That's an aristocratic point of view and I don't believe it. Truth comes as you or I or any human being genuinely feels something in her own self, with her own pulse, in her own heart. . . . Authentic lovers are always reaching out toward each other. One asserts himself and perhaps goes too far. He is answered and responds, sensitively, to the answer and either backs away or moves forward. Lovers are always on the edge of exploration.

"But lovers, like poets, are a menace on the assembly line. Who is going to get adjusted to a world like this? The world today is crazy. If you keep your cool and really get adjusted to it, you're the sickest person imaginable."

What Rollo May is trying to tell us, I reflected as I rode the elevator down from his serene crow's nest into the noisy Manhattan night, is very old and very new:

To love, one must risk being bruised and buffeted by this crazy world. Indeed, one can almost count on being bruised and buffeted. So be it. Be open and vulnerable, like a flower. Only then will you live — and love.

The street was spooky and dark. As a reporter, I am used to venturing out alone at night in Manhattan. As a reporter, yes; but as a woman, no. I have to do it, but I don't like it. There were no taxicabs in sight. I dialed my husband, Gideon, a busy and always-fatigued doctor, from the pay telephone in Rollo May's lobby. It was after midnight and I knew that my husband had gone to bed. What I feared far more than any rapist or mugger who might be lurking in the streets was Gideon's annoyance. What if he said to me, "Why the devil did you wake me up?"

Dr. May had given me the courage to rely on our relationship. "You are a nut," Gideon said fondly. "I've gone to bed, but I never *sleep* until you get home."

Fifteen minutes later our car pulled up in front of Rollo May's building. Gideon, in his pajamas, leaned over and kissed me. "I'm glad you called," he said.

So was I.

Thank you, Rollo May.

Unit Study Guide

A.   *Terms to Review*

Aphrodisiac	Institutionalized	Proprioceptive
Games (re Berne)	exclusiveness	Intimacy (inter-
Sensations	Gemeinschaft	personal)
Possession impulse	relations	Video-culture

B. *Questions for Discussion and Study*

1. Distinguish between instrumental and expressive orientation in intimate relations between marital partners. Illustrate and discuss.

2. Carefully read each article to identify both general and specific problems and issues connected with sexuality and affection in the marital partnership. List the issues and rank them in order of importance as you see it.

3. For each of the problems and issues which you listed above, suggest alternative courses of action or problem-solving approaches.

4. Citing sociological, cultural, and psychological factors, show why intimacy-deprivation is ordinarily construed as a "problem" in marriage.

5. "The private-property syndrome operative even in human relations is the single strongest barrier to authentic intimacy in American marriage." Explore the possible sources of this statement in the central themes emerging from the sexual equality and human potentials movements. Discuss the proposition in terms of validity and with regard to relevant social science data.

6. It has been said that "gestures are as important as words in the communication of intimacy between persons." Discuss the significance and functions of non-verbal communication and body language in the intimate behavior of marital partners.

C. *Topics-Ideas for Papers and Projects*

1. It has been suggested that quarreling and conflict over economic and marital matters is often a "cover-up" for underlying and unspoken sexual and affectional difficulties, eg. problems of intimacy. Interview several counselors and get their viewpoint on this interpretation.

2. "Vestiges of Patriarchal Norms in Current Marital Sexuality Patterns."

3. In your region, are there clinics devoted to treatment of marital sexual problems? Do a mail survey, getting information on their personnel, size of operation, sponsorship, evaluation studies under way, etc. Write up your findings and present to the class.

4. In the 1950's, research on college campuses explored the range and impact of the Kinsey studies and received wide coverage in mass media. Review the literature on that research and conduct a similar study on your own campus, with a focus on the work of Masters and Johnson (cf. Himelhoch and Fava, *Sexual Behavior in American Society,* New York: Norton, 1955).

5. Using the problems-category list discussed in they introduction to Unit 5, prepare a sheet on which students in your class can rank the problems from greatest to smallest importance. Count and graph the rankings; summarize, and use as the basis for a discussion of the relative importance of intimacy-related problems in marriage.

Unit 8
Reproduction and Parenthood

Unit 8

Reproduction and Parenthood

Children begin by loving their parents; after a time they judge them; rarely, if ever, do they forgive them. –
Oscar Wilde

Hail, wedded love, mysterious law, true source of human offspring. – Milton

---

Introduction

The encounter of the married pair with reproductive and parenting roles today has both positive and negative aspects. Generally speaking, the traditions, culture and current social organization of American society positively reinforce the assuming of reproductive and parenting roles by married persons. However, selective experience and subcultural differences in values regarding parenthood have led to a contemporary scene which is conflicting and ambiguous. Both within the marriage partners and in their immediate social environment there may exist views, feelings, and norms which tend to devalue reproductive and parenting roles. The decision to reproduce, if indeed a thoughtful approach to parenting is used, is increasingly less likely to be concerned merely with the timing of the first pregnancy, selection of a physician, or other secondary matters. Indeed, assuming of parental roles is, for many couples today, a culmination of serious, thoughtful discussion of psycho-socio-ethical aspects of creating and bringing into the world another human being. Whether or not the reproductive and parenting process is preceded by careful thought, abundant study makes it clear that persons entering these roles today will confront a variety of potential problems. In this unit we will examine and discuss some of these problems along with related issues and alternatives.

In past generations, it was apparently an almost universal norm that marriage would be followed by reproduction and parenthood. However, as we implied in the above discussion, this view of parenting as a "normal" outcome of marriage has been questioned seriously in recent years. Thus, a position paper circulated to members of the National Council on Family Relations was prefaced by a statement which held that, "Because of concern for the quality of life, family well-being, and

personal fulfillment, there is a growing concern over population pressures, environmental impairment, and the large number of unwanted
and unloved children." The paper went on to propose several objectives, the gist of which was to develop family planning and educational
services which could help potential parents to insure their "newborn's
birthright of love and full acceptance." Such planning would presumably contribute to ". . . a population level consistent with natural resource limitations and the preservation of human dignity."[1] Clearly, a
consciousness of social responsibility has now entered a domain which
was once almost totally within the prerogatives of the marriage partners.

Despite the rather negative tone of much recent discussion of the
reproductive role, the cultural impetus toward voluntary parenthood
per se remains quite strong. In 1955, a study showed that only about
one percent of the women responding wanted *no* children; most
wanted from two to four offspring.[2] In a study conducted seventeen
years later (1972) well over half the subjects considered two as the ideal
number of children and, as in the 1955 study, only about one percent
felt that it was best not to have any children.[3]

As we have seen in other aspects of marital experience, the environing society has great impact on what happens in the familial group. We
could expect, therefore, that the changes taking place throughout the
institutional web of society would constitute a potent source of problems for those entering reproductive and parenting roles. LeMasters
has identified the following aspects of social change in American society which may have made the parenting role more difficult than
formerly.[4]

1. *Higher standards for parents.* Inadequacy feelings in parents
may stem mainly from increasing levels of expectation in society
and the corollary tendency of parents to judge themselves more
harshly.

2. *The concept of progress.* Not only must parents be *super* to fit the
cultural expectation, but they must also rear children who will
surpass their own achievements — social, economic, etc.

3. *The cult of the child.* Americans have strongly internalized the
notion that children are intrinsically more important than any
other age-group. This may interfere with reality training for
children and lead to the view that parents are expendable while
children are not.[5] Connected with the cult of the child is the
emergence of semi-formalized youth peer group structures —
perhaps a youth subculture — with social, political, and economic
power.

4. *Emergence of professionals and experts on childhood.* Parents today
may find themselves judged by child-rearing concepts developed
by those having little or no contact with the "average" family

situation. Conflicting views among professionals and experts and changes over time in their views may foster much confusion among well-meaning parents.

5. *Marital instability.* Tentativeness in social relationships is widespread. Its impact on parents, as manifested in divorce, probably makes the child-rearing process more difficult. Few women, for example, probably ever consider the possibility of their becoming head of a one-parent family.

6. *New roles for women.* Women who assume the mothering role may also be employed outside the home, doing volunteer work or helping in community projects, and playing a role of leadership in some organization. Added to all this activity may be continuing responsibility for handling traditionally wife-related tasks within the home. In addition to the emergence of new roles for women, the parenting function has itself become more complex and demanding. Women bear a disproportionate amount of the burdens associated with these more complex demands.

7. *Increasing urbanization.* Simply put, change in the social and physical environment calls for increasingly complex adaptation patterns between family and society. Greater interdependence of the family with society is fostered by urbanization.

8. *Rise of the mass media.* Marked discrepancies may exist between values imparted in the mass media — especially television — and those considered important by the parents. The derogation of adults frequently conveyed in "childrens' " television programs may also add to the difficulty of those in parenting roles.

9. *Limited preparation for parenting.* In contrast to earlier generations, those entering parenthood today are likely to have much less exposure to various aspects of reproduction and child-rearing. Thus, while parenting continues to be highly valued, personal opportunities for adequate preparation for it are very limited.

These, as LeMasters saw it, constitute some of the more general social factors related to difficulties experienced by many persons in the parenting process. We can now turn to some discussion of practical problems which are more related to the quality of interaction in the partnership.

From the perspective of the married pair, three potentially troublesome aspects can be mentioned. The first of these concerns *motivations for reproduction.* Critical questions arise at this point. Is the motivation mutual or does it represent only one partner's wishes? Is reproduction seen as instrumental (e.g. to hold the marriage together, provide an heir, carry on a family name, give the mother status or acceptance with peers, help the father to get or hold a job, etc.)? Does the motive for reproduction reflect neurotic personality needs of the parents (e.g. to prove that he is a "real man," to show that she is a "real woman," to fulfill ego-extension needs, etc.)? There are doubtless many other questions that could be raised. The point is that ample research suggests that each of these kinds of motivation may enter into reproductive behavior. Failure of parents to examine honestly their motives can result in a familial scene that is psychologically damaging to offspring and parents alike.

A second potentially troublesome aspect of entry into parenting roles is connected with the *planning and distribution of responsibilities in parenting*. Are the predictable stresses — social, psychological, physical, economic — taken into account? Is there recognition of the greater range of stresses likely to be borne by the wife? Are both partners mature enough to assume the burden of highly-stressful responsibilities? Have the partners dealt realistically with their changing roles? Most research shows that the average couple has an extremely low level of preparation for becoming parents. Getting themselves together psychologically and interactionally for the parental role may, in itself, prove to be extremely demanding. In fact, as Rossi has pointed out, for most partners ". . . adjustment to parenthood is potentially more stressful than marital adjustment."[6]

A third and last aspect to be mentioned deals with *changes in interaction between partners* which may occur as a consequence of becoming parents. Considerable research and data based on counselor's files suggest that the intimacy patterns in the partnership may be significantly, and often adversely, affected by the coming of children. This seems especially true in regard to the birth of the first child and it is obviously strongly affected by the quality of the partners' relationship prior to pregnancy. Perhaps the ultimate reflection of pessimism on this effect is found in a statement attributed to Hegel: "The birth of children is the death of parents." Such an extreme view may be unwarranted. But the fact remains that, for many if not most couples, the coming of children probably constitutes an interpersonal crisis situation; this theme will be explored further in our readings for this unit.

The problems at the partnership level in regard to reproduction and parenthood seem in themselves quite enough without adding more. However, there are still other problems and issues implicitly connected with this area of marital encounter. Some of these will be cited below along with some alternatives which have been proposed, and in some cases implemented. Let us begin with reproduction.

Reproduction

Societal control. As we have noted in discussions in previous units, there are fundamental issues revolving around the balance of individual freedom versus societal coercion existing in a given society. This issue is relevant to virtually every area of marital experience and it is especially important here. Reproduction is not, by any stretch of the imagination, a private matter. For example, environmentalists argue that the basic problem affecting survival on planet Earth is overpopulation. The family thus constitutes, in its reproductive behavior, the prime source of problems for the survival of the human species. Sub-issues can be expressed in the form of questions: Is reproduction a right, or a privilege to be controlled by the state and extended to individuals as the needs of society require? Should infertility as well as fertility be subject to control? Argentina, for example, has recently banned the sale of contraceptives, on the grounds that the nation is underpopulated. Should the state be involved in the distribution of contraceptives or in the funding of contraception research? What kinds of steps could the state legitimately take in this area of reproduction without jeopardizing individual rights? There are numerous other unresolved issues regarding societal control.

Nature versus technology. A persistent argument revolves around the question of the extent to which mechanical or chemical technology should be used in the reproductive process. There is a persisting cultural tendency to regard interference with human reproductive-biological processes as *bad*; non-interference with "natural" processes is construed as *good*. While the limitation of birth per se is no longer a vital issue, the same cannot be said on the question of *how* human fertility is limited. There are unresolved issues on the extent to which intervention in "natural" processes may be damaging to health, the human psyche, the social order, and morals. An important sub-issue is concerned with the point at which intervention in the control of fertility takes place. The continuing, heated discussion of abortion is illustrative of this issue.

The decision to be non-fertile. One issue, and also an alternative to traditional behavior, concerns the right of couples to abstain from reproduction. Such couples may experience varying degrees of resentment, rejection, and "shaming." Even in contemporary society, one hears voluntarily-childless couples described as "selfish" or hears the partners described as individuals lacking in certain physical or psychological capacities.

Some alternatives in reproduction. Various alternatives, many of which are based on far-reaching developments in biochemistry, are emerging. Some could fit within the present structure of family life; others are more reflective of societal control in their function. This is merely a beginning list:

Improvement of reproductive education.

Predetermination of sex of offspring.

Artificial insemination.

Ex utero reproduction — using mechanical uterus.

Contraceptive "vaccine" for individual or mass use.
Proxy or surrogate mothers.
Asexual reproduction through cloning.
Development of ova and sperm storage banks.
Licensing of reproduction.
Prenatal determination of offspring characteristics.
Selective administration of sperm or ova to competing applicants.
Communal reproduction.
Selective awards for reproducing or non-reproduction.

Now that we have briefly reviewed some of the issues and alternatives associated with reproduction, let us turn to the question of the parenting function. As is the case for the preceding discussion, the listing below will begin with some issues and then proceed to cite some alternatives.

Parenting

Parenting as a social control mechanism. Critics of the society have suggested that the current parenting process is mainly a tool of the established order, insuring that offspring are imbued with a tendency to accept what they find in their objective world and to "adjust" to it. From this point of view, the conventional parenting process tends to perpetuate the injustices, the inhumanities of a "sick society." In preparing the child to "adjust," do parents thereby vitiate any tendencies to challenge the established order? What are the minimal kinds and levels of "adjustment" necessary for offspring?

The possession tendency. Just as in other relations, the private-property ethic finds its way into the parent-child relationship. Consequently, children may implicitly be regarded as property rather than persons. Children may thus be victimized as an outgrowth of the parents' need to control and possess. Adding to this problem is the tendency to view the child in terms of its future role in a production-oriented, materialistic society. Parents may thus be part of an exploitation tendency toward children. It has been contended that such exploitation ". . . can only be brought to an end in a socioeconomy in which the development of the individual is the highest social purpose and satisfaction of wants is understood to be possible in the absence of increased material production."[7] There are many subissues here. One concerns the question of childrens' rights as compared with the rights of other social groupings in the society.

Disproportionate parenting responsibilities for women. Documentation of the over-burdening of women with child-rearing responsibilities is so readily available that it needs no repeating here.[8] Issues here concern the appropriateness of men asuming greater parental responsibilities., the possible damage to women's actual child-rearing effectiveness through the assumption of too many such responsibilities; and the extent to which extensive involvement of both parents is essential to the optimum development of social, economic, and psychological health for the family and the offspring. LeMasters, Friedan, and others have suggested that it is high time for the misogynists and other critics to stop laying the blame for disfunctional child-rearing on the mother. Instead, they content, it is time for the father to assume his share of the burdens as well as the joys of the parental role.

Cultural norms regarding parenthood. Since the norms and culture of a society tend to be in flux and are thus characterized by discontinuity and conflict, they may in themselves contribute significantly to problems and issues in the parental area of family life. We will cite only a few which seem especially important. "Time with the children" is one such norm. Is the amount of time spent with children equally as important as the quality of interaction with them? If one must choose between being with one's children or being absent from them in order to provide for their physical, educational, and other needs, which option should be taken? Another norm suggests that there can be no "real" substitutes for a child's "real" parents. Why is it possible to get violent reactions from middle-class parents by merely suggesting that day-care centers just might do a much better job of caring for their children? Why is the fact of fertility often equated with readiness for parenting? Serious issues are contingent to the fact that cultural norms have gradually expanded the concept of "child" to ever-higher chronological age brackets. Thus, a dependent child of fifteen today would have been regarded as a miniature adult three generations ago. To what extent do the norms of dependency inhibit growth and maturation processes in the offspring? Subissues involve questions about how much shielding from reality should be afforded to a child. Or, somewhat differently, at what point should children learn that pain and burdens of various kinds are a normal part of life-experiences? These are merely a sampling of the issues connected with culture.

Some alternatives in parenting. Following is a brief listing of alternatives which have been proposed. The list is not intended to be comprehensive, as we shall see from our readings.

Licensing of parenthood, based on qualifications.
Separation of parenting from reproducive function.
Federally-supervised and certified day-care centers in every community, based on population and open to families of all economic levels.
Neighborhood-level parental-health centers with paid compulsory attendance.

Parental leaves-with pay from work.
Rearing of children by specially trained surrogate parents.
Communul child-rearing and parental responsibilities.

As we have seen thus far, problems and issues confront every major area of marital encounter. And it is amply clear that this holds true for the marital partners' encounter in reproductive and parenting processes. In addition, since these processes so effectively tie together the family and its environing society, it is expected that the problems, issues, and alternatives would reflect that interdependence. The readings to follow will help to illuminate the dimensions of the expanded interdependency which occurs when the married pair enters the parenting process.

REFERENCES

1. Huffman, Dean K., "Position Paper on Population and Family Planning," National Council on Family Relations, 1971.

2. Freedman, Ronald *et al. Family Planning, Sterility, and Population Growth* (New York: McGraw-Hill, 1959), pp. 46, 224.

3. Editors, Better Homes and Gardens, *A Report on the American Family* (Meredith Corp., 1972), p. 81.

4. LeMasters, E.E. *Parents in Modern America,* Rev. Edit. (Homewood: Dorsey Press, 1970), pp. 5-12.

5. Lerner, Max, *America As A Civilization* (New York: Simon & Schuster, 1957), pp. 560-570.

6. Rossi, Alice S. "Transition to Parenthood," *Journal of Marriage and the Family* 30 (February 1968): 26-39.

7. Meyer, Peter B. "The Exploitation of the American Growing Class," in David Gottlieb, (Ed.) *Children's Liberation* (Englewood: Prentice-Hall, 1973), pp. 35-52

8. Peck, Ellen. *The Baby Trap* (New York: Bernard Geis Associates, 1971).

Parenthood as Crisis

E. E. LeMASTERS

INTRODUCTION

In recent decades the impact of various crises on the American family has been subjected to intensive analysis. Eliot,[1] Waller,[2] Angell,[3] Komarovsky,[4] Cavan and Ranck,[5] Koos,[6] Hill,[7] and Goode[8] have published what is perhaps the most solid block of empirical research in the field of family sociology.

In all of these studies of how the modern family reacts to crisis, it appears that the shock is related to the fact that the crisis event forces a reorganization of the family as a social system. Roles have to be reassigned, status positions shifted, values reoriented, and needs met through new channels.

These studies have shown that crises may originate either from within the family itself or from the outside. It has also been demonstrated that the total impact of the crisis will depend upon a number of variables: (1) the nature of the crisis event; (2) the state of organization or disorganization of the family at the point of impact; (3) the resources of the family; and (4) its previous experience with crisis.[9]

These studies report a sequence of events somewhat as follows: level of organization before the crisis, point of impact, period of disorganization, recovery, and subsequent level of reorganization.

This study was conceived and designed within the conceptual framework of the above research.

THE PRESENT STUDY

In the study being described in this report, the main hypothesis was derived through the following line of analysis:

A. If the family is conceptualized as a small social system, would it not follow that the *adding* of a new member to the system could force a reorganization of the system as drastic (or nearly so) as does the *removal* of a member?

B. If the above were correct, would it not follow that the arrival of the *first* child could be construed as a "crisis" or "critical event?[10]

To test this hypothesis, a group of young parents were interviewed, using a relatively unstructured interviewing technique. In order to control socio-economic variables, couples had to possess the following characteristics to be included in the study: (1) unbroken marriage; (2) urban or suburban residence; (3) between twenty-five and thirty-five years of age at the time of the study; (4) husband college graduate; (5)

husband's occupation middle class; (6) wife not employed after birth of first child; (7) must have had their first child within five years of the date interviewed. Race and religion were not controlled.

Using these criteria, forty-eight couples were located by the device of asking various persons in the community for names. As a precaution, the exact nature of the study was not stated in soliciting names for the sample—the project was described as a study of "modern young parents."

Once a name was obtained that met the specifications, every effort was made to secure an interview. No refusals were encountered, but two couples left the community before they could participate, leaving forty-six couples for the final study group. The couples, then, were not volunteers. All of the intervewing was done by the writer during the years 1953-1956. Both the husband and wife were interviewed.

Typical occupations represented include minister, social worker, high school teacher, college professor, bank teller, accountant, athletic coach, and small business owner.

Various definitions of "crisis" are available to the worker in this area. Webster, for example, states that the term means a "decisive" or "crucial" period, a "turning point."[11] Koos specifies that crises are situations "which block the usual patterns of action and call for new ones."[12] Hill defines as a crisis "any sharp or decisive change for which old patterns are inadequate."[13] This is the definition used in this analysis.

A five point scale was used in coding the interview data: (1) no crisis; (2) slight crisis; (3) moderate crisis; (4) extensive crisis; (5) severe crisis.

The Findings

The essential findings of this exploratory study are as follows:

1. Thirty-eight of the forty-six couples (83 per cent) reported "extensive" or "severe" crisis in adjusting to the first child. This rating was arrived at jointly by the interviewer and the parents.

In several cases there was some difference of opinion between the husband and wife as to what their response should be. In all but two cases, however, the difference was reconciled by further discussion between interviewer and the couple. In the two cases, the wife's rating was recorded, on the theory that the mother makes the major adjustment to children in our culture.

For this sample, therefore, the evidence is quite strong in support of the hypothesis. The eight couples (17 per cent) who reported relatively mild crisis (values 1-2-3 in the above scale) must be considered the deviants in this sample.

Stated theoretically, this study supports the idea that adding the first child to the urban middle class married couple constitutes a crisis event.

2. In this study there was strong evidence that this crisis reaction was *not* the result of not wanting children. On the contrary, thirty-five of the thirty-eight pregnancies in the crisis group were either "planned" or "desired."

3. The data supported the belief that the crisis pattern occurs whether the marriage is "good" or "poor"— for example: thirty-four of the thirty-eight in the crisis group (89 per cent) rated their marriages as "good" or better. With only three exceptions, these ratings were confirmed by close friends. By any reasonable standards, these marriages must be considered adequate.

4. There is considerable evidence that the crisis pattern in the thirty-eight cases was not the result of "neurosis" or other psychiatric disability on the part of these parents. Judging by their personal histories, their marriages, and the ratings of friends, it seemed clear that the vast bulk of the husbands and wives in the crisis group were average or above in personality adjustment.

5. The thirty-eight couples in the crisis group appear to have almost completely romanticized parenthood. They felt that they had had very little, if any, effective preparation for parental roles. As one mother said: "We knew where babies came from, but we didn't know *what they were like.*"

The mothers reported the following feelings or experiences in adjusting to the first child: loss of sleep (especially during the early months); chronic "tiredness" or exhaustion; extensive confinement to the home and the resulting curtailment of their social contacts; giving up the satisfactions and the income of outside employment; additional washing and ironing; guilt at not being a "better" mother; the long hours and seven day (and night) week necessary in caring for an infant; decline in their housekeeping standards; worry over their appearance (increased weight after pregnancy, et cetera).

The fathers echoed most tf the above adjustments but also added a few of their own: decline in sexual response of wife; economic pressure resulting from wife's retirement plus additional expenditures necessary for child; interference with social life; worry about a second pregnancy in the near future; and a general disenchantment with the parental role.

6. The mothers with professional training and extensive professional work experience (eight cases) suffered "extensive" or "severe" crisis in every case.

In analyzing these cases, it was apparent that these women were really involved in two major adjustments simultaneously: (1) they were giving up an occupation which had deep significance for them; and (2) they were assuming the role of mother for the first time.

Interpretation of the Findings

There are, of course, various ways of interpreting the findings in this study. It may be, for example, that the couples obtained for the sample are not typical of urban middle class parents. It might also be true that the interviewing, the design of the study, or both, may have been inadequate. If we assume, for the present, that the findings are reliable and valid for this social group, how are we to interpret such reactions to

464 Reproduction and Parenthood

parenthood? It is suggested that the following conceptual tools may be helpful.

1. That parenthood (and not marriage) is the real "romantic complex" in our culture. This view, as a matter of fact, was expressed by many of the couples in the study.

In a brilliant article some years ago, Arnold Green[14] suggested as much—that urban middle class couples often find their parental roles in conflict with their other socio-economic commitments. If this is true, one would expect to find the reconciliation of these conflicts most acute at the point of entering parenthood, with the first child. Our findings support this expectation.

2. Ruth Benedict has pointed out that young people in our society are often the victims of "discontinuity in cultural conditioning."[15] By this she means that we often have to "unlearn" previous training before we can move on to the next set of roles. Sex conditioning is perhaps the clearest illustration of this.

Using this concept, one can see that these couples were not trained for parenthood, that practically nothing in school, or out of school, got them ready to be fathers and mothers—*husbands* and *wives*, yes, but not *parents*. This helps explain why some of the mothers inteviewed were actually "bitter" about their high school and college training.

3. One can also interpret these findings by resorting to what is known about small groups. Wilson and Ryland, for example, in their standard text on group work make this comment about the two-person group: "This combination seems to be the most satisfactory of human relationships."[16] They then proceed to pass this judgment on the three-person group: "Upon analysis this pattern falls into a combination of a pair and an isolate. . . . This plurality pattern is the most volatile of all human relationships."[17] This, of course, supports an earlier analysis by von Wiese and Becker.[18]

Viewed in this conceptual system, married couples find the transition to parenthood painful because the arrival of the first child destroys the two-person or pair pattern of group interaction and forces a rapid reorganization of their life into a three-person or triangle group system. Due to the fact that their courtship and pre-parenthood pair relationship has persisted over a period of years, they find it difficult to give it up as a way of life.

In addition, however, they find that living as a trio is more complicated than living as a pair. The husband, for example, no longer ranks first in claims upon his wife but must accept the child's right to priority. In some cases, the husband may feel that he is the semi-isolate, the third party in the trio. In other cases, the wife may feel that her husband is more interested in the baby than in her. If they preserve their pair relationship and continue their previous way of life, relatives and friends may regard them as poor parents. In any event, their pattern of living has to be radically altered.

Since babies do not usually appear to married couples completely by surprise, it might be argued that this event is not really a crisis—"well adjusted" couples should be "prepared for it." The answer seems to be that children and parenthood have been so romanticized in our society that most middle class couples are caught unprepared, even though they have planned and waited for this event for years. The fact that parenthood is "normal" does not eliminate crisis. Death is also "normal" but continues to be a crisis event for most families.

4. One can also interpret the findings of this study by postulating that parenthood (not marriage) marks the final transition to maturity and adult responsibility in our culture.[19] Thus the arrival of the first child forces young married couples to take the last painful step into the adult world. This point, as a matter of fact, was stated or implied by most of the couples in the crisis group.

5. Finally, the cases in this sample confirm what the previous studies in this area have shown: that the event itself is only one factor determining the extent and severity of the crisis on any given family. Their resources, their previous experience with crisis, the pattern of role organization before the crisis—these factors are equally important in determining the total reaction to the event.

CONCLUSION

In this study, it was hypothesized that the addition of the first child would constitute a crisis event, forcing the married couple to move from an adult-centered pair type of organization into a child-centered triad group system. Of the forty-six middle class couples located for this study, thirty-eight (83 per cent) confirmed the hypothesis.

In all fairness to this group of parents, it should be reported that all but a few of them eventually made what seems to be a successful adjustment to parenthood. This does not alter the fact, however, that most of them found the transition difficult. Listening to them describe their experiences, it seemed that one could compare these young parents to veterans of military service—they had been through a rough experience, but it was worth it. As one father said: "I wouldn't have missed it for the world."

It is unfortunate that the number of parents in this sample who did not report crisis is so small (eight couples) that no general statements can be made about them. Somehow, however, they seem to have been better prepared for parenthood than was the crisis group. It is felt that future work on this problem might well include a more extensive analysis of couples who have made the transition to parenthood with relative ease.

If the basic findings of this study are confirmed by other workers, it would appear that family life educators could make a significant contribution by helping young people prepare more adequately for parenthood.

REFERENCES

1. See Thomas D. Eliot, "Bereavement: Inevitable but Not Insurmountable," in *Family, Marriage, and Parenthood,* edited by Howard Becker and Reuben Hill, Boston: D.C. Heath and Company, Second Edition, 1955.
2. Willard Waller, *The Old Love and the New,* New York: Liveright, 1930.
3. Robert C. Angell, *The Family Encounters the Depression,* New York: Charles Scribner's Sons, 1936.
4. Mirra Komarovsky, *The Unemployed Man and His Family,* New York: Dryden Press, 1940.
5. Ruth Cavan and Katherine Ranck, *The Family and the Depression,* Chicago: University of Chicago Press, 1938.
6. E. L. Koos, *Families in Trouble,* New York: King's Crown Press, 1946.
7. Reuben Hill, *Families Under Stress,* New York: Harper and Brothers, 1949.
8. William J. Goode, *After Divorce,* Glencoe: The Free Press, 1956.
9. See Hill, *op. cit.,* for an excellent review of this research.
10. To some extent, the original idea for this study was derived from Hill's discussion, See *op. cit.,* ch. 2.
11. *Webster's Collegiate Dictionary,* Springfield: G. and C. Merriam Co., Second Edition, 1944, p. 240.
12. Koos, *op. cit.,* p. 9.
13. Hill, *op. cit.,* p. 51. See also his review of definitions in ch. 2.
14. Arnold W. Green, "The Middle-Class Male Child and Neurosis," *American Sociological Review,* 11 (February, 1946), pp. 31-41.
15. Ruth Benedict, "Continuities and Discontinuities in Cultural Conditioning," *Psychiatry,* 1 (May, 1939), pp. 161-67.
16. Gertrude Wilson and Gladys Ryland, *Social Group Work Practice,* Boston: Houghton Mifflin Company, 1949, p. 49.
17. *Ibid.*
18. Leopold von Wiese, *Systematic Sociology,* adapted and amplified by Howard Becker, New York: Wiley, 1932.
19. This is essentially the point of view in Robert J. Havighurst's analysis, *Human Development and Education,* New York: Longmans, Green, 1953.

Childrearing in the United States

JAMES H. S. BOSSARD
ELEANOR STOKER BOLL

. . . broad social changes have a way of expressing themselves in specific movements and attitudes, and the changing status of childhood has been no exception. During this century a variety of ideas have crystallized concerning how children should be treated by the larger society, and how they should be reared by their parents. Most of these ideas are reflections of definite changes in our society and have resulted in new experiments in rearing children. This chapter seeks to examine some of the trends, in this respect, in the United States during the 1900's.

THE CONCEPT OF RIGHTS

The best-known statement of human rights is the American Declaration of Independence. "We hold these truths to be self-evident, that all men are created equal, that they are endowed by their Creator with certain unalienable rights, that among these are life, liberty and the pursuit of happiness. That to secure these rights, governments are instituted among men, deriving their just powers from the consent of the governed." This statement, together with the French Declaration of the Rights of Man and of the Citizen (1789), marked the inauguration of the modern age and inspired the triumph of modern democracy.

Recent years have witnessed a resurgence of interest in the subject of human rights, and some notable attempts have been made to revise the historic formulations. These have been directed chiefly toward the inclusion of economic and social rights, on the basis of the claim that we are living in a new world in which the central problems arise from new pressures of power, production, and population which our forefathers did not face. The proposed new rights center about the development of personality, the basic implication being that there are certain social and economic rights which are as essential as the civil and political rights already established.

The concept of the rights of childhood is a product of the larger program of human rights. When first applied to children, the alleged rights were little more than claims which children were said to have

From pp. 535-541 and 544-549 in *The Sociology of Child* Development, 4th Edition, by James H. S. Bossard and Eleanor Stoker Boll. Copyright © 1966 by Eleanor Stoker Boll. By permission of Harper & Row, Publishers, Inc.

upon the consideration of society, especially if that society was blessed with social feelings and intelligence. These rights might be spoken of as a series of ethical insistences. Gradually, however, these claims found expression in organized efforts, first private and then public; in the "amiable purposes" of the philanthropic; in goals formulated by professional workers; in standards set by official and quasi-official bodies, as the White House Conferences; and lastly, in legislative enactments.

It is often contended that these rights are not "true rights" and that they have no validity in scientific treatises or in government documents, at least not until they become the specific statement of some legislative act. To this Merriam replies as follows: "That rights have not yet been fully recognized or realized does not remove them from the field of the political, for politics deals with ideals as well as with realities. Ideals indeed are themselves realities. The rights of man provide the domain of faith and hope in government, the court of appeal which is never closed, the law beyond the law and the jurists, the lawmakers, the managers, and the adjudicators. The rights of man go deeper and higher than institutional devices for interpreting or applying them."[1]

To clarify the point of view in this volume, it will suffice to say that the rights of childhood are conceived of as social values in process of translation into the realities of daily living. This process begins with the crystallization of the ideas on which these values rest; it passes through many forms of social expression; and each manifestation in its history is but another index of the changing status of childhood. Some of these rights or social values will be considered briefly.

The Right to Life. The basic right is the right to life. It involves the biological insistence for life expression, a social recognition of the eternal worth of the individual. Concretely, emphasis upon the child's right to life has been translated into the movement against infant mortality, one of the historic tragedies of childhood. Being a child has always been a dangerous occupation, and the earlier the stage in the life span, the greater has been the hazard. In all cultures and throughout the centuries, the first year was the most crucial one. A century ago, in this country, one out of every four babies born alive died before the end of the first year. As late as 60 years ago, a baby born in the United States had less chance to live a week than a person 90 years old, and less chance to live a year than an individual 80 years of age.

Following the series of fundamental discoveries in the second half of the nineteenth century which laid the foundation for the modern science of bacteriology, individual leaders like Pierre Budin in France, Benjamin Broadbent in England, and L. Emmet Holt in the United States began to develop and advocate new techniques which revolutionized pediatric practice. These in turn led to organized move-

---

[1] Charles E. Merriam, "Essential Human Rights," *Annals of the American Academy of political and Social Science,* January, 1946, p. 12.

ments, first developed through private initiative and financial support, like the Strauss milk depots in New York City, and then through publicly authorized and financed efforts, like the establishment of the federal Children's Bureau, the passage (1921) of the Sheppard-Towner Act, and the Social Security Acts, beginning in 1935. As a result of these efforts and changes in attitude which they indicated. infant mortality rates today are roughly one-sixth of what they were at the turn of the century. Social effort has gone far in guaranteeing the child's right to life.

The Right to Be Wanted. The desire to control fertility apparently is age-old and universal, and it has taken a variety of forms. Once infanticide was widely practiced, with full consent of society and its leaders. The milder form of abandonment once was a recognized device. Abortion seems universal and frequent, by means of either bodily violence or internal concoctions. In primitive society, infanticide and abortion are the chief substitutes for control of conception. Most of the modern methods used are preventive, in that they seek control through the prevention of conception.

The past century has witnessed marked changes in the ability of parents to limit the size of their families. First, there have been great improvements in the techniques of contraception, and in their effectiveness. Today more than 200 mechanical devices are used in Western culture, in addition to chemical and other agents, Second has been the widespread diffusion and democratization of contraceptive knowledge, resulting both in its wider diffusion at upper-class levels and in its widespread penetration into the lower classes.

The third development has been the rise of cultural pressures favoring the limitation of family size. Particularly outstanding has been the stress upon its social and economic desirability. Four of these pressures might be mentioned briefly. (1) The maintenance of a large family in an industrial culture is much more precarious than in the older handicraft or agricultural system. (2) The economic value of a child to his parents has changed enormously. Formerly, the child, measured in economic terms, was an asset. His early and certain introduction to employment, often in his own family, resulted in his maintaining himself and being a source of income to his parents over a long period. Our contemporary industrial-urban pattern has changed all that. City life offers few opportunities for early and gradual employment. Industry eliminates the opportunities for homework. Child labor laws establish age limits for entering gainful occupations, and compulsory school requirements supplement these nonemployment factors. As a result, the child is today an economic liability to his parents, and definitely so, rather than an asset as formerly. (3) A relatively open class system is an important even if intangible factor. In any country where a considerable number of persons believe that they can raise their status by their own efforts, prudence combines with ambition to lead many families to seek to limit their size. (4) The status of women and their conception of their role in life has changed greatly during the past century. In former times, the chief or one of their chief functions was to serve as a breeding machine. In recent decades many factors have revolutionized the status of women — education, employment opportunities, changing functions of the family, etc. This changed status has expressed itself nowhere more than in sex attitudes and behavior. The modern woman refuses to have her sex exploited. She has definite and often precise ideas concerning the number of children she will have, and the space that shall separate their births.

The Child's Right to an Education. The right to an education which prepares the child for life is perhaps the most completely established and accepted of all the rights accorded American children. Its development has been an integral part of our national history. While it had its beginning in the transplanting of English practices and systems, its subsequent unfolding came in answer to ideas and needs peculiar to the New World. Following the Revolutionary War, the idea grew that the continuity and welfare of the new republic depended upon the enlightenment of its people, and that the nation must educate its youth as a duty to itself. By 1900, the period of pioneering in public education was over, for it was required in nearly all states outside of the South. From that time on, enrollments in schools and colleges have steadily increased, and the current quest is for equal quality in education for all children.

The Child's Right to Health. The child's right to health may be said to be on the road to public acceptance. Compared with developments in public education, those in the field of child health make an unsatisfactory showing in large areas of this country; but when contrasted with the child health work of two or more generations ago, the advances made in recent years are striking. Two developments in the latter half of the nineteenth century in particular focused attention upon this aspect of child development. One was the evolution of public health work to the stage where the economy of the preventive approach was recognized. Once this approach was made, it was quickly seen that all the diseases which, from the point of view of medicine or public health, were known to be preventable, occurred in the early part of life; that to prevent disease, the beginnings must be made in the age span when it an be prevented; that if the individual's resistance was to be utilized to fight disease, this resistance must be built up in the years of childhood; and that if health education was to be made an effective instrument in public health work, the foundations for it had to be laid in the years when persons were most educable. These ideas, now seemingly so simple and obvious, were hailed in this earlier period with all the enthusiasm given a new discovery.

The Children's Charter. Other rights have been advanced by various persons interested in child development. The standard statement of all of the rights of children is contained in the Children's Charter, drawn up in 1930 by the third White House Conference on Child Health and Protection. Its provisions follow:

I. For every child, spiritual and moral training to help him to stand firm under the pressure of life.

II. For every child, understanding and the guarding of his personality as his most precious right.

III. For every child, a home and that love and security which a home provides; and for that child who must receive foster care, the nearest substitute for his own home.

IV. For every child, full preparation for his birth, his mother receiving prenatal, natal, and postnatal care; and the establishment of such protective measures as will make childbearing safer.

V. For every child, health protection from birth through adolescence, including: periodical health examinations and, where needed, care of specialists and hospital treatment; regular dental examination and care of the teeth; protective and preventive measures against communicable diseases; the issuing of pure food, pure milk, and pure water.

VI. For every child, from birth through adolescence, promotion of health, including health instruction and a health program, wholesome physical and mental recreation, with teachers and leaders adequately trained.

VII. For every child, a dwelling place, safe, sanitary, and wholesome, with reasonable provisions for privacy, free from conditions which tend to thwart his development; and a home environment harmonious and enriching.

VIII. For every child, a school which is safe from hazards, sanitary, properly equipped, lighted, and ventilated. For younger children, nursery schools and kindergartens to supplement home care.

IX. For every child, a community which recognizes and plans for his needs; protects him against physical dangers, moral hazards, and disease; provides him with safe and wholesome places for play and recreation; and makes provision for his cultural and social needs.

X. For every child, an education which, through the discovery and development of his individual abilities, prepares him for life; and through training and vocational guidance prepares him for a living which will yield him the maximum of satisfaction.

XI. For every child, such teaching and training as will prepare him for successful parenthood, homemaking, and the rights of citizenship; and, for parents, supplementary training to fit them to deal wisely with the problem of parenthood.

XII. For every child, education for safety and protection against accidents to which modern conditions subject him — those to which he is directly exposed, and those which, through loss or maiming of his parents, affect him indirectly.

XIII. For every child who is blind, deaf, crippled, or otherwise physically handicapped, and for the child who is mentally handicapped, such measures as will early discover and diagnose his handicap, provide care and treatment, and so train him that he may become an asset to society rather than a liability. Expenses of these services should be borne publicly where they cannot be privately met.

XIV. For every child who is in conflict with society, the right to be dealt with intelligently as society's charge, not society's outcast; with the home, the school, the church, the court, and the institution when needed, shaped to return him whenever possible to the normal stream of life.

XV. For every child, the right to grow up in a family with an adequate standard of living and the security of a stable income as the surest safeguard against social handicaps.

XVI. For every child, protection against labor that stunts growth, either physical or mental, that limits education, that deprives children of the right of comradeship, of play, and of joy.

XVII. For every rural child, as satisfactory schooling and health services as for the city child, and an extension to rural families of social, recreational, and cultural facilities.

XVIII. To supplement the home and the school in the training of youth, and to return to them those interests of which modern life tends to cheat children, every stimulation and encouragement should be given to the extension and development of the voluntary youth organizations.

XIX. To make everywhere available these minimum protections of the health and welfare of children, there should be a district, county, or community organization for health, education, and welfare, with full-time officials, coordinating with a state-wide program which will be responsible to a nation-wide service of general information, statistics and scientific research. This should include: (a) Trained full-time public health officials, with public health nurses, sanitary inspection, and laboratory workers. (b) Available hospital beds. (c) Full-time public welfare service for the relief, aid, and guidance of children in special need due to poverty, misfortune, or behavior difficulties, and for the protection of children from abuse, neglect, exploitation, or moral hazard.

*   *   *

There is a final group of questions that is being asked. These concern the complementary part of child development. For example, we have just discussed the rights of children. What now are their responsibilities? In return for the years of their rearing and preparation to play their role as adults, what do children owe in return? In contrast to the current emphasis upon the rights of children, the necessity for maintaining high standards for their development, and the need for ever prolonging the period of their preparation, one finds very little reference to reciprocal responsibilities. Is this a proper balance? Is life all take, and little or no give? What do children owe their parents? Their schools? Their college? Their community? The larger society? Are these questions not equal in importance to the standards of their development? Is not the price of early development that of subsequent responsibility? Does not the balance scale of life demand this? Does anything less spell inevitably the anomaly of social bankruptcy?

We talk constantly about developing the individual child. Into what sort of child are we developing him?

Are there abiding verities in life which could serve as the basic goals of child development? Is self-discipline one of these? In a society in which the role of the intimate primary groups has given way largely to the impersonal specialized controls of secondary groups, must not much more reliance for the behavior of the individual rest upon the inner springs of conduct? Is consideration for one's family one of these verities? The family is not only a vehicle for the development of the personalities of its individual members, but it is also the connecting link between successive generations, a group device for the perpetuation both of life and of civilization. Can a society survive without the general acceptance of familism as a supreme value?

Is consideration of one's fellows one of the eternal verities? Is the revival and detailed expression of this the basic remedy to the "institutional chaos" and "moral anarchy" which modern scholars decry? Does the right to one's own development inevitably involve recognition of the rights of others to their growth and development? Is one possible, in the last analysis, without the other? After all, the developing individual is surrounded by other individuals who also seek their respective developments.

This problem of values is one which social scientists in general, and sociologists in particular, tend to evade. While the role of the learned man in the past was generally that of emphasizing and conserving traditional values, the modern scientist claims that values "may not be derived by science, and therefore science should have nothing to do with them. . . . It prefers to say that for science the word 'ought' ought never to be used, except in saying that it ought never to be used."[2]

Actually, this is a good deal of a pose, without foundation of fact. Values inhere in everything the scientist does — the problems which he selects, those which he avoids, his evaluation of data, his methods of research, and his treatment of conclusions. "Research without an ac-

2. Robert S. Lynd, *Knowledge for What?*, Princeton University Press, Princeton, 1939, p. 181.

tively selective point of view becomes the ditty bag of an idiot, filled with bits of pebbles, straws, feathers, and other random hoardings."[3]

Yielding to no one in the insistence that the sociologist be pure in his lack of bias and detached in his gathering and appraising of data, it still seems relevant to us to point out that the values of society are what give direction, scope, and significance to scientific analysis, whatever its particular value may be. The concepts, the methods, and the content of the sociology of child development all take meaning from their relation to the needs and values of children *and of the society* in which they live. The determination of these needs and values may well constitute the next stage in the development of the sociology of childhood.

Trends in Childrearing Theory

Since 1900, with the tremendous growth in mass communications of all kinds, including books and magazines, the American public has been bombarded with advice and theories on childrearing, as no public has been at any time or in any place before.

Theories do not arise out of a vacuum, but are related to social movements and ideologies of the times. Often they are ephemeral and seem more like fads than theories when they have passed away for a newer one. This is especially true in a fast-changing culture. Rapid change means also that a theory of childrearing may not be tested out long enough to assess accurately its results. Certain unfavorable aspects of it may appear and a frequent reaction to it sets in—if this way of rearing children does not seem effective, the opposite way must be the correct way. Thus, the possible good is thrown out with the suspected bad and another extreme is launched upon for a time, even though the results of that cannot be predicted either.

That much of this cyclical change of childrearing theory has existed in the United States had been spelled out by Celia Stendler in a survey of materials in popular women's magazines from 1890 to 1950.[4] During the early period of this century the articles stressed the physical development of the child, specific behavior problems, and the instilling of good moral character through such traits as "courtesy, honesty, orderliness, industriousness, and generosity; character, not personality development, was the focal point."[5] A "Christian" atmosphere in the home was stressed as an essential, and the mother was thought of as the keystone of the home. Although they were given advice, "Mothers occupied a position of importance which they have never since recovered. This was the day when Mother knew best; there was no book, no scientific authority to shake her maternal self-confidence, and she could tend her flock with the calm assurance that her 'instincts' were

3. *Ibid.,* p. 183.
4. Celia B. Stendler, "Sixty Years of Child Training Practices," *The Journal of Pediatrics,* January, 1950, pp. 122-134.
5. *Ibid,* p. 125.

right." [6] The modes of operation suggested were setting a good example for the children to imitate; invoking God's help; and disciplining through love.

By 1910 a change was taking place. Apparently love, spiritual influences, and imitation were not effective enough. Now the advice turned to strict upbringing through punishment for misbehavior, and this was to be started early by rigid schedules, letting the baby cry it out instead of being picked up, and by being restrained in demonstrations of affection. The medical profession, during this period, were concerned over the high rate of infant mortality and urged careful regimens in order to combat it. Their advice on physical regimen, in itself not tested out, was taken over by the literary "experts" and extended to the general area of childrearing.

In the 1920s period, J. B. Watson began to influence theories about raising children. Their behavior, he said, was conditioned by very specific stimuli. If parents catered to them in moments of bad behavior they would be conditioned to continue it. Thus, strict regulation of the child continued to be the advice although it was not merely for their physical benefit but also for the sake of rearing properly conditioned human beings.

Under the growing influence of Sigmund Freud, G. Stanley Hall, and others, the advice of the 1930s softened greatly toward children. Fixations can occur at any point in life and the budding personality of the baby must not be repressed. That would inevitably mark the kind of adult he is to become. At the same time nutritionists were coming into their own and mothers became vitamin and diet conscious. "Interestingly enough, along with increased interest in scientific feeding in the twenties and thirties went more attention to feeding problems. There were more articles devoted to finicky eaters and slow eaters during these two decades than at any other time." [7] (Quite recently, pediatricians have been pointing out that too much anxiety in the mother concerning feeding can definitely cause eating problems.) Also, at this time, the moral behavior of children took second place to their personality development, a concept almost unheard of in the earlier literature.

By the 1940s, the change from toughness to permissiveness in rearing was almost complete. Permissiveness would produce two important things, a sense of security and a healthy personality. It was during this period that developmental theory also became popular. Arnold Gesell and Frances Ilg's writings became bibles for many parents who watched with interest, and sometimes with dismay, the process of maturation in their children as compared with the children in the studies.

Orville Brim has interpreted these variations against the background of cultural change rather than explicit scientific knowledge

6. *Ibid.*, pp. 126-127.
7. *Ibid.*, p. 130.

about children and their rearing.[8] The first part of this century, he says, witnessed the beginning of women coming into their own after a nineteenth-century male aggressive attitude toward children. The 1910-1930 period represented "the age of mother"—women coming, perhaps, too much into their own, and resulting in a subjugation of baby to her own needs. The rigid scheduling may have worked out better for mother than for baby. Dr. Brim calls the after 1935 period "the baby's decade" when the child came into his own.

. . .there are voices being raised suggesting that the child has now come too much into his own, and that some balance should be struck between developing their personalities and giving them discipline and good character—a word that was almost lost in the literature for a long period. No less a figure in advice to parents than Dr. Spock has recently been spelling out a modified program of childrearing aimed at these very things. There are, also, many voices, not always professional ones, advocating a return to the "get-tough-with-them" school of thought. Enough are heard in order to indicate that what was considered the proper way in one era may be thought of as entirely foolish in another. A superintendent of police has recently blamed the increasing delinquency in suburban areas to parental lack of discipline. A poll of more than a thousand young people, from coast to coast, revealed that those who had the most lenient discipline were the very ones most in favor of the get-tough theory. A similar poll of college students showed that when they themselves become parents they expect to give their children more responsibility, more discipline, and more spankings. More than one teen-ager has construed the lack of limitations put on him as meaning that his parents do not care enough about him to concern themselves. A teen-age girl asked her mother to *tell* her what she could and could not do. "Then I can tell them I'm not allowed to and can blame it on you, instead of having to decide against the other kids on my own!"

Another recent trend is a theory that there is no specific right or wrong way to rear a child. Neither permissiveness nor strict discipline are the things that affect the child. Rather, it is the manner in which the parents administer their discipline and the way in which they and the child relate to each other. The "atmosphere of the home" is the all-important thing. Unfortunately, no one has so far spelled out very concretely just what "manner" and what "atmosphere" are conducive for proper childrearing, nor, indeed, what is our desired end in the childrearing process. An attempt to define these things and explain them may be the next step toward new advice for parents.

8. Orville G. Brim, Jr., "Changes and Trends in Child-Rearing Advice," *Child Study,* Fall, 1959, pp. 23-27.

Children in the Family: Relationship of Number and Spacing to Marital Success

HAROLD T. CHRISTENSEN

"The Principle of Value Relevance" says that the values people hold are relevant to their behavior and to the consequences of this behavior. Applied to the problem at hand, it means that sheer number and spacing patterns within the family are less determining of marital success than are the degrees of convergence between actual and desired patterns. Values are an important part of the equation; they are intervening variables and, as such, must be taken into account. At least this is the hypothesis. Now let us examine the evidence.

How Family Size Affects the Marriage

In many societies — particularly those of the historical past and of the non-Western world today — blood bonds are stronger than marital bonds, and hence the parent-child relationship is considered more important than the husband-wife relationship. Not so in the contemporary Western family system, however, and particularly "not so" within the United States today. Here, the consanguine or extended family, which cuts across several generations, has given ground to the nuclear family of husband, wife, and immediate children; kinship ties have been greatly weakened, and children have come to be regarded almost as an appendage to, rather than the reason for, the marriage. In other times and places, asking how parenthood affects the marriage would likely be considered inappropriate. Here and now the question is quite relevant.

It is popularly assumed that children and marital happiness go together and are causally related. This notion is part of our folklore, and at first glance it seems to be given support by the fact that over half of all divorces involve childless couples, suggesting that children hold a marriage together. But these statistics are deceptive, since most divorces occur in the early years of marriage before many couples would normally start their childbearing and, furthermore, since the association of divorce with childlessness does not prove that these are causally related, only, perhaps, that they are "concomitant results of more fundamental factors in the marital relationship."[1] At any rate, the widely held belief that children serve to bring husband and wife closer together needs to be carefully reexamined. Perhaps they do in some

cases, while in other instances children may be destructive to the
marital relationship. And, if this latter is *ever* the case, we need to know
what it is that makes the difference.

There can be little question but that parenthood in some ways affects
the quality of marital interaction. Both LeMasters[2] and Dyer[3] have
demonstrated that the birth of the first child constitutes a crisis for
parents: by turning the twosome into a threesome and by adding extra
chores, especially demanding of the mother, which reduce the time
and energy that husband and wife have for each other. Before the
advent of parenthood there is only one relationship, husband and wife.
With the first child the number is increased to four: husband and wife,
father and child, mother and child, and the interacting triad composed
of all three. Furthermore, with each additional child, relationship
combinations within the family increase in this same exponential fashion, making for greater and greater complexity and fundamentally
changing the interactional pattern of the original married pair.

Though the ways in which family size may affect marital interaction
need to be further researched, some generalizations can be at least
tentatively identified. As number of children to the couple increases,
husband and wife experience more interference with their sexual
relationship; find less time for shared activities; and move toward
greater role specialization, often including a shift in power from an
equalitarian toward an authoritarian, or even patriarchal, base. If this
latter is true, that is, that the husband's influence goes up with size of
family, as some research suggests, this may be because the mother of
many children has less bargaining power, since, because of her children, she is in greater need of a husband and in a poorer position to
remarry or to find work.[4]

There have been more than a dozen studies testing the possibility of
a relationship between family size and marital adjustment — with
contradictory results. Several of these studies have reported no relationship, some a relationship in the positive direction, others a relationship in the negative direction, and still others have ended up with
irregular and/or ambiguous generalization.[5] Why is there such a confused picture, since, in most cases, the scholars are reputable? Undoubtedly part of the explanation lies in the variety of samples used and the
differing research designs employed. But surely if there is a general
relationship between these variables it would have shown up more
consistently, even granting divergent samples and designs. Perhaps the
key to our question is to be found in the conclusion of Lewis M.
Terman: he reported, for his sample, no correlation between presence
of children and happiness in marriage, but suggested that this may be
because opposing influences tend to balance each other out in a large
sample and that the presence of children may actually affect any given
marriage either way.[6]

After reviewing the literature and noting the contradictory results,
Udry said, "there is no reliable relationship between presence or ab-

sence of children and marital adjustment"[7]; and Burgess and Wallin concluded:

> The research evidence presented in this chapter establishes with considerable if not complete conclusiveness that the fact of having or not having children is not associated with marital success. What is associated with marital success is the attitude of husbands and wives toward having children. Persons with higher marital success scores to tend to have a stronger desire for children, whether they have them or not, than those with lower marital success scores.[8]

Yet both of these sets of writers elsewhere recognized that disproportionately low marital adjustment goes along with having children that are not wanted.[9] Evidently the decisive factor is not number of children, in and of itself, but the extent to which children are desired.

Nevertheless, it is our contention that desires (or values) can be most productive of understanding on this problem if they are treated as an intervening variable, rather than as a separate independent variable. To say that couples who desire children tend to be better adjusted than those who do not is one thing; it supports the reasonable assumption that family-mindedness contributes to marital harmony. But what of the connection between desires and practice, and of the effect of *this combination* (balance of desires with practice) upon marital success? We would hypothesize that if the parental values of husband and wife were adequately taken into account and treated as intervening variables against which the relationships between family size and marital adjustment were studied, the research results of the various studies would be more consistent and the relationship sought would show up more clearly. Continuing research is likely to reveal that it is not either values (desires for children) or behavior (children actually born) considered alone that are the crucial variables affecting the marriage, but rather the "value-behavior discrepancy"[10] (or lack of it) which leaves married couples in varying states of harmony or dissonance.

Support for this view was offered in an article by Christensen and Philbrick published more than a decade ago.[11] From an interview study of married college students, it was demonstrated that, for the sample involved, a positive relationship existed between *desired* number of children and marital adjustment score, while a negative relationship (up to two children and for wives, especially) existed between *actual* number of children and marital adjustment score. This apparent contradiction is to be explained by the fact that, though family mindedness (desire for children) is normally associated with marital adjustment, when the desired children come before the couple is ready for them (because of the pressures of school in this case), values are violated and marital maladjustment results. Reinforcement of this interpretation was provided by several additional findings: disproportionately low marital adjustment scores were discovered for couples (a) with "unplanned" children, (b) who said they would have fewer children if starting over again, or (c) would wait until after college either to marry or to start their families if they had it to do over again, or (d) who regarded their dual activities of college attendance and parenthood as interfering with each other. In other words, by whichever measure used, marital adjustment was lowest where there was a discrepancy between what was desired and what actually happened. This was the overall conclusion, and it was presented as being in harmony with Reed's earlier finding, in the Indianapolis Fertility Study, that marital adjustment increases according to the ability of couples to control fertility in line with their desires.[12]

How Child-Spacing Affects the Marriage

The Indianapolis Fertility Study also presented evidence to suggest that married couples are more successful in controlling the number of their children than the spacing of them. Regarding spacing, it was shown in that study that while some two-thirds of the wives in all groups thought the most desirable interval to first birth would be from two to three years, only a relatively small proportion of them actually had the first child at that time. The discrepancies between desire and practice were in opposite directions according to degree of planning success: about two-thirds of the "number-and-spacing-planned" wives waited longer than three years, while some three-fifths of the "number-planned" and the "too-many pregnancies" groups (higher in the latter) had the first child in less than two years. And the same general patterns showed up for the spacing of second and subsequent children.[13] Thus, when planning is successful, child-spacing intervals tend to overshoot the couple's desires, whereas when planning is unsuccessful actual intervals turn out to be shorter than desired intervals.

But, though the Indianapolis Fertility Study demonstrated a clear relationship between marital adjustment and the ability to control the *number* of children in line with desires, no evidence was presented on the possibility of a similar relationship between marital adjustment and the ability to *space* the children according to the couple's desires. It is to this latter problem that attention is now directed.

It will be recalled that, typically, American couples today space their first child about 18 months from the marriage, with second and subsequent births coming after progressively longer intervals and with the smaller families showing the larger intervals and vice versa. But the most important questions for our purposes have to do with the *effects* of the various alternative spacing patterns, and most especially their effects upon the marriage. Is it better to start the family as soon as possible or to postpone childbearing for a while after the marriage? Is it better to leave the children close together so that they can be companions to each other and so that parents can get their childrearing burdens over within a shorter but more concentrated period, leaving more time free later on for other things; or is it better to have them far apart to reduce sibling rivalry and strain on the mother and to permit parents to enjoy children at home at a more leisurely pace and for a longer portion of the family cycle?

Parents and prospective parents debate these questions, while at the same time being exposed to advice from physicians and varieties of child specialists. Obstetricians, with a primary concern for the mother's health, tend to recommend spacing intervals of from two to three years. Pediatricians and child development specialists look more toward what is best for the health and development of the offspring, but their counsel with reference to spacing seems less consistent. In neither instance has there been much concern with the effects of spacing patterns *upon the marriage;* and in both instances reliance for the positions taken has been more upon clinical experience and logical deduction than upon quantitative research. At any rate, there is a crying need for more and better reserach on this problem. And, it is our hunch that, when the necessary data are in, the crucial variable will be shown to be, not child-spacing pattern standing alone, but how successful parents are in controlling spacing to fit their desires. In other words, we hypothisze here, as we did earlier when dealing with family size, that values are an intervening variable and that it is value-behavior discrepancy that makes the difference.

There is at least some evidence to support this hypothesis. In their study, *Family Growth in Metropolitan America,*[14] Westoff and colaborators found the following: (1) twenty-one percent of the wives said that the first child came too soon, and ten percent that it came too late according to their desires. (2) As one moves from very short to increasingly long intervals between marriage and first child, the percent thinking that this child came too soon decreases and the percent thinking it came too late increases. Where the interval was less than eight months, for example, 55 percent thought that the timing was too soon and none thought it was too late; whereas, with an interval of 42-53 months, none thought the timing was too soon and 31 percent thought it too late. A similar relationship was found to hold between the interval separating first and second child and percentages of couples thinking the timing was either too soon or too late. (3) Of those who thought the timing of the first child was too soon, 19 percent said that it interfered with marital adjustment, 26 percent with enjoying things with husbands, and 41 percent with readying finances. Furthermore, with respect to each of these problems, the interference was deemed greatest by the wives experiencing the shortest intervals and smallest by the wives experiencing the longest intervals to first child. (4) Desired interval between first and second child involved a balancing of wanting children far enough apart to ease the burden of infant care with wanting them close enough together to insure that they become playmates. The tendency was to consider two to two and one-half years as the interval of optimum balance. (5) Preferred intervals to first, second, and third births showed considerable variation, which suggests a high degree of flexibility or adaptability regarding child-spacing. Respondents perceived "a broad span of interval length as not causing serious inconvenience." [15]

It will be noted that the Westoff study of preferred birth intervals was based upon retrospective judgments and, furthermore, that it did not relate actual spacing patterns to any objective measure of marital success. The closest it came to our present problem is represented in the third point of the above paragraph, namely, that those who thought the first child came too soon saw this as interference with one or more aspects of marriage adjustment—subjectively decided. Nevertheless, this does support our notion of maladjustment resulting from value-behavior discrepancy.

The writer's previously reported cross-cultural research on timing of first pregnancy[16] throws some additional light upon the problem at hand. It was a record-linkage analysis of marriage, birth, and divorce files based on samples from sexually permissive Denmark, sexually restrictive Mormondom in the intermountain region of the United States, and midwestern United States, which is in between but was found to be nearer the restrictive than the permissive end of the continuum. Bringing the three-set records together on a case-matching basis produced a neat longitudinal design having distinct methodological advantages. Since official vital records were used and the matching was done without the knowledge of subjects, problems of distortion through nonresponse and of falsification by respondents were largely eliminated, and other errors were confined to those already in the official records.

Child-spacing patterns were found to differ considerably across the three cultures studied. In the Danish sample some 24.2 percent of all first births came within the first six months of marriage (indicating premarital pregnancy), 36.5 percent within the first year of marriage, and 54.1 percent within the first two years of marriage. Comparable percentages for the Indiana sample were 9.4, 41.8, and 73.4 respectively; and for the Utah sample 3.4, 40.9, and 77.1, respectively. Thus, Denmark shows up disproportionately high on premarital conception and low on early postmarital conception, while in the United States samples—and especially Utah—the picture is just the reverse of this.

Of particular significance was the finding that the overall relationship between pregnancy timing and divorce rate is negative. Specifically, premarital pregnancy was more frequently followed by divorce than was postmarital pregnancy, and early postmarital pregnancy was more frequently followed by divorce than delayed postmarital pregnancy. Reasons for the association of divorce with premarital pregnancy seem to be, first, the fact that some premarital conceivers are pressured into marriage and lack either love or background preparation and, second, the probability that substantial numbers in this category harbor guilt feeelings or fear discovery or disapproval, any of which can make anxiety and interfere with adjustment. Similarly, there appear to be at least two good reasons for the association of divorce with early postmarital conception. In the first place, larger proportions of early conceivers may be presumed to have been unsuccessful in their birth-control attempts,[17] and there is strong evidence, as pointed out earlier in this paper, that couples with unplanned children have below-average marital adjustment.[18] In the second place, it may be tentatively assumed—though there is need for careful testing on this point—that the very early postmarital conceivers may be complicating their adjustments by having a child before there has been time for their own marital relationships to achieve stability.

Now, how do values intervene to qualify this picture of an overall negative relationship between length of interval to first birth and subsequent divorce rate? Since the vital records which provide the data told nothing of the couples' *desires* regarding the spacing of their children, the problem could not be approached on an individual case basis. But, since the differing fertility norms of the three societies are rather well know, it was possible to get at the problem by means of cross-cultural analysis. As to premarital pregnancy, it was expected that (though each of the three cultures showed somewhat higher divorce of these cases than for the postmarital conceivers) the *difference* in premarital versus postmarital conceiver divorce rates would be least in the most permissive culture (Denmark) and greatest in the most restrictive culture (Utah), simply because premarital pregnancy is closer to the norm of Denmark and most divergent from the norm of Utah; hence, more easily coped within the former while resulting in strains and dislocations in the latter. Research findings gave clear support to this hypothesis: *divorce-rate differentials* between premarital and postmarital conceivers turned out to be 62.2 percent in Denmark, 141.4 percent in Indiana, and 405.9 percent in Utah.[19]

As to early versus later postmarital conception, it was hypothesized that (though each of the three cultures showed somewhat higher divorce for the early starters) *divorce-rate differentials* would be greatest in the culture whose norm is to delay conception after marriage (Denmark) and least in the culture whose norm encourages early postmarital conception (Utah). Reasons for this expectation were similar to those relating to premarital pregnancy: it was thought that behavior which deviates from the norm would cause more difficulty than behavior which is in line with the norm of its group. Support for this hypothesis was only partial. Divorce-rate differentials between early (birth during 10-12 months of marriage) and later (birth during second year of marriage) postmarital conceivers turned out to be 17.1 percent for Denmark, 30.0 percent for Indiana, and 2.9 percent for Utah.[20] Why the differential was lower for Denmark than Indiana cannot be determined from the data. But at least it was lowest of all in Utah, where early postmarital conception has the most cultural support.

Recapitulation of the Theory

This brings us to a resting place in our story, at least for now. Both number and spacing of children in the family have been seen as affecting the quality of the marriage. But they do not affect marriage in precisely the same way for all couples. Though most husbands and wives want at least one child, some are "allergic" to even that one; and, though most want some delay before starting the family and some control over the spacing of children after that, not all couples do. People vary considerably in their desires concerning both family size and child-spacing. Hence, number and spacing patterns may affect any given marriage either way, which can help explain why statistical studies that ignore the value variable are often inconclusive and/or contradictory.

The evidence we have strongly suggests that marital success is affected by both number and spacing of children, but that even more crucial than these factors, considered by themselves, is the degree to which couples are able to control number and spacing according to their desires. Values, in other words, are an important part of the equation; they constitute an intervening variable which cannot be ignored. The key questions then become, not: "How many children?" but "Does the number one has line up with the number he wants?" not: "How are the children spaced?" but: "Does the spacing pattern conform with the desires of the couple?" It is value-behavior discrepancy that works against the marriage—more than either values or behavior considered alone. This was demonstrated for family size by taking into account in a limited sample the personal values of the respondents, and for child-spacing by taking into account differing social norms and comparing them cross-culturally.

REFERENCES

1. Paul H. Jacobson, "Differentials in Divorce by Duration of Marriage and Size of Family," *American Sociological Review*, 15:2 (April, 1950), p. 244.

2. E. E. LeMasters, "Parenthood as Crisis," *Marriage and Family Living*, 19:4 (November, 1957), pp. 352-355.

3. E. D. Dyer, "Parenthood as Crisis: A Re-study," *Marriage and Family Living*, 25:2 (May, 1963), pp. 196-201.

4. Cf. J. Richard Udry, *The Social Context of Marriage*, Philadelphia: Lippincott, 1966, pp. 360-361; 452-453; 489-495. In addition to his own discussion, this author cites the following research reports as bearing on the problem: Robert O. Blood and Donald M. Wolfe, *Husbands and Wives*, New York: Free Press, a division of the Macmillan Co., 1960; James H. S. Bossard, *The Large Family System*, Philadelphia: University of Pennsylvania Press, 1956; and several articles by David M. Heer, including "The Measurement and Bases of Family Power: An

Overview," *Marriage and Family Living*, 35:2 (May, 1963), pp. 133-139.

5. Brief reviews of these various studies can be found in: Udry, *op. cit.*, pp. 488-489; Ernest W. Burgess and Paul Wallin, *Engagement and Marriage*, Philadelphia: Lippincott, 1953, pp. 713-715; and Harold T. Christensen and Robert E. Philbrick, "Family Size as a Factor in the Marital Adjustments of College Couples," *American Sociological Review*, 17:3 (June, 1952), pp. 306-312.

6. Lewis M. Terman, *Psychological Factors in Marital Happiness*, New York: McGraw-Hill, 1938, pp. 171-173.

7. Udry, *op. cit.*, p. 489.

8. Burgess and Wallin, *op. cit.*, p. 722.

9. Udry, *op. cit.*, pp. 456, 488; Burgess and Wallin, *op. cit.*, pp. 715-719.

10. A phrase first used in the writer's (with George R. Carpenter) "Value-Behavior Discrepancies Regarding Premarital Coitus in Three Western Cultures," *American Sociological Review*, 27:1 (February, 1962). pp. 66-74. The concept is as relevant to the present analysis on family size and child-spacing as it was to the earlier one on premarital coitus; in fact, it *may be generally applicable* to problems of human behavior and its consequences.

11. Christensen and Philbrick, *loc. cit.*

12. Robert B. Reed, *Social and Psychological Factors Affecting Fertility*, VII, "The Interrelationship of Marital Adjustment, Fertility Control, and Size of Family," New York: Milbank Memorial Fund, 1948, pp. 383-425.

13. P. K. Whelpton and Clyde V. Kiser, *Social and Psychological Factors Affecting Fertility*, VI, "The Planning of Fertility," New York: Milbank Memorial Fund, 1950, pp. 209-257.

14. Charles Westoff, Robert G. Potter, Philip G. Sagi, and Elliot G. Mishler, *Family Growth in Metropolitan America*, Princeton, New Jersey: Princeton University Press, 1961, pp. 116-135.

15. *Ibid.*, p. 134.

16. Harold T. Christensen, "Timing of First Pregnancy as a Factor in Divorce: A Cross-Cultural Analysis," *Eugenics Quarterly*, 10:3 (September, 1963), pp. 119-130. Several earlier articles are referenced in this one.

17. Cf. S. Poffenberger, T. Poffenberger, and J. T. Landis, "Intent Toward Conception and the Pregnancy Experience," *American Sociology Review*, 17:5 (October, 1952), pp. 616-620.

18. Christensen and Philbrick, *loc. cit.*

19. Christensen, *op. cit.*, p. 126.

20. *Ibid.*, p. 126.

Non-Sexist Childrearing: De-Mythifying Normative Data

GLORIA TISHLER HIRSCH

Introduction

This paper presents a rationale for focusing on breaking down sex-role stereotypes through group process in order to help individual human beings realize their optimum human growth and potential. The potential of human beings for becoming unique and self-actualized along multi-dimensions, not constrained by biological sex, is evident from individual instances of "thinking" women and men, and "feeling" women and men. Each exception raises a challenge to the use of rigid role stereotyping on the basis of sex.

Hidden Assumptions Underlying Socialization for Normative Behavior

Western religio-philosophy is predicated upon patriarchal, male-dominated assumptions. Because philosophy provides the underpinning for science, much research in the behavioral sciences has unknowingly acted upon or within this structure.

From philosophy:

> We may thus conclude that it is a general law that there should be naturally ruling elements and elements naturally ruled . . . the rule of the free man over the slave is one kind of rule; that of the male over the female another . . . (Aristotle, *Politics*)
> Women may be said to be an inferior man. (Aristotle)

From religion:

> For a man . . . is the image and glory of God; but the woman is the glory of the man. For the man is not of the woman, but the woman of the man. Neither was the man created for the woman, but the woman for the man. (I Corinthian, 11:14)
> Let the woman learn in silence with all subjection. But I suffer not a woman to teach, nor to usurp authority over the man, but to be in silence. For Adam was first formed, then Eve. And Adam was not deceived, but the woman, being deceived, was in the transgression. Notwithstanding, she shall be saved in childbearing, if they continue in faith and charity and holiness with sobriety. (I Timothy, 2, 11-15)

Scientific positivism was developed by individuals who had been steeped in those assumptions, values, and biases. Even the so-called objective, scientific approach has hardly been objective, but has, in fact, reinforced the prevailing constraints and parameters of Western civilization.

From science:

> If the feminine abilities were developed to the same degree as those of the male, her (woman's) maternal organs would suffer and we should have a repulsive and useless hybrid. (Moebius, 1907)

NORMATIVE DATA AND MYTHS

Normative data are that information behavioral scientists obtain by looking at the "product" around them, "what is." Derived from persons already enculturated in the assigned sex-roles, such data tell no more about the "real" nature of woman and man than did the ancient myths. We ask the "product" to involve itself in the investigation and check off interests and inclinations and then make lists of attributes which are considered "natural" or innate for females and males. In so doing we ignore the fact that we have not separated what is biological from the result of the biological organism interacting with and receiving the impact of society.

If the subtle biases and hidden assumptions were not held so strongly and unconsciously, we might use information about human flexibility and capability more productively, instead of adapting uncritically tenets which make "male" superior and healthy and "female" inferior and deviant.

Whenever people move to change their social environments, the defenders of tradition tend to rise to the occasion by proclaiming the natural or "instinctive" basis for traditional patterns. As Thomas Huxley said, "Every great advance in natural knowledge has involved the absolute rejection of authority." Although biological differences have often been associated with differences in social opportunity or social power, this does not prove that differences in social power or social behavior between men and women are in themselves innate or immutable.

There are many mechanisms of social control, some more subtle than others. The socialization process, the climate of opinion in which people live, the group ideology (political or religious), the available social structures, the mass media, the popular literature, the legal system and the formal educational system are only some of the means society has at its disposal to channel people into the roles it finds necessary for its maintenance.

There is a real question about the validity of using normative data as a basis for sex role definition and sex role assignment. Gender and the functions of physical parts which determine biological sex are more free of cultural contamination. The tentativeness with which we hold what we formerly took to be scientific fact — e.g., because females are biological mothers, they also need to serve in mothering roles — is beginning to be widely acknowledged. Even Dr. Benjamin Spock has reversed his previous position about male and female inherent proclivities and no longer claims that women and men have predetermined roles and tasks based on biology (1972).

The contemporary myths of normative behavior — predetermination of people's choices in life on the basis of sex without regard to individual differences — is damaging to the humanity of all. Not only is deviance from the normative standard punished, but, even more damaging, the feminine standard itself is negatively perceived. The "normal" woman is considered by society to be deviant from a normal, healthy, functioning adult person (Broverman, 1970). Despite the fact that certain "feminine" traits attributed to females are valuable and desirable traits for all human beings, (tenderness, sensitivity) a negative value is placed on them because they are considered female. Despite the fact that domestic work and child rearing are necessary, valuable, and useful skills, they are widely perceived as secondary and degraded in importance.

An important characteristic of normative behavior is its forced nature — rigid roles for boys and men, rigid roles for girls and women — which ignores the common humanity and overlap of potentials and capabilities. However, such forcing and coercion is so very subtle (Bem and Bem, 1970) that all of us, male and female, come to adulthood believing we have chosen freely to do the tasks and wear the masks of our socialization.

Here the "scientific" data used to support the present societal roles is most insidious and sexist. It not only predetermines the shape of socialization, but it also places a higher value on male characteristics, values, and tasks. Yet, even men in their superior positions have a very hollow circumstance, because the very dichotomy prevents all concerned, even "superior" parties, from attaining full humanity.

SOCIAL-PSYCHOLOGICAL RESEARCH

One of the present imperative needs is for open research, the kind that acts as if we had empty notebooks, blank journals, and only questions. Some available research does raise questions about present practices of using stereotyped role designations and point toward the need for changes.

In 1968, an important series of studies was done by Inga K. Broverman and associates at Worcester State Hospital in Massachusetts. They constructed a "Sex-Stereotype Questionnaire" consisting of "122 Bipolar Items" — characteristics socially known or socially tested as male or female (aggression, independence, logic, ambition, opposed to tact, gentleness, quiet, dependence). Their studies indicated that stereotypically masculine traits are more often perceived as socially desirable than those considered feminine.

The Worcester researchers used their 122 items to test the assumptions of clinical psychologists about mental health (Broverman, 1970). Three matched groups of male and female clinical psychologists were given three identical lists of the 122 items unlabeled and printed in random order. Each group was given a different set of instructions: One was told to choose traits that characterize the healthy adult male; another to choose those of the healthy adult female; the third to choose those of the healthy adult — a person. The clinically healthy male and the clinically healthy adult were identical, and totally divergent from the clinically healthy female. The authors of the study concluded that "a double standard of health exists for men and women" (1970, 5). That is, the general standard of health applies only to men. Women are perceived as "less healthy" by those standards called "adult." At the same time, if a woman deviates from the sexual stereotypes prescribed for her — if she grows more active or aggressive, for example — she does not grow healthier. She may, in fact, be perceived as sick.

The distortions become so great, according to psychologist Phillip Goldberg, that by the time girls reach college they have become prejudiced against women. Goldberg (1968) asked female college students to rate a number of professional articles from traditional male, female, and neutral fields. The articles were identical, but the names of the authors were not. One set of articles was attributed to a male author, "John T. McKay," and another set was attributed to a female author, "Joan T. McKay." Each student was asked to read the articles in her booklet and to rate them for such factors as value, competence, persuasiveness, and writing style. The male authors fared better in every field, even in such "feminine" areas as art history and dietetics. Goldberg concluded that "women are prejudiced against female professionals and, regardless of the actual accomplishments of these professionals, will firmly refuse to recognize them as equals of their male colleagues" (1968, 30).

Since most counselors, psychologists, and psychiatrists are agreed that a feeling of self-value is a necessary attribute for a positively functioning human being (Maslow, 1954, rev. 1970; Rogers, 1961) it can be assumed that this refers to both women and men. One psychologist, Robert White (1961), has posited an innate drive for "competence" in human beings, the expression of which is necessary to mental health and feelings of self-worth. Sociologist Jean Lipman-Blumen (1972) found that most women will "think in terms of marrying a doctor rather than in terms of going to medical school." She suggests that women will not seek out opportunities for themselves if they perceive the seeking to be "inappropriate" behavior. Since social control agencies encourage and reward for personal success and achievement, vicarious achievement obviously is not the accepted basis for success, nor does it fulfill the need for "competency behavior."

Matina Horner, an experimental psychologist at the University of Michigan, has done testing and studies which indicate that women exhibit an active, anxious desire to avoid success (1970). Dr. Horner administered a series of thematic apperception tests to 90 female and 88 male undergraduates at the University of Michigan. Women showed significantly more evidence of the motive to avoid success than did men, 59 of them scoring high on this variable, as contrasted with only eight of the men.

What happens to most women, says Dr. Horner, is simple. Parents encourage their daughters to fulfill their entire potential and allow them some of the advantages given to men. The encouragement, however, is essentially hollow. The contradictory message that the girl gets, from society as well as her parents, is that if she is too smart, too independent, and above all, too serious about her work, she is "unfeminine" and will therefore never get married. The implication, clearly, is that the girl is predisposed to accept this notion that "feminity" and academic achievement are incompatible. She goes into a tailspin of anxiety as she struggles to reverse her appetite for human fulfillment, an appetite she learns is in direct contradiction to her "feminine fulfillment."

Non-Sexist Childrearing: New Directions

Non-sexist childrearing demands completely open possibilities for developing the "human" potential in both females and males. It attempts to create the equality (not sameness) of the sexes—legally, socially, educationally, psychologically, politically, religiously, economically —in and out of the home. The subtle variables which produce individuals known as "feminine" and "masculine" need to be defined and described. Behavorial scientists have an obligation to help families ascertain and question what is considered natural and what is possible in the development of whole human persons.

The Power Variable. Children learn about sex roles very early in their lives. They form their first responses in the context of how they are handled as infants and babies. They learn from a pervading feeling-climate who (which sex) is more/most important, and learn about the power-dynamic of the household (Sampson, 1965).

"Power" is a crucial variable, probably the most influential one affecting the child's growth and development. It is related to the development of feelings of self-worth and self-esteem because both of these require the individual to feel in charge and in control of his or her own life.

Bandura, Ross, and Ross (1963) in a study to explore identificatory learning found that children ages 33 to 665 months clearly identified with the source of rewarding power.

> Even at this young age a number of these children were firmly
> convinced that only a male can possess resources and, therefore,

the female dispensing the rewards was only an intermediary for the male model. (For example, 'He's the man and it's all his because he's a daddy. Mommy never really has things belong to her ... He's the daddy so it's his but he shares nice with the mommy ... He's the man and the man always really has the money and he lets ladies play, too'.) This view of resource ownership within the family constellation was often directly reinforced by the mothers. (For example, 'My mommy told me and Joan that the daddy really buys all the things, but the mommy looks after things.') (Bandura, Ross and Ross, 1963, 533)

This element is expressed through an authority male (head of household) who has a subordinate wife and children. It is written into our legal systems as well as embodied in our axioms for enculturation, e.g., family law reflects the encoding of this dynamic and job opportunities and rewards reflect the same power bias. The result is a continuous reinforcement of the status quo whereby young males are reared to be in charge and young females to cooperate as subordinates.

Sincere questions can be asked about what is wrong with such a system. After all, in every society there must be division of labor. The response is that if the division of labor resulted in equal respect and regard for both males and females, then perhaps our present system would be acceptable. The enormous range of behaviors which homo sapiens is capable of producing, because of the structure of the higher cortex, frees humans from the necessity of rigid adherence to stereotyped assignment of roles on a sexist basis.

A Group Program. As a practitioner, I work with clients who are seeking to rear their children in a non-sexist manner and live in non-sexist ways themselves. Group sessions seem to be the most effective approach for producing dissonance, awareness, and behavioral change.

Twelve such groups of interested parents, with fourteen participants per group, have met for periods of five to fifteen months. They met once a week for two-and-a-half hours. Group processes include discussion and encounter of practices, goals, and attitudes of the members about childrearing.

The groups have operated on the following explicit assumptions:

1. Every human being prefers to act caringly and to be cared for by others.
2. Role stereotypes get in the way of caring behavior because they are "un"-natural.
3. In an open, neutral climate clients can describe a healthy human being. When they list the behavior characteristics they wish their offspring to manifest in adulthood, for example, the list includes:

curiosity	leadership	independence
sensitivity	caring	dependence
adventuresome	courage	initiative

compassion	tenderness	intelligent
competence	self-assertion	goal-oriented
originality	considerate	honest
creativity	loving	

4. Clients need practice in confronting the contradictions between their actual descriptions of healthy human beings and their hidden assumptions about men and women. The hidden assumptions and unconscious biases rooted in the parents' own socialization maintain a continued influence on their childrearing practices. That is, even those parents who wish to rear their children in ways that develop individual potential—as opposed to stereotyped behavior—find that they socialize their children toward stereotypical sex-role patterns.

5. Clients need to build awareness and recognize the continual presence of conscious choice in their behavior.

6. In a nonthreatening environment, individuals will practice going against stereotypical patterns because the payoff consists of increased feelings of caring and being cared for, as well as growth toward fulfilling their human potential.

Uses of the Group. The group was used as a vehicle for self confrontation. Each member, in the non-threatening milieu, willingly and openly stated his or her priority personality traits (value choices). Discussion and relationship intra-group allowed members to self-disclose inner feelings, attitudes, biases, many of which were in contradiction to their stated ideals. These self-revelations, insights, resulted in an "aha" feeling—a cognitive recognition that dissonance exists between the traits they said they desired for their offspring (and themselves) and the traits they, in fact, were supporting and encouraging. At these moments, with critical, cognitive awareness, self-activated, they were able to begin to work on changing their attitudes, their biases, and most importantly, their behaviors.

Implications. As normative data are demythified it becomes possible to facilitate and nuture human offspring in totally human ways; to be encouraging of each child's feeling needs and competency needs; to provide the most optimum climate for the development of whole persons. The possibilities for a citizenry of mutually understanding women and men who can, in fact, share responsibilities and respect one anothers idiosyncrasies (including biological differences) are steps toward strengthening society and family.

CONCLUSIONS

The normative data presently used in studying males and females are culturally contaminated because what we turn to has been derived from research done by persons strongly enculturated in the assigned societal roles. It is time that behavioral scientists and others checked this information for hidden assumptions and biases.

Data collected from clinical practice indicate that many persons wish their infants to acquire healthy, mature, self-actualizing character traits. It is during the process of childrearing that stereotypical role characteristics are taught and caught.

It is time to identify the crucial variables which would result in non-sexist individuals who could actualize their human potential.

The infinite variety of alternative styles available to humankind dictates that behavioral scientists and mental health facilitators ought/need to look anew at the recorded data and bring to their clients in practice this questioning attitude. It dictates that we help families and individuals who come for guidance to "operate" as the unique individuals they are. If we implement this new, questioning perspective, we have the opportunity to facilitate individual growth so that females and males are primarily human beings, sure in ego strength, and capable of making actualized, caring relationships.

REFERENCES

Bandura, A., D. Ross and S. A. Ross. A Comparative Test of the Status Envy, Social Power and Secondary Reinforcement. Theories of Identificatory Learning. *Journal of Abnormal Social Psychology*, 1963, 67, 6, 527-534.

Bem, S. L. and D. J. Bem. Case Study of a Non-Conscious Ideology: Training the Woman to Know Her Place. In Bem, D. J. (Ed.) *Beliefs, Attitudes and Human Affairs.* Belmont, California: Brooks/Cole, 1970

Broverman, I. K., D. M. Boverman, F. E. Clarkson, P.S. Rosenkranz and S. R. Vogel. Sex-Role Stereotypes and Clinical Judgements of Mental Health, *Journal of Consulting and Clinical Psychology*, 1970, 34, 1-7.

Goldberg, P. Are Women Predjuiced Against Women? *Trans-Action*, April 1968, 28-30.

Horner, M. Femininity and Successful Achievement: A Basic Inconsistency. In Bardwick, J. M. et al. *Feminine Personality and Conflict.* Belmont, California) Brooks/Cole, 1970.

Lipman-Blumen, J. How Ideology Shapes Women's Lives. *Scientific American*, 1972, 226, (1) 34-42.

Maslow, A. H. *Motivation and Personality.* New York: Harper and Row, 1954 rev. 1970.

Rogers, C. R. *On Becoming a Person.* Boston: Houghton Mifflin, 1961.

Rosenkrantz, P., S. Vogel, H. Bee, I. K. Broverman, and D. Broverman. Sex-Role Stereotypes and Self-Concepts in College Students, *Journal of Consulting and Clinical Psychology*, 1968, 32, 287-295.

Sampson, R. V. *The Psychology of Power.* New York: Pantheon Books, 1966.

Spock, B. M. Should Girls Expect to Have Careers? *Redbook,* March 1972, 50-54.

White, R. W. Motivation Reconsidered: The Concept of Competence. *Psychological Review,* 1959, 66, 297-333.

A Peaceable Revolution in Parenthood

JOHN W. WEISS

"You've got exactly thirty seconds, Buddy. Then I have to take my cookies out of the oven."

This rather indignant remark coming from a 220-pound, six-foot-three-inch hulk, clad in denims and a flour-dusted apron, clearly startled the vacuum cleaner salesman who had been knocking on my front door. His ingratiating smile faded into a look of wonder and disbelief.

After knocking on dozens of doors, asking to speak to the lady of the house, the poor fellow had come upon me — a man who has taken over the child-rearing and housekeeping chores while his wife pursues a career in the outside world. I don't recall exactly how the salesman managed to get his foot inside the door — it is a knack they all seem to possess — but nonetheless, there he was, sampling my cookies, and soon the conversation shifted from vacuum cleaners to my occupation.

No, I explained, I didn't feel any threat to my male pride as a result of relinquishing the "masculine" world out there for which I had been prepared during my 28 years on earth. Nor did my wife Marianne feel any less feminine for having chosen to resume her professional career as a nurse. The truth is that both of us had begun to feel thwarted by our traditional roles and so, more as a gradual process than a radical shift, we had changed places.

When Marianne and I were married, she had completed her nursing education and was already working. I, on the other hand, was just preparing to enter graduate school. So it seemed perfectly natural for her to continue working for a while. Then a couple of years later when our daughter Lisa, now four, was born, it seemed entirely sensible for me to help out with baby care while studying at home.

Shortly after, I realized that the career in education I had been working toward was not for me. After I got my Master's in Education, I became increasingly dissatisfied by the jobs available to me. Writing, hunting, fishing, camping, and cooking were my first loves. I particularly enjoyed writing about my outdoor adventures, and some of my articles and stories had already found their way into the pages of leading sports magazines. With each passing day, however, I found that more and more of my time was being devoted to my conventionally-chosen profession, and less time was available for doing what I really liked to do. I wanted to be a free-lance writer.

Marianne, on the other hand, sorely missed her work and the sense of accomplishment it brought her. I finally decided, with her enthusiastic support, to make a break with the past and to start doing what

I wanted to do. I would no longer devote my energies to fulfilling traditional expectations.

The fact that I am not the primary breadwinner (even though I did sell nearly 40 feature articles and two dozen photos to outdoor magazines last year) is not threatening to me nor does it make Marianne uncomfortable. She and I believe there should be no such thing as the head of a household or a boss in the family. Our marriage has from the start been an equal partnership.

Very likely, a great number of American men and women today are in a predicament similar to the one Marianne and I were chafing under until we rearranged our lives to suit ourselves, rather than unhappily following the tyranny of "I should." From the very beginning of their lives, too many young boys and girls are trained to assume a certain role in society, and deviation from the accepted norm of homemaker-wife or breadwinner-husband is frowned upon. Such rigidity is gradually being abandoned by young married couples today. We no longer raise our eyebrows when a married woman returns to school or takes a job, or when a young man elects to become a nursery school teacher instead of entering a "male" profession. But few couples feel secure enough yet to undertake the kind of role reversal that Marianne and I did.

Of course the barrage of criticism directed toward our present style of life is never ending. But comments like "Why don't you get a nine-to-five job like everyone else" pass unregistered through my ears like inaudible sounds from a high-pitched dog whistle. Actually, I may well spend more hours working than these critics, and my free-lancing does in fact contribute a good number of dollars to the family till. Even more important, I think, are my solid effects at child-rearing, house-keeping, and shopping.

My typical day begins at dawn. I love to watch the sun rise, even on mornings when I choose not to go fishing or quail hunting. Breakfast may last an hour or more, as I delight in preparing healthy foods for my wife and Lisa. Standard fare includes orange juice, eggs, hash-browns, ham, homemade bread slathered with apple butter, and a pot of steaming coffee. As I pour a third cup of coffee, I amuse myself by watching the wrens flitting about the feeder outside our kitchen window.

After Marianne has gone to work, my first activity is a leisurely stroll with Lisa. We usually walk a few hundred feet to a nearby stream to see if any trout are running. Sometimes there are a few, but they usually dart away at our first appearance. We listen to the wind blowing through a nearby grove of aspens and watch the clouds moving across the sky.

It's usually not long before this brief interlude with nature is interrupted by Lisa, tugging at my arm, demanding that we go next door to visit the neighbor's puppies. The rest of the morning presents a variety of possibilities. My daughter and I may pack a lunch and hike to a nearby meadow where I can photograph mourning doves to illustrate a forthcoming article. While there, Lisa gathers black walnuts, which we'll later use in baking. Or perhaps we'll devote the morning to baking our own bread, with Lisa cracking the eggs and greasing the pans. Whatever we decide to do, we try to enter each activity fully, savoring it for what it has to offer and not just rushing through it to get to something else.

During Lisa's afternoon naptime I get out a few business letters to magazine editors and attend to any telephone calls or other paper work related to my writing. By late afternoon I've made the beds, vacuumed the rugs, bandaged a scraped knee or scratched hand, selected produce from a roadside stand, and have dinner — perhaps a duck shot on a recent hunting trip — underway.

When Marianne arrives home from the hospital, she is usually in good spirits but tired from being on her feet most of the day. A warm and compassionate person, she thrives on helping others, and would want to continue her career even if we had a million in the bank.

Most evenings a glass of wine plus a few minutes to sit down and read the mail are all Marianne needs to unwind. But if she has had a trying day, I find that listening patiently is usually enough to make the tensions and frustrations of her day slowly subside. Having held jobs myself, I can sympathize with the occasional setbacks Marianne experiences, and having managed a household, she can sympathize with me on days when Lisa has been fussy or the cheese soufflé has fallen flat.

After dinner I have a stretch of writing time while Marianne gives Lisa her bath, reads to her, and puts her to bed. Sometimes, when I've just finished an article and want to relax, this time finds me playing three-cushion billiards with the guys downtown.

Weekends are usually reserved for family outings and activities. From time to time, Marianne takes a few days off at a stretch and I go on pack trips of several days' duration. Not only do such ventures provide raw material for articles, but they also give me a chance to be with other men and thus compensate for the male companionship I miss in my domestic world.

Though Lisa is occasionally puzzled about why her daddy is home all day while other daddies are away at work, she seems to be flourishing under my care. She has a special relationship with her father that most children her age do not. Seldom is the conventional father in a position to participate in his youngster's everyday learning and play activities.

How does Marianne rate me as a housekeeper and child-tender? She knows that I am content with my new-found role in life and feels strongly that a person is most successful when he delights in what he is doing. It would be naive to expect my days to be perfect, but the difficulties that do occasionally arise usually prove to be inconsequential rather than catastrophic.

I would never suggest that every man quit his job tomorrow and stay home with the kids while his wife goes out to work. What I do hope is that, in the future, couples will feel free to choose a way of life that best suits their interests and abilities. Only then will we have truly satisfying marriages and a rewarding sense of personal fulfillment.

Biological Revolution

NICK PANAGAKOS

If someone had peeked into the Harvard laboratory of Dr. John Rock a few years ago, he would have seen the noted gynecologist staring intently at a pinhead-sized chunk of matter under glass. The speck was a human embryo, growing in an artificial womb that Dr. Rock devised. Using deft surgical technique, he had lifted an egg from a human womb and at the precise moment when the egg was in its most receptive state, he introduced human sperm obtained from a sperm bank. One sperm fertilized the egg, and the egg was then transferred to the artificial womb, where under laboratory nurturing it grew into an embryo.

The embryo died at the end of a week, but the important point is that what Dr. Rock almost achieved — the creation of life outside the human womb — no longer seems an impossible achievement. Indeed, discoveries made in recent months suggest that it is alarmingly close.

We are witnessing the start of a biological revolution that will affect life far more profoundly than the great industrial revolution of the 19th century or the technological revolution through which we are now passing. Serious research today will produce a world tomorrow where thousands of babies may owe their existence to a long-dead father, where men and women may no longer need unite to procreate, and where individuals may be tailor-made to specifications drawn up in advance.

The opening guns of the revolution are now being heard: Recently, Dr. E.S.E. Hafez, an experimental biologist at Wayne State University, asked a colleague from Germany to send him 100 head of prize sheep. His friend did. The entire herd was air-mailed to Dr. Hafez in a box that could be carried in one hand. The package contained a live female rabbit with 100 potential rams and ewes, all of them embryos a few days old, nestling in the rabbit's womb as if still in their natural mother. Upon the rabbit's arrival in the United States, each embryo was implanted in a ewe and was born a few months later, while its "real" mother grazed contentedly in Germany.

Dr. Hafez sees no reason why these techniques of artificial inovulation could not work just as well with human beings. He believes that in 10 or 20 years it will be possible for a woman to choose her own offspring by "prenatal adoption." She might walk into an embryo bank, look down a row of packets and pick her baby by label. Each packet would contain a frozen embryo, and each label would clearly identify the qualities of the egg donor — outstanding gifts of mind, disposition, character and physical fitness. After choosing, the woman could go to her doctor and have the embryo implanted in her womb, where it would grow and be born nine months later, like any baby of her own — but carrying the inherited characteristics of neither of the "adopted" parents.

Such experiments were originally begun as a means of improving breeds of livestock. All animals — including humans — are capable of producing more eggs than they could ever fertilize. By injecting FSH, the hormone that normally causes eggs to be released from the ovary, animals such as cows can be induced to release 50 to 100 eggs in a single cycle. The eggs are then fertilized by way of artificial insemination while still in the same animal. Several days after the mass conception, they are flushed out. They can then be implanted directly in the wombs of cows, or, as an interim measure, the embryos can be transplanted into small animals, such as rabbits, where they will grow as long as two weeks before they have to be implanted in cows to be brought to term. By using this method of artificial inovulation, prize-winning offspring can be produced by the hundreds.

The human implications are obvious. Genetically desirable women could be stimulated by hormones into producing a quantity of eggs each month instead of only one, and this could provide eggs for other women. A barren woman who could never have hoped to be pregnant could obtain the emotional satisfaction of having babies after all. And women who did not want to go through the demanding ritual of pregnancy would be able to hire surrogate mothers who would have the baby for them. A woman with a serious illness whose doctor forbade her to bear children might, by donating an egg, have her child carried by someone else. (The role of the surrogate mother would parallel that of the "wet nurse," a trade which once flourished among aristocrats.) The first representative of the Test Tube Generation may be gestating in the womb even as you read this. It is no longer a secret that two independent investigators, Dr. Landrum B. Shettles of Columbia-Presbyterian Medical Center in New York and Dr. R. G. Edwards of Cambridge University have grown an embryo in a test tube and will soon attempt to implant it in a human uterus (if they haven't already done so). And Edwards and Shettles are not alone in the medical race. Researchers in no less than half a dozen countries, including the Soviet Union, are known to be working along similar lines.

The most serious problem is the lack of an effective technique for storing fertilized eggs over long periods. Unlike sperm, the delicate embryo suffers in the freezing, and none have been successfully frozen for more than two weeks.

When freezing techniques are perfected, frozen sperm and egg banks will be established. And in such a world, a woman living in the 21st century could conceivably select as father of her child a 20th-century philosopher, an Olympic athlete or a brilliant scientist —

provided, of course, that these favored people had been willing to act as donors. The biologists have already coined a term for this concept — paleogenesis. Eventually, science may even make it possible to eliminate the need for any woman to carry a fertilized egg during its development into a child.

According to the respected British journal, "New Scientist," the development of an artificial womb that will serve as a satisfactory home to a test-tube embryo, all the way through to birth, is "only a matter of time."

The idea is to build a mechanical womb similar to one already constructed by Dr. Robert Goodlin at Stanford University — a steel chamber with a viewing porthole through which the progress of tiny embryos is observed. Designed along the lines of heart-lung machines, the device is built so the umbilical cord from the fetus passes through a lightly coiled cellulose tube, that bathes it in fluid, and oxygen is bubbled through.

The transfer of a fetus to an artificial womb presents a considerable technical problem. It is extremely difficult to join plastic tubes to the tiny and delicate veins, and experimenters must be careful not to damage the blood cells, which seem to be adversely affected by contact with artificial substances.

But in spite of these problems, such machines are already keeping human fetuses (the product of miscarriages) alive for 48 hours or more.

Scientists are confident that the machine will be improved to the point where it can bring an embryo to term without mishap.,

When will all this happen? It has taken scientists five years to understand the way gases are exchanged between fetus and environment. They expect it will take another 10 years to thoroughly understand the exchange of liquids and solids.

Once a "perfect" artificial womb has been evolved, someone, somewhere is going to bring forth a true "test-tube baby." The prospect of such an event cannot help but bring to mind the kind of "Baby Factory" visualized by Aldous Huxley 40 years ago, where conveyor belts carried embryos from conception to delivery in a fully automated plant at the rate of 1,000 a day. In Huxley's "Brave New World," the word "mother" was a vulgar term, reminding citizens of primitive days when women suffered needless pain and anguish for nine months to bring forth an heir.

The thought of a baby factory seems too bizarre, even in an era when far-fetched ideas become commonplace events in the blink of an eye. But what will our attitude be toward a baby that can be brought to term through the agency of a machine? Will there be indignation and furor? Probably — at the beginning.

But strong pressures for the acceptance of birth outside the womb will certainly come from medical researchers. Through actual examination of the embryo outside the human womb, birth defects could be noticed and corrected before it was too late. Surgery could be performed much more easily, and drugs could be administered. Moreover, the embryo would be protected from any harmful effects that might arise from drugs taken by the mother, or from any disease she might acquire, such as German measles. Pressures may also come from Women's Liberation groups, career girls, and others who would want children without any of the restrictions or "indignities" of pregnancy.

It is almost certain, too, that parents of the future, when they are about to create a new baby, will be able to specify its sex. We know now that sex is determined by the type of sperm that fertilizes the egg, and that the two kinds of sperm — male-producing and female-producing — differ slightly but definitely from each other. Under phase-contrast microscopy, one type shows up with elongated, oval-shaped heads; the other has more compact, rounded heads. The latter produces the male. There is another difference: The "male" sperm is less massive than the "female" one, and scientists believe they can separate the two types by exploiting this difference in mass. Once the two types are separated, it should be a relatively easy matter to fertilize an egg with sperm of the desired gender and bring the resulting embryo to term.

Sex by sedimentation has already been demonstrated with animal sperm, and works this way: Fluid containing sperm is allowed to sit in a cooled container for 12 hours; the heavier, female-producing sperm sinks to the bottom, while the lighter male floats near the top. By skimming the fluid off the top and using the sperm it contains to fertilize rabbit eggs in a test tube, experimenters are able to produce 77 percent male rabbits. Other experiments have produced results which are not as clear-cut but scientists see no reason why the technique, once perfected, could not work on humans.

It might be argued that to go to such lengths to satisfy the desires of some couples for a child of a particular sex is "unnatural" — but there are valid reasons for pursuing research in this area. Certain types of hereditary disease could be bred out of the population forever through sex determination. The defective gene for example, is carried by the woman — but the disease is expressed only in male offspring. If such women confined themselves to having male children, this defect would eventually be bred out through a sheer absence of female carriers.

Dr. Hafez of Wayne State University is certain that these techniques are the only sensible means to employ when man begins to colonize the outer planets in earnest. Considering the $500 per pound cost of launched payload — not to mention the other logistical difficulties of manned space flight — why send full-grown men aboard spaceships to colonize planets? Instead, Hafez argues, why not ship tiny embryos in care of a biologist or two who can grow them into people and livestock after they arrive at their extraterrestrial destination?

As science-fictionish as these techniques may seem, they may someday be regarded as primitive ways of growing human beings. For studies already are under way that open the possibility of producing a replica of a human being using only a piece of tissue from his or her body.

This phenomenon, known as "cloning," is based on the fact, established only recently, that each cell in the body, not only the united male and female sex cells, is capable of growing into a new individual.

At the Institute for Cancer Research in Philadelphia, Dr. Robert Briggs and Dr. Thomas King did some delicate surgery on a frog embryo. Using tiny surgical tools, they managed to lift out the nucleus of the original fertilized egg cell. The nucleus contained all the genetic information needed to build a tadpole. Normally, without this information, an organism would die. But in this case, Briggs and King replaced the missing nucleus with part of a cell from another part of the frog and the embryo kept right on growing as if nothing had happened. The tadpoles thus produced became frogs and, in spite of their unusual inheritance, reproduced normally.

The meaning was clear: The nuclei of the frog's other cells must also have contained the entire manual of instructions. Every cell in an organism — be it heart cell, liver cell or skin cell — still possesses all the genetic data transmitted by the first fertilized egg cell.

But the trick performed by Briggs and King works only during the first few days of the embryo's life. After that, transplanted nuclei will no longer function. Another point now becomes clear: Although every cell in the body contains all the genetic information to produce an individual, each cell employs only the specific instructions it needs at each step along the way to becoming specialized tissue such as muscle or nerve. The "unneeded" information is somehow switched off, but not destroyed. French scientist Jean Rostand says: "This new technique (cloning) would in theory enable us to create as many identical individuals as might be desired. A living creature could be printed in hundreds, in thousands of copies, all of them real twins."

Professor Frederick C. Steward demonstrated the cloning technique with carrots in experiments at Cornell University. Steward got more than 100,000 embryoids on one plate of agar jelly that had been injected with a solution of cells from a single carrot embryo. Of course, a carrot is hardly a person. To watch molecular biologists wrestle to understand the nightmarishly complicated electro-chemical switchboard that governs human cell growth is to obtain but a glimpse of the technical obstacles that lie ahead. But given enough time, biologists see no reason why cloning cannot become a reality. Stanford University's Nobel laureate Dr. Joshua Lederberg believes cloning will be accomplished in a time span of a few years. He says, with some apprehension: "There is nothing to suggest any difficulty about accomplishing (cloning) in mammals and man, though it will be rightly admired as a *tour de force* when it is first implemented."

In 1967, Baron Nathaniel Rothschild, the Cambridge physiologist turned businessman, told scientists at the Weizmann Institute in Israel that he regarded cloning as "a near possibility." The problem he foresees is whether everyone should be allowed to have himself cloned if he wishes, and he expects to see a commission for genetic control established to screen applicants.

One can imagine the maneuvers that egocentric individuals would go through to reduplicate themselves for posterity; for cloning confers a sort of immortality on the individual, since his offspring could be cloned in turn, with the process going on indefinitely.

Who, indeed, should be cloned? The late J.B.S. Haldane, one of the most brilliant scientists of our time, envisioned that most clones would be made from people at least 50 years old (except for athletes and dancers), who had excelled in some socially acceptable way. Equally useful, according to Haldane, might be the cloning of people with rare capacities, such as permanent adaptation to the dark (for resistance to radiation) or a high pain threshold.

Jean Rostand proposes storing, in deep freeze, the body cells of people of remarkable attainment, as insurance against fatal accidents. If, say, a great statesman were assassinated, doctors could simply produce a duplicate to replace him. Of course, there would be no guarantee that the clone would grow up to be exactly like the original. Environmental influences would play a great part. But the odds would be stacked in favor of greatness.

The similarity of minds among clones would make for better communication and generate greater sympathetic awareness of each other's needs and problems, much as is the case with identical twins. Such an advantage might be vitally important where teamwork is a matter of life and death, such as a space mission lasting several years, or teams doing long-term underwater exploration. If cloning does become a fact of life, we are likely to face pressing social and personal problems. How far can we integrate cloning into our culture?

Some countries may decide to prohibit such a mode of reproduction. As with many of the other biological developments which have been discussed, however, the decision may not be ours to make.

What if a Hitler-type dictator decided that he could produce more rugged soldiers, more brilliant statesmen or hardier workers by such techniques? The problem then facing the other nations would be whether to compete or face the possibility of being destroyed — or at least relegated to a low position in the world scheme of things.

Cloning could be a blessing or a curse. But there is yet another possibility with even greater implications: the creation of "tailor-made" human beings through the manipulation of the life-giving genes themselves. Estimates on when this will happen range from several decades to several lifetimes. But such terms as "gene insertion" and "gene deletion" are beginning to appear in scientific journals, and references to genetic engineering are common.

The potential control of genetic material stems from the molecular biologists' relatively recent ability to manipulate and experiment with the cell in its living state, rather than to merely observe it. We know now that the cell is more like a community than an individual, and that within the cell is a myriad of molecules carrying out thousands of complex chemical reactions every fraction of a second.

The seat of control and power is the nucleus of the cell, which contains genes, the materials that carry inherited traits from generation to generation. Genes are composed of molecules of deoxyribonucleic acid, or DNA, each of which consists of two strands of chemical compounds intertwined to form a double helix.

Using four specific chemical substances (given the code letters A, C, G and T by scientists to correspond to the initial letters of the chemicals' names), DNA sends messages to the cell telling it how to perform certain chemical functions and thereby determining characteristics of the organism. The order in which the four chemicals are arranged along the DNA molecule determines the message which will be sent, or the characteristic which will be exhibited.

Human DNA contains a billion of these letters of nucleotides, yet the DNA of all living creatures is built on the same general plan. Its basic combination of letters is responsible for the design of a snake, a pig or a man. Scientists have begun to be able to read the genetic code, but they are still in the elementary-school stage. When they are able to read the messages better, then perhaps they will be able to write the instructions themselves. And when this happens, man will presumably be able to write out any set of specifications he might desire for his ideal being.

One tool is already at hand: the laser beam, which can be focused to a diameter as small as one ten-thousandth of a centimeter. This incredibly precise "editing" device could be used to slice through the DNA molecule at given points, knocking out small sections so as to "erase" the unwanted genes.

Some scientists suggest that perhaps "repressor" molecules will be found that can be introduced to block the functioning of certain genes. For gene insertion, Nobel-laureate Professor Edward L. Tatum envisions the use of nuclear grafts from other cells. Other scientists foresee the programming of viruses to carry desired information into cells. But it may well turn out to be that detailed genetic tinkering is unnecessary. If a whole DNA molecule can be manufactured, carrying all the desired genes, then it could be copied in unlimited quantitites. The DNA molecule could then be inserted as a whole. A DNA-type molecule has already been manufactured in the laboratory, although the genetic message cannot yet be controlled.

Implicit in the ability to manipulate the genes themselves is the control of cancer and other degenerative diseases. Such an ability may also provide the platform for solving one of nature's most puzzling riddles: What causes us to grow old and die?

Over the last few years, it has become clear that aging is due to the failure and eventual death of individual cells, one after another, throughout the tissues of the body. This failure particularly affects those tissues where the cells lose the power to replace and renew themselves by division: that is nerve and muscle cells, including the heart.

What causes cell death? Various reasons have been suggested. One approach says we age and die because of genetic errors that cause our "switchboard" (or its operator) to give out. According to this idea, injuries to DNA — as the result of radiation, wear-and-tear or other causes — disorganize the stored collection of genetic information. In younger people, such injuries are quickly repaired, but as we grow older, repair is slow and our body cells no longer get the message of survival.

Are there any steps that can be taken to prevent this? Dr. Howard J. Curtis, senior biologist at Brookhaven National Laboratories, has proposed that it might be possible to control aging by "stabilizing" the DNA; that is, by halting its gradual modification which brings about the diseases associated with old age.

Another theory of aging suggests that cells contain some self-destroying mechanism that is an evolutionary rather than a biological necessity. Death becomes part of life's plan because evolution favors creatures that die — provided they do it after they have passed the reproductive age. As Sir George Pickering put it: "Insofar as man is an improvement on monkeys, this is due to death. . . . A new species, for better or for worse, can only start with a new life."

According to this idea of "planned obsolescence," there is a progressive switching-off of youthful functions and, in accordance with a genetic timetable, a programmed switching-on of functions that age us. If this is true, it is reasonable to suppose that men some day will discover how to tinker with the control or substitute a longer-running program to halt the onset of aging and even reactivate "youth genes" in older people.

It must be emphasized that at the moment the precise processes of development and aging in humans remain mysterious, but not hopelessly so. Just as the "impossible" four-minute mile served as a spur to trackmen to try to beat it, so the seeming impossibility of working out the intricacies of aging and death is resulting in a massive research assault. More than 1,000 teams of genetic engineers clock in on such work in the United States alone, and the nature of the problem has been defined much more clearly than ever before.

Dr. Alex Comfort, director of the Medical Research Council of London's University College, reflecting the attitude of many experimenters, believes that the enormous power of American science might uncover the secrets of aging within a decade if sufficient energy is devoted to the task.

You Can Choose
Your Baby's Sex

DAVID M. RORVIK
LANDRUM B. SHETTLES, M.D.

Over the centuries, man has devised at least 500 "formulas to help satisfy his overwhelming desire to choose the sex of his offspring. Aristotle advised the Greeks to have intercourse in the north wind if males were desired, in the south wind if females were wanted. Women of the Middle Ages didn't get off so easily. When boys were desired, they were required to down gamy concoctions of wine and lion's blood mixed by an alchemist and then, while an abbot prayed, to copulate under the full moon. When girls resulted despite these heroics, local wise men were usually ready with obscure "explanations." Some European peasants to this day wear their boots to bed when they want to conceive boys and in some rural American communities men still hang their pants on the right side of the bed if they want a boy and on the left side if they want a girl.

Interest in choosing sex remains as high among prospective parents today as it ever was, despite the almost universal unconcern of baby doctors. And failure to produce the desired sex still creates as much anguish as it did in the past—perhaps more, since we have come to expect so much from modern medical science. As one young housewife from Virginia who has three boys put it, "My doctor said I was being silly and immature when I begged him to help me have a little girl. He has children of both sexes and can't understand the deep hurt of having children of the same sex over and over."

One doctor who does understand the anguish of such parents is Landrum B. Shettles, M.D., Ph.D., D.Sc. (He is an assistant attending obstetrician-gynecologist at Columbia-Presbyterian Medical Center and an assistant professor of clinical obstetrics and gynecology at Columbia College of Physicians and Surgeons.) Sitting in his office, he recalls the night in the early 1960s when he made the discovery that may help millions select the sex of their offspring.

"Medical science had known for some time," he says, "that it is the male that determines the sex of the offspring. The man who leaves his wife because she brings him nothing but girls or nothing but boys is only kidding himself. If the man's fertilizing sperm carries an X chromosome, the child will be a girl; if it carries a Y, the child will be a boy."

The trouble was, he adds, doctors had always been unable to tell the difference between "male" sperm and "female" sperm. About all that was known was that the Y chromosome is smaller than the X. Dr. Shettles had long felt that this difference should be reflected in the overall size of the sperm heads. With ordinary microscopy, however, killed and permanently fixed sperm specimens failed to reveal the presence of two distinct sperm populations.

"Then one night," Dr. Shettles continues, "I decided to examine some *living* sperm cells under a phase-contrast microscope." The relatively new technique of phase-contrast microscopy throws eerie halos of light around dark objects, revealing details that ordinary microscopes miss. The living sperm cells under the microscope flashed through the field of vision like luminescent eels. Dr. Shettles put them into slow motion by exposing them to carbon-dioxide gas. The results were almost as electrifying as the "charged" sperm cells themselves: almost *immediately,* Dr. Shettles noticed that the sperm came in two distinctive sizes and shapes.

"I was so excited," he recalls, "that I ran upstairs and grabbed the first lab technician I could find. I had to show somebody what I'd found."

Now, after examining more than 500 sperm specimens, he is convinced that the two sizes correspond to the two sexes: small, round-headed sperms carry the male-producing Y chromosomes, and the larger, oval-shaped type carry the female-producing X chromosomes. He noticed that in most cases, the round sperm far outnumbered the oval-shaped sperm.

Dr. Shettles failed to find anyone who produced only the oval-shaped female sperm, but he did encounter some men whose specimens contained almost nothing but the round-headed variety. In each of the latter cases, his physiological sleuthing revealed a man who had produced nothing but male offspring. In cases in which the long-headed sperm prevailed, he generally found fathers surrounded by little girls (and wives who wanted boys).

Dr. Shettles stresses here, however, the rarity of cases in which the husband produces sperm that is predominantly of one type. And even in cases in which a man may produce unusually more sperm of one type than the other, *he can very often still produce offspring of both sexes,* provided he follows certain procedures. Individuals who have repeatedly fathered children of the same sex are more often the victims of bad luck than of genetics.

After making his discovery, Dr. Shettles published his findings in the scientific journal *Nature* and suddenly found himself in the middle of a controversy.

Not everybody has agreed with his findings, and he does not claim scientific infallibility. But he does stand on his record, on observations he has made in the laboratory and, most important, on his results to date. Other researchers have provided some impressive corroboration of Dr. Shettles' work.

As soon as he had made his initial discovery, Dr. Shettles had only one thing in mind: to find some means of exploiting this new knowledge to help parents choose the sex of their children. Since there definitely seemed to be a difference in the overall size of the two types of sperm, he reasoned, there must be other differences as well. Perhaps one type was stronger than the other or faster—or both. Perhaps one type could survive longer in a certain environment than the other. There were all sorts of intriguing possibilities that could lead to a means of selecting sex—simply by interfering, even slightly, with the environment in which the sperm seek out the egg.

It seemed fairly certain that the larger, female-producing sperm (now called gynosperms) must be more resistant than the other type. Why should there be nearly twice as many of the smaller, boy-producing variety (known as androsperms) in the ejaculate of the average male if not to compensate for some inferiority in coping with the environment beyond the male reproductive tract? There may be as many as 170 boys conceived for every 100 girls, and for every 100 female births, there are about 105 male births. In terms of longevity, resistance to disease and stress, the adaptability to environment, it has long been conceded, at least by scientists, that the male is the weaker of the two sexes. This fact now appears to be borne out even at the most elemental level; the male-producing sperm begin with a substantial head start (perhaps a 2-to-1 margin) but end up only slightly ahead of the female-producing sperm in the number of babies born each year.

What accounts for the great slaughter of androsperms within the womb? To find out, Dr. Shettles began studying the environment that exists inside the vagina and uterus at about the time of conception. He took transparent capillary tubes and filled them with cervical and vaginal secretions. Then he turned millions of sperm loose at the opening of the tubes and watched their activity through his microscope.

"It was a little like watching the races at Belmont," he said. When the secretions in the tubes were more acidic than alkaline, the gynosperms seemed to prevail. But when the tubes were filled with cervical mucus removed from a woman very close to the time of ovulation, the small androsperms were clear-cut winners every time. Why?

Acid inhibits both gynosperms and androsperms, but it harms the androsperms first and most, cutting them out of the herd and thus out of competition. The gynosperms' greater bulk seems to protect them from the acid for much longer periods than their little brothers are able to survive.

Alkaline secretions are kind to both types of sperm and generally enhance the chances for fertilization. But in the absence of hostile acids, the androsperms are able to use the one advantage they have over their sisters: the speed and agility that their small, compact heads and long tails give them.

As a gynecologist, Dr. Shettles knew that the environment within the vagina is generally acidic while the environment within the cervix and uterus is generally alkaline. And the secretions within the cervix and womb will be highly alkaline, more so even than in the vagina, in spite of the alkaline douch, and an alkaline environment is most favorable to androsperms. He knew that the closer a woman gets to ovulation the more alkaline her cervical secretions become.

All of this told him that *timing of intercourse* is a critical factor in choosing the sex of children. His findings suggested that intercourse at or very close to the time of ovulation, when the secretions are most alkaline, would very likely result in male offspring. Intercourse two or three days before the time of ovulation, on the other hand, when an acid environment still prevails, would be likely to yield female offspring. The female-producing sperm cells can survive those two or three days, while the androsperms rarely last longer than 24 hours.

Certain now that he was on the right track, Dr. Shettles began looking through scientific and historic literature for further confirmation. He found that Orthodox Jews produce significantly more male offspring than does the general population, and he began consulting rabbis and poring over the *Talmud*, a compilation of Jewish beliefs and laws. One of the passages he found was this: "The determination of sex takes place at the moment of cohabitation. When the woman emits her semen before the man [meaning when she experiences orgasm before her husband], the child will be a boy. Otherwise, it will be a girl." If a boy was desired, the *Talmud* directed the husband to "hold back" until his wife experienced orgasm. Dr. Shettles also found another clue in Orthodox Jewish law: women must not engage in intercourse during their "unclean" period (menstruation) or for one week thereafter.

Both of these directives coincided very neatly with Dr. Shettles' findings. Orgasm is the less important of the two factors, but it can play a part in sex selection. Female orgasm helps provide additional alkaline secretions. Of course, many women (perhaps 4 percent) never experience orgasm. These women should not think that their chances to conceive boys are diminished, because there are other ways of increasing the alkalinity that favors male offspring. The other point—abstaining from intercourse until at least a week after the conclusion of menstruation—is more significant, for this puts coitus very close to the time of ovulation in most women.

Dr. Shettles also sifted through the data on artifical insemination. Doctors specializing in artifical insemination try to pinpoint the time of ovulation in their patients so that fertilization can be achieved on the first try. It occurred to Dr. Shettles that an unintended side effect of this practice ought to be an abundance of male offspring. In a series of several thousand births achieved by artificial insemination, he found that the sex ratio was 160 males for every 100 females. In another series, 76 percent were boys, and 24 percent were girls!

Elated that his hunch seemed to be correct, Dr. Shettles began startling some of his patients by telling them that they no longer had to rely on the whims of Mother Nature—at least not entirely—when it came to the sex of their children. He also began working with Dr.

Sophia Kleegman, professor of gynecology at New York University's Medical School and director of its Infertility Clinic. Dr Kleegman has long been a leader in the field of artificial insemination.

Dr. Shettles also noted in the course of his early research that low sperm count seems to be associated with a preponderance of female offspring. Men with a high sperm count, on the other hand, tend to father a greater number of male offspring. This suggested that building up the sperm count through abstinences might be another way of increasing chances of begetting male offspring.

As a result of these findings, Dr. Shettles has formulated two procedures—one to be used if a female child is desired, the other if a male is wanted. These procedures can be used in the home *without* prior semen analysis.

The Procedure for Female Offspring

1. Intercourse should cease two or three days before ovulation. Timing is the most important factor.

2. Intercourse should be immediately *preceded,* on each occasion, by an acidic douche consisting of two tablespoons of *white* vinegar to a quart of water. The timing might be enough to ensure female offspring, but the douche makes success all the more likely, since the acid environment immobilizes the androsperms.

3. If the wife normally has orgasm, she should try to avoid it. Orgasm increases the flow of alkaline secretions, and these could neutralize or weaken the acid environment that enhances the chance of the gynosperms.

4. The face-to-face, or "missionary," position should be assumed during intercourse. Dr. Shettles believes that this makes it less likely that sperm will be deposited directly at the mouth of the cervix, where they might escape the acid environment of the vagina.

5. Shallow penetration by the male at the time of male orgasm is recommended. Again this helps make certain that the sperm are exposed to the acid in the vagina and must swim through it to get to the cervix.

6. No abstinence from intercourse is necessary, until after the final intercourse two or three days before ovulation. A low sperm count increases the possibiity of female offspring, so frequent intercourse, prior to the final try two or three days before ovulation, cannot hurt and may actually help. This may be why Dr. Shettles says that "having girls is more fun."

The Procedure for Male Offspring

1. Intercourse should be timed as close to the moment of ovulation as possible.

2. Intercourse should be immediately preceded on each occasion, by a baking-soda douche, consisting of two tablespoons of baking soda to a quart of water. The solution should be permitted to stand for 15

minutes before use. This allows the soda to become completely dissolved.

3. Female orgasm is not necessary but is desirable. If a woman normally has orgasm, her husband should time his to coincide with hers or let her experience orgasm first.

4. Vaginal penetration from the rear is the recommended position. This, Dr. Shettles says, helps ensure deposition of sperm at the entrance of the womb. This is desirable.

5. Deep penetration at the moment of male orgasm will help ensure deposition of sperm close to the cervix.

6. Prior abstinence is necessary; intercourse should be avoided completely from the beginning of the monthly cycle until the day of ovulation. This helps ensure maximum sperm count, a factor favoring androsperms.

All of this means," Dr. Shettles observes, "that if the first intercourse of the month takes place right at ovulation time, the male sperm will race along like a cab going through Broadway on a green light." If, however, intercourse takes place two or three days before ovulation, most of the male sperm will be incapacitated by the time the egg arrives. "For the female sperm," Dr. Shettles continues, "it's like flying into LaGuardia on a foggy night. They have to hover around and wait for the signal. Then they zoom right in."

Dr. Shettles does not *guarantee* that these procedures will be successful on *every* occasion. But, in his words, "The procedures are safe and simple. There's nothing distasteful about them, nothing any religious body has objected to. They can be carried out in the home, and they are entirely harmless. Clinical results show at least 80 percent success. And I believe that if the couple is conscientious with the douche and the timing, they can achieve success 85 to 90 percent of the time."

Dr. Shettles reports that all babies born after use of these techniques have been completely normal. Neither douche is harmful to mother or offspring. The safest applicator for either douche is the hot-water-bottle type. Let the fluid flow under the force of gravity alone. It is not harmful to use the douches repeatedly, before *each* intercourse during the fertile period. Remember, though, that douching should be used in conjunction with timing of intercourse and may not, by itself, be sufficient to tip the balance in the desired direction.

Pinpointing the time of ovulation is of vital importance. Most women ovulate between days 11 and 15 of the average menstrual cycle, but each woman must determine her own ovulation time. Generally, women are told to keep a temperature chart. Your doctor is familiar with this procedure and can instruct you in it. This procedure involves a special but inexpensive thermometer scored in tenths of a degree so that even tiny variations aren't missed. Temperature is taken orally each day before getting out of bed in the morning and then is recorded on the chart. Typically, temperature will remain about even throughout menstruation and will probably rise or fall two- or three-tenths of a degree over the next several days. A sudden dip of perhaps two-tenths of a degree or more in temperature over a period of a day usually indicates that ovulation is at hand, though no one is certain whether ovulation takes place at the bottom of the dip or as it begins to rise again. The temperature will rise sharply again, usually within a day, and remain high, indicating that ovulation has taken place.

Women should maintain records for two or, preferably, three or four months before using them for sex-selection. Women who have been on the birth-control pill should wait four to six months after discontinuing use of the pill before attempting to select sex. These months can be used to determine the exact time of ovulation each month. If the woman is emotionally upset, ill, or if she smokes, eats or moves about before taking her temperature each morning, the charts are not likely to be very accurate.

Because of the instability of the temperature approach Dr. Shettles recommends this newer and more accurate procedure to women: if you want to use it, buy a fertility test kit (available at most drugstores for about $7) or, for less money, but equally good, a little roll of Tes-Tape, also available in most drugstores without prescription. Tes-Tape is a roll of special yellow paper that comes in a Scotch Tape-type dispenser; the tape turns varying shades of blue and green when exposed to glucose, which is abundant in cervical mucus at the time of ovulation.

Beginning at the end of menstruation, start off each day by tearing off a three-inch strip of tape. Bend the strip over the index finger and secure it with a small rubber band. Now guide the finger into the vagina so that the tip of your finger and the tape make contact with the cervix, which will feel something like the tip of your nose. Hold the finger gently up against the cervix for ten to fifteen seconds, then withdraw it. Note the color of the tape at the tip of your finger. Early in the cycle it probably won't change color at all. Or it might change to a light green. As you approach ovulation, each new tape will be darker and darker. Consult the color chart on the Tes-Tape or fertility-kit dispenser. When the color of the tape matches the darkest color on the scale (a deep, greenish blue), you will know that ovulation is at hand. (The Tes-Tape chart is coded for the urine test — used by diabetics — but it works for ovulation as well.)

Dr. Shettles recommends that you experiment with the procedure through three or four cycles before using it for the critical intercourse. In this way, you can determine the day on which you normally ovulate and what color the tape is two or three days before it turns its darkest blue. This latter information will be important if you are trying for a girl. Keep careful records of the approximate color that turns up each day. Five different color bars are indicated on the Tes-Tape chart, so you may want to number these one through five, starting with yellow, and jot down the applicable number each day.

Test the cervical mucus two or three times a day as it approaches its darkest hue, so that if a boy is wanted, you can time coitus as closely as possible to ovulation. Always use the Tes-Tape before intercourse and, of course, before either of the two douches. If you feel that you are using the Tes-Tape or fertility kit (which comes equipped with an applicator) incorrectly, consult your doctor.

According to both Dr. Shettles and Dr. Kleegman, *Mittelschmerz* is the best indicator of ovulation. It is a pain that is felt in the lower abdomen, often on the right side, at the time of ovulation. Some women experience a small amount of bleeding at the same time. About 15 percent of all women have precise pains and thus are able to pinpoint ovulation almost to the exact second. In other women, the pains are nonexistent or vague. Dr. Kleegman has taught 35 percent of her patients to bring the pain out by practicing the "bounce test." From the ninth day of the cycle, both morning and night, the woman is instructed to bounce on a hard surface, such as a wooden chair, by sitting down abruptly three or four times. If she feels the pain, she should note the day and repeat the test during the next cycle to see if a pattern emerges. Women with vague mid-cycle pains should also use another method for pinpointing ovulation, and even women with well-defined *Mittelschmerz* should try to confirm with one of the other tests.

"The stretch test" is another means of determining the moment of ovulation. The cervical mucus is generally thick and rather milky in appearance. But it becomes increasingly thin and clear as ovulation approaches, until it reaches the consistency and transparency of raw egg white. At ovulation time, it can be stretched easily. The test itself is usually administered by doctors, but some women may notice the changing nature of their cervical mucus and use this to help determine the time of ovulation.

The further before ovulation that one times intercourse, the more difficult it is to achieve pregnancy. But it is also true that when one does achieve pregnancy in these cases, the offspring is very likely to be female. If a couple wants a girl, it's wise to time intercourse three days prior to ovulation. If, after three or four months, they have still not achieved pregnancy on this schedule, they should move to a two-and-a-half-day interval, and then, if that also fails, a two-day interval. At two days, it is still far more likely that female offspring will result (provided the other procedures are also followed). But the couple wanting a girl has nothing to lose by starting out with the more cautious three-day interval. Pregnancy can and does occur in a significant number of cases under these circumstances. If intercourse takes place up to seven hours after ovulation, a boy will most likely result. Cervical secretions are generally still very abundant and highly alkaline during this period — but always test the secretions before intercourse to be sure.

The clinical results of these timing procedures are encouraging. "With exposure to pregnancy two to twenty-four hours before ovulation," Dr. Keegman reports, "the babies were predominantly male [78 percent]. With exposure to pregnancy 36 or more hours before ovulation, the babies were predominantly female."

In another study, Dr. Shettles reported that one group of 22 couples who wanted female offspring took up to six months to conceive by timing intercourse two to three days before ovulation. "Of 22 offspring," he notes, "19 were girls. In a group of 26 women anxious to have boys, the first coitus occurred at the time of ovulation or within 12 hours thereafter. To these women, 23 boys were born."

Some observers believe that our new ability to choose the sex of our children will result in a bumper crop of boys, but Dr. Shettles is personally convinced that parents will not use his techniques to produce either mostly males or mostly females. "Over the years, parents have expressed only one desire," he says, "and that is to have families that are well balanced in terms of sex. Most find an equal number of boys and girls ideal."

Many couples have told Dr. Shettles they had initially planned for a family of two children, hoping for one of each. But when both offspring turned out to be the same sex, they made a third attempt and so on. So it is not too farfetched to envision sex-selection making a significant contribution in the effort to control the population explosion. How much better it would be to achieve the ideal family balance in two tries instead of three or four or more or never. The advantages of sex-selection are manifest: parental satisfaction, balanced families, very possibly smaller families and, healthier families.

Sometimes health—or lack of it—is attached to our sex chromosomes. Only males, for example, suffer from hemophilia, the grim and often fatal "bleeder's disease." Similar hereditary, sex-linked diseases include one type of muscular dystrophy and numerous enzyme-deficiency disorders that can kill, cripple and retard for life.

Though most of these diseases remain incurable, they can be prevented if carriers of sex-linked diseases could simply avoid conceiving children of the vulnerable sex.

The value of sex-selection in helping to overcome these diseases motivates many researchers in this field, such as Drs. Robert Edwards and Richard Gardner of Cambridge University. Writing in *New Scientist,* they point out that "the elimination of these disorders in one generation, by a judicious choice of the sex of the offspring, would not only be of direct benefit to that generation, but would benefit the race for generations to come."

Nothing about Dr. Shettles' method of sex-selection is morally or ethically objectionable. Protestant ministers have inquired about the procedures with the intention of incorporating them into their own family planning, rabbis have cooperated with Dr. Shettles in his research, and the Roman Catholic Church has bestowed its blessing. Msgr. Hugh Curran, director of the Family Life Bureau of the Archdiocese of New York, says that the Church has no objections to Dr. Shettles' sex-selection procedures "as long as the intent of these efforts is not to prevent conception." For the first time in all time, parents have the opportunity to make a scientific attempt at choosing the sex of their children and to make that attempt with a high expectation of success.

Parents Bring Up Your Children!

URIE BRONFENBRENNER

Many changes have occurred in ways of child-rearing in the United States, particularly since World War II, but their essence may be conveyed in a single sentence: Children *used* to be brought up by their parents. Families were bigger—not in terms of more children so much as more adults—grandparents, uncles, aunts, cousins. Those relatives who did not live with you lived nearby. You often went to their houses. They came as often to yours. Everybody minded your business. They wanted to know where you had been, where you were going, and why. And if they did not like what they heard, they said so.

And it wasn't just your relatives. Everybody on the block minded your business too. If you got into mischief, the phone would ring at your house, and your parents would know what you had done before you got back home. Sometimes you didn't like it—but at least people cared.

As the stable world of the small town or the city block has become absorbed into an ever-shifting suburbia, children are growing up in a different environment. The extended family has been reduced to a nuclear one with only two adults, and the functioning neighborhood has withered to a small circle of friends. For millions of American children, the neighborhood is nothing but a row of buildings where "other people" live. One house, or apartment, is much like another —and so are the people. They all have more of less the same income, and the same way of life. But the child does not see much of that life, for all that people do in the neighborhood is to come home to it, have a drink, eat dinner, mow the lawn, watch television and sleep. Before, the world in which the child lived consisted of a diversity of people in a diversity of settings. Today, housing projects often have no stores, no shops, no services, no adults at work or play. Rarely can a child see people working at their trades. Mechanics, tailors or shopkeepers are either out of sight or unapproachable. Nor can a child listen to the gossip at the post office or on a park bench. To do anything at all—go to a movie, get an ice-cream cone, go swimming or play ball—he has to travel by car or bus.

All that does not really matter, however, for children are not at home much. They leave early on the school bus, and it is almost suppertime when they get back. And there may not be anybody home when they get there. If their mother is not working at least part-time (and over a third of American mothers are), she is out a lot—not just to be with friends, but to do things for the community. The men leave in the morning before the children are up. And they do not get back until after the children have eaten supper.

Consequently, American parents do not spend as much time with children as they used to. This development does not imply a decrease in the affection or concern of parents for their children. Nor is it a change that we have planned or wanted. Rather, it is the by-product of a variety of social changes, all operating to decrease the prominence and power of the family in the lives of children. Urbanization, child-labor laws, the abolishment of the apprentice system, the working mother, the experts' advice to be permissive, the delegation and professionalization of child care—all decrease opportunity for contact between children and parents, or, for that matter, adults in general.

If a child is not with his parents or other adults, where does he spend his time? First and foremost, he is with other children—in school, after school, over weekends and on holidays. But even this contact is restricted. Housing projects, even entire neighborhoods, cater to families in a particular stage of their life or career. Social life becomes organized on a similar basis; and, as a result, contacts become limited to persons of one's own age and station. Whereas invitations used to be extended to entire families, with all the Smiths visiting all the Joneses, nowadays, every social event has its segregated equivalent for every age group down to the toddlers. While the adults take their drinks upstairs, the children have their "juice time" in the rumpus room downstairs. In short, *we are coming to live in a society that is segregated not only by race and class, but also by age.*

It doesn't take children very long to learn the lesson the adult world teaches: "Don't bug us! Latch on to your peers!"

That is exactly what children do. In a recently completed study, 766 sixth-grade children reported spending during the weekend, an average of two to three hours a day with their parents. Over the same period, they spent about twice as much time with peers, either singly or in groups. Moreover, their behavior apparently reflects preference as well as practice. When asked with whom they would rather spend a free weekend afternoon, many more chose friends than parents. Then, the characteristics of predominantly "peer-oriented" and "adult-oriented" children were compared in an attempt to find how the peer-oriented children got that way.

The study concluded that the peer-oriented youngster was more influenced by a lack of attention and concern at home than by the attractiveness of the peer group. In general, the peer-oriented children held rather negative views of themselves and the peer group. They also expressed a dim view of their own future. Their parents were rated as lower than those of adult-oriented children both in the expression of affection and support, and in the exercise of discipline and control. Finally, the peer-oriented children report engaging in more antisocial behavior such as "doing something illegal," "playing hooky," lying, teasing other children, etc. It would seem that the peer-oriented child turns to his age-mates less by choice than by default. The vacuum left by the withdrawal of parents and adults from the lives of children is filled with an undesired—and possibly undesirable—substitute of an age-segregated peer group.

In my study of middle-class adolescents, children who reported that their parents were away from home for long periods of time rated significantly lower on such characteristics as responsibility and leadership. Perhaps because it was more pronounced, absence of the father was more critical than that of the mother, particularly in its effect on boys. In general, father absence contributes to low motivation for achievement, inability to defer immediate rewards for later benefits, low self-esteem, susceptibility to group influence and juvenile delinquency.

In 1959, investigators studied the ages at which children turn to parents or peers for opinions, advice or company. There was a turning point at about the seventh grade. Before that, the majority looked mainly to their parents as models and companions; thereafter, the children's peers had equal or greater influence. A recent study shows a substantially greater percentage of peer "dependence" at every age and grade level than the previous one. It would appear that the shift from parents to peers occurs earlier than it did a decade ago and is now much more pronounced.

The effect of a peer group on the child depends on the attitudes and activities prevailing in that peer group. Where group norms emphasize achievement, the members perform accordingly; where the prevailing expectations call for violation of adult norms, these are as readily translated into action. In short, social contagion is a two-way street.

How early in life do children become susceptible to such contagion? Prof. Albert Bandura and his colleagues at Stanford University have conducted experiments which suggest that the process is already well-developed at the pre-school level. In the basic experimental design, the child finds himself in a familiar playroom. There is a person playing with toys in another corner of the room. This other person behaves very aggressively. He strikes a large Bobo doll (a bouncing inflated figure), throws objects and mutilates dolls and animal toys, using language to match. Later on, the child who "accidentally" observed this behavior is tested by being allowed to play in a room containing a variety of toys, including some similar to those employed by the aggressive model. Without any provocation, perfectly normal, well-adjusted preschoolers engage in aggressive acts, not only repeating what they had observed but elaborating on it.

The influence that peers have on the young is rivaled, perhaps, only by television. Many American children spend as much time watching television as they spend in school, and more than in any other activity except sleep and play. As with the peer group, they are propelled there in part by parental example and parental pressure.

During his experiments, Professor Bandura made films with essentially identical scripts: one with an actor, a second of a cartoon cat. The films were presented on a television set. When the children were tested, the television films turned out to be just as effective in arousing aggression as experiences with live people.

When Bandura's work was published in LOOK (October 22, 1963), the television industry issued a statement, questioning his conclusions on the interesting ground that no parents were present. "What a child will do under normal conditions cannot be projected from his behavior when he is carefully isolated from normal conditions and the influences of society."

Evidence for the relevance of Bandura's laboratory findings to "real life" comes from a study of more than 600 third-graders. The children who were rated most aggressive by their classmates were those who watched television programs involving a high degree of violence.

Another study tested the reactions of various groups to violence on the screen. The subjects were shown a knife fight between two teenagers from *Rebel Without a Cause*. Then they were asked to assist in an experiment on the effects of punishment in learning by giving an unseen person an electric shock every time he made an error. One version of the experiment employed 15-year-old high school boys as subjects. With this group, the designers wondered what would happen if no film were shown. Would the everyday environment of adolescents — who see more movies and more television programs and are called on to display virility through aggressive acts in teen-age gangs — provoke latent brutality?

The results were sobering. Even without the suggestive power of the aggressive film, the teen-agers pulled the shock lever to its highest intensities. A few of the boys made remarks that suggested they were enjoying the experience of administering pain; for example, "I bet I made that fellow jump."

The peer group need not act as an impetus to antisocial behavior — if it is properly influenced by the adult society. American children, however, are relatively cut off from the adult world, and the family, primarily because of changes in the larger social order, is no longer in a position to exercise its responsibilities. The role of the church in moral education has withered in most cases to a pallid Sunday school session. The school — in which the child spends most of his day — has been debarred by tradition, lack of experience and preoccupation with subject matter from concerning itself in any major way with the child's development as a person. The vacuum, moral and emotional, is then filled — by default — on the one hand by the television screen with its daily message of commercialism and violence, and on the other by the socially isolated, age-graded peer group, with its limited capacities as a humanizing agent.

If the current trend persists, we can anticipate increased alienation, indifference, antagonism and violence on the part of the younger generation in all segments of our society — middle-class children as well as the disadvantaged. From this perspective, the emergence of the hippie cult appears as the least harmful manifestation of a process that sees its far more destructive and widespread expression in the sharp rise recently in juvenile delinquency.

Why should age segregation bring social disruption in its wake? It is obvious that such qualities as mutual trust, kindness, cooperation and social responsibility are learned from other human beings who in some measure exhibit these qualities, value them, and strive to develop them in their children. It is a matter of social rather than biological inheritance. Transmission cannot take place without the active participation of the older generation. If children have contact only with their own age-mates, there is no possibility for learning culturally established patterns of cooperation and mutual concern.

We are experiencing a breakdown in the process of making human beings human. What is needed is a change in our ways of living that will once again bring adults back into the lives of children and children back into the lives of adults.

Some ways of accomplishing this change were presented at the White House Conference on Children in a report prepared under my chairmanship. It is well within the resources of our society to act on the Conference recommendations. What will happen if we don't?

In *Lord of the Flies,* William Golding describes events among a group of boys marooned on an island. Patterns of civilized human relationships, epitomized in the boy "Piggy," are as yet too shallowly rooted in the others, and are soon destroyed by the quickly rising sadism of peer power. Piggy is brutally killed just before the adult rescuers arrive. Their first question: "Are there any adults — any grown-ups with you?"

The message of the allegorical ending is clear. If adults do not once again become involved in the lives of our children, there is trouble ahead for American society.

Trial Parenthood

MARGARET MEAD

Young couples today are faced with a new challenge: Should they have children? Marriage has committed them to a partnership in life, a partnership based on their loving choice of each other. But they have another choice to make as well. Should they become partners in parenthood? Should they commit themselves to the task of bringing up children together?

The possibility of choice is entirely real and is rapidly gaining strong social backing. But it seems to me that this choice becomes meaningful only as those who are making it have gained some sense of what the prospects are for themselves, for each other and for the children to whom, as parents, they would commit themselves.

And yet how can they know? How can any two people know what kinds of parents they might become? Are there ways of trying out parenthood without becoming parents? This is the real challenge.

Six years ago I proposed that we move toward two kinds of marriage—an individual form of marriage for those who did not intend to have children then—or perhaps ever—and a second form, more binding and much more cautiously approached, for couples who were preparing to become parents. I thought of this proposal as one way of illuminating the choices that were opening up before us. But there are other ways too. One of these might be called trial parenthood. Young couples who hope someday to have children can try out how good they are at the kind of marriage into which children can be safely welcomed.

As there are many kinds of parenthood, adoptive as well as biological, and also foster and godparental relationships, a couple can explore thoroughly their aptitudes and mutual capacities *before* they elect to have children. Although they cannot be trial parents in fact, they can be parents in prospect and discover what having children would mean to their lives.

Even in the very recent past such an idea would not have made much sense. In a social setting in which almost everyone was expected to marry, it was assumed that all those who married wanted to have a family. In recent years we have argued furiously over a woman's right to delay having a child and her right to accept or reject a particular pregnancy. But we have continued to take it for granted that every couple sooner or later wanted a family and that only those who suffered from some tragic defect or disability would remain childless. So it was those who deliberately chose not to have children who had to justify their decision. Parents and parents-in-law—candidates for grand-parenthood—speculated about, admonished and scolded the childless, and many of those who remained childless. So it was those who deliberately chose not to have children who had to justify their decision. Parents and parents-in-law—candidates for grand-parenthood—speculated about, admonished and scolded the childless, and many of those who remained childless eventually considered adoption.

Now all this is changing. Although marriage still provides a way for young people to get away from parental homes into a home of their own, there is no longer extreme social pressure to make every marriageable person marry. And in light of our better understanding of the population explosion and what it implies for children now being born, social rewards are beginning to go to those who have few children or none at all. No longer pressured into marriage and parenthood, and consequently freer to make a choice, young couples can ask: Would we make good parents?

At the same time, of course, our ideas about parenthood and bringing up children are changing quite radically. Living as a family no longer means a simple division of labor in which Father is a good provider and Mother cares for the home and children. Being good parents now means something that could hardly have been imagined 100 years ago, when the continuity of the family was always threatened by the catastrophe of early death, though divorce was virtually unknown. Considering marriage, our grandparents in dark hours asked themselves: Is he strong? Might he die before our children grow up? Is she sturdy enough to bear and rear children?

Today the basis of good parenthood is the capacity of a man and a woman to live together in amity—to have the mutuality of feeling and the will necessary to stay married to each other at least until the children are grown—until the youngest child has left home. And the questions young couples ask are very different ones: Will he stay? Will she stay? Can we keep in communication with each other? Can we carry the responsibilities of parenthood together?

So the first step for parents in prospect is to try out the expectation of a long-term commitment and their mutual willingness to make the necessary adjustments and sacrifices to get—and keep—the commitment going. Such sacrifices may take many forms. A wife as well as a husband may be engaged in a long period of study and preparation for a career; this may mean a new style of living—and many minor crises—for both of them. Preference for a specific kind of work may necessitate living in a particular place, perhaps thousands of miles from home and familiar friends and diversions.

Daily living together—especially where both partners join in caring for the home—means an inner acceptance of each other's idiosyncrasies—her never being on time, his continual mislaying of his small possessions, her briskness in the morning and his wakeful discussions at night—as well as the inevitable bickering over where to stop for gas or lunch on an auto trip or whether to watch a sports program on television or go to the movie. These are not the kinds of things that can be settled in the glow of courtship or the first experience of living together. It takes time, too, to find out how much boredom each partner can stand, and in every relationship one has to come to terms with some boredom as one or the other tells the same story or makes the expected observation not twice but 100 times.

Can marriage endure through sickness and health, in good fortune and bad, on vacations as well as during the working months, on blue Monday as well as on Sunday? Until this seems to be a realistic expectation, parenthood may be tried out in imagination—fantasied children can be born, named, played with, sent to school and projected into a world of the future. But real children need not be conceived until the prospective parents feel reasonably certain that they will have a continuing home together.

And what about the children around whom young people build fantasies? How does a couple's picture of childhood match the actuality of children growing up today? The question is not only whether prospective parents can more or less agree with each other in their expectations about bringing up a child. Even more crucial, perhaps, is the problem of how well their most cherished fantasies of childhood accord with changed realities. For even parents who do not recall their own childhood with nostalgia—who want something very different for their own children—tend to relate what will be "different" to the remembered past rather than to the living present.

So I think it is important for young couples, as part of the process of making up their minds, to spend a good deal of time with children in their daily activities as one way of exploring their own reactions to contemporary childhood. Serious volunteers are in great demand, and nowadays men as well as women can be drawn into contact with even the smallest children in community centers, in play groups, in day-care centers, in day camps and summer camps and many other settings. Finding time for this will take planning and certainly will mean giving up desirable alternatives—but far less than living with one's own children.

If possible, I think, a couple should work together at such activities, and so enrich each other's perceptions of how they feel and react in a children's world. Some will discover unexpected talents for teaching and play and care. Others may conclude that they would certainly want to swim against the current in bringing up their own children—but at least they would have some idea of how strong the current is. Still others may realize, however reluctantly, that they fit best in a wholly adult world.

At the same time a couple can find out how strong an interest in—and a toleration of—children at different stages of growing each of them has. Both parents don't have to be easy with children of all ages, but one or the other of them has to be able to cope at each stage. And if by chance the husband is better than the wife at soothing a restless baby, this had better be known and faced in advance.

Many parental situations can be tried out for a few hours, a day, a weekend, a month. A couple can spend Saturday afternoon with a sister's new baby while she gets her hair done. They can have a child at home overnight or for a week while a friend takes his wife with him on a business trip. They can spend a vacation in a house full of youngsters. Prospective parents can discover how they respond to an evening dominated by a crying child, perhaps, or the calls of an insistent three-year-old; to the impossibility of discussing an urgent problem because the whole house, turned into a playpen, provides no place where parents can have a quiet talk; or to the miseries of a long cross-country trip with two restless children and a dog.

They then can get some sense of the balance—for them—between inevitable adult frustrations and the delights of discovering the often-unexpected directness and humor of children and their uninhibited imagination in response to the everyday world.

Young people may feel that these "tests" still are not like the actual situations of parenthood, and in a sense they are right. Standing them well is no guarantee that one can stand the long, unremitting years of parenthood. But if a couple—or one of them—cannot stand such "as-if" experiences knowing that the duration is limited, it is time to stop and think again. Living through difficult periods with their own children, parents cannot depart. They can only help a child reach another stage of growth, and sometimes this takes a very long time.

Realistically, there is another possibility that cannot be left out of account. Suppose that, after all, the marriage—undertaken with the best intentions and the deepest commitment—does not endure? What would each be like as a separated parent, singly responsible over long stretches of time for the care of the children? How willing would each one be to share the love and trust of children who no longer were part of a united home? How willing would either one be to join some form of community living with neighbors and friends to share the burdens of single parenthood?

There is no way, I think, of trying out a failed relationship—nor would anyone want to do so. But it is a possibility, however remote, that should matter to parents in prospect. All they can go on, perhaps, is their own and each other's responses to other couples who are in trouble.

All these are considerations for the future for those who do not yet have children. Young couples have a choice to make, and since they cannot turn to the past for precedents, they must find ways of using the present to set a new style of living as husband and wife alone or as partners in marriage who also consciously choose parenthood and the life of a family.

But how about the millions of men and women who did not so much

choose parenthood as simply accept it as an inevitable part of marriage? Do they have to mull over what they might think or say or do if
they were getting married today instead of ten years ago?

Of course not. Nothing is so fruitless as trying to relive one's life on
the basis of what one might have done at some other time and in a
different world. Ten years ago the dangers of the population explosion
had not been generally recognized, there was no effective Women's
Liberation Movement to raise consciousness levels and young men and
women alike accepted marriage with parenthood as a matter of course.
And where simply getting married meant accepting the children that
came, parents and children together shared in the fate of a kind of
family over which individuals had little control.

But this need not cut children off from the future. I do believe that
each generation *can* choose—if not for themselves, then for the benefit
of their children. Those who married in the older style can bring up
their children to believe that parenthood is a vocation for which not all
individuals have an aptitude and which may be as responsibly rejected
as it should be accepted. They can encourage their daughters and sons,
as they grow up and prepare to marry, to think of elective parenthood
as a choice they have the freedom and the responsibility to explore.

And finally, bridging past and present in their experience and that
of their young children, those who already know a great deal about the
hazards and rewards of parenthood can—if they are deeply honest
become a principal resource for parents in prospect. They too have an
important part to play in developing a style of living in which the
children who are born are positively wanted and welcomed by both
parents, who have put parenthood on trial and have decided for it.

Parenthood Training or Mandatory Birth Control: Take Your Choice

ROGER W. MCINTIRE

Few parents like to be told how to raise their children, and even fewer will like the idea of someone telling them whether they can even have children in the first place. But that's exactly what I'm proposing - - the licensing of parenthood. Of course, civil libertarians and other liberals will claim this would infringe the parents' rights to freedom of choice and equal opportunity. But what about the rights of children? Surely the parents' competence will influence their children's freedom and opportunity. Today, any couple has the right to try parenting, regardless of how incompetent they might be. No one seems to worry about the unfortunate subjects of their experimenting.

The idea of licensing parenthood is hardly new (see "It's Time We Taught the Young How to Be Good Parents" by Robert P. Hawkins, PT, November 1972). But until recently, our ignorance of environmental effects, our ignorance of contraception, and our selfish bias against the rights of children have inhibited public discussion of the topic. In recent years, however, psychologists have taught us just how crucial the effect of the home environment can be, and current research on contraception appears promising.

Contraception by Capsule

Successful control of parenthood will require a contraceptive that remains in effect until it is removed or counteracted by the administration of a second drug. Sheldon Segal, director of Rockefeller University's Biomedical Division of the Population Council has developed (with others) a contraceptive capsule implant and has clinically tested it. Inserted under a woman's skin by hypodermic needle, the capsule leaks a steady supply of progestin, which prevents pregnancy. A three-year capsule is now being perfected. A doctor could terminate the contraceptive effect early merely by removing the capsule.

Several scientists are currently conducting research on a contraceptive by which a man's sperm could be rendered inoperable.

Leslie A. and Charles F. Westoff, authors of *From Now to Zero: Fertility, Contraception and Abortion in America,* describe a procedure that strengthens the fluids that surround the sperm cells and prohibit fertilization. (Ordinarily, female enzymes in the uterus destroy this protection so that the sperm may fertilize.) Philip Rumke, head of the Department of Immunology at the Netherlands Cancer Institute, and

Roberto Mancini, professor of Histology at the Buenos Aires Medical School have both been experimenting with contraceptive vaccines that would inactivate male sperm.

THE CHILD VICTIM

Clearly, we will soon have the technology necessary to carry out a parenthood licensing program, and history tells us that whenever we develop a technology, we inevitably use it. We should now be concerned with developing the criteria for good parenthood. In some extreme cases we already have legal and social definitions. We obviously consider child abuse wrong, and look upon those who physically mistreat their children as bad parents. In some states the courts remove children from the custody of parents convicted of child abuse.

In a recent review of studies of child abusing parents, John J. Spinetta and David Rigler concluded that such people are generally ignorant of proper child-rearing practices. They also noted that many child-abusing parents had been victims of abuse and neglect in their own youth. Thus our lack of control over who can be parents magnifies the problem with each generation.

In the case of child abusing parents, the state attempts to prevent the most obvious physical mistreatment of children. At this extreme, our culture does demand that parents prove their ability to provide for the physical well-being of their children. But our culture makes almost no demands when it comes to the children's psychological well-being and development: Any fool can now raise a child anyway he or she pleases, and it's none of our business. The child becomes the unprotected victim of whoever gives birth to him.

Ironically, the only institutions that do attempt to screen potential parents are the adoption agencies, although their screening can hardly be called scientific. Curiously enough, those who oppose a parent-licensing law usually do not oppose the discriminating policies practiced by the adoption agencies. It seems that our society cares more about the selection of a child's second set of parents than it does about his original parents. In other words, our culture insists on insuring a certain quality of parenthood for adopted children, but if you want to have one of your own, feel free.

Screening and selecting potential parents by no means guarantees that they will in fact be good parents. Yet today we have almost no means of insuring proper child-rearing methods. The indiscriminate "right to parent" enables everyone, however ill-equipped, to practice any parental behavior they please. Often their behavior would be illegal if applied to any group other than children. But because of our prejudice against the rights of children, we protect them only when the most savage and brutal parental behavior can be proved in court. Consider the following example:

SUPERMARKET SCENARIO

A mother and daughter enter a supermarket. An accident occurs when the daughter pulls the wrong orange from the pile and 37 oranges are given their freedom. The mother grabs the daughter, shakes her vigorously, and slaps her. What is your reaction? Do you ignore the incident? Do you consider it a family squabble and none of your business? Or do you go over and advise the mother not to hit her child? If the mother rejects your advice, do you physically restrain her? If she persists, do you call the police? Think about your answers for a moment.

Now let me change one detail. *The girl was not that mother's daughter.* Do you feel different? Would you act differently. Why? Do "real" parents have the right to abuse their children because they "own" them? Now let me change another detail. Suppose the daughter was 25 years old, and yelled, "Help me! Help me!" Calling the police sounded silly when I first suggested it. How does it sound with a mere change in the age of the victim?

Now let's go back to the original scene where we were dealing with a small child. Were you about to advise the mother or insist? Were you going to say she shouldn't or couldn't? It depends on whose rights you're going to consider. If you think about the mother's right to mother as she sees fit, then you advise; but if you think about the child's right as a human being to be protected from the physical assault of this woman, then you insist. The whole issue is obviously tangled in a web of beliefs about individual rights, parental rights, and children's rights. We tend to think children deserve what they get, or at least must suffer it. Assault and battery, verbal abuse, and even forced imprisonment become legal if the victims are children.

When I think about the issue of children's rights, and the current development of new contraceptives, I see a change coming in this country. I'm tempted to make the following prediction in the form of a science-fiction story:

MOTHERHOOD IN THE 1980s

"Lock" was developed as a kind of semi-permanent contraceptive in 1975. One dose of Lock and a woman became incapable of ovulation until the antidote "Unlock" was administered. As with most contraceptives, Lock required a prescription, with sales limited by the usual criteria of age and marital status.

Gradually, however, a subtle but significant distinction became apparent. Other contraceptives merely allowed a woman to protect herself against pregnancy at her own discretion. Once Lock was administered, however, the prescription for Unlock required an active decision to allow the *possibility* of pregnancy.

By 1978, the two drugs were being prescribed simultaneously, leaving the Unlock decision in the hands of the potential mother. Of course, problems arose. Mothers smuggled Lock to their daughters and the daughters later asked for Unlock. Women misplaced the Unlock and had to ask for more. Faced with the threat of a black market, the state set up a network of special dispensaries for the contraceptive and its antidote. When the first dispensaries opened in 1979, they dispensed Lock rather freely, since they could always regulate the use of Unlock. But it soon became apparent that special local committees would be necessary to screen applicants for Unlock. "After all," the dispensary officials asked themselves, "how would you like to be responsible for this person becoming a parent?"

Protect Our Children

That same year, 1979, brought the school-population riots. Overcrowding had forced state education officials to take some action. Thanks to more efficient educational techniques, they were able to consider reducing the number of years of required schooling. This, however, would have thrown millions of teen-agers out onto the already overcrowded job market, which would make the unions unhappy. Thus, rather than shortening the entire educational process, the officials decided to shorten the school day into two half-day shifts. That led to the trouble.

Until then, people had assumed that schools existed primarily for the purpose of education. But the decision to shorten the school day exposed the dependence of the nation's parents on the school as the great baby sitter of their offspring. Having won the long struggle for daycare centers, and freedom from diapers and bottles, mothers were horrified at the prospect of a few more hours of responsibility every day until their children reached 18 or 21. They took to the streets.

In Richmond, Virginia, a neighborhood protest over the shortened school day turned into a riot. One of the demonstrators picked up a traffic sign near the school that cautioned drivers to "Protect Our Children," and found herself leading the march toward city hall. Within a week that sign became the national slogan for the protesters, as well as for the Lock movement. It came to mean not only protecting our children from overcrowding and lack of supervision, but also protecting them from pregnancy.

Because of the school-population riots, distribution of Lock took on the characteristics of an immunization program under the threat of an epidemic. With immunization completed, the state could control the birth rate like a water faucet by the distribution of Unlock. However this did not solve the problem of deciding who should bear the nation's children.

Congress Takes Over

To settle the issue, Congress appointed a special blue-ribbon commission of psychologists, psychiatrists, educators, and clergymen to come up with acceptable criteria for parenthood, and a plan for a licensing program. The commission issued its report in 1984. Based upon its recommendations, Congress set up a Federal regulatory agency to administer a national parenthood-licensing program similar to driver-training and licensing procedures.

The agency now issues study guides for the courses, and sets the required standards of child-rearing knowledge. Of course, the standards vary for parents, teachers, and child-care professionals, depending upon the degree of responsibility involved. The courses and exams are conducted by local community colleges, under the supervision of the Federal agency. Only upon passing the exams can prospective parents receive a prescription for Unlock.

Distribution of Lock and Unlock is now strictly regulated by the Federal agency's local commissions. Since the records of distribution are stored in Federal computer banks, identification of illegitimate pregnancies (those made possible by the unauthorized use of Unlock) has become a simple matter. Parents convicted of this crime are fined, and required to begin an intensive parenthood-training program immediately. If they do not qualify by the time their child is born, the child goes to a community child-care program until they do.

Drawing the Battle Lines

As might be expected, the parent-licensing program has come under attack from those who complain about the loss of their freedom to create and raise children according to their own choice and beliefs. To such critics, the protect-our-children or Lock faction argues: "It's absurd to require education and a license to drive a car, but allow anybody to raise our most precious possession or to add to the burden of this possession without demonstrating an ability to parent."

"But the creation of life is in the hands of God," say the freedom-and-right-to-parent-faction (referred to by their opponents as the "far-right-people").

"Nonsense," say the Lock people. "Control over life creation was acquired with the first contraceptive. The question is whether we use it with intelligence or not."

"But that question is for each potential parent to answer as an individual," say the far-right people.

The Lock people answer: "Those parents ask the selfish question of whether they want a child or not. We want to know if the child will be adequately cared for — by them and by the culture."

The far right respond, "God gave us bodies and all their functions. We have a right to the use of those functions. Unlock should be there for the asking. Why should the Government have a say in whether I have a child?"

"Because the last century has shown that the Government will be saddled with most of the burden of raising your child," say the Lock people. "The schools, the medical programs, the youth programs, the

crime-prevention programs, the colleges, the park and planning commissions — they will be burdened with your child. That's why the
Government should have a say. The extent of the Government's burden depends on your ability to raise your child. If you screw it up, the
society *and* government will suffer. That's why they should screen
potential parents."

From the right again: "The decision of my spouse and myself is
sacred. It's none of their damn business."

But the Locks argue: "If you raised your child in the wilderness and
the child's malfunctions punished no one but yourselves, it would be
none of their damn business. But if your child is to live with us, be
educated by us, suffered by us, add to the crowd of us, we should have a
say."

FACE OF THE FUTURE

I can understand how some people might find this story either far-
fetched or frightening, but I don't think any prediction in it is too far in
the future. Carl Djerassi suggested the possibility of a semipermanent
contraceptive such as "Lock" and "Unlock" (although he didn't use
those brand names) as early as 1969, in an article in *Science.* And as I
described earlier, other scientists are currently making significant
strides in contraceptive research.

Throughout history, as knowledge has eroded away superstition
about conception and birth, humans have taken increasing control
over the birth of their offspring. Religious practices, arranged marriages, mechanical and biochemical contraception have all played a
role in this regulation of procreation. Until now, however, such regulation has dealt only with the presence or absence of children, leaving
their development to cultural superstitions. Anyone with normai biology may still produce another child, and, within the broadest limits,
treat it anyway he or she chooses.

We have taken a long time in coming to grips with this problem
because our society as a whole has had no demonstrably better ideas
about child-rearing than any individual parent. And until now, people
couldn't be stopped from having children because we haven't had the
technology that would enable us to control individual fertility.

HOW TO REAR A CHILD

The times are changing. With the population problem now upon us,
we can no longer afford the luxury of allowing any two fools to add to
our numbers whenever they please. We do have, or soon will have, the
technology to control individual procreation. And, most important,
psychology and related sciences have by now established some child-
rearing principles that should be part of every parent's knowledge (see
"Spare the Rod, Use Behavior Mod," by Roger W. McIntire, PT,

December 1970). An objective study of these principles need not involve the prying, subjective investigation now used by adoption agencies. It would merely insure that potential parents would be familiar with the principles of sound child-rearing. Examinations and practical demonstrations would test their knowledge. Without having state agents check every home (and of course, we would never accept such "Big Brother" tactics) there could be no way to enforce the use of that knowledge. But insistence on the knowledge would itself save a great deal of suffering by the children.

The following list suggests a few of the topics with which every parent should be familiar:

1. Principles of sound nutrition and diet.
2. Changes in nutritional requirements with age.
3. Principles of general hygiene and health.
4. Principles of behavioral development: normal range of ages at which behavioral capabilities might be expected, etc.
5. Principles of learning and language acquisition.
6. Principles of immediacy and consistency that govern parents' reactions to children's behavior.
7. Principles of modeling and imitation: how children learn from and copy their parents' behavior.
8. Principles of reinforcement: how parent and peer reactions reward a child's behavior, and which rewards should be used.
9. Principles of punishment: how parents' reactions can be used to punish or discourage bad behavior.
10. Response-cost concept: how to "raise the cost" or create unpleasant consequences in order to make undesirable behavior more "expensive" or difficult.
11. Extinction procedures and adjunctive behavior: if rewards for good behavior cease, children may "act up" just to fill the time.
12. Stimulus-control generalization: children may act up in some situations, and not in others, because of different payoffs. For example, Mommy may give the child candy to stop a tantrum, whereas Daddy may ignore it or strike the child.

Most of us have some familiarity with the principles at the beginning of this list, but many parents have little knowledge of the other topics. Some psychologists would obviously find my list biased toward behavior modification, but their revisions or additions to the list only strengthen my argument that our science has a great deal to teach that would be relevant to a parenthood-licensing program.

MISPLACED PRIORITIES

Of course the word licensing suggests that the impersonal hand of Government may control individual lives, and that more civil servants will be paid to meddle in our personal affairs. But consider for a moment that for our safety and well-being we already license pilots, salesmen, scuba divers, plumbers, electricians, teachers, veterinarians, cab drivers, soil testers and television repairmen. To protect pedestrians, we accept restrictions on the speed with which we drive our cars. Why, then, do we encounter such commotion, chest thumping, and cries of oppression when we try to protect the well-being of children by controlling the most crucial determiner of that well-being, the competence of their parents? Are our TV sets and toilets more important to us than our children? Can you imagine the public outcry that would occur if adoption agencies offered their children on a first-come-first-served basis, with no screening process for applicants? Imagine some drunk stumbling up and saying, "I'll take that cute little blond-haired girl over there."

We require appropriate education for most trades and professions, yet stop short at parenthood because it would be an infringement on the individual freedom of the parent. The foolishness of this position will become increasingly apparent the more confident we become in our knowledge about child rearing.

The first step toward a parenthood law will probably occur when child abuse offenders will be asked or required to take "Lock" as an alternative to, or in addition to, being tried in court. Or the courts may also offer the child abuser the alternative of a remedial training program such as the traffic courts now use. The next step may be the broadening of the term "child abuse" to include ignorant mistreatment of a psychological nature. Some communities may add educational programs to marriage-license requirements, while others may add parenthood training to existing courses in baby care.

When the Government gets around to setting criteria for proper child rearing, these must be based upon a very specific set of principles of nutrition, hygiene, and behavior control. They cannot be based on bias and hearsay. Some of the criteria now used by adoption agencies, such as references from neighbors and friends, cannot be considered objective. We don't interview your neighbors when you apply for a driver's license, and it shouldn't be done for a parent's license either. But just as a citizen must now demonstrate knowledge and competence to drive a car, so ought he to demonstrate his ability to parent as well. Proof of exposure to education is not enough. We are not satisfied merely with driver-training courses, but demand a driver's test as well. We should require the same standards of parents.

We can hope that as progress occurs in the technology of contraception and the knowledge of child-rearing principles, the currently sacred "right to parent" will be re-evaluated by our society. Perhaps we can construct a society that will also consider the rights that children have to a humane and beneficial upbringing.

Marriage as a
Human-Actualizing Contract

VIRGINIA SATIR

When I was asked to write this paper, the idea excited me. I have many thoughts about this subject. As I sit down now to write, I am overwhelmed at the enormity of their implications. My power of imagination fails me in visualizing how all these changes could be accomplished, given this world as it is today, with its vast numbers of people and prevailing low image of a human being; this world, where love and trust are rarities and suspicion and hate are expected.

Person-person, male-female, adult-child relations, as they exist today, seem pretty inhuman and many times even anti-human. The current legal and social structure frequently acts to aid and abet these inhuman contacts. Given the state of human relations today, it is not hard to understand current human behavior in marriage, the family, and other human transactions.

The effect of these inhuman and anti-human relations seems abundantly obvious in the widespread presence of mistrust and fear between human beings. If relationships are experienced as mistrust and fear, how can love and trust come about? Statistics on alcoholism, drug addiction, suicide, murder, mental illness, and crimes against persons or property are more specific indications of inhuman and anti-human treatment. Continuing wars between nations, racial strife, and poverty are global evidences of these same practices.

While these statistics do not include every person in our population, enough are included to make it more than just a random or accidental occurrence. This raises the basic question: *Is this how man really is inherently or is this the result of how he has been taught?* I would have to stop this paper right now if I believed that man's present behavior is the result of what he is, inherently. I believe man's behavior reflects what he has learned and I take hope in the fact that anything that has been learned can be unlearned and new learning can be introduced.

This, of course, raises another basic question: *What are these new learnings?* To talk about a change in the marriage relationship without talking about making changes in the human beings who make the marriage is, in my opinion, putting the cart before the horse. I would like to present some ideas which might go a long way toward moving us

Virginia Satir, "Marriage as a Human-Actualizing Contract," in Herbert A. Otto, Ed., *The Family in Search of A Future,* ©1970 by Meredith Corporation. Reprinted by permission of Prentice-Hall, Inc., Englewood Cliffs, New Jersey.

all a notch forward in our whole human existence and consequently in the marriage relationship.

WHAT WOULD HAPPEN IF:

1. *Children were conceived only by mature adults?* If these parents felt prepared and knew, beyond few questions of doubt, that they had the skills to be wise, patient, and joyful teachers of human beings, of creative, loving, curious, real persons? Further, if this conception were an active mutual choice representing a welcome addition, instead of a potential deprivation or a substitute for a marital dissappointment?

2. *Parenting were seen as probably the most crucial, challenging, and interesting job for each adult engaged in it?*

a. The business and the working world would manage in such a way that young fathers would not be asked to be gone from Monday to Friday. Men are essential; their non-presence hands child-rearing almost exclusively over to women. This skews the kind of parenting a child gets, which is reflected in his image of himself and others. An integrated person needs to have an intimate, real familiarity with both sexes. For many children, fathers are ghosts, benign or malevolent. If they are males, this leaves them with a hazy and incomplete model for themselves. If they are females, their relations and expectations of men evolve more from fantasy than reality. It seems to me that knowledge about, and familiarity with, the other sex in the growing-up years is a large factor in satisfaction in married life. Furthermore, male absence overdraws on the woman's resources, paving the way for all kinds of destructive results for herself, her children, and her husband. However we slice it, we come into the world with life equipment, but it remains for our experiences to teach the uses of it. After all, the husbands and fathers, the wives and mothers of today are the boys and girls of yesterday.

b. Women who are mothers and men who are fathers could have auxiliary help without stigma in their parenting. Parenting for the first five years is a twenty-four-hour-a-day job. This gets pretty confining if there is no relief. Auxiliary help might go a long way toward the real responsibility of developing the child's humanity.

c. There would be family financial allowances to people who needed them, not on the basis of being poor and just making survival possible, but because it was needed to facilitate optimum growth.

d. Preparation for parenting would be seen as something to be actively learned instead of assuming that the experience of conception and birth automatically provided all the know-how one needed. Nobody calling himself an engineer would even be considered for an engineering job if all the preparation he had consisted of his wish to be one, and the knowledge he gained by watching his engineer father.

3. *The idea of developing human beings was considered so important and vital that each neighborhood had within walking distance a Family Growth Center which was a center for learning about being human, from birth to death.*

These might well replace public welfare offices, among other institutions. In my opinion, this process, learning how to be human, will never end: I believe the human potential is infinite. We have barely scratched the surface.

4. *The literal context surrounding the birth event included full awareness for the woman giving birth, the active witnessing of the birth process by father of the child, and the rooming-in of all three for at least the first two weeks.* Everyone would get a chance to be in on the getting-acquainted process that necessarily takes place. In a first birth, the female would meet her husband in his father role for the first time; the male would meet his wife in her mother role for the first time; each would meet a slightly new person. Many men and women feel like strangers to each other when they meet as fathers and mothers despite the fact that they have previously been husband and wives.

The subsequent celebration following the birth could celebrate not only a birth of a new human being, but a birth of new roles for the adults as well. (The way some celebrations have gone would suggest immaculate conception.) Men often feel like useless appendages at this time. No wonder there are fears of replacement on their part. I wonder whether it would be as possible for men who are fathers to leave their families as readily as they now do if they were part of the literal birth proceedings, openly hailed and honored as being and having been essential, as are women. I wonder too, if this were done, whether the birth of a baby would create as much estrangement between husband and wives as it often does.

5. *Child-rearing practices were changed.*

a. The emphasis in child rearing would be on helping the child find out, crystal-clearly, how to find out how he experienced others and affected them, instead of only the admonishment to be good and find out how to please others.

b. From the moment of birth he would be treated as a person with the capacity to hear, see, to feel, to sense, and to think, different from the adult only in body development and, initially, in putting his sensory and thought experiences into words.

c. He would have a predictable place in time and space.

d. He would have real and openly welcomed opportunities to feel his power and his uniqueness, his sexuality and his competence as soon as his resources permitted it.

e. He would be surrounded by people who openly and clearly enjoyed each other and him, who were straight and real with one another and with him, thus giving him a model for his own delight in interacting with people. Thus, the joy in relationships might overcome the grimly responsible outlook "becoming an adult" often has for a child.

f. "Yes" and "no" would be clear, reliable, appropriate, and implemented.

g. Realness would be valued over approval when there had to be a choice.

h. At every point in time, regardless of age or label, he would always be treated as a whole person and never regarded as too young to be a person.

i. Every child's feelings would be regarded with dignity and respect, listened to and understood; those around him would do the same with each other. There would be a basic difference between his awareness and expression of his feelings and thoughts, and the action he took in relation to them.

j. Every child's actions would be considered separately from his expressions, instead of linking expressions of feeling with an automatic specific act. He would be taught that actions had to be subject to time, place, situation, other persons, and purpose, rather than being given a stereotyped "should" that applies universally.

k. Difference from others would be seen clearly as an opportunity for learning, holding an important key to interest in living and real contact with others, instead of being seen primarily as something to be tolerated, or destroyed, or avoided.

l. Every child would have continuing experience that human life is to be revered, his and that of all others.

m. Every child would openly receive continuing knowledge of how he and all his parts work — his body, his mind, and his senses. He would receive encouragement for expressing, clarifying, and experimenting with his thoughts, his feelings, his words, his actions, and his body, in all its parts.

n. He would look forward to each new step in growth as an opportunity for discovery, encompassing pain, pleasure, knowledge, and adventure. Each phase of growth has special learnings that could be particularly planned for; evidence showing that a new growth step had been achieved would be openly and obviously validated, like celebrating with a party the onset of menstruation for girls and maybe a change of voice party for boys at the time of puberty. Further examples would be: parties for the first step, first tooth, first day at school, first overnight visit with non-familial members, first date, first sexual intercourse, and the first obvious and costly mistake. Mistakes are an inevitable part of risk-taking, which is an essential part of growth, and needs to be so understood.

o. He could see males and females as different, yet interesting and essential to each other, free to be separate instead of being implicit enemies or feeding on each other.

p. He could get training in male-female relations, could prepare openly for mating and parenting in turn, which would be explained as desirable, and demonstrated as such.

q. He would be openly let in on the experiences of adults in parenting, maritalling, and selfing.

6. *He could freely experience in an openly welcoming way the emergence of the sexual self.* This would require lifting the cover of secrecy on the genitals and all that it entails.

7. *The goal of being human was being real, loving, intimate, authentic, and alive as well as competent, productive, and responsible.*

We have never had people reared anything like this on a large enough scale to know how this would affect marriage, the family, and, in general, people-to-people relationships. We have never realized what impetus to a really better world and a socially more evolved people might be created for tackling the "insurmountable" problems of suicide, murder, alcoholism, illegitimacy, irresponsibility, incompetence, war, racial and national conflicts. I think this is worth trying.

In our society, marriage is the social and legal context in which new humans originate and are expected to grow into fully developed human beings. The very life of our society depends upon what happens as a result of marriage. Looking at the institution of marriage as it exists today raises real questions about its effectiveness.

*   *   *

If we were all to see the sexual act as the renewal value of the other and the increase of self-esteem in the self, if the decision to procreate was a voluntary, mutually-shared one entered into *after* the intimate, satisfying, renewing experience had been achieved by a male and female pair, what magnitude of revolution might we stimulate in a new model for person-to-person relations?

Anyone who has studied family process at all can see with one eye how (1) the sexual relationship is symbolic of the heterosexual interrelationship and thus carries the significance of the person-to-person relationship, and (2) that the fate of the child hangs on this interrelationship.

Intercourse is a fact, not a symbol. Conception, pregnancy, and birth are also facts, not symbols. The child is a result of these facts, but his maturing is guided by the feelings that surround these facts.

I am implying three changes:

1. That the cover of secrecy be removed from the sexual part of the human being. With this cover off, ignorance can be removed.

2. That there be as much attention, care, and implementation, openly, creatively and confidently given to the care, maintenance, and use of the genitals as there is, for instance, to the teeth.

3. That a couple have a means to know when they have achieved intimacy in their relationship, which is based on their experience with, and awareness of, each other as real persons whom they value, enjoy, and feel connected with.

If we were taught from childhood on that our most important goal as human beings is to be real and in continuing touch with ourselves, this in turn would ensure a real connection with others. Were we taught that creativity, authenticity, health, aliveness, lovingness, and productivity were desirable goals, we would have a much greater sense of when this was achieved, and would also find it much easier to do so.

With the expectation of the age of marriage being around twenty and life expectancy being around seventy, close to fifty years of a person's life can be expected to be lived under the aegis of a marriage contract. If the contract does not permit an alive, dynamic experience, with growth possible for both, the result is outrage, submission, destructiveness, withdrawal, premature death, or destructive termination. Maybe this type of marriage contract is impossible. If it is, then perhaps what we need to do is to find a way to conceive and bring up children that does not depend on a permanent relationship between the parents. The act of conception and birth could be entirely separated from the process of raising children. We could have child manufacturers and child raisers. We have much of this now except that it is socially stigmatizing. We work awfully hard to make adoption unsuccessful. "He is not my real child," or "She is not my real mother." Actually most of us know that the significance of the blood tie is mostly in our heads.

Maybe the most important thing is that new humans get born and then they are raised. Who does either or both may not be as important as that it is done and how it is done. Maybe if such a "division of labor" were effected, the energies of all the adults of the world would be more available for work and joy and less tied up with what they "should" be.

Procreation — coming about as it does, with little evidence that it will change much in the near future — guarantees that there will always be males and females around, and that they will be attracted to one another, in or out of marriage. Maybe this could be openly acknowledged and we could find ways to use it for our mutual benefit.

As for me, I think a relationship of trust, worth, and love between people is the highest and most satisfying way of experiencing one's humanity. I think this is where real spirituality takes place. Without it, humans become shrivelled, destructive, and desolate.

Right now, our current forms of human interaction, our fears, our suspicions, and our past are working against us. We have all the resources for the needed change, but we do not yet know how to use them. Our survival as a society may well depend upon finding these uses.

Unit Study Guide

A. Terms to Review

Androsperms	Cultural dis-	Reinforcement
"Bounce test"	continuity	Romantic complex
Cloning	Family allowances	Schettles technique
Couvade	Gynosperms	Sperm bank
Crisis	Indianapolis	Trial parenthood
	Fertility Study	(Mead)
	Intrauterine	
	device	

B. Questions for Discussion and Study

1. Considerable research suggests a debilitating effect of reproductive activity on the intimate behavior of marital partners. Account

for this, drawing on pertinent sociological, psychiatric, and psychological theory and research. Is a negative effect inevitable? If not, what intervention techniques or interpersonal changes could be induced to reduce the possible negative impact of reproduction?K

2. Suppose a group of three men and three women are entertaining the idea of forming a communal reproduction and parenting situation among themselves. Leaving aside the legal aspects, assume that each is about age twenty-three. What would be the minimal prerequisites (physical, social, behavioral, etc.) for persons forming such an arrangement? Could it be truly communal? Discuss and indicate the factual and ethical bases of your conclusions.

3. To what extent and in what ways do we already have some forms of state intervention in reproduction, especially regarding quality and quantity? Cite your sources in answering.

4. Suggest and describe ome practical steps that could be taken to promote the development of a humanistic, growth-oriented child-rearing process in the American family. Cite and discuss actual, concrete proposals and show how they might be implemented.

5. Briefly review each of the alternatives regarding parenthood which are listed in the introduction to this unit. Discuss their feasibility, their strengths and their weaknesses.

6. Discuss the possible influence of ideas from the sexual equality and human potential movements on the formulation of reproduction and parenting alternatives which are listed in the introduction to this unit.

7. Bronfenbrenner has argued that parents should take a much more active role in influencing the activities of their offspring, including the setting of limits and the enforcement of expectations. Do you agree with this? Describe your position and show why you hold that point of view.

C. *Topics-Ideas for Papers and Projects*

1. Develop an estimate of the cost in dollars of reproducing and rearing one child to age eighteen. Show the various kinds of expenses you anticipate, and cite your sources for the estimate.

2. "The relationship of family size to the incidence of child-abuse."

3. Research: "Sex differences in the Perception of Expectations about Forthcoming Parental Roles."

4. Make a list, in ranked order, of the five most important characteristics you consider essential in a "good" parent. Compare your list with others, tabulate the rankings developed by the whole class, and discuss the patterns

5. Construct a five-point scale (from "very high" to "not at all") on which each member of the class would rate the feasibility of each of the reproductive and parenting alternatives listed in the introduction to this unit. Next have each person rate these same alternatives on the personal acceptability of each one. Tabulate and compare the two rankings for the group, and discuss the patterns of congruence and divergence.

6. Invite a representative of a local-area family planning agency to speak to your class on the work of that agency.

7. Do a content analysis of local newspaper coverage of familial-marital topics. How does the topic of reproduction and parenthood compare in frequency of appearance and coverage size with other topics (eg. marriage, divorce, mate-selection, sexuality, etc.)?

8. Administer the "Attitudes toward freedom of children" scale (Shaw and Wright, *Scales for the Measurement of Attitudes,* McGraw-Hill, 1967) in your class. Next have each class member administer a copy of this same scale to his or her same-sex parent. After getting all responses, compare similarities and differences in responses and discuss the findings in class.

PART FOUR

MARITAL RELATIONSHIP CRISIS: PROBLEM-SOLVING RESPONSES

Unit 9
Termination and Remarriage: The American Pattern

. . .a second marriage represents the triumph
of hope over experience.–Samuel Johnson

What dire offence from amorous causes springs!
What mighty contests rise from trival things!–Pope

Introduction

Two distinctive but related features of the American marriage scene which continue to be the interest of social scientists are the processes of voluntary termination and remarriage. Voluntary termination is represented by the processes of divorce, separation, desertion, and annulment. In our examination of voluntary termination in this unit, we will focus mainly on divorce process. Divorce cannot, however, be adequately discussed without introducing the topic of remarriage. As we shall see in later discussion, the two processes are closely linked. A large proportion of divorces are followed very rapidly by remarriage of one or both partners. Americans seemingly "try . . . try again" in their quest for personal happiness. Thus, one of the features most interesting to sociologists studying voluntary marital termination is the apparent tendency of many persons to use the divorce mechanism as a problem-solving technique.

Although the trend runs counter to the traditional concept of marriage as a life-long union, there is increasingly wide usage of divorce as a legitimate technique of dealing with a marriage that is unhappy or which has failed to meet the partners' expectations. The magnitude of the voluntary termination phenomenon is suggested in statistics gathered nationally by the U.S. Census Bureau. Consider, for example, that there are at least fifteen million living Americans who have been through the divorce process at one time or another, Or that approximately four million persons currently list their marital status as "divorced." A conservative prediction is that as many as one-fifth of all adult Americans will experience divorce during their lifetime.[1] The trend in the incidence of legitimized marital termination could graphically be shown as a continuously rising curve. Thus, in 1895 one couple was divorced for every twelve who were married. Today, it is close to one couple divorcing for every three who are married. Examining data for more recent years, we find that the facts are no less startling. In 1971 there were 768,000 divorces and a termination rate of 3.7 per one thousand population; compare this with 1960 when there were 393,000 divorces and a 2.2 rate. Today's rate is more than double the 1953 divorce rate.[2]

At least passing comment ought to be made on the phenomenon of voluntary marital termination in a broader sense. Namely, while we have referred only to divorce thus far, it would probably be quite erroneous to assume that it constituted alone the major source of voluntary terminations of marriage. On the contrary, it seems highly probable that the number of desertions and separations occurring each year is at least equal to, and perhaps exceeds, the total annual number of divorces.[3]

So much, then, for the statistical overview. Most of us need little persuasion to convince us that voluntary marital terminations are occurring at a very high rate. And in terms of its qualitative aspects, a plethora of explanations and attributed "causes" of divorce are found in mass media, books, sermons, and classroom. Since a basic assumption in this introduction is that divorce serves as a problem-solving technique, we will not take time to review the many "causal" arguments and explanations; they range from sources in institutional-societal breakdown or complexity to individual neurotic motivations. Many thousands of couples enter the divorce process and probably as many thousands more contemplate divorce at some point in their marriage. The weight of religious tradition as well as hopeful optimism about marriage's durability continue to cast the divorce process in a somewhat negative light in this society. But given a society where both freedom of choice and the pursuit of happiness are extolled, it is likely that divorce will continue to be a widely-used technique for terminating an unhappy or unsatisfactory marital partnership.

Implicit support for the concept of divorce as a problem-solving mode is seen in the tendency of Americans to remarry following divorce. Thus, divorce per se does not imply a repudiation or even a belittling of the marriage institution. Instead, it releases individuals to pursue happiness in still another marital relationship. In 1969, for example, nearly one-fifth of all persons marrying had been married and divorced at least once before. Research also shows that little time is lost in the transition from one marital relationship to another. Twenty-five percent of divorcing men and women are remarried within five months; fifty percent of them are remarried within one year.[4] The statistical picture of remarriage can be rounded out somewhat further: (1) One of every five marrying couples involves a remarriage for one or both partners; (2) The probability of marriage for divorced persons is higher, at every age level, than for single persons;

and (3) About half of those remarrying are in their early thirties or younger.

It is readily seen that divorce and remarriage are closely related. in fact, there is probably much less randomness in remarriage than might be supposed. Many divorce actions probably represent, somewhat in the manner of "serial monogamy," a deliberate movement by one partner from an unsatisfactory marriage to a pre-selected partner in a subsequent relationship.[5] This transition is not likely to occur without some costs to those involved.

It is often claimed, and with probable validity, that most persons enter into the divorce process either too hastily or without sufficient pondering of its possible impact on their lives. High levels of aspiration may lead to disillusionment rather than fulfillment in the subsequent relationship ; and, as one divorced person put it, "Once you've torn down the structure of your marriage, it's impossible to put all the pieces together again—even if you want to desperately." Shakespeare put it well when he said: "Striving to better, oft we mar what's well." Thus, while the termination process may be conceived as a problem-solving technique, it may of itself be problem-laden or induce various difficulties. What are some of the problems associated with the divorce process? From the perspective of the marital partners involved, several can be briefly cited.

A major difficulty is found in the emotional upset and unhappiness connected with the decision to terminate the marriage. Few marriages are totally bad, utterly without redeeming qualities. Indeed, it might be contended that many marriages are terminated not because they have been so terrible for the partners, but as Farson has said, because ". . . by the very fact of being good, they generate discontent." This sort of discontent arises from a discrepancy between what persons experience in their marriage and what they believe is possible for people to experience in the marital partnership. Exposure to new ideas of personal fulfillment in intimate marital relationships may lead to "high-order discontent." In contemporary society, many persons may proceed to terminate their marriage, *with sincere regrets.* Thus, in making the decision to divorce, it is not surprising that "Many persons suffer the mingled emotions of love, hate, guilt, shame, foreboding, and carry the heavy lump of gnawing indecision waiting for some turn of events which might mercifully tip the scales."[6] Seen and unforeseen dilemmas thus confront those at the brink of the termination process.

Both in the accumulated repertory of individual experience and in the organization of contemporary society, there are potentially negative forces bearing on the divorce decision and the ensuing process of termination. These are sufficient to almost guarantee that some discomfort will be experienced by persons terminating a marriage. Some important ones can be categorized below for brief comment.

1. *Legal complications.* Despite the increasing use of a "no-fault" concept and its presumable corollary of simpler access to divorce,

there are still complications in the divorce process. In almost all states, an attorney must be obtained to initiate the divorce process. Questions of property and settlements, maintenance, and child support may enter the picture. Migratory divorces may be filled with difficulties even for those who obtain them without financial difficulty. Those who wish to remarry may find their plans blocked by required time periods of several months between divorce and remarriage. Unfortunately, there are few resources available to ease the legal complications.

2. *Ambiguity of the divorced status.* Simply put, many persons involved in the divorce process seem not to know what to expect from others nor what is expected of them. There may be an intermixture of blame and praise, conflicting motives and expectations, and uncertain movements of avoidance and involvement regarding one's friends, relatives, and acquaintances. This can add up to monumental confusion and uncertainty for many divorcing persons.

3. *Trauma of separation.* Despite the unsatisfactory state of affairs that may have preceded it, the actual splitting of the married pair may be accompanied by serious "withdrawal pains." Routines, habit patterns, and accustomed ways of interacting with a predictable marriage partner will have provided some structuring for personal and pair-identity. Even the undesirable traits or reactions of the former partner may lend nostalgic worth to the former partnership when one is experiencing initial loneliness, isolation, and feelings of confusion.

4. *Ambivalence toward the former mate.* Mixed feelings toward the former mate characteristically occur among those in the divorce process. Opposites such as repugnance and attraction or love and hostility persist as one mentally reviews the termination process. Divorced persons frequently find themselves doing the very things that previously were so irritating in the behavior of the former mate. Frequently connected with ambivalence is the trauma of injured pride. Where divorces are not mutually sought, one partner may experience feelings of lessened worth or personal rejection; thus rejected, one may tend to overcompensate in attempts to change the image supposedly held by the other. This mixed bag of feelings contributes to the general confusion and emotional maladjustment frequently associated with the termination of a marriage.

5. *Social and economic consequences.* Divorce process is almost always accompanied by disorganization of the pre-existing social patterns of the married pair. Interaction with friends and kin may undergo subtle or drastic change. Dissolution of the partnership may lead to a termination of individual friendships. The embarrassment and super-tactfulness of friends may be keenly

felt by the divorced person. The person who has gone through the termination process may be rather rudely awakened to the extent to which this society is pair-oriented. A social structure heavily oriented to husband-and-wife is not likely to be readily re-structured for an ex-husband and an ex-wife. Added to the social factors which may have undergone drastic change are the economic difficulties which are likely to be numerous and varied. Costs of the divorce itself can be devastating to those with modest incomes. It also seems clear that divorced women with small children are likely to experience considerable economic deprivation. While she struggles to keep her head above water, so does her ex-husband who may be laboring under the economic burden of establishing a new residence, making support and maintenance payments, and perhaps supporting a new family.

Although divorce today is much more widely accepted and lacks the stigma that it once carried, it can still be a source of much grief. However, despite their disenchantment with a particular marriage and the difficulties associated with the process of its termination, Americans tend to value the married state over the single life. Thus, a large proportion of divorced people will, as we saw earlier, "try again" by remarrying. Remarriage itself carries the probability of experiencing certain difficulties which deserve comment at this point.

For one thing, remarried persons may tend to demand more from their new marriage than from the previous one; furthermore, they may tend to dissolve them rather soon if they turn out to be unsatisfactory. On the other hand, those remarriages which survive may be relatively more satisfying than the previous partnership. There is some statistical evidence to this effect, in that ". . . those who remarry are much more likely to remain married until death intervenes than they are to become divorced." [7] The relatively greater maturity of experience among the remarrying plus the motivation to work doubly hard to ensure the success of the remarriage may lend considerable strength to the new partnership. On the other hand, there are a number of possible problems confronting those who remarry. Some of these can be briefly cited below.

1. *Continuity of problem-causation.* Remarrying persons frequently transfer irritants from their prior relationship over into their new marriage. Obviously, unless there is a profoundly different pattern of relations and strengths in the new partnership, as compared with the old, such problems may turn out to be quite as corrosive and damaging as they were previously.

2. *Focusing blame for psychological discomfort.* The divorce process, as we have seen, may be quite disorganizing. Persisting discomfort may impel one partner in the remarriage to blame the other for loss of the former mate or for the social stigma resulting from the divorce. Husbands may tend to blame the new spouse for

their being deprived of their children or for the heavy economic burdens they must bear. Often one partner may feel that the other is not sharing equally in the "emotional costs" of the divorce and remarriage. Similarly, arguments may occur over "who gave up the most."

3. *Unshared and unsharable experience.* The exclusiveness component of contemporary traditional marriage and remarriage may block the sharing of deeply-repressed guilt, grief, or occasional loneliness for the former mate. Likewise, one can not easily share the joys of peak experiences in the past marriage. Another problematic aspect here is the selective remembering which filters out the unpleasantness of the past; this may result in casting the present mate in a comparatively unfavorable light.[8]

4. *Continuity of habit systems and expectations.* Inappropriate behavior in the new situation may simply reflect the persistence of habit patterns. Examples would be calling the new mate by the name of the old, assuming common memories, making errors in anniversary and other dates, etc. In general, there may occur a playing of roles for which there are no counter-roles. Expecting the other to "read" one's gestures or understand the nuances of one's joking may obviously be very unfair expectations. Another bothersome tendency may consist in the partners' feeling that they are being compared with a former mate. A wife may feel concerned about her attractiveness, home-making skills, or ability to evoke love and interest relative to her husband's former mate. Or a husband may wonder about his sex prowess, earning capacity, or other personal traits relative to his wife's former spouse. In one marital counseling case, interaction between the partners had become stifling and tension-ridden due to the husband's nightly insistence that his mate give detailed accounts of her sex life with her former husband.

5. *Expanded family interaction network.* Since approximately sixty percent of all divorces involve children, many remarriages are confronted by the demands of expanded kinship relations. In many remarriages, the apt phrase is "My children, your children, and our children." The presence of children from a former marriage may, in itself, pose a variety of adjustment problems for all concerned. In addition, their presence may require extended contacts with two sets of in-laws and with former mates in their parental roles. Such an extended range of contacts is probably not inherently damaging to the new partnership. However, there is potential for stress in the scheduling difficulties, conflicting claims on time to be spent with the children, and the general stretching of available resources and energy.

As we have seen in this brief review, a variety of potential problems are connected with the termination and remarriage processes. On inspection it appears that most of these problems represent fundamental interpersonal difficulties of the types which we have discussed in earlier units.[9]

Just as is true in today's conventional marital relations, the termination process and subsequent remarriage may be fraught with difficulties in the maintenance of individual integrity and in establishing communication that is honest and open. Acceptance of the other as a person, neither in terms of possession nor in terms of ascribed status, is as critical in these processes as in an ongoing, stable marriage. Speculation suggests that most interpersonal problems associated with divorce and remarriage stem from the maladaptive aspects of this society's culture which have been learned and reinforced in individual experience. Thus, from the human potentials perspective, it could be hypothesized that remarriages which turn out well are likely to have been preceded by a considerable amount of evaluation and reorganization of self-concept in both partners. In an optimistic vein, we could speculate that the turbulence and change associated with termination of an established relationship may be a prelude to personal growth —growth which may improve the potential for meaingful interpersonal relations. In Jourard's words,

> Growth is the disintegration of one way of experiencing the world, followed by a re-organization of this experience, a re-organization that includes the new disclosure of the world. The disorganization, or even shattering, of one way to experience the world, is brought on by new disclosures from the changing being of the world, disclosures that were always being transmitted, but were usually ignored.[9]

Issues surrounding divorce and remarriage are interlaced with the personal problems experienced in connection with these processes. For example, difficulties involving legal complications reflect basic issues and questions regarding society's control of the termination process. Certain of the issues and questions listed below will, therefore, overlap somewhat with the preceding discussion.

The role of the state. Until the very recent development of a movement toward "no-fault" divorce proceedings, one of the most troublesome aspects of the legal system was in its operation under the "adversary" concept; under the law, one divorcing spouse had to be guilty and the other innocent. Divorce actions could be dismissed by the court if collusion were proved — that is, if the partners had mutually agreed on termination of their marriage and were acting in concert to obtain it. While gradual changes have been taking place over the past thirty years in divorce law, certain questions and issues persist. Among childless couples, assuming that property matters and distribution of economic resources are mutually agreed on, should any court action at all be required? Why not simply register such terminations, much as births or deaths are registered? To what extent do divorce laws reflect particular religious views and bias? Does this influence constitute discriminatory treatment of some? How can we justify, for example, interlocutory decrees and related prohibition against remarriage for a legally prescribed period of time? Numerous other such issues could be cited.

Termination – should it be easy or difficult? This issue is closely related to the foregoing one involving societal control. Some take the view that if divorce is made extremely difficult to obtain, more married persons would simply have to stay together and "work out" their problems. A similar view holds that "easy divorce" threatens the "sacredness" of the marriage institution. Opposing these views is a position which holds that some problems in interpersonal relations and expectations virtually defy any "solution." Furthermore, some partners may desire amicably and mutually to terminate a marriage for reasons other than the existence of serious problems. Thus, it is argued, making the termination process more difficult will not guarantee problem-resolution in troubled marriages; also, such a course may increase human suffering and may have the effect of detracting from the perception of marriage as a meaningful partnership.

Children and divorce. A persisting question in matters of marital dissolution has centered on its effects on children. Some argue that disintegration of the family group is invariably damaging to offspring. Others contend that living in a continued disruptive family situation is equally or more harmful. The state has asserted that its role in divorce is an expression of its duty to protect the child. Critics, however, would contend that it is not so much the humanitarian motives but the need to protect the state from assuming economic responsibility for the child that lies at the bottom of most actions of the court. To what extent do the legal ramifications of divorce contribute to disorganization and ill effects on children of divorce? An issue relates to the dominant custom of awarding child-custody to the mother. Should children's views be taken into account in the custody decision? Should the quality of the parents' life-style or remarriage be a determinant factor in the final custody decision? These are but a few of the persisting questions and issues in this aspect of divorce.

Negative social definitions. Social and economic difficulties, as we have seen, are likely to confront those entering the divorce process. Some such issues seemingly stem from relatively negative imputations to those who divorce. Although there exists a covert and somewhat tactful acceptance of divorce as a problem-solving technique, there are lingering implications of "failure" for the divorcing. This is especially true for those whose marriages have lasted several years. Tradition dies hard and terms such as "irresponsible," "immature," etc. are often used in describing those persons terminating marriage. Similarly, it is still difficult for Americans to view the termination process as an outcome of mutual choice or design rather than a situation characterized by unilateral action or mutual rejection. Speculation suggests that negative perceptions of divorce are reflected in such matters as the divorced person's employability, job opportunities, ability to obtain loans, and insurance premium rates. Perhaps the issue concerns the justifiability of humanistic versus actuarial decisions.

These are but a few of the issues and problems surrounding divorce and remarriage. It seems that the drama of divorce is played against a backdrop of lingering cultural commitment to the ideal of permanence in marriage. This ethic of permanence is deeply rooted in this society's Judeo-Christian heritage which also has had an immense influence on our laws. It must be acknowledged, of course, that the ideal of permanence has been greatly eroded. But it would be quite erroneous to conclude that the ideal of lifelong commitment is dead. Clearly, some relatively conservative religious organizations have become quite flexible about marriage procedures and ceremonies. Inspection of their new provisions, however, is likely to reveal that the permanence concept is honored. Thus, in announcing its new provisions for marriage, one church said: "Provision should be made for those who want to write their own form of the promises, provided that they always mention the complete sharing which is marriage and an indication that the promises are to be *a lifelong commitment.*"[10]

It is fairly safe to assume that some form of termination process, regardless of its name, will be a permanent feature of American marital-familial experience. Similarly, remarriage is but one aspect of this society's strong valuation of the married status and can be expected to closely parallel the frequency of divorce.

Given these assumptions, we can examine some *alternatives* which have emerged with the aim of reducing negative aspects of these processes. The listing below can be considered as an introduction only.

1. *Non-adversary legal divorce system.* This would imply such things as "no-fault," "dissolution" rather than divorce, and "maintenance" rather than alimony. There would be no presumptions about guilt or innocence of the parties.

2. *Divorce on demand.* This would call for little more than registration of the marriage's termination by the partners. No "grounds" would be required — not even "irreconcilable differences." Either or both partners could initiate the process.

3. *Conciliation Courts.* Before being granted a dissolution of their marriage, both partners would be required to consult with a counselor to ascertain whether divorce is their best solution.

4. *Divorce counseling.* Its purpose would be to reduce trauma, emphasize the positive aspects of the process, and enhance the persons' comprehension of various dimensions of the divorce process. It could help partners in deciding whether to divorce and how to handle it if they decide in the affirmative.

5. *Divorce pro per.* In this arrangement, one or both partners file their own divorce or dissolution papers, without the services of an attorney. Only a modest filing fee would be required. Similar to this is "mutual dissolution by affidavit through the mails," as is available to residents of Contra Costa County, California.

6. *Celebration of dissolution.* The celebration of amicable parting could pave the way for humane relationships between former mates. It might also help to reduce the tendency for labeling of "guilty" and "innocent" parties in divorce. Connected with this might be "gift showers" for the partner who is moving out, or other such activities.

7. *Divorce insurance.* At their marriage, couples could provide insurance against the financial hazards of a possible divorce in their future.

8. *Development of social support groups.* Emotional and social support could be developed through participation in various community groups. This alternative is not well-developed; but currently groups such as Parents Without Partners or Remarriage, Inc. indicate the possibilities.

9. *Education for remarriage or singlehood.* Through schools, churches, and other organizations classes could be organized to prepare people for dealing with the stresses of their new situation.

The termination of any established intimate social relationship is likely to be accompanied by some stress for the participants. But there is little justification for the level and extent of difficulty experienced among Americans in the divorce process. The belief underlying most of the alternatives mentioned above is that much, though not all, of the trauma experienced is produced by the nature of the traditional divorce processes. The aim of alternatives such as those cited above (as well as others not mentioned, e.g. the uniform marriage and divorce law reform movement) is to humanize the termination process and to reformulate the interpersonal connotations attached to it. The implications of this aim are rather well expressed in the words of one neighborhood sage: "People get married *loving,* but that doesn't mean they have to part *hating!*" The wider dimensions of some of the above alternatives will be developed in your readings for this unit.

REFERENCES

1. Williams, Robin. *American Society: A Sociological Interpretation* 2nd Edit. (New York: Knopf, 1960), p. 83.
2. U.S. Bureau of the Census, *Statistical Abstract of the United States, 1972* (Washington: U.S. Govt. Printing Office, 1972), p. 50.
3. Benson, Leonard. *The Family Bond* (New York: Random House, 1971), pp. 275-276.
4. Williams, Kristen M. *et al. Remarriage: United States* (Rockville: National Center for Health Statistics, Dec. 1973).
5. Bernard, Jessie. *Remarriage: A Study of Marriage* (New York: Dryden Press, 1956), p. 66.
6. Kirkpatrick, Clifford. *The Family As Process and Institution* (New York: Ronald Press, 1963), p. 605. The following discussion is based on Kirkpatrick's categories of difficulty.
7. Glick, Paul. Quoted in Betty Rollin, "The American Way of Marriage: Remarriage," Look 35 (Sept. 21, 1971): 62-67.
8. Leslie, Gerald. *The Family in Social Context,* 2nd edit. (New York: Oxford University Press, 1973), pp. 643-644. Much of this discussion is based on Leslie's chapter on "Remarriage."
9. Jourard, Sidney. In Herbert A. Otto and John Mann (eds.). *Ways of Growth* (New York: Viking Press, 1968), p. 2.
10. Loving v. Virginia, 388 U.S. 1 (1967). Also Cf. Thomas P. Monahan, "National Divorce Legislation: The Problem and Some Suggestions," *The Family Coordinator* 22 (July 1973): 359-362.
11. Associated Press, "Lutheran Group Proposes a New Marriage Ceremony," cited in Courier-Journal and Times, May 21, 1972.

The Dilemma of Divorce:
Disaster or Remedy

RONALD CHEN

SOS, as we know, is the international signal of distress. It cries "Help!" Recognizing divorce as a focal area of urgent problems, the Parents Without Partners Association has been developing an SOS program for divorcees as a means of providing help in the form of a mutual aid. Parents Without Partners is a national organization of divorced and widowed men and women with local chapters in most cities throughout the United States.

The SOS program was first sponsored by Parents Without Partners in Palo Alto, California, in 1963, through the efforts of one suffering divorcee. This mother of two young children was divorced in 1962, having been badly shaken by the psychological and practical problems in divorce. She first sought psychiatric help and was referred to a group therapist. Through her own experience in group therapy and what she learned from other patients in the group, she conceived the idea of having divorcees talk in the group so as to focus on the psychological and socio-economic issues which confront every divorcee. She promoted the idea in the Palo Alto community and received support from clergy and mental health specialists in the area. The Palo Alto Chapter of Parents Without Partners supported her idea by appointing a committee to assist her with a community-wide effort.

In 1963 a series of five free lectures was presented at a church under the auspices of Parents Without Partners. This was to bring interested people together leading to their involvement and commitment in group process sessions following the lectures. Responses were good and several groups began under the direction of a group therapist. In the past three years, over 50 local chapters of SOS have followed this lead, including chapters in Chicago, San Francisco, Oakland, and Washington D. C. Most participants are divorcees, but occasionally a married person in distress is granted membership.

Currently, the method used in providing help in most of the chapters is a form of group process short of formalized group therapy. Although psychological issues are discussed freely, an important fact remains that the participants are not psychiatric patients, at least not in these group sessions. Each participant pays a token fee (in most instances $1.50) which collectively reimburses the group leader for his efforts. In some localities (such as in Topeka) the group processes are conducted by voluntary mental health specialists in the community. The project has no formal funding.

The SOS groups have recognized and validated the value of mutual aid in alleviating distresses and torments, not only of the divorce itself but also the aftermath. The participants know of the common feelings of failure, guilt, censure and pain, and, because of the mutuality, they know how to talk about these feelings and concerns in a way that frankly faces the problem, focusing on the realism of future planning, consequent loneliness, and the potential problems of children of divorced parenthood.

In California alone, 400 persons have engaged in regular weekly sessions of SOS groups of PWP; the groups are generally composed of ten members. The process, which has been guided by trained psychiatric workers, does not claim the ability to solve all problems of divorce. They do not give positive advice, such as encouraging the still-married to take steps to divorce or advocating reconciliation. The aim is, rather, to answer the distress signal by providing a means of empathetic "sharing" of problems and circumstances, through candid and reflective discussion. This form of group participation points the way to clarification in many cases, and clarification often may result in the most effective solution.

The increasing magnitude of the problem is reflected in state and nation-wide statistical changes. In Kansas, according to the State Official of Vital Statistics, there were 18,806 marriages and 5,683 divorces during 1965, or 8.6 marriages and 2.6 divorces per 1,000 population. In percentage terms, there were approximately 30 divorces versus 100 lasting marriages. These figures, which are comparable to national figures, are a useful index to contrast the proportion of marriages and divorces in the past and present decades.

In 1860, the divorce rate per 1,000 population in Kansas was 1.2; in 1940, it was 2.2; in 1944, 3.1; in 1946, 5.0; in 1947, 4.0; in 1950, 2.6; in 1960, 2.2; and in 1965, 2.6. In the United States, there were 249,000 divorces in 1937, 502,000 divorces in 1945, and 450,000 divorces in 1964. The total number of divorced individuals in 1960 was three million, which represented an increase of 28 percent from the 1950 figure.

Variations in the patterns of divorce found in this country reflect differing laws in the states. The South and West, where it is easier to obtain a divorce, have higher rates of divorce than the North and East. A sizeable proportion of the divorces from the North and East go to out-of-state plaintiffs. There are other variations, true for all sections of the United States. Divorces are more common in urban than in rural communities. Lower socio-economic and less educated couples resort to the courts more readily than those who are culturally and financially better off. Persons in certain occupations and professions seem to be more divorce-prone than in others; for example, service workers and physicians have more divorces than business men; and clergymen have the least of all (Ogg, 1965).

Over 50 percent of divorced families have children under the age of 18 years. The proportion of divorces involving minor children has also risen from 42 percent in 1948 to 57 percent in 1960. Since so many divorces are sought in the first few years of marriage, the very young children affected are apt to constitute a large percentage of the total number of children involved (463,000, 1960).

The significant increase in the divorce rate in recent years reflects not only the decreasing sense of responsibility to remain married when the marital relationship presents difficulties, but also it represents social and cultural changes. An example is the increasing non-dependent attitudes in women who often prefer to pursue careers of their own. These changed practices have met general social approval, and in some instances they enhance the separation process. Our highly industrialized, diverse, and mobile society, in which 70 percent of us live in urban areas, offers more opportunities than formerly for men and women of different backgrounds to meet and marry. Such relationships have built-in stresses that couples who have grown up with a common outlook largely escape. In the small, self-centered family units of today, with few, if any, kin close by, relationships tend to become more intense. Yet, paradoxically, most husbands and wives spend much of their time in separate circles and in different activities. As they lose emotional touch with one another, the relative anonymity of big-city living perhaps makes it easier for them to contemplate divorce—at least they will be free from neighborhood gossip. Stronger emotional bonds, greater maturity, and continual renewal seem necessary to keep a modern marriage intact. The absence of these may be, in part, the reason for many more divorces today than in 1900, as many persons now believe in escaping from an unhappy marital situation instead of resigning themselves to it.

At times the decision to consider getting a divorce is merely the beginning of a painful, complicated, and emotionally overwhelming process. Usually common to all divorces is an element of disappointment, the feeling of letdown over a major life endeavor. This failure leads to self-reproach, a blow to self-esteem, and, as a result, to a sense of guilt and frequently results in depression and emotional instability. There is always this dilemma: continuation with the marriage because of the children or other conveniences, under unbearable tension, increasing hatred and hurtful action, or acceptance of divorce as the only apparent way out. During the decision-making process, soul-searching questions are raised and attempts are made to understand in what ways the relationship has gone sour. Alternatives may be sought in turning to persons in a position to help. There is no single formula to follow in looking for an answer in regard to divorce. However, competent advice in order to better understand the problems as well as possible solutions, before taking drastic action, would certainly help.

To consider the basic problem of divorce, we might begin by questioning whether man was made for marriage, or whether marriage became an institution to satisfy primitive man's biological, economic, social, and emotional needs. Marriage, we recognize, provides constant and assured sexual fulfillment; it promotes mutual comfort, maintenance and survival; it provides a stable family setting for the reproduction and rearing of children; and it serves to relieve psychic tensions by replenishing personal self-esteem and the confidence eroded in a grueling struggle with a hostile environment. Even though the persistence of marriage as a social institution reflects cultural influence, there still appear also to be strong psychological needs and emotions that lead to marriage and tend to hold marital partners together. These needs may be rational or irrational; the bond may be genuine affection or feelings of guilt, duty, and fear, combined with pleasurable expectations. The desire for a relationship based on domination or submission rather than mutual regard may tie certain persons together. In any event, the preservation of marriage — despite obvious lack of harmony in most instances, and the presence of extreme discord in many — seems to be governed in our society by emotional needs as well as socio-economic factors. The true nature of these needs is frequently exposed by marital conflict (Goldfarb, 1967).

Some Examples of Types of Marital Relationships:

1. *The dependent relationship.* Dependency is primarily a complex, exploitative maneuver employed by the "weak" person against the "strong" one, who is regarded as a possible protector. The weak person's self-esteem, confidence, and sense of purpose — his concept of life's meaning — are contingent upon his ability to find, attach, and hold a partner suitable to his needs. His aim, in essence, is to convert the designated protector into a surrogate parent who will relieve his anxieties and tensions, and provide gratification and pleasure. A crisis arises only when the protector behaves in a manner that threatens to destroy the image; he must then be persuaded to live up to his role, or the dependent mate will search for another protector. The roots of adult dependency are deeply planted in early infancy and childhood. In the matrix of the infant-parent relationship, a patterned expectation arises of obtaining from adults relief from anxiety or tension, and the gratification of needs. This often persists in memory as an emotional core upon which subsequent experience is grafted. Much of the varied pattern of dating, courtship, and marriage in our culture becomes clear when interpreted in terms of a search for a strong, supportive parental figure.

2. *The non-dependent relationship.* Marriage and parenthood represent culturally defined goals of pleasurable self-fulfillment in a cooperative social transaction. Marriage between two non-dependent individuals may yield a relatively superficial bond in which each may preserve a great deal of autonomy and make little or no effort to communicate with the other. The non-dependent relationship, unlike the dependent one, in which happiness is not contingent upon security and pride, in some instances actually enhances separation. Quite ironically, what contributes most to security is the interdependent couple's conviction that each partner really needs the other to depend upon him. In this sense, dependency can be a cohesive force in marriage.

3. *Serious individual problems.* In some cases one or both individuals in

the relationship have so many problems that without extensive reconstruction of each personality by some such means as psychotherapy, the relationship will continue to be incompatible and intolerable and may appropriately be terminated. Certain persons, in a constant effort to appease the spouse by being agreeable, lose their individuality; and individuality is necessary to provide feedback for the partner in this emotionally interdependent experience. In other instances, a certain extreme personality may make life miserable for the spouse. If there is no motivation for change, satisfactions in marriage cannot be achieved.

Distressed couples need not decide that continuation of the relationship is beyond hope before their situation is fully discussed with marital counselors, ministers, and workers in the mental health profession. While the quick step of divorce may actually end the protracted unhappiness, it may also bring about unforeseen consequences. It is imperative, therefore, that both partners give an ample amount of time to explore possible alternatives as well as to prepare for the eventual divorce.

To focus on constructive solutions to the problem of divorce, continued study and improvement of our divorce laws is essential, and acquaintance of couples in crisis with the aftermath — feelings of depression, resentment, loneliness, guilt, and temptations for reconciliation — is needed. And what about children? Preventive approaches which go back as early as child rearing must be explored; for example, expressed interest in and consistent attention to the children, guidance toward positive mental health, education on a more realistic approach to marriage, and premarital counseling, particularly in the cases of adolescents and younger adults. There is much more to be achieved in terms of educational efforts, public concern, and social actions.

REFERENCES

Ogg, Elizabeth. Divorce. *Public Affairs Pamphlets*, no. 380, 1965, New York.

Goldfarb, Alvin I. Marriage, Dependency, and the Search for Aid. *Medical Opinion and Review*, 1967, 3.

The Trauma of Children
When Parents Divorce

JUDSON T. LANDIS

The present research was undertaken in an effort to gain further insights and to answer some questions arising out of two previous studies of children of divorced parents.[1] The sample was composed of 295 University students, all children of divorced parents.[2] Each student was asked to complete an eight-page anonymous questionnaire covering certain items of his family background, his evaluation of the home before he learned of the prospect of his parents' divorce, his reactions to the divorce, a postmarital history of the parents, including remarriages, and the adjustment of the child to the parents' divorce and remarriage. Half of the students were registered in the family sociology course. The others were university students not presently registered in the family sociology course. No attempt was made to get a random sample of children of divorced parents, since such a small proportion of university students are from divorced families. (Data from student information files collected by the author from 1950-1959 shows that approximately 10 percent of the family sociology students are from divorced or separated homes.) One-third of the student respondents were men and two-thirds were women. Thirty-two percent were from one-child families; 48 percent were from two-child families; and the remaining 20 percent were from families of three or more children. Fifty-three precent of the fathers were in a profession or in business and 52 percent had some education beyond high school; one-third had a college or graduate degree. One-third of the mothers had some education beyond high school and 23 percent had a college or graduate degree. The parents had been married an average of thirteen years before the divorce. The average age of the 295 children had been 9.4 years when the parents divorced.

In analyzing the data it became clear that children of divorce cannot be treated as homogeneous group. Divorce of parents affects children in various ways, depending upon such factors as the age of the child at the time of the divorce and how the child viewed the home situation before he learned of the possible divorce.

There are cerain potentially traumatic situations existing for the child of divorcing parents. First, there is the necessity to adjust to the knowledge that divorce will probably take place; (2) there is the necessity to adjust to the fact of divorce; (3) there is the possibility that in the predivorce or postdivorce years one or both parents may "use" the child as a weapon against the other, with traumatic effects upon the child: (4) there is the necessity for a redefining of relationships with parents; (5) the new status of being the child of divorced parents may necessitate new adjustments with the peer group; (6) some trauma may result for children who recognize the implications of their parents' failure in marriage; and (7) there may be problems of adjustment for the child if the parents remarry. Our data will be considered in terms of these seven potentially traumatic situations for the child of divorcing parents.

Preliminary analyses of the data on the 295 children indicated that it was necessary to separate the sample into two groups—those who remembered the time preceding their parents' divorce and those who did not. Thirty-eight percent of the children (112) were too young at the time of the divorce to remember the circumstances in the home before the divorce took place. This does not mean that there was no trauma for this group of children, only that they were too young at the time of the occurrences to be able to furnish information later. However, many of these children could give information on their adjustment following the divorce.

The remaining 183 children were divided into three groups, according to how the child viewed the home situation before he learned of the possible divorce. A surprisingly large percentage of the children considered their homes happy or very happy before they learned that their parents would separate or divorce. Data from this group led us to hypothesize that parental divorce itself might be traumatic for some children, but for others the parents' divorce might mean relief from tension and the beginning of the child's emotional recovery: if the child had considered his home to be happy, the prospect and the fact of divorce might be traumatic; but if there had been continued hostility and conflict in the home, the divorce might mean relief fron tension for the child.

Each respondent was asked to rate his home on a four-point scale as he remembered it before he learned of the possible separation or divorce. The rating was in terms of his sense of family unity, his feeling of security or insecurity, and his evaluation of the general happiness or unhappiness in the home. The three variables probably all measured one thing—the general happiness of the home from the child's point of view before he sensed there would be separation or divorce. The top third of the sample felt there was family unity, believed that it was a happy family, and felt secure in the family. The children in the lowest third felt there was little or no family unity, believed the home to be unhappy or very unhappy, and had little or no security. In our analysis we shall report upon differences between the responses of the top third and the lowest third concerning their experiences in the seven potentially traumatic experiences of the child whose parents are divorcing (See Table 1).

1.

THE DESCRIPTION OF THE HOME BY 183 CHILDREN OF DIVORCED PARENTS AS REMEMBERED BEFORE THEY LEARNED OF A POSSIBLE SEPARATION OR DIVORCE

DESCRIPTION OF HOME AND SELF	1/3 HAPPIEST N = 61	1/3 UNHAPPIEST N = 61	TOTAL* N = 183
In terms of family unity:			
Closely united family	54.1	—	18.6
Moderate unity in family	44.3	11.5	39.3
Little family unity	1.6	55.7	31.1
No family unity	—	32.8	10.9
	$X^2 = 96.00$	df = 3	P<.001
Your feelings of security:			
Very secure	78.7	—	30.1
Secure	21.3	24.6	41.0
Little security	—	62.3	24.6
No security	—	13.1	4.4
	$X^2 = 94.28$	df = 2	P<.001
In terms of general happiness or unhappiness in the home:			
Very happy family	32.8	—	10.9
Happy family	65.6	9.8	50.8
Unhappy family	1.6	67.2	30.6
Very unhappy family	—	23.0	7.6
	$X^2 = 97.24$	df = 3	P<.001
In terms of your personal happiness or unhappiness as a child:			
Very happy	67.2	3.3	29.7
Happy	31.1	46.7	52.7
Unhappy	1.6	40.0	14.3
Very unhappy	—	10.0	3.3
	$X^2 = 65.95$	df = 2	P<.001
			(N = 61, 60, 182)
The relationship between your father and mother:			
Constant open conflict	1.7	46.7	22.0
Moderate open conflict	13.8	41.7	30.5
Little open conflict	17.2	8.3	15.8
No open conflict	53.4	1.7	24.3
No open conflict, but I sensed their unhappiness	13.8	1.7	7.3
	$X^2 = 68.84$	df = 3	P<.001
			(N = 58, 60, 177)

* Total represents two-thirds shown, plus one-third of sample not shown.

Findings of the Study

It is often assumed that divorce is almost always preceded by great unhappiness and open conflict, but our findings bring out rather clearly that from the viewpoint of the child the predivorce home may be quite satisfactory. Of the 183 children who could remember their homes before they learned of a possible divorce, 19 percent considered the family closely united; 30 percent reported that they felt very secure; 11 percent rated the home as very happy; 30 percent reported their childhood as very happy and 24 percent reported no open conflict in their family. A minority, 22 percent, reported constant open conflict between parents.

Table 2 summarizes the most common reactions of the children when they learned of the possible divorce. The first potentially traumatic experience is this first awareness of the prospect of a parental divorce. In this sample it was the mother, in more than half the cases, who told the child of the impending divorce. It will be observed that a significantly larger percentage of the children who thought the home unhappy reacted by thinking the divorce was the best for all concerned, and the third who thought the home was happy found it hard to believe. In general the first knowledge of divorce seemed to be a traumatic experience for those who believed theirs to be a happy home. Those who believed their homes to be happy were caught by surprise and were unprepared to accept the divorce; whereas open conflict and unhappiness in the other type of home seems to have prepared the child for the possibility of divorce.

The second adjustment for the child comes with the actual occurrence of divorce. Approximately one-third of the sample indicated one of the following reactions: "upset, worried, confused"; "acceptance, best solution for all"; "relief that it was over with and settled." Again, the children who considered their homes happy had the greatest difficulty adjusting to the fact of divorce. None of those who considered their homes happy, but one-fifth of those who considered their homes unhappy, reported that they were glad when the divorce was a fact. Those from unhappy homes reported greater relief that it was settled and greater acceptance of a view that the divorce was the best for all concerned.

Table 3 summarizes how these respondents felt the divorce had affected their feelings of security and personal happiness. It will be observed that for the entire group the effect of the divorce was to make the children feel less secure and less happy than was true before the divorce. When we study the two groups of children according to how they viewed the homes before knowledge of divorce, we see that those from apparently happy homes indicate either no change in feelings of security and personal happiness or they shift to feeling less secure or less happy. On the other hand, those who saw the homes as unhappy report greater security and happiness after the divorce. Again, the

TABLE 2

THE IMMEDIATE REACTION REPORTED BY 183 CHILDREN OF
DIVORCED PARENTS WHEN LEARNING THEIR PARENTS
WOULD PROBABLY SEPARATE OR DIVORCE

REACTION	1/3 HAPPIEST N = 61	1/3 UNHAPPIEST N = 61	TOTAL N = 183
Thought it was best for all concerned[1]	19.7	54.1	34.4
Couldn't believe that it had happened to us[2]	42.6	16.4	33.3
Fought against it and tried to prevent it	13.1	11.5	14.2
I was happy	1.6	14.8	6.0
I was unhappy and upset	52.5	57.4	51.9
I was worried and anxious about my future	14.8	27.9	20.2
Hated father[3]	4.9	19.7	8.7
Hated mother	1.6	8.2	3.3
Did not understand	18.0	8.2	12.0
Indifferent	6.6	3.3	4.9
Miscellaneous reactions	19.7	11.5	15.3

[1] $X^2 = 8.89$ $df = 1$ $P<.01.$
[2] $X^2 = 6.23$ $df = 1$ $P<.2.$
[3] $X^2 = 4.26$ $df = 1$ $P<.05.$

TABLE 3

PERCENTAGE DISTRIBUTION OF FEELINGS OF SECURITY AND
PERSONAL HAPPINESS OR UNHAPPINESS FOLLOWING
PARENTS' DIVORCE AS REPORTED BY 183
CHILDREN OF DIVORCED PARENTS

DESCRIPTION OF FEELINGS	⅓ HAPPIEST NU61	⅓ UNHAPPIEST N=61	TOTAL N=183
Your feelings of security:			
Much more secure	—	14.5	1.9
Somewhat more secure	—	27.3	14.3
No change in feelings of security	45.0	21.8	34.3
Less secure	36.7	20.0	30.9
Much less secure	18.3	16.4	14.9
	$X^2=32.57$		DF= $P<.001$
	(N=60, 55, 175)		
In terms of your personal happiness or unhappiness:			
Much happier than before	3.3	11.9	6.7
Somewhat happier	5.0	37.3	21.9
No change in happiness	46.7	23.7	36.0
Less happy	30.0	18.6	25.3
Much less happy	15.0	8.5	10.1
	$X^2=24.24$		$df=3$ $P<.001$
	(N=60, 59, 178)		

greater trauma occurred among children who thought their homes were happy before they learned of the divorce.

When the respondents were asked concerning any changes in their attitude toward the divorce with the passing of time, 28 percent of those who had thought they had a happy home and 64 percent of those who had considered the homes unhappy reported that they now believed that the marriage was a mistake in the first place. Of those who saw the home as happy 16 percent now felt the divorce was a mistake, while only 3 percent of those who saw the home as unhappy thought the divorce was a mistake.

The third potential trauma for the child comes if he is "used" by one or both parents in the pre- or post-divorce period. Forty-four percent of all of the 295 respondents reported that they felt they had been "used" by one or both parents. This included children who were too young to remember the home before the divorce but old enough to

TABLE 4

PERCENTAGE DISTRIBUTION OF SPECIFIC WAYS IN WHICH
295 CHILDREN OF DIVORCED PARENTS REPORTED THEY
WERE "USED" BY ONE PARENT AGAINST THE OTHER
BEFORE, DURING, OR AFTER THE DIVORCE

WAY IN WHICH PARENT "USED" CHILD	⅓ HAPPIEST N=61	⅓ UNHAPPIEST N=61	TOTAL* N=295
One tried to get information from me about the other	21.3	41.0	21.0
Asked to testify against one parent in court[1]	4.9	21.3	7.8
Asked to back up arguments of other in family quarrels[2]	1.6	31.1	9.8
Not permitted to talk to one parent	—	3.3	1.0
Not permitted to see one parent	3.3	8.2	4.1
One told untrue things about the other[3]	18.0	42.6	17.6
One gave messages to me to give to the other	9.8	11.5	7.1
I was used as a go-between in quarrels	—	13.1	3.7
One or both played on my sympathy[4]	14.8	52.5	25.8
Neither ever used me[5]	60.7	24.6	44.4
Miscellaneous responses and too young to remember	4.9	9.8	20.0

*Total represents two-thirds shown, plus one third not shown, plus 112 respondents who were too young to remember family before divorce but old enough to remember post divorce years.
[1]$X^2=6.25$ df=1 P<.02.
[2]$X^2=16.20$ df=1 P<.001.
[3]$X^2=6.08$ df=1 P<.02.
[4]$X^2=23.00$ df=1 P<.001.
[5]$X^2=12.10$ df=1 P<.001.

TABLE 5

PERCENTAGE DISTRIBUTION OF RELATIONSHIPS WITH
MOTHER AND FATHER BEFORE LEARNING OF POSSIBLE
DIVORCE AND AFTER DIVORCE WAS A FACT AS REPORTED
BY 183 CHILDREN OF DIVORCED PARENTS

RELATIONSHIP BEFORE DIVORCE	% HAPPIEST N=61	% UNHAPPIEST N=61	TOTAL N=183
Your relationship with your mother:			
Very close	55.7	28.3	40.9
Close	37.7	36.7	40.3
Not close	6.6	6.7	15.5
Distant	—	8.3	3.3
X²=17.34			df=2 P<.001
(N=61, 60, 181)			
Your relationship with your father:			
Very close	36.1	10.0	17.7
Close	50.8	31.7	43.6
Not close	9.8	40.0	29.8
Distant	3.3	18.3	8.8
X²=29.17			df=3 P<.001
(N=61, 60, 181)			

RELATIONSHIP AFTER DIVORCE AS COMPARED TO BEFORE DIVORCE			
Your relationship with your father:			
Much closer to mother	33.7	23.0	7.6
Somewhat more close	21.7	32.8	32.6
No change in closeness	23.3	27.9	24.9
Less close	13.3	9.8	11.0
Much less close	5.0	6.6	3.9
X²=2.56			df=3 P<.50
(N=60, 61, 181)			
Your relationship with your father:			
Much closer to father	11.7	3.3	8.8
Somewhat more close	10.0	11.5	10.4
No change in closeness	18.3	31.1	25.3
Less close	31.7	13.1	23.1
Much less close	28.3	41.0	32.4
X²=7.09			df=3 P<.10
(N=60, 61, 182)			

remember experiences following the divorce. Table 4 summarizes how these 295 respondents felt they had been "used" by their parents. It will be observed that on all items children who were from homes considered unhappy before the divorce were more likely to report being "used" during and after the divorce. The trauma associated with being "used" by parents appears to be more severe among those children who saw the home as unhappy before the divorce.

The fourth potentially traumatic experience is the necessity for redefining feelings and attitudes toward one or both parents. The children in this study felt closer to their mothers than to their fathers. The effect of divorce seemed to be to increase the emotional distance between children and their fathers. Table 5 summarizes how close respondents felt toward mothers and fathers before and after the divorce.

For a child to have to shift from a close to a distant relationship with one or both parents may be a traumatic experience. There may also be considerable disillusionment if the child accepts what one parent says about the other. The child may come to believe that the one he has felt close to and has looked up to is in reality one he cannot trust and respect. The shift away from the father is explained in part by the child's coming to accept the views of the mother about the father. Of the 295 children in this study 74 percent went to live with the mother and only 9 percent went to live with the father. One would expect the closer relationship with the mother as the father drops out of the home and the mother and children reunite.

The children who thought their homes happy before the divorce were much closer to their mothers and fathers than were those children who thought their homes unhappy. However, after the divorce both groups were drawn closer to their mothers and both groups became less close to their fathers.

The fifth potentially traumatic situation comes in reconciling the divorced status of one's parents with peer group associations. Two-thirds of the respondents reported that the parents' divorce did not affect their confidence in associating with friends. Among the third who did feel self-confidence was affected, some reported that confidence was increased while others reported it was decreased. It was those children from homes considered happy who reported greater trauma. Seven percent of these reported greater confidence while 22 percent reported less confidence in associating with friends. On the other hand, of those children who reported their homes unhappy, 25 percent reported feeling more confident and 17 percent reported feeling less confident in associating with friends after the divorce. This may mean that with the conflict past some children feel they can associate more freely and invite friends to their homes, while others would be reluctant to invite friends home and ill at ease with peers because of the changed parental status.

Each respondent was asked to report on how he felt his parents' marital status had affected his social acceptability and whether he had used "face-saving" techniques after the divorce. A summary of this information is given in Table 6. All 295 respondents are included, since children very young at the time of divorce seem, later, to have about the same reactions in associating with friends as do children older at the time of the divorce. Differences are not significant on this point between the third of the respondents who thought their homes happy and the third who thought their homes unhappy.

It might seem that if a child is very young when the parents divorce, and if both parents remarry quickly, the child might not feel a loss of face. Yet the data show that such a child may feel as different from other children as the child who has only one parent, because he has to explain two sets of parents and possibly four sets of grandparents as well as step-brothers and sisters. The child with one parent can say that the other parent is dead but the child with two sets of parents may find it difficult to explain his extra family members.

Some trauma may result for children who recognize the implications of parental failure in marriage. Table 7 gives a summary of how the respondents believed their feelings and attitudes toward their own future marriage had been affected. Responses here did not differ significantly among the different groups. The response to the items in Table 7 show that it was those from the unhappiest homes who indicated that their attitudes toward marriage had been affected most by their parents' divorce. They expressed caution about marriage, deter-*mination to make a better choice, and so on throughout most of the items.

Since it is not generally known among young people that there is a high relationship between the failure of parents in marriage and the failure of children in marriage, it would seem that this potentially traumatic phase of adjustment to divorce might not be traumatic for many children of divorce. However, other research shows that children of divorced parents have much less confidence in their ability to have successful marriages than do children from happy homes.[3]

Our final analysis was to relate the reported feelings and reactions of the children to the postdivorce status of the parents. The data seem to show that marriages which the children viewed as unhappy before they knew of the divorce are also the cases in which neither parent or only the mother remarries. Marriages which the children viewed as happy before they knew of a possible divorce are cases in which the father or both mother and father are more likely to remarry. If neither parent remarried, or if only the mother remarried, a larger percentage of the children reacted to the knowledge that divorce would probably take place by thinking it was for the best of all concerned, and fewer were unhappy and upset. A larger percentage of these children felt more secure after the divorce and fewer felt less secure after the divorce; also, they reported being "used" much more extensively in the ways parents "use" children in marital discord than did children from cases in which only the father or both parents remarried. Sixty-one percent of those from cases in which neither parent remarried reported being "used"; 50 percent, if only the mother remarried; 43 percent, if the father remarried; and only 36 percent, if both parents remarried. If neither parent remarried the children generally reported a greater variety of ways in which their parents "used" them.

TABLE 6

PERCENTAGE DISTRIBUTION OF ADJUSTMENTS REPORTED WITH FRIENDS AND ASSOCIATES BY 295 CHILDREN OF DIVORCED PARENTS

DESCRIPTION OF ADJUSTMENT	1/3 HAPPIEST N = 61	1/3 UNHAPPIEST N = 61	TOTAL N = 295
Did you feel that your parents' marital status had any effect upon your social acceptability with friends and associates?			
I felt different from other children	23.0	29.5	22.7
I felt inferior to other children	13.1	23.0	16.3
Embarrassed to face friends	11.5	11.5	10.2
Was ashamed that parents were divorced	29.5	23.0	21.4
It was a blow to my pride	8.2	8.2	6.8
Had no effect at all upon me	49.2	41.0	42.4
We moved and new friends did not know[1]	3.3	19.7	10.2
Envious of those with happy homes	1.6	4.9	5.4
Friends from divorced homes, so accepted	6.6	6.6	3.4
Did not tell friends or talk about it	1.6	—	2.0
Miscellaneous responses	4.9	1.6	13.6
Did you feel the need of "face-saving" techniques when discussing or having to give information on the marital status of your parents?			
Sometimes lied about where one parent was	11.5	8.2	9.5
Said one parent was dead	4.9	8.2	3.7
Said one parent was on a trip, at sea, or would be with us later	4.9	1.6	4.4
Talked as though parents were not divorced	19.7	16.4	15.3
Associated largely with other children who were from separated or divorced homes	3.3	3.3	3.7
Did not mention divorce except to those who came from broken homes	3.3	4.9	6.8
Never felt need to "save face"— just told the truth	72.1	75.4	70.5
Avoided subject, but truthful if asked	16.4	11.5	14.9
Never had to give information	—	1.6	1.4
Miscellaneous responses	—	—	.7

[1] $X^2 = 5.74$ df = 1 P<.02.

TABLE 7

PERCENTAGE DISTRIBUTION OF WAYS IN WHICH PARENTS'
DIVORCE HAS AFFECTED CHILDREN'S ATTITUDES
TOWARD MARRIAGE AS REPORTED BY 295
CHILDREN OF DIVORCED PARENTS

ATTITUDE TOWARD MARRIAGE	1/3 HAPPIEST N = 61	1/3 UNHAPPIEST N = 61	TOTAL N = 295
It has made me more cautious about marriage	72.1	77.0	67.5
I am bitter about marriage	—	3.3	1.7
Determined to make a better choice	47.5	72.1	60.0
It has made me more aware of the problems of marriage	80.3	82.0	76.9
I have a more realistic picture of marriage	50.8	63.9	53.9
I never want to get married	—	1.6	1.0
It has made me more willing to compromise in getting along with others	47.5	67.2	53.9
It has given me more determination to work a* making a success of my marriage	75.4	80.3	76.6
I will wait until I am older to marry	13.1	19.7	14.9
I have little confidence in making a success of my marriage	1.6	4.9	2.7
Aware of the consequences of failure	11.5	—	3.7
No effect	1.6	1.6	1.7

SIBLING ORDER AND THE TRAUMA OF DIVORCE

We hypothesized that sibling order and number of siblings would have some effect upon the extent to which the experience of parental divorce was traumatic. Responses were analyzed by whether those responding were oldest, youngest, in-between, or onlies. There were no significant differences in how the four different groups described the homes before divorce and the divorce experience as it affected them.

AGE OF CHILD AND THE TRAUMA OF DIVORCE

The respondents were next divided into three groups, by age at the time of the parental divorce: 5-8 (81), 9-12 (63), and 13-16 (59), and then considered by their description of the home before they knew of the possible divorce and their description of the trauma of divorce. This analysis revealed some significant differences between the age groupings. In general the 5-8 age group tended to feel more secure, to rate themselves happier, and to have been less aware of the conflict between their mothers and fathers before they knew of the divorce.

Fewer indicated they were unhappy and upset by the divorce and more indicated they did not understand what was going on. More of the 5-8 age group indicated there was no change in their feelings of security, and fewer indicated that their parents tried to "use" them in the divorce and postdivorce years. This group also expressed fewer feelings of inferiority in associating with friends than did those in the older groups at the time of divorce. There were no significant differences in how the three age groups felt the experience of going through divorce had affected their attitudes toward their own future marriages.

SUMMARY OF FINDINGS

1. This study of 295 young people, all of whom were from divorced homes, brings out rather clearly the unsoundness of grouping together and discussing all children of divorced homes as if they were a homogeneous group affected in the same ways by the divorces of their parents. In this group of 295 children of divorced parents, 38 percent were too young to remember the home before and at the time of the divorce.

2. Of children old enough to remember the home before the divorce there are several situations and relationships which seem to be traumatic for the child as he "goes through" divorce with his parents. For those who saw their homes as happy the divorce and adjustment to divorce was more traumatic than it was for those children who found themselves in unhappy homes characterized by open conflict between parents.

3. Children too young to remember the home before the divorce may feel different from other children and thus resort to "face-saving devices" in the postdivorce years.

4. It appears that the worst predivorce situations from the viewpoint of the child are the cases in which the parents are less likely to remarry.

5. Sibling order analyses did not reveal significant differences in how the children viewed the divorce and their adjustment of divorce.

6. Younger children who were old enough at the time of divorce so that they remembered events tended to be less aware of the traumatic effects of divorce than older children.

REFERENCES

1. Judson T. Landis, "The Pattern of Divorce in Three Generations," *Social Forces*, XXXIV (March, 1956), 213-216; and "A Comparison of Children of Divorced and Children of Happy or Unhappy Non-Divorced Parents on Parent-Child Relationships, Dating Maturation, and Sex and Marriage Attitudes," paper read before the Annual Meeting of the National Council on Family Relations, Minneapolis, August 27, 1955.

2. Cases of separation or of remarriage of the same spouse after divorce were eliminated from the study.

3. Landis, *op. cit.*

Divorce Adjustment:
A Woman's Problem?

VICKI L. ROSE
SHARON PRICE-BONHAM

INTRODUCTION

Waller's (1967) *The Old Love and the New,* initially published in 1930,[1] constituted the only major research dealing with adjustment after divorce until the publication of Goode's (1956) study of divorced women in Detroit. Since Goode's study, research in the area of divorce has been concerned only tangentially with the problem of adjustment. The primary purpose of this paper, therefore, is to review the literature and consolidate the major findings relative to divorce adjustment. Even though volumes have been written regarding the impact of divorce on children, the topic will be considered only insofar as it might affect the adjustment of the divorcing spouse-parent.

The concept of adjustment is applied to many aspects of social behavior. Adjustment is defined as a basic requirement of social participation (Bell, 1967). However, it is among the most controversial concepts dealt with in the study of the family. Divorce adjustment has been used in a variety of ways. It is beyond the scope of this paper to define divorce adjustment. However, it is necessary to caution the reader there is no stated consensus upon the usage of the term in the works which are cited in this paper.[2]

It is also pertinent that articles dealing with the general topic of divorce affects the general adjustment of women more than that of men. Likewise, Goode (1956) in his survey of postdivorce adjustment interviewed only mothers (95 percent had custody of their children) as he assumed that greater hardship is involved for the divorced woman with children than for the divorced man.

---

1. Although Waller's study is certainly a classic in the field and provides "an untapped source of hypotheses pertaining to personal adjustment" (Farber), it should not be included in the present paper. *The Old Love and the New* may more properly be considered an historical backdrop for more contemporary studies. The reader is referred to the 1967 edition in which Professor Bernard Farber, in the introduction, provides a valuable analysis of Waller's contribution to the study of postdivorce adjustment in terms of indicating the extent to which later investigation confirmed, denied, or modified Waller's hypotheses. Implicit in Farber's discussion are the limitations of any current application.

2. See Bell, 1967, Goode, 1949, Waller, 1967, Bernard, 1956; Locke, 1951, Goode, 1956, Hunt 1966; Burgess, Locke, and Thomes, 1965.

The Divorce

A divorce often comes as a crisis, even if desired by both spouses. Burgess, Locke, and Thomes (1963) contend that a crisis may not be experienced when the emotional involvement between the spouses is relatively weak, while it may be experienced as an extreme crisis when there is strong community opinion against it. Bernard wrote:

> . . . the whole trend in current social life is in the direction of demands for *laissez faire* in personal relationships. The issues that do arise will tend to be in the direction of making divorce as non-traumatic as possible for partners and for children (1970, 28-29).

Gurin et al. (1960) reported that persons who were relieved by divorce often suffered ample disorganization to the degree that they sought professional help. The trauma resulting from divorce includes both personal disorganization and behavior definitions such as unhappiness generated by conflict and the "unraveling of marital habits," which in turn affect the actions of divorcees (Goode, 1956, 185).

Goode (1956) measured the degree of trauma (high, medium, low) experienced by women in his study according to behavior items including difficulty in sleeping, poorer health, greater loneliness, low work efficiency, memory difficulties, increased smoking, and increased drinking. Using these criteria Goode found higher trauma to be positively related to: (1) having the husband first suggest divorce; (2) being given a short time for consideration of divorce; (3) having the idea of divorce come unexpectedly; (4) continuing to have attachment or emotional involvement with the ex-spouse after the divorce; (5) possessing a desire to punish her former husband; (6) being ambivalent about obtaining a divorce; (7) being personally disapproving of divorce; (8) having divorce disapproved of by her reference groups (family and friends); (9) experiencing discrimination as a divorcee; (10) coming from a rural background; and (11) her former husband having a middle or upper class occupation. In regard to age, Goode found the degree of trauma varied according to the length of time the divorcee had been married:

> . . . for younger people there is an association between a long marriage and a higher trauma index. However, for older people this pattern is reversed; a long marriage seems to be less traumatic . . . the possibility that in the case of older people the marriage has itself become somewhat stale and there are relatively few attractions in it for them . . . when the marriage is a short one, there is little association between age and trauma (1956, 193).

Goode also found that the decision to divorce was generally a reluctant decision which was reached over a long period of time, ". . . on the average of about two years" (1956, 137). For the *Significant Americans,* divorce was viewed as an "end of the rope" decision after a period of three or four years or even as long as ten or twelve years (Cuber and Haroff, 1965, 90). As a result of the fact that the decision to divorce is reached over a long period of time, it can be assumed that much of the adjustment relative to the divorce occurs before the divorce decree is granted. Therefore, Goode's (1956) finding that the greatest amount of trauma occurred at the time of the final separation rather than following the final decree was not unexpected.

Similarly, Bohannon distinguished between "emotional divorce" which is the deterioration of a marital relationship, and the "legal divorce:"

> ... the legal processes do not provide an orderly and socially approved discharge of emotions that are elicited during the emotional divorce and during the early parts of preparation for the legal processes (1970a, 48).

Several authors have stressed the fact that many times it is the adversary legal system that increases the trauma experienced by divorcing and divorced couples. Davis (1957) pointed out that the gap between theory and practice is perhaps greater in the field of divorce law than in any other area of legal practice. According to Hunt (1966) the grounds for divorce are molded to fit with the permissible grounds in any given state, and the charade-type nature of the suit is recognized by all who participate. In addition, Hunt contended that the laws require the divorcing spouses to become adversaries. The law's insistence on an adversary system tends to exacerbate the conflict (Kay, 1970), with disastrous moral and emotional consequences for everyone concerned (Lasch, 1966, 58). This adversary system could result in detrimental consequences for adjustment to divorce.

Several parallels have been drawn between loss of a spouse by divorce and loss of a spouse by death, as trauma and loneliness result from the loss of an intimate tie in either case. Weiss (1969) advised that new relationships be established; Hunt (1966) advocated "divorce work" to alleviate "role disturbance" including tears, reflection, and talk, therefore discharging feelings and slowly modifying one's habits and expectations in order to establish a new life. However, several students of divorce (Bernard, 1956; Bohannon, 1970a; Davis, 1957; Goode, 1956; Hunt, 1966; and Waller, 1967) noted differences between the two. Even though structural factors in the positions of the widow and divorcee are similar, the widow generally receives greater sympathy and support (Goode, 1956). According to Bernard ". . . no one . . . can take the sting or heartache out of divorce. That can perhaps never be institutionalized, as bereavment can" (1970, 16-17). In addition, loss of a spouse by divorce "involves a purposeful and active rejection by another person, who, merely by living, is a daily symbol of the rejection" (Bohannon, 1970a, 42).

Goode (1956) concluded that while society permits divorce, post-divorce institutional arrangements are inadequate. He outlines the failure of the kinship structure to provide unambiguous arrangements after divorce in material support, emotional support, readmission into the kinship structure, formation of families, and proper behavior and emotional attitudes. Society affords no clear definition as to the proper relationship between the divorced spouses. In spite of feelings of bitterness, love, or defeat, divorced persons "are obliged by convention to behave as though they were indifferent to it all" (Bernard, 1956, 202). Goode also noted the lack of prescriptions regarding reaction to divorce. Hunt agreed "the novice FM[3] does not know with any certainty what is expected (of him)" (Hunt, 1966, 46). Bohannon (1970a) contended that because of this ignorance concerning the requirements of divorce, the adjustment is more likely to be difficult.

Thus we see that difficulty in adjusting to a divorce may be largely a result of the ambiguous status of the divorced person because of the lack of institutionalized norms. The individual's attitudes toward their status as a divorcee will have an influence upon their adjustment and upon the performance of their new role as a divorced person (Bell, 1968).

Goode (1956) found a higher degree of adjustment after divorce among the women who: (1) had been the first to suggest divorce in their previous marriage; (2) held an attitude of indifference toward their former spouse; (3) could depend on regular child support payments from their former spouse; (4) had a full time job (thereby affording opportunities for meeting people); (5) had greater opportunities to date and develop new social relations. In addition, themes of complaint against the ex-husband were analyzed for their relationship to adjustment, but "other items, such as . . . age or dating behavior will shape . . . post-divorce experience far more definitely" (Goode, 1956, 131).

Hunt suggested "it is what the FM sees or believes about his own case that most affects his . . . adjustment or maladjustment to his new status" (1966, 25). However, Goode pointed out that a realistic "definition of the situation" facilitated adjustment.

A redefinition of identity was seen as required by Bohannon. New activities and behavior change his focus from past to present to future. The "psychic"[4] divorce, described as "the separation of self from the personality and the influence of the ex-spouse" is difficult, but "personally constructive" (1970a, 60).

The implication is clear; opportunities to date and meet new people are all-important for adjustment to divorce. Therefore, the approval of one's circle of family and friends is significant for the adjustment of the divorcee, as they will be helpful in meeting new people (Goode, 1956). Goode also reported that friends' acceptance of and reflection back to the divorcee of her new self-identity will facilitate her adjust-

3. Hunt utilizes the abbreviation FM to denote "the Formerly Married," a category including both the separated and the divorced, but omitting the widowed.

4. The reader will note that Bohannon's concept of the "psychic divorce" and its outcome is closely in line with Goode's definition of postdivorce adjustment in terms of a reorientation to the divorcee's present and future status.

ment. Goode also found that divorcees who have some divorced or divorcing friends are slightly more likely to fall into the low trauma classification.

Bohannon (1970a) and Cuber and Haroff (1965) reported divorcing persons often find themselves "dropped" by their married friends as they are viewed as introducing problems in social activities. Hunt (1966) pointed out that this alienation of the divorced person from married friends is at least partially because of difference in interests. He introduced the concept of "the world of the formerly married"—a subculture of the divorced and separated with its own rules, market mechanism, and adjustment patterns. "In general . . . continued relationships with friends and their children can make the disrupted home a less lonely and sad one" (Miller, 1970, 85).

Children. Children are involved in the majority of divorces and the custody of children is generally awarded to the mother. Children are often viewed as greatly complicating their mothers' postdivorce adjustment (Bernard, 1970). In contrast, Burgess, Locke, and Thomes (1963) suggest that the custodial parent experiences less crisis than does the parent who is cut off from his children.

Nearly all divorcing parents are concerned with the possible ill effects divorce may have on children, and according to Bohannon, "We do not know very much about it" (1970a, 55). In Goode's study the higher trauma group of women more often reported there had been some period during the divorce when the children had been harder to manage. At the same time, most of the mothers felt that the divorce had not been detrimental to their children; almost all believed that their children were "no worse off after the divorce than before" (1956, 318).

Kay (1970) and Bernard (1970) agree that research indicates that children of divorced homes suffer less than children living in homes torn with constant conflict. Bernard (1970, 12) continued: "To a woman concerned about the effect of divorce on her children, such findings are reassuring," and therefore, should have a positive effect upon her adjustment to divorce.

Dating and Other New Activities. Dating as an index of adjustment indicates a willingness to start a new life and serves as both "an introduction and stimulus to that new life" (Goode, 1956, 258). Hunt (1966) viewed the dating experience as one of reevaluation and one which renews self-esteem.

Friends and/or relatives provided help in meeting eligible suitors for almost half of Goode's respondents, while Hunt's respondents found such "conventional" methods to be of limited value and were willing to try more "unconventional" methods. Hunt concluded, "it is part of the way of life of the Formerly Married to violate conventions and take risks in order to increase the changes of readjustment and the opportunities for remarriage" (1966, 108).

Activities such as dating or taking a new job have similar beneficial effects. In either context, the divorcee's primary status is redefined; in the dating situation or work situation, the divorcee is "courted" or treated as a "co-worker" rather than someone's "ex." Likewise, even though the divorcee is strongly ambivalent in regard to loving again, both casual sex and love affairs are viewed as potential forms of aids in repairing the ego and leaving the individual more ready for remarriage (Hunt, 1966).

Remarriage as a Form of Adjustment. The statistics as to the rate and rapidity of marriage after divorce vary according to the source.[5] However, within any age group the divorced have a better chance for remarriage than either the widowed or the never married (Bernard, 1956; Goode, 1956).

Bell (1968) reported that the majority of the divorced view remarriage as the best means of postdivorce adjustment; and Goode (1956) concluded that remarriage represents a solution to the ambiguous status of the divorced. Hunt noted that his respondents whom even considered themselves reasonably successfully divorced "will not consider themselves wholly successful until they remarry" (1966, 285). Furthermore, it is held that "contemporary community attitudes appear to be receptive toward remarriage . . . for the divorced" (Bernard, 1956, 36). Reasons for remarriage include the fact that American adult society allows little latitude for the unmarried person, especially unmarried female parents; and social pressures for remarriage, though they may vary in intensity, are recurrent and include the couple-based nature of our society, the symbolic threat which the divorcee represents, the idea that children need two parents, and pressures from the children themselves (Goode, 1956).

Although Barnard (1956) reported that dependent children had a negative effect on the eligibility of women, Goode stated that "the remarriage rate of divorced mothers is not much lower than that of female divorcees generally" (1956, 207). Goode (1956) found that the number of children seemed to have no significant effect on the divorcee's courtship activities. However, women with fewer children did not remarry as rapidly as did those with more children.

Earlier remarriage was found more often among those women who (1) deliberated a longer period of time between first serious consideration of divorce and filing of the lawsuit; (2) experienced greater loneliness during the period of separation; (3) experienced high trauma; and (4) reported being in love with another man prior to divorce. Remarriage will be discussed only in the light of how it may affect the overall postdivorce adjustment.

Bonds between Ex-Spouses. Divorce, although it legally terminates the husband-wife relationship, never completely severs the ties between the individuals involved (Bohannon, 1970a; Burgess, Locke, and

[5] See Hunt, 1966; Bernard, 1956; Locke, 1951; Goode, 1956; Rollin, 1971.

Thomes, 1963; David, 1957; Mead, 1970; Hunt, 1966; Schwarz, 1968). Marriage has been referred to as "terminable and interminable" (Hunt, 1966) and the divorce process, just as it begins prior to the decree, "so may continue long afterwards" (Goode, 1956, 286). Vestigial bonds remain between the pair, especially when the marriage produced children:

> ...our present divorce style often denies the tie between the child and one of the parents, and it permits the parents to deny that—through their common child—they have an irreversible, indissoluble relationship to each other (Mead, 1970, 120-121).

This relationship with the ex-spouse could definitely affect adjustment in a remarriage. Bohannon refers to the chaotic situation in households of remarriage, i.e., the pattern of "divorce chains." These "chains" are "pseudokinship groups ... formed on the basis of links between the new spouses of ex-spouses" (1970b, 129), and are not uncommon, particularly when children are present as mediating influences. For example, ex-spouses are linked to each other as parents and as part of a kind of extended family, and a man's present wife and his ex-wife may become friends.

On the other hand, bitterness—or civility, at best—may characterize the relationship between ex-spouses. Hunt (1966) stated that continuing anger is more often found among divorced women than among divorced men. Goode's divorcees were most unhappy if their ex-spouses had remarried when they had not and least unhappy when they themselves had remarried while their ex-husbands had not. Thus, "in a certain sense, it may be said that the cost of a successful second marriage after divorce is often borne by the unmarried spouse" (Bernard, 1956, 203).

It is frequently the case that the crisis experienced by one member of the divorcing couple is prolonged by his attachment to the ex-spouse (Burgess, Locke, and Thomes, 1963). Although the general concession that some form of ties remain between the divorced spouses, it is at the same time true that disengagement from emotional involvement with the ex-spouse is imperative if adjustmental progress is to be made (Hunt, 1966).

Adjustment Other than Remarriage. The divorced persons who do not eventually remarry are in the minority. They are described as "long-terms" by Hunt (1966) and "hard core divorced" by Bernard (1956). The tendency of "long-terms" to remain in the "world of the formerly married" is explained by Hunt in terms of their more severe trauma and their need to progress through the process of adjustment more slowly; he further suggests the possibility of a "comfortable long-term adjustment to divorced life" (1966, 266).

NEED FOR FURTHER RESEARCH

This review of literature quickly reveals that much research is needed in the area of postdivorce adjustment.

It is evident that although Goode asserted, "the distortions created by interviewing only the wife are not extensive or many" (1956, 26) and the work of Bernard (1956), Hunt (1966), and Bohannon (1970) provide insights as to the postdivorce adjustmental process among men, research dealing with the male divorcee is very much needed. An investigation of divorcing and divorced *couples*, even though it may involve many prohibitive factors, would provide invaluable information. Likewise, the possibilities for cross-analysis of such data are extensive. In addition, it has been nearly a quarter of a century since the collection of Goode's data; this is approximately the same amount of time which passed between the publication of Waller's and Goode's studies. Also, replication of Goode's work would provide much information, especially in terms of empirical support (or lack of support) for possible changes in attitudes toward divorce and divorcees.

We must agree with Bernard that "no amount of research can wholly eliminate the emotional price exacted by divorce" (1970, 140). However, if, as she further alleges, research can "help lighten the load (and) . . . mitigate the accompanying feeling of guilt and shame," (1970, 104) then, clearly, more research in this area can do much to facilitate the process, as well as the understanding, of postdivorce adjustment.

REFERENCES

Barnett, James H. and Rhoda Gruen. Recent American Divorce Novels, 1938-1945: A Study in the Sociology of Literature. *Social Forces*, 1948, 26, 322-327.

Bell, Robert R. *Marriage and Family Interaction.* Homewood, Illinois: The Dorsey Press, 1967.

Bell, Robert R. (Ed.) *Studies in Marriage and the Family.* New York: Thomas Y. Crowell Company, 1968.

Bergler, Edmund. *Divorce Won't Help.* New York: Harper and Brothers, 1948.

Bernard, Jessie. No News, but New Ideas. In Paul Bohannon (Ed.) *Divorce and After.* Garden City, New York: Doubleday and Company, Inc. 1970, 3-29.

Divorce and After, Garden City, New York: Doubleday and Company, Inc., 1970, 3-29.

Bitterman, Catherine. The Multimarriage Family. *Social Casework,* 1968, 49, 218-221.

Bohannon, Paul. The Six Stations of Divorce. In Paul Bohannon (Ed.) *Divorce and After.* Garden City, New York: Doubleday and Company, Inc., 1970(a), 33-62.

Bohannon, Paul. Divorce Chains, Households of Remarriage, and Multiple Divorcers. In Paul Bohannon (Ed.) *Divorce and After.* Garden City, New York: Doubleday and Company, Inc. 1970 (b), 127-139.

Bohannon, Paul. Some Thoughts on Divorce Reform. In Paul Bohannon (Ed.) *Divorce and After.* Garden City, New York: Doubleday and Company, Inc., 1970 (c) 283-299.

Bohannon, Paul (Ed.) *Divorce and After.* Garden City, New York: Doubleday and Company, Inc., 1970.

Bossard, James H. S. Previous Conjugal Condition. *Social Forces,* 1939, 18, 243-247.

Bowerman, Charles E. Assortive Mating by Previous Marital Status: Seattle, 1939-1946. *American Sociological Review,* 1953, 18, 171.

Burgess, Ernest W., Harvey J. Locke and Mary Margaret Thomes, *The Family.* New York: American Book Company, 1963.

Chen, Ronald. The Dilemma of Divorce: Disaster or Remedy. *The Family Coordinator,* 1968, 17, 251-254.

Cuber, John F. and Peggy B. Harroff. *Sex and the Significant Americans.* Baltimore, Maryland: Penguin Books, 1965.

Davis, Kingsley. Divorce and its Effects. In Morris Fishbein and Ruby Joe Reeves Kennedy (Eds.) *Modern Marriage and Family Living.* New York: Oxford University Press, 1957, 100-113.

Gebhard, Paul. Postmarital Coitus among Widows and Divorcees. In Paul Bohannon (Ed.) *Divorce and After.* Garden City, New York: Doubleday and Company, Inc., 1970, 89-106.

Glick, Paul. First Marriages and Remarriages. *American Sociological Review,* 1949, 14, 726-734.

Goode, William J. Problems in Postdivorce Adjustment, *American Sociological Review,* 1949, 14, 394-401.

Goode, William J. *Women in Divorce.* New York: The Free Press, 1956.

Goode, William J., Elizabeth Hopkins, and Ellen M. McClure. *Social Systems and Family Patterns: A Propositional Inventory.* Indianapolis: Bobbs-Merrill, Inc., 1971.

Gurin, Gerald, Joseph Veroff, and Sheila Feld. *Americans View their Mental Health.* New York: Basic Books, Inc., 1960.

Hunt, Morton M. *The World of the Formerly Married.* New York: McGraw-Hill Book Company, 1966.

Ilgenfritz, Marjorie P. Mothers on their Own—Widows and Divorcees. *Marriage and Family Living,* 1961, 23, 38-41.

Jacobson, Paul H. *American Marriage and Divorce.* New York: Rinehart and Company, Inc., 1959.

Jourard, Sidney M. Reinventing Marriage: the Perspective of a Psychologist. In Herbert A. Otto (Ed.) *The Family in Search of a Future.* New York: Appleton-Century-Crofts, 1970, 43-50.

Kay, Herma Hill. A Family Court: the California Proposal. In Paul Bohannon (Ed.) *Divorce and After.* Garden City, New York: Doubleday and Company, Inc., 1970, 243-281.

Kushner, Sylvia. The Divorced, Noncustodial Parent and Family Treatment. *Social Work,* 1965, 10, 52-58.

Landis, Judson T. The Pattern of Divorce in Three Generations. *Social Forces,* 1956, 34, 213-216.

Lasch, Christopher. Divorce and the Family in America. *Atlantic Monthly,* 1966, 218, 57-61.

Levinger, George. Marital Cohesiveness and Dissolution: An Integrative Review. *Journal of Marriage and the Family,* 1965, 27, 19-38.

Litwak, Eugene. Three Ways in which Law Acts as a Means of Social Control: Punishment, Therapy, and Education: Divorce Law a Case in Point. *Social Forces,* 1956, 34, 214-223.

Locke, Harvey J. *Predicting Adjustment in Marriage: A Comparison of a Divorced and a Happily Married Group.* New York: Holt, Rinehart and Winston, 1951.

Locke, Harvey J. Predicting Marital Adjustment by Comparing a Divorced and a Happily Married Group. *American Sociological Review,* 1947, 12, 187-191.

Mead, Margaret. Anomalies in American Postdivorce Relationships, In Paul Bohannon (Ed.) *Divorce and After.* Garden City, New York: Doubleday and Company, Inc., 1970, 107-125.

Miller, Arthur A. Reactions of Friends to Divorce. In Paul Bohannon (Ed.) *Divorce and After.* Garden City, New York: Doubleday and Company, Inc., 1970, 63-86.

Mills, C. Wright. *The Sociological Imagination.* London: Oxford University Press, 1959.

Monahan, Thomas P. How Stable Are Remarriages? *American Journal of Sociology,* 1952, 58, 280-288.

Monahan, Thomas P. The Changing Nature and Instability of Remarriages. *Eugenics Quarterly,* 1958, 5, 17-85.

O'Neill, William L. *Divorce in the Progressive Era.* New Haven, Connecticut: Yale University Press, 1967.

Otto, Herbert A. *The Family in Search of a Future.* New York: Appleton-Century-Crofts, 1970.

Popenoe, Paul. Remarriage of Divorcees to Each Other. *American Socilolgical Review,* 1938, 3, 695-699.

Rollin, Betty. The American Way of Marriage: Remarriage. *Look Magazine,* 1971, 35, 62, 64-67.

Schlesinger, Benjamin. Remarriage: An Inventory of Findings. *The Family Coordinator,* 1968, 17, 248-250.

Schlesinger, Benjamin. *The One-Parent Family.* Toronto, Ontario: University of Toronto Press, 1970.

Schwartz, Anne C. Reflections on Divorce and Remarriage. *Social Casework,* 1968, 49, 213-217.

Waller, Willard, *The Old Love and the New: Divorce and Readjustment.* Carbondale, Illinois: Southern Illinois University Press, 1967.

Weiss, Robert S. The Fund of Sociability. *Trans-Action,* 1969, 36-43.

A Matter of Right

DAVID J. CANTOR

Divorce is an everyday cruelty. It is perpetrated upon our population by legal concepts which are archaic and illogical and perpetuated by legislatures which think that way. The damage which our law inflicts on the divorcing spouses and upon their children is incalculable, but it is deep and lasting.

The reasons why our divorce laws are this way are easily understood; the solution is not difficult to grasp. But to our profound shame the energy, courage and intelligence necessary to bring about this solution are rare and not yet successfully harnessed in any jurisdiction.

The primary fault of our law is fault itself. The fault concept ruling most of American jurisdictions decrees that a divorce may be granted only upon a showing that the defendant spouse has committed an offense against the marriage. There are exceptions, such as insanity, but they are insignificant. This requirement is embedded in an adversary system of jurisprudence, the result being that fault is determined, indeed can *only* be determined, upon the charge and proof of same by the other spouse.

No degree of kindness or civility or generosity on the part of spouses can avoid the necessity of assuming the posture of combatants and at least performing superficially like antagonistic gladiators. The process of battle for those who seek it is, because of the fault concept and the adversary system, rich in ways to traumatize, impoverish and enrage spouses; in ways to delay decisions and cripple children; and, if used to the most disgusting limits, in ways to defeat the divorce and thus maintain in law marriages which are dead in fact.

The consequence is bargaining. Because the defendant can always delay a divorce and often defeat it, the divorce itself becomes an object of trade. If the defendant decides not to contest the action, the plaintiff obviously will have little problem getting a divorce. The uncontested "trial" consists solely of the presentation of the plaintiff's claims and, with no rebuttal, this generally is sufficient evidence. The defendant therefore negotiates by offering the plaintiff an uncontested hearing — for a price. This price will normally be agreement to terms of alimony, support, custody, visitation or division of joint assets which the plaintiff, if not under duress, would not accept. These issues then become determined not on the basis of objective fairness, but rather on the basis of the plaintiff's desperation. The "agreement" is then submitted to the judge at the time of the uncontested divorce hearing, accepted by him and made the order of the court. Judges hardly ever refuse to accept terms agreed upon by the parties.

The bargaining process is wrong because it prevents justice, and it is evil because it too often works great harm on children. I have seen custody given to an inferior parent as the price of divorce — a result that is admittedly rare but which this sytem makes possible. More often, and very common, alimony and support payments will be either exorbitant or inadequate due to bargaining; assets will be inequitably divided; and visitation rights will be too broad or too constricted. All of these, in varying ways, adversely affect the children. The point is, and it cannot be made too emphatically, these questions are too important to be decided improperly. So long as a divorce is up for barter they will be.

There is only one way to take divorce out of this bargaining context. A divorce should be available as a matter of right to any spouse upon the filing of a petition. There should be no defenses and no means of delay. With the divorce itself extracted from bargaining, the ancillary matters of alimony, support, custody, visitation and division of assets could be decided fairly by a court. The parties would probably still reach agreements on these subjects, but under these circumstances a fair compromise could be expected because the spouse most desiring the divorce would not be at a disadvantage.

Making divorce available as a matter of right has other considerations to commend it besides eradicating the divorce barter. It would prevent the fighting that the bargaining engenders. It is an observable truth that tempers rise as bargaining intensifies, and divorce bargaining can be very intense. By reducing the level of animosity, the post-divorce relations of the spouses would have a better chance of being at least civilized, to the advantage of the children. With no divorce trials possible, the high lawyer's fees and, occasionally, detective's charges would be greatly lessened; in the latter case, perhaps eliminated. With no trial, the opportunity for each to attack and besmirch the other would cease to exist, again to the benefit of the children, who would be spared hearing all the dirt and possibly having to testify themselves.

The objections that would be raised against this type of reform may be easily anticipated. The first would most probably be that divorce would become too easy and endanger our prime social institution — marriage. The answer is that marriages which are no longer viable are not worthwhile social institutions. Once they cease to be viable, society is better off if they are dissolved peacefully and with as much good will as can be salvaged. Moreover, spouses generally do not seek divorce until after a long period has elapsed wherein they have sought to make the marriage work. The concept of frivolous divorce is a myth, blown utterly out of proportion because of the actions of a publicized few. I am frequently astounded at how much unhappiness spouses absorb *before* they decide to break up a marriage.

The second objection would probably be voiced on behalf of the spouse against whom a divorce petition is filed, if he or she did not want a divorce. Shouldn't this spouse have any rights? The answer is simply that no one should have the right to force the legal continuation of a marriage which has ceased to exist in fact. Society serves no useful purpose if it allows the law to be used as the servant of malice, delusion or unrealistic reluctance — and one or more of these must be present in a spouse who wishes to fight for the perpetuation of a dead marriage.

The third objection would be on behalf of the children. Wouldn't easy divorce endanger children by breaking up families and depriving them of one of their parents? Of course, divorce has this result and, of course, it's deplorable. But modern psychology and common sense both understand that children are more healthfully reared in a one-parent home free of tension and animosity than in a two-parent home where the spouses fight, or simply don't like each other, and show it. This concern for the children also overlooks the fact that under our present system divorce is very easy *if the spouses agree to it,* but this process of agreement, as we have seen, endangers the children by making their interests trade goods in negotiations for the divorce. The way to protect the children is not to make divorce harder, but to make it as easy as possible.

We will eventually have divorce on demand in the United States. The trend is as clearly this way as it is laudable. But fundamental social change, especially in the area of sexual relations, comes slowly. It also tends to come in stages. Thus, we are not likely to see any jurisdiction switch from the fault concept directly to divorce as a matter of right. What we have seen and what we shall see more of are switches away from the fault concept to intermediate formulations. These will not be solutions, but they will protect their backers from being deemed too radical.

One type of modest reform has been the creation of "incompatibility" as a ground for divorce. New Mexico, Oklahoma, Alaska and the Virgin Islands have adopted this ground. On its face, "incompatibility" would appear to allow a divorce to a plaintiff upon merely showing that plaintiff and defendant can't live together happily, or at least without rancor. Although the logic of the idea would seem to eliminate the relevance of defenses, nonetheless the New Mexico Supreme Court has held that actions by the plaintiff which "shock the conscience" of the trial judge may disqualify him or her from receiving a divorce despite the existence of incompatibility.

Many states have added varying forms of separation requirements as grounds, the most germane and the most liberal being those of Alabama, Arizona, Arkansas, Idaho, Kentucky, Louisiana, Puerto Rico, Texas, Virginia and Washington. In these states the physical separation of the parties is all that must be proven to qualify for divorce, though the time periods vary from two to seven years, and in Alabama only the wife may assert this ground as a plaintiff. No defenses exist, except to deny the fact of the separation for the requisite period, misbehavior of the plaintiff and the opposition of the defendant to the separation being irrelevant. The amount of time necessary for the separation, however, makes this ground unacceptable to most persons.

California has recently altered its law fundamentally so that the sole ground now, save only incurable insanity, is "irreconcilable differences, which have caused the irremediable breadown of the marriage." This has achieved the fine result of retiring the fault concept to pasture, but it still retains the adversary procedure and still preserves the possibility of trial and bargaining. Whether or not "irreconcilable differences" exist is, like incompatibility, an arguable question of fact under existing law, and is therefore susceptible of debate and trial.

These three innovations — incompatibility, separation, and irreconcilable differences — are all basically of the same philosophy. Each forms an inquiry into the viability of the marriage. The wording is different and the approach is different, but each forswears the concept of fault for an examination into the health of the relationship. Where each fails, and where all the other marriage breakdown theories similarly fail, is in the assumption that a marriage can be viable where one spouse persists in the view that it is not. Only after the parties have lived apart for an unconscionably long period of time prior to divorce do any of our laws consider the question of viability no longer debatable.

What our legislators and marriage "experts" must learn about divorce is that the only real experts in any marriage are the spouses themselves. It is pure arrogance for the state to intrude itself into the marriage with the power to decide whether or not it should continue. It is preposterous that a judge should be empowered to tell a spouse who wishes to cease living with a husband or wife that divorce would be an error, that the spouses really are or can be compatible, viable, happy or reconcilable. Of course, a minority of spouses will misjudge their own desires; this follows from the simple fact of human fallibility. But the possibility of error and mischief is much greater when someone outside the marriage is able to judge it viable over the objection of a spouse.

We will get divorce on demand eventually, not only because of the ineluctable logic of it, but because society more and more is tiring of those who presume to view people as sheep with the government as shepherd. The entire sad and absurd story of American legal restrictions on adult consensual sexual behavior is ascribable to the theory that the population needs moral guidance from the social shepherds — those who know right from wrong and arrogate to themselves the right to impose their tenets upon the entire polity. This paternalism is under attack and will fall because time and experience have shown that the shepherds do not guide their flocks well, or really at all. To those who followed they have brought guilt and unhappiness; the rest have simply ignored the shepherds' advice and sought illegal abortions; have violated adultery, fornication, and sodomy laws; have gotten Mexican divorces or, in another context, ignored prohibition — all these with deleterious social effects that would not have occurred had the shepherds stayed home and tended to their own problems.

We live in a time of erupting assertive egos. All the diverse groups which were heretofore deemed inferior by definition are not only asking but demanding the right of self-determination. In this the Black, the student, the homosexual, the migrant worker are united.

They are as one with others, too — the woman who seeks an abortion, the spouse who wants marital freedom. The day of sexual dogma has passed; old sexual taboos are dying. In a world teetering on the edge of obliteration, men are maturing through danger. The freedom to make basic, personal decisions is becoming an irreducible demand. Marriage will not long be a prison, with the state as jailer. The function of the state with regard to marriage should be and will be only to record its birth and its death. This will come in our lifetime.

UNIT STUDY GUIDE

A. *Terms to Review*

Annulment	Divorce on demand	Plaintiff
Conciliation Courts	Incompatibility	P.W.P.
Dilemma	Migratory divorce	Proper divorce
Dissolution (marriage)	No-Fault divorce	Rate (divorce)

B. *Questions for Discussion and Study*

1. What changes, if any, have been made in the divorce laws of your own state in recent years? Summarize and discuss their implications.

2. Dedate: "The decision to discontinue a marital partnership should be totally within the power of the participants to decide, not the state."

3. In one recent year, nearly one-fourth of all persons filing for divorce had been married for fifteen years or more (U.S. data). Discuss salient sociological, economic, psychological and other factors that may be involved in this phenomenon.

4. The sexual equality movement's influence has frequently been cited as a strong contributing factor in the general turbulence characterizing American family life today and in the increasing rate of marital disintegration as well. Explore this contention objectively within the framework of a socio-cultural analysis.

5. It has been frequently observed that there are discrepancies between actual and stated grounds for legal termination of marriage. Describe and explain this pattern.

6. Define and give an example of a "re-constituted family group." Discuss the roles and experiences of children living in a re-constituted family and discuss the particular kinds of stresses the marital partners may face in this type of family.

7. List and discuss the different pairing combinations among re-marriage partnerships in terms of age factors, prior marital experience, etc. Elaborate on the potential assets and liabilities of each combination.

8. In 1971 the U.S. Supreme Court ruled that persons too poor to pay filing fees and court costs must have these costs borne by the state. Discuss the implications, social and otherwise, of this development.

C. *Topics-Ideas for Papers and Projects*

1. Using records available in the court clerk's office, construct a map showing the distribution, by census tract or other area, of divorces or dissolutions in your county.

2. Research: "Expectations About Re-Marriage and its Qualities: A Comparison of Younger and Older Divorced Persons.

3. Divorce has been described as "death in sixty days." Interview a sample of recently-divorced men and women to ascertain emotions, feelings, and motivations similar to bereavement process which were possibly experienced in the termination process.

4. Do an analysis of the divorce rates in your state for the years 1900- 1970. Speculate on the influence of social, economic, and other conditions on observed fluctuations and trends in the rates.

5. Research: "A Study of Motives and Outcomes Among Persons Who Cancel Their Divorce Proceedings."

6. Research: "The Portrayal of Remarriage Success and Failure in Modern Fiction."

7. Survey the divorce laws of the U.S. with regard to those states which impose restrictions on remarriage following divorce. Describe these restrictions and discuss the rationale involved.

Unit 10
Improving the Marital Relationship

So advantageous are all forms of mutual service that the question may be fairly asked, whether after all Cooperation and Sympathy–at first instinctive, afterwards reasoned– are not the greatest facts even in organic nature. —Henry Drummond

Man, like the generous vine, supported lives:
The strength he gains is from the embrace he gives.
—Pope

Introduction

As we observed in the preceding unit, one widely used technique of problem-solving among unhappily married persons is voluntary termination of the partnership. Some, however, complain that the mass media coverage of the family scene tends to over-emphasize the admittedly high rate of marital breakup; and there may be good grounds for this charge. For despite the high level of marital disintegration, the fact is that there are comparatively many more cases in which the partners in a troubled-but-valued relationship attempt to solve their problems. In addition, there are doubtless many thousands of couples consciously seeking to improve their marriages. A disproportionate emphasizing of "social pathology" may exist to a degree even in the research and scholarly writing on the family and marriage. Too often, perhaps research is directed toward "deviant" family behavior (eg. divorce, maladjustment, etc.) rather than toward the customary patterns of problem-solving found in relatively happy and stable marriages. Much more needs to be done by family scholars toward assessing familial strengths and assets.

This unit focuses on improvement of the marital relationship. The impetus to improvement can be in the form of a response to an existing problem or it can be a conscious, ongoing process within a growth-oriented partnership. In both cases there are certain underlying assumptions. For one thing, it is assumed that most interpersonal difficulties confronting a marriage can be resolved if both partners truly value their relationship. A second assumption is that a great many of the serious problems encountered in a marriage turn out to be interpersonal problems within the partnership rather than, say, problems of economics, religious conflicts, or difficulties with in-laws or kin.

This is not to imply, of course, that situational conditions are of no importance. As we saw in an earlier unit, economic deprivation, physicial disability, and the intrusion of the job or other institutional sectors may induce problems and severely damage the functioning of the marriage. However, the very best conditions of existence cannot in themselves guarantee the emergence or maintenance of person-oriented, growth-oriented marital partnerships. In this connection, two related premises can be stated. First, optimal conditions of existence can significantly enhance the growth of a loving, caring, sharing relationship in which the partners are committed to growth in the partnership and within themselves as individuals. Secondly, such a relationship can continue to provide meaning, sustenance, and worth to the partnership despite the incursion or presence of potentially stressful situational conditions such as those cited above. The intention here is not to roll out the simplistic, romantic view that "love conquers all." Instead, the assumption underlying the materials in this unit is that a healthy partnership consists in a strong, resilient interpersonal bond and that such relationships are likely to fare relatively well in most situations; they have interpersonal strength and potential which can sustain the partnership "in good times and bad."

An inspection of some of the specific problems of marriage as presented in earlier units will show that many of the interpersonal problems in each area of marital encounter were defined in terms of changing ideals and norms concerning marriage. These changing perceptions of the desirable have, to a large extent, reflected this influence of ideas diffused by the sexual equality and human potentials movements. Let us assume that, whatever happens to these movements, the ideas which they promulgated about the nature and quality of marriage are likely to persist. If the assumption is valid, we are faced with significant implications for any effort to improve the quality of marriage. Let us review these implications.

For one thing, the significance of the drive toward equality in human relationships, and specifically in marriage, must be acknowledged. Inequality is the prime requisite of a dominant-subordinate, master-slave, superior-inferior form of relations; many Americans are coming to believe that this kind of relation has no place in a marital partnership. For another thing, increasing support is given to the belief that marriage *should not* and *need not* be suffocating to the individuals within it. A related implication is that the growth and development of the mates, as individuals, is as important as the maintenance of the partnership per se. While this is not a totally new idea, thanks to the history of individualism in American social thought, it has received great impetus with the emergence of the human potentials movement. That movement, as we have seen earlier, stresses self-actualization, social and individual cultivation of awareness and trust, and the maximizing of the individual's capacity for growth and love. Finally, there is a significant congruence of ideas in the sexual equality and human potentials movement regarding situational conditions within which modern marriage exists. Namely, implicit in both their ideologies is the need to reformulate and modify the roles of organizations and institutions which impinge on family life and marriage. The purpose of such change is to develop societal conditions within which true familial-marital partnerships, based on the principles cited above, can flourish. The materials in your readings for this unit explore each of these aspects to some degree.

Unlike other areas of marital encounter which were covered in earlier reading, this unit's materials call for little discussion in terms of issues. The pragmatic, instrumental social tradition in American thought supports and promotes the concept of improvement, whether it is focused on productive work or on the functioning of families and marriage. Very few would disagree that improvement is needed in the quality of today's marital relationships. There are, on the other hand, differences of opinion as to (1) where the improvement efforts should be focused — whether individual or group-oriented procedures are most effective, (2) how much and what kinds of improvement should be expected, (3) whether such efforts should be crisis-oriented or built into the ongoing partnership agreements, and (4) what specific techniques ought to be employed. These differences of opinion probably spring as much from variation in the views and orientations of professionals as from the actual needs of marriage itself.

One aspect of marital improvement does come close to being an issue; this is the question of whether improvement techniques and change-processes ought to be developed and applied from within the marriage, or whether such change-processes should be introduced from outside the group, drawing on professional or other help-sources. This issue, such as it is, stems in part from the long tradition of a "self-help" ethic in American culture and in part from the persisting notion of marriage as private and sacrosanct. An example: a counselor will often see a husband who is infuriated because his wife, having initiated contact with a family or marriage counselor, is "telling the whole world about our problems!" Such reactions may imply vestiges of patriarchal, male-supremacy tendencies; to the extent that counselors become privy to intimate marital processes, to that extent there is also a threatened loss of control over the situation.

For troubled families of an earlier era, dealing with marital unhappiness was usually construed as a matter of applying the power of will, of "toughing it out." In contemporary society, however, the intertwining of marital roles with one's other functions in an interdependent society seriously questions sole reliance on that technique. As Goode said, "Since family life is suffused with emotion, those who are unhappy in their family relationships usually learn that this kind of misery, like a toothache, cannot easily be set apart, compartmentalized, or controlled by an effort of will. It affects much of their lives."[1] Almost opposite to this view is the notion that somehow the state could prevent or reduce problems of interpersonal relations, presumably including family-related ones, by careful indoctrination of "adjustment" motivations and beliefs in the citizenry. Though not directing their remarks specifically to the improvement of interpersonal relations in families, Foote and Cottrell's work in interpersonal competence suggests the importance of developing in-group capacities for meeting and dealing with a changing world. Thus, while not rejecting the idea that valuable resources lie outside the familial group, it would be dangerous to rely too heavily on rigid institutional sources and the norms that emerge from them. Thus,

> The incessant problem of equipping human beings to handle their affairs and progress toward the discovery of new values and new means is not solved by authoritarian indoctrination of static attributes and beliefs. To rely upon such methods would not only be subversive of the most fundamental of American democratic values but would ultimately result in failure of the system which sought to maintain itself by these means.[2]

It is obvious that these maladapting forms of socialization could be as characteristic of particular family practices as of those emanating from any direct agency of the state. For many marriages, the issue of self-help versus outside help for problem-solving or marital improvement is probably quite real. For a growing number of marriages, however, the problem-solving and improvement processes draw from strengths and potentials both within the partnership and from a variety of external resources. Some of these will be evident in your readings for this unit.

Some *alternatives* in the improvement of marriage can now be listed. It should be noted that most of those cited below are calculated to build and enhance the development of partnership strengths; their orientation is thus toward fostering a continuous process of improvement and couple enrichment. They are thus not crisis-oriented; furthermore, they do not value the formation of great dependence by the marriage on external problem-solving sources. On some of the items below, references have been supplied in case you wish to explore some related literature.

1. Community-Operated Marital Health Centers.[3]
2. Marriage-Oriented Growth and Enrichment Groups.[4]
3. Encounter and Awareness Groups for Married Couples.[5]
4. Couples' Communication-Enhancement Training.[6]
5. Intimate Family Networks.[7]
6. Marriage and Family Counseling.[8]
7. Continuing Education for Marriage.

8. Written Contracts of Expectations Between Partners.
9. Mass Media Programming for Marital Improvement.
In each of the alternatives posed above, and for those cited in your readings which follow, it would be well to raise two questions: their relative feasibility and their likelihood of acceptance.

REFERENCES

1. Goode, Wm. J. "Family Disorganization," in Robert K. Merton and Robert A. Nisbet (eds.), *Contemporary Social Problems* (New York: Harcourt, Brace and World, 1961), p. 390.

2. Foote, Nelson and Leonard S. Cottrell, Jr. *Identity and Interpersonal Competence* (Chicago: U. of Chicago Press, 1955), p. 49.

3. Cf. Vincent, Clark. "Marital Health: A Needed Specialty," in *Journal of Marriage and the Family* 29 (Feb. 1967): 18-39; Herbert A. Otto, "Is Monogamy Out-Dated?," *Saturday Review* (April 25, 1970): 23 ff.

4. Anderson, Douglas A. "The Family Growth Group: Guidelines for an Emerging Means of Strengthening Families," *The Family Coordinator* 23 (Jan. 1974): 7-13.

5. Cf. Appendix in Herbert A. Otto (Ed.), *The Family in Search of A Future* (New York: Appleton-Century-Crofts, 1970).

6. Cf. Miller, Sherod *et al. Alive and Aware: Improving Communication in Relationships* (Minneapolis: Interpersonal Communications Programs, Inc., 1974).

7. Stoller, Frederick H., "The Intimate Network of Families As A New Structure," in Herbert A. Otto (Ed.). *The Family in Search of A Future* (New York: Appleton-Century-Crofts, 1970), p. 145.

8. These national organizations can provide information about certified marriage counseling in your area: American Association of Marriage and Family Counselors, 27 Woodcliff Drive, Madison, N.J. 07940; Family Service Association of America, 44 East 23rd St., New York, N.Y. 10010; National Council on Family Relations, 1219 University Avenue, S.E., Minneapolis, Minn. 55414.

Reconciliation or Resignation:
A Case Study

B. JEANNE MUELLER

Family court procedure is often legally based on the sentiment that suggests that ardent efforts should be made to effect reconciliation. In many courts both special commissioners and clinical facilities are used in an effort to avoid divorce although few studies have been made of what the reconciliation looks like when it does occur. This study involved an effort to learn in some detail about the perceptions of reconciled spouses concerning various aspects of their marriage relationship, including their satisfaction with the reconciliation. The study especially was aimed at providing information on the perceptions of the marriage relationship from the point of view of husbands as well as wives. Many reports in the literature dealing with marital relationships or marital conflict, such as those by R.O. Blood and D.M. Wolfe (1960) or by William Goode (1956), were based on data secured only from women and, therefore differences in perceptions between husbands and wives could not be assessed. This is a sampling bias which should not be overlooked or underestimated.

THE COUPLES

In the study reported here 28 reconciled husbands and wives were interviewed separately by a team of interviewers. The fourteen couples in the study were chosen from a list of all cases of divorce action dismissed during the four year period January 1964-December 1967 in a rural midwestern county. The county which provided the setting for the study was composed of farms and small towns located between two metropolitan areas. The population of about 50,000 was increasing through immigration. Median family income at the time was $5,590, near the state average of $5,926. Farming and related industry were an important part of the economy, but twice as many workers were employed in diversified manufacturing as in farming. Median age was 32 years and the population, evenly divided between males and females, was predominately Protestant. Of the total of 210 cases which were dismissed during the four year period chosen for this study 147 were subsequently separated again or divorced and two cases suffered death of a spouse. Interviewers sought to locate the remaining 61 couples through letters sent to last known addresses and by making inquiries of former neighbors, cross-roads storekeepers, postmasters, township chairmen, and the county sheriff. Thirty couples were located who lived in the county and who were still together ten months or more after reconciliation. Fourteen of these 30 couples were interviewed during this study. The remaining sixteen couples who were not readily accessible for interviewing, were similar in demographic characteristics, according to the court records.

Four of the husbands interviewed were business or professional men and the other ten were in blue-collar occupations. Half of the wives were employed, all in service occupations. Level of education ranged from seventh grade to graduate degree; the mode was high school graduation. Five wives had more education than their husbands, but this was not related to satisfaction with reconciliation. Median family income was in the $7,000-$9,000 range, well above the county median. Range for income was from less than $3,000 to more than $15,000. Age range was between 20 and 66 years with about a third of the couples in each of the three age groups, 25-35, 36-50, and 51-66. Six of the fourteen husbands were from nine to seventeen years older than their wives. Duration of marriage ranged from two years to 32 years. Five couples were married two to four years, five were married seven to twelve years, and four couples were married more than twelve years.

Of the 28 respondents, 20 had been married once, six had been married twice, and three had been married three times. At the time of the interviews all of the couples were parents and at the time of filing suit for divorce all but one couple had children living at home. Twelve couples were Protestants, one Catholic, and one represented a mixed marriage between Catholic and Protestant.

FINDINGS

Seven couples reported they were satisfied with the reconciliation, but three of the fourteen had reservations about the future duration of the marriage: (1) "Maybe when the children are grown we will go our separate ways;" (2) "Next time she files suit, I'm not coming back;" and (3) "I'll stay unless he beats me again." The other seven couples were dissatisfied but resigned to the reconciliation: "It's a sad situation," or "It's bitter-sweet." One wife explained that she did not want to be a divorcee, that she thought her husband would change in response to separation, "But he didn't." From her point of view major problems still remained and she believed he thought so, too. She took a job to avoid being at home. "Things won't get better, but I won't be there so much of the time."

For those seven husband and wife pairs who, as individual spouses, reported themselves to be currently satisfied with the reconciliation, the range of response agreement across all areas of inquiry was from 52 to 72 percent. For those couples in which one or both members expressed dissatisfaction with the relationship, response agreement was lower, ranging from 40 to 65 percent.

Conflict resolution was a difficult problem for the seven dissatisfied couples both before and after the court action. The greatest discrepancy in response, however, between these unhappily reconciled husbands and wives was related to family decision-making. for example, one husband reported that he decided on finances and discipline of the children and his wife decided on when to have sexual intercourse. His wife, to the contrary, said that he decided on sex and finances and that she decided on child discipline. Another wife whose husband reported that he was satisfied with the decision-making arrangements in the family told of her own dissatisfaction because "he makes all the decisions." These couples also showed an increase in differences in responses to questions about sexual relations after reconciliation compared to their reported recall of the sexual relationship during the period of their marriage prior to filing suit for divorce. That is, they were further apart in their perceptions of what was currently going on in their sexual relationship than in their perceptions of what had happened in the past before court action was taken.

For happily reconciled couples, convergence in perceptions and role expectation reportedly increased over all categories after reconciliation. The fewest differences in response between satisfied husbands and wives were in response to questions relating to conflict resolution. Knowing how to resolve differences was felt to be more critical by the spouses than the fact that conflicts occurred.[1]

Unmet Expectations. One third of the respondents said that his or her spouse did "not show affection as much as I would have liked" in the years of marriage prior to filing suit for divorce, and those who were satisfied with reconciliation said there had neen an increase in the amount of affection shown. Husbands freely volunteered that their wives had expected more affection than they were given before the separation, but few wives indicated that their husbands had wanted more demonstrations of love and affection. Affection had different meanings for husbands and wives. For a wife, affection was a diffuse term which meant talking for sociability, telling her that she was doing a good job with home and children, and backing up her decisions about family matters such as child discipline and budgeting. When the men said they needed more affection they meant something very specific, namely, more sexual responsiveness and more willingness by the wife to intitiate sex play.

Husbands expressed satisfaction with their own sense of adequacy in the sexual relationship both before and after reconciliation. Only four of the fourteen wives, however, reported viewing themselves as adequate sex partners after reconciliation. In general, wives were less satisfied with the sexual aspects of their marriage and said they were even less satisfied currently than in the earlier years of marriage. Husbands did not seem to reciprocate these feelings; most said they had been satisfied with their wives as sex partners during both periods of the marriage, i.e., before the divorce suit was filed and since recon-

[1] For further discussion of techniques of conflict resolution in marriage see G. R. Bach and Peter Wyden, *The Intimate Enemy.* New York: Wm. Morrow and Company, 1969.

ciliation. Either the husbands' expectations were more easily met or they were less willing to admit criticism of their wives on this sensitive topic. Reportedly, the men "frequently" or "always" experienced orgasm but nearly half of the wives said that they "seldom" or "never" or "don't know." Seven of the fourteen couples said sex tended to hold the marriage together during troubled times in those years before the divorce suit was filed. What the wives meant when they made this remark, however, was that sex held the husband in the marriage and husbands' comments verified this opinion.

Sexual infidelity, real or fantasied, was a frequent source of conflict. Four wives and eight husbands were openly involved in extramarital relationships and two other spouses were suspected of infidelity. Moreover, there was a definite lack of tolerance of any more legitimate interests or friendships developed outside the husband-wife relationship. Husbands complained if their wives wanted a night out to bowl with the girls and wives complained if husbands wanted a night out to play poker with the boys. There was little feeling that a spouse might need time off, and an expressed need for privacy was viewed not as a right but as an affront. Those couples who achieved a better relationship after reconciliation spent more time together doing things for fun.

Only two husbands complained about the wife's extravagance. One put his wife on a personal allowance and the other finally refused to give his wife grocery money until she changed her spending habits. More frequent, however, were wives' complaints about husbands who "squandered" money for recreation that did not include their joint participation. Twelve of the fourteen wives said their spouse spent too much time away from home drinking, gambling at card games, on hunting trips, or at sports events such as auto races which have limited feminine appeal. One husband, who reported that recreation with his wife was very satisfying, said they "went on trips, fishing, deer hunting, and to basketball, football and baseball games." His wife's version, however, was that "he never took me out and he didn't like it if I went out with my girl friends." This husband also reported that since the reconciliation they had gone together on an overseas holiday and that they went out for dinner once a week. The wife minimized this: "We took a trip and go out to eat. That's about all."

Alcoholism was a factor in only one marriage in which both spouses had a drinking problem. The husband persuaded his wife to join Alcoholics Anonymous while he joined the spouses' group of A.A. Complaints about drinking, therefore, were related not to excesses but to socializing in a neighborhood tavern which often included buying drinks for and dancing with other women. In the small town and rural neighborhoods which were the settings for this study, the cross-roads tavern functions as a kind of community center, a common meeting place for neighbors and friends who convene there once or twice a week to play cards or dance and to enjoy sociability over a few drinks. This was a respectable pastime for married couples, but in these cases wives complained because (1) their husbands did not take them along and (2) the money spent there was needed to pay bills.

Both husbands and wives were viewed as being more sympathetic and helpful when the partner was physically ill than when he or she was sad or emotionally upset. Only two husbands and one wife said the spouse tried to be helpful in the latter instance. As one husband wryly explained: "It's usually the way she's acting that makes me angry or upset and that's not a time when she's being helpful!"

Agreement on Expectations. When asked, "What does your husband most appreciate about you as a wife?" most women answered in terms of their homemaking and skills as a parent. One respondent, typical of others, said her husband thought of her as "a good housekeeper in his employ," but that he was angry when there was no money left after she had paid the bills. Not one of the wives mentioned companionship in answer to the question on what husbands appreciate although respondents represented middle class as well as working class families. The family structure represented in these marriages was one of segregated or parallel roles and it exemplified traditional rural values. Role specifications for wives called for good housekeeping, care of children, sexual acquiescence, and a minimum of nagging. Husbands were expected to be good providers and moderate in their sexual demands. Both men and women in this group agreed on these role definitions, but the women would have preferred a more interactional pattern with a greater emphasis on intimacy and meeting affective needs. Interestingly, none of the seven husbands who had a working wife mentioned her work as an appreciated contribution to the family.

The major expectation by both husbands and wives for the woman's performance as mother was that she should be a good housekeeper, seeing to it that the children were dressed and fed, a focus on instrumental task (Parsons, 1964) rather than on relationship. Only two out of the total group of 28 respondents mentioned giving love or affection. This was true not only for both spouses, but for both time periods in the marriage, i.e., before separation and after reconciliation.

Differences in Perceptions of Husbands and Wives. More mothers than fathers viewed their children as affecting and being affected by marital conflict and more fathers than mothers felt their children were better off since the reconciliation. This may be a reflection of the amount of time mothers spent with their children, and therefore, their greater exposure to the problems of children, or it may indicate that mothers are more ready to discover problems.

Women were heavily invested in child discipline and none attributed primary responsibility in this area to her husband. Only two husbands claimed they had control of discipline. As a group, however, husbands were more likely to say that they shared control than to indicate that the wife had the final say.

More husbands than wives claimed the husband made decisions about finances. None of the husbands said this was primarily the wife's responsibility; four of the wives said finances was their sole responsibility, but they wished their husbands would help them with budgeting and keeping accounts. As a group, husbands said they were involved in joint decisions in all areas more often than wives as a group said husbands were jointly involved in decisions. In fact, nine wives complained that husbands were negligent in sharing responsibility with them, but only two husbands mentioned conflicts over decision-making.

Twelve husbands but only three wives reported themselves to be in good health during the year before the divorce suit was filed; however, ten women reported their health had improved since reconciliation. Wives complained that husbands were not very perceptive about their state of health, and this was reflected in the fact that all except one husband said his wife was in either "good" or "very good" health prior to the separation. At issue here, of course, was not actual health status, but the differences in perceptions between spouses about health status.

Separation and Reconciliation. Some spouses became aware of serious marital problems within the first six months of marriage, but five respondents were married more than eight years before they began to think the marriage might fail. One husband said he was unaware of any conflict until legal notice was served on him. More frequent, however, was the use of threat of divorce by a husband or wife as a way of trying to get their spouse to change undesirable behaviors. Especially for the unhappily reconciled couples, separation seemed to be just another tactic in an overall strategy of war, an escalation of aggressive behavior shown in threats to take court action rather than any actual intent to desert the field of conflict. Half of the respondents said they never actually discussed the subject of filing suit. Once the decision had been made, six wives and one husband filed without announcing their intention so that the first their spouses knew about it was when the summons was served. One husband said, "I still don't know what she was mad about, but I think she's over it now." Another said, "Some little misunderstanding got exaggerated;" and still another explained, "She threatened divorce from time to time but I didn't know she meant it until she just left." Another said, "I threatened divorce, but he never said anything. I couldn't talk to him. I just went ahead and did it." This wife went on to explain that she had to fill out a complaint form at the courthouse. When her husband read it, "he first realized how I felt and he made the first move." They talked things over and decided to try again.

Eight wives and three husbands said they took steps to avoid divorce. By this they meant that they took initiative for talking things over with their spouses. Only one respondent, a husband, contested the suit. Twelve respondents (six couples) tried to work out difficulties together, nine other respondents said they thought things out alone, and five said that court-ordered marriage counseling helped them to achieve a reconciliation. Ministers, lawyers, friends, and relatives as well as marriage counselors were used by many as advisors, but most respondents did not credit advice or counseling as being the primary factor in their decision to try again. It was their children who lowered vulnerability to divorce. All but one couple had children at the time of separation and three women had married a second time in order to make a home for children by a previous marriage. The single most important factor in decisions to reconcile was reported by both men and women to be "for the sake of the children." Underlying this was an economic factor. Only one husband could have supported two households adequately. Before separation most wives had been greatly concerned with getting out of debt or buying a home or adding capital to the husband's small business. They disliked the added costs of separation and seemed to feel they were being disloyal to common family goals. Furthermore, few women were prepared for the kind of jobs that would both support their living expenses and cover the cost of child care. Independence and individualism were strong community values and there was aversion to applying for public aid. Only one mother received Aid for Dependent Children during the period of separation and after reconciliation she tried to repay the amount received to the county welfare department. Another wife said, "We got together again because I had no place else to go. No job and no money. One Sunday my husband came and packed me up and carried me home." Under such circumstances, "for the sake of the children" was an easy rationalization for reconciliation.

One of the tactics used to minimize conflict after reconciliation was for the husband to take a second job or for the wife to work during part of the time he was at home. This helped to stabilize their marital relationship in several ways. More family income, for instance, meant fewer worries over unpaid bills or being able to finance a new car or a home. This made husbands feel more adequate because both husbands and wives defined his role primarily in terms of providing material goods. Every husband who was satisfied with reconciliation mentioned having resolved conflicts over family finances. More time spent working also meant that time available to be together was limited mostly to weekends so there was less time spent fighting and more willingness to do something for fun such as inviting friends over or going out to eat. These shared enjoyments promoted good feelings and a few wives even became more sexually responsive.

Future Expectations. Future expectations for these marriages were modest: mentions were made of "a routine comfortable life without conflict" or of "an acceptable relationship." Half of the respondents had sought advice from marriage counselors prior to reconciliation and one wonders why some had not returned for additonal help. Perhaps it was because they thought of counseling only in terms of avoiding divorce.

SUMMARY AND CONCLUSIONS

Fourteen couples whose suits for divorce had been dismissed were interviewed concerning their current assessments of various aspects of their marital relationship. Information was gathered on perceptions of two time periods: (1) the time preceding filing suit for divorce, as recalled by the respondents; and (2) the current situation, ten months or more subsequent to reconciliation. Each spouse was interviewed simultaneously by a team of interviewers using the same schedule appropriately modified for husband or wife. In comparing responses for pairs, there was a bi-modal distribution comprised of those who were satisfied with the reconciliation and whose marital relationship had improved and others who were only resigned to the reconciliation, whose relationship had stabilized at some lesser level of satisfaction. Among those who were unhappily reconciled, there was less agreement on responses than for those who were happily reconciled. The fewest differences were found between happily reconciled husbands and wives in the area of conflict resolution. The greatest discrepancy in response was between unhappy pairs in answers to questions about family decision-making.

Wives, as a group, were less well satisfied, than husbands; they saw major conflicts remaining. Six of the fourteen were dissatisfied either with themselves or their husbands as sex partners. All couples had children and wives were more likely to believe the children had been adversely affected by marital conflicts, even after the reconciliation. Half of those wives who worked still experienced conflicts between the demands of work and family responsibilities. However, most wives said they were better appreciated since the reconciliation and they were better satisfied with the way in which family decisions were made.

Husbands said they valued affectionate response more often than wives reported this as role expectation. On the other hand, husbands perceived correctly that wives wanted more emotional support than they, the husbands, gave. Many husbands blamed themselves and said they were not very good spouses during the earlier period of the marriage. As a group, husbands tended to say their health was good and to report a higher rating for the health of their wives than the wives reported for themselves. Husbands tended to say that the reconciliation was a good idea; they believed the children were getting along better; they felt more appreciated by their wives; and they reported fewer remaining conflicts. The men said they had learned to handle disagreements by talking things over instead of by disruptive fighting. They also claimed to be satisfied with their sexual relationship. All in all, reconciliation seemed better to husbands than to wives.

Differences in perceptions concerning what was being experienced in the marital relationship was evident when comparing the paired responses of a specific couple or in comparisons between groups of husbands and wives. That is, expectations of the spouses for themselves and for their partners were often at variance with the expectations of the "other." These unmet expectations often left uncommunicated and unclarifed, were the bases for disappointments, anger and persistent conflict. Some respondents defined the major source of marital failure in terms of a breakdown in communication and nearly all had sought outside mediation for their problems after the suit for divorce was filed.

Those couples who were still dissatisfied with marriage after reconciliation also continued to show lack of agreement on expectations and perceptions of both self and spouse across many dimensions of the relationship. For them reconciliation had meant only resignation rather than increased satisfaction in the marriage. Such situations suggest that for some couples divorce counseling might be more appropriate than marriage counseling. Other couples may continue to need counseling help even after reconciliation. From this study it is not clear why unhappy couples did not ask for marital counseling; perhaps it had not occurred to them that counseling might be used to improve a relationship as well as to prevent a divorce.

Finally, the number and variety of differences in responses between the group of husbands compared to wives and between specific marital pairs suggests there may be a serious bias in those many studies which have allowed wives to answer for their husbands.

REFERENCES

Blood, R. O., Jr. and D. M. Wolfe. *Husbands and Wives.* New York: Free Press, 1960.

Goode, William J. *Women in Divorce.* New York: Free Press, 1956.

Parsons, Talcott. *The Social System.* New York: Free Press, 1964.

Counseling A Troubled Marriage

RICHARD MERYMAN

The marriage counseling hour was almost over. David and Lynn Maxwell were in their second month of therapy—and making little progress. The counselor, Mrs. Marcia Lassell, was talking. "David, what if five years from now Lynn still dislikes sex? Are you willing to live without it the rest of your life?"

"Absolutely not!" said David.

"Well, what will you do then, have an affair?" asked the counselor.

"No, by God, I want sex with my wife."

"It sounds like you're saying you may get another wife."

"Well, I sure think about it a lot," answered David.

"Okay, how does that make you feel, Lynn?" asked the counselor.

"I don't want to lose my marriage," answered Lynn. "I guess I'll have to work on my problem. But don't I get anything? I want some emotion from him—and damn it, I want some freedom to be *me*!"

Such voices, such dilemmas, such angers sometimes seem to be beyond every doorstep. Forty percent of U.S. marriages now end in divorce. In southern California, the national trend barometer, the rate is over 50%. A federal study found that since last year the divorce rate for marriages of 20 years and over has shot up 38%. Is marriage an anachronism in today's America? What *has* happened?

There is an answer in the story of the Maxwells. They live—under a different name—in Pomona, Calif. At 40, David is a $20,000-a-year computer programmer. He is a curly-haired man of medium height, in top physical trim from volleyball and fencing at his local YMCA. Lynn, at 36, is a good-looking, solidly built blond woman a little taller than her husband. They have been married 12 years and have two boys, Peter, 10, and Duncan, 8. And though they do have occasional good times —camping, going to the beach, working on crossword puzzles—the Maxwells' marriage mostly is lacerated by battles.

Some of their quarrels are as old as the oldest marriage joke. But those ancient, almost reflexive collisions between two human natures are taking place in a new world. The Maxwells' struggles are occurring in this "age of self-fulfillment," in which selfless commitment to being the perfect wife and mother, the ultimate provider and father, the ideal son or daughter is just no longer the be-all of life.

So for Lynn Maxwell, like many, many women in every part of America, a new theme has been amplifying virtually all of her problems. "The inner me," it goes, "is more important than serving society's traditional commandments. If that me can be fulfilled, I will be a better person, and everybody close to me will benefit. Therefore I am morally justified in doing whatever is necessary to liberate myself." Out of this philosophy has come, of course, the counterculture of the youth and the women's liberation movement.

The Maxwells' experience can be distilled in three periods of their marriage. In 1965 Lynn had an affair with a man in her amateur theatrical group. Her state of mind in that time is a classic description of how marriage can destroy a woman's self-confidence and self-esteem. In 1968 David had an affair with a secretary at his job. His behavior is an example of what often happens when a wife pushes hard for more freedom and identity, and a husband tries to recharge his ego. This past January, the Maxwells started counseling with Mrs. Marcia Lasswell. The understandings they arrived at through her quesioning offer important insights into much of what troubles marriages in America today.

LYNN'S AFFAIR

Lynn got to know a married television executive when they were together in an amateur production of *Life with Father*. She saw him as "very sensitive, artistic. He wrote poetry and painted, and I felt there was a tremendous vulnerability, the need to be protected—you know, my compulsion to mother men. And wow, I jumped. I asked him out for coffee and, God, I floored him. I told him I felt very sexually attracted to him. I had figured out that the way you got a man was sex. Then I could go to what I really wanted, what I wasn't getting from David: emotional satisfaction. It was the first time that I really stood on my own two feet and did what I wanted regardless of the consequences."

In her relationship with her husband, Lynn says, "The only use I felt David had for me was in bed. We had a social marriage. He could chat intellectually just delightfully—you know, from now till hell freezes over, about everything except what is really important. But there is no real warmth between people unless there is a sharing of emotion.

"If I tried to talk about how I felt in a situation between us, that immediately threatened him. Like I was trying to explain what I felt was the problem with our oldest boy, Peter, and how things in David's and my relationship were hurting him. David just closed up, and as soon as he could said, 'Well, you're probably right,' and made an excuse to leave.

"If he felt angry or upset or depressed, I could tell by little signs, but he's never express his emotions. I used to fight so much and so hard to get a reaction out of him, and I so seldom did. He'd argue beautifully and on such a logical plane. And I'd get so emotional I'd be tongue-tied—or didn't even know what I was saying. Then I'd get frustrated, and I'd end up crying. That made me feel beneath him, very inadequate.

"After our fights I would always end up feeling miserable. I was sure it was my fault that the marriage was in the situation it was in. David wasn't happy; the kids weren't happy. I had been taught as a child that the perfect wife has a very happy husband and this in turn is her fulfillment. And I was constantly aware that society expected me to be a good wife, a good mother, a good woman, active in the community. And I just didn't fit into that slot."

Before her marriage, Lynn had had a very successful college career: good grades, president of the drama club, a starter on the field hockey team. When David married her she was a research assistant at a local TV station. In those days she felt strong, confident, and herself. But like most girls getting married, Lynn was full of vague dreams. As usual, there had been no realistic, explicit discussion of marriage at school, at home, or with David. Many of her expectations came from the stereotypes of young people's books, the movies and magazines. "I felt," says Lynn, "marriage would be some great romantic thing, a wonderful freedom from being under my mother's thumb—that I'd be able to do what I wanted and go where I wanted with somebody I wanted to share those things with."

Lynn found instead that she was often the lonely focus of tremendous pressures—decisions to be made, repetitious tasks stupefyingly tiresome. She felt wrung between her yearnings for an independent sense of self and all those weighty obligations drilled into her since childhood. "Of course, I was doing no worse than anybody else, but I always assumed that everybody else on the street had their house running and in order and were solving their problems creatively—and I'm not. I'm inadequate. I felt guilty feeling that housework wasn't challenging, wasn't productive. But it's true. I tried to tell myself, 'You can find dignity in anything you do.' I'd fix a special dish and spend hours at it. I'd put it on the table and the kids would say, 'Yuuuk! Are we having that?' Of course, I had set myself up. I should have been able to fix a meal and not see it as a love offering.

"I tried very hard to sell myself on the idea that what ultimately mattered was my family. But the other side of me still said, 'Okay, but when you started out all those years ago, here was this circle which was me as a person. And in came that big chunk which was wife. And in came another big chunk and that's mother. And now there's just a little itty-bitty sliver left of the circle that is still me.'

"It's pretty hard to be your own person when you're running the whole show for everybody else. It seemed like if I didn't nag David constantly, the bills didn't ever get paid. When the school principal called to say Peter was in trouble, I felt I didn't have anybody to depend on to help me decide what to do. And all the small things. God, if I left getting up in the morning to David, all three of them would still be in bed at noon. Even the cars were my job. I felt like nothing ever happened in that house unless I made it happen. I remember I would look at David and think, 'Who are you to place this burden on me and sit there smug, eating your meal and then reading a magazine afterwards?" And I hated myself because I was letting it be done to me.""

The parents, grandparents, aunts, uncles, cousins who might have been a sympathetic sounding board for Lynn were all in the East, where she grew up. And this type of isolation is among the most crucial of all factors affecting marriage today. In the past 70 years all the social forces surrounding marriage have drastically changed. When America was essentially rural and people stayed put, the values and voices of Lynn's larger family would have enveloped and supported her. And there was not the concern then about identity; on the farm the family was more of a team, working together on almost every aspect of living and survival, including education and religion.

But now, Lynn's marriage existed in an urban, anonymous mobile world. And today, aside from child-rearing, the prime job of marriage is to provide emotional contact. Isolated in their shifting, rootless world, the members of the nuclear family—mother, father and children—are asked to answer every emotional need for each other. As a result, the family often turns in upon itself, and the members consume each other.

"Just before I had my affair," says Lynn, "I was really desperate — seemed like every day there were moments when all I wanted to do was curl up into a little ball in a corner and escape everybody and everything. I guess one big reason I got involved with another man was that I thought it took another person to prove I was somebody. You know, a man is willing to lie or cheat because he finds me exciting and interesting.

"It was very important to discover that I wasn't frigid. I could be sure the problem came mainly from my mother. She was an extremely domineering woman and I spent an awful lot of my childhood doing things I hated because I was obliged to. Before we were married, David and I had a great sex life because then I thought I was being a person in my own right — doing something my mother didn't approve of. After we were married sex was one more obligation — you know, like it was right there in the marriage contract. And also, we had so little emotional contact that making love was a very empty thing, and afterwards I would get so depressed. I would get the feeling that what I was doing was really nothing more than masturbation, because he really wasn't there for me.

"There was this terrible paradox in me that I wanted to be normal; I hated feeling like a failure as a wife, and yet I didn't want to change. Looking back on my affair, I realize there really wasn't anything happy about that time — just two people not knowing how to swim, drowning and hanging onto each other for support. All the lying — I wasn't very good at it. I was terrified that David would wonder why I was going to such a lot of school meetings and why the drama club rehearsals were lasting so god-awful late. I'd get home and I'd be sure it showed on me somehow. It was like living on the edge of a cliff waiting for the wind to push you over. And it's pretty hard to feel guilty like that and good about yourself at the same time."

David never did learn about the affair until it was over — and Lynn never had to choose between the two men. The television producer got a job offer in another city and simply moved away with his family. "Lousy as things were at home," Lynn says, "being married was still better than being lost in a sea of people. It's funny, but just having another warm body in the house . . . I mean, even if you're fighting all the time — or maybe because you are — there's a kind of connection you feel. And also, my ego was so shot, I felt I had to have somebody to provide for me, take care of me. Somehow, I felt as though my marriage created my identity, and without it, I'd just be a big zero. And when you think, 'I've got to stay in this marriage,' even that is debasing. It's more proof that you're nobody.

"When my affair was over, I felt devastated. It was like an adolescent in her first love — this feeling of longing and desperation and never seeing the person again. It must have been a year before I got over it. Of course, I didn't really want to get over it. I wrote him several times — and got one business-like letter back."

DAVID'S AFFAIR

"We always seemed to have our fights on Saturday mornings," says David, "and always about something trivial. On this particular Saturday afternoon we went sailing with friends and by then we weren't speaking. Lynn was steaming and I was like an iceberg. And . . . well, I happen to think marital problems should be kept strictly inside the home, so I tried to act natural.

"That evening, Lynn just ripped into me. You know, 'You lousy bastard. Big phony. Pretending like everything is just swell and I'm your dear little wife — sweetie — all that stuff — it makes me sick because it's such a lie.' She went on and on like that. She ended up saying I should start having some honest emotions and show them — or just get out.

"And suddenly I felt, 'Oh my God, here we are — the 9,000th argument and it's going to lead nowhere for the 9,000th time' — and it was like everything I'd ever felt at those moments came at me all at once. So I just walked out and went and stood alone in the garage to try to keep control of myself.

"Lynn followed me out there, and before she could lay something else on me I said, 'I want a divorce.' And I really meant it. She just kind of stood there and the skin all around her mouth got tight-looking. Then she said, 'Is there somebody else?' I guess I just smiled. 'Cause for six weeks I'd been in love with another woman.

"The girl I'd taken up with was my boss's secretary. We'd been in a car pool together, and I guess, compared to her husband, I was a literate, educated genius. We began having lunch and sharing a lot of feelings. And, you know, she hadn't heard all my stories before.

"One Saturday we both had to go to the office, and driving home she suddenly slid across the seat, put her head on my shoulder. And I felt,

'Oh, my God. Terrific. What's happening? What have I gotten myself into?' But, man, I was really ready for something like that!"

At that moment David was sure an affair would heal his unhappiness — but it is the experience of counselors that when people want to improve the quality of their lives, but are uncertain what they want from life, then their attempts at fulfillment are going to be confused and often destructive. They will try to reshape their worlds to fit their fantasies, laying all blame outside themselves.

"The marriage was bleak, really in a rut. I was closed up tight. Lynn was closed up tight. I felt really lonely. A man has to have a woman he can unload to, talk to, somebody who isn't always running him down and hassling him about things.

"It's amazing how important it is to come home and be welcomed, be greeted, you know, warmly. Mostly it was come home, go find Lynn, say, 'Hi, how are you? What's happened today?' She'd be sort of unresponsive — so then it was just find the newspaper, see what the mail was. And, I suppose, she was probably standing there thinking, 'That son of a bitch. He comes home and doesn't thank me for all the . . . practically doesn't see me.' But you expect to find your wife there. She's been there all day, you know."

A major friction which had readied David for his affair was Lynn's increasing involvement with women's liberation ideas. For six months before his affair, Lynn had been attending a weekly meeting with other restless wives at their church. It was, in effect, an informal women's liberation consciousness-raising group. They used as their "text" a special issue of their Methodist magazine devoted to the ideas of the movement. There were titles such as "The Dancing Dog" and "Women's Will to Fail." The tidal wave of popular literature describing what a good marriage ought to be is one of the modern stresses on marriage. It almost always insinuates that nobody should settle for less than total success.

Lynn would always deny she was in a women's liberation group; she feared belittling, crude remarks and jokes. And David frequently managed little digs at Lynn and her friends — like "Well, you liberated women, what's on for today?" He delighted in pumping Lynn for intimate details about the other women in the discussion group. But when he learned that one was having a secret affair, he was suddenly fearful that they might be urging Lynn to do the same again. He also began to wonder what would happen if these women did indeed help make Lynn confident and self-reliant, which he had often silently disparaged her for not being.

As Lynn began to apply more and more of the liberationist doctrine to herself, housework, typically, became one of the tensest topics with David. "Sometimes," says David, "I'd come home tired out from my day at work and find her sitting there reading some book of plays, and see a sinkful of dirty dishes and the house a mess. And I'd think, 'Damn it, why doesn't she get about her business — which is *not* reading.' She'd see me look at the dishes and say, 'If you want the dishes clean — clean them.'

"I remember once Lynn was off at her meeting with those women, and I was up to my elbows in soapsuds. And I thought, 'What the hell am I doing here? I'm a respected professional with a full-time job that brings in all our money — and Lynn is just off talking. Damn it, what I do is life, and what she's doing is amusement.'

"Somebody has to take the responsibility for the home, and since I'm gone at work and Lynn is home, she's the person. It's not that I didn't agree she should be fulfilled. I agreed that there are no socially redeeming features about housework. That's why I didn't want to do it either, and why I didn't see why I should be her only alleviation from drudgery. And I might add that things I was doing in my job were not an unmitigated joy. A lot of it was as crappy as laundry.

"My time is worth money. And that includes unaccounted time at home just staring out the window sort of recharging my batteries. If she thinks running the house is tough, she should try the whole financial responsibility for a while."

The confrontation in the garage — David's demand for a divorce — had a dramatic effect. Lynn was suddenly affectionate, and interested in sex. Simultaneously, tells David, "My girl friend said, 'This can't go on.' How's that for an original line?" Two weeks later, David and the woman he was having the affair with sat in his car at a vacant construction site in the woods. David told her he would stay with Lynn. "It was the hardest thing I've ever done," says David. "Whether it was guilt or fear, God knows. It wasn't chivalry."

A week after David's decision, Lynn's desire for sex disappeared as abruptly as it started. "It really was not conscious," says Lynn, "and I felt terribly, terribly guilty about it." A month later, Lynn woke David at one a.m. "Would it be all right with you," she said, "if I got a job?" "We'll talk about it in the morning," said David.

But they did not talk. And a week later Lynn announced that she had a part-time job at a real estate office, fitted in while David and the children were gone at school and work. "That meant," says Lynn, "that I had to move twice as fast and be twice as careful so I'd be working — but it would be like I wasn't working. See, I was willing to push for my freedom, but I was not ready to risk my marriage. And part of me was really hung up on guilt, on the idea that my real responsibility was still to David and the kids.

"But, wow, that job was great. I was very scared that I'd be incompetent. But I learned. And my boss trusted me and depended on me, which was terrific and really made me feel like a person again. And the other people in the office seemed to find me interesting and made me feel fun."

Though David was still making digs at Lynn — "Seems like all the career women I've ever met are always competing and arguing" — he also quite liked the idea that she was bringing in some money, even though he sometimes disapproved of how she spent it. Also, they now had more to talk about. Her mind and anger were not so concentrated on him and the household.

Perhaps out of guilt over his affair, David began helping more around the house — and feeling very virtuous about it. But he was also playing the politics of housework. "I never disagreed aloud with the principle," admits David, "but I sure dragged my feet. I'd agree the hell out of Lynn, but wind up saying something like, 'I don't have compulsive, middle-class standards. I don't mind a dirty house.' Or I'd do jobs shoddily or wastefully so I wouldn't be asked to do them again."

David was playing the same game he always had. He never had talked Lynn into taking all the household responsibility, but had steered her into those responsibilities by the familiar stratagem of default — an extremely common ploy among personality types like David, known as "passive-aggressives." Often such men learned to be dominated by women during boyhood, when mothers and female teachers and Cub Scout den mothers literally taught them passivity by forbidding roughhousing, fighting and emotional outbursts. As adults, these men get their way by that subtle, infuriating monolithic aggression of passive resistance.

"I had a sort of British-type upbringing," says David, describing his childhood in Pennsylvania. "Where it was 'Don't show caring. Don't show feeling. Be the great stone face. Nothing fazes you.' So I had this mechanism that blocks out even thinking. When Lynn got mad at me, it was 'I'm in my own shell. Screw you. I've got my wall up.' Then I'd sulk."

The marathon of job and home soon began to leave Lynn feeling almost as oppressed as before. And she put even more pressure on David to help. "What I couldn't understand," says David, "was why hiring help wasn't the perfect solution. But she just got all upset over that. Her point was that I should be willing to share, that we're homemakers together, parents together, everything together. But she wouldn't spend her salary on getting help — said having some money of her own was part of being free. I felt if she wouldn't sacrifice, I was damned if *I* was going to sacrifice."

It was a familiar marital contest, one of the most destructive attitudes in marriage: "Am I giving up more than I am getting?" One of Lynn's complaints was that David always got to do whatever he wanted. Once David asked Lynn, "Where do you want to go to dinner?" She said, "Oh, I don't care." David said, "Well, let's go to such and such." Suddenly Lynn was furious. "Jesus, we always go where you want to go."

"Society had pretty much spelled out my role," David says, "and now I was being attacked for it on all fronts, the awful things I was supposedly doing were because I'd been trained to do them. But that didn't mean I wasn't likable, that I wasn't a good person — you know, good old . . . I really wanted to treat Lynn fairly. I really am a person of goodwill."

The Maxwells in Counseling

One night early in January of this year, two policemen knocked on the

Maxwell's door to quiz their son Peter about some vandalism in the neighborhood. Lynn suspected Peter was guilty, and she was overwhelmed by the feeling that their problems were out of control. Torn on one hand by her need for the same liberation at home she felt at work and on the other by her vision of herself as a bad mother and wife, Lynn was desperate for someone who might help. David, himself frustrated and embattled, acquiesced. Lynn chose as a marriage counselor a woman who seemed completely liberated: Marcia Lasswell, who is successfully married, a mother and, in addition to her private counseling practice, is a professor of psychology at California State College, Pomona.

To the counselor, the Maxwells were a very familiar case. When David and Lynn met, they had been drawn to each other by their differences — David's calm passivity meshing with Lynn's impatient strength. "But," says Marcia Lasswell, "people lose respect for differences, and begin to defend themselves against the differences. Then the qualities that made them different become their defense mechanisms." David got more and more passive as Lynn got more aggressive to overcome his passivity. So finally their behavior became so exaggerated that they were almost caricatures of where they started out. "They were poles apart," says the counselor, "with a battleground in between — and they'd ceased communicating."

So the first step was to teach David and Lynn to communicate with each other. And the counselor quickly found a classic sample of garbled communication. The tension between the Maxwells over sex would periodically build until Lynn felt so guilty she would decide that, okay, she would give in tonight. And she would be furious at David when, after she had talked herself into it, he then misread her cues and stayed downstairs watching television.

"I was watching TV," David said in the second counseling session, "and I heard Lynn say, 'I'm tired! I'm going to bed.' And that meant to me, 'I'm going to sleep, don't bother me.' "

"Okay, Lynn," asked Marcia Lasswell, "what *did* you mean?"

"He should have known I wanted him to come upstairs pretty soon," answered Lynn.

"Now then, David, could Lynn have meant that?"

"Well, why didn't she *say* so?"

"Okay," said Marcia Lasswell, "suppose she did say, 'I'm going upstairs; are you coming up?' Then what would you have said?"

"I might have said, 'I'm going to wait until the news is over.' "

"What would that have means to you, Lynn?"

"I'd have figured he wasn't interested and I'd have gone to sleep."

"No," said David, "I would have meant, 'I'll be up when the news is over. Don't go to sleep.' "

"You get the point?" finished the counselor. "I'm trying to show you how ambiguous you are most of the time and how everybody tries to read minds. People jump to conclusions and read meanings which are simply wrong, then act on the basis of those misinterpretations, and when their expectations are not delivered, they feel rejected and not loved."

The Maxells met Marcia Lasswell one evening a week for an hour — at a cost of $25 per hour. For four weeks they detailed their complaints about each other, defended themselves, let Marcia Lasswell lead them through self-analysis of their motives and feelings. They did not, however, make any effort at home to use their new understandings to solve problems.

The counselor decided to take drastic action: the use of confrontation technique to jolt them into taking aggressive steps to help themselves. "I am willing to listen for a few weeks," she says, "to people playing that 'poor me' song over and over. But that's as long as I'll listen."

One night, Lynn got a bawling out from the counselor. "I am tired," Marcia Lasswell said, "of listening to you talk about how hard life is, and how rotten you feel about it. I'm trying to help you see through some of these problems and agree on some solutions. If you want to come in here and work, all right. But please don't come in here and take up my time sulking."

Lynn got up and stalked out. Out in the car, Lynn wept in David's arms. Several days later, Marcia Lasswell telephoned Lynn, and despite an icy reception they agreed that she would return to counseling. "I think that was the turning point in my therapy," says Lynn. "It was a revelation to me that somebody can get mad at you because they care about you, and it doesn't mean they have rejected you. It gave us a tremendous closeness."

The next confrontation came when David threatened Lynn with a divorce unless the sex problem eased, and Lynn in return demanded more emotions and more freedom from David. Shaken up they then went to work on their sex difficulties.

The counselor felt that Lynn's disinterest in sex had always been present. Therefore, Lynn could use sex as a weapon to punish David, while getting out sex herself. "Women who enjoy sex," says Marcia Lasswell, "rarely withold sex because they are also depriving themselves. They'll find some other way to punish their husbands."

She applied a technique called "desensitization." Every other night would be "open" for sex or not as the Maxwells wished. But on the alternate nights no sex was allowed. Instead, they would have tender physical contact doing whatever they enjoyed such as hold each other close, rub backs, brush hair, bathe together. Hopefully, when Lynn did not have to worry that David was "trying to march me off to bed," she would be able to relax enough to rediscover sensual feelings with him. "They were so jittery with each other," says Marcia Lasswell, "that they couldn't even hold hands anymore. Lynn wouldn't touch David because it might encourage him. And, unless he was desperate, David wouldn't touch her for fear of being rejected." Two weeks later, Lynn triumphantly announced they had made love very happily that Saturday night and again the next morning.

Each counseling session usually began with the question, "What do you want to talk about today?" Lynn for some time had wanted to attack the question of women's liberation directly. And she assumed that the counselor would be her eager ally in thumping David. But although Marcia Lasswell is in complete sympathy with the movement, she consciously avoids pushing those ideas on her clients, feeling that tackling their basic emotional conflicts will also tackle problems of liberation. "It could really mess up a couple," she says, "if I said, 'Hey, look. Love the way I do and you'll be happy.' "

So the day Lynn brought up the subject, the counselor guided her into an analysis of just how much liberation she was actually ready for. Lynn was explaining that there was a rule that the boys had to put their dirty clothes into the hamper, or their laundry did not get washed. "I was telling myself," said Lynn, "that I'd be damned if I'd keep picking up after them. But then I feel terribly guilty when they don't have clean clothes." Ten questions and answers later, Marcia Lasswell said, "If you really, deep, deep down believe that a good mother always picks up the clothes and the child doesn't need to respond by putting laundry in a hamper, that if you are a good person you will do this — then how can I help you?"

"Well," said Lynn, "when you say it that way, I'm being ridiculous. But getting myself to believe it is a lot harder."

Trying to alter the emotional reflexes of a lifetime is obviously a slow process, but David and Lynn did feel they were learning about themselves. One evening Marcia Lasswell, probing David, steered him to an important insight into why he pushed all responsibilities onto Lynn. They concluded that David feared getting angry because he was afraid he might say unforgivably hurtful things to people. And he believed that getting angry was a necessary part of taking responsibility.

When the Maxwells were some three months into their counseling, it suddenly came out that their desensitization program had gradually drifted into disuse. They had fallen back into their old routines — watching TV until David, full of good intentions early in the evening, would often fall asleep in the couch, and Lynn would go up to bed.

Lynn was angry at David for being lazy about the program, which to her secret astonishment had been working so well for her. In fact, the counseling had eased the Maxwell's marriage a great deal — which is why they had become overconfident and momentarily lapsed. Lynn's guilt was much lighter, and there was not the steady, grinding tension between her and David. Even in public they held hands and would greet each other with a kiss and a one-arm hug. Lynn's anger was less frequent; David was taking a heavier hand with the children. Understanding themselves better, they were able to handle or head off collisions. And they would never again return to their original despair.

But what ultimately happens to the Maxwells depends on how hard they are willing to work — and they still have a distance to go to achieve a happy marriage. Still missing for the Maxwells is that crucial element lacking in virtually all troubled marriages today: Lynn must fulfill her potential as a woman, and David must fulfill his as a man. Only through an affectionate blend of independence and sharing can a couple and a marriage have the strength to withstand the awesome stresses of modern society. Otherwise, maintains Marcia Lasswell, David and Lynn will always depend on each other to satisfy every need — for gratitude, esteem, emotion, companionship, etc., etc. — and no one human being can supply another with all that.

"We are talking," says Marcia Lasswell, "not about women's liberation, but human liberation." She considers "human liberation" the key to the future of marriage in this changing society. Almost certainly, marriage will always be there in some form. And it is equally certain that men and women in marriages will always behave like hedgehogs, moving close to each other for warmth, pricking each other, moving apart into the cold, then back to closeness.

And it is certain, too, that the most illusive, indefinable and unpredictable element in marriage will always be love. During her affair, Lynn kept a diary, recording all her activities and longings and aches and desperations. She left it in her top bureau drawer. A month after the affair ended, David inevitably found the small volume. He read it and was overcome with fury and humiliation. But when he came to the end, David took a pen and wrote after the last entry, "Lynn, I have read this. And I love you."

To Love, Honor and Negotiate

SUSAN EDMISTON

One evening long ago, when my husband and I were doing what used to be called courting, we came across a quiz in a magazine. The quiz, to be taken by both husband and wife or girlfriend and boyfriend, was designed to test how couples felt about some of the basic issues involved in marriage—whether or not a wife should work, how the couple's money should be handled, how each felt about marital fidelity, and so one.

As a lark, chuckling all the way through, we took the quiz.

In the process, I learned what then seemed some rather surprising things about the man who was to become my husband—among them that he definitely wanted a wife who worked outside the home, that he was willing to help make it possible for her to do so, and that he wasn't interested in having children until he could really become involved in their upbringing. I decided right then and there that though men might be like buses in that there's always another one coming, this was one model I'd better not miss. Not that he would have suited everyone, but he was just right for me.

Two years later we were married. More than anything else, that silly quiz, taken in jest, was the basis of the agreement that underlay our marriage. You might call it a marriage contract, although we've never written it out or lived by any rigid rules.

Most people wince when they hear the phrase "marriage contract," because it sounds cold and hard, but I use the term advisedly. Marriage itself is essentially a contract—an agreement about rights, responsibilities and loyalties. If you look in a dictionary that's old enough, you'll find that at one time the two words were almost synonymous. Marriage is still a contract under the laws of the state, one which we cannot dissolve without going through another legal process—divorce. And certain religions, orthodox Judiasm for one, emphasize the contractual aspects of marriage by having the signing of a document a part of the ceremony.

Of course, most of us marry thinking of a higher agreement. Presumably the reason we marry at all—other than the blind force of convention—is that we see some value in a sustained commitment to life with another person. Marriage, at its best, is a partnership in which two people support, sustain, encourage and stimulate one another. It provides the conditions for a special kind of lifetime adventure—the profound personal interaction and development possible only in a long, intimate and committed relationship.

But in addition to these kinds of marriage contract—the religious, the legal, the idealistic—there is another: the traditional one that deals with the practical side of marriage. Tradition tells us that the husband supports the wife and family and the wife rears the children and takes care of the house. Tradition prescribes sexual exclusivity and togetherness. And tradition dictates a particular kind of relationship, in which the husband is the protector and authority—the "head of the household"—and the wife is the compliant and supportive helpmeet and "dependent." Many couples today find that this traditional "fine print" in their unwritten marriage contracts needs revision.

Marriage—like everything else—is not what it used to be. We used to know what we wanted from it and what we owed one another within it. Women sought a good provider, men a woman skilled in the household arts—and both expected that a major purpose of their marriage and justification for their labor would be the rearing of children. But today, all is confusion.

To begin with, the realities of life in the twentieth century conflict with the particulars of the traditional marriage arrangement, which was created for the social needs of past centuries. Today, more mothers of minor children work than stay home. Obviously, they can't take on all the traditional responsibilities of housewives as well. Years ago when women exhausted themselves in bearing children and often died young, they had no opportunity, not to mention *need*, for careers beyond child-rearing. But today we have the Pill and the IUD and we no longer have an economy in which large numbers of children constitute a family's wealth or fill the needs of the society. Most women live so long that child-bearing and -rearing take up only a relatively small proportion of their lifetimes.

These new realities have created new ideas and expectations. Many people believe that both women and men should have *both* family and work—or some kind of sustained serious involvement—outside the home. More and more people feel it's essential for women to be economically and psychologically independent. The idea that marriage should be an equal partnership has ceased being a platitude and is now a serious goal for many couples. And we have in marriage, as in other areas of life, a crisis of rising expectations. We now expect to be happy and to be emotionally and sexually fulfilled where our grandmothers may have expected simply to be kept and protected.

We don't have a new contract that covers all this—and we couldn't because we don't all want the same thing. But some husbands and wives have begun to work out individual arrangements that they think are just right for them. By probing and comparing what they really want from marriage—as opposed to what friends, in-laws, society or the law expect them to want—they can come to agreements that help their marriages work.

The first and most basic issue is whether or not they accept the traditional marital roles—wife as homemaker, husband as breadwinner. If they don't, and the wife works, they next quesion is equally **thorny:**

Have they made adjustments in other areas of the marriage so that she gets a fair shake? . . . or is she just doing two jobs instead of one?

When the discussion gets down to specifics, questions about role often turn out to be questions about the aspects of marriage that may seem to be the most trivial—housework and the day-to-day details of child care. As Norman Mailer said in *The Prisoner of Sex,* "It all comes down to who does the dishes." Because whoever does the dishes . . . and the laundry . . . and the thousand little services children require . . . is to a large extent prevented from doing anything else.

When novelist Alix Shulman and her husband were first married, they had an equal partnership in which both worked and both shared housework, but the birth of their children completely transformed their lives. Alix gave up her job in a publishing company in order to be able to stay home with the children. Soon the Shulmans found that almost without realizing it they were slipping into the traditional marriage: he was spending the whole day at the office and she was working from six a.m. to nine p.m. taking care of the children and the house—with almost no time left for the career she had planned to pursue at home.

One day they realized that even though they loved one another very much, they just weren't living the life they wanted to. Alix, who had been active in the women's liberation movement, decided that it might be possible to change it by abolishing the traditional sex roles. She sat down and wrote out a detailed, intricate agreement based on the principle that, as parents, she and her husband should share all work and responsibility for the care of their children and home. Their agreement, which her husband accepted, said, among other things, that Alix would continue to take care of the children during the day, but her husband would do all the housecleaning in exchange. Cooking and child care in the morning were to be divided equally, week by week. To some people the Shulmans' agreement might seem to dot more i's than are necessary, but it did the job for them. It freed Alix to develop a career—she's written or edited six books since then—and gave her husband the chance to become truly involved with his children.

Other women I know have attempted to work out some sharing of housework simply because they've found, all rumor to the contrary, that they work longer and harder than their husbands. My friend Jane, who used to be a book editor before she married and had her daughter, tells me, "I get up an hour before my husband and I don't really finish till nine thirty at night. Yet when he comes home he expects me to serve him dinner. I adore him, so, of course, really I'd do anything for him, but at the same time I know what it is to work and I know that compared to what I do now, he has an easy job."

Another friend, Linda asks, "Why should a woman's day go on so much longer just because she works at home?"

A Westchester woman with two pre-school children tells me, "Sometimes I put in a twelve-hour day and don't sit down once." She always wanted to have children and stay home with them, and she takes great pleasure in her husband's advancement. But it irks her when her husband arrives and finds the house messy and says, "What's the matter? You've had nothing to do but stay home all day."

Despite all protestations that "there is no more important job than being a mother and a housewife," that women are the "backbone of the country," and that "behind every great man there is a great woman," many people — even husbands — behave as if the work women do in their homes is not important and their time is not valuable. The telltale symptoms of this attitude are that a woman finds herself working longer hours than her husband (her work is considered less important and therefore she must compensate by putting in longer hours) and she ends up doing all the trivial, time-consuming errands (her time is less valuable so it doesn't matter whether it's wasted on meaningless tasks).

The woman who works outside the home to help support her family is often the most in need of a renegotiated marriage contract. She may find that although she is now sharing the role of breadwinner, her husband is unwilling to share housework and child care. He's still operating under the old contract, although the realities of their life together make it obsolete.

Of course, the converse holds true as well: a wife may not realize that her husband would like to have the same flexibility she has to choose between work and home (or school or time to pursue a special interest). He may envy her freedom to do things at her own pace and choice. Some couples today find that the best thing for them is to exchange roles completely: the husband stays home with the children and the wife earns the money. Other couples follow the same principle in less extreme forms. My husband knows that if he ever wants to take a year off from work or go back to school, I'll happily support him. He was the first man I'd known who wholeheartedly approved of *my goals*. If it hadn't been for his emotional, as well as financial, support, I never would have gotten my writing career off the ground.

Closely allied to the question of role is the question of financial control. Traditionally, the husband made the major financial decisions and controlled the purse strings. Today, more and more women take care of monthly bill-paying and share in the decision-making. But money still rates as a major area of marital conflict. One couple I know always fell into arguments because the wife thought that the husband was unnecessarily extravagant. "I felt that if he didn't spend so much money on the eight dozen book clubs he belongs to, we'd be able to save more money," she said. Her husband argued that it was she who didn't know how to handle money. Fortunately, they hit on a way of resolving their argument — alternating responsibility. One month the husband paid all the bills and the next month the wife did. Through the concrete experience of handling the money, the wife found that she was spending just as much on little extravagances as her husband was on book clubs. And he learned that she was just as capable of handling the money as he was. They haven't had a single financial argument since.

Sometimes the opposite treatment is necessary. My friend Melinda has always loved beautiful clothes and spent a large part of her salary on them. When she married David, she kept working but they began pooling their money and paying bills jointly. When David found out how much Melinda spent for clothes he was amazed and annoyed. "But," says Melinda, "I never stopped *buying* clothes; I just started hiding the clothes I bought." Finally they solved their problem by separating their bill-paying. She opened a separate account and used it to pay some of the household bills and all of her clothing bills. Since David doesn't see them, they no longer upset him.

Other traditional "male" or "female" prerogatives also need reexamination. For example, women have traditionally done the decorating of the house. Sometimes their husbands are so excluded that they feel like strangers in their own homes. One husband I know was far more concerned about decorating than his wife. "He likes total neatness," she says. "Not only do I have trouble keeping things neat but I'm not even happy in a neat room!" They solved this conflict by finding an apartment big enough so that she could have a room of her own. "We call it my mad room. He's not allowed to complain about it or straighten it up. If he sees anything lying around the house looking messy, he throws it in my mad room." The same couple split up the decoration of their house. She planned the kitchen, since she wanted it to be efficient, and the baby's room. He did their bedroom and the living room and the dining room. "He likes an apartment that's decorated and looks right. I don't care about that; I just want it to be functional."

Another couple reversed the traditional roles in entertaining. The husband loves to give parties but his wife hates worrying about all the details. Now he arranges them, theme and all, and she appears at six thirty and says, "Who's coming?"

There are other areas where couples may find that their wants conflict with society's unwritten marriage contract. They should ask themselves some serious questions:

● How many children do they want? Are they sure they want any at all? Who will take care of them?

● Do they accept the traditional total togetherness of marriage or would they prefer a relationship with a little more breathing space? Separate bedrooms? Separate vacations? Should each have a day every week to spend on his or her own?

In short, anything a couple really cares about should be brought out and discussed. There are no longer any pat answers, any traditional contracts that work for everyone. Today's couples really have to invent their own marriages.

When it comes to negotiating their own marriage agreement, many couples find that their main disagreements center on housework. Here are some techniques that can help.

First, eliminate. The women I talked to found it worked to start cutting out things that weren't really important to them but were sapping their precious time. They asked themselves, "Do I really care about being a gourmet cook? A flawless housecleaner? A chauffeur? A gardener?" Studies have shown that a woman who takes on an outside job or a vital new interest can cut the time required to do her housework to one sixth(!). Anyone for whom housecleaning isn't a pleasure should do it faster and more efficiently and do less of it. Most women are always apologizing for the way their houses look. Unless what they want in life is to be a superduper housecleaner, they should stop apologizing and relax. If housecleaning is your *bête noir*, get your husband to write two lists: On one should go everything around the house that really matters to him. On the second should go everything you're doing that he really doesn't care about. Make the same two lists yourself. Eliminate everything that neither of you cares about. I know at least half a dozen highly respectable couples who never make the bed. "It's better to let it air out anyway," says one European-born woman.

The same with cooking. Many women get involved in time-consuming gourmet cooking to make a job they don't really find rewarding "creative." Unless what you want written on your tombstone is "She was a fabulous cook," don't spend your whole day in the kitchen. If you *want* to be a gourmet cook, build up a repertoire of fast gourmet meals. Julia Child has some that take only thirty minutes from beginning to end. Be inventive. One couple I know stopped eating their big meal at night. The husband eats high-calorie business lunches every day and needs a big dinner like a straight shot of cholesterol. Nutritionist Adelle Davis says, "Eat breakfast like a king, lunch like a prince and supper like a pauper." Breakfasts are easier to cook.

Get your children to do things. It's good for you and it's good for them. If there's a bus, you don't have to chauffeur them. Or maybe they can walk.

Eliminate time-consuming comparison shopping unless you consider your life (that's what your time is) less important that the pennies you save. Too many women act as if their time is worthless. Find stores with reasonable prices and stick to them.

When you've finished eliminating, divide. Some couples divide up household chores and child care in excruciating detail. Though some may find it necessary to write down in black and white what each specifically agrees to do, you may not consider this an appealing way of going about it. And your husband may balk at overnight, total change. In the beginning you may only be able to get him to take on one new responsibility. Most of the couples I know who've worked out agreements have spent several years settling into them. When my husband and I were first married he left a trail of towels from shower to bedroom, considered dishwashing one of the deeper mysteries of life, and had two culinary specialties—hamburgers and chicken livers with burnt onions. Obviously, despite his best intentions, he wasn't equipped to plunge right into a full share of housekeeping. Now, four years later, he can do just about everything around the house I can and takes great pride in his repertoire of recipes, which includes several spectacular party meals. We still don't have a rigid schedule. In fact, we have no schedule at all, but we do have a basic understanding. If he has a lot of work or is under a lot of pressure, I may do everything—all cooking, dishwashing, shopping and cleaning (in addition to my own full-time work)—for a week or so, and then he'll take over. If I'm feeling low or facing a deadline, he does the same for me.

When Betsy McLaughlin first married, she worked as assistant producer for a radio show. "Every night I'd bring home magazines and books to read as part of my job. But Jack would sit down, start reading the magazines and say, 'Where's my dinner?' Afterwards he'd say, 'Thank you darling, that was delicious.' But I really wanted to read those magazines too.

"When our first child was born, Jack still wasn't very helpful. On weekends, I couldn't go anywhere because he didn't want to change diapers. We had gone through natural childbirth together and I would wonder, 'How could he be in on all that and *still* not want to change a diaper?' But I didn't want to challenge his assumption that he didn't have to."

Today, seven years later, Betsy has a second child and works full time. Gradually, after years of calm discussions, strong demands and stronger challenges, her husband has come to participate more and more in raising their children and taking care of their home. "Now Jack makes the morning coffee, gives our older child Billy his breakfast and gets him dressed for school," says Betsy. "Lots of times I don't like the way Billy is dressed but I don't say anything. If I did, the responsibility would fall back on me. I give the baby his bottle, change him and take Bill to the school bus. I do most of the getting up when the baby wakes up during the night. I don't mind it—it makes up for the tender moments missed during the day when I'm at the office."

Whenever possible, chores should be done by the person to whom they're most important. If the husband complains about meals, he should be the one who plans the week's menus. My husband doesn't seem to care about carpentry and little repairs around the house as much as I do. After storming around trying to get him to do them, I finally said to myself, "Why should he have to do these things just because they're supposed to be men's work? I'll do them myself."

Once negotiations are open on a marriage contract, it may be necessary to fall back on some well-thought-out negotiating techniques. Some husbands, being reasonable, will yield to sweet reason. Seeing that their wives are putting in more hours than they are or that their wives need more time for themselves—or agreeing in principle that housework should be shared—they may willingly take on their shares.

Most husbands, however, will resist. There are several classic resistance techniques. The first and greatest of these is feigned ignorance. When Alice and George lived in an apartment they had a catacomb of a laundry in their basement and George always did the wash. Now that they have a house and their very own eighteen-cycle, harvest gold, super-fantastic washer-dryer, George claims he can't operate the machine. One day my friend Bob, who's a neurosurgeon, came home to find his wife sick in bed with the flu. She asked if he'd get her some tea and toast. When he came back a full forty-five minutes later, she asked why it had taken so long. "Well," he said, "I had to go down to the luncheonette."

The night before Richard and Judy's second child was born, their two-year-old began to cry. "All he wants is a bottle of milk. Will you get it for him?" asked Judy, who wasn't feeling too well.

"Where do you keep the milk?" asked Richard.

The answer to the ignorance ploy is simple: teach him. Teach him sweetly and gently and if he doesn't learn, teach him again. If you give in and do it yourself because "it's easier," you'll never get out from under.

A related technique is incompetence. Jane, the woman you heard about earlier whose husband has the easy job, finally got him to agree to do the dishes after dinner every night. He does them, but he does them badly. If there's a covered pot on the stove, he'll pretend he thought it was clean. Or he'll leave other pots to soak in the sink till morning. To deal with such tactics, explain what he's doing wrong. Complain. Explain again, but don't give in and do it yourself. If he can't get you to give in, eventually he'll start doing it right.

When husbands don't yield to gentle requests, sweet reason, and unshakable patience, when what the political scientists call gradualism doesn't work, stronger action is necessary. You'll need the courage to demand, and the inner conviction that what you're asking for is right. One tactic is simply to stop doing anything you don't think you should do. My fondest idle fantasy is of having a personal servant who'll pick up my clothes where I drop them, hang them up, wash the ones that need washing, take the others to the cleaner and sew on any buttons that have fallen off. One day I realized that this, my most extravagant dream, is taken for granted by most men. My friend Rachel realized the same thing, so she stopped. Her husband's clothes accumulated on the bedroom chair for four days. Finally on the fifth day, he began hanging them up and putting the dirty ones in the hamper. Rachel had won a real victory. She was no longer his personal maid.

Another friend decided one day she just *had* to get a job, even though her husband objected to her working. She stopped asking and pleading, went out and found the job, hired a babysitter and simply announced one evening at dinner that she was starting work on Monday. Ultimately it may come to this, that it is necessary to *act* without asking for permission, to begin behaving like an autonomous person, not a dependent, an inferior or an unsalaried employee.

When a husband agrees to take on new tasks, he should be given breathing room. His wife must be willing to give up control as well as responsibility. "In the beginning I would always be telling Jack when to do things and exactly how they should be done," says Betsy. "He'd say to me, 'You just want a maid.' But now when he does something, I keep out of it and let him do it his way."

One couple who decided to split the care of they young daughter faced the same problem. "I finally realized," the mother said, "that although my husband was going to do it differently, he was going to do it all right."

When change comes, most husbands enjoy it. Many a man has discovered the pleasures of his children by taking care of them. Or found new talents and sources of pride in himself. Faced with Betsy's demands that he take on some of the cooking, Jack learned to make soufflés. Now he has a city-wide reputation as a great soufflé-maker. And he adores it!

But the greatest reward of negotiating a new marriage contract, of course, is a better marriage. Hopefully, even talking and thinking about it should bring husband and wife to a better understanding. And, if they can come to new agreements that make them loving, sharing equals—not an inferior dependent resentful of her role and an omniscient provider trapped by his responsibilities—they can truly support, encourage, stimulate and enjoy one another in fulfillment of the highest contract of marriage.

How To Make
A Good Marriage Better

JOYCE TAYLOR
RICHARD TAYLOR

Joyce: Friday morning at eight o'clock the phone rang: on such short notice, could we make the Marriage Encounter that weekend? The rest of the day was full of the machinations necessary to get out of the house (baby to grandmother, clothes to wash and pack for the weekend, etc.) that I had no time to think of what Richard and I were heading into. The newspaper had said something about "trying to make good marriages even better." I felt as I imagine I would feel if I were going off to have minor plastic surgery done. Ashamed to admit — not the need, exactly, but an awareness of the need. It seemed contradictory to like the marriage we had yet be on the lookout for change. A betrayal.

Richard: I felt pretty smug about us; I was humoring Joyce by agreeing to go to the encounter. I expected that we would come away rating ourselves somewhere near the top of the list of all-time-great marriages. I planned to sit there, listen to lectures, smile knowingly at my wife from time to time. I thought probably everyone else would have serious problems, we would enter into it only on an intellectual level.

Joyce: I didn't mind the idea of us changing, except that change always comes from an unpleasant direction you least expect. I tried to think of what I didn't expect. Impossible.

Richard: Friday night when we arrived, there was a sort of ski house atmosphere: lots of first-name welcomes, nametags, cookies and coffee, help carrying suitcases to rooms. It was an old rambling Catholic retreat house.

Joyce: I remember hanging up our clothes carefully so that Richard wouldn't be put off by a mess — I was so nervous about how he might react to the weekend that I wasn't taking chances on an added irritant.

The big room we were to meet in was done in Basic Fraternity House: lots of overstuffed couches and chairs; big poster-like banners drooping on the walls. Twenty couples divided into two camps: those socializing a little frantically around a table, and those sitting isolated, unspeaking, wall-eyed with apprehension. That was us: front right corner, closest to the wall. We would have been by the door if it hadn't been for the draft.

A couple and a priest took chairs at the front and we all shushed obediently like children. It was a larger version of the first natural childbirth class Richard and I had gone to: everyone sitting stiffly, united only by a common predicament. The couple and priest began an unmemorable pitterpat of welcome which had a lulling effect and then suddenly the girl turned to her husband and said, "The most endearing thing about my husband is that when he smiles he lights up clear down to his toes and he makes me light up too." I thought, "Oh, dear." Her husband said the most endearing thing about her was that she was beautiful and belonged to him and Richard and I squirmed in my chairs. And then they asked each person to say what was the most endearing thing about his/her spouse beginning — oh, God — in the front right corner of the room closest to the wall.

I expected Richard to slide past it, but he answered perfectly straight: "The most endearing thing about Joyce is that I have never, in all the time I've known her, heard her say something deliberately unkind about another person."

It was so untrue that I wanted to cry, but instead I had to say something, something as real as Richard had. I said that his most endearing trait was his ability to be honest even in the bad times when it might hurt one of us. Then we leaned back and clutched hands like survivors.

Richard: Aside from that trauma, I was chiefly embarrassed for the lead couple since they didn't seem to have sense enough to be embarrassed for themselves. My first impression was that they were overselling the Marriage Encounter; they seemed to be afraid of a mass exodus. After all, everyone came voluntarily. Or did they? We were the only ones who came through reading about it, and I wasn't exactly a volunteer. Everyone else had heard through church, evangelical friends, family. I was glad we hadn't; there would be a certain pressure: I have to have as deep an experience as my older brother did, etc.

Anyway, however and whyever we had come, all the other men looked as uneasy as I felt. The women looked determined.

Joyce: We had expected chiefly a get-acquainted session Friday, and instead they immediately began the heavy stuff. First that awful public announcement of how endearing we all were to shake us up, then each of us was given our very own pen and our very own little black composition book with space for our name on the front; we were told to write our names in immediately. It was all too brownie-scout for words. And then began the plan that would be followed all weekend: one of three lead couples and a priest would talk about certain areas of marriage, interpreted through their marriage or the priest's experience with people — loneliness, sex, pressures of the outside on the couple. Never children; for the weekend we were all childless. The talk — called a presentation — would end with questions which (hopefully) would encourage us to think about what had been said in terms of our separate marriages. The first talk was called "Orientation and Focus" — generalities about how people with supposedly good marriages think about marriage. Then the questions pulled it down from the general to a one-to-one level: "What are my feelings about what I find most attractive in you? What I find I like best in me? What I find most attractive in us?" Then all the couples split, one to stay in the big room, one to return to the bedroom while each wrote on the questions. At the end of an unannounced time period the priest rang a bell and the halves of the couples met in their bedroom to trade notebooks and discuss what each had written.

My first reaction was, Richard will never forgive me for getting him into this.

Richard: I was caught off guard by the whole technique, which they called, "Reflection and Dialogue." We've never been far enough apart to write letters, so I wasn't used to talking that way — and I didn't have much practice in deciphering Joyce's handwriting — it takes practice.

But I appreciated the technique of splitting the couples up. The priest said that otherwise you each kept wondering what the other was writing. It's true. If I had to sit and watch Joyce scribbling away I wouldn't be able to put two complete sentences back to back.

Joyce: We each found it easier to talk about the other's attractive qualities — hadn't we just announced in public why we were endearing? Discussing it privately was easy. But we were skittish talking about our own good qualities. Richard said something about his ability to make me happy, which isn't really a quality at all. I said nothing. When it came to talking about our strength as a couple, Richard was very solid: "What a fantastic relief it was to find somebody who thinks" — he meant that we both brought this capacity to the relationship.

But I got very confused by the question of our strength as a couple. You are so aware of what your spouse wants or thinks (or what you *think* he/she wants or thinks) that by the time you actually say anything it is already a compromise of what you really feel.

Richard: It was a relief that they began with something that helped us to see ourselves in a positive way: if they had started right off with problems the whole weekend would have gone zap.

And I began to see the point in the way the lead couple ran on. There they were gushing out all the things they felt; it made you feel you couldn't possibly say anything more foolish or more damning. I wasn't sure we were keeping up with their program — they said that sleep was a copout and that the cookies and coffee would be there all night for whoever wanted them — but we just didn't have that much to say. It was quite a turn-around from the smug outlook I had had a few hours before, to feel that I might not be measuring up.

We were all a little aloof at the meeting after breakfast, as if the encounter was slightly on trial. But the next presentation was a body blow.

It was called "Encounter with Self." Nothing startlingly new was said, although they had a lot of points pulled together: that a person is separate from what he/she does, so your achievements don't really define you. That everyone puts on the masks of acting this way or that as a way of hiding from others and from oneself. Something about the basic worth of every person unmasked: "God doesn't make junk." And the questions, really, were general: "1. What are my good points? What are my bad points? 2. What are my masks that cause me to behave as I do? 3. Do I really like myself?"

But the answers couldn't be general. They had to come out of my head. And I had to write something because Joyce was off somewhere trying to. That really got to me. There was nothing to do but write — no books, couldn't go outdoors, no television, no retreat but the bathroom next door. I wrote things I had never said to anyone, hardly even admitted to myself. Like I had always prided myself on my ability to get along with people but suddenly I wondered if I were a weathervane. Secondly, I realized I had always had to have the best house, the most expensive electric drill, best skis of all my friends. And the best wife. When Joyce was unhappy, she threatened that image. Where did her need leave off and my need to be a superhusband begin? And — hardest to face — since my masks seemed to be in good working order, would I really make the effort to throw them off?

Joyce: I've always envied people who seem to float along the surface of life, even though I could never manage it: I rehash the things I do and castigate myself endlessly. It seemed that for once I was in a place where that quality would be of use.

But rehashing the stupid things you do is different from just sitting down and writing about yourself non-stop

So I didn't get far in that reflection. I didn't like it and I couldn't think of anything good and everything I did think of began conflicting with everything else and I got very unhappy.

It was a relief to have that over and go on the next topic: "Marriage in the Modern World." The negative way people, including married people, think of marriage. You aren't supposed to talk to your husband too much at parties or sit too close to him. Jokes about yourselves ("He always does this, ha ha," "She always does that, ha ha") that shield affection and subtly continue fights. The world's standard of marriage is so low that all you have to do is survive to be considered successful. "We love each other 'enough'."

Richard: Two unrelated things chiefly impressed me here. One was the statement "The enemy of a better marriage is a good marriage." That was worth the whole weekend. The second was a list of rules for fighting. I was amused to discover later on that Joyce had unconsciously left out the second and sixth on *my* list:

1. Find out what the subject is.
2. Stick to the subject.
3. Don't be a historian—no past incident.
4. No third parties—no reference to outsiders.
5. No hitting below the belt.
6. Don't wear your belt around your neck.
7. No name-calling.
8. Hold hands.

The guy reading off my rules came to the last one, looked at his wife, looked at us and said. "Have you ever tried holding hands with a clenched fist?"

Joyce: At lunch for the first time someone mentioned his job. So far as I know no one has used the telephone; we are all assuming that our children are alive and healthy. I felt as if we were snowed in. We rushed obediently to the big room after lunch to begin again—it was already a habit—even though no one seemed to be having a pleasant time and most of the women, like me, were carrying a rolled up bunch of toilet paper, having come inadequately stocked with tissues.

Richard: Saturday afternoon was the most important part for me. "Areas for Reaching Out to Each Other," the presentation was called; and I think it was chiefly for the men because it took dead aim at the stock male retreat: logic. The priest talked about feelings—what was the instinctive response to another person's feelings, how that usually fouled things up, and what one should try to do instead. You aren't responsible for feelings after all, they have no positive or negative value, they just are. But the instinctive reaction is rejection: "You're wrong to feel that way." Not that one says that, it's usually, "I'm sorry you feel that way." Implication: You have your feelings and I have mine, and I can't help you. Or—my favorite trick—you try to rationalize it to problem-solve.

Up to the encounter, I liked to get wrapped up in some project so that I didn't have to think about problems at all. If Joyce did get through to me about some problem that was making her unhappy, I analyzed it, rationalized it, sermonized it, and decided that she shouldn't have a problem since I wouldn't have one in her place. My first reaction was count your blessings and don't bother me.

Joyce: At last! For the emotional, a comeback to refute the logical: "You're not trying to understand, you're just problem-solving." "Problem-solving" is such a tidy term for what goes wrong when we try to discuss something. Richard always has a reason and a cure for everything. Knowing there is an answer to whatever is wrong ("All mothers lose their tempers," "If you were more efficient about house-cleaning it wouldn't take so long," "If you just didn't listen to Nixon, you wouldn't get upset") does nothing to dilute how I feel, it only turns it inward. Twice the grief.

At the same time, I retaliated to problem-solving by using my feelings as weapons—my downfall. When I said "I want" it wasn't merely a feeling, it carried the unspoken appendage ". . . so do something about it."

Suddenly is a word that should be used sparingly but it was that way: as the priest spoke about feelings, suddenly I could see things I was doing, Richard was doing, behind our words, I thought of how often the baby bugged me and I saw suddenly that it wasn't what he did but my feelings about it. Then there was guilt at not measuring up to my own standards, fear that I wasn't measuring up to Richard's, trying to do what he wanted without ever having the nerve to ask straight out what it was. Unacknowledged resentment at my own loss of privacy, and family relationships, too, that we had discussed with intellectual calm but that I could see now were really full of unadmitted jealousy and guilt.

What we wrote began to change about that time. Instead of being polite and little apologetic, he became straight, visceral and at times uncomfortable in what was implied for one or the other. It was as if we felt suddenly released to have bad feelings and were spilling them out, not meaning to accuse but still the fact that they existed was a kind of accusation. At last I was admitting to myself and to Richard how uncertain I was about the wife image and how much I hated parts of it and how hostile I felt when he pushed it at me. And at last he was admitting how hostile *he* felt when I couldn't manage something simple like picking up after the baby.

Richard: It was inevitable that a note of finger-pointing crept in now and then. Because we were new at listening to feelings too. I kept thinking I had to take responsibility for Joyce's feelings—meaning I got defensive. When she told me how housecleaning got to her, it was like I was being told to stop wanting a clean house. When she said she was lonely, I immediately felt guilty about going to work every morning. But that wasn't fair, I had a right to my feelings too. I had to learn to stop, back up, try to wipe away all those reactions, try instead to feel the same way Joyce was feeling. Without asking why. Just accepting. Then she had to try the same for me. It was punishing physically.

That was why the next topic came in like fresh air. The title was unpromising: "Marriage in the Plan of God." But the question was great: "Name three specific instances where I have felt closest to you. Describe fully in loving detail those feelings of closeness." I think I could have come up with a lot more than three. It made me realize that we hadn't done so badly.

Joyce: Whenever people reason about religion my mind wanders. I found myself studying the banners in the room.

But I came alive answering the question. I knew that *numero uno* for us both would be our son's birth, so that we would both be thinking of it at the same time; it was almost like a physical link, like repeating some of the absolute exhilaration.

Richard: This subject was obviously stuck in to get us thinking positively again, just like the first subject Friday started us off on a good note. I'm surprised that I avoided feeling that I was being manipulated up and down the emotional scale Saturday.

Joyce: What was happening between us was beginning to seem bigger than the questions we were writing about. We were getting a sense of what it was like to be the other person. Who could have more going for him than a bachelor in his early thirties, which is what Richard was when we met? But now I tried to feel the loneliness, not visiting married friends because there was no girl who fit in, watching your godchildren grow up, and finally, when you did marry, wishing you could celebrate your tenth anniversary instead of your first. There was another question focused on the problems we might have revealing feelings, which seemed to open up to a hundred different pesonal revelations between us, I don't quite know why. I remember telling Richard about being so unhappy as a child that I started a savings account for running away in the third grade. Admitting for the first time the 110 percent failure I had been in high school, of the time I had tried to kill myself and chickened out with the glass of ammonia in front of me and carried away a feeling not of survival but of failing on yet another count. Someone had said something to the effect that when you said things thay you had never heard or thought before, you were getting down to feelings. But by Saturday night I felt strongly that any more of the same general soul-probing would be, for us anyway, a kind of wallowing. We needed to turn the same kind of exploration to some real point of stress in our lives, to see if it held up.

So we set up our own dialogue, formally, with question and separation to write a reflection. There was a sort of mock-solemnity to it, trying our fledgling wings. We wrote about keeping house, a loaded issue on both sides, and all kinds of things surfaced of which neither of us had been aware — including the fear, which I suppose we'll run into again, that what you feel can be too hurtful to say no matter how much any outsider has assured you otherwise. Richard is ashamed of me — there, it's out — because he finds cleaning so easy that he doesn't understand how it can be a problem to anyone but a slob. But he isn't defined by it, I am: housewife. I realized for the first time how I was tied to the past: subconsciously I had always wanted to "show" the people who made me unhappy as a child and now I could feel them laughing at me whenever I pushed a mop around. You can't explain or problem-solve feelings like those. The only thing that helps is for the other person to try to understand.

We wrote, read, talked — and it worked! I could feel pressure dissipating. Sharing something that opens up such wells of tenderness toward the other person.

Richard: They had told us we might want to set up our own dialogues — all night long, if it seemed useful, and cookies and coffee would be there like the night before.

In spite of that, when we actually did it, I was sure no one else was. It was a feeling I'd had all weekend long. Although we were following exactly the pattern everyone else was, it was just impossible to believe that other couples were having the same experiences. I know it was true. I could see the changes as we sat in the big lecture room — couples sitting with linked hands leaning toward each other where Friday night they — we — had been leaning away. But it was easier to believe that all the other red eyes and sniffs and sodden lumps of tissue were because everyone except us had colds.

Joyce: I couldn't understand why there were so many tears. Nervous tension? Self-pity? Relief at getting something out in the open? It was a convalescent kind of easy tears, as if one had been very ill and was still fragile. After Saturday, anything more would have had to have been a miracle. It wasn't. The Sunday morning talk was titled "Sacrament and Its Graces," a beginning attempt, I think, to apply the couple experience to a bigger group, i.e., a church.

It was the first thing all weekend that I couldn't relate to in any way. And it was also the first attempt to talk to us as a group rather than an aggregate of couples. But what Richard and I had shared had nothing to do with thirty-eight other strangers, it was no basis to become instant friends.

The priest and the lead couple talked as if this morning were some kind of watershed. But it wasn't the first time that I had been less than impressed by the presentation; yet away from them, writing, the questions still worked. Perhaps this time too, I thought, pen poised to answer: "Why do I go on living?"

Were we supposed to be so open by then that that kind of absolute topic would be moving instead of self-conscious? I hadn't made it. There was something so pointed and personal about the previous questions, that was their strength; but this one seemed to lose focus.

But maybe it would all seem to be worth it when we exchanged notebooks and talked, so I pushed the feeling away and wrote.

Richard: It was impossible not to be trite. You knew what the answer was supposed to be so all you could do was repeat what they said in a different way. What could I say: "I want to go on living because I enjoy poisoning pigeons in the park?" I wrote all the acceptable nice things and it sounded like a catechism.

I was beginning to get mad at them. I think they expected a kind of humility of us here which wasn't the right note — not for me, not for us. We were proud and exhilarated by what we had accomplished together the day before, we didn't want to back away from that into something acceptably meek.

When we met to discuss what we had written, we couldn't say much of what we felt. We had trusted them this far, we didn't want to say that this hadn't worked for fear of denying the whole weekend. Here we were with an ideal little crisis to share feelings about and we flubbed it.

Joyce: I had expected Sunday to end on some romantic crisis, like repeating our marriage vows. Instead we all filed trustfully into the big room after lunch and whoosh! — like a cold douche we were plunged into the business end of the Encounter.

I knew the Marriage Encounter was run by amateurs, couples who had encountered themselves, plus priests. We had been told so over the course of the weekend. I had fantasized that some amateurs were so moved by the experience that they volunteered. Not so. It took a great deal of dexterity to avoid being commandeered for something. For example, the gaudy wall banners I had assumed were someone else's leftovers in fact belonged to Marriage Encounter and volunteers were needed to sew more, please sign the list as it was passed around. There was an official Marriage Encounter symbol available in jewelry (14k gold, gold-filled, sterling), decals for cars (passed out free), rubber stamps.

Volunteers were needed to man telephones, baby-sit, work on the Encounter Newsletter, run bloodbank drives. Presumably after enough of this behind-the-scenes work one worked one's way up to lead couple.

There was also the Rookie Renewal (a meeting one month hence to cement our experience), a celebration in three months for Ninety Day

Wonders. (That was the term for those who had managed for three months without once missing to have a daily "reflection-and-dialogue." But it wasn't called that anymore, it had become the "ten and ten" — ten minutes for each.) Sometime later in the year there was to be a rally for all people who had ever Encountered.

Richard: What I couldn't understand was the response of the other people. I thought everyone would react with the outrage we did. Instead they leaped joyously into the organizing bit, as if glad to escape into it.

Joyce: Ironically, the day *did* end with a repeat of marriage vows. Again it seemed to work for everyone but us.

Richard: If we hadn't been cowards, we would have left.

Joyce: The drive home seemed long and lonely. Writing-and-talking — my mind self-consciously refused to say "reflection and dialogue" — had worked so well for us that Sunday morning I had pictured a serene unrolling of days and months and years of exchanged conversations, all the things I was going to learn about Richard and share with him. Now I was cheated of my comfortable vision — by the same Encounter people who had shown me its existence in the first place. There was no way I could ask Richard to try a daily reflection and dialogue after Sunday afternoon's histrionics. It wasn't fair.

Richard: I had been angry when they started pressuring everybody to do their daily ten and ten. They made an article of faith out of it: there is no other way. But I could hardly deny the value of the two little black books we carried home with us. I thought we might as well give it a try.

Joyce: It was a dubious beginning. I was grateful to Richard for being so magnanimous and agreeing to try. Then I got mad at myself for feeling grateful about something which should, after all, be equally important to both of us. And that in turn put a chip on my shoulder — for days I lost my temper at the smallest comment I could interpret as a putdown to my important new personhood.

Richard: We were both self-conscious. Who was going to pick the topic each day? Did we have to choose topics fifty-fifty? How close to home did they have to be? Should we stay away from heavies like death and sex?

Joyce? I didn't have any great hopes. I was waiting for the first flush of energy to die away and the dialogue to seem like another nightly burden, like picking up after the baby. Which of us would be the first to suggest skipping?

Richard: But then little plusses began to show up. Like the time Joyce was telling me about something that made her unhappy and I said, "It really hurts me when you feel that way" — and she stopped me. Told me I was being defensive instead of listening. It startled us. We hadn't realized what a lot of supposedly warm-sounding statements really mean "Stop feeling that way."

Richard: We began to notice that we were seeing other people differently too. Like the baby. Thinking of him in terms of his feelings instead of reacting incident by incident may — *may* — get us through his Terrible Twos. The books all explain how a two-year-old tests authority, but when he keeps it up hour after hour it's hard to stay on that abstract plane — the tendency is to brain him now and think about insights later when he's asleep. But with an outlet like dialogue Joyce and I can take it one day at a time, let off steam without accusing each other of anything, which seems in turn to take the pressure off when we deal with him. (Easy for me to say, I'm not home with him all day.)

As we continue, my opinion of the Encounter is inching upward. The Marriage Encounter is insensitive to — doesn't depend on — any particular lead couple or priest. Or even what they say. Because you aren't relating to them, you are simply lifting their method to relate to your spouse. I think that's the key to its success. It's like a franchise — it's the basic formula for fried chicken that counts, not who's running the store.

Joyce: The logic of it got to Richard pretty quickly. For me the turning point came from one of those incidents that pressure me into the role of suburban housewife. In this case it was a department store that refused to issue a charge plate to *me* because their policy is to use the name of the husband, i.e., billpayer. Logical, I suppose. Infuriating.

I began my usual kicking and screaming, and Richard said, as he usually did, "But, honey, it just isn't that—"

Stopped.

Drew in a deep breath and let it out.

Said in a dogged voice, "I understand how you feel."

One of these days you may find us embroidering banners.

Has Monogamy Failed?

HERBERT A. OTTO

Never before in the history of Western civilization has the institution of marriage been under the searching scrutiny it is today. Never before have so many people questioned the cultural and theological heritage of monogamy — and set out in search of alternatives. The American family of the 1970s is entering an unprecedented era of change and transition, with a massive reappraisal of the family and its functioning in the offing.

*　　*　　*

The weight of tradition and the strong imprinting of parental and familial models assure that for some time to come the overwhelming bulk of the population will opt for something close to the family structures they have known. In view of this strong thrust, it is all the more surprising that preventive programs (other than didactic approaches) that center on the strengthening of the family are almost unknown. Also sadly lacking is massive federal support for programs designed to help marriages and families beset by problems. A network of federally supported marriage-counseling clinics making marital and premarital counseling services available throughout every state in the Union could accomplish a great deal toward reducing marital unhappiness and divorce.

Present day medical science widely recommends that we have an annual physical check-up as a means of prevention. In a similar manner, annual assessment and evaluation should be available to couples interested in developing and improving their marriages. The goal would be to identify, strengthen, and develop family potential *before* crises arise, with the main focus on helping a family achieve an even more loving, enjoyable, creative, and satisfying marriage relationship. The plan of a marriage and family potential center was developed in 1967 and 1968 by a colleague, Dr. Lacey Hall, and myself during my stay in Chicago. The project was supported by the Stone Foundation, but, owing to a number of complex reasons, the program was never fully implemented. As a part of the work in Chicago, and also under the auspices of the National Center for the Exploration of Human Potential, a number of "More Joy in Your Marriage" groups and classes have been conducted and have shown considerable promise as a preventive approach.

Another highly promising field of inquiry is the area of family strengths. Little or no research and conceptualization had been done in relation to this area until the work of the Human Potentialities Research Project at the University of Utah, from 1960 through 1967. Paradoxically, family counseling and treatment programs have been offered for decades without a clearly developed framework of what was meant by family strengths, or what constitutes a "healthy family." In spite of extensive efforts to obtain foundation or government support for this research, no financial support was forthcoming. Ours remains a pathology-oriented culture saddled with the bias that the study of disorganization, illness, and dysfunction is the surest road to understanding the forces that go into the making of health and optimum functioning.

The emergence of alternative structures and the experimentation with new modes of married and family togetherness expresses a strong need to bring greater health and optimum functioning to a framework of interpersonal relationships formerly regarded as "frozen" and not amenable to change. There is no question that sex-role and parental-role rigidities are in the process of diminishing, and new dimensions of flexibility are making their appearance in marriage and the family. It is also evident that we are a pluralistic society with pluralistic needs. In this time of change and accelerated social evolution, we should encourage innovation and experimentation in the development of new forms of social and communal living. It is possible to invent and try out many models without hurting or destroying another person. Perhaps we need to recognize clearly that the objective of any model is to provide an atmosphere of sustenance, loving, caring, and adventuring. This makes growth and unfoldment possible.

It is in this light that the attention of an increasing number of well-known humanistic psychologists has been drawn to the institution of marriage. A new recognition of the many dimensions and possibilities of monogamy is beginning to emerge. For example, Dr. Jack Gibb and Dr. Everett Shostrom have each been conducting a series of couples groups at Growth Centers designed to revitalize and deepen love in the marital relationship.

Another eminent psychologist and author, Dr. Sidney Jourard, suggests that we "re-invent marriage" by engaging in "serial polygamy to the same person." He points out that many marriages pass through a cycle of gratifying the needs of both partners, and are experienced as fulfilling until an impasse is reached. One partner or the other finds continuation in that form intolerable, and the marriage is usually legally dissolved at that point. He believes it is possible for the couple at this juncture to struggle with the impasse and to evolve a new marriage with each other, one that includes change, yet preserves some of the old pattern that remains viable. This is the second marriage that, whatever form it takes, will also reach its end. There may then be a time of estrangement, a period of experimentation, and a remarriage in a new way — and so on for as long as continued association with the same spouse remains meaningful for both partners.

One of the originators of the group marathon technique, Dr. Frederick Stoller, has another interesting proposal to add new dimensions to marriage and family relationships. He suggests an "intimate network of families." His intimate network consists of a circle of three or four families who meet together regularly and frequently, share in reciprocal fashion any of their intimate secrets, and offer one another a variety of services. The families do not hesitate to influence one another in terms of values and attitudes. Such an intimate family network would be neither stagnant nor polite, but would involve an extension of the boundaries of the immediate family.

Another possibility to introduce new elements of growth and creativity to monogamy is contained in my own concept of the "new marriage," i.e,, marriage as a framework for developing personal potential. This concept is based on the hypothesis that we are all functioning at a small fraction of our capacity to live fully in its total meaning of loving, caring, creating, and adventuring. Consequently, the actualizing of our potential can become the most exciting adventure of our lifetime. From this perspective, any marriage can be envisioned as a framework for actualizing personal potential. Thus, marriage offers us an opportunity to grow, and an opportunity to develop and deepen the capacity for loving and caring. Only in a continuing relationship is there a possibility for love to become deeper and fuller so that it envelops all of our life and extends into the community. However, growth, by its very nature, is not smooth and easy, for growth involves change and the emergence of the new. But growth and the actualization of personal potential are also a joyous and deeply satisfying process that can bring to marriage a *joie de vivre,* an excitement, and a new quality of zest for living.

There are a number of characteristics that form a unique Gestalt and distinguish the new marriage from contemporary marriage patterns:

> There is a clear acknowledgment by both partners concerning the *personal relevance* of the human potentialities hypothesis: that the healthy individual is functioning at a fraction of his potential.

> Love and understanding become dynamic elements in the actualization of the marital partners' personal potential.

> Partners in the new marriage conceive of their union as an evolving, developing, flexible, loving relationship.

> In the new marriage there is planned action and commitment to achieve realization of marriage potential.

> The new marriage is here-and-now oriented and not bound to the past.

> There is clear awareness by husband and wife that their interpersonal or relationship environment, as well as their physical environment, directly affects the actualization of individual potential.

> There is clear recognition by spouses that personality and the

actualization of human potential have much to do with the social institutions and structures within which man functions. The need for institutional and environmental regeneration is acknowledged by both partners as being personally relevant, leading to involvement in social action.

Husband and wife have an interest in exploring the spiritual dimensions of the new marriage.

Since it is often difficult for two people to actualize more of their marriage potential by themselves, participants in the new marriage will seek out group experiences designed to deepen their relationship and functioning as a couple. Such experiences are now being offered at Growth Centers that have sprung up in many parts of the United States. Extension divisions of institutions of higher learning and church organizations are also increasingly offering such group experiences. Based on my many years of practice as marriage counselor, it has long been my conclusion that every marriage needs periodic rejuvenation and revitalization. This is best accomplished in a couples group that focuses on the development of greater intimacy, freedom, joy, and affection.

The challenge of marriage is the adventure of uncovering the depth of our love, the height of our humanity. It means risking ourselves physically and emotionally; leaving old habit patterns, and developing new ones; being able to express our desires fully, while sensitive to the needs of the other; being aware that each changes at his own rate, and unafraid to ask for help when needed.

Has monogamy failed? My answer is "no." Monogamy is no longer a rigid institution, but instead an evolving one. There is a multiplicity of models and dimensions that we have not even begun to explore. It takes a certain amount of openness to become aware on not only an intellectual level but a feeling level that these possibilities face us with a choice. Then it takes courage to recognize that this choice in a measure represents our faith in monogamy. Finally, there is the fact that every marriage has a potential for greater commitment, enjoyment, and communication, for more love, understanding, and warmth. Actualizing this potential can offer new dimensions in living and new opportunities for personal growth, and can add new strength and affirmation to a marriage.

Open Marriage: Implications for Human Service Systems

NENA O'NEILL
GEORGE O'NEILL

We, ourselves, as individuals from two different backgrounds, as developing personalities with distinct identities, as husband and wife, and as mother and father of two grown sons, have in the half century of our lives witnessed the profound alternations in our social and technological organizations. They have influenced us in a deeply personal manner as individuals, as parents, as a family, and as members of our society, just as they have influenced other individuals and families living in a world of rapid social change. For many, these changes have raised questions concerning commitment to marriage. The meaning of commitment in marriage and family life today *is* being modified and both the individuals and the systems that service their needs require review as to the meanings and goals of their mutual involvement in the institution of marriage.

In response to the rapid changes in our social, psychological and physical environment, many variant and experimental family and marriage forms have emerged, not all of them monogamous. We frankly believe that monogamy provides the potential for the most fulfilling of human relationships. It is to this potential that we addressed ourselves in our book, *Open Marriage: A New Life Style for Couples* (O'Neill and O'Neill, 1972a, 1972b).

In researching contemporary marriage since 1967, we found that many of the expectations for traditional monogamy, which we term "closed marriage," limited this potential and were out of step with changes in a contemporary world where technological and sociological conditions have inevitably altered our needs for flexibility and had changed our perspectives on human equality. The rigidities of a patriarchal and monolithic style of marriage, based on an agrarian past with husband and wife roles solidified into stratified positions, did not readily permit growth or change. In our contemporary world many factors including a longer life span, education, greater mobility, and technological innovations have changed the position of women and have created new needs for greater parity in marriage and in man-woman relationships.

Open Marriage presents a model for a marital relationship that *is* based on equality and that is flexible enough to not only permit but encourage growth for both partners. It is directed to the individuals upon whom the marital relationship depends—the husband and wife.

Inherent in this model is our belief that individuals can and ought to be the focus for change. Also inherent in the way we have presented *Open Marriage* is our belief that in a complex and bureaucratic society the best human service system may well be your own.

While *Open Marriage* attempts to demythologize the unrealistic ideals and expectations of our traditional closed marriage, its primary objective is to delineate the elements that contribute to a more vital and egalitarian marital relationship and to outline some methods and skills for attaining such a relationship. The open marriage model offers insights and learning guides for developing more intimate and understanding marital relationships.

Open marriage can be defined as a relationship in which partners are committed to their own and to each other's growth. Supportive caring and increasing security in individual identities makes possible the sharing of self-growth with a partner who encourages and anticipates his own and his mate's growth. It is a relationship that is constantly being revised in the light of each one's changing needs, through consensus in decision-making, by acceptance and encouragement of individual development and in openness to new possibilities for growth.

The first step is for partners to reassess the marriage relationship that they are in or hope to achieve, in order to reevaluate expectations for themselves and for their partner. Former expectations, such as the belief that woman's primary role is wife, mother, and child-raiser and that man's primary role is provider and part-time father, limits both spouses in their full expansion into personhood. Another major expectation of closed marriage—namely, that one partner will be able to fulfill *all* of the other's needs—presents obstacles to growth and attitudes that foster over-dependency and conflict between partners. Awareness of these expectations and a realignment more in accord with a realistic appraisal of each partner's capabilities is fundamental to instituting change and to solving problems in the relationship.

The open marriage model embodies eight guidelines for achieving more openness and growth in the marriage relationship. Living for now involves relating to self and partner in the present rather than in the past or in terms of future goals which are frequently materialistic rather than emotional or intellectual ones wherein growth is possible. The granting of privacy is essential for examination of self and for psychic regeneration. A way out of the role-bind involves working toward greater role flexibility, both in terms of switching roles temporarily or on a part-time basis and as a therapeutic device for greater understanding of self, the other, and the dynamics of their interaction. Open and honest communication is perhaps the most important element in an open relationship. Lack of communication skills creates a formidable barrier between husband and wife, yet these skills are the most important in sustaining a vital relationship, promoting understanding and increasing knowledge of self. Open companionship involves relating to others, including the opposite sex, outside the primary unit of husband and wife as an auxiliary avenue for growth.

Equality involves relating to the mate as a peer in terms of ways to achieve stature, rather than in terms of the status attached to the traditional husband and wife roles. Identity involves the development of the individual through actualizing his own potentials rather than living through the mate or the child. Trust, growing through the utilization of these other guidelines and based on mutuality and respect, creates a climate for growth. Liking, respect, sexual intimacy, and love grow through the dynamic interaction and use of these elements.

Each progressive guideline becomes increasingly abstract. The system can be seen as an expending spiral of evolving steps in complexity and depth in the marital relationship. The system operates on the principle of synergy, which means that two partners in a marriage, or in any relationship, can accomplish more personal and interpersonal growth together while still retaining their individual identities, than they could separately. Synergic buildup is the way in which the growth of both partners, women as well as men, provides positive, augmenting feedback that can continuously enhance mutual growth and fulfillment. It is not assumed that most couples can or would want to utilize all of these guidelines simultaneously. Open marriage, then, can best be understood as a resource mosaic from which couples can draw according to their needs and their readiness for change in any one area.

What then are the implications of this new and revitalized open relationship in monogamy for human service systems? We believe they will develop in two directions. One is the way service systems can help effect and support more egalitarian marriage relationships, and the other is the effect an increasing number of open marriages will have on these service systems, thus setting up a feedback situation based on cybernetic dynamics. We feel that open marriages and the values they engender are conducive to building healthier, more dynamic, and stronger family units. In this way we see social change occurring through micro-cultural changes which stem from the strength of the basic family unit. It can happen in three ways.

First: Open marriage is designed to strengthen the marriage and at the same time strengthen the individual in the marriage. A more vital and understanding marital relationship gives more meaning to shared commitment. Rather than harboring deepseated resentments or splitting when problems arise, couples may be able to resolve differences, to cope with change, and to find greater joy and challenge in sharing life together.

Second: We feel that the children of open marriages will tend to be responsible, confident, self-reliant individuals. If husband and wife grow in emotional maturity through open marriage, and if their relationship is one of equality, respect, mutual problem-solving through consensus, and supportive love, these values can then be transmitted to the child. Through an enculturation process that emphasizes the values of respect for individual differences, personal responsibility, self-actualization, and growth in interpersonal relationships, family ties will be more meaningful, thus providing the foundation for creating an open family. Utilizing the elements and themes of open marriage within the family should encourage dialogue between generations and minimize the conflict and gaps in understanding.

Third: Because couples have an open marriage they can open up to other families. By being open within, they can be more open without. Because they have established the meaning of commitment to each other within the family, they can better relate to other couples and families and explore the meaning of mutual commitment and a greater intensification of humanness with others. The can create strong local groups which might be called "initiator groups" and increase community solidarity in terms of goals and thus provide the foundation for creating family-based social networks. In this way they can direct their strength toward obtaining needed services and toward dealing with bureaucratic inadequacies in existing services.

However, the reality today is that no matter how open some marriages, families, and communities are, they still operate in a societal context where human service systems have not caught up to their needs and where substantial structural revisions are necessary to meet these needs. We have mentioned the need for supportive structures in our book: "While each of us can modify roles to suit our needs, the success of sharing parenthood and interchanging husband and wife roles will depend on the creation of new patterns in work and family arrangements which offer broader bases than the nuclear family for sharing and mutual support" (1972a, 158). Obviously it will be difficult for couples to achieve an open marriage in a society that does not provide means or opportunities for individual growth for both partners at the same time that the needs of children and family life are considered.

What can human service systems do in innovative ways to help effect greater parity in the marriage relationship, to provide for developing individual potential for all members of the family, and at the same time encourage closer family ties and greater community support? Change can occur on two levels: one concrete, the other in value orientation.

We shall mention some of the concrete proposals first, many of which have already been suggested by members of this group and others (Osofsky and Osofsky; Rossi 1970, 1972a, 1972b; Steinem, 1972; Stoller, 1970; Sussman 1971a). They occur primarily in the area of change in residence, work, child care, and educational patterns. Some are directed toward facilitating the movement of women into the mainstream of American life, some toward sharing parenthood and family responsibilities, and others for changes in education.

1. An expansion of equal opportunities for women in education, jobs, and professions, including, of course, equal salaries.
2. Minimization of sex role stereotyping in all media and in our educational institutions.
3. Networks of child care centers under voluntary, private, community, industrial, university, and other institutional auspices. We have excluded state auspices from this list because of

the recent proposals for 24-hour nurseries. We do not endorse group child care during the crucial first two years of infancy, since our interpretation of developmental and primate studies indicates that a one-to-one or one-to-two relationship of close physical intimacy and affectionate response provides optimum benefits for the infant. Whether this care is maternal, paternal, or surrogate or whether it occurs in a nuclear, single, or extended family context does not seem to be as significant as the maintenance of the quality of intimacy and the level of interaction and response. After these early years, the benefits of broader socialization patterns are clearly acknowledged.

4. An upgrading of the nurturing professions and the increasing utilization of men and older men and women in teaching and child-care facilities.

5. An expansion of opportunities for continuing and alternating sequences of education throughout life.

6. Encouragement of arrangements and innovations conducive to shared parenthood between husband and wife and community. There have been many suggestions in this area; some are for time off with pay, alternating work weeks or days, or interchangeable jobs, such as those which are being experimented with in Scandinavia where the same job is held by husband and wife who alternate weeks at work and home.

7. Decentralization of many delivery systems. The new telecommunications inventions (Goldmark, 1972) may well facilitate mechanical delivery of services to the families of the future, but in the present we still need more personalized and direct service. The mechanical communications revolution and the implications it has for the loss of intimacy and for fragmentation may result in an even greater necessity to focus on the fulfillment and depth that interpersonal relationships have to offer.

8. Dissemination of contraceptive and sex information both to reduce the number of unwanted children and to encourage responsible family planning.

9. Education for parenthood, sex, human biology, and infant development. This education need not be in terms of how the child is to be raised, which may be unduly restrictive, but could be in the areas of imparting knowledge about the relevant biological and cognitive stages of child and adolescent development, and basic elements in the role of parenting.

10. The establishment of parity for men and women in legal codes affecting marriage, sex, and human rights, including those of the child. Upon ratification, the new Equal Rights Amendment will have far-reaching effects on marriage and parenthood. Until such parity is effected, persons entering marriage should be made aware of the implicit legal aspects of the marriage contract they are signing and of the legal statutes affecting their rights in marriage.

11. A movement of women into policy-making positions on governmental and institutional levels.

12. A change in work and residence patterns designed to effect more family contact hours and contiguity between work and family living.

13. A revamping of the policies of industry and employers regarding job offers and job relocation will be necessary in order to accommodate an increasing number of dual-career families and couples.

14. An increase in planned built-in environments accommodating many life styles and encouraging community interaction, solidarity, and support. Suburban sprawl and anonymous urban cubicles isolate the family and its members from facilities as well as community support.

15. Encouragement of kin and non-kin peer family networks for mutual aid and support.

16. Encouragement of discussion groups and experiential therapy for couples. Six years ago, Dr. Clark Vincent (1967) suggested that marital health become a legitimate field of specialization. In line with his suggestion, there could be an increase in couple counseling as well as an increase in discussion groups for couples who may not need therapy but who want to clarify issues and attain better relationship skills.

17. An increase in creative premarital counseling.

18. In general, non-directive counseling designed to reduce the pressure of conformity to traditional role expectations in marriage, and to help couples and individuals to clarify their own goals and to understand and maximize the choices available to them. Many systems could focus on providing the individual, the marital couple, and the family unit with new coping mechanisms for meeting change in life events through experimental and emotional education. Coping mechanisms, however, should evolve into more positive ways of providing creative and growth experiences.

19. Changes in home maintenance and housework patterns. The answer is not to put every husband in an apron and a lunch bucket or executive pen in every wife's hand, but to encourage everyone to share in home maintenance, including our children who currently expect Mom to do it all. Less of an emphasis on material possessions and goals would contribute to a more relaxed style of living and housekeeping that values creative work and play arrangements. Certainly our technological know-how could be applied to making household maintenance simpler and more efficient instead of grinding out dubious technological marvels and an avalanche of material possessions that threaten to bury us all in ecological overkill.

20. A deliberate focus on the problems of men in adjusting to our new equalities. Ten years of the women's movement and, of

course, other conditions in our society have brought many changes and have altered our conceptions of marriage and the role of men and women in it. Its impact has prepared many women for new adjustments, but little has been actively initiated to help men adjust to the changes in masculine and feminine expectations, or to promote the man's understanding of these changes. Both men and women as well as therapists report the doubts, conflicts, and confusion centering around current changes in the concepts of masculine and feminine identity. Although courses in women's studies now number 670 across the country (Rossi 1972b) there has been no similar expansion in the number of courses dealing with both masculine and feminine role changes. A new course designed to explore the problems of both men and women in adjusting to new role expectations might be helpful for both sexes. In addition, there could be an emphasis on education, research, and modes of therapy in this area.

We have two additonal suggestions in the area of education which are closer to the heart of the matter and have implications far beyond marriage. One of these is education for a full life for everyone. By this we mean a man is not a full person if he is educated just for a career or job, and a woman is not a full person if she is educated just for the expectation of homemaking and raising children or careers which are in conflict with these roles. All of us anticipate multiple roles in career, family, social, civic, and leisure areas. Our life span is too long, too varied, and too subject to change today for education to be devoted to rigid role specialization and to be limited only to the early years. There should be education for the whole person. Spontaneity, innovation, and creativity should be encouraged in addition to the acquisition of skills needed for specific careers.

Efforts should be made to make a child's education more participatory and relevant to his experiences and needs in our culture. The recent Foxfire project in Georgia (Johnston, 1972; Wigginton, 1972) is one example of how this can be done, while the free school movement is another expression of this need. In preliterate, small-scale societies, a child's education for living and parenthood is coeval with growing up. In ours it is not. Therefore we should educate our population for a new kind of thinking that incorporates the whole person and that is devoted to maximizing individual potential and responsibility. Education should provide individuals with experience and skills in dealing with the problems of the world we live in. Experiential training should and can be combined more effectively with didactic methods. In a recent article Alice Rossi (1972b) made some suggestions along this line for incorporating in the school curriculum specific training for young people in carrying combined home, civic, and school responsibilities.

Another suggestion we have in this area is to implement courses in human relations in our school systems from primary grades through college. This education would not only be valid as preparation for marriage, but would be basic for conducting any human relationship — that between person and person, child and adult, and person and group.

The need to learn skills in conducting interpersonal relationships and to maintain those values we consider most important to being human is paramount in today's world. Many of our satisfactions and dissatisfactions in life hinge on our ability to sustain and benefit from rewarding interpersonal relationships. Certainly there are factors in our mass technological society which are beyond an individual's control yet which affect his personal development, growth, and fulfillment. As Useem has commented: ". . . people are in trouble if that with which they are imprinted does not enable them to live emotionally satisfying lives in those social conditions which are blueprinted" (1971, 223). Obviously there are problems today in both the imprinting and the blueprinting process — both of which need comprehensive revision. Although individuals may feel that they have little direct control over social conditions or the blueprinting process, they *can* improve their own interpersonal relationships. Change in this area, whether gained through individual motivation and efforts or in school curricula could have widespread effects. The seed from which social responsibility grows can be found in how we care for and relate to others. As David McClelland (1970) has suggested, even leadership and power can have an S-power or social component, i.e., a concern for the welfare of others.

If we can educate our young in career and literacy skills, certainly it should be possible to educate them in acquiring skills for conducting beneficial and synergic human relationships which could be more emotionally satisfying and growth enhancing. Logically, parents could impart these skills beginning in the home with the new infant, but husband and wife are frequently caught in emotional and habitual patterns of relating and communicating carried over from their own parental, kinship, and social models. Without re-education in relationship skills, parents perpetuate the negative aspects of their childhood models in raising their children. We have tried to provide guidelines in *Open Marriage* for achieving awareness and relationship skills, but the exercise of these requires strong motivation and, most important, practice. So there is a need for experiential training, not only for couples in a marriage relationship, but at an age much earlier than when marriage occurs.

The elements and content of such training and courses would not be difficult to define once value orientations were stated and kept clearly in mind. The major focus could be on re-education and communication skills. We do not mean the techniques of persuasion and manipulation so popular in our advertising-dominated media and too frequently mirrored in our interpersonal relations. We do mean the skills of true dialogue and of competence in distinguishing between such elements as feeling, intention, interpretation, and expression in communication (Miller, Nunnally, Wackman, 1971) which lead to knowing one's self and others and helps in working out differences in constructive ways. Over and over, our research pointed out this pressing need for skills in communication, not only in marriage, but in other areas as well (O'Neill, 1964). Misunderstanding and lack of skills in communication repeatedly impeded understanding and the attainment of mutual goals. In our days of an astounding revolution in communication technology we are still living in the dark ages of personal, face-to-face communication. Billions of dollars are invested in new communication marvels, yet few are invested in teaching husband and wife, parent and child, worker and employer, or person and person to communicate in ways that clarify feelings, encourage mutual decision-making, and promote self-esteem, human dignity, respect, and compassion.

Many of these needs have been ignored through the imperatives of our technological and market-oriented society. To counteract this there should be a positive thrust for education in those values we consider to represent humanness. Although man is born with the capacity to be human, he nevertheless has to be taught to be human. The emphasis in this kind of education would not be on what types and forms of human relations people should have, but only on how to conduct the ones we do have so that everyone's needs are considered and the relationship can provide optimum benefits for all.

These suggestions for education for human relationships thus have ramifications for many social problems in our society, most of which are simply not subject to technological solutions. In the face of computer projections, such as those of the Club of Rome (Meadows, 1971), which demonstrate the possible fate of a technological and overpopulated future, it is apparent that we need both technological *and* human solutions. Better and more responsible human relations would certainly contribute a new factor and parameter for the computer calculations, and incidentally might help us in designing a different future.

All of which brings us to the value orientation we spoke of earlier. Since we live in a pluralistic society, the effectiveness of our human service systems will be a function of their capacity to become more flexible, to acknowledge new directions, and yet to keep intact certain basic core values. For instance, the emphasis of human service systems could be less on favoring only one dominant family form and more on discovering those values which are universal to all family forms, both variant and experimental. (For a review of these forms see Sussman 1971b). In marriage, the emphasis could be less on perpetuating a dominant mode of marriage which favors one partner, and more on discovering the values and needs of both partners in a marriage.

One of the ways in which this can be done is to facilitate a closer interaction between service systems and the people they service. The flow in the past has been from the top of the service pyramid — that is, from the institution and blueprinters — down to the individual. The flow must be reversed from the individual upwards in a synergistic process between individuals and institutions. Individuals can and do shape their culture, but they cannot do it effectively against institutional rigidities or against blueprints they did not help design. People on all levels must be drawn into the decision-making process that directly affects their lives and their interpersonal relationships.

Wherever we start, whether on an individual level as in open marriage or on an institutional level, the priorities are the same: an emphasis on human values that encourage cooperation through recognition and acceptance of individual differences and needs. Perhaps our human service systems could profit from a new focus on what we call "people systems." Quite realistically people systems would be expected to be inefficient and creative human systems rather than direct analogs of mechanical and thermodynamic models so favored by the systems analysts. While "trade off," "payoff," "input," and "output" might occasionally be valuable systems terms in analyzing interpersonal and group dynamics, we prefer to believe that there is something more to human relationships than input and output and that there are values that are not efficiency-oriented. A recognition of people systems would enable human service systems to concentrate on helping individuals integrate their multiple roles and to deliver services with an understanding that human interaction is more than a sum of its parts.

The concept of open marriage both explicitly and implicitly delineates and spells out certain basic values in the marital relationship. Perhaps our central message is that human service systems will also and necessarily have to do the same: they will have to search out the universal values to be maintained in all human relationships. We believe that certain fundamental values are common to any good human relationship no matter the variety or form. That these basic values revolve around equality, responsible freedom, personal growth, respect for self and others, and a desire for more rewarding interpersonal relationships appears self-evident. Once having declared these values, both individually and institutionally, we can then perhaps more clearly see that there are many routes to perpetuating them and upholding them, and that there are many paths to joy, sharing, and cooperation in an open world that has a place for everyone.

REFERENCES

Goldmark, Peter C. Tomorrow We Will Communicate to Our Jobs. *The Futurist,* 1972, 6 (2), 55-58.

Johnston, Donald. 'Foxfire': They Learned, and They Loved It. *The New York Times,* April 9, 1972.

Meadows, Donella, Dennis L. Meadows, Jorgen Randers and William W. Behrens, III. *Limits to Growth.* New York: Universe Books, 1971.

McClelland, David D. The Two Faces of Power, *Journal of International Affairs,* 1970, 24, 29-47.

Miller, Sherod, Flan W. Nunnally and Daniel B. Wackman. Awareness and Communication Training for Engaged or Married Couples.

646   *Improving the Marital Relationship*

Presented at the Annual Conference of the American Association of Marriage and Family Counselors, Salt Lake City, Utah, October, 1971.

O'Neill, George Catavena and Nena O'Neill. *Vocational Rehabilitation Needs of Disabled Puerto Ricans in New York City: A Pilot Study.* New York: Puerto Rican Social Services, Inc., 1964.

O'Neill, Nena and George O'Neill, *Open Marriage: A New Life Style for Couples.* New York: M. Evans and Co., 1972a.

O'Neill, Nena and George O'Neill. Open Marriage: A Synergic Model, *The Family Coordinator,* 1972b, 21, 403-410.

Osofsky, Joy D. and Howard J. Osofsky. Androgyny as a Life Style. *The Family Coordinator,* 1972, 24, 414-418.

Rossi, Alice S. Equality Between the Sexes: An Immodest Proposal. In Mayer Baresh and Alice Scourby (Eds.). *Marriage and the Family.* New York: Random House, 1970, 263-309.

Rossi, Alice S. Family Development in a Changing World. *American Journal of Psychiatry,* 1972a, 128, 1057-1066.

Rossi, Alice S. Letter to The Editor under heading "Practicing Beliefs," in *The New York Times Magazine,* April 9, 1972b, 6, 8, 18.

Steinem, Gloria. What it Would Be Like if Women Win. In Frank D. Cox (Ed.). *American Marriage: A Changing Scene?* Dubuque, Iowa: Wm. C. Brown, 1972, 214-219.

Stoller, Frederick H. The Intimate Network of Families as a New Structure. In Herbert A. Otto (Ed.). *The Family in Search of a Future.* New York: Appleton-Century Crofts, 1970, 145-159.

Sussman, Marvin B. The Experimental Creation of Family Environments. Presented at the Annual Meeting of The Groves Conference on Marriage and the Family, San Juan, Puerto Rico, May 8, 1971a.

Sussman, Marvin B. Family Systems in the 1970s: Analysis, Politics, and Programs. *The Annals of the American Academy of Political and Social Science,* 1971b, 396, 40-56.

Useem, Ruth Hill. The New Woman. In Paul B. Horton and Gerald R. Leslie (Eds.). *Studies in the Sociology of Social Problems.* New York: Appleton-Century Crofts; 1971, 217-228.

Vincent, Clark L. Mental Health and the Family, *Journal of Marriage and the Family,* 1967, 29, 18, 39.

Wigginton, Eliot, (Ed.). *The Foxfire Book.* New York: Doubleday, 1972.

UNIT STUDY GUIDE

A. *Terms to Review*

Affective needs	Gestalt	Role specifications
Contracts within marriage	Imprinting	Serial monogamy
Divorce culture	Instrumental tasks	Subclinical
Encounter group	Interpersonal competence	

B. *Questions for Discussion and Study*

1. As Mueller's article indicates, reconciliation does not necessarily imply the rebuilding of a viable, satisfying relationship between partners. Discuss factors most likely to be associated with successful coping in a troubled marriage.
2. Compare and contrast "marriage counseling" with individual or group "therapy."
3. "If a couple can just get through the first five years, they're not likely to have any really serious problems after that." Discuss the assumptions, validity, and implications of this claim.
4. Discuss the assets and liabilities of non-verbal communication patterns in marital problem-solving or marital improvement processes.
5. It has been suggested that "Ideally, a marriage should have resources within itself for coping with everyday realities and for dealing with most of the ongoing interpersonal problems encountered in family living." Cite some examples and illustrate how application of congruent, basic principles from the sexual equality and human potentials movements might contribute to the development of strong problem-solving and coping resources within new marriages.

C. *Topics-Ideas for Papers and Projects*

1. Develop a descriptive listing of all agencies in your area which do marr age counseling.
2. Prepare a list of five or six hypothetical problems covering the major areas of marital encounter. Have each person describe how he or she would deal with each problem. If help outside the marriage is visualized, what forms would it take? Why? Discuss the similarities and differences of answers for given problems in the class responses.
3. Compile a listing of group-oriented resources for marital improvement and enrichment available in your area (e.g. marriage enrichment seminars, retreats, growth groups focused on marriage, marriage-focused encounters, marathons, etc.).
4. Beginning with the alternatives cited in the introduction to this unit, list and describe as many additional ones as you can. For each one, consider feasibility, assets and liabilities, and its probability of acceptance.
5. Research: "Variation by Sex in the Evaluation of Probable Efficacy of Counseling for Selcted Types of Marital Problems."
6. "The history of marriage counseling in the U.S.A."

PART FIVE

PROSPECTS AND
POSSIBILITIES

Unit 11
Alternatives, Change, and the Future of Marriage

The surest way to lose truth is to pretend that one already possesses it. – Gordon Allport

In the long run the fate of a civilization depends on . . . what we believe and feel about . . . the possibilities of human nature. – Joseph Wood Krutch

---

Introduction

The contemporary spate of serious discussion and debate on familial topics is not a novel occurrence in human history. Discussions of the infirmities and failures of family life, as well as proposals to set things right, have been recurrent themes since at least the times of Plato. The closest that contemporary discussion comes to truly evincing a new development lies largely in the extent to which it tends to focus on the forms and processes of marriage and the corollary tendency to view problems from the perspective of the married pair. Thus, if there is a singular theme, it may consist in the emergent fact that marriage per se is no longer taken for granted universally. Clearly, marriage today faces a mounting barrage of questions and issues, some of which would have appeared incredible to Americans of only two generations ago. For, while some of these questions are peripheral and concerned with everyday mechanics of marital functioning, others are focused on the very nature and validity of the marriage institution.

Judging by the discussions which we have covered in our earlier reading, there are indeed some very heavy questions confronting every aspect of marriage in this society. And, thus far, many of the answers reflect only caustic criticism of our present marital arrangements and deep pessimism about the future of marriage. However, not all students of contemporary marriage possess such a bleak outlook. For example, the following statement is found in a widely used college textbook on marriage:

> Marriage is not paradise in the United States, it is just better

651

than man has been accustomed to. It fulfills deep social and personal needs, perhaps more fully than ever before, and the family is more lasting, seeing more children through to maturity before the death of either parent.[1]

Needless to say, perhaps, is that one's evaluation of the quality of contemporary marriage reflects always the criteria of excellence which are applied.

While the overall tone of this unit regarding marriage is rather optimistic, it is also tinged with realistic assessment of the turbulent familial scene in this society. A realistic appraisal suggests that there is widespread dissatisfaction with various aspects of marriage today and that this condition has furnished a fertile ground for the budding of alternative marital forms and processes. Such alternatives as have emerged in theory and practice do not always match well with the needs of persons or groups; hence, solutions may lead to further questing for better solutions. One purpose of this concluding unit is to illustrate that serious questions remain to be asked about marriage and family life; we can begin by briefly considering some questions about alternatives per se.

Before reviewing some questions connected with alternatives, one point will bear repeating, namely, that the quest for family improvement and the development of proposals for modifying family or marital relations are not really new phenomena. Many of the seemingly "revolutionary" proposals currently under discussion are found to have existed in practice or theory in much earlier times.[2] Polygyny is not new, nor is the idea of companionate marriage. Communality in sex relations and in child-rearing also can be found recorded in the history of past epochs. There are, of course, some differences in the motives and conditions associated with utopian arrangements in the past as compared with current alternatives. One such difference is exemplified by the presence of a strong religious-mystical component in many utopian ventures in the past. Most persons experimenting today with, say communal arrangements, need no justification on religious grounds nor do they feel any need to make the experiment a reflection of "divine will." Another difference lies in the conception of who would benefit by the new arrangements. Experimentation in the past tended to focus on the alleged benefits for the group, or society, or humankind; in contrast, much of today's experimentation in variant family or marital forms and relations seems designed to enhance primarily the worth and functioning of the individual. Finally, in contrast to most proposals of the past, a particular variant marriage form today is likely to be held forth merely as an example of but one alternative mode of living; no one form is seen as "the" way for all people. The current potential for cultural pluralism in American society thus enhances the emergence and organized promotion of variation in marital forms and processes.

In earlier units, we considered alternatives in the major areas of interaction encountered in marital partnership. Without reviewing all those proposals specifically, we will simply consider some general questions which persistently arise, or perhaps ought to, in discussions of alternatives for contemporary marriage. Let us consider these:

1. *The question of feasibility and acceptability.* The *feasibility* question asks, "Is it workable or can the alternative form be implemented in real life?" The *acceptability* question asks whether community or societal norms and organization will tolerate this variation from the traditional and whether those who participate in it will be harassed so extensively as to cancel the benefits from the alternative lifestyle.

2. *The question of expectation levels.* In general, Americans tend toward high levels of aspiration in many aspects of familial experience — including marriage. The correspondingly high possibility for disillusionment constitutes a serious problem. Experimentation with alternatives to conventional marriage is not immune to this problem. For example, to expect that communal child-rearing will solve all problems typically associated with parent-child communication, disproportionate parenting responsibilities for females, adequate socialization, etc. virtually ensures that this variant form will bear much too heavy a burden and will likely be disillusioning to participants. A related question could ask, "Are the expectations engendered by the alternative form realistic?"

3. *The question of shortcomings in theory or practice.* Many of the currently-discussed alternatives for marriage emerged presumably as reflections of new viewpoints and philosophies fostered largely by the sexual equality and human potentials movements. Thus, individuals who are sensitive to the promise of these movements are likely to be serious disillusioned if, as a participant in an experimental life-style, they encounter sexism, vestiges of the possession syndrome, or stringent group pressures to conform. One writer who spent nearly a year seeking "the better life" in hippie communes concluded dolefully that, "The major problems of the commune were male chauvinism, insensitivity, and stagnation."[3]

These are but three fairly general questions; substantive questions are probably as numerous as the alternatives themselves. Maybe, in short, the questions of over-arching importance should be: "Do they work?," and "What is the *least* we should expect from an alternative for conventional marriage?" Relative to the latter question is a comment by human potentials leader Herbert Otto who concludes that ". . . the objective of *any* model is to provide both an atmosphere and a sustenance of loving, caring, and adventuring. This makes human growth, actualization, and unfoldment possible."[4]

The topic of *change* in marriage and the family is also confronted by many questions. From one point of view, it appears that drastic change is occurring in familial patterns. From another perspective, it is contended that radical change is really not taking place, that most of our appraisals of great change stem from our lack of attention to stable factors in family life. In other words, we may be overly sensitized to change, since it has immediate impact on us as individuals. Since some general considerations regarding social and familial change were reviewed in Unit 2, we will not explore the topic to any great length here. However, at least one major principle could be stated; namely, at any period in history, the forms of marriage and familial interaction are much more a transitive process than a finished product. Thus, a fundamental question must be, "From what to what?" Numerous questions could be raised regarding *capacity* for change, both in the social arrangements constituting marriage and in the values of individuals who form partnerships. Miscellaneous questions can be cited to illustrate the broad ramifications of changes in familial styles. Can change effectively occur in marital forms without corresponding change in marital processes? Is change induced from without more or less effective than change patterns built upon processes normally occurring within the family group? A related question is, "How extensively can the state or the community function in the production of socially-approved change in family forms and processes? What aspects of change in marriage and family life are likely to come about as a consequence of "revolutionary" forces, which are more likely to evince "evolutionary" patterns of development? Such questions could go on almost endlessly. Rather than pursue them, however, we will comment briefly on the significance of prevailing attitudes toward changes in familial patterns.

We have discussed resistance to change in earlier units; for various reasons, as we saw, opposition to purposive change (in the form of alternatives for contemporary marriage) ranges from disdain to destructive or coercive actions against their proponents. But since change in every aspect of life — including familial — seems inevitable, perhaps it is not so important merely to recognize and bewail the existence of opposition to any kind of change. For in terms of the survival of marriage and family life as a source of meaningful existence, the crucial factor may well lie in the society's positive acceptance of purposive change. In other words, a society can optimize its capacity for building a truly loving, caring family system ". . . only by welcoming innovation, experimentation, and change. . . ." Thus, survival of the family as a meaningful, worthwhile unit implies constructive change in our institutions and in our social relationships. For "What will destroy us is not change, but our inability to change — both as individuals and as a social system."[5]

The emphasis of most materials in this book has been on understanding and coping with marital encounters in the "here and now," rather than on speculation as to what the future holds. Regardless of the term used to describe the activity — forecasting, secular prophecy, futuriz-ing — attempts to predict what lies ahead for marriage and the family have become common in family textbooks and journals. The scope of "futurology" is, of course, not limited to studies of marriage and the family.[6] Most major institutions and the society as a whole have been scrutinized by the futurologist.[7] Let us turn briefly to some speculation on the nature and functions of forecasting.

According to the arguments of some futurologists, we could reason-ably conclude that much of today's discussion on the future of mar-riage reflects the deep extent to which *change is desired* in the forms and processes currently typical of marriage. Indeed, the construction and testing of alternatives in the present probably reflects an impetus gained by looking ahead to what marriage ideally could be with im-proved relationships and greater satisfaction for individuals. In de Jouvenal's words,

> Time future is the domain able to receive as "possibles" those representations which elsewhere would be "false." And from the future in which we now place them, these possibles "beckon" for us to make them real.

From this perspective, then, ". . . the future is the domain into which a man has projected, and in which he now contemplates, the possible he wishes to make real. . . ."[8] Margaret Mead makes somewhat the same point in a discussion which emphasizes the potential of the "here and now" orientation of youth for infusion of positive change into an adult-controlled society.

> If we are to build a prefigurative culture in which the past is instrumental rather than coercive, we must change the location of the future. Here again we can take a cue from the young who seem to want instant Utopias. They say: The Future is Now. This seems unreasonable and impetuous, and in some of the demands they make it is unrealizable in concrete detail; but here again, I think they give us the way to reshape our thinking. We must place the future, like the unborn child in the womb of a woman, within a community of men, women, and children, among us, already here, already to be nourished and succored and protected, al-ready in need of things for which, if they are not prepared before it is born, it will be too late. So, as the young say, The Future is Now.[9]

If the lifestyles of marriage in the future are seen, then, as rich in freedom, openness, choice, equality, and rationality, the dimensions of marriage in the near future — and increasingly the present — will be progressively affected by emergent alternatives which bring such "fu-tures" into contemporary reality, even if in limited form.

Before turning to our readings, we can summarize a few central assumptions about marriage which have emerged in earlier discussion. If we accept the principle that our knowledge of the future is inversely proportional to the societal rate of change, such assumptions may be fairly adequate forecasts. (1) Personal happiness, or the quest for it, will continue to be the most dominant individual factor in the formation, the quality, and the stability of marriage. (2) There will be an increase in the utilization of objective research data in developing marital strengths and assets and a corollary increase in planned, purposive change in the marital institution. (3) Marriage will predominantly continue to take the form of a dyadic partnership, but this form will be only one of a variety of forms which will be possible within the law. (4) Finally, it seems safe to forecast that marriage as an intimate, committed partnership, is here to stay. And, if we accept family sociologist F. Ivan Nye's conclusion, we can anticipate that the familial group:

> . . . will become an even more competent instrument for meeting human needs, and as a consequence, will become more highly and generally valued throughout society in that fascinating and ever more rapidly changing world of tomorrow.[10]

REFERENCES

1. Landis, Paul H. *Making the Most of Marriage,* 4th Edit. (New York: Appleton-Century-Crofts, 1970), p. 14.

2. Review of pertinent materials can be found in: Gerald R. Leslie, *The Family in Social Context,* 2nd Edit. (New York: Oxford University Press, 1973), "Utopian Family Experiments," pp. 123-151; David A. Schulz, *The Changing Family: Its Functions and Future* (New York: Prentice-Hall, 1972), "Pathways in Utopia," pp. 379-409.

3. Estellachild, Vivian. "Hippie Communes," *Women: A Journal of Liberation* 2 (Winter, 1971): 40-43.

4. Otto, Herbert A. (ed.) *The Family in Search of A Future* (New York: Appleton-Century-Crofts, 1970), p. 9.

5. Otto, *op. cit.,* p. 9.

6. Cf: John N. Edwards, "The Future of the Family Revisited," *Journal of Marriage and the Family* 29 (August, 1967): 505-511; Ivan F. Nye, "Values Family, and A Changing Society, *Journal of Marriage and the Family* 29 (May, 1967): 241-248; Robert R. Parke, Jr. and Paul Glick, "Prospective Changes in Marriage and the Family," *Journal of Marriage and the Family* 29 (May, 1967): 249-256; Carle C. Zimmerman, "The Future of the Family in America," The 1971 Burgess Award Address, *Journal of Marriage and the Family* 34 (May, 1972): 323-333; Jessie Bernard, *The Future of Marriage* (New York: World Pub. Co., 1972).

7. For a listing of 50 books about the future, see Alvin Toffler, *The Futurists* (New York: Random House, 1972), pp. 311-313.

8. de Jouvenal, Bertrand. *The Art of Conjecture* (New York: Basic Books, Inc., 1967), pp. 27, 28.

9. Mead, Margaret. *Culture and Commitment* (New York: Doubleday & Co., Inc., 1970), p. 175.

10. Nye, F. Ivan. "Values, Family, and A Changing Society," *Journal of Marriage and the Family* 29 (May 1967): 241-248.

If You Look to Marriage As an Instrument for Personal Growth

MICHAEL KORDA

The institution of marriage is everywhere on the defensive. They young rebel against it, women's liberationists attack it, exponents of liberated sexuality from Hugh Hefner to R.D. Laing recoil at its implications of sexual exclusivity. Even those who *are* married deny it by the simple process of divorcing at a rapidly increasing rate. And yet people still marry. The old rituals of the ring, the exchange of vows, the religious blessing, still hold their magic power, even though they are now very frequently the prelude to a short union and quick divorce.

The radical and even liberal attitude toward marriage today recalls St. Paul's Epistle to Corinthians: "It is better to marry than to burn," an early and pessimistic view of the state. He meant of course that a life of chastity and prayer was the proper state for man (possibly even woman) but that human weakness being what it is, there existed an outlet for mankind's carnal instincts that was acceptable to God though with some reluctance. The early Church blessed marriage but without enthusiasm—an attitude which survives today in our secular view of the relationships between the sexes, though our point of view has changed diametrically. Among Christians in St. Paul's time sexual relationships were reason enough to damnation, and marriage a haven for those weak enough to indulge in them. In our day, of course, we worship sexual relationships, and marriage is seen often as a haven for those whom cannot compete successfully in the Darwinian struggle of sexual freedom.

St. Paul being an apostle naturally had a secondary meaning when he made his famous comment. To be married was to involve yourself in the world—a man with a wife, a house, children could hardly keep his mind on God. Therefore, it became necessary to create a Church that would keep its mind on God for him. Those who prayed in monasteries in the Dark Ages did not pray for themselves but for the souls of those who had elected to live in the world, with all its moral dangers. Now, to young radicals, marriage seems a similarly and anachronistic flight from reality. Virtue consists of immersing yourself in the problems of other people, the ghettos, Vietnam, the Palestinian refugees, Chicano grape pickers; to marry today is turn away from the world to opt for your own small fortress of illusory security. Like St. Paul, young radicals see the world as a dangerous place, but they find their religion in its dangers, in which they rather resemble the early Church Fathers, who had the singular good fortune to be both bearded prophets and the establishment at the same time. Is it moral to settle down to the cultivation of one's own garden as Voltaire put it in *Candide,* while the world around one burns with war and injustice? Is marriage relevant? What is it all about?

—A married woman in her thirties says, "I've had it. All my husband does is work and when he isn't working he has this *image* of the Beautiful Life, and it's my job to provide it; the right kind of pepper in the peppermill, *fresh* herbs for the omelette, the lapels on his suits rolled, not pressed, flat, I'm not a person, I'm a *service.* The children are old enough to survive a divorce, and that's what I'm getting. There's a man who loves me and doesn't fly into a rage if his eggs are cooked thirty seconds too long. That's where I'm going and I don't know if we'll marry. Maybe I never want to be married again."

—A noted young woman married with one child, "It's not that I don't *love* him but up to three years ago I had a *life* sometimes lousy, sometimes great, and now I'm trapped like a held *prisoner* by this *stranger* who wants to go camping when I want to go to the beach, who simply goes to bed with me because that's the way things are instead of having to talk, compete, win to treat me as I were a human being. I mean when I worked in New York things were sometimes terrible. I went through some really bad scenes, sure but they were *my* scenes and I met some really terrific people as well as some bastards. And now there's this guy with whom I'm supposed to spend the rest of my life, and he doesn't even know who I *am* or care that I've given up my music because of the baby, because what counts for *us* is his law degree. I keep telling myself one day I'll wake up and be free, the rest of my life isn't going to be this. Who is this stranger whose bed I'm sleeping in, who am I and what the hell happened to me?"

—A noted woman, with five (yes, five) children, "I thought we had a *marriage,* and love was part of the package, along with sex, children, the mortgage on the house. Then he quit his job as a journalist, wrote a successful book, and suddenly he's off on publicity trips, and I know, I *know* he's sleeping around. I mean, why wouldn't he, all those twenty-two-year-old Sarah Lawrence girls saying, 'Oh, tell me more about the radical consensus' with five inches of thigh showing. Okay, sleeping around is sleeping around—maybe I would myself, if I weren't stuck to the kids and the house—but then he gets involved with this girl, younger, prettier than I am, one of those publishing secretaries who lives in a West Side one-room apartment with one good dress, ten pairs of pantie-hose, a subscription to *The New York Review of Books,* and a cat. Suddenly there isn't any marriage, the kids would be happier if we faced our problems frankly, all those years of paying the mortgage off and making ends meet don't count a good God damn and neither do I. I mean I'm not an idiot or a prude. If he wanted to sleep around I don't say I'd have been happy but I thought we had a *marriage*, that we had something here that counted more than a quick lay. He says he has 'grown', she's smarter than I am, she's been to parties with Norman Mailer, she understands his work. She's twenty years younger and hasn't had five children, and didn't see him through the years when he was nobody. His success gives him the right to have a younger body in bed with him that's all. But then what's marriage *for*? It's not *my* fault we decided to make a life together and had children and bought a house we couldn't afford. I thought that was life, but it turns out that for him it was just an *experience*, part of becoming a person, he says. Well, I'm a person and look where it got me!"

"Becoming a Person. . ."

Until recently, people divorced each other for the traditional reasons of incompatibility: "Your Honor: He beats me . . . She drinks like a fish and hides the bottles all over the house . . . He's impotent . . . She's frigid . . . We haven't got a marriage." The notion that there exists some God-given right to be a "person" is a relatively new one and has only recently filtered down to ordinary people. As late as the nineteenth century, the egocentric pursuit of one's own individuality at the expense of other people was the privilege of the very rich or the very talented—everybody else was expected to take his place in the hierarchy of work and marriage and counted himself lucky, no doubt, to survive.

Ordinary people of all social classes were horrified by Lord Byron's behavior, for example, but doubtless felt that a man who was at once a peer and a great poet was entitled to a certain measure of irresponsibility and eccentricity. A great poet might well feel himself trapped by marrriage and Lord Byron would probably have been forgiven for separating from his wife if it had not been generally believed that he was leaving her because he was in love with his own half-sister. What people emphatically did *not* believe was that one was entitled to behave like Byron without Byron's talent. And that is the problem of our age when a remarkable combination of Freudian simplification and democratic attitudes have made the sorrows of Werther and the agonies of Childe Harold, all the Romantic *Sturm und Drang* of the search for oneself, available to millions of perfectly ordinary people whose potential for "human growth" is perhaps not as great as they have been led to believe, and who might be better off making what they *have* work rather than torturing themselves with the thought that they ought to become something else.

Now, people get divorces because they feel that marriage is preventing them from "growing." This feeling has become so widespread that divorce and re-marriage are becoming a *means* of growth—those who have gone through the experience look down on those who haven't. As one man said, "I didn't *know* myself at all until I left Nico. When we went through the whole business of the divorce, I began to understand her and our feelings about each other for the first time. Now I think I'm a better person for the experience and she is too. We were stifling each other. I don't regret my first marriage because the experience made it possible for me to really *love* my second wife, to relate to her as a person, I'm a better husband, a better father, I can see the mistakes I made last time and I know our baby is going to be brought up in a different way from the children of my marriage to Nico. It's a very maturing experience." Yes, but to the outside observer the children of the first marriage do not seem very happy, Nico is stuck with two growing boys, a small apartment, alimony, and it is *she* who is paying the price of her husband's experience and new "maturity." If he has "grown," she has shrunk.

If you look to marriage as an instrument for personal growth and character development you will I fear be disappointed. Marriage is a tribal and social institution and while its customs are capable of infinite variation—there is no reason why men shouldn't do housework, why women can't be the wage-earners, no law that says a marriage must be an instrument of male chauvinism—the obligations and the purpose of marriage are precisely and rigorously defined by tradition, by necessity and in the words of the marriage ceremony itself, not to speak of the Bible's forceful simplicity on the subject: *Therefore shall a man leave his father and mother and shall cleave into his wife and they shall be one flesh.*

Living Beyond Eden

Women's liberations will be happy to note that God was less than explicit in defining the roles of the sexes in the institution he had just invented for Adam and Eve. What he was saying in effect, was that life was going to be very harsh out of Eden, and that the only way to survive would be for a man and woman to share the hardships together splitting the task of survival in whatever way might seem best suited to the circumstances. Among the Pygmies of the Congo, who are gatherers of fruit and seeds, women and men are equal, share the same tasks and live pretty much free from any form of male chauvinism. In hunting tribes, where man has traditionally been the adventurer, the warrior, the killer of food, woman is relegated to domestic concerns, but is not thought of as being any the less important for that: the functions are considered separate but equal. The notion of woman's inferiority is, paradoxically enough, a modern one. The primitive man and woman married because marriage created a unit that enabled husband, wife and children to survive in a harsh and hostile world. They created a unit of survival. There was nothing romantic about it, though romance need not have been excluded: it was simply a pragmatic and defensive mechanism.

We have come to think of "freedom" as being a natural and necessary goal, and if you define freedom as the right to do just what you want to do, to be yourself at any cost to others, then marriage is automatically reduced to a claustrophobic system of restraints. But men and women do not give up "freedom" when they marry in tribal societies. The right to be alone, to do whatever one pleases, to avoid responsibility, is quite simply the right to die—to have to fight other males for the possession of a woman, to lie uncared for when one is ill, to die of starvation when one is too old to hunt or plant or search for food. If St. Paul was right to say that it is better to marry than to burn, a tribesman might say with equal truth, "It is better to marry the wrong woman than to die alone in the wilderness."

Today, our wealth, our complex society, our institutions, all contrive to make it possible for a man to live alone if he wants to, and the same is true for a woman. Blue Cross will care for you if you are sick, the dry cleaner will repair your clothes, food need not be hunted, planted, gathered, the police are paid to protect you from the enemy, Social Security will look after you marginally in your old age. You can, if you like, be "free." But to what extent? And is such a "freedom" really desirable? Hardly. Our cities are full of miserable and unhappy people who have escaped from the obligations and responsibilities of that ancient social contract, or failed to live up to them, and while they may not be starving to death, they scarcely seem any the happier for their freedom.

Many of the young see little real meaning in marriage today because there is simply no reason for them to be married. They see no valid reason why people who love one another shouldn't live together without going through a ceremony or accepting the whole complex legal situation that marriage represents. For the Third Party to every marriage is the State, which has set up an endless amount of laws defining the rights and obligations of marriage, laws which may seem meaningless when one signs the marriage certificate, but assume weightier meaning ten years later when one is thinking of divorcing. It is then that the true nature of marriage asserts itself forcibly: it is a binding legal contract between a man, a woman and the State, and it is wise not to forget this, for the good reason that the State won't.

So long as you live in the Eden defined as being young, solvent, healthy and free, marriage is probably a mistake. Marriage properly comes with the first intimation of mortality. We may hope to share our pleasures in marrying, and if we are lucky we do, but we have contracted to share our pain, our defeats, our sickness and our old age as well. In effect, we are mortgaging a certain amount of our freedom and our individuality in the present against some future repayment, agreeing to pay for certain pleasures and shared experiences now by devotion in the future, when the bargain, as in all contracts, may not look so good in hindsight. For marriage is the realization of a paradox: life is a tragic experience that can be enjoyed. We might have been happy alone in Eden, but cannot survive alone outside it.

THE HEARTLESS SOCIETY

The customs of marriage can change, should change, for women in a post-industrial society can hardly be expected to live with the restraints and in the traditional roles of a Victorian marriage. Nor is there any sense in a man playing out the role of an autocrat/breadwinner if in fact his wife can go out and earn twice as much money as he does. To turn away from marriage itself, however, is another matter altogether, with far more dangerous implications. This makes it all the more important to proceed as soon as possible to restructure the institution so that it fits our needs, rather than being a Procrustean bed into which we must all fit.

The importance of marriage has nothing to do with your happiness or mine, and not much to do with the way in which we choose to define the rules of marriage. Our human society is founded on the *idea* of marriage. Even today, it performs those timeless functions that the human condition imposes. It is the primary institution we have created to cope with sexual needs and competition, to provide for the rearing and education of children, to look after the old and the sick as if they were people instead of abstract social problems. It is, in short, the basic building block of society, the institution where all problems begin and end.

The more we shift the responsibilities of life from ourselves to the community at large, the more we give up the right to define the nature of our society. The family as an institution has come in for much abuse recently, some of it well deserved, but if we abandon it, we shall have to invent something to take its place, and the chances are that it will not be replaced by communal living or creative anarchy but by "1984" of "Brave New World." When we are sick, we do not want to be passed into the hands of people who do not know who we are, who care for us without caring *about* us, and on the most selfish level, all marriages are attempts to carve out a niche of security in the blank wall of an increasingly depersonalized society. Marriage implies the recognition that human nature is inconstant and untrustworthy, that promises are not enough, that in an accidental and slippery world we are willing to make an attempt at stability.

An observer of The American Way of Love, recently returned from a trip around the country, reports that most of the women she interviewed were sleeping around with men other than their husbands, and that few of them had anything good to say about their marriages or their spouses. This is depressing, but hardly surprising. Marriage is the most existential of institutions, but people have never managed to treat it existentially. We have mythologized it, merchandised it, destroyed its real meaning by making it a national illusion — love, "togetherness," his and hers bath towels, all the tawdry commercialization that surrounds the marital state in twentieth century America.

"Sometimes I just sit in the bathroom and cry. It's not that I don't love him, I guess I do, really I do, but we've been married nearly two years now, and I still love this other man. Sometimes I just shut myself up in this fantasy world — not sex fantasies, you know, just fantasies of being someone else, somewhere else. It's not that I'm not happy, a lot of the time I guess I *am*, I'm just not sure that this is what I wanted. I don't think he understands who I am, and when I'm in one room reading, and he's in the other one building something, I suddenly find myself thinking he doesn't know me, I don't know him, I wish I were dead."

Our culture has trained us to look for the wrong things in marriage: passion and sentiment, instead of affection and care; excitement, instead of stability; individual gratification, instead of the difficult task of building a life together and creating a world of one's own making, however small. Above all, marriage has no room for fantasies: by its very nature it deals with very basic realities of life — sex, birth, age, death — and married people very soon find out that they cannot afford to have fantasies about each other. In marriage, as in some dangerous sports, it is essential to make the running with someone you trust. You may not trust your husband's fidelity should he be tempted on a business trip; he may not trust your financial judgment (or vice versa) — but can you trust each other over the long haul of a married life, in, as they say, the crunch? It's a long trip, after all, meant to last a lifetime (though that's less and less the case now that marriages evaporate, unable to survive the heat of our desire to grow our characters, our personalities, as if they were exotic hot-house orchids); and fantasies are no substitute for shared interests, the hand that heals, the voice that tells you you're a human being when the whole world tells you you're not.

We are all able to recognize the heartlessness of modern society — the corroded and decaying cities, the hopeless poverty, the hypocrisy on a national scale, the sense of impermanency, the alienation — but the institutions of our government have perhaps grown beyond the size that would render them susceptible to humane reform. It is the ancient institution of marriage and family that calls for reform and offers hope, and because of its small size, its personal nature, its *scale,* it allows for an extraordinary creativity and endless innovation. It has been said that every marriage is a battle, in which our friends, our acquaintances, or family, are waiting to see which side will win, ready to applaud the victor and damn the loser, ready, if necessary, to spur on the combat if it seems likely to bore everybody by flagging. Doubtless this is true to a certain extent, but in a larger sense marriage is a social experiment whose effects reach out far beyond the confines of an apartment, a hut, a house, to touch the larger world. Just as Marshall McLuhan sees each television set as a link in a vast chain of global communications, so each marriage is a cell in the complex honeycomb of our society, exerting its influence on the whole, rendering more humane and sensible the nature of our national life, filtering politics through domestic discussion, putting the State's decisions about education or health care to the test of several million semi-autonomous and very different human groupings, reducing great social decisions to the practical, family level.

MAKING IT WORK

For these reasons, I am disenchanted with the idea of "alternatives" to marriage. Marriage is power, and if we give up those powers to determine our lives within our own social unit, they will be transferred to a larger entity. The commune of the American young is a form of anarchy, attractive as an idea, but not very practical as a social organization for a major industrial state. Societies that opt for communal living rarely do so out of any desire to give people greater freedom. Israel's *kibbutzim* impose their own very strict rules and philosophy on the *kibbutznik,* and while these are voluntarily accepted, they are nevertheless highly restrictive. Communal living in China, the country that has taken the most ambitious steps in abolishing family and regulating marriage, is firmly directed from above. Whatever the faults of the modern American idea of marriage, it seems more viable than the alternatives that are being developed elsewhere.

The major factor is, of course, *children.* Do you want them? Do you *need* them? If you have them, do you want to bring them up as reflections of yourselves, or to pass them over to a larger entity? Without children, a marriage is merely a legal compact in which both parties look to each for protection and shelter, a very sensible arrangement for all those who would just as soon not leave their emotional and sexual needs to the chancey business of meeting the right person for the night in a swinging singles bar, and who, if they pool their belongings and their hopes, would very sensibly like to have something in writing to confirm the arrangement.

With children, marriage assumes a very much more crucial importance. "Who has children has given hostages to fortune." Children tie us down, force us to behave as if our lives had a permanency, even if, at heart, we suspect they don't. We are connected to the notion of immortality by our children, forced to accept that our very importance as parents is the sign of our mortality.

The strength of marriage lies in the fact that it enables us to cope with so complex a phenomenon as the bearing and raising of children. I don't mean that we have to have them, necessarily — the population crisis would seem to indicate the contrary. Nor do I mean that marriage must inevitably lead to a woman's accepting the traditional role of child-carer. But marriage as an institution is flexible enough to deal with an infinite variety of problems, including that of reproduction, which is more than can be said of most of the artificial institutions we have created in the centuries since the decline of tribal living.

For two people to attempt to make a life together seems to me on the whole a good and hopeful pledge, a vote of confidence in our ability to survive somehow. For them to bring up children is a triumph of hope over realism, given the state of the world today, but without such decisions we may as well give up and settle for anarchy, in which the strongest will thrive and the weak go to the wall. What is needed then is not the abolition of marriage, but a sensible *progression* of relationships. My own theory is a simple one: People who have no intention of bearing children should be able to marry without assuming all the crippling obligations of the current marriage and divorce laws. They might be able to pledge themselves to a lesser form of marriage for a limited period of time, say five years. During this time, their rights and obligations would be laid down, but would be of a less drastic nature — that is, divorce should be easier and less catastrophic, requiring merely a hearing at which they express their desire to separate, an equitable sharing of their property, and a reasonable assurance of support for a limited period. After five years they would automatically have the choice of escalating their marriage into a more permanent and binding relationship, and this agreement could then be reviewed every five years. However, if they want to have children, they must accept a far more stringent definition of marriage, enforceable by either party and by the State until the children have reached a certain age, unless there are exceptional circumstances that mitigate against this: cruelty, incompatibility, insanity, non-support, etc., the "traditional" reasons for divorce in most states today.

Within any of these categories of marriage, there should be the maximum opportunity for self-definition, each partner being allowed to work out a relationship that provides for equality and a rational sharing of tasks and responsibilities.

In short, a man and woman should be able to *test* their marriage before making it permanent, should be able to accept a greater responsibility toward each other as they pass through the various stages of marriage, should be given every chance to settle on the *right* marriage. Once they have decided to have children, however, they must be presumed to have established the conditions necessary for raising children — they should not be in a position to have children, then walk away from them.

In the words of one young woman, "I thought having a baby would fix things up, but it hasn't changed anything. Things were bad between us — nothing terrible, you understand, just the general feeling that we really didn't like each other much, that I was a drag on him, from his point of view; that I'd given up someone who loved me and a life of my own, from my point of view, and that somehow adding the two of us together made us less than one person. So now we have a kid, and the other guy has a kid, and we're all stuck. I don't want to take our child away from my husband, the other guy doesn't want to take his away from his wife, and probably doesn't want to have someone else's child added to his problem either, and all of a sudden we're parents without ever having become *people*."

The problem of marriage is not so much to decide who will do the dishes and wash the underwear (though I do not underrate such domestic problems), as to prevent people from accepting its full obligations until they are ready to do so, giving them a chance to find the right person, the right relationship, the right situation, before signing on the dotted line for that most demanding of promises, the marriage oath.

As for the institution itself, it looks like it is surviving somehow. A couple in Virginia have just been married in an open-air ceremony in a field full of flowers, with an organic wedding feast. A young couple have recently been married by a nine-year-old boy. Girls who have reached the age of nineteen having known few clothes other than bell-bottom jeans and T-shirts, are even now shopping for wedding dresses. Even those who are divorced show their confidence in the institution by re-marrying at a dizzying rate. There is hope.

As one young married said, "I always put it down, but now I'm married, and it isn't what I thought it was going to be at all. I'm on the defensive about a lot of things, but it's just different than living with someone. You live with someone and you look around for someone better, it's unconscious, automatic. But once you're married, you walk away from the world a little bit, you slow down, you start to say, OK, I put myself here, can I make it work? I don't know how to put it — it's, like, *reality*."

Marriage of the Future: Revolutionary or Evolutionary Change?

DAVID H. OLSON

*The land of marriage has this peculiarity,
that strangers are desirous of inhabiting it,
whilst its natural inhabitants would willingly
be banished from thence.–Montigue.*

The paradoxical nature of marriage has intrigued and perplexed scholars and laymen alike for centuries. Psychologists such as John B. Watson in 1927 prophesized that marriage would not survive by 1977. About the same time, sociologists like Pitirim Sorokin and Carl Zimmerman also predicted its demise. (Barnard, 1970)

A rather common statement one hears nowadays is that "The last fifty years have apparently changed the marriage relation from a permanent and lifelong state to a union existing for the pleasure of the parties. The change thus swiftly wrought is so revolutionary, involving the very foundations of human society, that we must believe it to be the result not of any temporary conditions." (Thwing and Thwing in Reiss, 1971, 317) The only surprising thing about this statement is that it was made in 1887.

In spite of all the predictions regarding the collapse of the institution of marriage, it continues to survive. In fact, marriage still continues to be the most popular voluntary institution in our society with only three to four percent of the population never marrying at least once. And national statistics on marriage indicate that an increasing number of eligible individuals are getting married, rather than remaining single. (Vital Statistics, 1970) For the third consecutive year, in 1970 there were over two million marriages in the country. The rate of marriage has also continued to increase so that the 1970 rate of 10.7 marriages per 1000 individuals was the highest annual rate since 1950. There has also been very little change in the median age of first marriage between 1950 and 1970, 22.8 to 23.2 years for males, and 20.3 to 20.8 years for females, respectively. (Population Census, 1971)

While getting married has increased in popularity, so has the number of individuals who have chosen to terminate their marriage contract. In 1970, there were 715,000 divorces and annulments in the United States, which is almost double the number in 1950 (385,000). Since 1967, the divorce rate has increased by 30 percent. (Vital Statistics, Vol. 19, 1971) The rate has progressively moved toward a cumulative rate, one divorce for every four marriages. The rate of divorce among those married under 18 is close to 50 percent. The ratio of divorced individuals compared to those married has increased in the last ten years. In 1960, there were 28 divorced men for every 1000 men married, and 35 in 1970. Comparable figures for females were 42 in 1960, and 60 in 1970. (Population Census, 1971) The number of divorces for married women over 15 years of age changed from 9.3 per 1000 in 1959 to 13.4 in 1969 (Vital Statistics, Vol. 20, 1971) Also, the average length of marriage has declined to an average of 7.1 years.

THE DATING-MATING GAME

In spite of the fact that quantitatively marriage continues to be very popular, the quality of the husband-wife relationship is often far less advantageous than individuals either expect or desire. One of the reasons that the marriage institution does not live up to its expectations is because of the many myths and unrealistic expectations that individuals bring to marriage. Another major factor that contributes to problems in marriage is the lack of preparation that society provides for this major decision in life. Whereas one expects that individuals will take years of schooling to adequately prepare for their occupation choice, it is assumed that individuals need no guidance in making what is probably the most significant decision in their life. For unlike a job, or even an occupation, which is relatively easy to change, it still is legally and emotionally much more difficult to change, or at least dissolve, a marital relationship. Individuals are given few useful guidelines to follow and then wonder why marriages are not as fulfilling as expected or desired.

From the vantage point of society, the present dating system which has evolved in this country is successful in that it effectively places most people into marriage at least once. But one of its major limitations is that it is too effective in that it pushes many into marriage who would not, and perhaps should not, get married. In other words, there are rather strong implicit sanctions against anyone who would prefer to remain single. Society does this by labeling individuals as deviant and maladjusted if they do not conform to societal expectations in this regard. The continuous push by parents and friends alike is rather persuasive and very effective. A more complete discussion of the third parties' influence on marriage is described in greater detail in a recent paper. (Ryder, Kafka and Olson, 1970)

This encouragement of heterosexual involvement begins so early that it is becoming more realistic to talk about dating beginning as early as elementary school. Broderick (1968) has documented a rather advanced level of heterosexual development and activity in fifth and sixth grades. Many children (84 percent of the females and 62 percent of the males) at this stage were already accepting the idea that they would eventuallly be married. Also, a high percentage (74 percent) of those wanting to eventually marry already has a girlfriend or boyfriend, and of those already having a friend, 66 percent reported having been in love.

What has developed, therefore, in this society is a *laissez faire* approach to the mate-selection process and this has helped to turn the process into a dating-mating game. The goal or major objective in this game is finding a suitable marital partner. The rules of the game are usually implicit rather than explicit and this results in a friendly confrontation, with increasing sexual intimacy (which is used as one of the most lethal weapons). The participants use strategies and counterstrategies within the limits of the unwritten rules in order to attain their goal, i.e., a suitable marital partner. While dating has turned out to be fun for some, it is often a hurtful and destructive game for many.

Although dating has been successful from a functional point of view, of facilitating the mate selection process and placing individuals into marriage, it has failed in a most essential way. It has failed because it does not assist couples in learning how to develop and maintain vital and meaningful relationships. Only recently have more of the youth become aware of the time inadequacies of the current dating system which has evolved in this country. They have become aware of the superficiality of dating and the over-emphasis and misuse of the purely sexual aspects of these relationships. As a result, there are increasing numbers who are trying to break away from the traditional dating-mating game by living together, either as couples or in groups. But simply living together is not *alone* going to prepare them to learn how to relate meaningfully, to adequately cope with differences and conflict, or to deal with long-term commitment. However, it is becoming increasingly clear that alternative models of mate selection are needed to prepare couples for lifelong commitment.

Fortunately, there are a few innovative programs that are just beginning to be used to train couples in more functional communication skills. (Miller and Nunnally, 1970) In some ways, however, this is really like giving birth control pills to a woman who just became pregnant—it is too little, too late. Dramatic changes are needed in the education and emotional preparation provided and changes in the social climate that continues to pressure individuals into marriage so early, so unaware, and so unprepared.

DEMYTHOLOGIZING THE MYTHS ABOUT MARRIAGE

One of the reasons that the marriage institution does not live up to its expectations is because of the many myths and unrealistic expectations that individuals bring to marriage. One of the most prevalent myths about marriage is the belief that "if an intimate relationship is *not* good, it will *spontaneously* improve with time." This myth not only leads couples into marriage but may keep many couples together in anticipation of change in their relationship. Initially, dating couples begin by saying, "If only we go steady, things will improve and he (or she) won't act this way." At a later stage they say, "If my steady and I were having difficulties, engagement might help resolve some of our problems." The same theme continues during engagement with the assumption that "marriage will help change or reform my fiancé." However, most newlyweds soon find greater difficulty in marriage than they antici- pated, for not only do their past problems continue to exist, usually in greater intensity than before, but they also encounter new areas of conflict which result from living together. And many couples then feel that: "Our relationship isn't very fulfilling now that we are married, but if we only had a child, that would bring us closer, and resolve many of our difficulties." I have even heard couples optimistically carry this theme further and admit that: "This one child had *not* helped our marriage, but if we had another child, our relationship would really improve." In general, all these myths are examples of the general theme that a relationship will spontaneously improve with increasing commitment and time.

Several other common myths have been described by Lederer and Jackson (1968) in their book on the *Mirages of Marriage.* Myths abound regarding the relationship between love and marriage such as: "People marry because they are in love," "Most married people love each other," "Love is necessary for a satisfactory marriage," and "All prob- lems can be solved if you're really in love."

In search of a fulfilling life, many individuals falsely assume that "marriage is easy, the difficulty is finding the right person." Further, "who they marry is more important than when they marry," and therefore, "there is one best person for them to marry." They also assume that "the only way to be truly happy is to marry." They wish- fully assume that "marriage will alleviate their loneliness." What they do not realize is that marriage often intensifies rather than eases loneliness. It is important to realize that if individuals cannot live with themselves, they will probably have considerable difficulty trying to live with someone else. (Ryder, 1970) Couples also assume that their partner will be able to satisfy all their needs" and, therefore, "the more time and activities that are spent together, the better the marriage relationship."

Once couples begin having difficulty in marriage they falsely assume "that patterns of behavior and interaction they develop are easy to change" and "that a quarrel or disagreement can only be detrimental to their relationship." Many further maintain that "it is best *not* to express negative feelings about one's spouse." Couples assume that "if their spouse loves them, they will know what they are feeling or what they want." When marital problems become more extreme many believe that "for the sake of the children, keeping a conflicted family together is preferable to divorce."

In regard to their sexual relationship, many couples falsely assume that "a good sexual relationship is easy to develop" and that "if there is a good sexual relationship, other problems will take care of themselves" and "sexual adjustment in marriage will result more from proper techniques than from proper attitudes." Couples also overemphasize the value and significance of sex in marriage and believe "sex will be one of the most fulfilling aspects of their marriage."

Unfortunately, too many individuals accept many of these myths about marriage and little is currently being done to demythologize these ideas. As a result, many couples enter marriage with idealistic and unrealistic expectations about what marriage can and will provide. It is usually not until after they have become disappointed and frustrated with their partner that they begin to face the realities of the marital relationship.

For further details about the prevalence of these and related myths, a Premarital Attitude Scale (PMAS) was developed and used to assess the attitudes of family specialists and college students on many of these issues. (Olson, 1967; Olson and Gravatt, 1968)

A SEXUAL REVOLUTION OR EVOLUTION?

In 1938, Terman predicted that: "The trend toward premarital sexual experience is proceeding with extraordinary rapidity. . . . In the case of husbands the incidence of virginity at marriage is 50.6 percent in the oldest group and only 32.6 percent in the youngest. The corresponding drop for wives is from 86.5 percent to 51.2 percent. If the drop should continue at the average rate shown for those born since 1890, virginity at marriage will be close to the vanishing point for males born after 1930 and for females born after 1940." (321-22)

Kinsey's data on females (1953) indicates the rate of premarital sex (PMS) was about 49 percent. Comparable data from the Burgess and Wallin research (1953) found about 68 percent of the males and 47 percent of the females had premarital sex. A recent study by Kaats and Davis (1970) has indicated similar results of PMS, 60 percent for males and 41 percent for females. Another recent study (Bell and Chaskes, 1970) of female premarital sex patterns in 1958 and 1968 found only a small increase in rate for females from 31 to 39 percent, respectively. One of the best designed studies of sexual attitudes and behaviors of young people in three cultures was conducted in 1958 and replicated in 1968 by Christensen and Gregg. (1970) They found in their midwest sample a rather prominent increase in PMS in females between 1958 and 1968, 21 to 34 percent respectively, but no change in the rate for males, 51 to 50 respectively. All of these recent studies actually are underestimates of the actual rate of PMS because the individuals studied were middle class college students who were not yet married. These studies are not representative because it is known that lower class individuals have higher rates of PMS than college students. Further, the actual rates of PMS cannot accurately be assessed until the individuals are actually married. This latter fact is particularly important since PMS still occurs most frequently with one's potential spouse. (Bell and Chaskes, 1970)

On the basis of these studies, it is clear that Terman's prediction that virgin marriages would be only a historical fact has not been realized. However, there have been noticeable changes in female attitudes and behavior. The most dramatic change, which might even be called a female revolution, is the increasing PMS rates for females, which Christensen and Gregg (1970) found changed in the last decade from 21 to 34 percent. This has resulted in a growing convergence in the rates of PMS between the sexes (50 and 34 percent for males and females respectively). This study also showed considerable liberalizations in the attitudes toward PMS in the last decade, again most dramatically in females. This has resulted in fewer differences between PMS attitudes and behavior, so that fewer people are violating their own values and, therefore, there is less guilt associated with PMS. Although the rate of PMS increased, there was an increasing tendency to limit their sexual activity to one partner.

Another trend found in the study of Bell and Chaskes (1970) was that PMS was less dependent on the commitment of engagement than it was a decade ago. While more PMS occurred during engagement, from 31 percent in 1958 to 39 percent in 1968, the PMS rates increased more drastically in dating, from ten to 23 percent, and going steady, from fifteen to 28 percent, stages.

Marital Sex. While there is considerable data on premarital sexual behavior, there is a dearth of empirical data on the sexual relationship in marriage. In fact, little has been done since Kinsey's intitial data on the male (1948) and female. (1953) Cuber and Harroff (1965) have described the sexual relationships of *Significant Americans* within the context of a relationship typology. However, they did not provide specific normative data about these couples' sexual relationships. Perhaps the largest sample of data on early marriage and sexual behavior is contained in a longitudinal study of 2000 couples conducted by Robert Ryder and the author. Unfortunately, the data on marital sexual behavior has not yet been analyzed. The major source of information, therefore, comes from therapists who find sexual problems to be both a *cause* and a *symptom* of most marital difficulties. We can only hope that the next decade will provide more substantive normative data on this significant aspect of marital behavior.

Extra-Marital and Group Sex. Unlike the lack of research on sex in marriage, there have been several recent investigations into the *extra* in extra-marital sex (EMS). Kinsey (1948) provided the first extensive data on EMS and reported that by the age of 40 about one-quarter (26 percent) of the females and one-half (50 percent) of the males had at least one such affair. A more recent study by Whitehurst (1969) was done on 112 upper middle class business and professional men. He found that 67 percent had no EMS, nine percent played around but had no serious sexual involvement, sixteen percent had limited affairs, and only about three percent had rather lengthy affairs. He found that those with the highest levels of EMS more often were alienated, especially showing high levels of social isolation and powerlessness.

Another recent study of EMS was conducted by Johnson (1969) in which 100 middle class couples were investigated. He found 28 percent of the marriages were involved in at least one affair. The marital adjustment of the couple was not related to EMS, for an equal number of couples with high marital adjustment had affairs or passed up the opportunity. However, it was found that husbands, but not wives, who had lower levels of sexual satisfaction were more likely to become involved in affairs. An important finding was the significance of a "perceived opportunity" for having EMS. About 40 percent of those who "perceived" an opportunity took advantage of the situation.

A more expanded discussion on extra-marital sex is contained in a recent book, *Extra-Marital Relations,* edited by Neubeck. (1969) Neubeck offered a useful perspective on EMS when he discussed the unrealistic expectation that marriage will meet all the needs of both spouses at all times. While spouses permit each other some freedom to relate to others, "faithfulness is ordinarily seen as faithfulness in the flesh." (22) The unreality of such expectations is demonstrated by the number of involvements, sexual and emotional, that violate these ideals.

While married individuals typically have had unilateral affairs, recent evidence has indicated that more couples have jointly sought out another couple(s) for group sexual experiences. In a recent book by Bartell (1971) he describes a study of 280 swinging couples. He estimates that perhaps as many as one million couples are presently experimenting within this general context. Many are "respectable" suburbanites who use this experience to relieve boredom. Contacts are made purely for sexual reasons and are usually not maintained for more than a few meetings. It appears, however, that this style of life is seldom maintained permanently because of the large amount of time and energy which is needed to simply locate new partners. Also many come to realize that the experience does not provide the degree of satisfaction they expected.

In conclusion, it appears that while new patterns of relating sexually are evolving, there is not a significant change in the sexual behavior of individuals or couples to label any changes as revolutionary. However, it does appear that there are several trends that have implications for sexual behavior in the future. First of all, there appear to be noticeable changes in both attitudes and behaviors of females which will lead to a greater convergence with the male in society. This could lead to a further decline in the traditional double standard of sexual behavior. Secondly, the openness and frequency with which sexual matters are discussed is increasing, not only in the mass media but also interpersonally. As a result, the discrepancy between attitudes and behaviors in both sexes shows signs of diminishing and as this continues there will be less guilt feelings associated with sexual behavior. Thirdly, there is a trend away from restricting the sexual experience only to a relationship where there is some type of mutual commitment, i.e., engagement or marriage. While a good sexual relationship might still be confined to a love relationship, love has also become more broadly defined to include more than just a marriage relationship. While these are only trends and do, in fact, reflect evolutionary changes in both sexual attitudes and behaviors of individuals in society, they do not indicate any type of sexual revolution that would dramatically affect the institutions of marriage and the family.

ALTERNATIVE STYLES OF LIVING

In an attempt to change the qualitative aspects of marriage, there is a growing interest in re-structuring the mate seiection process and the traditional monogamous conjugal marriage where husband and wife live alone in their own apartment or home. Discussion of alternative living styles has lately become rather prominent in the mass media. (*Futurist,* April, 1970)

One trend is the increasing numbers of college students and other young people living in arrangements other than segregated male-female dormitories or sorority or fraternity houses. Some are collectively renting large houses and forming communal arrangements. While the housing arrangement is communal, there is a great deal of diversity in the interpersonal life styles these individual residents adopt. Some legitimately qualify as communal arrangements where expenses, tasks, and experiences are shared. But many communes often revert to being more like traditional boarding houses where there is little cooperative interest or emotional commitment to others in the house.

Likewise, heterosexual cohabitation takes a variety of forms, from simply sharing a room with one or more individuals, to sharing a bed and a room as a couple, either alone or with other individuals. Macklin (1971) found in a survey of 150 under-classmen at Cornell Universith that 28 percent had recently lived under some form of cohabitation. Some of the reasons for cohabitating given in the Macklin study included: a search for more meaningful relating, avoidance of the dating game, avoiding the loneliness of a large university, and the testing of the relationship. In most of the relationships there was a strong affection but marriage was not seen as an immediate possibility. Macklin indicated that about three-quarters of the relationships involved a girl moving in to share a boy's room in an apartment or house he shared with other males. Usually these arrangements were not planned but simply conveniently available at the time they made the decision. Students in the Macklin survey (1971) had mixed feelings about the success of the experience, but over half felt the advantages outweighed the numerous problems they encountered. Of the problems, a variety of sexual problems was the most pervasive issue. Parental disapproval also was frequently encountered, as was interpersonal issues relating to commitment, communication of feelings, and lack of privacy.

It appears that colleges and universities are becoming more responsive to these changes in student attitudes and behaviors. Universities are now becoming more lax in enforcing their regulations regarding *locus parentis.* There are also increasing numbers of coeducational dormitories that permit a variety of living arrangements.

In addition to new styles of living among unmarried individuals, there are others who are forming multilateral marriages in which usually three or more individuals form a group marriage arrangement. An active proponent of group marriages is Robert Rimmer, author of *The Harrad Experiment* and *Proposition 31,* who feels that new experimentation in sex and marriage is needed to break way from the problems with monogamous marriage. Larry and Joan Constantine (1970; 1971) have attempted to study most of these marriages they could locate, which to date numbers approximately 35 to 40. On the average, these arrangements have not lasted more than a year. The Constantines stated that "We must conclude . . . that multilateral marriage, though a promising growth-oriented form of marriage, is itself a structure limited to a relative few." (1970, 45)

Recently more research has also been done on a small sample of approximately 20 to 30 unconventional marriages that were found in the total sample of 2000 couples who were part of the longitudinal study of early marriage conducted at the National Institute of Mental Health by Robert Ryder and the author. Details of this clinical investigation are contained in a paper entitled Notes on Marriage in the Orbit of the Counter-culture. (Kafka and Ryder, 1972) There are several characteristics which define the ethos espoused by these unconventional couples. There is an intended dominance of feelings over cognition, a present versus future orientation, avoidance of conventional role expectations and traditional patterns of marriage, a high evaluation in "working things out," an intense concern with increasing and maintaining openness and heightened intimacy, disavowal of materialistic goals, and high evaluation of play and travel. In spite of their attempts to build this ethos into their daily lives, they were not able to maintain these ideals without, at times, unwittingly slipping back into many of the traditional problems they wished to avoid. For example, their attempts at role reversal were often difficult to maintain and proved to be at times more than either could cope with and consequently there was a "return to the conventional." Although sexual possessiveness was devalued they found that "hang ups" often interfered; for example, the jealousy they experienced when their partner had an affair with a friend. These couples generally exhibited a more meaningful vital and working relationship than the majority of conventional couples sampled in this study. Both their satisfactions and frustrations were experienced with greater intensity and both extremes occur with greater frequency than in conventional marriage. These couples seldom achieved what they desired and they often found themselves "reverting to the conventional style." These marriages also had a higher rate of divorce than the more conventional sample. Paradoxically, one might conclude that the most vital relationships are the ones that do not last.

In conclusion, although increasing numbers of young people are experimenting with alternative styles of relating as a substitute for the traditional dating game, there is little evidence that this is more than a newly emerging developmental stage in the mate selection process. This newly emerging stage would perhaps come as an extension of the engagement period and might appropriately be called experimental marriage. While this experimentation might delay marriage temporarily for some of them, the vast majority will still adopt a more or less conventional conjugal marriage. While this experience might not result in radically different types of marriages, it might contribute to assisting couples in developing a qualitatively different type of marriage relationship or, at least, more adequately prepare them for the types of problems they will encounter in marriage. According to present evidence, there is only a small percentage of couples who actually attempt to develop and permanently maintain a more unconventional marriage from the traditional monogamous conjugal type.

If any single aspect of marriage is in the greatest state of change, it is the expectations regarding the appropriate role relationship between a husband and wife. And as was true in the area of changing premarital sexual behavior, it is primarily a female revolution. Women, spurred on by women's liberation groups, are increasingly demonstrating against their second class status in marriage in this society. It is true that our society has prescribed roles for husbands and wives that are based not on interest or ability, but on tradition. Tradition has also helped maintain the double standard in sexual and nonsexual areas.

However legitimate the criticisms regarding the woman's role in marriage, changing expectations do not necessarily result in changing actual role relationships that couples adopt. What is happening as a result of these changing expectations is that couples are increasingly being forced into a situation, primarily by the wife, where they must negotiate or renegotiate the way they will structure their role relationships rather than simply accept the traditional definitions. Although this is creating a crisis situation for some, it is providing the opportunity for others to create a new and, hopefully, more vital relationship for both individuals. If these expectations are not realized, it will cause increasing role conflict and growing dissatisfaction with marriage, especially for women, who have traditionally been the defenders of the marriage institution. This is the revolution in marriage. And to paraphrase Otto (1970), what will destroy marriage is not change but the inability of indivuals within it to change.

Redefining a Successful Marriage

While a successful marriage has often been determined by its longevity (i.e., those having twenty-fifth anniversaries) or by how well it fulfills the traditional roles prescribed by society (husband being a good provider and wife being a good housekeeper and mother), there is an increasing awareness that these criteria are not necessarily associated with a successful marriage. Youth has begun to seriously question these criteria and they have become somewhat cynical about marriage because of the alienated, conflicted, and devitalized marriages they see their parents and other adults tolerate. Perceptive as they are, they increasingly see marriage as a relationship that is less often cherished than simply tolerated and endured.

In recent years, there seems to be some change in the criteria used to evaluate the success of a marital relationship. Increasingly, individuals are seeking a relationship that will provide growth for them as individuals and as a couple. More than a companionship marriage as defined by Burgess, there is a search for an authentic and mutually actualizing relationship. Ideally, the successful marriage is seen as a relationship context in which growth and development of both partners is facilitated to a greater extent than it could be for either of these individuals outside the relationship. While this has been one function of marriage that has been implicitly assumed, it has not been explicitly demanded until recently.

Ironically, although more individuals are beginning to evaluate marriage in respect to this criterion, most couples have been unable to achieve this idealized type of relationship. One of the main reasons for this is that society has not adequately prepared individuals to relate in a meaningful way that will facilitate mutual growth within a relationship. As a result, if growth occurs, more commonly it occurs in only one of the individuals. And paradoxically, the greater the growth in one partner in a relationship, the greater the chance the couple will grow further apart rather than closer together. This is often true when both individuals grow also, because they usually do not share the same growth experience and do not use the experience to further develop their relationship. As a result, many couples today are becoming increasingly frustrated because they have rejected the more traditional definition of a successful marriage and yet are having difficulty achieving the type of mutually actualizing relationship that they are striving to achieve. It, therefore, appears that a successful marriage continues to be a difficult and elusive objective to achieve.

NEEDED: A NEW LEXICON ABOUT MARRIAGE

If nothing else productive comes from considering the alternative styles of marriage, it has certainly demonstrated the inadequacy of our present language for describing and classifying marriage and nonmarriage relationships. Even the language used by anthropologists is insufficient to describe the varieties of heterosexual or homosexual relationships and the range of new life styles and communal arrangements on the contemporary scene. This might be a primary reason that family professionals have been unable to develop an adequate typology of marital relationships and another reason why there has been so little substantive research in this area.

Marriage research has, unfortunately, been too concerned with describing marriage along the elusive dimensions of "marital happiness" or "marital satisfaction" or "marital adjustment." The numerous problems with conceptualizing and operationalizing concepts have been reviewed elsewhere (Hicks and Platt, 1970), but their inadequacy becomes even more apparent when describing and classifying unconventional life styles. Family researchers and theorists alike have also limited themselves to simplistic concepts such as "family decision making" and "family power structures." Recent evidence suggests that not only is family power a difficult concept to define and operationalize, but that the various measures used have almost no relationship to each other (Turk and Bell, 1972), and that these measures also lack validity. (Olson and Rabunsky, 1972)

General dimensions that have emerged from this renewed focus on marriage indicate a need for concern with commitment to a relationship rather than primary attention being given to simply whether the couple remains married, i.e., permanence. Attention also needs to be given to a typology of relationships rather than simply classifying a couple as happy. Some preliminary work in this regard was done by Cuber and Haroff (1965) when they classified marriages according to five relationship categories of vital, total, conflict-habitual, passive-congenial, or devitalized. One also needs to know more about the actual interpersonal dynamics in marriage. Newly emerging system concepts such as circular causality, homeostasis, and transaction may aid in this regard.

What is meant by the concepts of marriage and family must also be clearly defined. Are these relationships best defined as legal contracts, verbal commitments, or a definition based on the structure and functions these relationships develop? There need to be new distinctions, such as between emotional monogamy and sexual monogamy. Also, the adaptability (Vincent, 1966) of individuals and relationships needs to be better understood. Attention should also be given to the effects of institutionalizing affection and commitment. Rather than focusing so exclusively on the type and degree of maladjustment that exists in marriage, more attention also needs to be given to marital health (Vincent, 1967) and ways in which individuals and relationships can be helped to become more self-actualizing.

RECOMMENDATIONS REGARDING MARRIAGE

After surveying marriage from a variety of perspectives, it is readily apparent that this institution, like many in this society, has not been the panacea that many have envisioned. Rarely is marriage found to be vital and fulfilling relationship for both spouses. In part, this might be caused by the way we have institutionalized this affectionate relationship. But it also is a reflection of the inability of individuals to relate in meaningful ways and the unrealistic expectations individuals bring to marriage. The following proposals are offered as guidelines and recommendations that might help make marriage a more meaningful and vital relationship.

1. Individuals should not be encouraged to marry at an early age but should wait until they have matured emotionally and have established themselves in their chosen profession.
2. All individuals should not be encouraged or pressured into marriage.
3. Individuals and couples should be encouraged to experiment with a variety of life styles in order to choose the style which is most appropriate for them.
4. Couples should be encouraged to openly and honestly relate rather than play the traditional dating-mating game.
5. Couples should not get married until they have established a meaningful relationship and resolved their major difficulties; for marriage will only create, rather than eliminate, problems.
6. The decision of parenthood should be a joint decision which should follow, rather than precede (as it does in about one-third of the cases), marriage.
7. Couples should not have children until they have established a strong and viable marriage relationship.
8. Couples should be creative and flexible in how they work out their changing roles and mutual responsibilities, not only during their initial phases of marriage, but throughout their marriage relationship.

Individuals would have greater freedom to develop in these ways if they were given societal support rather than implicit and explicit restrictions and constraints. There are a few specific ways in which legal and legislative reform would facilitate these opportunities.

1. Marriage laws should be made more stringent in order to encourage individuals to take this major decision more seriously. Presently it is easier in most states to obtain a marriage license than a license to drive a car.
2. No fault divorce laws should be developed while still providing for adequate support for children. California and Florida have already taken constructive steps in this direction.
3. Premarital, marital, and divorce counseling should be offered to all individuals regardless of their ability to pay.
4. Tax laws should be changed so as not to unduly discriminate against any particular life style.
5. Sex laws which prohibit any form of sexual behavior between consenting individuals should be changed to allow for individual freedom and development.

FUTURE EVOLUTION OF MARRIAGE

Historically, the types and variety of ways in which couples arrange their marriages have always been changing and evolving. These emerging styles have been both responsive to societal change and a cause of change. In fact, in some ways the marriage institution is an emotional thermometer of contemporary society and also an indicator of future trends. The fact that there are beginnings of a female revolution is already, and will continue to be, reflected both in marriage and society. There are also indications that youth are increasingly questioning many of the institutions in our society, including the marriage institution. Both these groups are challenging marriage as it has been traditionally defined and they have been actively experimenting with alternative ways of arranging their lives and marriages. This might lead to a greater variety of ways in which couples define their relationship, arrange their living styles, and carry out the traditional functions of marriage.

While some may feel that these attempts at change are the cause of society's problems, these behaviors might more appropriately be seen as a solution to problems in marriage and also in society. Some unrealistically fear that the institution of marriage might be radically changed. There is, however, little need to be concerned because institutionalized forms of behavior are difficult to dramatically change. In addition, highly industrialized society offers strong support for the style of marriage that has evolved. Lastly, emotional development will tend to minimize any excessive change. As Reiss (1970) stated:

> Our emotions will continue to close off many avenues of change and our habits will further reinforce this. Thinking is a time-consuming activity that often leads to painful revelations. Habit and emotional responses are our ways of easing that pain. (397)

But one must not be afraid of change or afraid to challenge ideas and traditions, no matter how sacred. A great concern is with facilitating the growth and development of individuals in and out of marriage, as Otto (1970) appropriately stated:

> What will destroy us is not change, but our inability to change — both as individuals and as a social system. It is only by welcoming innovation, experiment, and change that a society based on man's capacity to love man can come into being. (9)

REFERENCES

Bartell, Gilbert D. *Group Sex.* New York: Peter H. Wyden, 1971.

Bell, Robert R. and Jay B. Chaskes. Premarital Sexual Experience among Coeds, 1958 to 1968. *Journal of Marriage and the Family,* 1970, 32, 81-84.

Bernard, Jessie. Woman, Marriage, and the Future. *Futurist,* 1970, 4, 41-43.

Broderick, Carlfred B. and George P. Rowe. A Scale of Preadolescent Heterosexual Development. *Journal of Marriage and the Family,* 1968, 30, 97-101.

Christensen, Harold T. and Christina F. Gregg. Changing Sex Norms in America and Scandinavia. *Journal of Marriage and the Family,* 1970, 32, 616-627.

Constantine, Larry L. and Joan M. Constantine. Where Is Marriage Going? *Futurist,* 1970, 4, 44-46.

Constantine, Larry L. and Joan M. Constantine. Group and Multilateral Marriage: Definitional Notes, Glossary and Annotated Bibliography. *Family Process,* 1971, 10, 157-176.

Cuber, John F. and Peggy B. Harroff. *The Significant Americans.* New York: Appleton-Century, 1965.

Hicks, Mary W. and Marilyn Platt. Marital Happiness and Stability: A Review of the Research in the Sixties. *Journal of Marriage and the Family,* 1970, 32, 553-574.

Hill, Reuben. The American Family of the Future. *Journal of Marriage and the Family,* 1964, 26, 20-28.

Johnson, Ralph E. Some Correlates of Extramarital Coitus. *Journal of Marriage and the Family,* 1970, 32, 449-456.

Kaats, Gilbert R. and Keith E. Davis. The Dynamics of Sexual Behavior of College Students. *Journal of Marriage and the Family,* 1970, 32, 390-399.

Kafka, John S. and Robert G. Ryder. Notes on Marriage in the Orbit of the Counter-Culture, Unpublished manuscript, 1972.

Kinsey, Alfred C., Wardell B. Pomeroy, Clyde E. Martin, and Paul Gibbard. *Sexual Behavior in the Human Female.* New York: Sanders, 1953.

Kinsey, Alfred C., Wardell B. Pomeroy, Clyde E. Martin, and Paul Gibbard. *Sexual Behavior in the Human Male.* New York: Sanders, 1948.

Lederer, William J. and Donald D. Jackson. *The Mirages of Marriage.* New York: W. W. Norton, 1968.

Maslow, A. H. A Theory of Human Motivation. *Psychological Review,* 1943, 50, 370-396.

Maslow, A. H. *Motivation and Personality.* New York: Harper and Row, 1954.

Miller, Sherod and Elam Nunally. A Family Developmental Program of Communication Training for Engaged Couples. Monograph Family Study Center, University of Minnesota, 1970.

Neubeck, Gerhard (Ed.) *Extramarital Relations.* Englewood Cliffs, New Jersey: Prentice-Hall, 1969.

Oldon, David H. Student Attitudes Toward Marriage. *College Student Survey,* 1967, 1, 71-78.

Olson, David H. and Arthur G. Gravatt. Attitude Change in a Functional Marriage Course. *The Family Coordinator,* 1968, 17, 99-104.

Olson, David H. and Carolyn Rabunsky. Validity of Four Measures of Family Power. *Journal of Marriage and the Family,* 1972, 34, 224-234.

Otto, Herbert A. (Ed.). *The Family in Search of a Future.* New York: Appleton, Century and Crofts, 1970.

Reiss, Ira L. *The Family Systems in America.* New York: Holt, Rinehart, and Winston, 1971.

Ryder, Robert G., John S. Kafka, and David H. Olson. Separating and Joining Influences in Courtship and Early Marriage. *American Journal of Orthopsychiatry,* 1971, 41, 450-464.

Ryder, Robert G. An Opinion on Marriage. *Mademoiselle*, (January) 1971.

Satir, Virginia. Marriage as a Human-Actualizing Contract. In Herbert A. Otto (Ed.) *The Family in Search of a Future*. New York: Appleton, Century and Crofts, 1970.

Sussman, Marvin B. and Lee Burchinal. Kin Family Network: Unheralded Structure in Current Conceptualizations of Family Functioning. *Marriage and Family Living*, 1962, 24, 231-240.

Sussman, Marvin B. Relationships of Adult Children with their Parents in the United States. In Ethel Shanas and Gordon F. Streib (Eds.). *Social Structure and the Family: Generational Relations*. Englewood Cliffs, New Jersey: Prentice-Hall, 1965.

Terman, Lewis M. *Psychological Factors in Marital Happiness*. New York: McGraw Hill, 1938.

Turk, James L. and Norman W. Bell. Measuring Power in Families. *Journal of Marriage and the Family*, 1972, 34, 215-223.

Vincent, Clark E. Familia Spongia: The Adaptive Function. *Journal of Marriage and the Family*, 1966, 28, 29-36.

Vincent, Clark E. Mental Health and the Family. *Journal of Marriage and the Family*, 1967, 29, 18-39.

Whitehurst, Robert N. Extra-Marital Sex: Alienation of Extension of Normal Behavior. In Gerhard Neubeck (Ed.) *Extra-Marital Relations*. New York: Prentice-Hall, 1969.

The Future of Marriage

MORTON HUNT

Over a century ago, the Swiss historian and ethnologist J.J. Bachofen postulated that early man lived in small packs, ignorant of marriage and indulging in beastlike sexual promiscuity. He could hardly have suggested anything more revolting, or more fascinating, to the puritanical and prurient sensibility of his time, and whole theories of the family and of society were based on his notion by various anthropologists, as well as by German socialist Friedrich Engels and Russan revolutionist Peïr Kropotkin. As the Victorian fog dissipated, however, it turned out that among the hundreds of primitive peoples still on earth—many of whom lived much like early man—not a single one was without some form of marriage and some limitations on the sexual freedom of the married. Marriage, it appeared, was a genuine human universal, like speech and social organization.

Nonetheless, Bachofen's myth died hard, because it appealed to a longing, deep in all of us, for total freedom to do whatever we want. And recently, it has sprung up from its own ashes in the form of a startling new notion: Even if there never was a time when marriage didn't exist, there soon will be. Lately, the air has been filled with such prophecies of the decline and impending fall of marriage. Some of the prophets are grieved at this prospect—among them, men of the cloth, such as the Pope and Dr. Peale, who keep warning us that hedonism and easy divorce are eroding the very foundations of family life. Others, who rejoice at the thought, include an assortment of feminists, hippies and anarchists, plus much-married theater people such as Joan Fontaine, who, having been married more times than the Pope and Dr. Peale put together, has authoritatively told the world that marriage is obsolete and that any sensible person can live and love better without it.

Some of the fire-breathing dragon ladies who have given women's lib an undeservedly bad name urge single women not to marry and married ones to desert their husbands forthwith. Kate Millet, the movement's leading theoretician, expects marriage to wither away after women achieve full equality. Dr. Roger Egeberg, an Assistant Secretary of HEW, urged Americans in 1969 to reconsider their inherited belief that everyone ought to marry. And last August, Mrs. Rita Hauser, the U.S. representative to the UN Human Rights Commission, said that the idea that marriage was primarily for procreation had become outmoded and that laws banning marriage between homosexuals should be erased from the books.

So much for the voices of prophecy. Are there, in fact, any real indications of the mass revolt against traditonal marriage? There certainly seem to be. For one thing, in 1969 there were 660,000 divorces in America—an all-time record—and the divorce rate seems certain to achieve historic new highs in the next few years. For another thing, marital infidelity seems to have increased markedly since Kinsey's first surveys of a generation ago and now is tried, sooner or later, by some 60 percent of married men and 30 to 35 percent of married women in this country. But in what is much more of a departure from the past, infidelity is now tacitly accepted by a fair number of the spouses of the unfaithful. For some couples it has become a shared hobby; mate-swapping and group-sex parties now involve thousands of middle-class marriages. Yet another indication of change is a sharp increase not only in the number of young men and women who, dispensing with legalities, live together unwed but also in the *kind* of people who are doing so; although common-law marriage has long been popular among the poor, in the past few years it has become widespread—and often esteemed—within the middle class.

An even more radical attack on our marriage system is the effort of people in hundreds of communes around the country to construct "families" or group marriages, in which the adults own everything in common, and often consider that they all belong to one another and play mix and match sexually with total freedom. A more complete break with tradition is being made by a rapidly growing percentage of America's male and female homosexuals, who nowadays feel freer than ever to avoid "cover" marriages and to live openly as homosexuals. Their lead is almost certain to be followed by countless others within the next decade or so as our society grows ever more tolerant of personal choice in sexual matters.

Nevertheless, reports of the death of marriage are, to paraphrase Mark Twain, greatly exaggerated. Most human beings regard whatever they grew up with as right and good and see nearly every change in human behavior as a decline in standards and a fall from grace. But change often means adaptation and evolution. The many signs of contemporary revolt against marriage have been viewed as symptoms of a fatal disease, but they may, instead, be signs of a change from an obsolescent form of marriage—patriarchal monogamy—into new forms better suited to present-day human needs.

Marriage as a social structure is exceedingly plastic, being shaped by the interplay of culture and of human needs into hundreds of different forms. In societies where women could do valuable productive work, it often made sense for a man to acquire more than one wife; where women were idle or relatively unproductive—and, hence, a burden—monogamy was more likely to be the pattern. When women had means of their own or could fall back upon relatives, divorce was apt to be easy; where they were wholly dependent on their husbands, it was generally difficult. Under marginal and primitive living conditions, men kept their women in useful subjugation; in wealthier and more leisured societies, women often managed to acquire a degree of independence and power.

For a long while, the only acceptable form of marriage in America was a life-long one-to-one union, sexually faithful, all but indissoluble, producitve of goods and children and strongly husband-dominated. It was a thoroughly functional mechanism during the 18th and much of the 19th centuries, when men were struggling to secure the land and needed women who would clothe and feed them, produce and rear children to help them, and obey their orders without question for an entire lifetime. It was functional, too, for the women of that time, who, uneducated, unfit for other kinds of work and endowed by law with almost no legal or property rights, needed men who would support them, give them social status and be their guides and protectors for life.

But time passed, the Indians were conquered, the sod was busted, towns and cities grew up, railroads laced the land, factories and offices took the place of the frontier. Less and less did men need women to produce goods and children; more and more, women were educated, had time to spare, made their way into the job market—and realized that they no longer had to cling to their men for life. As patriarchalism lost its usefulness, women began to want and demand orgasms, contraceptives, the vote and respect; men, finding the world growing ever more impersonal and cold, began to want wives who were warm, understanding, companionable and sexy.

Yet, strangely enough, as all these things were happening, marriage not only did not lose ground but grew more popular, and today, when it is under full-scale attack on most fronts, it is more widespread than ever before. A considerably larger percentage of our adult population was married in 1970 than was the case in 1890; the marriage rate, though still below the level of the 1940s, has been climbing steadily since 1963.

The explanation of this paradox is that as marriage was losing its former uses, it was gaining new ones. The changes that were robbing marriage of practical and life-affirming values were turning America into a mechanized urban society in which we felt like numbers, not individuals, in which we had many neighbors but few lifelong friends and in which our lives were controlled by remote governments, huge companies and insensate computers. Alone and impotent, how can we find intimacy and warmth, understanding and loyalty, enduring friendship and a feeling of personal importance? Why, obviously, through *loving* and *marrying*. Marriage is a microcosom, a world within which we seek to correct the shortcomings of the macrocosm around us. Saint Paul said it is better to marry than to burn; today, feeling the glacial chill of the world we live in, we find it better to marry than to freeze.

The model of marriage that served the old purposes excellently serves the new ones poorly. But most of the contemporary assaults upon it are not efforts to destroy it; they are efforts to modify and remold it. Only traditional patriarchal marriage is dying, while all around us marriage is being reborn in new forms. The marriage of the future already exists; we have merely mistaken the signs of evolutionary change for the stigmata of necrosis.

Divorce is a case in point. Far from being a wasting illness, it is a healthful adaptation, enabling monogamy to survive in a time when patriarchal powers, privileges and marital systems have become unworkable; far from being a radical change in the institution of marrige, divorce is a relatively minor modification of it and thoroughly supportive of most of its conventions.

Not that it seemed so at first. When divorce was introduced to Christian Europe, it appeared an extreme and rather sinful measure to most people; among the wealthy—the only people who could afford it—it remained for centuries quite rare and thoroughly scandalous. In 1816, when president Timothy Dwight of Yale thundered against the "alarming and terrible" divorce rate in Connecticut, about one of every 100 marriages was being legally dissolved. But as women began achieving a certain degree of emancipation during the 19th Century, and as the purpose of marriage changed, divorce laws were liberalized and the rate began climbing. Between 1870 and 1905, both the U.S. population and the divorce rate more than doubled; and between then and today, the divorce rate increased over four times.

And not only for the reasons we have already noted but for yet another: the increase in longevity. When people married in their late 20s and marriage was likely to end in death by the time the last child was leaving home, divorce seemed not only wrong but hardly worth the trouble; this was especially true where the only defect in a marriage was boredom. Today, however, when people marry earlier and have finished raising their children with half their adult lives still ahead of them, boredom seems a very good reason for getting divorced.

Half of all divorces occur after eight years of marriage and a quarter of them after 15—most of these being not the results of bad initial choices but of disparity or dullness that has grown with time.

Divorcing people, however, are seeking not to escape from marriage for the rest of their lives but to exchange unhappy or boring marriages for satisfying ones. Whatever bitter things they say at the time of divorce, the vast majority do remarry, most of their second marriages lasting the rest of their lives; even those whose second marriages fail are very likely to divorce and remarry again and, that failing, yet again. Divorcing people are actually marrying people, and divorce is not a negation of marriage but a workable cross between traditional monogamy and multiple marriage; sociologists have even referred to it as "serial polygamy."

Despite its costs and its hardships, divorce is thus a compromise between the monogamous ideal and the realities of present-day life. To judge from the statistics, it is becoming more useful and more socially acceptable every year. Although the divorce rate leveled off for a dozen of years or so after the postwar surge of 1946, it has been climbing steadily since 1962, continuing the long range trend of 100 years, and the rate for the entire nation now stands at nearly one for every three marriages. In some areas, it is even higher. In California, where a new ultraliberal law went into effect in 1970, nearly two of every three marriages end in divorce—a fact that astonishes people in other areas of the country but that Californians themselves accept with equanimity. They still approve of, and very much enjoy, being married; they have simply gone further than the rest of us in using divorce to keep monogamy workable in today's world.

Seen in the same light, marital infidelity is also a frequently useful modification of the marriage contract rather than a repudiation of it. It violates the conventional moral code to a greater degree than does divorce but, as practiced in America, is only a limited departure from the monogamous pattern. Unfaithful Americans, by and large, neither have extramarital love affairs that last for many years nor do they engage in a continuous series of minor liaisons; rather, their infidelity consists of relatively brief and widely scattered episodes, so that in the course of a married lifetime, they spend many more years being faithful than being unfaithful. Furthermore, American infidelity, unlike its European counterparts, has no recognized status as part of the marital system; except in a few circles, it remains impermissible, hidden and isolated from the rest of one's life.

This is not true at all levels of our society, however: Upper-class men—and, to some extent, women—have long regarded the discreet love affair as an essential complement to marriage, and lower-class husbands have always considered an extracurricular roll in the hay important to a married man's peace of mind. Indeed, very few societies have ever tried to make both husband and wife sexually faithful over a lifetime; the totally monogamous ideal is statistically an abnormality. Professors Clellan Ford and Frank Beach state in *Patterns of Sexual Behavior* that less than 16 percent of 185 societies studied by anthropologists had formal restrictions to a single mate—and, of these, less than a third wholly disapproved of both premarital and extramarital relationships.

Our middle-class, puritanical society, however, has long held that infidelity of any sort is impossible if one truly loves one's mate and is happily married, that any deviation from fidelity stems from an evil or neurotic character and that it inevitably damages both the sinner and the sinned against. This credo drew support from earlier generations of psychotherapists, for almost all the adulterers they treated were neurotic, unhappily married or out of sorts with life in general. But it is just such people who seek psychotherapy; they are hardly a fair sample. Recently, sex researchers have examined the unfaithful more representatively and have come up with quite different findings. Alfred Kinsey, sociologist Robert Whitehurst of Indiana University, sociologist John Cuber of Ohio State University, sexologist/therapist Dr. Albert Ellis and various others (including myself), all of whom have made surveys of unfaithful husbands and wives, agree in general that:

> Many of the unfaithful — perhaps even a majority — are not seriously dissatisfied with their marriages nor their mates and a fair number are more or less happily married.
> Only about a third — perhaps even fewer — appear to seek

extramarital sex for neurotic motives; the rest do so for non-pathological reasons.

Many of the unfaithful — perhaps even a majority — do not feel that they, their mates nor their marriages have been harmed; in my own sample, a tenth said that their marriages had been helped or made more tolerable by their infidelity.

It is still true that many a "deceived" husband or wife, learning about his or her mate's infidelity, feels humiliated, betrayed and unloved, and is filled with rage and the desire for revenge; it is still true, too, that infidelity is a cause in perhaps a third of all divorces. But more often than not, deceived spouses never know of their mates' infidelity nor are their marriages perceptibly harmed by it.

The bulk of present-day infidelity remains hidden beneath the disguise of conventional marital behavior. But an unfettered minority of husbands and wives openly grant each other the right to outside relationships, limiting that right to certain occasions and certain kinds of involvement, in order to keep the marital relationship all-important and unimpaired. A few couples, for instance, take separate vacations or allow each other one night out alone per week, it being understood that their extramarital involvements are to be confined to those times. Similar freedoms have been urged by radical marriage reformers for decades but have never really caught on, and probably never will, for one simple reason: What's out of sight is not necessarily out of mind. What husband can feel sure, despite his wife's promises, that she might not find some other man who will make her dream come true? What wife can feel sure that her husband won't fall in love with some woman he is supposed to be having only a friendly tumble with?

But it's another matter when husband and wife go together in search of extramarital frolic and do their thing with other people, in full view of each other, where it is free of romantic feeling. This is the very essence of marital swinging, or, as it is sometimes called, comarital sex. Whether it consists of a quiet mate exchange between two couples, a small sociable group-sex party or a large orgiastic rumpus, the premise is the same: As long as the extramarital sex is open, shared and purely recreational, it is not considered divisive of marriage.

So the husband and wife welcome the baby sitter, kiss the children good night and drive off together to someone's home, where they drink a little and make social talk with their hosts and any other guests present, and then pair off with a couple of the others and disappear into bedrooms for an hour or so or undress in the living room and have sex in front of their interested and approving mates.

No secrecy about that, certainly, and no hidden romance to fear; indeed, the very exhibitionism of marital swinging enforces its most important ground rule — the tacit understanding that participants will not indulge in emotional involvements with fellow swingers, no matter what physical acts they perform together. Though a man and a woman make it with each other at a group-sex party, they are not supposed to meet each other later on; two swinging couples who get together outside of parties are disapprovingly said to be going steady. According to several researchers, this proves that married swingers value their marriages: They want sexual fun and stimulation but nothing that would jeopardize their marital relationships. As sociologists Duane Denfeld and Michael Gordon of the University of Connecticut straight-facedly write, marital swingers "favor monogamy and want to maintain it" and do their swinging "in order to support and improve their marriages."

To the outsider, this must sound very odd, not to say outlandish. How could anyone hope to preserve the warmth and intimacy of marriage by performing the most private and personal sexual acts with other people in front of his own mate or watching his mate do so with others?

Such a question implies that sex is integrally interwoven with the rest of one's feelings about the mate — which it is — but swingers maintain that it can be detached and enjoyed apart from those feelings, without changing them in any way. Marital swinging is supposed to involve only this one segment of the marital relationship and during only a few hours of any week or month; all else is meant to remain intact, monogamous and conventional.

Experts maintain that some people swing out of neurotic needs; some have sexual problems in their marriages that do not arise in casual sexual relationships; some are merely bored and in need of new stimuli; some need the ego lift of continual conquests. But the average swinger, whatever his (or her) motive, normal or pathological, is apt to believe that he loves his spouse, that he has a pretty good marriage and that detaching sex — and sex alone — from marital restrictions not only will do the marriage no harm but will rid it of any aura of confinement.

*   *   *

In contrast to this highly specialized and sharply limited attitude, there seems to be a far broader and more thorough rejection of marriage on the part of those men and women who choose to live together unwed. Informal, nonlegal unions have long been widespread among poor blacks, largely for economic reasons, but the present wave of such unions among middle-class whites has an ideological basis, for most of those who choose this arrangement consider themselves revolutionaries who have the guts to pioneer in a more honest and vital relationship than conventional marriage. A 44-year-old conference leader, Theodora Wells, and a 51-year-old psychologist, Lee Christie, who live together in Beverly Hills, expounded their philosophy in the April 1970 issue of *The Futurist*: " 'Personhood' is central to the living-together relationship; sex roles are central to the marriage relationship. Our experience strongly suggests that personhood excites growth, stimulates openness, increases joyful satisfactions in achieving, encompasses rich, full sexuality peaking in romance. Marriage may have the appearance of this in its romantic phase, but it settles down to prosaic routine. . . . The wife role is diametrically opposed to the personhood I want. I [Theodora] therefore choose to live with the man who joins me in the priority of personhood."

What this means is that she hates homemaking, is career oriented and fears that if she became a legal wife, she would automatically be committed to traditional female roles, to dependency. Hence, she and Christie have rejected marriage and chosen an arrangement without legal obligations, without a head of the household and without a primary money earner or primary homemaker — though Christie, as it happens, does 90 percent of the cooking. Both believe that their freedom from legal ties and their constant need to rechoose each other make for a more exciting, real and growing relationship.

A fair number of the avant-garde and many of the young have begun to find this not only a fashionably rebellious but a thoroughly congenial attitude toward marriage; couples are living together, often openly, on many a college campus, risking punishment by college authorities (but finding the risk smaller every day) and bucking their parents' strenuous disapproval (but getting their glum acceptance more and more often).

When one examines the situation closely, however, it becomes clear that most of these marital Maoists live together in close, warm, committed and monogamous fashion, very much like married people; they keep house together (although often dividing their roles in untraditional ways) and neither is free to have sex with anyone else, date anyone else nor even find anyone else intriguing. Anthropologists Margaret Mead and Ashley Montagu, sociologist John Gagnon and other close observers of the youth scene feel that living together, whatever its defects, is actually an apprentice marriage and not a true rebellion against marriage at all.

Dr. Mead, incidentally, made a major public pitch in 1966 for a revision of our laws that would create two kinds of marital status: individual marriage, a legal but easily dissolved form for young people who were unready for parenthood or full commitment to each other but who wanted to live together with social acceptance; and parental marriage, a union involving all the legal commitments and responsibilities—and difficulties of dissolution—of marriage as we presently know it. Her suggestion aroused a great deal of public debate. The middle-aged, for the most part, condemned her proposal as being an attack upon and a debasement of marriage, while the young replied that the whole idea was unnecessary. The young were right: They were already creating their own new marital folkway in the form of the close, serious but informal union that achieved all the goals of individual marriage except its legality and acceptance by the middle-aged. Thinking themselves rebels against marriage, they had only created a new form of marriage closely resembling the very thing Dr. Mead had suggested.

If these modifications of monogamy aren't quite as alarming or as revolutionary as they seem to be, one contemporary experiment in marriage *is* a genuine and total break with Western tradition. This is group marriage—a catchall term applied to a wide variety of polygamous experiments in which small groups of adult males and females, and their children, live together under one roof or in a close-knit settlement, calling themselves a family, tribe, commune or, more grandly, intentional community and considering themselves all married to one another.

As the term intentional community indicates, these are experiments not merely in marriage but in the building of a new type of society. They are utopian minisocieties existing within, but almost wholly opposed to, the mores and values of present day American society.

Not that they are all a piece. A few are located in cities and have members who look and act square and hold regular jobs; some, both urban and rural, consist largely of dropouts, acidheads, panhandlers and petty thieves; but most are rural communities, have hippie-looking members and aim at a self-sufficient farming-and-handicraft way of life. A very few communes are politically conservative, some are in the middle and most are pacifist, anarchistic and/or New Leftist. Nearly all, whatever their national political bent, are islands of primitive communism in which everything is collectively owned and all members work for the common good.

Their communism extends to—or perhaps really begins with—sexual collectivism. Though some communes consist of married couples who are conventionally faithful, many are built around some kind of group sexual sharing. In some of these, couples are paired off but occasionally sleep with other members of the group; in others, pairing off is actively discouraged and the members drift around sexually from one partner to another—a night here, a night there, as they wish.

Group marriage has captured the imagination of many thousands of college students in the past few years through its idealistic and romantic portrayal in three novels widely read by the young—Robert Heinlein's *Stranger in a Strange Land* and Robert Rimmer's *The Harrad Experiment* and *Proposition 31*. The underground press, too, has paid a good deal of sympathetic attention—and the establishment press a good deal of hostile attention—to communes. There has even been, for several years, a West Coast publication titled *The Modern Utopian* that is devoted, in large part, to news and discussions of group marriage. The magazine, which publishes a directory of intentional communities, recently listed 125 communes and the editor said, "For every listing you find here, you can be certain there are 100 others." And an article in *The New York Times* last December stated that "nearly 2000 communes in 34 states have turned up" but gave this as a conservative figure, as "no accurate count exists."

All this sometimes gives one the feeling that group marriage is sweeping the country; but, based on the undoubtedly exaggerated figures of *The Modern Utopian* and counting a generous average of 20 people per commune, it would still mean that no more than 250,000 adults—approximately one tenth of one percent of the U.S. population—are presently involved in group marriages. These figures seem improbable.

Nevertheless, group marriage offers solutions to a number of the nagging problems and discontents of modern monogamy. Collective parenthood—every parent being partly responsible for every child in the group—not only provides a warm and enveloping atmosphere for children but removes some of the pressure from individual parents: moreover, it minimizes the disruptive effects of divorce on the child's world. Sexual sharing is an answer to boredom and solves the problem of infidelity, or seeks to, by declaring extramarital experiences acceptable and admirable. It avoids the success-status-possession syndrome of middle-class family life by turning toward simplicity, communal ownership and communal goals.

Finally, it avoids the loneliness and confinement of monogamy by creating something comparable to what anthropologists call the extended family, a larger grouping of related people living together. (There is a difference, of course: In group marriage, the extended family isn't composed of blood relatives.) Even when sexual switching isn't the focus, there is a warm feeling of being affectionally connected to everyone else. As one young woman in a Taos commune said ecstatically, "It's really groovy waking up and knowing that 48 people love you."

There is, however, a negative side: This drastic reformulation of marriage makes for new problems, some of them more severe than the ones it has solved. Albert Ellis, quoted in Herbert Otto's new book, *The Family in Search of a Future,* lists several categories of serious difficulties with group marriage, including the near impossibility of finding four or more adults who can live harmoniously and lovingly together, the stubborn intrusion of jealousy and love conflicts and the innumerable difficulties of coordinating and scheduling many lives.

Other writers, including those who have sampled communal life, also talk about the problems of leadership (most communes have few rules to start with; those that survive for any time do so by becoming almost conventional and traditional) and the difficulties in communal work sharing (there are always some members who are slovenly and lazy and others who are neat and hard-working, the latter either having to expel the former or to give up and let the commune slowly die).

A more serious defect is that most group marriages, being based upon a simple, semiprimitive agrarian life, reintroduce old-style patriarchalism, because such a life puts a premium on masculine muscle power and endurance and leaves the classic domestic and subservient roles to women. Even a most sympathetic observer, psychiatrist Joseph Downing, writes, "In the tribal families, while both sexes work, women are generally in a service role. . . . Male dominance is held desirable by both sexes."

Most serious of all are the emotional limitations of group marriage. Its ideal is sexual freedom and universal love, but the group marriages that most nearly achieve this have the least cohesiveness and the shallowest interpersonal involvements; people come and go, and there is really no marriage at all but only a continuously changing and highly unstable encounter group. The longer-lasting and more cohesive group marriages are, in fact, those in which, as Dr. Downing reports, the initial sexual spree "generally gives way to the quiet, semipermanent, monogamous relationship characteristic of many in our general society."

Not surprisingly, therefore, Dr. Ellis finds that most group marriages are unstable and last only several months to a few years; and sociologist Lewis Yablonsky of California State College at Hayward, who has visited and lived in a number of communes, says that they are often idealistic but rarely successful or enduring. Over and above their specific difficulties, they are utopian—they seek to construct a new society from whole cloth. But all utopias thus far have failed; human behavior is so incredibly complex that every totally new order, no matter how well planned, generates innumerable unforeseen problems. It really is a pity: group living and group marriage look wonderful on paper.

• • •

All in all, then, the evidence is overwhelming that old-fashioned marriage is not dying and that nearly all of what passes for rebellion against it is a series of patchwork modifications enabling marriage to serve the needs of modern man without being unduly costly or painful.

While this is the present situation, can we extrapolate it into the future? Will marriage continue to exist in some form we can recognize?

It is clear that, in the future, we are going to have an even greater need than we now do for love relationships that offer intimacy, warmth, companionship and a reasonable degree of reliability. Such relationships need not, of course, be heterosexual. With our increasing tolerance of sexual diversity, it seems likely that many homosexual men and women will find it publicly acceptable to live together in quasi-marital alliances.

The great majority of men and women, however, will continue to find heterosexual love the preferred form, for biological and psychological reasons that hardly have to be spelled out here. But need heterosexual love be embodied within marriage? If the world is already badly overpopulated and daily getting worse, why add to its burden —and if one does not intend to have children, why seek to enclose love within a legal cage? Formal promises to love are promises no one can keep, for love is not an act of will; and legal bonds have no power to keep love alive when it is dying.

Such reasoning—more cogent today than ever, due to the climate of sexual permissiveness and to the twin technical advances of the pill and the loop—lives behind the growth of unwed unions. From all indications, however, such unions will not replace marriage as an institution but only precede it in the life of the individual.

It seems probable that more and more young people will live together unwed for a time and then marry each other or break up and make another similar alliance, and another, until one of them turns into a formal, legal marriage. In 50 years, perhaps less, we may come close to the Scandinavian pattern, in which a great many couples live together prior to marriage. It may be, moreover, that the spread of this practice will decrease the divorce rate among the young, for many of the mistakes that are recognized too late and are undone in divorce court will be recognized and undone outside the legal system, with less social and emotional damage than divorce involves.

If, therefore, marriage continues to be important, what form will it take? The one truly revolutionary innovation is group marriage—and, as we have seen, it poses innumerable and possibly insuperable practical and emotional difficulties. A marriage of one man and one woman involves only one interrelationship, yet we all know how difficult it is to find that one right fit and to keep it in working order. But add one more person, making the smallest possible group marriage, and you have three relationships (A-B, B-C and A-C); add a fourth to make two couples and you have six relationships; add enough to make a typical group marriage of 15 persons and you have 105 relationships.

This is an abstract way of saying that human beings are all very different and that finding a satisfying and workable love relationship is not easy, even for a twosome, and it is impossibly difficult for aggregations of a dozen or so. It might prove less difficult, a generation hence, for children brought up in group-marriage communes. Such children would not have known the close, intense, parent-child relationships of monogamous marriage and could more easily spread their affections thinly and undemandingly among many. But this is mere conjecture, for no communal-marriage experiment in America has lasted long enough for us to see the results, except the famous Oneida Community in Upstate New York; it endured from 1848 to 1879, and then its offspring vanished back into the surrounding ocean of monogamy.

Those group marriages that do endure in the future will probably be dedicated to a rural and semiprimitive agrarian life style. Urban communes may last for some years but with an ever-changing membership and a lack of inner familial identity; in the city, one's work life lies outside the group, and with only emotional ties to hold the group together, any dissension or conflict will result in a turnover of membership. But while agrarian communes may have a sounder foundation, they can never become a mass movement; there is simply no way for the land to support well over 200,000,000 people with the low-efficiency productive methods of a century or two ago.

Agrarian communes not only cannot become a mass movement in the future but they will not even have much chance of surviving as islands in a sea of modern industrialism. For semiprimitive agrarianism is so marginal, so backbreaking and so tedious a way of life that it is unlikely to hold most of its converts against the competing attractions of conventional civilization. Even Dr. Downing, for all his enthusiasm about the "Society of Awakening," as he calls tribal family living, predicts that for the foreseeable future, only a small minority will be attracted to it and that most of these will return to more normal surroundings and relationships after a matter of weeks or months.

Thus, monogamy will prevail; on this, nearly all experts agree. But it will almost certainly continue to change in the same general direction in which it has been changing for the past few generations; namely, toward a redefinition of the special roles played by husband and wife, so as to achieve a more equal distribution of the rights, privileges and life expectations of man and woman.

This, however, will represent no sharp break with contemporary marriage, for the marriage of 1971 has come a long way from patriarchy toward the goal of equality. Our prevalent marital style has been termed companionship marriage by a generation of sociologists; in contrast to 19th Century marriage, it is relatively egalitarian and intimate, husband and wife being intellectually and emotionally close, sexually compatible and nearly equal in personal power and in the quantity and quality of labor each contributes to the marriage.

From an absolute point of view, however, it still is contaminated by patriarchalism. Although each partner votes, most husbands (and wives) still think that men understand politics better; although each may have had similar schooling and believes both sexes to be intellectually equal, most husbands and wives still act as if men were innately better equipped to handle money, drive the car, fill out tax returns and replace fuses. There may be something close to equality in their homemaking, but nearly always it is his career that counts, not hers. If his company wants to move him to another city, she quits her job and looks for another in their new location; and when they want to have children, it is seldom questioned that he will continue to work while she will stay home.

With this, there is a considerable shift back toward traditional role assignments: He stops waxing the floors and washing dishes, begins to speak with greater authority about how their money is to be spent, tells her (rather than consults her) when he would like to work late or take a business trip, gives (or withholds) his approval of her suggestions for parties, vacations and child discipline. The more he takes on the airs of his father, the more she learns to connive and manipulate like her mother. Feeling trapped and discriminated against, resenting the men of the world, she thinks she makes an exception of her husband, but in the hidden recesses of her mind he is one with the others. Bearing the burden of being a man in the world, and resenting the easy life of women, he thinks he makes an exception of his wife but deep-down classifies her with the rest.

This is why a great many women yearn for change and what the majority of women's liberation members are actively hammering away at. A handful of radicals in the movement think that the answer is the total elimination of marriage, that real freedom for women will come about only through the abolition of legal bonds to men and the establishment of governmentally operated nurseries to rid women once and for all of domestic entrapment. But most women in the movement, and nearly all those outside it, have no sympathy with the anti-marriage extremists; they very much want to keep marriage alive but aim to push toward completion the evolutionary trends that have been under way so long.

Concretely, women want their husbands to treat them as equals; they want help and participation in domestic duties; they want help with child rearing; they want day-care centers and other agencies to free them to work at least part time, while their children are small, so that they won't have to give up their careers and slide into the imprisonment of domesticity. They want an equal voice in all the decisions made in the home — including job decisions that affect married life; they want their husbands to respect them, not indulge them; they want, in short, to be treated as if they were their husbands' best friends — which, in fact, they are, or should be.

All this is only a continuation of the developments in marriage over the past century and a quarter. The key question is: How far can marriage evolve in this direction without making excessive demands upon both partners? Can most husbands and wives have full-time uninterrupted careers, share all the chores and obligations of homemaking and parenthood and still find time for the essential business of love and companionship?

From the time of the early suffragettes, there have been women with the drive and talent to be full-time doctors, lawyers, retailers and the like, and at the same time to run a home and raise children with the help of housekeepers, nannies and selfless husbands. From these examples, we can judge how likely this is to become the dominant pattern of the future. Simply put, it isn't, for it would take more energy, money and good luck than the great majority of women possess and more skilled helpers than the country could possibly provide. But what if child care were more efficiently handled in state-run centers, which would make the totally egalitarian marriage much more feasible? The question then becomes: How many middle-class American women would really prefer full-time work to something less demanding that would give them more time with their children? The truth is that most of the world's work is dull and wearisome rather than exhilarating and inspiring. Women's lib leaders are largely middle-to-upper-echelon professionals, and no wonder they think every would be better off working full time — but we have yet to hear the same thing from saleswomen, secretaries and bookkeepers.

Married women *are* working more all the time — in 1970, over half of all mothers whose children were in school held jobs — but the middle-class women among them pick and choose things they like to do rather than *have* to do for a living; moreover, many work part time until their children have grown old enough to make mothering a minor assignment. Accordingly, they make much less money than their husbands, rarely ever rise to any high positions in their fields and, to some extent, play certain traditionally female roles within marriage. It is a compromise and, like all compromises, it delights no one — but serves nearly everyone better than more clear-cut and idealistic solutions.

Though the growth of egalitarianism will not solve all the problems of marriage, it may help solve the problems of a *bad* marriage. With their increasing independence, fewer and fewer wives will feel compelled to remain confined within unhappy or unrewarding marriages. Divorce, therefore, can be expected to continue to increase, despite the offsetting effect of extramarital liaisons. Extrapolating the rising divorce rate, we can conservatively expect that within another generation, half or more of all persons who marry will be divorced at least once. But even if divorce were to become an almost universal experience, it would not be the *antithesis* of marriage but only a part of the marital experience; most people will, as always, spend their adult lives married — not continuously, in a single marriage, but segmentally, in two or more marriages. For all the dislocations and pain these divorces cause, the sum total of emotional satisfaction in the lives of the divorced and remarried may well be greater than their great-grandparents were able to achieve.

Marital infidelity, since it also relieves some of the pressures and discontents of unsuccessful or boring marriages — and does so in most cases without breaking up the existing home — will remain an alternative to divorce and will probably continue to increase, all the more so as women come to share more fully the traditional male privileges. Within another generation, based on present trends, four or five husbands and two of three wives whose marriages last more than several years will have at least a few extramarital involvements.

Overt permissiveness, particularly in the form of marital swinging, may be tried more often than it now is, but most of those who test it out will do so only briefly rather than adopt it as a way of life. Swinging has a number of built-in difficulties, the first and most important of which is that the avoidance of all emotional involvement — the very keystone of swinging — is exceedingly hard to achieve. Nearly all professional observers report that jealousy is a frequent and severely disruptive problem. And not only jealousy but sexual competitiveness: Men often have potency problems while being watched by other men or after seeing other men outperform them. Even a regular stud, moreover, may feel threatened when he observes his wife being more active at a swinging party than he himself could possibly be. Finally, the whole thing is truly workable only for the young and the attractive.

There will be wider and freer variations in marital styles — we are a pluralistic nation, growing more tolerant of diversity all the time — but throughout all the styles of marriage in the future will run a predominant motif that has been implicit in the evolution of marriage for a century and a quarter and that will finally come to full flowering in a generation or so. In short, the marriage of the future will be a heterosexual friendship, a free and unconstrained union of a man and a woman who are companions, partners, comrades and sexual lovers.

There will still be a certain degree of specialization within marriage, but by and large, the daily business of living together — the talk, the meals, the going out to work and coming home again, the spending of money, the lovemaking, the caring for the children, even the indulgence or nonindulgence in outside affairs — will be governed by this fundamental relationship rather than by the lord-and-servant relationship of patriarchal marriage. Like all friendships, it will exist only as long as it is valid; it will rarely last a lifetime, yet each marriage, while it does last, will meet the needs of the men and women of the future as no earlier form of marriage could have. Yet we who know the marriage of today will find it relatively familiar, comprehensible — and very much alive.

UNIT STUDY GUIDE

A. *Terms to Review*

Counterculture	Futurology	Premarital Attitude
Dating-Mating Game	Intentional	Scale (PMAS)
Emotional Monogamy	Community	Revolution
EMS Rates	*Mirages of Marriage*	Tribal Families
	PMS Rates	

B. *Questions for Discussion and Study*

1. As you see it, in which area of marital encounter is greatest change now occurring? Draw upon research sources to support your view.

2. The "here and now" orientation has been described and its significance assessed in the writing of the O'Neills, Margaret Mead, and others. Discuss critically the assets and liabilities of this orientation as it is related to marriage and family life.

3. It has been argued by futurists that forecasting is an integral component of true freedom-of-choice. In what way is this true? Or, is the assertion without foundation? Show why you agree or disagree.

4. Family literature frequently maintains that the sexual equality movement is certain to have a long-range effect on marital-familial forms. Select one aspect or area of marital interaction, cite and describe the measurable impact of this movement on it, and project any trends into the future. In playing the role of the futurist, draw upon both theory and research to substantiate your forecasting.

C. *Topics-Ideas for Papers and Projects*

1. Locate persons in your area who are currently involved in an alternative life style. Invite several to serve as a panel to discuss the positive and negative aspects of experimentation in marital-familial forms and processes.

2. "Utopian Communes in America's 19th Century."

3. Research: "Sex Differences in the Perceived Feasibility of Various Alternatives for Contemporary Marriage."
4. Using at least four of the areas of encounter discussed in this book, interview at least 10 each clergy, senior citizens, students, and newly-marrieds and ascertain their assessment of changes currently taking place and what they think the future holds. Rank their comments on an "optimism" scale. Are there group differences? Explain and discuss.

SELECTIVE BIBLIOGRAPHY

Since an abundance of articles are referenced in the readings, the entries here are limited to books. Furthermore, an effort was made to eliminate from this list any book titles which appear in the references to the reading selections. If papers or projects are planned, you should begin by consulting the available references in the relevant unit and then refer to this bibliography. To facilitate this process, the titles below have been grouped by unit topic.

1. SOURCES OF CHANGE IN FAMILY LIFE AND MARRIAGE

Bell, Gwen and Jaqueline Tyrwhitt. *Human Identity in the Urban Environment*. Baltimore: Penguin Books, 1973.

Bennis, Warren G. and Philip E. Slater. *The Temporary Society*. New York: Harper and Row, 1968.

Bernard, Jessie. *Women and the Public Interest*. Chicago: Aldine-Atherton, Inc., 1971.

Broderick, Carlfred B. (Ed.). *A Decade of Family Research and Action*. Minneapolis: National Council on Family Relations, 1972.

Buder, Leonard *et al. Where We Are: A Hard Look at Family and Society*. New York: Child Study Association of America, 1970.

Carr, Gwen B. *Marriage and Family in A Decade of Change*. Reading, Mass.: Addison-Wesley, 1972.

Dizard, Jan. *Social Change in The Family*. Chicago: University of Chicago Press, 1968.

Edwards, John N. *The Family and Change*. New York: Alfred A. Knopf, 1969.

Goode, William J. *The Contemporary American Family*. Chicago: Quadrangle Books, 1971.

Goode, William J. *World Revolution and Family Patterns*. New York: The Free Press of Glencoe, 1963.

Maslow, Abraham (Ed.). *New Knowledge In Human Values*. New York: Henry Regnery Co., 1959.

Schaff, Andrew. *Marxism and the Human Individual.* New York: McGraw-Hill, 1970.

Schulz, David A. *The Changing Family: Its Function and Future.* Englewood Cliffs: Prentice-Hall, 1972.

Sullerot, Evelyne. *Woman, Society and Change.* New York: McGraw-Hill, 1971.

The Editors, *Better Homes and Gardens. A Report on the American Family.* New York: Meredith Corporation, 1972.

Yablonsky, Lewis. *The Hippie Trip.* Indianapolis: Pegasus Books, 1968.

2. CURRENT SOCIAL MOVEMENTS AND MODERN MARRIAGE

Allport, Gordon W. *Becoming.* New Haven: Yale University Press, 1955.

Allport, Gordon W. *The Person in Psychology.* Boston: Beacon Press, 1969.

Andreas, Carol. *Sex and Caste in America.* Englewood Cliffs: Prentice-Hall, 1971.

Back, Kurt W. *Beyond Words: The Story of Sensitivity Training and the Encounter Movement.* Baltimore: Penguin Books, 1973.

Bird, Caroline. *Born Female: The High Cost of Keeping Women Down.* New York: Pocket Books, 1968.

Chafetz, Janet Saltzman. *Masculine/Feminine or Human: An Overview of the Sociology of Sex Roles.* Itasca, Ill.: F. E. Peacock Publishers, Inc., 1974.

Clinebell, Howard J., Jr. *The People Dynamic: Changing Self and Society Through Growth Groups.* New York: Harper and Row, 1972.

Cudlipp, Edythe. *Understanding Women's Liberation.* New York: Coronet Communications, Inc., 1971.

Fairchild, Johnson E. *Women, Society, and Sex.* Greenwich: Fawcett Publications, 1956.

Farber, Seymour and Roger H. L. Wilson. *The Potential of Women.* New York: McGraw-Hill, 1963.

Firestone, Shulamith. *The Dialectic of Sex: The Case for Feminist Revolution.* New York: Wm. Morrow & Co., 1970.

Flexner, Eleanor. *Century of Struggle: The Woman's Rights Movement in The United States.* New York: Atheneum Publishers, 1968.

Goble, Frank: *The Third Force: The Psychology of Abraham Maslow.* New York: Grossman Publications, 1970.

Greer, Germaine. *The Female Eunuch.* New York: McGraw-Hill, 1971.

Hanna, Thomas. *Bodies in Revolt.* New York: Holt, Rinehart and Winston, 1971.

Harbeson, Gladys Evans. *Choice and Challenge for the American Woman.* Cambridge: Schenkman Publishing Co., 1971.

Hole, Judith and Ellen Levine. *Rebirth of Feminism.* Chicaago: Quadrangle Books, 1971.

Janeway, Elizabeth. *Man's World, Woman's Place: A Study in Social Mythology.* New York: Dell Publishing Co., 1971.

Jourard, Sidney M. *Disclosing Man to Himself.* New York: Van Nostrand-Reinhold Co., 1968.

Mann, John. *Encounter: A Weekend With Intimate Strangers.* New York: Pocket Books, 1969.

Maslow, Abraham. *The Farther Reaches of Human Nature.* New York: Viking Press, 1971.

Millett, Kate. *Sexual Politics.* New York: Avon Books, 1971.

Mintz, Elizabeth E. *Marathon Groups: Reality and Symbol.* New York: Avon Books,1972.
Moustakas, Clark. *Personal Growth: The Struggle for Identity and Human Values.* Cambridge: Howard A. Doyle Pub. Co., 1969.
Neubeck, Gerhard. *Ways of Growth.* New York: Grossman Publications, 1968.
O'Neill, William. *The Woman Movement: Feminism in the United States and England.* Chicago: Quadrangle Books, 1969.
Otto, Herbert A. *Explorations in Human Potential.* Springfield: Chas. C. Thomas, Publisher, 1966.
Otto, Herbert A. *Human Potentialities: The Challenge and the Promise* St. Louis: Warren H. Green Co., 1968.
Perls, Frederick S. *In and Out of the Garbage Pail.* Lafayette, Cal.: Real People Press, 1969.
Peterson, Severin. *A Catalog of the Ways People Grow.* New York: Ballantine Books, 1971.
Reeves, Nancy. *Womankind: Beyond the Stereotypes.* Chicago: Aldine-Atherton, 1971.
Shostrom, Everett L. *Man, the Manipulator: The Inner Journey from Manipulation to Actualization.* Nashville: Abingdon Press, 1967.
Stambler, Sookie. *Women's Liberation: Blueprint for the Future.* New York: Charter Communications, Inc., 1970.
Tanner, Leslie B. *Voices from Women's Liberation.* New York: New American Library-Signet, 1970.
Yablonsky, Lewis. *Robopaths: People or Machines.* Baltimore: Penguin Books, 1972.

3. HUMAN SEXUALITY: POTENTIALITIES AND REALITIES

Bell, Robert R. *Premarital Sex in a Changing Society.* Englewood Cliffs: Prentice-Hall, 1966.
Bell, Robert R. and Michael Gordon. *The Social Dimension of Human Sexuality.* Boston: Little, Brown and Company, 1972.
Bohannan, Paul. *Love, Sex, and Being Human.* New York: Doubleday and Co., 1969.
Breasted, Mary. *Oh! Sex Education.* New York: Praeger Publishers, 1970.
Geddes, Donald P. *An Analysis of the Kinsey Reports.* New York: New American Library, 1954.
Hettlinger, Richard F. *Living With Sex: The Student's Dilemma.* New York: Seabury Press, 1972.
Hofmann, Hans F. *Sex Incorporated: A Positive View of the Sexual Revolution.* Boston: Beacon Press, 1967.
Kirkendall, Lester A. and Robert N. Whitehurst (Eds.). *The New Sexual Revolution.* New York: Donald W. Brown, Inc., 1971.
Lipton, Lawrence. *The Erotic Revolution.* Los Angeles: Sherbourne Press, 1965.
Packard, Vance. *The Sexual Wilderness.* New York: David McKay Co., 1968.
Petras, John W. *Sexuality in Society.* Boston: Allyn and Bacon, Inc., 1973.
Schur, Edwin M. *The Family and the Sexual Revolution.* Bloomington: Indiana University Press, 1964.
Winick, Charles. *The New People: Desexualization in American Life.* Indianapolis: Pegasus, 1968.

Wood, Frederic C. *Sex and the New Morality*. New York: Association Press, 1968.

Zubin, Joseph and John Money. *Contemporary Sexual Behavior: Critical Issues in the 1970's.* Baltimore: John Hopkins University Press, 1972.

4. GETTING TOGETHER: THE PARTNER-SELECTION PROCESS

Belgum, David. *Engagement*. St. Louis: Concordia Press, 1972.

Berne, Eric. *Sex in Human Loving*. New York: Pocket Books, 1971.

Fielding, William. *Strange Customs of Courtship and Marriage*. New York: Popular Library Eagle Books, 1956.

Gottlieb, David. *Youth in Contemporary Society*. Beverly Hills: Sage Publications, 1973.

Group for the Advancement of Psychiatry. *Sex and the College Student*. New York: Fawcett World Library, 1965.

Hamilton, Eleanor. *Sex Before Marriage*. New York: Bantam Books, 1970.

Kirkendall, Lester A. *Premarital Intercourse and Interpersonal Relations*. New York: Julian Press, 1961.

Kline, Arthur and Morris L. Medley. *Dating and Marriage: An Interpersonal Perspective*. Boston: Holbrook Press, 1973.

Reiss, Ira L. *The Social Context of Premarital Sexual Permissiveness*. New York: Holt, Rinehart, and Winston, 1967.

Rimmer, Robert H. *The Harrad Experiment*. New York: Bantam Press, 1966.

Segal, Erich. *Love Story*. New York: New American Library, 1970.

Turner, E. S. *A History of Courting*. New York: Ballantine Books, 1954.

Wallace, Karl M. *Love is More than Luck: An Experiment in Scientific Matchmaking*. New York: Wilfred Funk, 1957.

Winch, Robert F. *Mate-Selection: A Study of Complementary Needs*. New York: Harper and Row, 1958.

5. MARRIAGE TODAY: CHALLENGE AND CHOICE

Avery, Curtis and Theodore B. Johannis, Jr. *Love and Marriage: A Guide for Young People*. New York: Harcourt Brace Johanovich, Inc., 1971.

Barron, Milton L. *The Blending American: Patterns of Intermarriage*. Chicago: Quadrangle Books, 1972.

Besanceney, Paul H. *Interfaith Marriage: Who and Why*. New Haven: College and University Press, 1970.

De Wolf, Rose. *Bonds of Acrimony*. Philadelphia: Lippincott, 1970.

Eisner, Betty G. *The Unused Potential of Marriage and Sex*. Boston: Little, Brown and Company, 1970.

Geismar, Ludwig L. *555 Families: A Social-Psychological Study of Young Families in Transition*. Rutgers: Transaction, Inc., 1973.

Kieren, Dianne K., June Henton, and Ramona Marotz. *Hers and His: A Problem Solving Approach to Marriage*. New York: Holt, Rinehart and Winston, Inc., 1974.

Lederer, William J. *The Mirages of Marriage*. New York: W. W. Norton Co., Inc.,1968.

Libby, Roger W. and Robert N. Whitehurst. *Renovating Marriage: Toward New Sexual Life Styles*. Dannville, Calif.: Consensus Publishers, 1973.

Melville, Keith. *Communes in the Counter Culture: Origins, Theories, Styles of Life*. New York: Wm. Morrow and Co., 1972.

Scanzoni, John H. *Sexual Bargaining: Power Politics in the American Marriage.* Englewood Cliffs: Prentice-Hall, 1972.

Seidenberg, Robert. *Marriage Between Equals: Studies from Life and Literature.* Garden City: Doubleday Anchor, 1970.

Smith, James R. and Lynn G. *Beyond Monogamy: Recent Studies of Sexual Alternatives in Marriage.* Baltimore: Johns Hopkins University Press, 1973.

Stuart Irving R. and Lawrence E. Abt. *Interracial Marriage: Expectations and Realities.* New York: Grossman Publications, 1973.

6. SITUATIONAL STRESSES

Agee, James. *A Death in The Family.* New York: Bantam Books, 1971.

Bergler, Edmund. *Money and Emotional Conflicts.* Paterson, N.J.: Pageant Books, 1959.

Billingsley, Andrew, *Black Families in White America.* Englewood Cliffs: Prentice-Hall, 1968.

Davis, Fred. *Passage Through Crisis: Polio Victims and Their Families.* Indianapolis: Bobbs-Merrill, 1963.

Eisenstein, Victor W. (Ed.). *Neurotic Interaction in Marriage.* New York: Basic Books, 1956.

Feldman, Races Loman. *The Family in A Money World.* New York: Family Service Association, 1957.

Fritz, Dorothy B. *Growing Old is A Family Affair.* Richmond: John Knox Press, 1972.

Glasser, Paul H. and Lois N. Glasser. *Families in Crisis.* New York: Harper and Row, 1970.

Holmstrom, Linda Lytle. *The Two Career Family.* Cambridge: Schenkman Publishing Co., 1972.

Horowitz, Irving L. (Ed.). *American Working Class in the 1970's.* Rutgers. Transaction, Inc., 1974.

Hymovich, Debra (Ed.). *Family Health Care.* New York: McGraw-Hill, 1973.

Kriesberg, Louis. *Mothers in Poverty: A Study of Fatherless Families.* Chicago: Aldine Publishing Co., 1970.

Laing, Roger D. *The Politics of Experience.* New York: Ballantine Books, 1967.

Larsen, Donald E. and Lyle E. Larson. *Family, Health and Illness.* Calgary, Alberta: Sociology Dept., University of Calgary, 1973.

Lifton, Robert J. *Home from the War: Transformation of Vietnam Veterans.* New York: Simon and Schuster, 1973.

Mann, Michael. *Workers on the Move: The Sociology of Relocation.* New York: Cambridge University Press, 1973.

Parker, Richard. *The Myth of the Middle Class: Notes on Affluence and Equality.* New York: Harper and Row, 1973.

Strauss, Anselm L. (Ed.). *Where Medicine Fails,* 2nd Edition. Rutgers: Transaction, Inc., 1973.

7. INTIMATE INTERACTION

Bach, George R. and Peter Wyden. *The Intimate Enemy: How to Fight Fair in Love and Marriage.* New York: Avon Publishers, 1969.

Bartell, Gilbert. *Group Sex*. New York: Peter H. Wyden, Inc., 1971.

Burt, John J. and Linda B. Meeks. *Toward A Healthy Sexuality*. Philadelphia: W. B. Saunders Co., 1973.

Chapman, A. H. *The Strategy of Sex*. New York: G. P. Putnam's Sons, 1969.

Charney, Israel W. *Marital Love and Hate*. New York: The Macmillan Co., 1972.

Clinebell, Howard J. *The Intimate Marriage*. New York: Harper and Row, 1970.

Cuber, John F. and Peggy B. Harroff. *Sex and the Significant Americans: A Study of Sexual Behavior Among the Affluent*. Baltimore: Penguin Books, 1965.

Davis, Murray S. *Intimate Relations*. New York: The Free Press, 1973.

De Rougement, Denis. *Love in the Western World*. New York: Harper and Row, 1974.

Fast, Julius. *Body Language*. New York: Pocket Books, 1970.

Fromme, Allan. *The Ability to Love*. New York: Pocket Books, 1972.

Jourard, Sidney M. *The Transparent Self*. New York: D. Van Nostrand, 1964.

Koestenbaum, Peter. *Existential Sexuality: Choosing to Love*. Englewood Cliffs: Prentice-Hall, 1974.

Lehrman, Nat. *Masters and Johnson Explained*. Chicago: Playboy Press, 1970.

Levy, Ronald. *Self-Revelation Through Relationships*. Englewood Cliffs: Prentice-Hall, 1972.

May, Rollo. *Love and Will*. New York: W. W. Norton, 1969.

Mazur, Ronald. *The New Intimacy*. Boston: Beacon Press, 1973.

Moustakas, Clark E. *Loneliness and Love*. Englewood Cliffs: Prentice-Hall, 1972.

Neubeck, Gerhard. *Extramarital Relations*. Englewood Cliffs: Prentice-Hall, 1969.

Otto, Herbert A. *Guide to Developing Your Potential*. New York: Charles Scribner's Sons, 1968.

Otto, Herbert A. (Ed.). *Love Today: A New Exploration*. New York: Association Press, 1972.

Roy, Rustum and Della. *Honest Sex*. New York: New American Library, 1968.

Rubin, Isadore and Deryck Calderwood. *A Family Guide to Sex*. New York: Signet Books, 1973.

Rubin, Isadore. *Sexual Life After Sixty*. New York: Basic Books, 1965.

Singer, Irving. *The Goals of Human Sexuality*. New York: Schocken Books, 1974.

Updike, John. *Couples*. Greenwich: Fawcett Publications, Inc., 1968.

Watts, Alan W. *Nature, Man and Woman*. New York: New American Library, 1958.

8. REPRODUCTION AND PARENTHOOD

Beard, Ruth. *An Outline of Piaget's Development Psychology for Students and Teachers*. New York: Basic Books, 1969.

Berne, Eric. *What Do You Say After You Say Hello?: The Psychology of Human Destiny*. New York: Grove Press, 1972.

Bernhardt, Karl S. *Being A Parent: Unchanging Values in A Changing World.* Toronto: University of Toronto Press, 1970.

Braga, Joseph and Laurie, *Growing With Children.* Englewood Cliffs: Prentice-Hall, 1974.

Bull, Richard E. *Summerhill USA.* Baltimore: Penguin Books, 1970.

Callahan, Daniel J. *Abortion: Law, Choice, Morality.* New York: Macmillan Co., 1970.

Callahan, Sidney Cornelia. *The Working Mother.* New York: The Macmillan Co., 1971.

Corbin, Hazel. *Getting Ready to Be a Father.* New York: McGraw-Hill, 1964.

Denzin, Norman (Ed.). *Children and Their Caretakers.* Rutgers: Transaction, Inc., 1973.

Draper, Elizabeth. *Birth Control in the Modern World.* Baltimore: Penguin Books, 1965.

Farson, Richard. *Birthrights: A Bill of Rights for Children.* New York: The Macmillan Co., 1974.

Gordon, Thomas. *Parent Effectiveness Training.* New York: Peter H. Wyden, Inc., 1970.

Ingle, Dwight J. *Who Should Have Children?: An Environmental and Genetic Approach.* Indianapolis: Bobbs-Merrill, 1973.

Oakley, Ann. *Sex, Gender and Society.* New York: Harper and Row, 1972.

O'Connell, Dorothy *et al. Research Relating to Children.* Urbana: ERIC Clearinghouse, University of Illinois, 1973.

Polansky, Norman *et al. Roots of Futility.* San Francisco: Jossey-Bass, 1972.

Ritchie, Oscar W. and Marvin R. Koller. *Sociology of Childhood.* New York: Appleton-Century-Crofts, 1964.

Spiro, Melford. *Kibbutz: Venture in Utopia.* New York: Schocken Books, 1971.

Westoff, Leslie Aldridge and Charles F. Westoff. *From Now to Zero: Fertility, Contraception and Abortion in America.* Boston: Little, Brown and Co., 1971.

9. TERMINATION AND REMARRIAGE: THE AMERICAN PATTERN

Athearn, Louise M. *What Every Formerly Married Woman Should Know.* New York: David McKay Co., 1973.

Baer, Jean. *Second Wife: How to Live Happily With a Man Who Has Been Married Before.* Garden City: Doubleday and Co., 1972.

Becker, Russell J. *When Marriage Ends.* New York: Fortress Publications, 1971.

Bohannan, Paul (Ed.). *Divorce and After.* Garden City: Doubleday and Co., 1970.

Cantor, Donald J. *Escape from Marriage: How to Solve the Problems of Divorce.* New York: Wm. Morrow and Co., 1971.

Carter, Hugh and Paul C. Glick. *Marriage and Divorce: A Social and Economic Study.* Cambridge: Harvard University Press, 1970.

Duty, Guy. *Divorce and Remarriage.* St. Louis: Bethany Fell, 1967.

Frohlich, Newton. *Making the Best of It: A Common Sense Guide to Negotiating A Divorce.* New York: Harper and Row, 1971.

Goode, William J. *Women in Divorce.* New York: The Free Press, 1965.

Gould Staff Editors. *Marriage, Divorce and Adoption Laws in the U.S.* New York: Gould, 1974.

Grollman, Earl A. (Ed.). *Explaining Divorce to Children*. Boston: Beacon Press, 1972.

Israel, Stanley. *The Bibliography on Divorce*. New York: Bloch, 1973.

Jacobson, Paul H. *American Marriage and Divorce*. New York: Holt, Rinehart and Winston, 1959.

Krantzler, Mel. *Creative Divorce: A New Opportunity for Personal Growth*. New York: M. Evans and Co., 1973.

Lanier, Roy H. *Marriage, Divorce, and Remarriage*. Shreveport: Lambert Books, 1970.

Raush, Harold *et al*. *Communication, Conflict, and Marriage*. San Francisco: Jossey-Bass Inc.. 1974.

Reed, Angela. *The Challenge of Second Marriage*. London: Plume Press, Ltd., 1973.

Waller, Willard. *The Old Love and the New: Divorce and Readjustment*. New York: Liveright, 1930.

Young, Leontine. *The Fractured Family*. New York: McGraw-Hill, 1973.

10. IMPROVING THE MARITAL RELATIONSHIP

Barron, Frank. *Creativity and Personal Freedom*. New York: D. Van Nostrand, 1968.

Gardner, John. *Self Renewal*. New York: Harper Colophon Books, 1963.

Harris, Thomas A. *I'm OK—You're OK*. New York: Harper and Row, 1967.

James, Muriel and Dorothy Jongeward. *Born to Win: Transactional Analysis with Gestalt Experiments*. Reading, Mass.: Addison-Wesley, 1971.

Jud, Gerald and Elizabeth Jud. *Training in the Art of Loving*. Philadelphia: Church Press, 1972.

Koestenbaum, Peter. *Managing Anxiety: The Power of Knowing Who You Are*. Englewood Cliffs: Prentice-Hall, 1974.

Lewis, Howard R. and Harold S. Streitfeld. *Growth Games: How to Tune in Yourself, Your Family, Your Friends*. New York: Bantam Books, 1970.

Mace, David and Vera. *We Can Have Better Marriages*. Nashville: Abingdon Press, 1973.

Moustakas, Clark E. *The Self: Explorations in Personal Growth*. New York: Harper and Row, 1974.

New York Magazine Press. *Couples: A Magazine on the Art of Staying Together*. New York, 1973.

Otto, Herbert A. *Group Methods Designed to Actualize Human Potential*. Chicago: Achievement Motivation Systems, 1968.

Otto, Herbert A. *The Family Cluster: A Multi-Base Alternative*. Beverly Hills: The Holistic Press, 1971.

Otto, Herbert A. and John Mann (Eds.) *Ways of Growth: Approaches to Expanding Awareness*. New York: Grossman Publications, 1968.

Pearce, Jane and Saul Newton. *The Conditions of Human Growth*. New York: Citadel Press, 1969.

Perls, Frederick S. *Gestalt Therapy Verbatim*. Lafayette, Cal.: Real People Press, 1969.

Powell, John. *Why Am I Afraid to Tell You Who I Am?*. West Los Angeles: Argus Communications, 1969.

Reymond, Lizelle. *To Live Within*. Baltimore: Penguin Books, 1973.

Rodgers, Roy. *Family Interaction and Transaction*. Englewood Cliffs: Prentice-Hall, 1973.

Rogers, Carl R. *et al. Person to Person: The Problem of Being Human.* Lafayette, Calif.: Real People Press, 1967.

Satir, Virginia M. *Conjoint Family Therapy: A Guide to Theory and Technique.* Palo Alto: Science and Behavior Books, 1964.

Satir, Virginia M. *Peoplemaking.* Palo Alto: Science and Behavior Books, 1972.

Schutz, William C. *Joy: Expanding Human Awareness.* New York: Grove Press, 1967.

Snyder, Ross. *On Becoming Human: Discovering Yourself and Your Life World.* Nashville: Abdingdon Press, 1967.

Watts, Alan W. *The Book: On the Taboo Against Knowing Who You Are.* New York: The Macmillan Co., 1966.

11. ALTERNATIVES, CHANGE, AND THE FUTURE OF MARRIAGE

Blitsten, Dorothy R. *Human Social Development: Psychobiological Roots and Social Consequences.* New York: College and University Press, 1972.

Brown, Harrison and Edward Hutchings, Jr. (Eds.). *Are Our Descendants Doomed?: Technological Change and Population Growth.* New York: Viking Press, 1972.

Cooper, David G. *The Death of the Family.* New York: Pantheon Books, 1970.

Cottle, Thomas J. and Stephen L. Klineberg. *The Present of Things Future: Explorations of Time in Human Experience.* New York: Free Press, 1973.

Duberman, Lucy. *Marriage and Its Alternatives.* New York: Praeger Publishers, 1974.

Fairfield, Richard. *Communes USA: A Personal Tour.* Baltimore: Penguin Books, 1972.

Farson, Richard *et al. The Future of the Family.* New York: Family Service Association of America, 1969.

Flacks, Richard. *Youth and Social Change.* Chicago: Markham Publishing Co., 1971.

Frankl, Victor. *Man's Search for Meaning.* New York: Washington Square Press, 1968.

Fromm, Erich. *The Revolution of Hope: Toward A Humanized Technology.* New York: Harper and Row, 1974.

Gordon, Michael. *The Nuclear Family in Crisis: The Search for an Alternative.* New York: Harper and Row, 1972.

Gorney, Roderic. *The Human Agenda.* New York: Simon and Schuster, 1972.

Kanter, Rosabeth M. *Communes: Social Organization of the Collective Life.* New York: Harper and Row, 1973.

Kinkade, Kathleen. *A Walden Two Experiment: The First Five Years of Twin Oaks Community.* New York: Wm. M. Morrow and Co., 1973.

Kostelanetz, Richard (Ed.). *Social Speculation: Visions for Our Time.* New York: Wm. Morrow and Co., 1971.

Lopata, Helena Z. (Ed.). *Marriages and Families: Seeds of Social Change.* Rutgers: Transaction, Inc., 1973.

Maltz, Maxwell. *Psycho-Cybernetics and Self-Fulfillment.* New York: Grosset and Dunlap Co., 1971.

Michael, Donald N. *The Future Society.* New Brunswick: Transaction Books, 1970.

Rimmer, Robert T. *You and I . . . Searching for Tomorrow.* New York: New American Library, 1971.

Roberts, Ron E. *The New Communes: Coming Together in America.* Englewood Cliffs: Prentice-Hall, 1971.

Roszak, Theodore. *The Making of A Counter Culture.* New York: Doubleday Anchor, 1969.

Skinner, B. F. *Beyond Freedom and Dignity.* New York: Alfred A. Knopf Co., 1971.

Sussman, Marvin B. (Ed.). *Non-Traditional Family Forms in the 1970's.* Minneapolis: National Council on Family Relations, 1972.

TeSelle, Sallie (Ed.). *The Family, Communes and Utopian Societies.* New York: Harper and Row, 1972.

Theobald, Robert. *Futures Conditional.* Indianapolis: Bobbs-Merrill, 1972.

Toffler, Alvin. *Future Shock.* New York: Bantam Books, Inc., 1971.

Zablocki, Benjamin. *The Joyful Community.* Baltimore: Penguin Books, 1972.